Policing in Northern I

Delivering the New Beginning?

'*Since a multi-pronged approach to combatting 'Premier League' crime will have its rough edges at times, a mature democratic society must ensure the police act in a way that secures public confidence and support.*

The Northern Ireland Policing Board was created to ensure the accountability of the new Police Service of Northern Ireland. This book graphically sets out how this responsibility was consistently discharged – against a background of, at times, severe public and political pressures and complex, emotive criminal investigations.'

Sir Dan Crompton, former Chief Constable of Nottinghamshire and one of Her Majesty's Inspectors of Constabulary, who himself played a key role as an adviser to the Policing Board.

'*It was indeed a pleasure to review this remarkable tour de force. The authors have, in an evidential fashion, provided much more than a journey down memory lane. They have allowed us, through the prism of the Northern Ireland Policing Board, to glimpse the reality of the normative journey of change where the nexus between the political and peace process in Northern Ireland was not always evident. The Policing Board in these times served as a proxy for political progress. It was – and remains - a key institution linking the political and peace processes.*

This is an astute and scholarly recounting by the authors who were not only witnesses, but played a key role in the Northern Ireland peace journey. I commend this book to interested academics, historians, local and international practitioners of justice reform programmes, and of course others.'

Al Hutchinson, Former Police Oversight Commissioner and Police Ombudsman, Northern Ireland

'*I think this is a well-researched, carefully chronicled and humanely recited account of what was one of the most significant periods of change within UK policing. Much of what was pioneered and achieved over this period is now almost taken for granted in other policing settings; that it all happened so recently and so fast is testimony to the determination and dedication of those involved.*'

Fraser Sampson, Chief Executive and Solicitor at the Office of Police and Crime Commissioner for West Yorkshire

'"*The proposed revisions for the policing services in Northern Ireland are the most complex and dramatic changes ever attempted in modern [policing] history*".

Thus wrote the first Police Oversight Commissioner and American law enforcement expert, Tom Constantine. This book tells the tale of that fascinating – and highly successful – journey, largely through the 'eyes' of Northern Ireland's first cross-community police accountability body, the Policing Board. The reader will find it a comprehensive study that offers valuable lessons and insights for law enforcement officers, accountability 'bodies' and academics world-wide.

I was fortunate to have worked with the Policing Board. I saw first-hand how the Board worked collaboratively to resolve issues and overcome seemingly unsolvable challenges. This book captures the excitement and drama of the historical challenges of policing in a divided community and provides great lessons for others who face daunting challenges.

This should be required reading for anyone who cares about organisational change and what is possible when principled people are determined to make a difference.'

Chuck Wexler, Executive Director, Police Research Executive Forum, (Washington DC)

'*The changes recommended in the Patten Report to provide for a modern accountable police service in Northern Ireland were an essential ingredient of the political deal reached in the Belfast Agreement and the successful implementation of the Report resulted in cross community support for the PSNI which had never been given to the RUC.*

The implementing measures put human rights and accountability at the heart of the new policing.

That the PSNI story is a successful one, and that the police are supported across the community, owes much to the Northern Ireland Policing Board. The Board was at the core of ensuring accountability.

The authors detail the changes as they happened but they also place the reform in its international and political context and do not duck some of the difficulties which occurred and the problems, especially with the past, which remain.

This is an important book, one which could be of use to others involved in police reform. The authors are to be commended for an extremely authoritative account.'

Dáithí O'Ceallaigh, former Irish Ambassador in London, and current chair of the Press Council of Ireland.

Policing in Northern Ireland

Delivering the New Beginning?

Desmond Rea
and
Robin Masefield

LIVERPOOL UNIVERSITY PRESS

First published 2014 by
Liverpool University Press
4 Cambridge Street
Liverpool
L69 7ZU

British Library Cataloguing-in-Publication data
A British Library CIP record is available

ISBN 978-1-78138-150-2

Typeset by Carnegie Book Production, Lancaster
Printed and bound by Short Run Press Ltd.

Contents

Foreword

A S T H E title of this book suggests, progress in Northern Ireland since the 1998 Belfast (or Good Friday) Agreement is bound up with policing. The Police Service of Northern Ireland was born of the Agreement and in many respects the success or failure of the PSNI has come to symbolise the success or failure of the new beginning in Northern Ireland. And that brings the work of Northern Ireland's first ever cross-community Policing Board into very sharp focus.

This book tells the story of the PSNI and the Northern Ireland Policing Board so far. It is both a history book and a political book, which touches on something that sits at the very heart of a modern democracy: the accountability of the police to the community they serve. It is an insider's account, which brings both insight and authority.

The book begins, inevitably, with the Report of the Independent Commission On Policing For Northern Ireland, which was the blue print for the PSNI. As the authors make clear in the first chapter, the Independent Commission's Report sought not to highlight the past or to attribute responsibility or blame, but to point to the future. What was envisaged was a modern police service – accountable, responsive and transparent, held to account by an 'entirely new Policing Board'. As the make-up, political dynamic and early priorities of the Policing Board make clear, the description of the new police force as a 'service' and the emphasis on 'policing with the community' rather than 'community policing' (the description more often used in England and Wales) should not be underestimated. Accountability evolved within this framework and, as the authors make clear, sustaining accountability was probably the most important, as well as the most challenging, function of the Policing Board.

Sustaining accountability requires challenge to, and follow up on, all reports from the Chief Constable, something that was lacking in the arrangements between the Police Authority and the Royal Ulster Constabulary in the past. But it also requires support. The role of the Policing Board is not just to highlight failings but also to provide support where this is merited. And that takes me to the part of this book with which I am most familiar: human rights.

In the chapter on human rights the authors note that the previous chapters have considered the many key events, decisions, publications and people without which the progress that once seemed beyond reach could never have been achieved. They go on to say that, of all the developments in that chronology, the publication of the Human Rights Monitoring Framework by the Northern Ireland Policing Board was possibly one of the most significant indicators of just how far the communities and those who served them had come – and the direction in which those who came after would need to continue.

As the Human Rights Adviser to the Policing Board from 2002 to 2007, I was able to observe and contribute to the Board's work in this important area. Like so many other aspects of the transition to a new way of policing post-Patten, the approach to human rights contained a number of 'first of its kind' initiatives. The Code of Ethics was unique, combining as it did ethical statements and discipline regulations. The Monitoring Framework was similarly unique. It set out a demanding programme for human rights monitoring coupled with practical statements of how human rights applied to real policing decisions rather than abstract concepts which are of little or no use to police officers on the ground having to make real decisions in real time. But by far the most important aspect of all this was the reaction of the PSNI itself.

As the authors note elsewhere in the book, the Chief Constable from 2002 to 2009, Sir Hugh Orde, regularly made plain his belief that the PSNI was (and remains) one of the most inspected police services in the world. But, in my experience, he did not let that belief stand in the way of scrutiny. In exchange for open access to all officers and all documentation Jane Gordon and I, as the Board's Human Rights Advisers, offered to assess the performance of the PSNI as a whole (i.e., success as well as failure), a dynamic process which allowed problems to be resolved as they arose by positive dialogue between the PSNI and the Board, and on the basis that the process of monitoring should not be retrospective. First the Board, and then the PSNI itself, took us up on that offer and real progress was made – so much so that several police forces in England and Wales subsequently followed suit.

The non-retrospective nature of the Board's monitoring of the PSNI's human rights compliance was integral to its success. But, inevitably, on other matters a different approach had to be taken. As the authors note, issues relating to policing in a divided society such as Northern Ireland, especially those issues relating to the past, remain hugely toxic, with an immense capacity to impact adversely on comparative political consensus reached on other matters. For that reason, policing in Northern Ireland requires the Chief Constable and, of course, the Board itself, to manage the politics – in three dimensions – of the past, the present and the future. The chapter entitled 'Dealing with the Past – an Intractable Problem?' is one of the most insightful in the book. It spells out the very difficult balance that the Board had to achieve between acknowledging past failings and pursuing a new beginning. The problem with so much in policing is that so often the past reaches out to claim the present, and this has probably been the most difficult aspect of policing in Northern Ireland since the PSNI was created. By and large the Board has approached matters in a pragmatic way as they arose. Consensus about the past was impossible, but agreeing not to reach a collective viewpoint allowed the focus to remain on the present and future. And that is an achievement that should not be underestimated.

As Sir Hugh Orde noted, the transition in Northern Ireland to a new beginning in policing has probably been the ultimate challenge in European policing in recent years. That so much progress has been made in a relatively short time frame is largely down to the determination of the Northern Ireland Policing Board to break new ground, to ensure it was fully sighted on all important matters and to follow through. No one expects a police service that never makes a mistake (nor, for that matter, an oversight body that is always right). But what inspires confidence is the knowledge and belief that the accountability mechanisms work. At the end of this, the first chapter of its existence, the Policing Board has demonstrated that the accountability mechanisms work and thus inspired confidence in policing. The challenge thrown down in the Patten Report that there should be a modern police service, accountable, responsive and transparent, held to account by an 'entirely new Policing Board', has largely been met. That is no mean feat.

Sir Keir Starmer, KCB, QC

Abbreviations

ACC	Assistant Chief Constable
ACPO	Association of Chief Police Officers
AEP	Attenuating Energy Projectile
APA	Association of Police Authorities
ARA	Assets Recovery Agency
ARV	Armed Response Vehicle
ASBO	Anti-social Behaviour Order
BCU	Basic Command Unit
BME	Black and Minority Ethnic
CAB	Criminal Assets Bureau
CJINI	Criminal Justice Inspection Northern Ireland
CORE	Corporate Opportunity for Resilience and Efficiency
CRDP	Crime and Disorder Reduction Partnership
CSP	Community Safety Partnership
DCC	Deputy Chief Constable
DCU	District Command Unit (within the PSNI)
DPP	District Policing Partnership
DUP	Democratic Unionist Party
EMPA	Ethnic Minority Police Association
ECHR	European Convention on Human Rights
FTR	Full Time Reserve
GAA	Gaelic Athletic Association
Garda	Garda Síochána
GB	Great Britain
HET	Historical Enquiries Team
HMIC	Her Majesty's Inspectorate of Constabulary

IACP	International Association of Chiefs of Police
ICIS	Integrated Crime Information System
ICR	Institute for Conflict Research
IICD	Independent International Commission on Decommissioning
ILEF	International Law Enforcement Forum on Minimal Force Options
IMC	Independent Monitoring Commission
INLA	Irish National Liberation Army
IRA	Irish Republican Army
LGBT	Lesbian, Gay, Bisexual and Transgender
LVF	Loyalist Volunteer Force
MLA	Member of the Legislative Assembly
NAO	National Audit Office
NCA	National Crime Agency
NI	Northern Ireland
NIAC	Northern Ireland Affairs Committee
NIAO	Northern Ireland Audit Office
NICS	Northern Ireland Civil Service
NIHRC	Northern Ireland Human Rights Commission
NIM	National Intelligence Model
NIO	Northern Ireland Office
NIPS	Northern Ireland Prison Service
OCPA	Office of the Commissioner for Public Appointments
OCTF	Organised Crime Task Force
OOC	Office of the Oversight Commissioner
PBR	Plastic Baton Round
PCSO	Police Community Support Officer
PCSP	Policing and Community Safety Partnership
PERF	Police Executive Research Forum
PIRA	Provisional Irish Republican Army
PONI	Police Ombudsman for Northern Ireland (also known as OPONI)
POPT	Police Officer Part Time
PPS	Public Prosecution Service
PSNI	Police Service of Northern Ireland
PTR	Part Time Reserve
PUP	Progressive Unionist Party

RCMP   Royal Canadian Mounted Police
RIC   Royal Irish Constabulary
ROI   Republic of Ireland
RPA   Review of Public Administration
RUC   Royal Ulster Constabulary
SDLP   Social Democratic and Labour Party
SOCA   Serious Organised Crime Agency
TSG   Tactical Support Group
UDA   Ulster Defence Association
UDP   Ulster Democratic Party
UK   United Kingdom of Great Britain and Northern Ireland
UUP   Ulster Unionist Party
UVF   Ulster Volunteer Force

Introduction

T HE Belfast (or Good Friday) Agreement of 10 April 1998, in its section on Policing And Justice, stated:

'*The participants recognise that policing is a central issue in any society. They equally recognise that Northern Ireland's history of deep divisions has made it highly emotive, with great hurt suffered and sacrifices made by many ... They believe that the Agreement provides the opportunity for a new beginning to policing in Northern Ireland with a police service capable of attracting and sustaining support from the community as a whole.*'

The Agreement announced that:

'*An independent Commission will be established to make recommendations for future policing arrangements in Northern Ireland including means of encouraging widespread community support for the arrangements within the agreed framework of principles reflected in the [Agreement] and in accordance with the terms of reference at Annex A [of the Agreement].*'

The Independent Commission On Policing For Northern Ireland (hereafter the Independent Commission) was quickly established; it had eight members and was chaired by (now Lord) Chris Patten. The Independent Commission published its Report, '*A New Beginning: Policing In Northern Ireland*', in September 1999.

The Independent Commission devoted 14 chapters of its Report to the police service and two to accountability, though these included 36 of the Report's 175 recommendations. In terms of democratic accountability, the Independent Commission said:

'A new beginning for democratic accountability is key to a new beginning for policing and to involving the community as a whole in the delivery of policing. We recommend that an entirely new Policing Board be created ...'

Part of the title of this book is *Delivering the New Beginning*, to which we have added a question mark. We have sought to answer the question. While, therefore, this book is essentially about a police service, it is also tells the tale of Northern Ireland's first cross-community Policing Board, from its conception in 1999 and its establishment in 2001 through to the reconstitution of the membership in 2009. Drawing largely on publicly available material, it is an account by two individuals uniquely well placed to produce an authoritative record: Professor Sir Desmond Rea, the Policing Board's first Chairman – one of whose responsibilities was, under the Board's Standing Orders, to act as spokesperson for the Board – and Robin Masefield, the senior civil servant who headed the British Government's team implementing the recommendations of the Independent Commission.

The foreword to this book is written by Sir Keir Starmer QC, the former Director of Public Prosecutions for England and Wales, to whom we are most grateful. As the first Human Rights Adviser to the Policing Board, Sir Keir was extremely well placed to observe both the challenges faced by the Board and the ways in which it went about resolving them. (We wish to make clear that Chapter 10, on Human Rights, had been completed before the text was seen by Sir Keir.)

The book also includes valuable contributions from other expert commentators, all of whom have the necessary expertise to offer unique insights. Chapter 13, on Police Performance, was written by Edgar Jardine, a former head of the Northern Ireland Statistics and Research Agency and later a stand-in Chief Executive of the Policing Board. Other expert contributions have come from Dr Sydney Elliott (Queen's University) and Fraser Sampson (Chief Executive and Solicitor at the Office of Police and Crime Commissioner for West Yorkshire) in Chapters 11 and 10, on civil unrest and human rights, respectively. Sir Dan Crompton, a former Her Majesty's Inspector of Constabulary, has played a vital role in quality assuring the work from his particular perspective.

We wish to thank Tom Kelly, and through him Shona McCorry, of the Stakeholder Group for his generosity in the design of the cover.

His approach reminded us of his critical input to the design of the police emblem.

The book deals with a number of separate but closely inter-linked strands. At its heart is policing seen through the story of the Policing Board itself – the context, the challenges the Board faced and its manifest achievements. It is also a human story – one that brings out the personal and professional contributions made by so many individuals committed to bringing about a better and a safer Northern Ireland.

Almost as important, it is an account of the politics of policing in Northern Ireland, including – conversely – the impact that changes in policing arrangements had on political development. It shows how the work of the Policing Board positively influenced the path of both the *political* and the *peace processes*.

The individual policing topics that the book addresses are highly germane today, not just in these islands, but also internationally in America and elsewhere. They are reflected in the chapter titles. While the topics are the authors' choice, they have been selected as likely to be of most interest to a wide range of readers and audiences. They include:

a. the need for the composition of a police service to reflect the community that it aims to serve, together with the implications for public confidence in policing and policing with the community;

b. upholding human rights in the context of policing civil unrest and terrorism; and the lessons for effective policing;

c. how best in a democratic society to hold a police service effectively to account as well as providing that service with the support it requires; and

d. the challenge of dealing with the legacy of inter-communal violence over 40 years which included over 3,500 deaths and societal upheaval that left few families in Northern Ireland unaffected.

The authors have inevitably had to be selective about the examples and incidents which they have chosen to highlight. We recognise that commentators may find fault with those choices. However, we have always sought to strike a balance and to lay out the evidence in a way that allows the reader to make up their own mind.

The 1998 Omagh bombing, in particular, presented the policing institutions in Northern Ireland with challenges of considerable complexity which related to the following: the Omagh bombing investigation 'overview' and the scrutinising of the current inquiry; the review of murder investigation in general; the management and dissemination of intelligence; monitoring arrangements; and communicating with the victims of the bombing. All of these are a story in themselves but it is one for another day.

The authors are very clear on the importance of the Office of the Police Ombudsman in the policing architecture of Northern Ireland. The book does deal with – subject to the one major exception highlighted in the preceding paragraph – the impact of investigations by the Ombudsman on the Policing Board. However, the authors did not have the benefit of direct involvement with the day-to-day operation of the Ombudsman's office. Accordingly, we concluded that it would be better for other parties, better placed than we were, to complete a full account of the Ombudsman's work.

We wish to make clear that the period from the establishment of the Northern Ireland Policing Board in autumn 2001 to the stepping down from office of Professor Sir Desmond Rea as Chairman of the Board in summer 2009 is the particular emphasis of this work. We have dealt with events after 2009 to the extent that, had we not done so, unfinished business and issues would have been left hanging in the air. Again, the authors did not have access to as full a range of material for the subsequent period. We could not have done as much justice to it, and we hope that the task of writing up these years will be taken up by others.

We believe that it is important to record that the vast majority of the material on which we have drawn is publicly available. In many cases, it was public from the point of origin – such as, for example, published minutes of the *Public Sessions* of the Northern Ireland Policing Board, the Board's press releases or published reports. In other cases, the records are available in line with the Policing Board's Freedom of Information policy (as set out in section 5 of Chapter 5). A third category consisted of material subsequently published by third parties. The book also draws directly on one of the authors' experience and recollections, from his time as the Policing Board's first Chairman.

For the very large part, we have relied on the documentary evidence and let it speak for itself. In so doing, we trust we have done justice to all sides of the argument.

This book is a unique account that we believe vividly shows how elected representatives and others who hold fundamentally opposed views can work together to resolve problems affecting the most vital issues facing contemporary society. The names of some Board Members inevitably occur with more frequency in this account than others. This book is a tribute to all those who have been involved in the progress of policing in Northern Ireland over the past 15 years, whether as members of the police, elected or independent representatives on the Board and District Policing Partnerships, or public servants working on those bodies or in Government.

The Policing Board was, for several years, the only major institution in Northern Ireland, with elected representatives, operating on a cross-community basis. External events, of both a political and a security nature, buffeted the Board and on occasion raised challenges to its continued existence. But, through all that, the focus on accountability and delivery of effective policing was sustained, for which the police themselves, the Board Members, and, indeed, its staff, deserve huge credit. Moreover, even though some of the *Political Members* of the Board were opposed to the implementation of the Independent Commission on Policing, the recommendations in its report were put into practice. They still serve as a template for policing not just in these islands but also internationally.

In the light of our analysis set out in this book, we conclude that – notwithstanding some inevitable and some unforeseeable challenges – the new beginning to policing in Northern Ireland has indeed been delivered.

September 2014

CHAPTER ONE

Policing
in its Historical and Political Context

1.1 The Origins of Northern Ireland and its Police

This book aims primarily to set out the creation, efficacy and achievements of the Northern Ireland Policing Board. However, this has to be seen in the context of Northern Ireland's troubled history and divided community. It is almost as unthinkable to look at policing without an understanding of the politics as it is to understand the politics without appreciating the significance of the policing issue.

Northern Ireland is a small place; it is made up of six of the 32 counties that constitute the whole of Ireland. Its total population is currently just over 1.8m, which is a little greater than that of Hampshire – 1.3m – and rather less than that of West Yorkshire – 3.2m.

Again, to understand the politics of today, it is essential to study the past. When she visited Ireland for the first time, in May 2011, the Queen spoke of *'our troubled past'*. Whether one goes back as far as the Norman incursion of the 12th century, the struggles of the Elizabethan period 400 years later, the flight of the Earls and the Plantation (particularly of Northern Ireland by Scots and English settlers), the attacks initially by native Irish in 1641 and the response thereafter, or the largely Presbyterian-supported rebellion of 1798, relations have not been exactly harmonious. Against this background it is hardly surprising that in Northern Ireland there has been a history of a lack of total acceptance of the authority of the current government and a greater willingness to challenge State institutions, even through the use of force, than is apparent in many other countries, certainly in Western Europe.

Efforts by successive British Governments in the late 19th century and then in the early 20th century to introduce Home Rule for the whole of the island of Ireland were challenged particularly by the descendants of the English and Scottish settlers in the Northern counties and effectively thwarted. In turn, the Easter Rising in 1916, albeit focused on Dublin, achieved a wider level of support for Irish nationalism than had the previous efforts of the militant minority.

At the end of the First World War, the electoral rise of Sinn Féin and the first meeting of Dáil Éireann were followed by a period of guerrilla warfare against the British authorities. A truce was declared in July 1921 and a fresh attempt was made by the British Government, led by David Lloyd George, in discussion with the Sinn Féin leadership, to resolve the issue of self-determination. This led to an historic agreement, the Anglo-Irish Treaty, signed at Downing Street in London on 6 December 1921. It provided for the creation of the Irish Free State, out of which the six northern counties opted, with a Boundary Commission to clarify the actual border. The Treaty was ratified in the Dáil and then in a vote across the new country in June 1922, but it was followed by an intense civil war in the new State. Equally there was inter-communal rioting and attacks on the police in Belfast, with significant fatalities there too. Partition was finalised in 1925, when the delineation of the border was acknowledged in an amendment to the Treaty, leaving significant numbers of Roman Catholics in many parts of Northern Ireland, representing about 33.5% of the population (according to the 1926 Census). The Irish Constitution, promulgated in 1937, stated in Article 2 that 'the national territory consists of the whole island of Ireland' and successive Irish Governments made clear their desire for reunification, a position as consistently opposed by the Unionist majority in the north.

The Royal Irish Constabulary (RIC) came to an end in Northern Ireland in April 1922, having in effect split into the Garda Síochána (the Civic Guard) in the south and the Royal Ulster Constabulary (RUC) in the north. The Royal Ulster Constabulary formally came into being on 1 June of that year, with, initially, about 2,000 men. Although a new badge including the red hand of Ulster on a St George's Cross was designed, the harp and Crown insignia of the order of Saint Patrick as worn by the RIC was readopted. The composition of the Royal Ulster Constabulary included a significant proportion of Roman

Catholics, over 500 by 1925, although by statute a third of all posts were reserved for Catholics, broadly reflecting the population at that time. Thereafter the Royal Ulster Constabulary struggled to recruit Catholics, not least as Nationalist leaders discouraged members of their community from joining and the Irish Republican Army (IRA) targeted those who did. With the permission of the Minister of Home Affairs, Sir Dawson Bates, an Orange Lodge was formed within the Royal Ulster Constabulary. From the beginning its officers were armed, as the RIC had been. The Royal Ulster Constabulary was supported by the Ulster Special Constabulary, an auxiliary part time force.

As can be seen from the turbulent birth of Northern Ireland, the Royal Ulster Constabulary had from the first a contentious role, one very different from that of the Garda Síochána, which has traditionally enjoyed a much wider level of community support. It is interesting to note that historically the development of policing in the Western world had some of its origins in Ireland, with the passing of the Dublin Police Act 1786 and the extension of the Constabulary Police to the whole of the island from 1822. It was his experience of Irish policing that Sir Robert Peel took with him when he played a key part in setting up the Metropolitan Police in London.

1.2   The Troubles

It is not necessary, for the purposes of this book, to cover the period between the establishment of Northern Ireland and the start of the Troubles in the late 1960s. In 1968 and 1969 the Civil Rights Movement placed major challenges before the comparatively small (at just over 3,000 members) and not very well equipped Royal Ulster Constabulary. It was perhaps inevitable that these and other factors would lead to what was widely perceived as an overreaction by members of the Royal Ulster Constabulary, particularly in relation to the minority community and its representatives. In August 1969 the British Government deployed the Army on the streets of Northern Ireland in aid of the civil power.

That same month it established an urgent review of policing in Northern Ireland, led by Lord Hunt, who was to report just two months later. Some of the conclusions reached by Hunt proved a recurring theme for the still more radical recommendations in the Report of the Independent Commission On Policing In Northern Ireland (the Independent Commission) over 30 years later. Among Hunt's recommendations were the disarming of the Royal Ulster Constabulary, the abolition of the Special Constabulary (including the B Specials) and their replacement with what was to be the Royal Ulster Constabulary Reserve, and the creation of a Police Authority reflecting the proportions of different groups in the community. The report stressed that '*it is a truism that the police forces in any country operate within the context and in the climate of the political conditions and stability of that country*'. It was also stressed that

'*The police force can and should play a leading part, not only in enforcing law and order, but in helping to create a new climate of respect for the law, a new attitude of friendship between its members and the public, and a sense of obligation among all men of goodwill to cooperate with the police in fulfilling their civic duties in the Province, notwithstanding any wider political aspirations which they may have.*'

The report, however, referred to 'the police force' rather than a 'service' and made no explicit reference to the wider concept of policing that the Independent Commission was to highlight. In November 1969 the then head of the Royal Ulster Constabulary resigned and was replaced by the experienced Commissioner of the City of London Police, Sir Arthur Young. Within a year the Royal Ulster Constabulary had increased to 4,000 regular officers with a further 1,500 in the new Reserve, the B Specials having been disbanded in April 1970.

Direct Rule was established in March 1972, with the suspension of the Northern Ireland Government. The British and Irish Governments met with representatives of many of the Northern Ireland political parties, including the Ulster Unionist Party (UUP), the Social Democratic and Labour Party (SDLP), and Alliance at Sunningdale in December the following year. The 20-point communiqué issued on 9 December 1973 had two main sections relating to institutions – the creation of a new Council of Ireland and

'... *the question of policing and the need to ensure public support for and identification with the police throughout the whole community. It was agreed that no single set of proposals would achieve these aims overnight and that time would be necessary. ... It was broadly accepted that the two parts of Ireland are to a considerable extent inter-dependent in the whole field of law and order and the problems of political violence and identification with the Police Service cannot be solved without taking account of that fact.'*

The Irish Government undertook to set up a Police Authority, appointments to which would be made after consultation with the Council of Ministers of the Council of Ireland. An independent complaints procedure for dealing with complaints against the Police would also be set up. (N.B. The full text of the Sunningdale Communiqué is set out at appendix 1.A. below.)

The power-sharing Executive, established on 1 January 1974 following the elections the previous year, collapsed at the end of May 1974 after the Ulster Workers Council strike. The provisions in relation to the Council of Ireland and an Irish Police Authority fell into abeyance.

The level of violence during the period of office of the Executive had not greatly abated, with 205 deaths in Northern Ireland in 1974 as a result of the Troubles. Indeed, on 17 May Loyalist paramilitaries had set off bombs in Dublin and Monaghan, killing a total of 33 people. 1972 had been the worst year of violence in Northern Ireland, with no less than 467 fatalities, including 241 civilians, 146 members of the security forces, and 80 characterised as terrorists, according to the report of the Committee led by Lord Gardiner, published in January 1975.

Lord Gardiner's Committee had been set up *'to consider, in the context of Civil Liberties and human rights, measures to deal with terrorism in Northern Ireland'*. The report acknowledged *'the need for firm and decisive action on the part of the security forces; but violence has in the past provoked a violent response'*. It went on to recommend consideration of a Bill of Rights. In relation to policing, the Gardiner Committee was clear that

'Effective policing must derive from the community it serves and draw its strength, support and prestige from that community. We therefore hope that, in the very near future, the minority community as a whole will accept and support the police in normal policing duties throughout their areas, and that

the leaders of the minority community will find it possible to recommend that members of their community should join the Royal Ulster Constabulary in greater numbers.'

Lord Gardiner's Committee noted that while there was provision for a tribunal incorporating an independent element to be set up by the Police Authority under the Police Act (Northern Ireland) 1970, this had never been invoked. They recommended the introduction of an independent means of investigating complaints against the police. The report stressed that

'There is one aspect of the problem of communal conflict which should not be overlooked in this context. It involves the special international obligations of the Government of the United Kingdom. In the first place the United Kingdom and the Republic of Ireland are both members of the European Community, whose members explicitly recognise and even have a higher degree of obligation to cooperate than is the case between sovereign states in general.'

The report also noted the presence of influential communities of Irish descent in many parts of the English-speaking world which meant that a number of Britain's allies had a keen interest in the stability of communal relations in Northern Ireland, even though some of those same Irish communities had helped to sustain violence in Northern Ireland by their support for the paramilitary organisations.

In 1976 the Royal Ulster Constabulary re-established the principle of 'police primacy', in which the Army primarily provided support in policing, for example by accompanying police patrols in areas where the risk was greater, rather than taking the lead. While this restored a more normal institutional framework, it also meant that the Royal Ulster Constabulary had perforce to take on a more 'paramilitary' role itself in terms of the carrying of weapons and the strengthening of mobile support units equipped to deal with public disorder.

The *'Report of the Consultative Group on the Past'*, jointly chaired by the Archbishop of Armagh, the Right Reverend Robin Eames, and Denis Bradley, published in January 2009, included a section on the legacy of the conflict. Table 1.1, from that report, contains the breakdown of the figure of 3,523 people killed as a result of the conflict between 1969 and 2001.

Table 1.1   Northern Ireland: party responsible for persons killed 1969–2001

Responsible party	Number of deaths
Republican paramilitary groups	2,055
Loyalist paramilitary groups	1,020
Security forces	368
Persons unknown	80
Total	3,523

In percentage terms, 58% were killed by Republicans, 29% by Loyalists, 10% by British (and Irish) security forces, and 2% by persons or groups unknown.

The breakdown of those killed, according to the report, is shown in Table 1.2.

Table 1.2   Northern Ireland: breakdown of persons killed 1969–2001

Civilians	1,855
Members of the security forces	1,123
Republican paramilitary group members	394
Loyalist paramilitary group members	151

3,523 represents a significant proportion of the total population of Northern Ireland, around 1.7m during this period. Proportionately it would correspond to around 125,000 out of the total population of the United Kingdom or about half a million people in America.

Not all the deaths occurred in Northern Ireland, however, as shown in Table 1.3.

Table 1.3   Northern Ireland: where deaths occurred 1969–2001

Within Northern Ireland	3,267
In the Republic of Ireland	113
In Great Britain	125
In continental Europe	18

Of the deaths within Northern Ireland, just over one-third took place in either West or North Belfast.

Figure 1.1 plots the yearly fatalities due to the Troubles from 1969 right through to 2010.

Figure 1.1   Northern Ireland: yearly fatalities due to the troubles 1969–2010

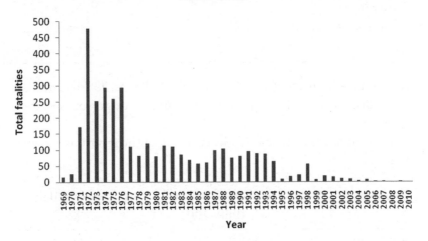

In addition, some 47,000 people in Northern Ireland sustained injuries in the same period in 16,200 bombing and 37,000 shooting incidents. A total of 19,600 individuals received a sentence of imprisonment for scheduled offences – that is, crimes that the legislation determined related to terrorism.

Large numbers of Northern Ireland residents worked for the security forces during those 40 years. They, with their immediate families, would have totalled perhaps some 200,000. At its maximum the actual strength of the Royal Ulster Constabulary totalled around 13,000, including some 8,500 regular officers and a further 5,000 Full Time or Part Time Reservists; this was in addition to its civilian cadre.

Specifically, by the end of the Royal Ulster Constabulary on 3 November 2001, a total of 301 Royal Ulster Constabulary members had been killed as a result of terrorism, all but some 25 at the hands of Irish Republican groups. (In addition, two Members of the Police Authority – William Johnston in 1972 and Oliver Eaton in 1976 – had been killed, as had two civilian police staff.) These figures, however, underplay the full extent of the impact of the Troubles on the police in

Northern Ireland and members' families, with a much greater number sustaining significant injuries while on duty and others taking their own lives, in part reflecting the pressures they were under.

Although no list of some of the worst violent incidents during the Troubles can be other than selective, it may help to frame the context for consideration of the *peace process*. The following list draws on the CAIN (Conflict Archive on the Internet) website of the University of Ulster:

'*9 August 1971 – 14 people were killed in separate shooting incidents in Belfast (10 Catholics and 3 Protestant civilians and 1 IRA member); 13 by members of the British Army and 1 by a Republican Group;*

4 December 1971 – 15 Catholic civilians were killed in a bomb attack on McGurk's Bar in North Belfast, carried out by the Ulster Volunteer Force;

30 January 1972 – 'Bloody Sunday', 14 Catholic civilians were killed in a civil rights march at Londonderry, shot by the Army;

21 July 1972 – 'Bloody Friday', 9 people were killed in 2 separate explosions in Belfast by the IRA – 5 Protestant and 2 Catholic civilians, and 2 Army members;

31 July 1972 – 9 civilians, 5 Protestant and 4 Catholic were killed in 3 car bombs at Claudy, carried out by the IRA;

4 February 1974 – 12 people were killed in an IRA bomb attack on an Army coach in Yorkshire;

17 May 1974 – 33 civilians were killed in Dublin and Monaghan in Loyalist Paramilitary car bombs;

21 November 1974 – 20 civilians were killed in two explosions in public houses in Birmingham;

5 January 1976 – 10 Protestant civilians were killed by a Republican Paramilitary Group in their minibus near Bessbrook, County Armagh;

17 January 1978 – 12 Protestant civilians were killed in a bomb attack on the La Mon restaurant in County Down;

27 August 1979 – 18 Army members were killed in 2 IRA bomb attacks near Warrenpoint, County Down;

6 December 1982 – 17 people were killed in an INLA bomb at the Droppin Well Bar in Ballykelly, County Londonderry;

28 February 1985 – 9 Royal Ulster Constabulary members were killed in an IRA mortar bomb attack on Newry Police station;

8 May 1987 – 8 IRA members and 1 Catholic civilian were killed by the Army in the course of an attack on Loughgall Royal Ulster Constabulary station, County Armagh;

8 November 1987 – 11 people, 10 Protestant civilians and 1 Royal Ulster Constabulary member, were killed in an IRA explosion at the Remembrance Day ceremony at Enniskillen, County Fermanagh;

21 October 1993 – 10 people, 9 Protestant civilians and 1 IRA member, were killed in an IRA explosion at a Shankill Road fish shop in Belfast;

30 October 1993 – 7 civilians, 6 Catholic and 1 Protestant, were killed at the Rising Sun Bar in Greysteel, County Londonderry, in an attack carried out by the Ulster Freedom Fighters;

18 June 1994 – 6 Catholic civilians were killed in a UVF attack on a bar at Loughinisland, County Down;

15 August 1998 – 29 civilians were killed as a result of a bomb attack in Omagh, County Tyrone, carried out by the Real IRA.'

Henry Patterson, in *Ireland's Violent Frontier*, has recently argued that the ethnic cleansing of Protestants living in Border areas over 20 years of the Troubles was, in part, a tool to stop Unionists coming to a political accommodation with the moderate Nationalist party, the SDLP, and, in part, a strategy to force Britain into doing a deal with Sinn Féin.

1.3   The Peace Process

Successive British Governments sought to tackle both the political and the security situations in tandem. However, neither the 1975 Constitutional Convention nor the Assembly established under the Northern Ireland Act 1982 made substantial progress. The death of ten hunger strikers in the Maze prison in 1981 played an important part in the development of Sinn Féin as an electoral force representing the political wing of the Provisional IRA.

In 1984 the Provisional IRA set off a bomb in the Grand Hotel at Brighton during the Conservative Party conference. On 15 November in the following year the British and Irish Governments reached the Anglo-Irish Agreement at Hillsborough Castle. This, for the first time, explicitly gave the Irish Government an enshrined right to put forward views on proposals on certain matters, critically including policing. The two Governments also agreed (article 7)

'That there is a need for a programme of special measures in Northern Ireland to improve relations between the security forces and the community, with the object in particular of making the security forces more readily accepted by the Nationalist community. Such a programme shall be developed, for the Conference's consideration, and may include the establishment of local consultative machinery, training in community relations, crime prevention schemes involving the community, improvements in arrangements handling complaints, and action to increase the proportion of members of the minority in the Royal Ulster Constabulary (RUC).'

A joint Secretariat was set up at Maryfield outside Belfast, which provided Irish officials with a direct channel through which to raise specific issues about policing and security matters and gave them a discreet location at which to develop in the ensuing years a direct personal relationship with senior police officers. Although the Anglo-Irish Agreement was condemned by many Unionist representatives, it was not a body, such as the 1974 Executive, that could be brought down in similar fashion. Nevertheless, a large number of Royal Ulster Constabulary officers and their homes were attacked by Loyalist paramilitaries at this time.

In 1991 inter-party talks were set up, initially meeting during a period of suspension of the Intergovernmental Conference under the Anglo-Irish Agreement. (It was in the same year that there was an historic first meeting between senior members of the UUP and the Taoiseach.) Before the talks ended in November 1992, a senior Australian figure, Sir Ninian Stephen, had been brought in to chair part of the proceedings. These were the first talks that identified three separate strands, the first dealing with relationships within Northern Ireland and the political institutions there; the second dealing with relationships between Northern Ireland and its larger neighbour on the island of Ireland; and the third dealing with East–West relations with Great Britain.

In this period the British Government was reaffirming that it '*had no selfish, strategic or economic interest in Northern Ireland*'; in other words, its primary role was in relation to 'holding the ring' between the political parties in Northern Ireland. (This was first stated by Peter Brooke, when he was Secretary of State for Northern Ireland, in a speech on 9 November 1990.) On the other hand, the Nationalist parties tended to look towards the Irish Government for direct political support.

For some years prior to this there had been informal, private contacts between John Hume, then leader of the SDLP and Gerry Adams, the President of Sinn Féin. It was also revealed subsequently that there had been confidential discussions between British Government officials and Sinn Féin. In March 1993 the British Government set out in a nine-paragraph note its position on the scope for political progress, and other changes in Northern Ireland, that an end to violence would offer. A joint statement by the Prime Minister and the Taoiseach in Brussels in October 1993 was followed on 15 December 1993 by the historic Downing Street Joint Declaration by Prime Minister John Major and Taoiseach Albert Reynolds.

The following month, US President Bill Clinton sanctioned a visa for Gerry Adams to enter the United States. On 31 August 1994 the Provisional IRA announced a 'complete cessation of military operations'; this was followed in mid-October 1994 by a ceasefire declaration from the Combined Loyalist Command. On 21 October 1994 the Prime Minister opened the way to talks with Sinn Féin, which began on 9 December 1994 and were followed by exploratory dialogue with Loyalist representatives on 16 December. The '*peace process*' might be said to be formally underway at this point.

It is, however, important to recognise at this stage that there were in effect two separate but inter-connected issues – the *peace process* and the *political process*. To achieve lasting progress the two must not just run in parallel but positively align; this was not always the case, the significance of which would become apparent in later years.

On 22 February 1995 the United Kingdom and Republic of Ireland Framework Documents were published, setting out the two Governments' proposals for relationships within the island of Ireland and between them, and also the British Government's proposals for the new democratic institutions within Northern Ireland. Reflecting the increasing recognition of the American dimension, Senator George Mitchell accepted the Governments' invitation to chair the International Commission for Disarmament in Northern Ireland. On 28 November 1995 the British and Irish Governments issued a joint communiqué outlining the proposed twin-track approach to the decommissioning of paramilitary weapons and all-party negotiations. This was reinforced by the first visit of President Clinton to Northern Ireland two days later.

In 1995 a Fundamental Review of the Royal Ulster Constabulary was set up, led by Ronnie Flanagan, who was then the Deputy Chief Constable. This was a wide-ranging and influential review of many facets of the Police in Northern Ireland in the context of its time, although the full report was not published.

On 21 January 1996 Senator Mitchell issued his report, which contained six important principles set out for adoption by the political parties. In the following month the Provisional IRA announced its return to violence, with the Canary Wharf bomb being set off in London on 9 February 1996. On 30 May 1996 elections were held to the Northern Ireland Forum; of the 110 seats, the UUP took 30, the Democratic Unionist Party (DUP) 24, the SDLP 21 and Sinn Féin 17. A week later Garda officer Jerry McCabe was killed by the Provisional IRA in an armed robbery in County Limerick.

On 10 June 1996 multi-party talks, excluding Sinn Féin, were begun at Stormont by Prime Minister John Major and Taoiseach John Bruton, subsequently chaired by George Mitchell. The policing of the annual Orange parade from the Church of Ireland church at Drumcree down the Garvaghy Road towards Portadown was particularly challenging that year. The Royal Ulster Constabulary initially decided that the parade should not be permitted on Sunday 7 July 1996, although after considerable violence across Northern Ireland, including several deaths, this decision was rescinded on 11 July 1996. An independent review of parades and marches in Northern Ireland, headed by Peter North, was set up in September; it reported the following January, recommending the creation of an independent Parades Commission to have responsibility for determinations in relation to parades, relieving the Royal Ulster Constabulary of that responsibility. In November 1996 Ronnie Flanagan took over as Chief Constable.

In March 1997, ahead of the United Kingdom General Election

on 1 May 1997, the multi-party talks were adjourned. A Labour Government was formed, with Marjorie (Mo) Mowlam MP as the Secretary of State for Northern Ireland. The Prime Minister, Tony Blair, made clear from the start that he regarded Northern Ireland as a priority. Among the Northern Ireland parties the UUP obtained 33% of the vote, the SDLP 24%, Sinn Féin 16% and the DUP 14%.

The momentum quickened. Multi-party talks resumed at Stormont on 3 June 1997. Three days later there was an election in the Republic of Ireland leading to a Fianna Fail majority government and to Sinn Féin's gaining their first seat in the Dáil. Although two Royal Ulster Constabulary officers were killed by the Provisional IRA in Lurgan on 16 June 1997, on 24 June the British and Irish Governments put forward proposals for the decommissioning of paramilitary weapons to be supervised by an international commission. On 19 July 1997 a renewed ceasefire was announced by the Provisional IRA. On 26 August 1997 the Independent International Commission for Decommissioning (IICD) was announced by the two Governments. On 9 September 1997 Sinn Féin IRA announced that they would sign up to the Mitchell principles; during the following week all-party talks began, chaired by Senator Mitchell. That autumn substantive nego-tiations began, involving the Irish Government as well, and dealing with all three strands: that is, within Northern Ireland, North–South and East–West. The first indication of a dissident republican position emerged, with the establishment late that year of the Real IRA and its political wing, the 32 County Sovereignty Movement.

The progress of those talks (which did not include the DUP) has been documented elsewhere and we do not rehearse it here. Again, some features of later talks were apparent – in January 1998 the two Governments produced the 'Heads of Agreement' document, which included areas such as a new Northern Ireland Assembly, an Intergovernmental Council and a North–South Ministerial Council, and changes to the Irish constitutional claim to Northern Ireland. On 9 January 1998 the Northern Ireland Secretary of State, Mo Mowlam, visited the Maze prison in order to talk to leading representatives among the Loyalist prisoners, following a ballot which had indicated minority support for the *peace process* among them. Some two weeks later the talks moved for a few days to Lancaster House in London, removing the participants from the intensity of scrutiny in Belfast.

On 29 January 1998 the British Government announced an inquiry into the deaths of 13 civilians in Londonderry on 30 January 1972, known as Bloody Sunday.

1.4   The Belfast Agreement of 10 April 1998

On Good Friday, 10 April 1998, the historic Belfast Agreement was reached. The signatories included all the Northern Ireland political parties except the DUP. The text of the Agreement included the outcome on each of the three strands. During the following month referenda were held simultaneously in Northern Ireland and the Republic of Ireland. In the North 71% voted yes, while in the South 94% did so.

It is not necessary to set out the text of the entire Belfast Agreement. However, the section on Policing and Justice, together with its associated Annex A, follows in full:

'POLICING AND JUSTICE

1. *The participants recognise that policing is a central issue in any society. They equally recognise that Northern Ireland's history of deep divisions has made it highly emotive, with great hurt suffered and sacrifices made by many individuals and their families, including those in the RUC and other public servants. They believe that the agreement provides the opportunity for a new beginning to policing in Northern Ireland with a police service capable of attracting and sustaining support from the community as a whole. They also believe that this agreement offers a unique opportunity to bring about a new political dispensation which will recognise the full and equal legitimacy and worth of the identities, senses of allegiance and ethos of all sections of the community in Northern Ireland. They consider that this opportunity should inform and underpin the development of a police service representative in terms of the make-up of the community as a whole and which, in a peaceful environment, should be routinely unarmed.*

2. *The participants believe it is essential that policing structures and arrangements are such that the police service is professional, effective and efficient, fair and impartial, free from partisan political control; accountable, both under the law for its actions and to the community it serves; representative of the society it polices, and operates within a coherent and co-operative*

criminal justice system, which conforms with human rights norms. The participants also believe that those structures and arrangements must be capable of maintaining law and order including responding effectively to crime and to any terrorist threat and public order problems. A police service which cannot do so will fail to win public confidence and acceptance. They believe that any such structures and arrangements should be capable of delivering a police service, in constructive and inclusive partnerships with the community at all levels, and with a maximum delegation of authority and responsibility, consistent with the foregoing principles. These arrangements should be based on principles of protection of human rights and professional integrity and should be unambiguously accepted and actively supported by the entire community.

3. *An independent Commission will be established to make recommendations for future policing arrangements in Northern Ireland including means of encouraging widespread community support for these arrangements within the agreed framework of principles reflected in the paragraphs above and in accordance with the terms of reference at Annex A. The Commission will be broadly representative with experts and international representation among its membership and will be asked to consult widely and to report no later than Summer 1999.*

4. *The participants believe that the aims of the criminal justice system are to:*
    - *deliver a fair and impartial system of justice to the community;*
    - *be responsive to the community's concerns, and encouraging community involvement where appropriate;*
    - *have the confidence of all parts of the community; and*
    - *deliver justice efficiently and effectively.*

5. *There will be a parallel wide-ranging review of criminal justice (other than policing and those aspects of the system relating to the emergency legislation) to be carried out by the British Government through a mechanism with an independent element, in consultation with the political parties and others. The review will commence as soon as possible, will include a wide consultation and a report will be made to the Secretary of State no later than Autumn 1999. Terms of reference are attached at Annex B.*

6. *Implementation of the recommendations arising from both reviews will be discussed with the political parties and with the Irish Government.*

7. *The participants also note that the British Government remains ready in*

principle, with the broad support of the political parties, and after consulta-
tion, as appropriate, with the Irish Government, in the context of on-going
implementation of the relevant recommendations, to devolve responsibility
for policing and justice issues.

ANNEX A
COMMISSION ON POLICING FOR NORTHERN IRELAND

Terms of reference

Taking account of the principles on policing as set out in the agreement, the
Commission will enquire into policing in Northern Ireland and, on the basis of
its findings, bring forward proposals for future policing structures and arrange-
ments, including means of encouraging widespread community support for
those arrangements.

Its proposals on policing should be designed to ensure that policing arrange-
ments, including composition, recruitment, training, culture, ethos and
symbols, such that in a new approach Northern Ireland has a police service
that can enjoy widespread support from, and is seen as an integral part of, the
community as a whole.

Its proposals should include recommendations covering any issues such as
re-training, job placement and educational and professional development
required in the transition to policing in a peaceful society.

Its proposals should also be designed to ensure that:

- *the police service is structured, managed and resourced so that it can be*
  effective in discharging its full range of functions (including proposals on
  any necessary arrangements for the transition to policing in a normal
  peaceful society);

- *the police service is delivered in constructive and inclusive partner-*
  ships with the community at all levels with the maximum delegation of
  authority and responsibility;

- *the legislative and constitutional framework requires the impartial*
  discharge of policing functions and conforms with internationally
  accepted norms in relation to policing standards;

- *the police operate within a clear framework of accountability to the law*
  and the community they serve, so:

  ○ *they are constrained by, accountable to and act only within the law;*

○ *their powers and procedures, like the law they enforce, are clearly established and publicly available;*

○ *there are open, accessible and independent means of investigating and adjudicating upon complaints against the police;*

○ *there are clearly established arrangements enabling local people, and their political representatives, to articulate their views and concerns about policing and to establish publicly policing priorities and influence policing policies, subject to safeguards to ensure police impartiality and freedom from partisan political control;*

○ *there are arrangements for accountability and for the effective, efficient and economic use of resources in achieving policing objectives;*

○ *there are means to ensure independent professional scrutiny and inspection of the police service to ensure that proper professional standards are maintained;*

  - *the scope for structured cooperation with the Garda Síochána and other police forces is addressed; and*

  - *the management of public order events which can impose exceptional demands on policing resources is also addressed.*

The Commission should focus on policing issues, but if it identifies other aspects of the criminal justice system relevant to its work on policing, including the role of the police and prosecution, then it should draw the attention of the Government to those matters.

The Commission should consult widely, including with non-governmental expert organisations, and through such focus groups as they consider it appropriate to establish.

The Government proposes to establish the Commission as soon as possible, with the aim of it starting work as soon as possible and publishing its final report by Summer 1999.'

A number of points should be noted at this stage. It is striking that, while the Belfast Agreement included a wide range of comprehensive detail on specific matters, the particularly sensitive issues relating to policing and criminal justice were too difficult to resolve in the context of those inter-party talks. To an extent this reflected the precedent of both the Sunningdale and Anglo-Irish Agreements. Put simply, issues relating to policing in such a divided society, issues covering the present, future and, perhaps especially, the past, remained hugely toxic, with an immense capacity to impact adversely on comparative political consensus reached on other matters.

It was, however, possible to reach agreement among those present on the creation of an Independent Commission that would address the policing issues. Indeed, in both the seven paragraphs of the main text and then the actual terms of reference for the Commission a comprehensive range of principles was set out which was to provide a clear lodestone for all those who subsequently played parts in bringing about the new policing in Northern Ireland.

Within the United Kingdom and, indeed, within the island of Ireland, issues relating to civil liberties and human rights have been more to the fore in Northern Ireland than elsewhere. This can be seen again from the 1973 Sunningdale Agreement and external reports such as the 1975 Gardiner Committee. There has been constant recognition of the vital importance of sustaining human rights in the context of a major conflict that involved the extensive use of force. The Bill that became the United Kingdom's Human Rights Act 1998 was making its passage through Parliament while these talks were progressing.

As early as 1973 the British Government was looking to work with its Irish counterpart in reaching a solution. This was reaffirmed in the Anglo-Irish Agreement of 1985. There was further recognition during the various stages of the *peace process* leading up to the talks that concluded in April 1998 of the benefits of international involvement, particularly the American dimension. This undoubtedly added an external perspective, as well as valuable diplomatic skills, that aided proceedings. It also provided some additional input into what could be an unbalanced equation. As noted already, Nationalists in Northern Ireland have looked to the Irish Government for support, whereas the British Government has seen its role as trying to hold the ring, not favouring any particular party or community.

The composition of the Northern Ireland parties involved in the talks, in particular the participation of parties seen as politically extreme, has varied over the years. The Belfast Agreement was significant in that, unlike previous discussions leading to Agreements, elected representatives from Sinn Féin and the two Loyalist political parties (the Progressive Unionist Party (PUP) and the Ulster Democratic Party (UDP)) were an integral part of the talks. On the other hand, the DUP were not present on that occasion. They did, however, attend the crucial talks at St Andrews in 2006 that led both to further political agreement and finally to Sinn Féin's support for policing.

Richard Haass, President of the US Council on Foreign Relations and, from 2001 to 2008, US Envoy to the Northern Ireland Peace Process, in the *Irish Times* of 23 November 2012, with reference to a recent ceasefire agreement between Israel and Hamas brokered by Egypt and the US, argued:

'However, there is a big difference between a truce that is an interlude between rounds of fighting and one that presages a promising political process. It might take a willingness to learn from Northern Ireland, of all places, to tip the scales towards the latter.

Decades of violence – "the Troubles" – set the backdrop to negotiations. Success had its roots in British policy. London's objective was to end the terrorism and bring about a political settlement.

Doing so required persuading the Provisional IRA that it would never be able to shoot or bomb its way into power and that there was a political path open to it that would satisfy some of its goals and many of its supporters, if it would act responsibly...'

In the end Gerry Adams and Martin McGuinness – the leaders of Northern Ireland's Hamas equivalent – met the British challenge ...

References

The Sunningdale Communiqué, 9 December 1973

The Conflict Archive on the Internet (CAIN), University of Ulster

Report of the Work of the Police Authority 1970–81

The Downing Street Declaration, 15 December 1993

Report of the Consultative Group on the Past, 23 January 2009

Powell, Jonathan, *Great Hatred, Little Room, Making Peace in Northern Ireland*, The Bodley Head, London, 2008

Patterson, Henry, *Ireland's Violent Frontier*, Palgrave Macmillan, London, 2013

Appendix 1.A

Extracts from the Text of the 20 Point Sunningdale Communiqué published on 9 December 1973:

'12. *The Conference also discussed the question of policing and the need to ensure public support for and identification with the police throughout the whole community. It was agreed that no single set of proposals would achieve these aims overnight and that time would be necessary. The Conference expressed the hope that the wide range of agreement that had been reached and the consequent formation of a power-sharing Executive would make a major contribution to the creation of an atmosphere throughout the community where there would be widespread support for and identification with all the institutions of Northern Ireland.*

13. It was broadly accepted that the two parts of Ireland are to a considerable extent inter-dependent in the whole field of law and order, and the problems of political violence and identification with the Police Service cannot be solved without taking account of that fact.

14. Accordingly the British Government stated that, as soon as the security problems were resolved and the new institutions were seen to be working effectively, they would wish to discuss the devolution of responsibility for normal policing and how this might be achieved with the Northern Ireland Executive and the Police.

15. With a view to improving policing throughout the island and developing community identification with and support for the police services, the Governments concerned will cooperate under the auspices of a Council of Ireland through their respective police authorities. To this end, the Irish Government would set up a Police Authority, appointments to which would be made after consultation with the Council of Ministers of the Council of Ireland. In the case of the Northern Ireland Police Authority, appointments would be made after consultation with the Northern Ireland Executive, which would consult with the Council of Ministers of the Council of Ireland. When the two

Police Authorities are constituted, they will make their own arrangements to achieve the objectives set out above.

16. An independent complaints procedure for dealing with complaints against the Police will be set up.

17. The Secretary of State for Northern Ireland will set up an all-party Committee from the Assembly to examine how best to introduce effective policing throughout Northern Ireland with particular reference to the need to achieve public identification with the Police.'

CHAPTER TWO

A New Beginning
to Policing in Northern Ireland –
The Report of The Independent Commission
On Policing For Northern Ireland

2.1 Introduction

The Independent Commission On Policing For Northern Ireland (the Independent Commission) was set up on 3 June 1998. The Chairman was the Right Honourable Christopher Patten, and the Commission's report, referred to in this chapter as 'the Report', is therefore commonly referred to as the Patten Report. There were in all eight members of the Commission, who provided a blend of practical policing expertise, familiarity with the issues in Northern Ireland, and academic understanding of critical concepts. Three members were appointed from overseas. (The full list of membership is at Appendix 2.A below.)

From the beginning the Commission signalled its intention to conduct the review both inclusively and comprehensively. The Commission, either collectively or individually, sought to meet all those who wished to make representations. In October 1998 the Commission began taking oral submissions in public meetings and then held a series of open meetings in each of the 26 District Council areas in Northern Ireland. The level of consultation was unprecedented – in all, more than 10,000 people attended the public meetings and around 2,500 individual written submissions were received. A survey was carried out of public attitudes to policing. The Commission visited the Garda Síochána in the Republic of Ireland and a number of police services in Great Britain, Canada, South Africa, Spain and the United States, as well as attending the Council of Europe in Strasbourg.

The Report of the Independent Commission was published on 9 September 1999. The work of the Independent Commission did not, of course, take place in a vacuum. There were developments affecting both the *peace process* and the *political process* over the 15 months of its existence. For example, a fortnight after the Independent Commission held its first meeting, elections were held for the Northern Ireland Assembly. On 15 August 1998 a bomb exploded in Omagh, killing 29 civilians and two unborn babies; it was Northern Ireland's worst terrorist atrocity. Responsibility was claimed by the Real IRA. The following month saw the first releases of paramilitary prisoners from the Maze prison under the terms of the Belfast Agreement. In November the Police (Northern Ireland) Act 1998 was enacted, setting up the Police Ombudsman's Office. In an interview on the BBC on 31 January 1999 the Chief Constable, Sir Ronnie Flanagan, said that

'When we see, as we're seeing, a significant change in the environment in which we operate, then of course there should be a significant change in the way we go about our business.'

It was not, however, until November 1999 that David Trimble and Seamus Mallon were appointed as First and deputy First Minister respectively, and the first power-sharing Northern Ireland Executive took office. This delay reflected some of the challenges that were still inherent in the *political process* at that time.

It is possible to summarise the main strands in the Report in a number of different ways. Writing more recently, Professor Clifford Shearing, in his essay in *Policing The Narrow Ground*, has highlighted three themes – the symbolically charged issues, conventional good policing, and the governance of policing. The Independent Commission's Report itself identified some seven different strands – the purpose of policing; police accountability; policing with the community; the structure and composition of the police; recruitment and training, along with the culture and ethos of the police service; relationships with other police services; and arrangements for overseeing the programme of change in policing arrangements in Northern Ireland. The Report concluded with 175 recommendations.

The Independent Commission saw the importance of the interrelationship between policing and politics:

'There is plainly a close relationship between the success of the overall *agreement and changes in policing. If the fresh start for politics founders, it will be more difficult to make changes in policing; and if changes in policing are resisted (or mishandled) then there could be a serious impact on the attempt to rebuild democratic politics in Northern Ireland.*' (Independent Commission Report, paragraph 1.7)

In Chapter One the Report set out the principles recorded in the Belfast Agreement and went on to state that '*these principles provided the benchmark against which we have tested all our proposals*'. The specific tests that the Independent Commission applied were:

' • *Does this proposal promote effective and efficient policing?*

• *Will it deliver fair and impartial policing, free from partisan control?*

• *Does it provide for accountability, both to the law and to the community?*

• *Will it make the police more representative of the society they serve?*

• *Does it protect and vindicate the human rights and human dignity of all?*'
  (Paragraph 1.10)

The Report emphasised that

'*The word that has occurred over and over again is accountability – police accountability to the law and the community. ... It is their task to uphold the rule of law, exercising their independent professional judgement in doing so... But the proper assertion of independence should not imply the denial of accountability. ... The debate about accountability has a particular resonance in Northern Ireland.*' (Paragraph 1.12)

The Report continued:

'*We make proposals for a new structure of accountability which should ensure effective and democratically based oversight of policing and the creation of a close partnership between the police and every local community.*' (Paragraph 1.15)

In the same chapter the Independent Commission made the point that policing should be a collective community responsibility: a partnership for community safety. Community policing should become the core function of the police. The Independent Commission made clear (in paragraph 1.17) that it was convinced that policing with the community was the best way to provide *'a new beginning'* for policing in Northern Ireland. It recognised that real community policing was not possible if the composition of the police service bore little relationship to the composition of the community as a whole. The Report noted that Anita Hazenberg, a Dutch police officer directing the 'Police and Human Rights' programme at the Council of Europe, had claimed that *'in no country in this world is the composition of the police representative of the society'*.

Two key statements begin Chapter Four of the Report:

'It is a central proposition of this report that the fundamental purpose of policing should be, in the words of the Agreement, the protection and vindication of the human rights of all.'

'There should be no conflict between human rights and policing. Policing means protecting human rights.'

The Report emphasised that human rights are not an impediment to effective policing but, on the contrary, vital to its achievement. While the Report made a number of specific recommendations relating to a comprehensive programme of action and a new code of ethics, training and monitoring of performance under this heading, it stressed that this human rights-based approach was more a matter of the philosophy of policing and should be seen as the core of the report.

It is interesting to reflect that this Report came at a time when the impact on policing of the Human Rights Act 1998 had barely been addressed by the police in the United Kingdom. On the other hand, some work had begun internationally, particularly under the auspices of the Council of Europe and in North America, on studying the relationship between human rights and policing.

2.2   Accountability

Chapters Five and Six of the Report in particular dealt with the critical issue of accountability. Here, unlike in the rest of the Report, there was an initial analysis of the past and present position. The

Report emphasised that there were many aspects to accountability, but stressed that accountability should run through the bloodstream of the whole body of a police service. Here, too, for the first time, the important proposition, especially in the context of Northern Ireland, that policing was not a task for the police alone was explicitly stated.

The Report noted the inadequacy of the then current tripartite arrangement involving the Secretary of State, a Police Authority (appointed by the Secretary of State, rather than consisting of elected representatives), and the Chief Constable. It pointed out that the Secretary of State exercised direct influence over the police, not least through direct links with the Chief Constable and through setting the annual policing budget. Importantly, the Report also brought out the lack of transparency, noting, for example, that while Police Authorities in Britain met in public, the Northern Ireland Police Authority did not, and that the annual Policing Plan produced by the Police Authority was not a costed plan.

An interesting perspective is provided by Dr Gerald Lynch in the book *Policing the Narrow Ground*; in a chapter on human rights and police reform he pointed out, in New York, regular historical examples of the inability of American law enforcement to police itself and noted that an independent civic commission had needed to be set up every 20 to 25 years during the 20th century to deal with police corruption scandals there. One of the key safeguards that he advocated (returned to below) was higher education for all police officers.

The Independent Commission Report was clear:

'We recommend that an entirely new Policing Board be created, to replace the present Police Authority.'

'We recommend that the statutory primary function of the Policing Board should be to hold the Chief Constable and the police service publicly to account.' (Paragraphs 6.2 and 6.3)

The Report's basic approach to the simplification of the tripartite arrangement was that the Secretary of State (or the appropriate Minister after devolution of policing) should set long-term governmental objectives, the Policing Board should set medium-term objectives and priorities, and the police should develop the short-term tactical plans for delivering those objectives. The Board should be responsible for adopting an Annual Policing Plan, developed by the Chief Constable through a process of discussion with the Board on the basis of objectives and priorities set by the Board and within the agreed three- to five-year strategy. Moreover the Board, not the Department, should be responsible for negotiating the annual policing budget, which it should then allocate to the Chief Constable, subsequently monitoring police performance against both the Annual Policing Plan and the budget.

The Policing Board should have responsibility for appointing all chief officers and their civilian equivalents. In addition, the Board should have the power to call upon the Chief Constable and other chief officers to retire in the interests of efficiency and effectiveness, subject to the approval of the Secretary of State (and successor after devolution).

The Report emphasised that the Commission's selection of the title 'Policing Board' was deliberate. The role of the body was to go beyond supervision of the police service itself, extending to the wider issues of policing and the contributions that people and organisations other than the police could make towards public safety. It recommended that the Policing Board should coordinate closely with a wide range of other agencies affecting public safety. The Commission had in mind not only arrangements being established in Britain but also those that existed in other countries, such as the Netherlands, which had a system of Community Safety Plans.

The Report then addressed the membership of the Board. The Commission members were clear that the Board would be *vital to the new beginning for policing and to the success of all the new policing arrangements recommended*'. They recommended a 19-person Board, of whom the majority – that is, 10 – should be Assembly members drawn from the parties that comprised the new Northern Ireland Executive. The *Political Members* could not at the same time be holding ministerial office in the Executive. The other nine members should be selected from a range of different fields – including business, trade unions, voluntary organisations, community groups, and the legal profession – with the aim of finding a group of individuals representative of the community as a whole. These *Independent Members* were to be appointed by the Secretary of State in consultation with the First Minister and the deputy First Minister. The Report noted that '*the first chairman of the Board will be a crucial figure, and a key determinant of whether the new Board rises to the challenge of the extensive reform programme set out in this report'* (Paragraph 6.14).

The first Chair was to be appointed by the Secretary of State to serve for four years, thereafter being elected by the Board.

The Report recommended that responsibility for policing be devolved to the Northern Ireland Executive as soon as possible, except in matters of national security. (Interestingly, the Commission did not seek to define 'national security' in the Report. There was then and still remains no legal definition of this term in United Kingdom legislation.) The Commission also recommended strongly that the powers of the Policing Board should in no way be diminished at the point of devolution.

At paragraphs 6.19 to 6.24 the Report addressed the important issue of operational independence. The Commission noted that it was not to be found or defined in any legislation, but was clear that the scrutiny of the police should not be impeded by any assertion that scrutiny was limited to matters outside the scope of operational independence. The Commission concluded that, in a democratic society,

'All public officials must be fully accountable to the institutions of that society for the due performance of their functions, and a chief of police cannot be an exception.'

The Report stated a preference for the term operational responsibility instead. This they defined as meaning that it was the Chief Constable's right and duty to take operational decisions, and that neither the Government nor the Policing Board should have the right to direct the Chief Constable as to how to conduct an operation. However, the Chief Constable's conduct of an operational matter should not be exempted from inquiry or review <u>after</u> the event. The Report recommended that the Policing Board should have the power to require the Chief Constable to report on any issue pertaining to the performance of his functions or those of the police service, with the obligation extending to explaining operational decisions. There were two important caveats: first, should the Chief Constable conclude that it was not appropriate for a report to be provided to the Board on a particular matter he could refer the question to the Secretary of State for a decision on whether the Board's requirement should stand; second, as in the rest of the United Kingdom, the Chief Constable's main accountability for the involvement of police in matters involving national security was to the Secretary of State rather than to the Policing Board.

The Report recommended that the Policing Board should meet in public once a month to receive a report from the Chief Constable. Further, it recommended that the Policing Board should have the power, on receipt of a report from the Chief Constable, to initiate an inquiry into any aspect of the police service or police conduct. The Board should also have the option to request the Police Ombudsman, the Inspectorate of Constabulary, or other bodies to conduct or contribute to such an inquiry.

2.3   District Policing Partnership Boards and Other Accountability Mechanisms

The Commission members were clear that policing should be decentralised and that there should be constant dialogue at local levels between the police and the community. They recommended that each District Council should establish a District Policing Partnership Board (DPPB) as a committee of the Council with a majority elected membership reflecting the political balance of the Council, with the remainder being independent members selected by the Council with the agreement of the Board. In Belfast the main DPPB was to have four geographical sub-groups. These Boards were to be coterminous with the police districts and correspondingly the 26 District Council areas. The Report noted that if the Assembly were to reduce the number of Councils the number of DPPBs should reduce correspondingly. The function of the DPPBs should be *advisory, explanatory and consultative*. They should represent the consumer, voice the concerns of citizens, and monitor the performance of the police in their Districts. They should be encouraged to see policing in its widest sense. There should be monthly public meetings with the police District Commander at which the police should present reports and answer questions. Additionally, the Report recommended that District Councils should have the power to contribute up to three pence in the pound towards the improved policing of the district, which could enable the DPPB to purchase additional services from the police or other statutory agencies, or the private sector. The Policing Board should maintain regular contact with the DPPBs through annual conferences, training courses and the provision of information.

The Report also considered the position of the Police Ombudsman. It contained a number of recommendations designed to strengthen the position of the Ombudsman beyond that set out in the previous report written by one of the Commissioners, Dr Maurice Hayes, in 1996 and enshrined in the Police (Northern Ireland) Act 1998. Importantly, one recommendation was that the Ombudsman should exercise the power to initiate enquiries or investigations even if no specific complaint had been received. The Ombudsman should also exercise the right to investigate and comment on police policies and practices where these were perceived to give rise to difficulties, even if the conduct of individual officers might not itself be culpable, and should draw any such observations to the attention of the Chief Constable and the Policing Board.

The chapter concluded with a section on covert policing, stressing that there should be much more comprehensive independent and local scrutiny of this important and sensitive area of policing.

2.4   Policing with the Community

The Report then addressed the important issue of the style of policing, noting that developments in the security situation could inevitably impact on the pace of progress. The Commission defined policing with the community as:

'The police working in partnership with the community; the community thereby participating in its own policing; and the two working together, mobilising resources to solve problems affecting public safety over the longer term rather than the police, alone, reacting short term to incidents as they occur.' (Paragraph 7.3)

The Report emphasised that the partnership that this entailed amounted to a profound shift in both police and community thinking. The structure of the police service should be organised so that neighbourhood policing was at the core of police work. The District headquarters and the specialist units should exist to support the neighbourhood teams, rather than the other way around. In short, it recommended that *'policing with the community should be the core function of the police service and the core function of every police station'* (Paragraph 7.9).

Members of neighbourhood policing teams should serve in the locality for longer, where practicable patrolling on foot, and should be trained in problem-solving techniques.

The Commission recognised that they could not at that time say that Northern Ireland had been transformed into a peaceful society. The Report contained a number of recommendations designed to normalise policing, relating to the appearance of police stations, the replacement of armoured Land Rovers with unarmed vehicles, the reduction of the role of Army support for the civil power, the closure of the three historic police holding centres, and the goal of moving towards a routinely unarmed police service.

The Commission addressed the particular sensitivities of public order policing in Northern Ireland, noting the challenge that it posed, particularly during the marching season, and the impact that it could have on relations between the police and the differing communities. The Report highlighted the use of plastic baton rounds as the most controversial aspect of public order policing. While making clear that the Commission did not wish to see a situation in which the police would have no choice but to resort to live rounds sooner than would be the case under the then arrangements, the Commission recommended that *'an immediate and substantial investment be made in a research programme to find an acceptable, effective and less potentially lethal alternative to the plastic baton round (PBR)'* (Paragraph 9.15).

The Report noted the initiatives being taken in developing non-lethal weaponry alternatives in America, particularly at Pennsylvania State University and the National Institute of Justice in Washington. It recommended that the use of plastic baton rounds (PBRs) be reported to the Policing Board and to the Police Ombudsman.

2.5 Human Resources Issues

The next section of the Report dealt with how the existing police service should be restructured to deliver the new style of policing. It recognised the scale of the challenge, which affected virtually all aspects of management and personnel, information technology, the structure of the organisation (including the support staff), the size of the service and – crucially – its composition, recruitment, and training. The Report again stressed the need for devolution and empowerment of local management, allied to greater internal accountability.

The Report recommended that there should be one District Command for each District Council area (although it recognised that this would make some commands unusually small). It recommended a slimmer-structured headquarters, including the bringing together of Special Branch and Crime Branch under the command of a single Assistant Chief Constable. There should be a substantial reduction in the number of officers engaged in security work in this new command, and officers should not spend such long periods in this work as before. The Report recommended that the future police service should not include a Full Time Reserve, but that there should be an enlarged Part Time Reserve.

The Commission considered at some length the appropriate size of the police service for Northern Ireland. The Report recommended that:

'*Provided the peace process does not collapse and the security situation does not deteriorate significantly from the situation pertaining at present, the approximate size of the police service over the next 10 years should be 7,500 full time officers.*'

It stressed that this figure was approximate, and that arrival at it was not a precise science, although the Commission said that they would find it difficult to justify a much higher figure.

The Report recommended an early retirement or severance package be offered to regular officers and Full Time Reservists aged 50 or above, including a generous lump sum payment and pension enhancement. They also recommended enhanced terms for officers leaving the service before the age of 50. Early retirement was to be on a voluntary basis. The Report contained some models of the changing size of the service, although it was not absolutely prescriptive about the number of officers who should leave each year and the number of their replacements.

The Report contained some controversial recommendations as to the composition of the police service. It stressed that real community policing was impossible if the composition of the service bore little relationship to the composition of the community as a whole, although it made clear that this was not a matter of having Catholic police officers to police Catholic people – that would be an unhealthy balkanisation of policing. The point was that communities as a whole should see themselves as having a stake in the police service as a whole. It was the imbalance between the number of Catholics/Nationalists and Protestants/Unionists which was the most striking problem in the composition of the RUC, the Report stated. It did not set a target for the proportion of women officers, noting rather the encouraging level of female interest in police work.

The Report recommended that the police should contract out the recruitment of both police officers and civilians into the police service, with the involvement of lay community representatives on recruitment panels. It recommended that:

'All candidates for the police service should continue to be required to reach a specified standard of merit in the selection procedure. Candidates reaching the standard should then enter a pool from which the required number of recruits can be drawn. An equal number of Protestants and Catholics should be drawn from the pool of qualified candidates.'

The Report also recommended lateral entry of experienced officers from other police services and secondments or recruitments from non-police organisations, stating that any police service can benefit from the infusion of diverse talent and experience from elsewhere.

In the section on training (at paragraph 16.4) the Report provided a useful summary of the objectives it set out:

'• *a police service dedicated to the protection of human rights and respect for human dignity;*

• *a police service that is accountable, responsive, communicative and transparent;*

• *a new policing style based on partnerships with the community;*

- *a decentralised police service with decision-making responsibilities devolved to beat teams and to district commanders;*
- *more flexible management and personnel practices.'*

The Report stressed that these objectives need to be matched by a training, education, and development strategy for both recruits and existing officers. One specific recommendation was that Northern Ireland police should have a new purpose-built police college the funding for which should be found in the next public spending round. Ideally, the college would have links with a university. Community awareness training should be integrated into all aspects of training. All existing members of the service were to take a course dedicated to enabling them to understand the impact of the new constitutional and policing arrangements and the reforms of the criminal justice system, as well as human rights issues. There should be some joint training with members of the Policing Board or DPPBs.

2.6 Culture, Ethos, and Symbols

Although contained in a short chapter nearly at the end of the Report, the recommendations relating to culture, ethos, and symbols proved highly controversial in the period after the publication of the Report, prior to the establishment of the Policing Board. The most significant recommendations (at paragraph 17.6) were as follows:

'• *while we have not accepted the argument that the Royal Ulster Constabulary should be disbanded, it should henceforth be named the Northern Ireland Police Service;*
- *the Northern Ireland Police Service adopt a new badge and symbols which are entirely free from any association with either the British or Irish states;*
- *the Union flag should no longer be flown from police buildings;*
- *on those occasions on which it is appropriate to fly a flag on police buildings, the flag flown should be that of the Northern Ireland Police Service and it, too, should be free from association with the British or Irish states.'*

The Report considered '*it important that the link between the Royal*

Ulster Constabulary (RUC) and the new Northern Ireland Police Service be recognised' and recommended that the colour of the current police uniform be retained, though the uniform itself should be updated. Memorials recording the dedication and sacrifice of officers of the RUC should remain in position. It was recommended, based in part on a cultural audit undertaken by the Commission, the maintenance of a neutral working environment should become an assessed management responsibility at all levels of management.

The Report contained a number of specific recommendations designed to enhance practical cooperation between the Northern Ireland Police Service and the Garda Síochána, as well as other GB services and police services overseas.

Finally, the Commission concluded that a new structure should be created to ensure that the recommendations in the Report were implemented comprehensively and faithfully. This was to be a mechanism to oversee the changes required of all those involved in the development of the new policing arrangements and to assure the community that the Report was being implemented. They recommended the appointment of an eminent person from a country other than the United Kingdom or Ireland as an oversight commissioner with responsibility for supervising the implementation of their recommendations. The Oversight Commissioner would report regularly on progress and make observations on the extent to which any failures or delays were the responsibility of the policing institutions themselves or due to matters beyond their control.

2.7   In Conclusion

Any review report inevitably reflects the composition of the team that produces it, the members' prior experience and expertise, and contemporaneous factors that may – or may not – prove ephemeral.

The Commission sought not to highlight the past or to attribute responsibility or blame, but to point the future direction. The Report explicitly recognised that the security situation in Northern Ireland was still evolving, and that future developments would directly impact both on the size of the service and in some respects on the style of its policing. They sought to build into the oversight mechanism an external monitoring function for that.

The Independent Commission's Report is remarkable as a comparatively succinct yet comprehensive blueprint for policing. There have been a number of assessments in recent years – for example, the international conference held in February 2007 hosted by the Police Service of Northern Ireland in partnership with the Northern Ireland Policing Board – of the extent to which the Report has stood the test of time. In the main, it has been judged to have done just that.

What are the areas where, with hindsight, it might have been preferable to take a different position? One concerns the dual role of the Policing Board in supporting the police service as well as holding it to account. This arguably fed through into a lack of clarity in the subsequent legislation which certainly was clearer on the accountability dimension.

Another point concerns the composition of the civilian element of the service. Unlike the recommendation in respect of police officers, the Commission did not advocate a 50:50 recruitment rule, and, while noting that the same principle of a balanced and representative workforce should apply, made no recommendation as to how that might be achieved. Nor was the Report costed or timetabled, save in a few areas. Given the scale of the change programme and its duration, the costs have been huge, almost certainly greater than the Commission or the Government appreciated at the time.

References

Doyle, John (ed.), *Policing the Narrow Ground, Lessons from the Transformation of Policing in Northern Ireland*, Royal Irish Academy, Dublin 2, Republic of Ireland, 2010

Appendix 2.A

The Membership of the Independent Commission on Policing

The Right Honourable Christopher Patten, formerly Governor of Hong Kong and a Cabinet Minister

Dr Maurice Hayes, a member of the Irish Senate and previously Northern Ireland Ombudsman and Permanent Secretary in the Northern Ireland Department of Health and Social Services

Dr Gerald Lynch, President of John Jay College of Criminal Justice, New York

Kathleen O'Toole, a career police officer, previously Massachusetts Secretary of Public Safety, and an administrator at Boston College

Professor Clifford Shearing, professor of criminology and sociology at the University of Toronto and a Professor within the School of Government at the University of the Western Cape

Sir John Smith, formerly Deputy Commissioner of the Metropolitan Police and a former Inspector of Constabulary

Mr Peter Smith QC, a barrister practising in Northern Ireland

Mrs Lucy Woods, former Chief Executive of British Telecom in Northern Ireland and BT Ireland

The secretary of the Commission was Mr Robert Pierce, of the Foreign and Commonwealth Office

From Publication of the Independent Commission's Report to the Establishment of the Northern Ireland Policing Board

3.1 Introduction

This chapter covers the two years from the publication of the Report of The Independent Commission On Policing For Northern Ireland (the Independent Commission) in September 1999 through to the establishment of the Northern Ireland Policing Board (the Policing Board or the Board) in October 2001. Both authors were directly involved in some of the key events during this time.

As before, to get a full understanding of the policing developments it is essential to consider the *political process* and the *peace process* at the same time. A number of strands, which provide the structure to this chapter, included:

- reactions to the publication of the Independent Commission's Report
- the British Government's legislation – the Police (Northern Ireland) Act 2000
- manifold discussions between the British Government and the political parties, some on a bilateral basis, but many also involving the Irish Government and representatives of the United States (US) Government
- contemporary political and security development
- steps taken by the Royal Ulster Constabulary (RUC) and the Northern Ireland Office (NIO) to establish and then take forward a major change programme
- the establishment of the Northern Ireland Policing Board

3.2   Reactions to the Publication of the Independent Commission's Report

Within Northern Ireland, there were three main responses to the publication of the Independent Commission's Report in September 1999. In summary, the British Government welcomed the Report and undertook to implement the recommendations; the Unionist parties were vehemently critical of a number of aspects of the Report; while the Nationalist parties commented that certain parts of the Report did not go far enough. The Irish Government in general reflected the position of the Nationalist parties and mostly sided with them in pressing the British Government to implement the recommendations in full. Representatives of the US Government also welcomed the Report and encouraged the British Government on implementation, while recognising the sensitivities and challenges that both intrinsic and external events posed.

Perhaps the most quoted response to the Report's publication came from David (now Lord) Trimble, then the Leader of the Ulster Unionist Party (UUP). In particular, he described the Report as 'flawed and shoddy'. As Independent Commission member Peter Smith QC has pointed out in his essay in *Policing the Narrow Ground*, in practice this criticism was directed principally at a handful of the 175 recommendations, in particular those relating to:

'The re-naming and re-badging of the Royal Ulster Constabulary to remove references to the British state, and to positive discrimination in the recruitment of Catholics in order to redress the existing religious imbalance of the Royal Ulster Constabulary in favour of Protestant.'

Smith goes on to say that he was 'shocked and puzzled' by Trimble's outburst. He saw it as inevitable that, if the objectives set out in the Commission's terms of reference were to be achieved, the British connotations of the name and badge of the RUC would have to go. (Dean Godson's *Himself Alone – David Trimble and the Ordeal of Unionism* and Frank Millar's *David Trimble – The Price of Peace* both contain further commentary on Trimble's position.) There was also criticism of Ken (now Lord) Maginnis's input as the UUP's policing spokesman. Virtually all shades of Unionist were united in the view that the Report failed to honour explicitly the 301 police officers killed at the hands of terrorists.

As pointed out above, on the Nationalist and Republican side there was criticism that the Report did not go far enough. As Clifford Shearing noted in his essay in *Policing the Narrow Ground*:

'Many on this side of the political divide, along with some academics, criticised the Patten Commission for not acting as a commission of inquiry and for not drawing conclusions about the rights and wrongs of the partisan conflict, and the role of the police in this conflict, which had characterised Northern Ireland for so long.'

It is important also to note the reaction of the RUC and the wider policing family. Here, too, there was criticism of the lack of recognition of the sacrifices made by them throughout the Troubles, and in some cases this overshadowed the more measured reflection that many of the Report's recommendations followed through on the approach taken in the RUC's own Fundamental Review, led by Ronnie Flanagan in 1995/96.

It can be seen already that there was a certain irony in one of the key conclusions reached by the Independent Commission, namely that policing should no longer be a *'political football'* in Northern Ireland. For, indeed, that was precisely what the Report became, both in itself as a hotly contested nexus of issues that caused division between the political parties (and indeed, to an extent, between the British and Irish Governments) and more widely in acting as a lightning rod for fundamental political differences.

It is essential to appreciate the degree of controversy over policing throughout the two years after the publication of the Independent Commission's Report running up to the establishment of the Policing Board. That it was so bitterly contested makes the subsequent success of the Board so noteworthy. It was all the more remarkable given contemporary security issues and the fact that, for many months of its existence, the Board was the only cross-community body consisting of elected (and independent) representatives that was functioning effectively at a time when the Northern Ireland Executive had been suspended by the British Government.

3.3   The British Government's Legislation

As noted above, the British Government had welcomed the Independent Commission's Report and had undertaken to implement its recommendations. It was constitutionally clear from the beginning that to do this would require a major piece of legislation – that is, a Parliamentary Bill at Westminster dealing with Northern Ireland policing exclusively. This was of itself slightly contentious, as a previous Bill making significant changes to Northern Ireland policing had been taken through Parliament as recently as 1998. It should also be noted that, in 2000, although it still had a very large majority in the House of Commons, the Labour administration did not command a majority in the House of Lords if the Opposition parties and enough cross-benchers voted against the Government's proposals. Moreover, there were close historical ties between the Conservative Party and the UUP. This meant that, notwithstanding the avowedly bilateral approach towards Northern Ireland traditionally adopted by the main parties throughout the Troubles, the Conservatives would be briefed by the Unionists and could be likely to adopt their approach on specific issues during the Bill's passage through Parliament. Moreover, the Liberal Democrat spokespersons in the House of Lords, while broadly supportive of the Government's overall stance on Northern Ireland, had some distinctive views on specific policing issues which meant that their support could not be taken for granted.

The process of preparing legislation is a traditional one. Once space is found in the Parliamentary timetable for legislation Government officials draw up instructions for the Parliamentary Counsel, based in Whitehall. On all the main issues and points of sensitivity officials will put up written submissions to Ministers to ensure that they are complying with Ministers' wishes. The instructions are themselves prepared, in line with Ministerial guidance, in liaison with the Departmental legal advisers. Then the legal advisers communicate with Counsel, passing the draft legislation as prepared by Counsel back to the officials and then, in turn, passing on to Counsel the officials' comments on the draft legislation. This fairly tortuous process places considerable weight both on getting the original instructions right and on the ability of Counsel to understand the political nuances and draft the legislation accordingly. Westminster legislation is not a vehicle well suited for enshrining the 'constructive ambiguity' that has so often been the outcome of political negotiations in Northern Ireland.

The Police (Northern Ireland) Act 2000 was introduced as a Bill in Parliament in spring of that year and not enacted until 23 November 2000, by which time a considerable amount of water had flowed under the proverbial bridge. As subsequent sections of this chapter demonstrate, the progress of the Bill and changes to its contents directly reflected not only discussions with political parties and other key players on policing matters but also wider developments such as the political pressure being experienced by David Trimble and his followers.

Clifford Shearing made the point that:

'The Bill brought before Parliament in early 2000 to set up the framework for the implementation of the Patten Report proved to be a far cry from what the Report had recommended... This was reversed to some degree by the time the Bill was enacted; in effect, once this gap between rhetoric and action became the subject of rigorous political debate.'

In some ways, the most controversial clause of the entire Bill was what became the very first clause, headed 'Name of the Police in Northern Ireland'. The Independent Commission had recommended (recommendation 150) that *'while the Royal Ulster Constabulary should not be disbanded, it should henceforth be named the Northern Ireland Police Service'*. This would have been abbreviated to the acronym NIPS, which was already appropriated by the Northern Ireland Prison Service. The controversy related not to the choice of the title 'Police Service of Northern Ireland' – often abbreviated to 'PSNI' – but to the legislative means of providing for moving from the RUC in a way that did not mean its disbandment but nevertheless complied with the Independent Commission's recommendation. Ken Maginnis, on behalf of the UUP, and Seamus Mallon, then deputy leader of the Social Democratic and Labour Party (SDLP), were key protagonists. The wording that was finally enshrined in section 1 of the Act, which owed a good deal to Ken Maginnis, effectively contained both the long and the short title for the new Service, with the former being set out in section 1(1), namely *'the body of constables known as the Royal Ulster*

Constabulary shall continue in being as the Police Service of Northern Ireland (incorporating the Royal Ulster Constabulary)'.

In essence, the Bill had passed its Commons stages by the summer recess in 2000, leaving the Lords for the autumn. It was not always the same issues that exercised their Lordships' minds. The Liberal Democrats probed particularly the tripartite structure and the role of the Policing Board, drawing on experience with Police Authorities in England and Wales. The contentious matter of 50:50 recruitment proved particularly hard-fought, with the Government securing a bare majority in the upper House.

As noted above, the Bill had been significantly amended by the end of its journey through Parliament. Nevertheless, the SDLP remained determined that further policing legislation was required to bring the provisions more closely into line with the Independent Commission's Report. For their part, the UUP would continue to oppose the renewal of the 50:50 arrangements at the three-yearly reconsideration.

3.4   Discussions With Interested Parties

Peter Mandelson MP had succeeded Mo Mowlam MP as Secretary of State for Northern Ireland in October 1999. He remained in this post until his resignation on 24 January 2001, when he was succeeded by Dr John Reid MP. Mandelson was thus at the helm throughout the key period for the shaping of the legislation and its passage through Parliament. He was rare in having a grasp of the detailed subject matter as well as a clear appreciation of strategy. Although Jane Kennedy MP was the Northern Ireland Office (NIO) Security Minister with responsibility for policing, it was Mr Mandelson who took the key decisions, directly involving himself in the many discussions with the Northern Ireland political parties and others. His interpretation of the interaction of politics and policing had a direct impact on not only the shape but also the content of the legislation and the Government's approach to implementation of the Independent Commission's Report. His capacity for attention to detail can be illustrated by two small anecdotes: on one day no less than eight submissions on different aspects of policing were put forward to the Secretary of State by the Patten Action Team, while he even took a close interest in the colour and design of the cover page for the Updated Implementation Plan.

In the SDLP, its then deputy leader, Seamus Mallon, and its justice spokesman, Alex Attwood, were regular interlocutors. They constituted the powerful combination of a deep understanding of the broad Nationalist position on policing and a forensic focus on the detail in the Independent Commission's Report and the developing legislation. It was certainly unusual for there to be so much discussion about the contents of a Bill away from Westminster (in Northern Ireland), and although the discussion at the meetings was often 'frank and robust' – that is, ending (if not starting) in a row – they did undoubtedly have an impact on the final shape of the 2000 Police Act.

At this time Seamus Mallon was the deputy First Minister. The regular disagreements with the Northern Ireland Secretary of State on policing matters cannot have helped either the relationship of the Executive with the British Government or indeed the internal dynamics of Mr Mallon's relationship with the First Minister, David Trimble. On the other hand, the SDLP were being asked, as the then leading Nationalist grouping in Northern Ireland in electoral terms, to sign up to participating in policing, the first time such a body would have done since the creation of the Northern Ireland State in 1922. The SDLP were very conscious of the electoral threat posed by Sinn Féin and the extent to which this totemic issue could alter forever the balance of power between the two Nationalist parties.

In the period between the publication of the Independent Commission's Report and the establishment of the Policing Board there were two main phases. During the first the focus was largely – though not exclusively – on the legislation. In the second, as closely contested as the first, the debate with the Northern Ireland parties and indeed others revolved largely around the revised Implementation Plan and the broader *political* and *peace processes*. In the first phase it was the SDLP that took the lead on behalf of Nationalism, although Peter Mandelson and the Northern Ireland Office did seek to reach out to other representatives, such as the Roman Catholic hierarchy. Indeed, the SDLP shared their critique with Sinn Féin as well as with the Irish Government.

Although the discussions with the SDLP covered many aspects of implementation of the Independent Commission's Report, there were a number of topics that particularly engaged them. Foremost among these was the tripartite relationship ('*the Policing Authority, the Chief Constable and central government share responsibilities*'). The SDLP argued powerfully that the Policing Board should be given explicitly as powerful a role as set out in the Report, and was concerned lest the British Government might seek to interfere in policing beyond its remit in the period prior to the eventual devolution of policing and justice. Other iconic issues for the SDLP included the closure of the three holding centres (Strand Road, Gough Barracks and Castlereagh), the role and position of Special Branch, inquiries, and the role of the Police Ombudsman.

The UUP had far fewer discussions on policing matters with Northern Ireland Office Ministers or officials, although there was nevertheless a degree of contact outside the Westminster context. The greater importance for the development of the policing proposals lay in the wider political situation. During the early summer of 2000 David Trimble was under severe pressure from members of his own party. It seemed quite possible that the 'power-sharing' Executive could fall. As Secretary of State, Peter Mandelson was determined to avoid this if at all possible. It was this factor that led to the approach in the Police Bill that was seen as a watering down or even a 'gutting' of Patten, as it was described by some external critics. These changes were not due to some perfidy on the part of British Government Ministers or – as has been alleged by some academics – reluctance on the part of Northern Ireland Office officials, commonly referred to as '*securocrats*', to give up their power over the police in Northern Ireland. They were principally a political calculation by the then Northern Ireland Secretary of State, ultimately supported by the Prime Minister, as to what was required at least in the short term to maintain stability in the institutions that were still so newly established in Northern Ireland.

Sinn Féin's first serious engagement with the British Government on policing matters, given their MPs' abstention from Westminster debates, took place at a different level in January 2001. There was to be a meeting with the Prime Minister, Tony Blair, at Chequers, and the day before Sinn Féin presented the Northern Ireland Office with a list of 20 'demands' in relation to policing. While he had taken considerable interest in the progress of implementation of the Independent Commission's Report, this was probably the Prime Minister's first excursion into the minutiae of the out-working. As a barrister, he demonstrated his ability to grasp the salient points of the brief swiftly and to put that position across articulately. He could also appreciate where there might be scope for give or manoeuvre. This particular session at Chequers also involved representatives of the Irish Government and the US Consul General in Belfast.

At this stage, unlike the SDLP, Sinn Féin was not so exercised about the policing institutions. For them, ending the use of plastic baton rounds was always a core issue.

The Irish Government had from the beginning taken a very close interest in the implementation of the Independent Commission's recommendations. Of course, their position was very similar to that of the SDLP; as the process developed, their relationship with Sinn Féin on policing issues was more ambivalent. Brian Cowen was then the Republic of Ireland's Minister for Foreign Affairs, and it was the Department of Foreign Affairs rather than the Department of Justice that took the lead on policing in Northern Ireland. Department of Foreign Affairs officials were well briefed and engaged closely in discussions with Northern Ireland Office officials and Ministers on all aspects of implementation, from the legislation through to the establishment of the Policing Board.

3.5   Political and Security Developments

July 2001 was a seminal period for the progress of policing in Northern Ireland. The British and Irish Governments held 'intensive' discussions over several days with the UUP, the SDLP, and Sinn Féin at Weston Park, a palatial country house in central England. The talks were adjourned over the 12 July 2001 Orange Parades which, incidentally but importantly, allowed for Northern Ireland Office officials to update Chief Constable Ronnie Flanagan before the talks were resumed.

Although policing was central to the Weston Park talks, the outcome was presented in a joint Northern Ireland Office/Department of Foreign Affairs text on 1 August 2001 as agreement on:

'The elements of a package which, we believe, will help deliver a full and early implementation of the Good Friday Agreement. The package covers all four

outstanding issues – policing, normalisation, the stability of the institutions and decommissioning.'

The text went on to say:

'*The outstanding issues relate to policing, the stability of the institutions, security normalisation and decommissioning. While each of these issues is best addressed in its own terms, rather than being seen as a precondition for progress on any other, the Agreement can only succeed if all parts of it are implemented together.'*

The document contained five paragraphs on policing which are set out at Appendix 3.A below. The key issues identified concerned a commitment by the British Government to publish a revised Implementation Plan; the Oversight Commissioner (Tom Constantine, who had been appointed in June 2000) being asked to review the new arrangements in the light of experience gained during the first year of the Policing Board's operation; and a commitment by the British Government to introduce further legislation '*to amend or clarify some provisions to reflect more fully the Patten recommendations'* and to set up the Police Fund and the Royal Ulster Constabulary George Cross Foundation. On this basis, the British Government would invite the parties to nominate *Political Members* to the new Policing Board and complete the process for the selection of *Independent Members*, so that the Board would be established by the end of September 2001.

The text demonstrates the efforts by the British Government to deal even-handedly between the two main traditions in Northern Ireland. Thus, for example, the range of commitments designed to reassure Nationalist representatives, including the references to the closure of Gough holding centre, to Special Branch and to plastic baton rounds is offset against references to the Police Fund (the way to which had now been cleared by the separate report by John Steele) and the Royal Ulster Constabulary George Cross Foundation.

Paragraph 18 of the document, although not directly related to policing, demonstrated once again how any attempt to move forward in Northern Ireland is inevitably challenged by the past, and how, without efforts to address the past, the Nationalist parties were unwilling to participate in the new policing arrangements. It is worth setting out here in full:

'Both Governments want the new policing arrangements now being estab-lished to focus on the future. But they also accept that certain cases from the past remain a source of great public concern, particularly those giving rise to serious allegations of collusion by the security forces in each of our jurisdictions. Both Governments will therefore appoint a judge of international standing from outside both jurisdictions to undertake a thorough investigation of alle-gations of collusion in the cases of the murders of Chief Superintendent Harry Breen and Superintendent Bob Buchanan, Pat Finucane, Lord Justice and Lady Gibson, Robert Hamill, Rosemary Nelson and Billy Wright.'

What had led to Weston Park? Certainly, the instability of the polit-ical institutions was a central factor. While the Northern Ireland Executive had taken office in late November 1999, the institutions had been suspended by the British Government as early as February 2000. Decommissioning was the lightning rod through which political divi-sions were played out. David Trimble came under great pressure within his own party for the lack of tangible progress, notwithstanding, for example, the statement by the Provisional Irish Republican Army (PIRA) in May 2000 (which followed talks held by Tony Blair and Bertie Ahern with the political parties in Belfast) that included the clause that it would *'completely and verifiably put its arms beyond use'*. The Executive remained in a state of suspended animation, although the Assembly continued to sit. British Ministers were recalled to act as head of Northern Ireland Departments. On 7 June 2001 a United Kingdom General Election had further weakened the position of the UUP through gains made by the Democratic Unionist Party (DUP). On 1 July 2001 David Trimble announced that he was standing down as First Minister, with a stand-in for six weeks.

The document of 1 August 2001 was put to all the political parties who were at Weston Park along with a draft statement which the parties would issue in the event that the overall package was accept-able. Although there had been some frank discussions into the small hours at Weston Park, both Governments had reluctantly accepted that Sinn Féin were not prepared at this stage to endorse the new policing arrangements.

Notwithstanding the challenges that parts of the document were to pose in the following years this text, and the subsequent clarifications, did crucially pave the way for the setting up of the Policing Board on the basis that it not only ensured the participation of *Political Members* on the Board from the SDLP but also encouraged applications to serve as *Independent Members* from others of a Nationalist persuasion.

It was not, however, all plain sailing in terms of the *political process* or indeed the *peace process*. There were 'technical' suspensions of the Assembly by the British Government in August and September 2001, reflecting the continuing political uncertainty at Stormont. On 16 August 2001 three individuals closely linked to Sinn Féin were arrested by the authorities in Colombia. However, on 23 October 2001 Gerry Adams announced the first act of decommissioning by the Provisional IRA. Its political significance was demonstrated less than two weeks later by the re-election of David Trimble as First Minister.

3.6   Steps taken by the Royal Ulster Constabulary and the Northern Ireland Office in Preparation for the Change Programme

Under the leadership of Ronnie Flanagan the RUC had not been slow in making preparations for change. Specifically, a dedicated Change Management Team had been set up under the highly experienced Assistant Chief Constable Tim Lewis and initial consultancy support had been provided by Professor Andrew Kakabadse from the Cranfield School of Management. To provide continuity and to ensure liaison between the police and the Northern Ireland Office Chief Superintendent Sheamus Hamill, who had facilitated liaison with the Independent Commission, now provided a similar invaluable role for the Northern Ireland Office.

Both the RUC leadership and Northern Ireland Office Ministers were clear that it was important to press on with aspects of implementation consistent with the Independent Commission's Report prior to the formation of the Policing Board. In January 2001, after an open competition procurement exercise, Consensia, a consortium headed by Deloitte & Touche, was selected to run the new 50:50 recruitment programme. (Lay assessors to sit on the recruitment panels and independent community observers of the process were appointed subsequently.) Just a month later, on 23 February 2001, the first recruitment campaign to the new Police Service of Northern Ireland was launched. The terms of the early severance programme recommended by the Independent Commission had been published during the previous summer and the first 483 police officers to depart under the scheme had left the RUC by 31 March 2001. On 1 April 2001 26 newly appointed Police Service of Northern Ireland District Commanders took up post, based on the existing District Council areas. On the same date Special Branch and the Crime Department were brought together under one Assistant Chief Constable.

The Northern Ireland Office had, similarly, been taking legislative and administrative steps. As mentioned briefly above and set out fully in Chapter 17, Tom Constantine had been appointed in June 2000 as the Oversight Commissioner. He was not slow in appointing a supporting team, principally composed of colleagues with extensive experience in North America, and drawing up the detailed criteria against which they would assess progress in the implementation of the recommendations of the Independent Commission. The Commissioner's first report was published in January 2001; Al Hutchinson (a former Canadian senior police officer) was appointed as the Commissioner's Chief of Staff.

On 6 November 2000 the office of the Police Ombudsman came into operation, with Nuala O'Loan (later Baroness O'Loan) as the first Ombudsman. On the same date, new Police Unsatisfactory Performance Regulations came into force.

In July 2000, in line with a recommendation in the Independent Commission's Report, the British Government launched a research programme into less lethal public order equipment. On 2 April 2001 the first report of this group was published. It included a literature survey and a framework document for future research (as described in Chapter 11).

3.7   The Advent of the Northern Ireland Policing Board

The Police (Northern Ireland) Act 2000 contained the legislative basis for the Northern Ireland Policing Board. Part II of the Act dealt mainly with the role and powers of the Board. Section 2 provided that *'There shall be a body corporate to be known as the Northern Ireland Policing Board.'* Section 3 set out the general functions of the Policing Board (see Appendix 3.B below). Schedule 1 of the Act contained provisions for the appointment of the Board and its staffing, funding and procedural arrangements.

The administrative preparations for the establishment of the new cross-community Board were themselves a major undertaking. The work entailed the ending of the 30-year-old Police Authority and the selection of new premises. While the new body would, of course, be very different, it was clearly essential to provide continuity in areas where this mattered, in relation, for example, to individual cases being handled by the Police Authority, and finance. The Chairman of the Authority stepped down in advance of the transition and was succeeded on an interim basis by Professor Herbert Wallace. Credit is due to Members of the Authority and its officers for the arrangements they made in what were not always easy circumstances.

Early in 2001 applications were invited from members of the public to serve as *Independent Members* of the new Policing Board. PricewaterhouseCoopers were appointed by the Northern Ireland Office to assist in the selection process run by the Department on behalf of the Secretary of State, which involved shortlisting and extensive interviews. The Department separately introduced the Northern Ireland Policing Board (Prescribed Period) Regulations 2001, which came into effect on 2 February 2001, providing the arrangements for nominating *Political Members* of the Policing Board.

References

Doyle, John (ed.), *Policing the Narrow Ground, Lessons from the Transformation of Policing in Northern Ireland*, Royal Irish Academy, Dublin, 2010, Chapter 2, 'The Curious Case of the Patten Report', by Clifford D. Shearing, pp. 27, 28

Doyle, John (ed.), *Policing the Narrow Ground, Lessons from the*

Transformation of Policing in Northern Ireland, Royal Irish Academy, Dublin, 2010: Chapter 6, 'Policing and Politics', by Peter Smith, p. 68

Godson, Dean, *Himself Alone – David Trimble and the Ordeal of Unionism*, Harper Collins, London, 2004

Millar, Frank, *David Trimble – The Price of Peace*, Liffey Press, Dublin, 2004

Powell, Jonathan, *Great Hatred, Little Room, Making Peace in Northern Ireland*, Bodley Head, London, 2008

Ensuring an Effective, Efficient, Accountable and Impartial Police Service, The Life and Times of the Northern Ireland Policing Board, 4 November 2001 to 31 March 2006, Northern Ireland Policing Board, 2006

Appendix 3.A

Extract from the Weston Park text
published by the Northern Ireland Office and
the Department of Foreign Affairs on 1 August 2001

Proposals on policing

8. Both Governments remain committed to a new beginning in policing on the basis set out in the Good Friday Agreement. The British Government reaffirms its determination to bring about such a new beginning by implementing the Patten Report.

9. The British Government will publish a revised Implementation Plan. This will set out in greater detail the plans for implementing, among other matters, Patten's recommendations on the Full Time Reserve, the Part Time Reserve, the closure of Gough holding centre and the future structure of Special Branch. It will also set out the intention to avoid the use of Plastic Baton Rounds, except where there is a serious risk of loss of life or serious injury, while Patten's recommendation for a major research programme on alternatives is completed.

10. The Oversight Commissioner is responsible for overseeing the implementation of the changes recommended in the Patten Report. These are momentous and wide-ranging: it is important to be confident that they are delivering the new beginning intended in the Good Friday Agreement. So, in addition, the British Government will ask the Oversight Commissioner to review the new arrangements in the light of experience. The review will start in March 2002. It will be conducted on the basis of experience during the first year of the Board's operation and report by October 2002. Legislation will be introduced as soon as practicable thereafter to amend or clarify some provisions to reflect more fully the Patten recommendations. These amendments will be set out in detail in the revised Implementation Plan.

11. On this basis, the British Government will invite the parties to nominate political members to the new Policing Board and complete the process for selection of independent members, so that the Board will be established by the end of September.

12. The British Government is also establishing the Police Fund, which will assist families of officers killed by terrorist action, and the RUC GC Foundation, which will mark the sacrifices and honour the achievements of the RUC.

Appendix 3.B

Section 3 of the Police (Northern Ireland) Act 2000

'3.- (1) *The Board shall secure the maintenance of the police in Northern Ireland.*

(2) the Board shall secure that-

    (a) the police

    (b) the police support staff, and

    (c) traffic wardens appointed by the Board under section 71,

are efficient and effective.

(3) In carrying out its functions under subsections (1) and (2) the Board shall-

    (a) in accordance with the following provisions of this Act, hold the Chief Constable to account for the exercise of his functions and those of the police, the police support staff and traffic wardens;

    (b) monitor the performance of the police in-

        (i) carrying out the general duty under section 32 (1);

        (ii) complying with the Human Rights Act 1998;

        (iii) carrying out the policing plan;

    (c) keep itself informed as to-

        (i) the workings of Part VII of the 1998 Act (police complaints and disciplinary proceedings) and trends and patterns in complaints under that Part;

        (ii) the manner in which complaints from members of the public against traffic wardens are dealt with by the Chief Constable under section 71;

        (iii) trends and patterns in crimes committed in Northern Ireland;

        (iv) trends and patterns in recruitment to the police and the police support staff;

(v) the extent to which the membership of the police and the police support staff is representative of the community in Northern Ireland;

(d) assess-

(i) the effectiveness of measures taken to secure that the membership of the police and the police support staff is representative of that community;

(ii) the level of public satisfaction with the performance of the police and of district policing partnerships;

(iii) the effectiveness of district policing partnerships in performing their functions and, in particular, of arrangements made under Part III in obtaining the views of the public about matters concerning policing and the cooperation of the public with the police in preventing crime;

(iv) the effectiveness of the code of ethics issued under section 52;

(e) make arrangements for obtaining the co-operation of the public with the police in the prevention of crime.

(4) In carrying out its functions, the Board shall have regard to-

(a) the principle that the policing of Northern Ireland is to be conducted in an impartial manner;

(b) the policing plan;

(c) any code of practice issued by the Secretary of State under section 27; and

(d) the need-

(i) to co-ordinate its activities with those of other statutory authorities; and

(ii) to co-operate with such authorities.'

CHAPTER FOUR

The Members of the Policing Board

4.1 The Membership of the Policing Board

The advertisement for *Independent Members* of the Northern Ireland Policing Board (the Policing Board or the Board) appeared on 3 October 2000 with a closing date of 13 November 2000, subsequently extended to 11 December 2000. The following is the main text of the advertisement:

'*The Good Friday Agreement established the principle of a new beginning for policing in Northern Ireland, with a police service capable of attracting and sustaining support from the community as a whole. As a fundamental part of this new beginning the police service will in future be held to account by a body, to be known as the Northern Ireland Policing Board, which is fully representative of the Northern Ireland community in terms of factors such as religious background, gender and geographic spread. The Secretary of State is now seeking nine individuals to act as Independent Members of the Policing Board. The Board collectively must have the expertise to carry out its functions, which will include:*

- *Setting objectives and priorities for policing;*
- *Adopting a policing strategy and annual policing plan;*
- *Overseeing the process of police reform;*
- *Overseeing and monitoring the human rights performance of the police;*
- *Negotiating the annual policing budget with the appropriate body;*
- *Monitoring police performance against budgets and strategy;*
- *Appointing chief officers and civilian equivalents; and*
- *Co-operating with the Oversight Commissioner.*

Applicants must be able to demonstrate previous experience in:

- *Setting targets or objectives for an organisation and in ensuring the achievement of these; or*

- *Managing an organisation's financial resources; and in addition*

- *Previous experience in a role which has required an independent and impartial contribution.*

However, in ensuring that the Board possesses the broad range of skills necessary, this experience may have been gained in any sector, and we encourage applications from the public, private, voluntary or community sectors, or from professional practice. Candidates must also be of undisputed integrity, having held no position of interest that might cast doubt on their ability to act impartially. They must have the expertise to probe and scrutinise different areas of police performance and should demonstrate a commitment to the way forward for policing and the promotion of equality of opportunity within the police service. In addition, applicants will be asked to demonstrate that they meet other criteria for the role, as fully outlined in the person specification.

The appointments will be made on a 4-year fixed term basis, with the possibility of renewal at the end of that term. The posts will attract remuneration of £12,000 per annum, on the anticipated basis of 2–3 days per month, which could comprise either full or part days depending on the situation. The Chairman and Vice-Chairman will subsequently be appointed by the Secretary of State from amongst the nineteen members of the Board, following consultation with the First Minister and deputy First Minister.'

The information pack supplied to interested parties contained:

- a main paper, which described the background for potential *Independent Members*; the powers and functions of the Board; the recruitment and selection process (in addition to public advertisement, '*a number of organisations and groups representing the local and broader community are being invited to nominate individuals who they believe have the expertise both to set policing priorities and to probe and scrutinise different areas of police performance*'); terms and conditions of appointments; and the principles of equal opportunity that will apply

- The Job Description for *Independent Members* of the Board

- The Role Profile and Person Specification for the Chairman and Vice-Chairman respectively

The Job Description for *Independent Members* stated:

'*Job Description for Independent Members*

Role: January 2001 – March 2001

It is envisaged that the Board will operate in shadow for a three-month period in preparation for the abolition of the Police Authority.

  During this period Board members will

- *Undergo training in, and familiarisation with, the powers and functions of the Board, the tripartite policing structure in Northern Ireland, the police organisation and any relevant policing legislation;*
- *Be briefed on the planned implementation of The Independent Commission On Policing For Northern Ireland;*
- *Create committee structures and regulate procedures; and*
- *Draft a future work programme.*

Role: from April 2001

When the Board comes fully into operation in April 2001 its key function will be to secure the maintenance of an efficient and effective police service and to hold the Chief Constable and the police service publicly to account. To achieve that objective the Board will have a wide range of functions, to include:

- *Setting objectives and priorities for policing;*
- *Adopting a policing strategy and an annual policing plan;*
- *Overseeing the process of police reform;*
- *Overseeing and monitoring the human rights performance of the police;*
- *Negotiating the annual policing budget with the appropriate body;*
- *Monitoring police performance against budget and against the annual plan and the longer term strategy;*
- *Appointing chief officers and civilian equivalents; and*
- *Co-operating with the Oversight Commissioner.*'

Desmond Rea was interviewed on 13 December 2000. In the letter of invitation to the interview he was informed (as no doubt were the other candidates) that:

'At this interview you will be asked to make a five minute verbal presentation, in response to one of the following topics:

"Please indicate where you see the major priorities for policing in Northern Ireland and show how, as a member of the Board, you would contribute to the advancement of these priorities".

OR

"Please describe to us how you have acted in a leadership role and the means by which, in the role, you built consensus amongst team members".'

He was informed by letter of 21 December 2000 from the recruitment consultants that 'We understand decisions relating to those candidates successful to the positions will not be agreed until the New Year.' On 14 March 2001 the Secretary of State for Northern Ireland announced a temporary extension of the Police Authority; he stated: 'It is important that while discussions on policing continue prior to establishing the ... Board, the police remain accountable for their performance.' By letter of 2 April 2001 Desmond Rea was informed: 'Following your interview for the above named position, we wish to advise you that the Secretary of State is continuing to consider his decision as to the successful appointees to the ... Board.' By letter of 17 August 2001 he was informed:

'I wanted to write to you now to bring you up to date on the current position. The package of measures announced by the British and Irish Governments on 1 August contained a commitment by the British Government to publish a revised Implementation Plan and to seek to make appointments to the Policing Board by the end of September. The Secretary of State has just published the revised Plan. It sets out how the Programme of Patten recommendations is being taken forward.

On appointments to the Board it says, given the passage of time and the prospect for greater cross-community support, that there is to be a supplementary competition for independent members. My client wants me to stress that this is not intended as a reflection on you, but is intended to increase the pool of potential appointees so that, as the Secretary of State is required to do by statute, he may have an increased opportunity to appoint a Board which is representative of the community in Northern Ireland.'

Subsequently a readvertisement for Independent Members was published on 24 August 2001.

The BBC reported on 25 September 2001 that '*a Government announcement on the nine Independent Members to the new ... Board has been delayed ... until later in the week.*' Nevertheless, the report added, '*however, most of the names are now in the public arena*'.

The Irish Times of 26 September 2001 clarified the reason for the most recent delay:

'*Mr Chris Patten's grand objective when he published his commission's report on police reform two years ago, was to take politics out of policing.*

An admirable ambition but judging by Nationalist annoyance over who should chair the new Policing Board very difficult to realise.

Senior SDLP figures were yesterday intensively lobbying the North's Minister of security, Ms Jane Kennedy, and her senior officials to appoint a perceived Nationalist rather than a perceived Unionist as chairman of the Policing Board.

One uses the term "perceived" because the row centres on two of the nine appointees to the 19-member board who are described as independent.

The British government, according to reliable sources, is anxious to appoint Prof Desmond Rea as chairman, with Mr Denis Bradley as his vice-chairman. The SDLP, however, wants Mr Bradley in the chair.

The SDLP is not questioning Prof Rea's bona fides – he has business exper-tise and is a member of the Labour Relations Agency, but argues that he comes from the Unionist "side of the house".

Prof Rea is very much on the liberal wing of politics. He was a central figure in the behind-the-scenes but influential and moderate cross-community JIGSA grouping of academics and professionals, which was one of the first – and prior to the IRA ceasefire – to open up dialogue with republicans.

He is a classic liberal Unionist with a small u, who would be basically supportive of David Trimble's approach to the peace process...

Neither are Ulster Unionists questioning Mr Bradley's bona fides but they believe he comes from the Nationalist "side of the house"...'

Also on 26 September 2001 the BBC reported that Ulster Unionist leader David Trimble had said:

'*... the two top posts on the new Police Board should be chosen from among the political appointees ... An Ulster Unionist member should be appointed Chairman and an SDLP member appointed Vice-Chair.*'

On 27 September 2001 the Irish Times reported:

'*The Northern Secretary, Dr John Reid warned he would not be lobbied by either side of the political divide in deciding who will chair the North's new Police Board.*'

On 29 September 2001 Secretary of State Dr John Reid announced the full composition of the Policing Board:

'*The appointment of the Independent members and the subsequent selection of the chairman and vice-chairman complete the process of creating the Board.*

Announcing the composition of the Board, Dr Reid said:

"*I am delighted to announce the full membership of the Board, including Professor Desmond Rea and Mr Denis Bradley, both independent members, as its first chairman and vice-chairman. Together they will play a key leadership role in ensuring the provision of a fully effective policing service which will enjoy the support of all sections of the community.*

I very much look forward to working with them and the rest of the Board in helping to shape the future direction of policing in Northern Ireland."

The other seven independent members are confirmed as:

> *Viscount Brookeborough*
> *Brian Dougherty*
> *Barry Gilligan*
> *Tom Kelly*
> *Pauline McCabe*
> *Rosaleen Moore*
> *Suneil Sharma*

The 10 members nominated by political parties are:

> *Fred Cobain MLA – Ulster Unionist Party (UUP)*
> *Ivan Davis MLA – UUP*
> *Lord Kilclooney MLA – UUP*
> *James Leslie MLA – UUP*
> *William Hay – Democratic Unionist Party (DUP)*
> *Ian Paisley Jnr MLA – DUP*
> *Sammy Wilson MLA – DUP*
> *Alex Attwood MLA – Social Democratic and Labour Party (SDLP)*

Joe Byrne MLA – SDLP
Eddie McGrady MLA – SDLP

[NB During devolved Government 10 members will be nominated from the
Northern Ireland Assembly using the d'Hondt method of selection.]'

The reason for the delay in announcing the full composition of the
Policing Board beyond those just referred to were explained in Chapter
3. In summary they were:

- 'The Patten Report was widely supported by the Nationalists, but it angered
  Unionists who regarded the proposed symbolic changes as a slur on the
  memory of the RUC.' (Paul Dixon and Eamonn O'Kane, *Northern Ireland
  Since 1969*, p. 100)
- Delay in PIRA's decommissioning of weapons and the political
  consequences for the UUP's leader David Trimble.

The first meeting of the Policing Board was held in private and in
public on 7 November 2001. The breakthrough on policing came at the
end of August 2001, when the SDLP signed up to the UK Government's
revised policing implementation plan. The next breakthrough came
in the last week of September 2001, when the UUP and the more
hard-line DUP signed up, albeit stressing that they would continue to
oppose many of the reforms proposed. Sinn Féin refused to join the
new Board, saying that the reforms did not go far enough to satisfy
the concerns of Republicans. Gerry Kelly said *'we will not sit on a flawed
Policing Board or support a force which remains flawed in significant ways'*.
Since Sinn Féin did not take up its two seats on the Board, the seats
were reallocated – one each to the UUP and DUP under the d'Hondt
system. As indicated above, this brought the former to four members
and the latter to three members.

At the *Public Session* of the first meeting of the Board, the Chairman
made the following statement on behalf of the Board:

*'Fellow members, Chief Constable, and representatives of the Police Staff
Associations good afternoon and welcome to the first public meeting of the
Northern Ireland Policing Board.*

*We welcome in particular the members of the public and the press who have
joined us today to observe and report on our meeting. I thank you for coming*

along to find out about our work, and hope that you will have a continued interest as we get down to business in the coming weeks and months.

We will shortly receive a report from the Chief Constable of the Police Service for Northern Ireland, but we would first like to take a few minutes to reflect on our journey to this point in time. This has been a momentous week for policing in Northern Ireland, and for all those touched by policing. Already it has been marked by the achievement of a significant number of changes.

The formation of the Police Service of Northern Ireland; the first balanced intake of trainees to the new Police Service, they have been selected and their training commenced; the creation of the Northern Ireland Policing Board, this Board, and today's historic first public meeting with the Chief Constable giving his address to the Board and to the wider community in Northern Ireland.

To arrive at this new beginning has of course not been without its controversy, it has required considerable work over the past months and years by many. Without such commitment we would not have witnessed the historic changes achieved in recent days and to which we have just referred. And we would not now be here ready to play our part in helping to define the future of policing within Northern Ireland.

However, as we look forward to the challenges ahead, it would be remiss not to reflect on the significant contribution made by the RUC and by so many police officers down the years. It would be remiss,

- *Not to remember all those officers who have lost their lives and their family circles.*

- *Not to remember all those officers who have been injured and who continue to carry the scars;*

- *Not to acknowledge the dedication and the commitment of those officers recently retired from their policing careers and those whose continued commitment is embedded in their willingness to move forward with the new police service;*

- *Not to acknowledge the contribution of the wider policing family who have provided support to the police in difficult times.*

*It is the contribution of all that we've referred to, which has enabled us to move with some confidence to **this new beginning**, and we thank them and all the others who have helped us to get here.*

Special thanks must also be extended to the Chairman and members of the former Police Authority for Northern Ireland for their help in recent weeks to ensure a seamless transition and for their words of encouragement to this Board as the future of police accountability in Northern Ireland. Perhaps the most significant fact about this new beginning is that it enables the police service to be embraced by the whole community. The essential goal of the police is to serve the whole community. The Northern Ireland Police Service and the Board will be seeking the whole-hearted support of the whole community. The police must be free to police with all of our communities, and we will be judged by the ability of officers to live with the people they serve.

Policing with the community is at the heart of the new service, the importance of the community, accepting their responsibility to support and work in partnership with the police service cannot be overstated. Community policing is about matching community expectation with day-to-day delivery of the Police Service. Community policing is about consulting with the community and working in partnership with them to solve local problems. Community policing is about the accountability of the police to their community. Community policing is the bedrock of the District Policing Partnerships and as we begin to establish these forums, we hope that the community will fulfil their responsibility to be fully participative in the Partnerships and to support their work. In the coming months we will also be consulting with the community to find out more about their policing needs. As a new body our role will evolve. We have an agenda to work to, within a fairly tight timetable.

As we commence our work we will have the ability to shape our future and the future of policing in Northern Ireland. We recognise and we accept our responsibilities. We are also realistic about the challenging and the sometimes difficult issues and decisions that we will consider and have to make. We will consider each issue carefully in a balanced way. Our decision making will benefit from the diversity of our members, who each have an enormous contribution to make to shaping the future of policing in Northern Ireland. We must self-consciously as a Board take ownership of the policing agenda, in so far as it is within our remit, and to try to remove the Service from becoming a political football. A significant amount of work has already been achieved, the enormity of the change process ahead has been recognised and we must work together with all those involved to progress the policing agenda. A recent report suggested that the ideal would be a marriage, between the required political pace of change and what can be achieved managerially. We must recognise and match what must be done, with community expectation, and with what is organisationally achievable.

This Board, Chief Constable, is very conscious that the past week has not been easy for you or for your colleagues. We commend you and all your Officers for your management of the situation, and for your willingness to embrace the changes demanded of you. I have much pleasure on behalf of the Board in inviting you to address the Board and the people of Northern Ireland, Chief Constable.'

For the SDLP Eddie McGrady said that the new Board represented

'... Another important step into the new beginning for policing. The Board is the central cog in the machinery of accountability to ensure policing is as Patten intended and as the community requires.'

For the UUP Lord Kilclooney (John Taylor) said:

'The UUP was taking part in the Board on the basis of our continuing opposition to parts of the Patten Report and its implementation plan.'

For the DUP Sammy Wilson said:

'There is great sadness that the setting up of the Policing Board sees the demise of the RUC. It is something which we predicted, something which the UUP said would never happen and something which has now come to pass.'

Meanwhile, 'outside the tent', Sinn Féin said:

'The SDLP is making a great mistake in trusting the British to change policing legislation. The new beginning to policing had not yet occurred ... the Secretary of State and the Chief Constable have too much power under the new arrangements.'

Before commencing his report the Chief Constable, Sir Ronnie Flanagan, made the following short opening statement:

'Thank you very much indeed, Mr Chairman, Vice Chairman and all members of the Board. Can I, on behalf of all my colleagues, thank you for the welcome here this afternoon, and can I particularly thank you for the comments you have made.

I'm delighted that particular mention was made of those colleagues who down through the years had their lives taken in the service of all the people

of Northern Ireland and of those many, many colleagues who suffered and continue to suffer the effects of serious injury. It is only their commitment, it is only the platform, the foundation that they built, that has allowed us to follow in their tradition and embrace the changes that have been recommended and are to be adopted for the benefit of all the people of Northern Ireland.'

In his report – among other matters – the Chief Constable

- Presented the Chairman with a copy of a draft Code of Ethics for the PSNI (refer Recommendation 3, Report of The Independent Commission On Policing For Northern Ireland);
- Updated the Board concerning progress towards the development of a Human Rights Programme (refer Recommendation 1, Report of The Independent Commission On Policing For Northern Ireland);
- Presented a source document on the new training programme for trainees to the Police Service of Northern Ireland just commenced (refer Recommendation 129, Report of the Independent Commission for Policing for Northern Ireland);
- Presented a paper to the Chairman concerning the range of uniforms to be provided to the new Service (refer Recommendation 154, Report of The Independent Commission On Policing For Northern Ireland).

The minutes of the Board's first meeting record that the Board:

- Received the report of its Agenda Working Group;
- Noted the arrangements, which had been agreed with the Chief Constable for its first 'public' meeting
- Adopted the committee structure and allocation responsibilities subject to review after a period of no longer than 12 months
- Agreed to adopt the media policy recommended by the Agenda Working Group subject to the following amendment:

  'The Chairman is the official spokesman of the Board. When it is considered desirable or appropriate the Vice-Chairman and other members may be charged by the Chairman with commenting publicly on specific subjects against a pre-determined brief.'

- Noted a paper concerning a training programme to assist members in carrying out their responsibilities
- Considered the Secretary of State's proposed three policing objectives for commencement in April 2002
- Noted two tabled papers concerning the Board's programme of work and agreed that more work was required to prioritise it
- Noted a paper and received a presentation on the development, procurement and outstanding issues associated with the new police uniform (NB In respect of the issue of the blackthorn or leather sticks to senior officers the motion that those officers should not carry a stick was carried by nine votes in favour to eight against)
- Noted the following statement by the Agenda Working Group in its report:

> 'The Working Group noted that the Secretary of State had a responsibility to consult the Board about badges and emblems for the Police Service and that the legislative and production time constraints were very tight. It was agreed that the Board should address the issue and attempt to reach a consensus view.
>
> It was agreed that it would be helpful for officials to arrange for the Board to receive a presentation on 7 November 2001 to further explain the existing badges of rank and the logistical and time constraints involved in the adoption of new badges/emblems.'

On the same day as the first meeting of the Policing Board the BBC reported that:

'The first batch of between 260–300 Police Service of Northern Ireland trainees – selected on a 50% Catholic, 50% Protestant basis – began training on Sunday and are expected to be on the streets by spring 2002.'

At the sixth meeting of the Policing Board, held on 21 February 2002, the Chairman confirmed that he had received a letter from the Secretary of State advising that Mr Sam Foster (UUP) and Mr Alan McFarland (UUP) would replace the two outgoing UUP political nominees, Mr Ivan Davis and Mr James Leslie. (NB The latter moved to be a Junior Minister.)

On 14 October 2002 the UK Government suspended the Northern Ireland Assembly. Dixon and O'Kane explain why:

'The IRA's first act of decommissioning allowed the UUP to return to government. The IRA carried out a second act of decommissioning in April 2002 and Sinn Féin performed very well in the Republic's general election the following month, winning five seats (a gain of four). This more optimistic phase of the peace process was, however, brought to an end by concerns over the apparent continued involvement by republicans in spying and targeting. The IRA was implicated in a break-in at the Special Branch office at Castlereagh police station in March 2002 and on 4 October the PSNI made a high-profile raid on Sinn Féin's offices at Stormont related to allegations that republicans were operating a "spy-ring". As a result of the raid both the DUP and UUP ministers threatened to resign unless Sinn Féin was excluded from government (the UUP had announced a month earlier that its members would resign in January if the IRA failed to demonstrate it had left violence behind for good). On 14 October the British government suspended the Assembly.'

On 14 October 2002 the Secretary of State wrote to the Chairman of the Board confirming suspension of devolved government in Northern Ireland:

'I take this action with considerable regret. I concluded, however, that the Government had no alternative, in the best interests of the peace process and the Agreement, and of good government in Northern Ireland.

I very much hope that this period of suspension will not be prolonged, but it provides an opportunity to find a basis on which to bring the institutions back, and the Government will make every effort to help find that basis.'

In the letter he pointed out that, under the Police (NI) Act 2000, there are separate provisions for membership during devolved government and during suspension of devolved government, and that, 'from the coming into effect of the Order suspending devolved government, the current Board members cease to hold office.' At that point the other provisions come into play, and that, accordingly, 'in looking to make appointments under the [relevant] Schedule [he] will be inviting all the existing members of the Board to take up an appointment during suspension of devolved government for a period of three years.' In a Board press release of 15

October 2002 the Chairman of the Board *described the agreement of Board members to continue their work following suspension of the devolved institution as good news for everyone in Northern Ireland.*

On 21 October 2003 Prime Minister Tony Blair announced Assembly elections to be held in November 2003 and the Independent International Commission on Decommissioning (IICD) confirmed a further act of decommissioning by PIRA. The elections took place on 26 November 2003: *'the long expected triumph of the hard-line Sinn Féin and the DUP was the outcome'*. However, the Assembly was to remain in suspension until 15 May 2006, as it took until then to get both the DUP and Sinn Féin on board.

Dixon and O'Kane record that:

- on 28 July 2005 the IRA announced the end of its armed campaign
- on 26 September 2005 the IICD Report confirmed that the IRA had met its commitment to put all its arms beyond use
- on 6 September 2006 an Independent Monitoring Commission report stated that the IRA was no longer involved in terrorist activity
- over 11–13 October 2006 multi-party talks were held at St Andrews, Scotland
- on 28 January 2007 a special Sinn Féin Ard Fheis (conference) voted to call for support of police forces on both sides of the border

And so the Assembly elections took place on 7 March 2007. The outcome was as follows: DUP (36 seats), Sinn Féin (28 seats), the UUP (18 seats), the SDLP (16 seats), Alliance (7 seats), Green Party (1 seat), Independent (1 seat), and Progressive Unionist Party (1 seat). Subsequently,

- on 26 March 2007, Rev Ian Paisley and Gerry Adams announced that DUP and Sinn Féin would share power in a new Executive
- on 8 May 2007, the Northern Ireland Assembly reconvened
- on 31 July 2007, the British Army's operation in Northern Ireland (Operation Banner) officially ended

Faced with the term of office of all 19 Board Members expiring on 16 October 2005, the Secretary of State announced on 2 August 2005 that he had decided to roll forward the current membership of all 19 Members for a period ending no later than October 2006, with no change to the position of Chairman or Vice-Chairman. This decision did not go down well with the DUP in particular, which wanted a new membership when the remit of the current member body ended on 16 October. The party believed that a new Board line-up should reflect its strong electoral showing. On 13 October 2005 the Secretary of State confirmed the continuation of the current membership of the Board until 31 March 2006 and indicated that the Board would be reconstituted on 1 April 2006 using the d'Hondt formula applied to the 2003 election results for *Political Members* and that a competition for *Independent Members* would be launched shortly. (NB In respect of the political membership this would mean the DUP (4 seats), Sinn Féin (2 seats), the UUP (2 seats), and the SDLP (2 seats.))

The following was the membership of the Policing Board as announced by the Northern Ireland Office on 14 March 2006:

Political Members:

- Arlene Foster MLA (DUP)
- William Hay MLA (DUP)
- Ian Paisley Jnr MLA (DUP)
- Peter Weir MLA (DUP)
- Fred Cobain MLA (UUP)
- Danny Kennedy MLA (UUP)
- Alex Attwood MLA (SDLP)
- Dolores Kelly MLA (SDLP)

Independent Members:

- Joe Byrne[1,2]
- Brendan Duddy
- Barry Gilligan[1]
- Deirdre Mac Bride
- Pauline McCabe[1]
- Rosaleen Moore[1]
- Dawn Purvis[3]
- Trevor Ringland[4]

- Professor Sir Desmond Rea[1]
- Brian Rea
- Suneil Sharma[1]

[1] On last Board
[2] Former elected representative of SDLP
[3] Chairperson of Progressive Unionist Party who had stood as a candidate for the party
[4] Member of UUP

At the Board meeting held on 6 April 2006 Professor Sir Desmond Rea was re-elected as Chairman (by ten votes to six for Mrs McCabe) and Barry Gilligan was elected unopposed as Vice-Chairman. As at the setting up of the Board, there had been publicised pressure, not least from the SDLP, for a Nationalist Chairman.

With Sinn Féin joining the Board in May 2007, the Board required to be reconstituted and another recruitment competition for independent members commenced. The Board Members as at May 2007 were as follows:

Political Members:

- Tom Buchanan MLA (DUP)
- Rt Hon Jeffrey Donaldson MLA (DUP)
- David Simpson MP MLA (DUP)
- Peter Weir MLA (DUP)[2]
- Martina Anderson MLA (Sinn Féin)
- Alex Maskey MLA (Sinn Féin)
- Leslie Cree MLA (UUP)
- Basil McCrea MLA (UUP)
- Dolores Kelly MLA (SDLP)[2]

Independent Members:

- Barry Gilligan[1, 2]
- Mary McKee
- Rosaleen Moore[1, 2]
- Gearóid O hEára
- Brian Rea[2]

- Professor Sir Desmond Rea[1,2]
- Trevor Ringland[2]
- David Rose
- Suneil Sharma[1,2]

[1] On first Board
[2] On second Board

Professor Sir Desmond Rea and Barry Gilligan were re-elected unopposed for a further two years as Chairman and Vice-Chairman respectively of the Board at its meeting on 31 May 2007. Speaking after his re-election, the Chairman said:

'This is an eventful time for Northern Ireland and I am honoured, along with my Vice-Chairman Barry Gilligan, to have been re-elected.

For nearly a decade policing has been one of the central issues of the peace process and of the political negotiations that have brought us to this point. While this is the third Policing Board to have been established since November 2001, it is the first that includes the community's elected representatives from across the whole political spectrum.

Previous Policing Boards, and the members who served on them, achieved much and I pay tribute to them today. However, we are entering a new era in the history of policing in Northern Ireland and this new Board will continue to ensure for all the people of Northern Ireland an accountable, effective, efficient and impartial Police Service. I believe that both the political and independent members of this Board intend to work for all the people of Northern Ireland in seeking to meet the Board's objectives.'

Vice-Chairman Barry Gilligan added:

'Policing in Northern Ireland still faces many challenges but my fellow members have indicated their full commitment to the job in hand. Engaging communities and building public confidence in policing will be a priority for the new Board – particularly where communities have been disaffected.

The Board has made a significant contribution to the policing reforms process to date; and as we move forward I, along with my fellow members, look forward to playing my part in helping make our communities safer and ensuring the delivery of a policing service which meets community need.'

At the meeting of the Board held on 6 March 2008 the Chairman informed Members that, as a consequence of his appointment as a Minister in the Office of the First Minister in the Northern Ireland Executive, the Rt Hon Jeffrey Donaldson MP MLA (DUP) was now disqualified from membership of the Board and that he had been advised that Ian Paisley Jnr (a Member of the first Board) had been appointed in his place.

At the meeting of the Board held on 3 July 2008 the Chairman advised Members that he had received a letter from Mr David Simpson MP MLA (DUP) enclosing a copy of his letter of resignation from the Board to the Secretary of State effective from 18 June 2008. The Chairman further advised that *appropriate administrative arrangements were being finalised by the DUP and the Northern Ireland Office to appoint Mr Jimmy Spratt MLA (DUP) to the Board.*

As stated above, Professor Sir Desmond Rea and Mr Barry Gilligan were elected Chairman and Vice-Chairman respectively of the Board from 1 May 2007 to 30 April 2009. Prior to election of the Chairman and Vice-Chairman at the Board's meeting on 7 May 2009 Professor Rea had intimated that he would not be seeking re-election. At that meeting Mr Barry Gilligan and Mr Brian Rea were elected unopposed as Chairman and Vice-Chairman respectively. At the same meeting the Chief Constable, Sir Hugh Orde, tendered his resignation as from 31 August 2009; he advised that he had been elected as President of the Association of Chief Police Officers of England, Wales and Northern Ireland. The same meeting was also the last meeting of the Deputy Chief Constable, who was retiring after some 29 years as a distinguished police officer in Northern Ireland and England. In his opening remarks at the 7 May 2009 *Public Session* of the Board the retiring Chairman noted that the Board had been very fortunate (as had the Chief Constable) to have had a stable Senior Command Team for over four years.

On 7 May 2009 the membership of the Board was as follows:

Political Members:

- Tom Buchanan MLA (DUP)
- Ian Paisley Jnr MLA (DUP)
- Jimmy Spratt MLA (DUP)

- Peter Weir MLA (DUP)
- Martina Anderson MLA (Sinn Féin)
- Alex Maskey MLA (Sinn Féin)
- Daithi McKay MLA (Sinn Féin)
- Leslie Cree MLA (UUP)
- Basil McCrea MLA (UUP)
- Dolores Kelly MLA (SDLP)

Independent Members:

- Barry Gilligan
- Mary McKee
- Rosaleen Moore
- Gearóid O hEára
- Brian Rea
- Trevor Ringland
- David Rose
- Suneil Sharma
- Desmond Rea

4.2   In Conclusion

The general functions of the Policing Board, as laid down in the Police (Northern Ireland) Act 2000, are:

- To secure the maintenance of the police in Northern Ireland
- To secure that the police and police support staff in Northern Ireland are effective, efficient and impartial
- To hold the Chief Constable to account for the exercise of his/her functions and those of the police and police support staff

Schedule 1 of the Police (Northern Ireland) Act 2000 states:

- The Board shall consist of not more than 19 members appointed by the

Secretary of State, 10 of whom shall be nominated from Members of the Assembly (*Political Members*) and nine of whom shall be appointed by the Secretary of State (*Independent Members*).

• The Secretary of State shall so exercise his/her powers of appointment under this paragraph as to secure that as far as is practicable the membership of the Board is representative of the community in Northern Ireland.

Above we have traced the membership of the Board from September 2001, when the SDLP's joining made its setting up possible, to Sinn Féin (seamlessly) joining the Board in May 2007, and through to May 2009, when Professor Sir Desmond Rea intimated that he would not be standing for re-election and Barry Gilligan, a member of the Nationalist identity, became Chairman. It is evident that the Secretary of State followed the letter of the law when nominating and seeking to nominate *Political Members* and appointing *Independent Members* in order to ensure that membership of the Board was representative of the community in Northern Ireland. Neither author of this book has any room for a Board made up solely of *Independent Members* nor one solely of *Political Members*. (This is not intended as any criticism of an Assembly Committee, such as the Justice Committee, which is more genuinely representative albeit in a rather different role, and which has been shown to work despite a testing agenda).

What the above account did not tell is that, first, the Board's *Political Members* were deeply divided on some of the Patten Report recommendations. In the *Belfast Telegraph* of 7 November 2001, Ben Lowry, in a perceptive article, quoted:

– Eddie McGrady: '*The SDLP have a clear agenda on the Board – to vigorously pursue Patten in policy and in practice and in every aspect of policing*'

– Lord Kilclooney: '*[I] and the other UUP members would continue to oppose aspects of Patten*'

– Ian Paisley Jnr: '*The DUP wants to move immediately away from the discrimination of 50/50 recruitment [of police officers]*'

– Gerry Kelly (NB Sinn Féin, and not taking seats on the Board at that time): '*Patten [was] unambiguous and the current Board did not have the power to hold the police to account*'

In addition to holding the Police Service of Northern Ireland to account through the Chief Constable, monitoring the performance of the police in carrying out its general duty, complying with human rights obligations, and carrying out the Policing Plan etc. as laid down in the Police (Northern Ireland) Act 2000, it was obvious that managing the Board's obligations under Patten was not going to be easy.

Second, the Chairman was soon to become aware that

- Difficult matters were best tackled when all the political parties were represented at the meeting and preferably when 'all' Members, *Political* and *Independent*, were present.
- It was better to have 'heavy hitters', especially among the *Political Members*, on each side of Northern Ireland's political divide – acceptable accommodations were more likely to be reached.

Third, it was important to get on with the job and, in doing that, the *Independent Members* had an important role to play. *Independent Members*, on an issue which was contentious between *Political Members*, if they were prepared to come together, could effectively influence the latter to seek and indeed achieve compromise.

References

BBC Radio Ulster, 25 September 2001

Irish Times, 26 September 2001

BBC Radio Ulster, 26 September 2001

Irish Times, 27 September 2001

Dixon, Paul and Eamonn O'Kane, *Northern Ireland Since 1969*, Pearson Education, Harlow, 2001

Ben Lowry, *Belfast Telegraph*, 7 November 2001

CHAPTER FIVE

Accountability – In Theory and Practice

5.1 Introduction

This chapter addresses the key principle of accountability – that is, the role of the Northern Ireland Policing Board (the Policing Board or the Board) in holding the Chief Constable to account, and through him the Police Service of Northern Ireland (the Police Service or the PSNI) as a whole. The chapter begins by setting out the importance of the issue as described in the Report Of The Independent Commission On Policing For Northern Ireland (the Independent Commission), summarises the legislation, and then shows the principle being worked through in a number of ways.

It was clear from the Report of The Independent Commission that accountability was an absolutely critical area not just for the development of policing but also for wider political progress in Northern Ireland. It was the one area for which the Independent Commission set out at length the then current position, before making recommendations for future arrangements. As noted in Chapter 3, the Report considered different headings under the same theme – democratic accountability, transparency, legal accountability, and financial accountability. Of these by far the most attention was given to the first, in particular the creation of a new Policing Board and its membership, functions, and powers. The Independent Commission's Report contained more recommendations on accountability (38) than on any other topic.

The section in the Report on the concept of operational independence, or operational responsibility as the Independent Commission preferred to term it, is an important one. The Commission was told by the Northern Ireland Police Authority that, under the previous arrangements, if the Chief Constable decided that a matter was operational and therefore within the scope of police independence, there was nothing they could do to pursue it. Members of the Commission consulted extensively in several countries, but concluded that the term operational independence was neither found nor defined in any legislation. It was an extrapolation from the phrase direction and control included in statutory descriptions of the functions of Chief Constable.

The Independent Commission concluded that:

'Operational responsibility means that it is the Chief Constable's right and duty to take operational decisions, and that neither the Government nor the Policing Board should have the right to direct the Chief Constable as to how to conduct an operation. It does not mean, however, that the Chief Constable's conduct of an operational matter should be exempted from inquiry or review after the event by anyone.' (Paragraph 6.21)

The Independent Commission's Report contained a number of key recommendations in this area:

'9 The statutory primary function of the Policing Board should be to hold the Chief Constable and the police service publicly to account.

24 The Chief Constable should be deemed to have operational responsibility for the exercise of his or her functions and the activities of the police officers and civilian staff under his or her direction and control.

25 The Policing Board should have the power to require the Chief Constable to report on any issue pertaining to the performance of his functions or those of the police service. The obligation to report should extend to explaining operational decisions. If there is a disagreement between the Board and the Chief Constable over whether it is appropriate for a report to be provided on a particular matter, it should be for the Chief Constable to refer the question to the Secretary of State for a decision as to whether the Board's requirement should stand.

26 The Policing Board should have the power, subject only to the same limitation set out in paragraph 6.22, to follow up any report from the Chief Constable by initiating an inquiry into any aspect of the police service or police conduct.'

These recommendations took account of perceived weaknesses in the relationship between the Police Authority and the Royal Ulster Constabulary (RUC) Chief Constable: for example, the Police Authority had no power to follow up on the receipt of any report from the Chief Constable. In its own commentary on the Independent Commission's Report, the Police Authority stated that:

'Although the power contained in Section 48 of the Police (NI) Act 1998 to call for reports is an obvious recognition of the Chief Constable's accountability to the Authority there has never been a clear statement in statute that the Chief Constable is accountable to the Authority ... The absence of a categorical statement of a Chief Constable's accountability to the Authority has been the source of dispute and difficulty in the past and we conclude that this recommendation must strengthen police accountability and clarify matters.'

The only exception to this accountability structure recommended in the Independent Commission's Report concerned national security matters, for which the Chief Constable would be mainly accountable to the Secretary of State for Northern Ireland (paragraph 6.22).

The Independent Commission also pointed to a perception that Police Authority members had *'strongly pro-police orientations'*, as exemplified by the way in which the Authority sometimes defended the police service in relation to allegations of wrongdoings before they had been properly investigated. Their Report also noted that the Police Authority had been hampered in its accountability function by having been responsible, until the implementation of the 1998 Police Act, for the provision of executive services to the police and the management of more than 3,000 civilian support staff working for the police. It concluded that *'The combination of being at once part of the policing service and also required to monitor that service and hold the police to account was seriously flawed'* (Paragraph 5.13).

The Report made the point (paragraph 6.10) that *'the title "Policing Board" is deliberate'*. The Independent Commission saw the role of the new body as going beyond supervision of the police itself and extending to the wider issues of policing and the contributions that people and organisations other than the police could make towards public safety.

The Report also made certain recommendations in relation to the annual planning process: these were designed to clarify the respective roles of the Policing Board, the PSNI, and the Secretary of State. That subject, including the relevant legislation and the outworking by the Policing Board, is dealt with later in this book.

5.2   The Legislation Underpinning Accountability

By its nature, legislation is usually more difficult to follow and understand than a narrative report, and the Police (Northern Ireland) Act 2000 (the Act) is certainly no exception to that rule. Sections 2 to 13 in Part II deal with the Northern Ireland Policing Board. Part IV provides for policing objectives, plans, and codes of practice. However, to understand the complexity of the application of the principles of operational responsibility and accountability to the Policing Board it is necessary to look also at Part VI, which deals with the general functions of the police; Part VII, which provides for reports and inquiries; and Schedule 1. The clauses relating to the powers of the Policing Board in regard to initiating an inquiry were some of those most closely probed and tested by the Social Democratic and Labour Party (SDLP) during the preparation of the legislation and its subsequent passage through Parliament.

It is not until section 33 that the general functions of the Chief Constable are clarified: the Act states that *'the police shall be under the direction and control of the Chief Constable'*. The section continues that: *'in discharging his functions, the Chief Constable shall have regard to (a) the policing plan; and (b) any code of practice under Section 27'*.

It is to be noted that there is again no legislative definition of the concept of operational responsibility, but section 33 does effectively confer on the Chief Constable the power to run the Police Service of Northern Ireland.

Section 3 of the Act is the key text setting out the general functions of the Policing Board (see Appendix 3.B, above). In summary, it requires the Board to *'secure the maintenance of the police in Northern Ireland, and to secure that the police are efficient and effective'*. In carrying out these functions the Board shall, in accordance with the other provisions of the Act, hold the Chief Constable to account for the exercise of his functions and those of the police. This section also requires the Board to have regard, in carrying out its functions, to *'the principle that the policing of Northern Ireland is to be conducted in an impartial manner'.*

This key role for the Policing Board might be summarised as holding the Chief Constable – and through him or her the PSNI – to account for the delivery of effective, efficient, and impartial policing, in accordance with the framework of the Act.

Paragraph 19 of Schedule 1 of the Act lays down certain requirements on the Policing Board under the heading 'Public Meetings'. Each year there must be at least 10 meetings held by the Board for the purpose of receiving and considering a report on policing from the Chief Constable. Members of the public may attend any meeting, but that does not prevent the Board from excluding the public from a meeting or from part of a meeting.

Part VII of the Act provides for reports and inquiries. Section 59 obliges the Chief Constable to submit to the Board, when so required, a report on any such matter connected with the policing of Northern Ireland as may be specified. However, there was an important and sensitive caveat in relation to this wide-ranging power, which was the ability of the Chief Constable to refer the Policing Board's request to the Secretary of State if he believed that a report would contain information which ought not to be disclosed on one or more of the following four grounds:

'*(a) in the interests of national security;*

(b) because it relates to an individual and is of a sensitive personal nature;

(c) because it would, or would be likely to, prejudice proceedings which have been commenced in a court of law;

(d) because it would, or would be likely to, prejudice the prevention or detection of crime or the apprehension or prosecution of offenders.'

The Northern Ireland Secretary of State might then modify or set aside the Board's requirement to exempt the Chief Constable from the obligation to report information which ought not to be disclosed on the grounds above. Furthermore, section 60 provides that the Board, when it has considered a report on the matters submitted by the Chief Constable, may cause an inquiry to be held '*by reason of the gravity of the matter or exceptional circumstances'*. Again, the Chief Constable may refer the decision of the Policing Board to hold an inquiry to the Secretary of State.

What, then, are the sanctions if the Policing Board concludes that the Chief Constable or the PSNI have acted wrongly? The legislation does provide for the Policing Board to have certain powers in relation to the removal of senior officers – in section 35 (3) 'the Board may, with the approval of the Secretary of State, call upon any senior officer to retire in the interests of efficiency or effectiveness'. The only other formal sanction available to the Board would be to initiate disciplinary proceedings against the Chief Constable. These are both clearly very hard-edged actions – indeed, they might be described as 'nuclear' options – and are ones that would not be taken lightly.

Legislation is often a comparatively blunt instrument. Thus the Act does not include any provision for the Policing Board to express its disapproval of a particular action in a more restrained fashion; it certainly contains no reference, for example, to moral suasion or to the ability of the Board as a corporate body or its Members as individuals to make public their concerns. This scope for making public comments on actions by the Chief Constable was clearly likely to be explored by the Political Members, especially in the close-knit community of Northern Ireland, where the media have easy and frequent access to elected representatives.

In the particularly febrile political atmosphere of the early days of the Policing Board a critical issue for the Membership, and the Chairman in particular, was to understand the operation of the legislation and its practical application, with its limitations, in this vital area of holding the Chief Constable to account. A subsequent section of this chapter sets out how the Policing Board went about this.

It is also worth noting that there is no specific provision in the 2000 Act requiring that the Board should be 'supportive' of the Police Service beyond the general requirement that it 'shall secure the maintenance of the police in Northern Ireland'. It is, however, logical that the Policing Board should support the Police Service in achieving the objectives for the police which it itself has set. It can also be supportive of instances of good policing, both through public comments and through explicit participation in activities that promote and endorse good policing, such as attending police awards ceremonies.

There is undoubtedly scope for tension between the explicit

legislative requirement of holding the Chief Constable to account and the assumption of a broadly supportive role. It is unlikely to be in the interests of any Policing Board or other police authority to be explicitly dismissive (taking that to be the opposite of supportive) of the chief officer and his or her police service, unless the relationship has broken down fundamentally or the police service is so 'broken' that the only alternative is radical reform for which there is widespread public support.

As this chapter makes clear, from a very early stage the Chairman of the Policing Board reached the conclusion that the other side of the coin of holding the PSNI to account through the Chief Constable for the delivery of effective, efficient, and impartial policing was supporting the Service through the Chief Constable toward the end of effective, efficient, and impartial policing.

As noted in Chapter 3, the British Government had undertaken in the discussions at Weston Park in July 2001 to introduce further legislation amending the Police (Northern Ireland) Act 2000. Some of these changes were foreshadowed in the Updated Implementation Plan, entitled 'The Community and the Police Service', published in August 2001. The Plan's Foreword by the then Secretary of State, John Reid, stated:

'The Government has indicated a number of areas where it intends to amend the legislation, following the review. They are identified individually in this Plan, but include the core function of community policing, the tripartite arrangements for accountability and the powers of the Policing Board, as well as the role of the Ombudsman.'

One lacuna in the original 2000 Act, principally perceived by the SDLP, although it did not in practice appear to restrict the powers of the Policing Board, was the absence of a provision requiring the Chief Constable to supply the Board with such information and documents as it might require. Accordingly, the Police (Northern Ireland) Act 2003 contained provision at section 32, inserting a new section 33A into the 2000 Act, which began as follows:

'Provision of information to the Board

(1) the Chief Constable shall supply the Board with such information and

> *documents as the Board may require for the purposes of, or in connection with, the exercise of any of its functions'.*

The rationale for this was that the Board might consider that the Chief Constable or his staff were being unnecessarily defensive in providing information or documents that the Board felt justified in requiring. To have to apply the full weight of section 59 in demanding a report felt to some as taking a sledgehammer to crack a nut. The new provision made it clear beyond doubt that the Chief Constable was to supply the Board with information on a day-to-day basis, as reasonably required.

It was, however, not until June 2005 that the Policing Board, on the foot of a recommendation from its own Human Resources Committee, seriously considered the use of the new section 33A. (This was in relation to three reports that had been provided by external consultants to the PSNI concerning the Police College which certain senior staff in the PSNI were perceived to be being dilatory in supplying. In the event, the documents were supplied without the need to invoke the new legal powers, though perhaps the knowledge that their use was under consideration ensured that there was no further delay.)

Changes were also made to the original provisions in the 2000 Act requiring the Chief Constable to submit to the Board a report on any matter connected with the policing of Northern Ireland, whenever so required, enabling the Board, when it has considered the report, to cause an inquiry to be held. Although the Chief Constable could in effect appeal to the Secretary of State against such a requirement on certain grounds, it provided the Board with a specific power unique to the Northern Ireland policing authority. At the instigation, primarily, of the SDLP, the British Government introduced an amendment in the Police (Northern Ireland) Act 2003 effectively reducing the grounds on which the Chief Constable might appeal and also reducing the number of Policing Board Members required to be present during voting for a proposal for an inquiry. In the Updated Implementation Plan the British Government also undertook to issue a best practice code (under section 27) setting out how the Secretary of State would approach proposals from the Board for an inquiry.

It is worth noting that the SDLP's concern about the wording in the original legislation was not substantiated in practice, as the Policing

Board neither requested a report from the Chief Constable under Section 59 nor sought to initiate an inquiry under section 60 prior to the amendments introduced in the 2003 Act.

5.3   The Tripartite Policing Structure in Northern Ireland

Elsewhere we have referred to what is often called the 'tripartite' or three-party structure in relation to policing; this term is used to describe the relationships between a particular police service, the relevant policing authority or Board, and the Government Department with legislative responsibility. These arrangements, established in Great Britain in the Police Act 1964, create a distinction between the police and the State and allow for public representatives to be responsible for police effectiveness and efficiency in their locality and to consult the public on policing matters. In England and Wales the relevant Government Department is the Home Office, headed by the Home Secretary; in Northern Ireland, until the devolution of policing and justice in April 2010, it was the Northern Ireland Office (NIO), headed by the Secretary of State for Northern Ireland.

The Independent Commission was clear that the balance of powers in the tripartite arrangements in Northern Ireland was skewed too strongly in favour of the NIO. The Commission noted that there was inevitably a difference between the arrangements in Northern Ireland and in England or Wales, where, with no less than 43 different police forces, and at that time a large number of Police Authorities – today it is Police and Crime Commissioners – the Home Secretary was inevitably a more remote figure, less able to take a hands-on role. This obliged the Chief Constable in any particular force to forge a working relationship with the respective Police Authority. Moreover, in Northern Ireland, the security situation had been a major factor in bringing about a situation in which, in effect, the Chief Constable was responsible to the Police Authority for what might be called ordinary crime policing but directly to the Secretary of State for security-related policing.

Specifically, the Independent Commission's Report recommended that the wide-ranging provision in Section 39 of the Police (Northern Ireland) Act 1998 that the Secretary of State might issue guidance to the police as to the exercise of their functions should be repealed. This particular power was unique to Northern Ireland – the Home Secretary had no such control. The report stated: *'We do not believe that the Secretary of State or a future Minister in the Northern Ireland Executive should even appear to have the power to direct the police'* (Paragraph 6.18).

While this specific provision was repealed in the Police (Northern Ireland) Act 2000, Section 27 provided for the Secretary of State to issue and revise codes of practice relating to the discharge

'(a) by the Board of any of its functions;

(b) by the Chief Constable of any functions which he exercises –

　　(i) on behalf of and in the name of the Board;

　　(ii) in relation to funds put at his disposal [by the Board];

　　(iii) under Section 26 or Part V.'

Before issuing a code of practice under this section the Secretary of State was required to consult the Board, the Chief Constable, and such other persons or bodies as the Secretary of State considered appropriate. In Section 33, as set out above, it can be seen that in discharging his functions the Chief Constable was required to have regard to any code of practice issued under section 27. This still retained a significant role for the Secretary of State.

In addition to this comparatively general power, the Secretary of State for Northern Ireland also had other specified powers under the 2000 Act, usually but not always in relation to the making of regulations. For example, he was empowered to make regulations relating to the recruitment of police trainees (Section 44) and to emblems and flags (Section 54).

A third general power for the Northern Ireland Secretary of State – again, somewhat different to that exercised by the Home Secretary in England or Wales, where part of the funding for policing comes from local authorities – derives from effectively holding the purse strings for policing. While in practice it is the staff of the Chief Constable who put forward proposals for the police budget for future years and the Policing Board has a role in considering those proposals, prior to the devolution of policing and justice it was the NIO that led the financial discussions with Her Majesty's Treasury in Whitehall. (Post-devolution in Northern Ireland it is primarily the Department of Justice that negotiates with the Department of Finance and Personnel within the Northern Ireland Government, although the NIO still has a residual function in relation to discussions with the Treasury about national security provision.)

Fourth, the Secretary of State – or now the Minister of Justice post-devolution – has a supervisory role in approving the choice of Chief Constable.

Fifth, the Department's role in creating legislation, albeit after consultation, could always exert influence over the work of the Policing Board and the PSNI. One example was a consultation paper published by the NIO in November 2002 entitled 'Race crime and sectarian crime legislation in Northern Ireland'. NIO Ministers concluded that the existing legislation in Northern Ireland was insufficient compared with the provisions of the British Crime and Disorder Act 1998. The views of the Policing Board were sought and, after discussion, a response was sent to the NIO, noting that some Members were uncomfortable with the proposals.

Furthermore, the legislation obliged the Policing Board to consult the Secretary of State in relation to many aspects of the Board's work.

It will be recalled that the Report of the Independent Commission recommended explicitly (Recommendation 22) that 'the provisions of the Police (Northern Ireland) Act 1998 should be simplified so that the respective roles of the Secretary of State (or successor), the Policing Board and the Chief Constable are clear.' It is open to debate how far the final provisions of the 2000 Police Act, and indeed the subsequent Police (Northern Ireland) Act 2003, complied with this requirement. While there was certainly an honest intention to do so on the part of the Secretary of State for Northern Ireland and the NIO, one inevitable consequence of the political negotiations surrounding the finalisation of the legislation was that some comparatively straightforward draft provisions in the Bill became more complex.

Finally, the Independent Commission's Report noted that, with the devolution of policing responsibility to the Northern Ireland Assembly and the advent of the Assembly's Justice Committee, the structure would become quadripartite (as came to pass in 2010).

5.4   Respective Financial Accountabilities

The Independent Commission's Report recommended a substantial strengthening of financial accountability, including a fully costed Annual Policing Plan, a strong audit department within the Policing Board, and a more systematic use of the Audit Office to study police resource management, at the behest of the Policing Board or on its own initiative. The Report said that, in allocating the police service budget to the Chief Constable, the Policing Board should agree expenditure subheads with the Chief Constable and should also be responsible for approving any major capital expenditure. It also recommended that the Chief Constable should be designated a sub-accounting officer in addition to the Chief Executive of the Policing Board, so that either or both might be called, together with the Permanent Under Secretary of the NIO as principal accounting officer, to give evidence to the Public Accounts Committee.

The Police (Northern Ireland) Act 2000 contained financial provisions in Part II requiring the Policing Board to prepare and submit to the Secretary of State for Northern Ireland estimates of the receipts and payments of the Board for police purposes, and for the Board in each financial year to put at the disposal of the Chief Constable an amount equal to the grant for police purposes received by the Board from the Secretary of State under section 9(1) of the Act. However, in addition, it was necessary to have new codes and documents setting out how the comparatively bare legislative provisions would operate in practice.

The NIO drew up separate draft Management Statements for the Chief Constable and the Policing Board together with a document entitled 'Conditions attaching to Grant to the Policing Board for Police Purposes' made under section 9(1) of the Police (Northern Ireland) Act 2000, to be issued to the Chief Constable. Part of the Conditions of Grant included delegated expenditure limits within which the Chief Constable must operate. (In addition, the NIO prepared a document entitled 'Conditions Attaching to Grant to the Northern Ireland Policing Board For Amounts To Be Put At The Disposal Of The Chief Constable under Section 10(5) Of The Police (Northern Ireland) Act 2000', covering the relationship with the Policing Board.) The Secretary of State determined that this would be treated as a code of practice under section 27 of the 2000 Act to provide clearer statutory underpinning.

The Policing Board had a key role in approving the financial estimates for the PSNI. The Chief Constable was required to prepare the estimates for police purposes and submit these to the Policing Board. The estimates were scrutinised by the Board in conjunction with the PSNI Director of Finance at a meeting of the Board's Finance and Resources Committee. Following finalisation and approval by the Board the estimates were submitted to the NIO. In addition to reviewing and approving the annual estimates, the Finance and Resources Committee also considered the three-year spending review for the Police Service.

In addition, Part V of the Police (Northern Ireland) 2000 Act related to 'economy, efficiency and effectiveness'. In particular, section 28 required the Policing Board to make arrangements to secure continuous improvement in the way in which its own functions, and those of the Chief Constable, are exercised, having regard to a combination of economy, efficiency, and effectiveness. The Board was required to conduct regular reviews of the way in which its functions, and those of the Chief Constable, are exercised. The Policing Board was to prepare and publish its performance plan, containing details of how these arrangements were to be implemented, for each financial year. This performance plan would identify the performance indicators and set performance standards (targets). The performance plan would be audited by the Comptroller and Auditor General.

It is important to note that the police are funded differently in Northern Ireland. In England and Wales the Council Tax levied by Councils provides over 20% of the costs of policing. In Northern Ireland all the costs of policing are met by central Government: through the NIO to the Treasury in Whitehall prior to the devolution of policing and justice, and principally through the Northern Ireland Department of Justice to the Northern Ireland Department of Finance and Personnel after that.

5.5   Public Accountability – Public Meetings and Questioning of the Chief Constable

Clearly the Policing Board needed to decide at a very early stage how it would execute the requirement to hold public meetings with the Chief Constable. It is remarkable that the arrangements established for the first such public meeting, held on 4 November 2001, broadly continued to be the favoured approach thereafter, although this was kept under constant scrutiny by the Members. The norm has been for the Chief Constable, accompanied by his senior colleagues and others he deemed appropriate, to meet the full Board for a private discussion prior to the *Public Session* scheduled to begin at noon. (Initially the *Private Session* was scheduled for just 30 minutes, but as, in practice, this often proved too short, it was extended to one hour.)

The *Public Session* would usually consist of a number of key elements: an update on the PSNI's performance against the targets in the Policing Plan, coverage of specific events that had occurred since the last Board meeting (which often were dominated by particular incidents that might be of an historic nature), and reflections on prime areas of concern over the medium term. This last passage often featured a presentation by a PSNI officer on a particular topic frequently in line with the Board's interests. Such presentations were seen by the Board Chairman as particularly valuable in underpinning the Board's role in informing the public through the vehicle of the *Public Session* (and the section later in this chapter on thematic examples includes reference to a number of presentations).

While *Public Sessions* of the Board might be attended by more or fewer members of the public, largely depending on the relative controversy or interest in policing matters at that time, they would always be attended by the media. It was likely, therefore, that at least some account of the contents of a presentation would be aired by the media for public consumption. While, as noted above, the Board is required to hold 10 such public meetings each year, it usually held more than that in practice (though normally not in August).

From the beginning it was apparent that the great majority of PSNI officers and staff understood the definition of operational responsibility as set out in the Independent Commission's report and the concomitant accountability role exercised by the Policing Board, and wanted to play a constructive part in making that role work.

Questions typically come from Board Committees and from Board Members in advance of this meeting; such questions may be put either in the *Public Session* or in the *Private Session*. Normally one supplementary question is also permitted. The Board's Chief Executive will liaise with the Board Chairman on the questions and may suggest to an individual Member whether a particular question is more suited to one or other of the two sessions. Common sense suggests that there may be topics, particularly for reasons of sensitivity, on which the Chief Constable may feel able to give a fuller answer in *Private Session* with the Board, rather than in *Public Session*. On the other hand, a Board Member, particularly a *Political Member*, may feel that he or she would wish to have the matter raised in public and for his or her name to be associated with that line of questioning. Indeed, a Board Member might wish to ask the same question in both the *Private Session* and the *Public Session*. While time constraints might in practice dictate the outcome, the choice has been largely the individual Member's prerogative – not the Board Chairman's, nor that of the Chief Constable (although the Chief Constable's staff might advise the Board in advance that they would suggest certain questions be better taken in the *Private Session*). A Board Member could also seek to insist that a particular question be answered in writing. In addition to this forum, of course, Board Members had the opportunity through their membership of Board Committees to probe PSNI police and staff officers in more depth on particular topics.

These issues were kept under regular review by the Board, in discussion with the Chief Constable. In April 2004 the Policing Board Chairman advised the Corporate Policy Committee meeting that he believed it was opportune to reappraise the Board's approach to supporting the PSNI and holding it to account through the Chief Constable to the ends of effective, efficient, and impartial policing. He noted that the Policing Plan would always be at the heart of the Board's role in holding to account the PSNI through the Chief Constable, and that there were other areas of monitoring required under the legislation, such as human rights compliance. However, he added that at any given time he considered that there were a small number of key areas on which the Board should particularly focus; at that time, he identified human resources, information technology, and best value, while in the longer term areas such as finance, estates, communications, corporate governance, and policing with the community could come to the fore. He reminded Members of the need to ensure that the Policing Board's involvement in these issues did not stray across the line into operational matters and in so doing compromise the Board's ability to hold the Chief Constable to account. He cited the example of the human resources strategy as a model of good practice – here an agreed strategy had been developed with clear objectives, targets, and timetables which had been independently validated, with the appointment of an agreed independent validator reporting to the relevant committee of the Board and the PSNI (in this case Dan Crompton, one of Her Majesty's Inspectors of Constabulary). In relation to information technology and best value he suggested exploring potential roles for Her Majesty's Inspectorate of Constabulary or the Police Information Technology Organisation and the Comptroller and Auditor General. Finally, he noted the value of requesting the Chief Constable or Deputy Chief Constable to attend the Board and its Committees when those particular strategies were being presented and reviewed.

In discussion, Board Members noted the Policing Board's entitlement to openness and frankness, as well as 'early warnings', from the PSNI. There was also value in advisers being appointed jointly by the Board and the PSNI. These issues were in turn taken into account in the development of the Policing Board's Corporate Plan for 2005/08 (see the following chapter).

Other issues included the acceptance of supplementary questions and the position in relation to questions received from members of the public. Arrangements were also made for the Board to adopt a procedure whereby when a question was received from a member of the public it would be addressed to the Chief Constable by a Policing Board Member. In the *Public Session* a place was provided at the table for a representative of the PSNI Superintendents Association, the Police Federation, and (later, at their request) the Northern Ireland Public Service Alliance (NIPSA).

In 2007, in agreement with the Chief Constable, the Policing Board agreed, initially for a trial period, to a further inclusion of questions from members of the public attending Board meetings. Under this arrangement a written question from the public provided in advance, if accepted, would be put by a Board Member to the PSNI, and the member of the public was to be given the opportunity to put one supplementary question from the public gallery. (However, anonymous questions would not be accepted and the Chairman would still retain the discretion to decide on the appropriateness of the question, including whether or not to seek a written response.) A suggestion by a Board Member the previous year to introduce the web-casting of Board meetings in public was not taken up.

The Policing Board determined early on that it should meet twice a year at venues outside Belfast. Although the Board had launched its second annual report in the centre of Derry/Londonderry on 30 September 2003, where a Board panel had responded to public questions, the first formal public meetings were held in Omagh (February 2004), Armagh, Derry/Londonderry, Ballymena, Enniskillen, and Newcastle (November 2006). At such meetings the Chief Constable was asked additionally to report on features pertaining to local policing in that area, as well as reporting on regional crime performance against the target set in the Policing Board's Policing Plan. The choice of Omagh was in part with a view to sending a positive message to support District Policing Partnership (DPP) Members in the west of Northern Ireland. One matter raised in the public session at Omagh, topical in terms of both timing and, to an extent, geography, was the critical report that had just been published by the Police Ombudsman into the RUC's investigation of the murder of Sean Brown in Bellaghy in 1997. In his response, the Deputy Chief Constable publicly accepted that there had been significant failings in this investigation and that it had not been carried out to the standards that the PSNI would now wish to see. The PSNI were committed to a full reinvestigation of the murder. The public meeting was a valuable opportunity for the PSNI to get this message across to an audience west of the Bann.

In terms of the lead given by the PSNI top management in their accountability relationship with the Policing Board, it is also interesting to note the following remarks of Deputy Chief Constable Paul Leighton at the Omagh *Public Session* in response to a question from *Political Member* Alex Attwood (SDLP):

'With regards to transparency before this Board, I have tried my best and the Chief has tried his best and we have all committed to transparency before this Board and we have brought things to this Board that previously would never have been brought to a public forum. I defended this top team as being very much in favour and committed to transparency and we will continue with that and where possible at all we will bring things before the Board.'

The meeting in Armagh, which took place on 4 November 2004,

was attended by the Primate of All Ireland, Archbishop Sean Brady. Speaking then, the Archbishop said:

'Real progress in policing has been made over the last three years. I am convinced that even greater progress could be made and indeed needs to be made, if the whole community took responsibility for the future success of policing. There can be no peace without justice and no justice without an effective and account-able system of law and order.'

Of course, there were other fora in which contact could be had by Policing Board Members with both the Chief Constable and a range of police officers. These included set pieces such as PSNI graduation ceremonies at Garnerville, DPP meetings and seminars with DPP and PSNI Members. In addition, the Board Chairman sought to provide additional opportunities to improve communications, including, for example, an evening Board meeting (not open to the public) with the Chief Constable and his senior officers held in late 2002. There were also visits to District Command Units (DCUs).

This chapter has already set out the comparative complexity of the legislative provisions relating to the tripartite relationship. It must be borne in mind that many of the Board Members had little prior experience of legislation concerning policing or its practical application in an accountability role. On the other hand, half of the Board Members were politicians, used to working with the media to put across their party's and their own political perspective. It was important that they were facilitated to reach a consensus understanding on the key elements of the new role as soon as practical. While the Board could turn for legal advice to the Crown Solicitor's Office, this was a matter on which it was very valuable for the Board to be able to turn to an outside individual who had both considerable relevant expertise and a clear personal grasp of the events that led to the creation of the Board and the legislation. Peter Smith QC, a member of the original Independent Commission, provided very helpful advice both during the Board's formative months and later on issues in relation to the legislation, the tripartite relationship, and corporacy.

Another of the issues considered from time to time by the Policing Board Chairman and others was the extent to which the Board should itself seek to undertake a research function in relation to best policing practice internationally. As noted elsewhere, the Chairman sought to ensure that positive policing developments outside the jurisdiction were drawn to the attention of Board Members; moreover, Members of the Board did themselves travel on official business to look at such developments at first hand.

There were for some time no formal arrangements for the Policing Board to meet regularly with either officials from the NIO or NIO Ministers, although in practice in the years after the Board's establishment the head of the relevant NIO Division attended the *Public Session* and was afforded the opportunity for informal discussion with Board Members after it. There were different types of interaction with NIO Ministers; as noted above, there might be exchanges between the Board Chairman and the Secretary of State or the Minister responsible for policing either in correspondence or in a meeting (usually with the Vice-Chairman also involved); there could be a meeting between some Board Members and the Minister with responsibility for policing, perhaps on a particular theme (as, for example, in May 2002, when the related issues covered included public order policing, particularly in North Belfast, the timetable of the CCTV scheme being introduced by the Department, and the approach of community leaders); and from time to time the Secretary of State or the Minister would attend a meeting with the full Board, accompanied by NIO officials. Such meetings provided a valuable opportunity for the Board to be briefed on matters for which, under the tripartite arrangements, the NIO was primarily responsible, and for Board Members to probe Government Ministers. (By 2007 there had come to be a regular meeting every two months between the Policing Board Chairman and Vice-Chairman and the NIO Minister with responsibility for policing.)

The Policing Board used a range of opportunities to put across the accountability agenda in terms not only of the PSNI's accountability to the Board but also the Board's own responsibility to the public at large. The Board had set up its own Press and Public Relations Sub-Committee and the Board had its own communications strategy. In 2002 an external review of the Board's Press and PR Department was commissioned, following which production companies were invited to bid for the production of a DVD explaining the role and work of the Board.

Many opportunities to promote the work of the Board arose in relation to activities by the PSNI. To give one example, in June 2003 the Policing Board Chairman issued a press release welcoming the new-style PSNI annual report. Commenting on the police performance against the objectives set in the 2002/03 Policing Plan, the Chairman said:

'*The Policing Board has a responsibility to support the PSNI in delivering effective and efficient policing. But it must also hold the service to account for delivery through the Chief Constable. Whilst the PSNI has demonstrated success in meeting some of the targets set in the Policing Plan, there is still much work to do. Crime and the fear of crime continues in communities throughout Northern Ireland, particularly among those that are vulnerable. Many initiatives undertaken by the PSNI to proactively tackle crime and other policing issues such as speeding and personal safety, have been very successful. But making communities safer is not the sole responsibility of the police. The community must also support and work in partnership with the police to help reduce crime and criminality.*'

The Policing Board Chairman was clear that the opportunity should be taken, at the personal level, to demonstrate visible support for the PSNI. Thus, for example, the Policing Board expressed concerns about serious attacks on community officers who had been targeted by dissident republicans using a rocket-propelled grenade in Fermanagh.

On 23 November 2008 four PSNI officers were tragically killed following a road traffic collision; they were Constables based at Kilkeel police station in the Newry and Mourne District. They were part of the neighbourhood and frontline community policing team in that area and had been travelling to the assistance of colleagues under attack late at night. In support of the PSNI the Policing Board Chairman and Vice-Chairman gave a personal lead in attending the funerals, as did other Board Members, and in visiting the DCU to convey the Board's sorrow and sympathy. A one-minute silence was held, along with the Senior Command Team of the PSNI, at the start of the December 2008 Policing Board. In media interviews the Chairman said: '*What is important is that we are supportive of the families; we are thinking of them and at the same time we are encouraging their colleagues to get on with the job that has to be done on behalf of the whole of this community.*' In addition, while it would not be appropriate to give the full details, an issue arose as to the entitlement of the partner of one of the Constables to a pension under the Police Pension (Northern Ireland) Regulations 2007. It is very clear that the Policing Board sought, alongside the Chief Constable, to do all that it could to see to it that the position of the Constable's dependants were considered within the 'spirit' rather than the 'letter' of the Regulations.

In October 2006 the Chief Constable wrote to the Policing Board Chairman in relation to potential topics for inspection by the Criminal Justice Inspector. The Chief Constable referred to the number of agencies which had a statutory responsibility to inspect the PSNI and proposed convening a meeting with all interested parties to discuss how the various inspection processes over the following 12 to 18 months were best organised. This would enable his staff to have clarity as to their workload, and hopefully ensure that there was no duplication of effort. The Chief Constable also raised the role of non-statutory agencies and agencies that had no direct remit in relation to policing who might be involved through other oversight bodies. A particularly significant phrase in the letter was this: 'It seems to me that as the Policing Board is the agency who at the end of the day helps me to account for policing, it would be appropriate for you to lead on this matter.' This suggested not only that the Chief Constable was clear on where the pre-eminent accountability responsibility lay but also that he saw the Policing Board as an important delivery body with which he and his staff could work to influence other agencies. It was a reflection of the positive relationship between the Chief Constable and the Board.

The Policing Board drew up a Publication Scheme which was agreed in March 2003 and publicly launched on 30 June 2003. In the accompanying press release the Chairman noted that the 'Policing Board's Core Values include commitments to accessibility and accountability.' Under the scheme the Board undertook to publish approved Board and Committee meeting minutes from 1 January 2004 onwards. The scheme was based on the model developed by the Association of Police Authorities. This was a further demonstration of the transparency of the new policing dispensation and further encouraged confidence in the new institutions. It should also be noted that this was a proactive move, over a year ahead of the statutory requirement under the Freedom of Information legislation, which took effect from 1 January 2005. When a request was received in the summer of 2003 for a copy of the minutes of Board meetings at which a particular issue had been discussed, the Board also agreed that:

'If a request was received after 1 January 2004 for all or part of minutes of a Board or committee meeting, which took place between November 2001 to December 2003 the request would be facilitated, subject to the exemptions of the Freedom of Information Act.'

The Policing Board regularly monitored compliance with Freedom of Information requests.

On occasions the PSNI team declined to be drawn into operational matters at the Policing Board. For example, in the *Public Session* of December 2003 one of the *Political Members*, Sammy Wilson (DUP), asked the Chief Constable what actions the police were now taking to investigate any allegations of Martin McGuinness's involvement in murders during the period when he had reportedly stated to the inquiry chaired by Lord Saville into the events of Bloody Sunday in Derry/Londonderry in 1972 that he was the local commander of the IRA at that time. The Chief Constable invited Assistant Chief Constable Sam Kinkaid to answer the question. Mr Kinkaid began with a general point about the PSNI approach to murder enquiries and followed with reference to the setting up of the Serious Crime Review Team, but then went on to state specifically that: '*it would not be appropriate for the PSNI to comment on whether a particular individual is a suspect, in either a historic or a current murder*'. (Chapter 20 deals with the PSNI's and Government's approach towards historic investigative inquiries.)

There were alternative ways of providing the information to the Board. For example, in the *Public Session* of May 2003 the Chief Constable declined to go into detail in response to a question about the failure of CCTV coverage but made clear that he was more than happy to give further information to the individual *Member* outside the public forum.

On occasions, especially if there were time constraints, the Chief Constable would send a number of letters to the Policing Board providing fuller written information, often to supplement an initial response in the *Public* or *Private Session*. For example, following the Board meeting of February 2006 letters from the Chief Constable dealt with the effectiveness in policing operations of the PSNI helicopter, the role of the PSNI Underwater Search Unit, the number of car rallies and motorcycle 'ride-outs' notified to the police, costs of the demolition of two West Belfast police stations, PSNI investigation of reports of people trafficking for prostitution, the number of police officers convicted of drink-driving offences, and the outsourced PSNI Vehicle Recovery Scheme. Following the June meeting, the Chief Constable wrote on the effectiveness of alternative methods of patrolling, including the rationale for the pilot usage of horses in Northern Ireland. As can be seen, these responses covered a wide range of different topics; some replies were short, while one was a three-page letter with a 20-page report attached.

Issues would also arise from time to time which merited a different, sometimes joint, approach. In 2005 a court case raised matters of concern in relation to a contract with the PSNI. The Policing Board were concerned about the circumstances surrounding the case, relating to procurement procedures, possibly inappropriate activities, and the use or misuse of public money. The Chairman reported in the *Public Session* of 3 November 2005 that, since the Judge's statement, the Board had met with the Chief Constable on two occasions to discuss the case and the arrangements for taking forward the criminal investigation and administrative review recommended. He stressed that both the Board and the PSNI were anxious to be sure that the public could be confident that the investigations were conducted in a thorough and objective manner and with appropriate oversight by the Board. To achieve this, a joint approach had been agreed between the Board and the Chief Constable.

The criminal investigation was to be run by the PSNI Crime Operations Department with the Assistant Chief Constable in charge, while an external expert with appropriate fraud investigation experience would be appointed to quality assure the process. That person would be available to brief the Board on any issues arising from the investigation. Five members of the Board, one from each political party together with the Chairman and Vice-Chairman, would form an independent advisory group and receive regular progress reports on the criminal investigation. An administrative review of PSNI procurement procedures would be undertaken by independent consultants. A joint Project Board, between the Policing Board and the PSNI, would be established in relation to the administrative review of procurement processes; the Project Board would include two members from the Policing Board's Audit Committee.

The outcome of the administrative review was presented to the Policing Board's Corporate Policy, Planning and Performance Committee on 22 November 2006. Those involved had included the PSNI's internal auditors, the National Audit Office, and Deloittes. The presentation advised the Board that, of the 15 recommendations that had been made, 12 had already been implemented. The Policing Board was provided with some assurances that the identified gaps in the procurement arrangements had been rectified. In lines to the media, the Board's Chairman stressed that it was essential for the whole community to have a police service that was effective, efficient, impartial, and accountable.

5.6   The Evolution of the Handling of Accountability Issues

The arrival of Sinn Féin on the Northern Ireland Policing Board, following its reconstitution on 22 May 2007, further changed the dynamic, internally as well as externally. To some extent this reflected change that was only to be expected as a result of inclusion of a new ingredient in the mix of representation that had remained broadly unchanged since the creation of the Policing Board in November 2001. However, that would understate the significance of what was, in effect, the final piece of the policing jigsaw, with the very tangible demonstration by Sinn Féin of the party's recognition of the new policing dispensation by taking their seats on the Policing Board and on the reconstituted District Policing Partnerships (DPPs), including the reorganised Belfast sub-groups.

The Board Chairman at that time, in referring to the position prior to Sinn Féin's advent, drew an analogy with the public sculpture in Geneva of a large three-legged chair: the chair of representation on the Policing Board was now complete.

At the Northern Ireland Police Federation annual conference on 12 September 2007 the chairman Terry Spence spoke about the Policing Board and the inclusion of Sinn Féin in the Membership:

'We welcome the fact that the Policing Board, whose performance over the past *six years has been surefooted, is now fully representative of the entire community. Two years ago the Federation signalled that we would meet Sinn Féin once they join the Policing Board as a consequence to being in the Executive. I look forward to their acceptance of our request to meet them.'*

It has already been noted that, especially during the period when the Assembly was not sitting, the Policing Board was the most high profile (and at times the only) political institution in Northern Ireland on which representatives of the two traditionally opposed communities were working together. This inevitably meant that the political representatives on the Board chose to publicise their contribution in ways that they believed would have most impact on their future electoral prospects within their broad constituency. On the Unionist side, the Democratic Unionist Party (DUP) representatives on the Board consistently took the line that they were not there to implement the Patten recommendations. The SDLP, coming to Board Membership from a position of opposition to the previous policing arrangements, sought from the beginning of the Board's business to demonstrate the changes for which it could claim credit in helping to deliver. Given that coming on board was effectively a still greater leap for Sinn Féin, it was likely that their *Political Members* on the Policing Board would be looking for opportunities to score their own points.

The impact of Sinn Féin can be seen, especially looking back after several years now, in two tangible ways. The first related to the nature of their questioning of the Chief Constable and his senior colleagues. There could be a level of detail and sharpness in the specific questions that had not always previously been present. To an extent this reflected the depth of research and administrative support available to their *Political Members* from their party's headquarters.

In spring 2008 a revised approach to the *Public Sessions* of Policing Board meetings, including the framing of the questions, was introduced for a pilot period. The PSNI commented, at senior officer level, that many of the questions asked were more operationally than strategically focused. They felt it would be better if operational questions were addressed outside the Board meeting or in a Committee, and the specific local issues should be referred to the relevant DPP. This would, they suggested, allow more time for discussion; in addition, Board Members were welcome to engage more informally through visits and escorting patrols. The Chief Constable wrote that the level of detail requested by some Board Members required a huge amount of activity within his organisation and that there were occasions when the questions the police were asked were more technical than strategic, in his view. However, he concluded:

'On balance, in my experience, I still believe that the Public Session Of Policing Board meetings remains a vital part of the accountability network. I think as a model within the United Kingdom, the combination of the Policing Board and the DPPs remains one of "Best Practice" which other police forces could benefit from.'

The second aspect of the arrival of Sinn Féin may be demonstrated in the robust exchanges in the *Public Session* at the meeting of the Policing Board on 3 April 2008. The Chief Constable accepted that '*the police service is not and should not be immune to criticism*', but he made clear his view that making Northern Ireland a safer place was not the sole responsibility of the police and criticised '*some commentators who should know better who suggest that this is the case*'. He referred to '*somewhat unfair criticism in the recent past*'. He drew a parallel with his time in the Metropolitan police, both as head of Operation Trident and, more recently, following the murder of a number of teenagers earlier that year in London, and noted the need to engage the wider community and the vital need for community cooperation. In his view, some of the criticisms from a small number of politicians and commentators in some of the media '*do not seem to be rooted in a desire to actually solve the overall issues and the clear problems we are facing*'.

At this point the Chief Constable noted the dreadful murders of two men in West Belfast and one more recently in Dungannon, adding that in every case individuals had been arrested, charged, and brought before the courts. Against this background he was advocating:

'Mature conversations between my local police commanders and local community leaders. The megaphone frankly as a means of communication is truly out of date.'

He concluded by accepting that his organisation still had some way to go and would continue, without doubt, to get things wrong on occasions. But, for him, the more informed and mature the debate was the more he thought we had a chance of moving Northern Ireland on more quickly.

The response came from a Sinn Féin *Political Member* on the Board who took issue with the Chief Constable's remarks. He said that, in his view, the criticisms that the party had levelled were very balanced, not only because he had personally made the point that he regretted having criticised the PSNI in the manner in which he had had to do in a very public way but he had also remarked that all of us, including ourselves, had to ask the very deep, soul-searching question: 'are we doing enough to tackle these problems?'. He accepted that many PSNI officers were genuinely committed to providing a public service, but he was also saying that, very often, that meant service was not joined up. The PSNI certainly, in his view, had not at all times responded in the way in which it should have responded, in a timely, effective, and efficient manner. This view was shared by retailers and persons who had been victims of burglary. There had been a number of discussions scheduled between representatives of the PSNI and Sinn Féin, right up to the top level, yet this issue had been brought into the public domain. It was very unhelpful to suggest that his party colleagues, at least in some instances, appeared to be anti-police. That was factually incorrect and not conducive to building the kind of working relationship that the party had been proactively engaged in, particularly in the previous 12 months. He asked if the Chief Constable would retract his remarks.

In response, the Chief Constable said that he stood by his words, which had been chosen carefully. For his part the Sinn Féin *Political Member* stressed that the Chief Constable was not giving proper acknowledgement to the efforts of the party in building trust and a working relationship with his officers at all levels.

Following this exchange, a DUP *Political Member* said that he found this

'Straight talk actually refreshing. I think it shows a maturity that we are now able to take this across the table and if there are issues which bother the Chief Constable, he has the right to put them to this meeting in a forthright manner. If there are matters then which members feel they have to hit back on, either as independents or as political representatives, then we can do it.'

A second Sinn Féin *Political Member* added that:

'*The role and responsibility of this Board to deliver effective and efficient policing and to hold the Chief Constable to account, allows us to be able to criticise you in a way publicly. There will be unhealthy tensions between ourselves, or healthy tensions, whatever way one wants to describe them, but we will be doing it within the context of our statutory responsibility and that is to hold you publicly to account.*'

In his response the Chief Constable said:

'*I do think it is important, not only that it is debated in the public, I am happy for that, but also my officers will be looking to their Chief Constable when they know they have done the right thing and the allegation is they have done the wrong thing, that someone stands up for them and that is also very much part of my role. I have no difficulty being held to account by this Board; that is exactly why I am here.*'

5.7   Accountability in Practice: Examples of Areas Probed by the Board

So far this chapter has primarily described the legislative and procedural aspects of accountability rather than the practical application of the principle to specific policing issues. The next section illustrates the practical application of accountability to policing issues through just a few of the topics or themes which the Board probed with senior PSNI representatives, either in the full Board or sometimes in a Board Committee, and also in connection with the newly created DPPs. It shows the use of *Public Sessions* of the Board, including presentations and specially commissioned reports, to bring issues to the attention of the wider public, as well as demonstrating accountability.

The examples which follow are very much in the field of 'ordinary' crime, which readers outside Northern Ireland will recognise, although there are inevitably some local variations. The main examples are hate crime, domestic violence, crimes against the elderly, and anti-social behaviour.

The first is the issue of hate crime – an important concern in

Northern Ireland and one which the Board regularly tackled. In 2004 incidents of hate crime across Northern Ireland came to the fore. The number of racist incidents in the first nine months of 2003/04, at 267, was 60% higher than in the previous year. Although much of the performance against target in the Policing Plan was positive, the media pressed on this issue.

The Policing Board gave a lead. On 12 February 2004 Members of the Board, accompanied by senior PSNI officers, invited representatives of ethnic minority communities to express their concerns. (This followed an earlier meeting in 2004 between the Policing Board Chairman and the Chief Constable with representatives of the Northern Ireland Council for Ethnic Minorities.) In a subsequent release the Chairman stressed the Board's legal responsibility to make sure that there was an effective and efficient police service which secured the confidence of the <u>entire</u> community. At the same time there was a need for the Board to acknowledge the concerns of the community and ensure that the PSNI's response met community needs. He referred to the specific indicators covering racist and homophobic incidents in the Policing Plan.

April 2004 saw the publication of a report entitled '*Racist harassment in Northern Ireland*', which had been prepared by the Institute for Conflict Research (ICR) on behalf of the Office of the First Minister and deputy First Minister. Later that year the Policing Board and the Police Ombudsman jointly commissioned the ICR to conduct two separate research projects that explored the views and experiences of individuals from (a) the black and minority ethnic population and (b) the lesbian, gay, and bisexual population towards the new policing arrangements in Northern Ireland. Two ICR reports, '*Policing, accountability and the black and minority ethnic (BME) communities in Northern Ireland*' and '*Policing, accountability and the lesbian, gay and bisexual (LGB) communities in Northern Ireland*', were published on 22 February 2006.

The Policing Board produced an action plan to deal with the recommendations relating to the Board and DPPs. In the Board's press release accompanying the reports' publication, an *Independent Member* who had been closely involved with the work pointed out that:

'*Consulting with the public to find out about their views on policing is a core function of the Policing Board and District Policing Partnerships. This means*

*engaging with all sections of the public, regardless of race, ethnic background
or sexual orientation... It is crucial that this research is used to further understand the policing needs of these communities so that the police can address
these needs more effectively. By doing this, we can help build these communities' confidence in policing, provide a policing service that meets their needs,
and make Northern Ireland a safer place for everyone to live.'*

One recommendation referred to a need to increase the number
of Black and Minority Ethnic (BME) recruits to the PSNI. The PSNI
response referred to previous research commissioned by the Service
on BME recruitment, noting that changes had been introduced to
the initial selection test in 2005. The PSNI also had in place Minority
Liaison Officers in each DCU, and had also brought in a new Service
hate incident policy, introducing minimum supervision and investigations standards, and investigation reviews by senior officers. The PSNI
undertook to explore how these developments could best be promoted
within the lesbian, gay and bisexual communities.

The Chief Constable was asked in the *Public Session* of the Policing
Board meeting on 1 March 2006 about the PSNI's response to the
reports. He undertook to provide a full written response, underlining that the PSNI took these issues extremely seriously, internally
and externally. Later that month the PSNI issued an updated policy
directive entitled '*Police response to hate incidents*'.

On 1 June of that year, following the murder the previous month of
15-year-old Michael McIlveen in Ballymena, the Chief Constable reiterated in the Board's *Public Session* that one of the biggest challenges
facing Northern Ireland was the rise in hate crime. An *Independent
Member* raised concerns that the issue of sectarianism was not being
fully addressed in the induction and training of new recruits. The
Deputy Chief Constable said there had been an issue in relation to a
course for new recruits, and the PSNI had carried out two reviews. The
conclusion was that the issues of racism and homophobia were not
being sufficiently addressed and needed to be included in a replacement training course. He had had a long discussion with the Board's
Committee on the issue and he invited Board Members to the initial
pilot of the new course. In September 2006 the Board Chairman
and Vice-Chairman met 11 members of the Coalition on Sexual
Orientation to discuss the follow-up to the ICR reports.

In May 2009 a Sergeant from the Community Safety Department of the PSNI gave a presentation on the issue of hate crime, including the historical perspective from 1997. She noted that both the PSNI and the Policing Board had been involved in a joint meeting with the Board's reference group, and the feedback had been very positive. In the most recent year the clearance rate for both racist and homophobic crimes had increased. The first question, which had been previously submitted by a member of the public, was: what changes did the Chief Constable think the PSNI had made since September 2002 as regards race relations in Northern Ireland? In reply he stressed the key themes of engagement, inclusiveness, and trust.

In May 2014 the PSNI set up a dedicated unit to tackle hate crime.

The second example is domestic violence – a concern to the Policing Board and indeed to DPPs. Lisburn DPP took an initiative with the local PSNI to arrange a major conference to address domestic violence. (Domestic violence accounted for 16% of violent crime in the city of Lisburn, with 1,650 domestic violence-related incidents in 2004/05.) The conference brought together over 90 delegates from DPPs and other statutory and voluntary groups from across Northern Ireland. The conference was told that 66 people had been charged with domestic violence-related offences during the period April–June 2005, compared with just two people during the same period in the previous year. This was due to the proactive arrest strategy adopted by the police in Lisburn, as outlined in their Domestic Violence Control Strategy.

Following this successful local event a wider two-day conference on domestic violence, including delegates from all parts of the United Kingdom and the Republic of Ireland, was held in February 2006.

At the Policing Board's *Public Session* on 3 November 2005 the PSNI gave a presentation on domestic violence. This covered an annual increase of just under 25% in the number of domestic violence incidents that had been reported to the police as well as a significant proportion of the respondents in the Northern Ireland Crime Survey 2003/04. While, on average, five people had been murdered in Northern Ireland in domestic violence-related incidents in each of the previous five years, the PSNI attended an average of 57 domestic violence incidents each day. On the other hand, the detection rate was nearly 75%. The presentation described the PSNI's new Domestic Violence Policy, introduced in September 2004 (which had almost certainly increased the level of recorded reports). It was also stressed that this was not an issue for the PSNI alone – partnership was required with a range of different agencies, with whom the police were very much involved.

At the Policing Board meeting on 2 April 2009 the Chairman referred to the publication by the Board on 24 March of the first of its Thematic Enquiries focusing on how effectively the PSNI dealt with incidents of domestic abuse. The report detailed the PSNI's compliance with the Human Rights Act 1998 in this area and included 14 recommendations for the police to consider as a means of further improving their service to victims of domestic abuse. The presentation by the PSNI that day was on domestic abuse. The Inspector noted that the Northern Ireland crime survey for 2007/08 had estimated that just one in four victims went to the police reporting their worst incident; it was clear that there were significant levels of both under-reporting and repeat victimisation. Across Northern Ireland police attended a domestic incident once every 23 minutes. The PSNI's approach was based on three principles – protection, prevention, and prosecution. There were now Domestic Abuse officers located in each of the Districts. The Inspector stressed again that the PSNI needed the assistance of other agencies – both Government and non-governmental – and had been working closely with them for a number of years.

Another issue to engage the Policing Board's attention for a sustained period was crimes against the elderly, and their fear of crime. In October 2003 the NIO launched a £2.5m campaign to tackle crime against older people, principally through the Department's Community Safety Unit, to be delivered in partnership with the Northern Ireland Housing Executive. During the following month the Chairman and Vice-Chairman of the Policing Board met representatives from a number of groups representing older people. They stressed that this was an issue high on the Board's agenda, not least in relation to recent DPP survey results which rated fear of crime among the elderly as an important issue. Following this, the Chief Constable was probed during the *Public Session* in the December Board meeting, to which representatives from the groups were invited. A presentation was given by the PSNI – the Service had just set up an Independent Advisory Group at Headquarters level to advise on its approach to crimes against the elderly. The PSNI arranged a two-day conference in March 2004 on Human Rights and Victims, with the second day devoted specifically to the issue of crimes against the elderly. Members of the Policing Board visited Merseyside in May to view their partnership arrangements, and the Board also raised their concerns about the limitations of the Government's scheme with the NIO.

The issue was raised again in the *Public Session* when the Policing Board met in Newcastle in November 2006, following the murder of an elderly lady in her home in North Down. The following month the PSNI were probed by Board members drawing on questions supplied by Age Concern and Help the Aged. The PSNI had launched an operation earlier in 2006 which had led to the arrest of 31 individuals suspected of involvement in this type of crime. It was also noted that all DCUs had ongoing initiatives in relation to this vulnerable section of the community, although the Assistant Chief Constable did point out that elderly persons were far less likely to be a victim of crime than other groups in society.

The Chief Constable was further probed by the Board on this matter in October 2007, and reported that there had been a 63% reduction in incidents in the first eight months of that year.

The issue of crimes against the elderly has continued to have a high profile; for example, the *Belfast Telegraph* of 25 April 2012 carried a feature on the subject. Statistics showed that every day four pensioners are burgled or robbed, but just one in 18 cases results in a person being arrested or charged. The issue was raised by the MLA Paul Givan, then the Chairman of the Assembly Justice Committee. The clearance rate appeared to be lower than that for other types of similar offence. The chair of Age Sector Platform in Northern Ireland, Patricia Donald, was quoted as saying that, in a survey of some 1,200 older people across the province, 64% were fearful of being a victim of crime. She accepted that the fear heavily outweighed the chances of actually being a victim, but stressed the importance of providing confidence.

Anti-social behaviour – predominantly committed by young people – was an important continuing issue. The Policing Board was consulted on the draft Anti-Social Behaviour (Northern Ireland) Order 2004 and the Policing Board's Human Rights Adviser gave a presentation to the following meeting of the Human Rights and Professional Standards Committee, which was open to all Board members.

Apart from the Government's policy and legislation, the issue of anti-social behaviour and disorder on the ground was also a concern for the Policing Board. For example, at the *Public Session* of the Board on 1 December 2004 a presentation was given by Assistant Chief Constable McCausland on the 2004 Christmas policing plan for South Belfast. Introducing the presentation, he explained that over 1m people would visit Belfast city centre during December. In the previous year a reduction in crime of one-third had been achieved using a specific Christmas policing plan. The objectives were to reduce crime, tackle anti-social behaviour and provide a safer city. The plans included a training session for city centre traders and a partnership approach adopted with Belfast City Council, Chambers of Trade and Commerce groups, traffic wardens, and outreach workers. Specific PSNI operations related to combatting illegal street trading, the 'Get Home Safe' campaign, crime prevention initiatives, and dealing with rough sleepers. Members of the Board encouraged the PSNI to extend the approach to other parts of Northern Ireland.

A Member of the Policing Board attended a conference in London on the Night-time Economy and Licensing Act in November 2004. As a result of his report, even though the legislation did not apply to Northern Ireland, the Policing Board arranged a similar conference in Northern Ireland, which was held in Derry/Londonderry on 7 June 2005.

The benefits of a partnership approach were highlighted. In January 2005 the same Policing Board member attended a conference in London on developing ways of tackling anti-social behaviour and reported back to the Board on the lessons that could be applied to Northern Ireland. Visible and locally known officers with an ability to enforce order were an important asset. Good neighbourhood policing should identify those crimes which acted as warning signals for an area, such as an increase in vandalism or attacks on elderly people – such activities had a disproportionate impact on the sense of security in an area.

At the *Public Session* of the Policing Board on 6 September 2006 the Chairman put a question to the Chief Constable on behalf of a member of the public as to why the PSNI were not making the best use of Anti-social Behaviour Orders (ASBOs) in Northern Ireland. The Chief Constable and his colleagues explained that there had been a judicial review of the very first ASBO that had delayed all other cases progressing by about eight months.

At the next *Public Session*, on 5 October 2006, the Chairman reiterated the question; as at April of that year, only six of nine ASBOs in Northern Ireland over the previous two years had had some PSNI involvement. In response, the Chief Constable noted that while the legislation had been three or four years behind the rest of the United Kingdom *'it was driven very much by us with the support of the Policing Board'*. In his remarks at the Policing Board's meeting in public held in Newcastle on 1 November 2006, the Chairman noted that at the previous week's Board and PSNI strategy day, during which they had discussed the policing priorities to be outlined in the Northern Ireland Policing Plan for 2007/08, at the top of the concerns from DPPs was the issue of anti-social behaviour and how best to tackle it. At their meeting, the Policing Board received a presentation from the local PSNI commander in relation to local initiatives to tackle anti-social behaviour. These included prosecutions for individuals drinking in the street and a number of initiatives with local off-licences. It was noted that there had been a significant reduction in crime over the previous year.

In October 2007 the Policing Board met in public in Bangor. The first topic that the Chairman highlighted related to the problems of anti-social behaviour. He stressed that the Policing Board were alive to the issue and that it was facilitating a round-table meeting on 15 October with a number of community representatives and key agencies across the criminal justice sector to ensure that a joined-up approach was being taken to tackle the problem. The Chief Constable was again probed on the PSNI response to anti-social behaviour. He accepted that there was more to do and that, in the context of discussions on the Policing Plan, he would be looking to include a harder edge to some of the performance targets around neighbourhood policing.

It was reported that the meeting convened by the Policing Board on 15 October, which had included, among others, church leaders and senior staff from statutory bodies, had contained an emphasis on the perceived failure by the police to deliver service to the required standard. As a consequence, it was agreed by the Policing Board that there would be further bilateral discussions prior to reconvening the main groups three months later.

At a meeting of the Policing Board on 6 March 2008 the Chief Constable reported on a number of operations that had been undertaken in the recent past. These included activities focused on tackling underage drinking, with a pilot in Lisburn being proposed for roll-out across Northern Ireland.

In April 2009 (not for the first time at that time of year) the Policing Board probed the Chief Constable and his senior officers on the anti-social behaviour and disorder witnessed in the Holylands area of south Belfast on St Patrick's Day, 17 March. In response, there was reference to the introduction of fixed penalty notices and penalty notices for disorder, which it was felt would give the PSNI the powers to nip certain anti-social behaviours in the bud before they got started. The Policing Board obtained a further update in May, with regard to the number of persons charged and reported in relation to the particular incident.

In November 2007 Members of the Policing Board met with the North Belfast DPP sub-group and the PSNI following the death of a 16-year-old who had taken his own life having taken illicit drugs. This death, following an earlier one in Strabane, led to public outcry regarding drug dealers. The discussion explored the measures that the police had taken to disrupt the supply of drugs and apprehend drug dealers, the role of the DPP in reassuring the public that the issue was being dealt with, and opportunities for the DPP and the PSNI, and where appropriate the Policing Board, to work together with other agencies to address the drug issues in North Belfast. The press release issued in the name of the Policing Board Vice-Chairman Barry Gilligan emphasised that, while the police undoubtedly had a crucial role to play, the community and other organisations must also address the problem. The police and the DPP agreed to meet again within two weeks to monitor the policing of drug dealing in the locality.

When the issue was raised in turn at the Policing Board meeting in December 2007 the Chief Constable reported that in the previous three months the PSNI Drugs Squad had arrested 36 people, impacting on 12 major crime gangs who were acquiring drugs from an international market; he gave a detailed report on some of the specific successes. A Sinn Féin *Political Member* welcomed the apparent increase in the number of drug raids, but sought an assurance that the PSNI would sustain a coordinated attack against all levels of the drugs trade.

The Board was given a thematic presentation on the PSNI alcohol and drug strategy at the public meeting in March 2008. In the previous year there had been 45 arrests and a significant seizure by the Garda, with PSNI cooperation, of heroin destined for the Dublin market. In addition, a major haul of cannabis had been stopped at Calais by the French authorities, again with PSNI cooperation. At the Board meeting in September 2008 the Chief Constable reported on a successful major operation that had led to arrests north and south of the border and the recovery of over £3m of illegal drugs along with a substantial quantity of firearms.

Another example was a briefing for the Community Involvement Committee on the work of the PSNI's Auto Crime Team, given in February 2004 by the relevant Chief Superintendent. The questioning included the Police Service's relationship with an important pressure group Families Bereaved Through Car Crime and the scope for rolling out to the rest of Northern Ireland good practice in dealing with car crime in West Belfast. The Policing Board Chairman had himself accompanied the PSNI's Assistant Chief Constable Urban during a police operation over-night on 19 December 2003 which had included the issue of car crime. In a press release issued after his experience the Chairman said:

'As a Board, we can support, praise and encourage the PSNI towards the end of effective and efficient policing; we can monitor police performance, and, from time to time, we can tell the PSNI to do better. But if we all want to live in safer times and in safer communities, the entire community must recognise their responsibility to support and work with the PSNI to achieve that goal, as they are here to serve.'

Knife crime was another issue of concern to the Policing Board. A culture of knife crime had become increasingly prevalent in Northern Ireland. The murder of Thomas Devlin in autumn 2005 and the subsequent stabbing of a schoolboy in Ballymoney highlighted the problem. The majority of offenders and victims were in the 11 to 18 age group.

In March 2006 the Policing Board's Community Involvement Committee met representatives from the PSNI and Genesis (the public relations company responsible for the proposed knife awareness and disposal campaign). It was noted that there were 1,000 knife-related crime incidents per year in Northern Ireland, resulting in an average of seven knife-related murders being recorded each year. In May 2006 the Government, the Policing Board, the PSNI, and other agencies announced their intention to confront knife crime in Northern Ireland. The Policing Board was a key strategic partner in the campaign, contributing a significant financial sum both to the initial campaign and then to an extension for the following year. The campaign also presented DPPs with the opportunity to emphasise, at a local level, their commitment to making their communities safer and to engaging with young people. It was arranged that the PSNI would provide a full brief to the Policing Board on the outcome of the campaign by the end of 2006.

A three-week amnesty was announced in which individuals were encouraged to hand knives in. At the *Public Session* of the Policing Board meeting in Enniskillen in June 2006 the Board's Chairman welcomed the initial report that just under 900 knives had been handed in during the previous three-week amnesty as part of the knife awareness campaign. The Board sought a report from the Chief Constable on the lessons learned, including whether the legislation needed to be expanded further. In September 2008 the Chief Constable reported that the PSNI had relaunched their knife awareness advertising campaign and that knife crime remained a concern, in line with the rest of the United Kingdom.

5.8   In Conclusion

As the Independent Commission had correctly foreseen, sustaining accountability was probably the most important, as well as the most challenging, function of the Policing Board. As an issue it had to be kept always under review, including the balance between the *Private* and *Public Sessions*. While the approach evolved over time, reflecting in part the make-up of the Board and the nature of its key players, it is also remarkable how the format adopted at the start of the Board's work broadly held up through the practical outworking in a range of different situations and events.

This chapter has dealt with the practical application of accountability to some thematic examples of what one might term 'ordinary policing'. In Chapter 15 we describe how the Board handled a number of high-profile incidents and events in the field of organised crime and national security.

Presenting accountability, both in theory and in practice, was also an issue that posed problems for the Board's relationship with the media, which inevitably tended to be quicker to highlight the perceived failings of the Police Service than to point out where it was doing well. As the Chairman noted from its beginning, a key function of the Policing Board was to support the PSNI where this was merited. As we observe in the concluding chapter of this book, it is interesting that the word 'support' is now specifically included in the job description of the Police and Crime Commissioners in England and Wales.

References

Shaping the Future Together, a response from the Police Authority for Northern Ireland to the Report of the Independent Commission on Policing, Police Authority

The Community and the Police Service, The Patten Report/Updated Implementation Plan 2001, Northern Ireland Office, August 2001

Racist Harassment in Northern Ireland, http://conflictresearch.org.uk/reports/hatecrime/OFMDFM-Racsim.pdf

Ensuring an Effective, Efficient, Accountable and Impartial Police Service – the Life and Times of the first Northern Ireland Policing Board 4 November 2001–31 March 2006, Northern Ireland Policing Board, 2006

Policing, accountability and the black and minority ethnic (BME) communities in Northern Ireland, Institute for Conflict Research, 2006

Policing, accountability and the lesbian, gay and bisexual (LGB) communities in Northern Ireland, Institute for Conflict Research, 2006

Framework Document for Governance of PSNI, dated 2009, Policing Board website

Belfast Telegraph, 25 April 2012

CHAPTER SIX

The Policing Board's Modus Operandi

6.1   Introduction

This chapter focuses on the arrangements that the Northern Ireland Policing Board (Policing Board or Board) made for going about its work and for communication with the public, and on the series of internal and external reviews of how the Board operated.

There was no clear template for the processes to be adopted by the newly established Policing Board in October 2001. While there were some precedents in the workings of the Northern Ireland Police Authority, the Policing Board clearly sought to distinguish its approach from that of its predecessor. And while the new Board could potentially look to models adopted by the Police Authorities in England and Wales or elsewhere, that would take time.

As one very early step, the Members of the Policing Board agreed to set up a Working Group to look at the agenda for the new Board. The membership of the Working Group was the Chairman and Vice-Chairman, Alex Attwood (Social Democratic and Labour Party (SDLP)), Barry Gilligan, Lord Kilclooney (Ulster Unionist Party (UUP)), Pauline McCabe and Ian Paisley Jnr (Democratic Unionist Party (DUP)). The preparation of the papers for the Working Group, and the preparation of a series of briefing papers, had been led by the interim Chief Executive, Ivan Wilson. This Working Group met on 30 October 2001 and presented its recommendations to the first meeting of the Board a week later on 7 November 2001.

The recommendations included interim Standing Orders, Committee responsibilities, and a media policy, all of which had been addressed by the Working Group and were broadly endorsed by the full Board. The draft interim Standing Orders were subject to considerable discussion and some amendment. It was agreed at this early stage to allow a Board Member to ask a supplementary question of the Chief Constable, but further consideration needed to be given to the process by which questions were put to the Chief Constable, this being a key element of the central Board function of holding the Chief Constable to account. The Chairman would have final discretion about what urgent matters could be raised. It was also agreed that the Standing Orders should be amended to express the Board's desire to reach decisions by consensus.

In the discussion on Committee responsibilities the Working Group addressed the process for appointing chief officers of the police service, and whether the appointment should be made by the full Board or a standing Committee, with their decision ratified by the full Board. In addition it was agreed that officials would write to Board Members seeking preferences for Membership of Board Committees.

The Working Group put proposals for Committee responsibilities to the first Board meeting. The agreed structure was as follows:

- Corporate Policy (of which public relations was a sub-Committee)
- Personnel and General Purposes
- Community Affairs
- Finance and Resources
- Audit
- Complaints Monitoring

The Corporate Policy Committee proved to be the key Committee; it was responsible for the coordination and oversight of the policies and strategies of both the Policing Board and the Police Service, including planning, organisational effectiveness, and delivery of the change programme. This Committee also took responsibility for Policing Board co-ordination with other agencies.

Thereafter the Board's Committee structure was kept under regular review; changes were effected in subsequent years reflecting developments in the policing agenda, recommendations made in reviews, and other factors. A fuller account of the evolving Committee structure is at Appendix 6.A below.

The paper on media issues recognised the importance of

establishing from the start the '*image of the Board as a strong, credible and independent body, setting this in the context of the overall new beginning in policing*'. Early action was to be taken to ensure that the public were aware of the Board's role, responsibilities, and Membership. While the Police Authority had had the benefit of both an in-house Press Office and external consultants, Weber Shandwick, the latter had resigned from the contract in August 2001, having been appointed as marketing consultants for the police service. After discussion, the media policy was amended to make clear that:

'*The Chairman is the official spokesperson of the Board. Where it is considered desirable or appropriate the Vice-Chairman and other Members may be charged by the Chairman with commenting publicly on specific subjects against a pre-determined brief.*'

Three options were put forward for the initial promotion of the Board – a 'big bang' approach, an 'incremental' approach, and deferring media activity for a period. It was recognised that the third of these was not practical given the intense media interest and the requirement to hold public meetings.

Careful consideration was given to the recording of the Policing Board discussions. The practice adopted was not to identify the names or voting position of individual Members or political groupings in minutes except where there was a specific request by the Member or Members involved. While the essence of discussion on substantive items of business was included in the minutes, the detail of discussions in both the *Private Sessions* of Board meetings and Committee meetings was not recorded; the *Public Sessions* of Board meetings were recorded in full with a verbatim minute prepared from an audiotape. While this approach was reviewed from time to time, most particularly after the reconstitution of the Board in 2007, no major change was made to it.

At its first meeting the Board discussed a paper on a training programme to assist Members in carrying out their new responsibilities. The programme included legislation and corporate responsibility, governance and risk management, equality and human rights issues, audit and finance, and aspects of the interface with the community.

Two papers were put to the Board with proposals for a programme of work. One noted the Change Management Programme within the Police Service of Northern Ireland (the Police Service or the PSNI), which included eight key work programmes, while the second identified 20 major areas of activity set out in the Implementation Plan.

As noted in Chapter 4, the Policing Board Chairman made an opening statement to the first *Public Session* of the Policing Board. He referred to the significant amount of work that had already been achieved and the enormity of the change process ahead.

Her Majesty's Inspector of Constabulary attended a meeting of the Policing Board for the first time on 12 December 2001 – the Board's third meeting.

On the appointment in September 2002 of the first permanent Chief Executive of the Policing Board, Bob McCann, the interim Chief Executive Ivan Wilson departed. As might have been expected from a former Under Secretary in the United Kingdom Treasury, the latter was a highly competent Chief Executive who richly enjoyed returning to his roots in Northern Ireland. In turn, on 3 December 2003, the Chairman welcomed Trevor Reaney as the new Chief Executive. (That was also the last meeting attended by Alastair McDowell, a senior official who had provided valuable continuity from the Police Authority to the Policing Board, including a period when he acted as interim Chief Executive of the Board.)

6.2   The Policing Board's Corporate Plan for 2002–2005 and its Code of Conduct

An important step in the public presentation of the Policing Board was the publication of a Corporate Plan for April 2002 to March 2005. It set out the Board's vision, objectives and targets. It included the following mission statement:

'*To secure in partnership with the Chief Constable, the Police Service and Staff Associations, for all of the people living in Northern Ireland an effective, efficient and impartial Police Service which will secure the confidence of the whole community and work in partnership with this community to contribute to the development of a safer, more harmonious and peaceful society. On behalf of the community, the Board will set high standards for the behaviour and performance of the Police Service, and hold the police to account for achievement of the standards. In addition, it will set high standards for itself in its dealings with the Police Service and the general public.'*

The Policing Board identified 10 core values – accessibility, accountability, responsiveness, objectivity/independence, impartiality, integrity, partnership, mutual respect, equality/human rights, and team working. The Foreword by the Chairman stressed that the Policing Board was independent of both government and the PSNI and was accountable to the Northern Ireland community for the delivery of its responsibilities and functions, which were set out in the Corporate Plan. In addition, there were 10 corporate objectives:

'1. to secure the maintenance of an effective, efficient and impartial Police Service and hold the Chief Constable and Police Service publicly to account for the performance of their functions;

2. to promote the concept of community policing;

3. to promote the principles of Human Rights, equality of opportunity and good relations in all that we do and to hold the Police Service similarly to account;

4. the implementation of the Police Service Management of Change Programme;

5. to appoint senior police officers and senior civilian employees in compliance with employment and equality legislation, and where appropriate to call upon these officers/employees to retire;

6. to increase public awareness about the role and responsibility of the Northern Ireland Policing Board and the importance of effective police accountability;

7. to create an environment of continuous improvement in which Board staff, Members and the Police Service are provided with the necessary skills and competencies to perform their respective roles and in which they feel that their contribution is valued;

8. to secure adequate resources to fund the services provided by the Northern Ireland Policing Board and manage these in line with the Police (Northern Ireland) Act 2000 and the Northern Ireland Office Management Statement and Conditions of Grant;

9. to secure an adequate Grant for Police Purposes and ensure that the Chief Constable manages this Grant in an appropriate manner; and

10. to secure continuous improvement in the way in which our functions and those of the Chief Constable are exercised.'

For each of these corporate objectives a series of key performance indicators and targets was published. The Policing Board held regular reviews of progress against the objectives in the Corporate Plan, so that, for example, a paper came to the Corporate Policy Committee in March 2004 detailing progress achieved in the first two years.

A code of conduct was prepared for Members of the Policing Board, which was then reviewed annually. In carrying out their statutory duties under the Police (Northern Ireland) Act 2000 and other related legislation, the code made clear that they should follow the Seven Principles of Public Life set out by the Committee on Standards in Public Life (Nolan). These relate to: selflessness, integrity, objectivity, accountability, openness, honesty, and leadership.

In terms of the principle of selflessness, one unwelcome facet of undertaking public responsibility in this sensitive area in Northern Ireland was the personal risk. From time to time there were threats against and even actual attacks on Members of the Policing Board, either individually or collectively. For example, at its meeting in September 2004 the Board noted details of two incidents in which letters addressed to Members and containing suspect powder had been received at the Board's headquarters. In addition, the Royal Mail had intercepted suspect mail at the sorting office. In September 2005 the Policing Board Vice-Chairman Denis Bradley was seriously assaulted by dissident republicans in his home city.

The code stated that the Chairman of the Policing Board had particular responsibility for:

' • *Providing effective strategic leadership on matters such as formulating the Board strategy in discharging its statutory duties;*

• *encouraging high standards of propriety, and promoting efficient and effective use of staff and other resources throughout the organisation;*

• *ensuring that the Board, in reaching decisions, takes proper account of guidance provided by the Secretary of State for Northern Ireland; and*

• *representing the views of the Board to the general public.'*

The code then made clear that Board Members must at all times:

' • *Observe the highest standards of propriety;*

• *maximise value for money;*

• *be accountable to users of services, the community, the Chairman of the Board and to Parliament;*

• *ensure that dealings with the public are in accordance with the Board's Code of Openness.'*

6.3 The Policing Board's Approach to Consultation and Communications

Consultation with the public and the Policing Board's media policy were kept under regular review. At its meeting in January 2003 the Policing Board took a paper on the Board's consultation policy. This followed an Omnibus survey which included a question on consulting with the public on policing issues which showed that only 27% of those surveyed thought that the Board carried out this function well or very well. The paper noted that the Board consulted with people in a variety of ways, including questionnaires on policing priorities, public information meetings, face-to-face meetings with groups and organisations, conferences, focus groups, press releases, and media interviews. However, it was considered that there had been an over-reliance on written consultation and that the public information evenings that had been adopted in the recent months had not succeeded proportionately in reaching some groups within the community.

The consultation policy, which was designed as practical advice and guidance for Board Members, stressed that there was no 'one size fits all' panacea. The first step must be to define clearly the aims and objectives of the consultation. Feedback should be built in. It was important that the arrangements for any meetings should be carefully thought through to avoid excluding certain categories of attendee. If a particular method was inappropriate for a particular group, what additional method might help to gather the views of those who would otherwise be excluded? The Policing Board's Equality Scheme contained a general commitment to a minimum of eight weeks' consultation on individual documents. The paper stressed the importance of using plain language in all communications.

The Board's consultation paper also noted the issue of 'consultation fatigue', with many groups stating that they were consulted on too many different topics. It was noted that establishing longer-term partnerships with groups would be one practical way of mitigating . this risk.

The Board paid particular attention to the issue of relating to young people and engaging their opinions. In 2003, together with the Police Ombudsman, the Board engaged the Institute for Conflict Research (ICR) to conduct a study of young people's attitudes and experiences of policing in Northern Ireland. Members noted that, at that time, there was no equivalent study of young peoples' attitudes to the police in Great Britain.

Later in 2003 the ICR report was published. While 65% of respondents had heard of the Policing Board a much smaller proportion had knowledge of what it did, although those who did appreciated that the role of the Board was to oversee policing and hold the Chief Constable and the PSNI to account. Around 20% agreed that the Board was independent and impartial and had made policing more effective, although more Protestants than Catholics held these views. The ICR recommended that the Policing Board begin an outreach programme to engage with young people through schools and youth organisations on policing issues.

In February 2004, at a conference in Coleraine, senior local police officers shared a platform with the Police Ombudsman and the Policing Board Chairman, taking questions from 120 teenagers on a range of issues. Speaking at the conference, the Chairman said:

'For me the conference is an investment in the future of our community and society, for each and every one of you are part of our future – but just as importantly you are also part of our present and you have the right for your voice to be heard on issues affecting our society – policing is a critical one of them.'

The Policing Board Standing Orders stated that it was the duty of the Human Rights and Professional Standards Committee to 'Consider complaints about the Board (as distinct from the police service) and to make recommendations to Corporate Policy Committee on them'. In February

2004 the Committee considered and endorsed a paper setting out how individual complaints should be handled. This was approved by the full Policing Board a month later.

In June 2004 the Policing Board considered how best to publicise the Policing Board's own 2003/04 Annual Report. Previously the Board had produced formal Annual Reports that had been circulated in hard-copy format to statutory bodies, key interest groups, schools, and libraries. In addition, in 2003 two public meetings were held to coincide with the launch of the Report. In 2004 the Policing Board considered how to reach and inform a wider audience. It was agreed that a 'supplement styled' 12-page Annual Report would be produced, to be inserted into the three main daily newspapers. This ensured delivery, on 21 September that year, to over 200,000 homes across Northern Ireland. This approach included a greater focus on the role of the Board and its emphasis on holding the police to account.

In March 2005 an analysis of media activity was carried out on behalf of the Policing Board. It fell broadly into three categories: proactive briefings from the Press Office (up to 75% of all activity), issuing formal written press releases (10–15% of activity), and providing official spokespersons for interview or broadcast comment (about 10–15% of activity). As regards the first category, clearance was usually sought from the Policing Board Chairman alone. Analysis of the 54 formal Board press releases issued in 2004 showed that the Chairman had been quoted in 41, the Vice-Chairman in six, the Chairman of the Human Resources Committee in three and the Chairman of the Audit and Best Value Committee in one. The Chairman and Vice-Chairman had featured in virtually all the interviews arranged by Policing Board officials, although on occasions, as nominated by the Chairman, other individual Members gave interviews on specific topics such as finance, hate crime and the Police College development. It was noted that when individual Members spoke on behalf of the Policing Board on a nominated basis, it was done only where the item under consideration enjoyed a broad consensus on the Board.

Also in 2005 the Policing Board's then Director of Communications, Peter Holt, brought forward to the Board's Corporate Policy Committee an updated draft communications strategy for the Policing Board. It set out the Policing Board's strategic aims and the statutory functions that were to be carried out, the themes, key issues and consistent messages to be addressed and delivered; appropriate ethics and standards, including the statutory requirements; audience identification (that is, the different groups and agencies with which the Board needed to communicate); the different media for communication; and a 15-month intensive prioritised programme of activity.

The strategic aims included raising understanding of the Policing Board and its role and building public confidence in community involvement in policing through an effective two-way dialogue between the Policing Board and community representatives and partner agencies. A number of current themes were identified, including policing with the community, confidence in the action of policing institutions while addressing and responding to the public's concerns, and the proposition that progress in policing was at risk without sufficient funding. It was proposed that future Policing Board communication activity should be geared to addressing one or more of the key themes, taking account of the key issues expected to pose challenges over the coming months.

There was considerable discussion of the draft communication strategy before it was adopted by the Board in summer 2005. Members concluded that the Board should seek to extend the boundaries of risk-taking in public relations activities to raise the Board's profile further, that there should be additional public relations initiatives, and that press releases and other media activity should be more creative. It was also agreed that individual Policing Board Committees should routinely consider a paper at each meeting addressing recent communication activity and forthcoming activities. The Corporate Policy Committee monitored performance as a whole on a quarterly basis.

There was recognition that there were opportunities that were not being fully taken for developing outreach initiatives and public affairs activity. A number of specific outreach initiatives were adopted late in 2005.

A further updated communication strategy came before the reconstituted Policing Board in November 2006. The paper noted that 'policing remains a hugely significant media and public issue and there exists a huge appetite for information locally, nationally and internationally'.

In January 2008 the Policing Board's Press and Public Relations Manager, Lorraine Calvert, initiated a quality of service review of the

Board's Branch, issuing a detailed questionnaire to a wide range of contacts.

In the following month, after a landmine attack on police officers in County Fermanagh, Policing Board Members agreed that consideration should be given to the development of a protocol regarding the Board's response immediately following serious incidents, in addition to that already in place for the Chairman as Board spokesperson. The issue was returned to in the meeting of the Corporate Policy, Planning and Performance Committee in January 2009, when the Chairman suggested that the question the Committee might wish to consider was how the Board might present itself more robustly in the media on operational issues – this topic having had an initial discussion at the November 2008 Board. There was recognition that, inevitably, by the time the Policing Board had met to discuss or consider an incident or report, quite often that issue had moved off the news agenda. In the first eight years of its existence it had not been the practice for the Board to respond or offer commentary in respect of what could be considered day-to-day policing issues, for example where there had been a murder or a violent robbery. However, it was recognised that these were the very issues that often led the news agenda and raised public concerns around effectiveness of policing and service delivery. In such cases *Political Members* of the Policing Board were frequently approached directly by the media for comment.

6.4   The Policing Board's Corporate Plan for 2005–2008 and Related Work

In September 2004 Members of the Policing Board held a corporate planning day. This included a review of the initial Corporate Plan for 2002–2005 (and the final outcome on each of the objectives), the preparation of the draft Corporate Plan for 2005–2008, feedback on consultation, and internal self-assessment of the Board's performance. The assessment of the outcome against objectives in the first Corporate Plan was broadly positive, with the great majority of items being scored as completed and substantial progress recorded against nearly all the others.

The 2005–2008 Corporate Plan again highlighted the role of the

Policing Board in holding the Chief Constable to account, in support for District Policing Partnerships (DPPs), in ensuring police effectiveness and efficiency, and in human rights, finance, and recruitment. The main challenges in relation to Government policy initiatives as identified by the Board were the implementation of the Criminal Justice Review, the potential devolution of policing, the Review of Public Administration, the Efficiency Review led by Sir Peter Gershon, and freedom of information. The Northern Ireland Office (NIO) reiterated the Public Service Agreement objective that the Department had negotiated with the Treasury – 'to build and sustain confidence in the effectiveness, efficiency, and capability of the police service and police oversight and accountability arrangements in Northern Ireland'. The Chief Constable had referred to the shaping of a post-Patten Police Service that ensured effectiveness and efficiency, was sensitive to the political environment, and addressed the demands of the National Intelligence Model and community safety.

The Policing Board's revised statement of purpose was briefer than the original mission statement: 'to secure an effective and efficient Police Service which gains the confidence of the whole community in policing'.

The Board decided on just three main objectives, under which the Board's key responsibilities were brigaded:

' • to encourage confidence in policing,

  • to ensure the delivery of an effective police service, and

  • to ensure the delivery of an efficient police.'

The Policing Board's 2005–2008 Corporate Plan was published on 7 April 2005. In line with the Corporate Plan, the Board operated to a yearly Business Plan. Measurement against targets in the Business Plan allowed progress on Corporate Plan objectives to be mapped over the period of the Corporate Plan. The official responsible for each performance indicator was identified. The Business Plan for each year was then rigorously reviewed in each subsequent year to assess performance against target. (For example, at the end of 2005/06 the Board assessed that 93% of targets were in the green category – target met or good progress – with the remaining 7% in the amber category – some progress, but not sufficient to meet green status. In the following year there were no less than 79 targets in the Business Plan, of which all but three were deemed to be on target or completed at the half-yearly review in October 2006.)

Another important outcome of the corporate planning day was the establishment of a Working Group to consider and define the role of the Board in the 'policing architecture' of Northern Ireland. The composition of the working group was the Chairman, the Vice-Chairman, Alex Attwood (SDLP), Fred Cobain (UUP), and Sammy Wilson (DUP). It was to consider the role of the Board both under the then obtaining political arrangements and also under arrangements which might be proposed for the devolution of policing and justice to the Northern Ireland Assembly. The Chairman invited Peter Smith QC to assist the Group in preparing a paper for consideration by the full Board. Some of the issues considered by the Working Group were challenging, including the added value that the Board had brought to policing, where the Chief Constable's operational independence began and ended, what involvement the Board should have in areas such as organised crime, and what issues were arising from the Police Reform White Paper in England and Wales (entitled *Building Communities, Beating Crime*'), published in November 2004.

While it was agreed subsequently that the Working Group would also consider the issue of '*dealing with the past*', the Group then concluded that no further action should be taken by the Policing Board on this particular issue at that time, given that the Parliamentary Northern Ireland Affairs Committee (NIAC) had just produced a report on ways of dealing with the past. (See Chapter 20, in which the past is dealt with more fully.)

In May 2005 the Board's Working Group considered two papers, one entitled '*Where does the Policing Board go from here?*', the other '*The Future for the District Policing Partnerships*'. The first looked at the potential for the development of the role of the Policing Board. Peter Smith suggested that there were a number of areas in which the Board might consider initiating its own research, so that it would be in a better position to hold the Chief Constable and the police to account and meet more effectively the 'best value' objective imposed on the Board. The paper also looked at the possibility of the Board having some representation on the Organised Crime Task Force set up by the NIO with the PSNI and other executive criminal justice agencies. That consideration is dealt with more fully in Chapter 16.

6.5   Reconstitution of the Policing Board in 2006

As noted in Chapter 4, the Policing Board was not reconstituted until 2006. At the end of March 2006, just ahead of reconstitution, the Board published a document entitled '*The Life and Times of the First Northern Ireland Policing Board*', which recorded the achievements of the Board since it was established in November 2001.

In 2006, at a gathering for Policing Board Members and representatives of its many stakeholders, the Board Chairman quoted the Latin saying – '*Respice, prospice et sursum corda*'. It may be translated as '*Look back, look forward, and do so with a stout heart*', an appropriate judgement on the work of the first Policing Board.

The final *Public Session* of that first Board took place on 1 March 2006. In his remarks, the Chairman stressed that the Policing Board had understood its role to be:

'*First, to support the Chief Constable and the PSNI towards the ends of effective and efficient policing, and*

secondly, through the Chief Constable to hold the PSNI to account for the delivery of those ends.'

He continued:

'*Given the nature of our history, the times that the Board found itself in, the absence of complete political support for policing, the threats and intimidation, the controversial issues Members had to deal with, and ongoing political uncertainty, one of the Board's most remarkable achievements is, perhaps, that it survived at all, and still accomplished what it was set up to do. If the Board has had a maxim it was and is, that regardless of the vicissitudes of the moment, to get on with the business and this is what the Board has done, and continues to do. ...*

Given the evolvement of policing in Northern Ireland and the requirement to deliver a substantial change programme, the level of scrutiny provided by the Board and the policing architecture in place has been a necessary requirement to build public confidence in policing and deliver an open and transparent policing service which is fully accountable to the community it serves. The model in place in Northern Ireland provides lessons on effective accountability mechanisms for policing. ...

But we are not standing still and in respect of oversight of policing we too are evolving and learning how we can further improve the oversight mechanisms in place. Both the PSNI and the Board must begin to think of even newer and even better ways of doing things, especially as we look down the road with the budgetary constraints likely to be pressing.'

Paying tribute to the outgoing Vice-Chairman, Denis Bradley, the Policing Board Chairman Desmond Rea said:

'Denis has been at the forefront of some of the most exciting, complex and at times difficult changes in Northern Ireland's recent history. His outstanding commitment to the work of the Board, often in the face of threats, intimidation and even physical attack, cannot be underestimated.'

It may be instructive to look briefly at the induction and training programme for the Members of the new Board. The arrangements had clearly evolved since autumn 2001. It is also true that, by 2006, there were fewer immediately urgent issues – the Members of the first Board were very much thrown in at the deep end and invited to swim. A paper on the training and development policy for Policing Board Members had been prepared and endorsed by the Board in February 2006.

Following an initial informal event for the new Board Members to meet, there were two induction days on 6 and 7 April 2006. (The first *Private Session* of the new Policing Board was held at the end of the first day, on 6 April, to elect the Chairman and Vice-Chairman.) A Members' Handbook, containing key briefing papers and background material, was prepared as part of the induction process, together with a compendium of background reading material.

On 11 April 2006 a full day's session was held at the Police College at Garnerville, with briefings from senior PSNI members. On 25 April there was a full Committee day. Officials briefed Board Members on the role of each Committee and current issues, including the provision of a first-day brief covering specific current topics. Urgent business was taken and initial consideration was given to a proposal for individual Members to take the lead on certain Committee issues, outside those on which the chair of the Committee would ordinarily take the lead. (This was a reflection of the increasingly complex range of issues being addressed within Committees. The idea had been developed by the Metropolitan Police Authority, where individual lead Members would keep themselves informed of key developments and issues in their specific area of work, contributing to policy development as appropriate and acting as champion for that particular matter. However, the lead Members did not have the authority to commit the Authority to a particular course of action or to make decisions on its behalf.)

In the months from appointment through to October 2006 PSNI site visits were arranged for new Policing Board Members. On 31 August 2006 there was a Members' workshop on developing strategic priorities for the Policing Board. (Work by the outgoing Policing Board in February 2006 had identified as the three highest priorities policing with the community, organised crime, and human resources planning strategy. Officials had prepared an analysis of the match between the priorities identified by Policing Board Members and the targets set in the Policing Plan.) The conclusions of the August workshop fed into a strategy event with the PSNI held in October that year, which had by then become an annual exercise.

Membership of the Policing Board's five standing Committees was decided at the Board meeting on 7 April 2006. The Board also determined that two Members, one of them an *Independent Member*, would be appointed as representatives of the Policing Board on the Organised Crime Task Force Strategy (or Stakeholder) Group (dealt with more fully in Chapter 16).

At the first *Public Session* of the reconstituted Policing Board on 3 May 2006 the Chairman reiterated his approach to his role. He would at all times aspire first to act in the best interests of policing, second to act on behalf of and in the best interests of the whole community, and third to interpret as far as possible the mind and will of the Policing Board in all that he did.

During 2006 the Policing Board decided to carry out a new equality screening exercise and published a report for consultation in May 2006 detailing the 82 separate policies existing at that time, giving their origin, a short summary, and the outcome of the screening process. This was done in line with the Equality Commission's guidance, which requires policies to be screened to establish if there is a differential impact on any of the nine categories or groups set out in Section 75 of the Northern Ireland Act 1998. The primary purpose of screening is to identify whether there is a differential impact on any of these groups, and whether it impacted adversely. While it might then be necessary to carry out a full equality impact assessment, the Policing Board concluded that none of its 82 policies did require that at that time, though a number of areas were to be kept under review.

The Policing Board unanimously decided at its meeting in September 2006 that the Chairman should write to the Secretary of State seeking a review of the allowances paid to Board Members. The annual revalorisation of the allowances from 1 April 2005 promised by the then Secretary of State, Paul Murphy, had not occurred. (It was regrettable that a well-informed article relating to the 'pay rise' being sought by the Policing Board appeared in the News Letter on 6 September even before the formal request had been made to the Secretary of State. It was another unhelpful leak.) Peter Hain, who had succeeded Paul Murphy as Secretary of State, wrote to the Chairman advising him that he had increased Members' remuneration with effect from 1 April 2006.

In December 2006 the Policing Board agreed in principle to publish on the Policing Board's website an information schedule detailing the attendance of Members at events other than Policing Board and Committee meetings during the period from 1 April to 31 October 2006. (Their attendance record at Board and Committee meetings was already published.) The schedule demonstrated the extraordinarily wide range of additional responsibilities of Members of the Board, including visits to police stations and DPPs, meetings with external bodies, contacts with Ministers and other politicians, seminars and workshops on policing themes, interviews, and presentations.

6.6   Reconstitution of the Policing Board in 2007

As noted in Chapter 4, the Policing Board was reconstituted in May 2007. The induction day for the new Board took place on 30 May 2007. Board Members were asked to identify strategic issues and future challenges which in turn fed into the Board's corporate planning process. On 31 May (coincidentally the day on which the Police Oversight Commissioner, Al Hutchinson, published his final report – see Chapter 17), elections to the post of Chairman and Vice-Chairman were held.

The Board decided to split the existing Community and Human Rights Committee, forming a separate Community Engagement Committee and a Human Rights and Professional Standards Committee; both had *Political Members* as Chairman – Alex Maskey and Basil McCrea. Jeffrey Donaldson became Vice-Chairman of the Corporate Policy, Planning and Performance Committee. Barry Gilligan was again the Policing Board's representative on the steering group for the new Police College.

The first meeting in *Public Session* of the new Board took place on 6 June 2007. The rest of that month included a range of events – a PSNI Graduation Ceremony at the Police College, an information event on the setting up of a lesbian, gay, bisexual and transgender reference group in Derry/Londonderry, a briefing on the PSNI's proposal for the introduction of Taser, and a briefing on the Organised Crime Task Force by the Minister with responsibility for policing. Members were also advised that the Home Secretary had commissioned Her Majesty's Chief Inspector of Constabulary, Sir Ronnie Flanagan, to undertake a Review of Policing focusing on four themes: reducing bureaucracy, neighbourhood policing, local involvement and accountability, and managing resources. It was proposed that the Policing Board would make a contribution to the review and consider its findings.

At the meeting of the Policing Board on 5 July 2007 it was resolved to adopt the gender-neutral terminology of 'Chairperson' and 'Vice Chairperson' when referring to those offices. (For the sake of consistency, the terms Chairman and Vice-Chairman are retained for use throughout this book.)

A meeting of the Policing Board's Corporate Policy, Planning and Performance Committee in July 2007 approved the Board's Statistical and Research Strategy 2007–11, for which it had delegated authority from the full Board. Many of the proposed activities within the strategy were to meet the Policing Board's statutory obligations under section 3(3)(d)(ii) of the Police (Northern Ireland) Act 2000 to *'assess the level of public satisfaction with the performance of the police and District Policing Partnerships (DPPs)'*. The strategy included continuing the Policing Board module in the biannual Northern Ireland Omnibus Survey to assess public satisfaction with the PSNI, the Policing Board, and DPPs. Other elements included a DPP public consultation survey held in 2008 and Best Value Review surveys. In January 2008 the

Policing Board ran a staff attitude survey, while, a year later, there was a survey of Board Members covering topics such as the quality of papers, minutes, and the service provided by officials.

On 30 August 2007 the Policing Board held an internal seminar to assess the strategic priorities. This time, funding issues were seen as a priority challenge, alongside community policing and community engagement. Following further discussions within the Board and consultation with external bodies, the Policing Board's third Corporate Plan 2008–2011 was published on 3 April against a very different backdrop to that of the previous Corporate Plans, as the foreword by the Board Chairman noted.

The revised wording of the corporate vision was:

'To ensure for all the people of Northern Ireland the delivery of an effective, efficient, impartial, representative and accountable police service which will secure the confidence of the whole community by reducing crime and the fear of crime.'

Nine core values were identified: 'accountable, inclusive, independent, innovative, integrity, openness and transparency, proactive engagement, respectful, and work in partnership', thereby introducing several new values. Three corporate objectives were stated:

' • police performance (to enhance and strengthen the Board's oversight role in order to achieve continuous improvement in police performance and service delivery),

• community engagement and confidence (to increase community support and confidence in policing and to increase the responsiveness of the police),

• service delivery (to ensure the most effective and efficient delivery of services and functions by the Board).'

The challenges ahead that were identified included: future resourcing, a Shared Future, policing the past, present and future, and the transfer of national security.

The Policing Board's Business Plan 2008/09 was distributed as an insert with the published Corporate Plan.

In February 2008 eight Members of the Policing Board, including the Chairman and Vice-Chairman, made a study visit to Edinburgh. The aims included exploring the comparative constitutional arrangements in Scotland, identifying the key challenges for policing in Scotland since devolution, understanding the role of the Scrutiny Committee of the Scottish Parliament, and learning about community policing and call management operations in the Lothian and Borders Constabulary.

In December 2006 the Department of Culture and Leisure issued a consultation paper on proposed Irish language legislation. Following a second consultation exercise, a paper on a languages policy for the Policing Board was brought to the Corporate Policy, Planning and Performance Committee in September 2007, recognising the need for a less piecemeal approach. Both Foras na Gaeilge and the Ulster Scots Agency were consulted by Policing Board officials. Following a critique by an *Independent Member* of the Policing Board, in summer 2008 a sub-group of the Policing Board was set up to consider the Policing Board's Minority Languages Policy. The sub-group consisted of the Board Vice-Chairman, Brian Rea, Peter Weir (DUP), and Gearóid O hEára. The following paragraph, as proposed by the sub-group, was agreed to be incorporated by the Policing Board:

'The Northern Ireland Policing Board recognises the existence within the wider community, of substantial, vibrant flourishing linguistic and cultural communities, including Irish Language, Ulster Scots language and a range of Non-Indigenous Communities. We welcome cultural diversity as a positive influence. The Board acknowledges our responsibility to those significant communities, recognising minority languages as an expression of cultural wealth. We also recognise that some of these communities have not traditionally been fully engaged with Policing. As a Board we will continue our commitment to engage with these communities.'

The policy reaffirmed that the Policing Board would, where possible, and subject to cost and value for money considerations, issue a reply in Irish using the Central Translation Service where necessary. (It noted also that while the 'European Charter' did not establish any individual or collective rights for the speakers of regional or minority languages, it would be in the spirit of the Charter to accept requests in Ulster Scots, though it might not always be possible to reply in that language.) Documents would be translated into Irish or Ulster Scots where they were likely to be read and used generally and were likely to be of particular relevance to Irish or Ulster Scots speakers.

Following initial discussions in the summer of 2007, in April 2008 a worked-up proposal came to the full Board for a research allowance for *Political Members* of the Policing Board at the rate of £20,000 to each political party. Initial approaches to the NIO and subsequently to the Secretary of State had been resisted, if extra funds were to be required – rather than the money coming from within the Policing Board's existing budget. The allowance was to provide for the appointment of a researcher on behalf of each party represented on the Policing Board. After consultation with the Northern Ireland Assembly, the NIO, and the internal auditors interim arrangements were approved at the Board meeting held on 5 June 2008, with the scheme to be reviewed at the end of that financial year. (A number of *Independent Members* did register concern at the lack of equivalent assistance available to them.) The allowance was in practice paid by the Assembly, in part as Assembly Members also benefited. The researchers were not to have access to <u>confidential</u> papers or information supplied by or through the Policing Board, although they would have access to an otherwise full range of Board and Committee papers. The scheme was endorsed for a further year at the review in April 2009.

In July 2008, with the support of the NIO Minister responsible for policing, Paul Goggins, an approach was made to the Home Office seeking agreement for a nomination from the Policing Board to the National Policing Board. This body had been established to advise on and consider strategic issues in respect of policing and the Northern Ireland Policing Board Chairman believed that representation on the National Board would be valuable.

On 4 March 2009 Adrian Donaldson, previously Chief Executive of Castlereagh Borough Council, was appointed Chief Executive of the Policing Board. (The Deputy Chief Executive, Dr Debbie Donnelly, had been acting as Chief Executive for some months, following Trevor Reaney's departure in summer 2008 to serve as the Clerk and Director General of the Northern Ireland Assembly.) Two years later Mr Donaldson resigned with effect from 1 March 2011. He was replaced on an interim basis by Edgar Jardine (who in turn was replaced on a permanent basis in 2013 by Sam Pollock).

6.7   Personal and Personal Security Concerns

One dimension of the accountability role that has arisen more often in Northern Ireland than in other jurisdictions in these islands is concerns about the potential implications of exchanges in a public forum or articles that appear in the media for individuals' personal security or prejudice to their position.

On 2 October 2007 there was a lengthy article in the *Irish News* reporting that more than 30 serving police officers were at that time currently suspended from duty because of alleged misconduct or involvement in criminal activity. A number of the cases were described in some detail (although no names were quoted). The Deputy Chief Constable wrote to the Policing Board expressing his grave concern that, as the information contained in the article had been provided to the Policing Board, a Member or Members of the Board might have provided that information to the media. The Chief Executive highlighted for Policing Board Members the implications under Data Protection and Human Rights legislation of such information appearing in the public domain. (In December 2005 the Policing Board had considered a paper on the handling of leaked documents that had been approved by the Board's Corporate Policy Committee.)

In February 2008 the Chief Constable raised concerns in relation to statements by certain Board Members in *Public Sessions* of Board meetings regarding potential issues in regard to obligations under the Human Rights Act 1998. He stressed that his concerns were not intended to limit the freedom of expression of Members of the Board or to seek to limit criticism of the PSNI:

'*Holding the police to account can involve robust expressions of opinion and difficult questions, especially in relation to matters of general public interest. However, it must be borne in mind that the exercise of freedom of expression carries with it the duties and responsibilities, in particular where it involves attacks on the reputation of individuals.*'

He went on to suggest that, where Board Members had matters which necessarily involved the discussion of sensitive issues concerning individuals, a closed session of the Board was the most appropriate forum. The Policing Board took a paper in April 2008 which included legal advice on the need to frame questions, and indeed answers, in a manner that avoided infringing any individuals' human rights. A paper was prepared for the Board Members later that year assessing the results of the revised pilot arrangements for questions. The Board agreed to tighter guidelines for the conduct of the *Public Session*, including strict adherence to timings, concise questions and answers, local issues being referred to the relevant DPP, and questions and answers that did not identify individuals and thus give rise to a breach of due process or human rights.

6.8   A Series of External and Internal Reviews of the Policing Board

As we have already noted, the Policing Board regularly reviewed its own business and decision-making processes. To give another example, papers were prepared by officials for the Board in October 2004 relating to a range of issues, including those concerning Standing Orders, the code of conduct, and the role of Committees (in particular the extent of delegation of authority to them). Moreover, some changes came about as a consequence of external developments: for example, Standing Orders were amended to reflect the '*Code of Practice on Reports and Inquiries*' issued by the Secretary of State in July 2004. In 2006, following an issue concerning communications between the Chair of one of the Policing Board's Committees and the acting head of the PSNI College, it was agreed to include a paragraph in a revision to the code of conduct concerning the role of Committee Chairs and Vice-Chairs. Other changes came about following Internal Audit reviews of corporate governance and procurement.

Looking back, it is striking how many more additional 'set-piece' reviews were conducted of the Policing Board, some internally commissioned and others conducted on the initiative of third parties. This section describes the main such reviews, though there were other reviews of part or ostensibly all of the Board's conduct of its responsibilities by statutory and non-statutory bodies in Northern Ireland, such as, for example, the Committee on the Administration of Justice.

The reviews covered in this section are as follows:

a. the 2002–03 NIO-sponsored review of remuneration and staffing

b. the 2003 Business Development Service review of Board staffing levels

c. the 2005 Northern Ireland Affairs Committee (NIAC) report on the functions of the Board

d. the 2005 Independent Assessment of the Policing Board

e. the 2006–07 Best Value Review of Accountability

f. the 2010 Independent Continuous Improvement Review of the Board

Of these, the NIAC Report and the Independent Assessment are treated at most length.

The overall conclusions of the reviews of the Board functions were, for the most part, similar: the Board had done well, given the challenging agenda it faced and the choppy political and security waters, but there was always scope for some fine-tuning to improve performance; the clusters of recommendations tended to relate to Board procedure and Committee roles, performance targets, training for Board Members, the Board's dealings with third parties, and the relationship between DPPs and Community Safety Partnerships (CSPs).

One point that most reviews perhaps did not fully recognise was that, with a majority of *Political Members*, it was inevitable that some would use their position on the Board to seek to further their own position or that of their party.

By spring 2002 some concerns were being expressed on behalf of Members of the Policing Board about the amount of time they were expected to spend on Board business and the remuneration provided. The exchanges culminated in an undertaking by the NIO in May 2002 that the Department would conduct a comprehensive review of the remuneration provisions at the end of the financial year by which time the Policing Board would have had a full year's operation after the initial start-up period.

On 7 November 2002 the Minister of State, Jane Kennedy, informed the Policing Board Chairman about the Steering Group that had been set up, comprising senior officials from the NIO with Tony Hopkins, formerly head of Deloitte & Touche Northern Ireland and himself a Chairman of non-departmental public bodies, as an independent member. The terms of reference required the Steering Group to make recommendations for April 2003 onwards, to take account of the roles undertaken by Members of the Policing Board, and to bench-mark against analogous bodies in Northern Ireland in Great Britain. Tony Hopkins then conducted a series of meetings with the great majority of Members of the Policing Board.

The review noted that the public advertisement for Policing Board Members had referred to a commitment of 2–3 days per month, with the Chairman and Vice-Chairman being appointed on the basis that a *'much greater time commitment will be required'*. While it also noted that a wide disparity existed within the Police Authorities in England and Wales, it placed considerable weight on a review recently carried out on behalf of the Association of Police Authorities (APA) and on the arrangements adopted for the Metropolitan Police Authority.

The report concluded that it was clear that the roles and func-tions which Members discharged went considerably beyond the job description in the application documentation. The report's basic recom-mendations were that the basic annual rate for *Independent Members* should be increased from April 2003, with the remuneration for the Chairman and Vice-Chairman also increasing then. (This recognised the features that made the Chairman's role *'the most taxing in Northern Ireland public life'*.) In addition, special responsibility allowances would be paid to up to six Committee chairs (other than the Policing Board Chairman, the Vice-Chairman, and those who are Political Members). Thereafter there should be an annual revalorisation.

On 8 April 2003 the then Secretary of State, Paul Murphy, sent the Board Chairman a copy of the review report, stating that he accepted the conclusions and that, in addition, he proposed that all 19 Members should receive a further £3000 for the commitment they had shown over the previous year. With some reluctance on the part of the Board, the recommendations were implemented in 2004.

In January 2003 the then Chief Executive of the Policing Board contacted the Government's Business Development Service (BDS – an in-house consultancy) to carry out a review of the staffing levels within the Policing Board. The review identified 60 current posts and included a further six, taking account of the anticipated workload in relation to DPPs and future initiatives such as freedom of information. While at November 2003, 23 of the 66 agreed posts remained unfilled, by August the following year this was rectified. The BDS review also recommended the creation of a post of Deputy Chief Executive, although this was not implemented until August 2006, following the report of the Independent Assessment Panel, which encouraged a further staffing review.

In 2004 NIAC, an inter-party Committee of the House of Commons composed of some 14 MPs, several of whom represented constituencies in Northern Ireland, which is constituted to examine a range of issues relating to Northern Ireland and the responsibilities of the Secretary of State, decided to hold an inquiry into the functions of the Northern Ireland Policing Board. The Committee stated that it intended to look into three particular areas:

' • *progress towards developing the Board's role since it was set up in November 2001;*

• *the performance of the Board in respect of its general functions; and*

• *the efficiency and effectiveness of the structure, administration and expenditure of the Board, including its performance against key indicators and targets.'*

The Policing Board made a submission to the Committee in September 2004. This submission stated that:

'The Board takes its accountability role seriously, and we have many powers given to us by the 2000 and 2003 Police Acts to allow us to carry out that accountability function. We do not believe in making knee-jerk reactions, they do not help policing and particularly not when they are made in relation to the policing of a contentious march. ... While people may not like our decisions or judgements we cannot be faulted for being too hasty. We will not jump to criticise or defend (a trap the previous Police Authority fell into) but rather we will discharge our accountability function in an even-handed manner.'

A meeting was held on 25 October 2004 between Members of NIAC and the Policing Board. In addition, the Chairman and Vice-Chairman of the Policing Board gave oral evidence to the Committee.

NIAC published its report on 10 March 2005. The key findings were that:

'The Northern Ireland Policing Board has made solid progress in establishing and developing its role, and its achievements since 2001 in establishing

a framework of accountability for policing in Northern Ireland have been significant. The Board has put in place mechanisms to monitor and assess the performance of the Chief Constable and the PSNI, including a human rights monitoring framework, human resources and training strategies, and a code of ethics for police officers. It has made difficult decisions successfully in a complex political environment.'

The Committee also welcomed the constructive relationship which had been developed between the Policing Board and the senior management of the PSNI.

The Committee's report did contain some criticisms, relating, for example, to the relationship between the Policing Board and the Police Ombudsman, the development of the relationship between the Board and the DPPs, the perceived level of understanding of some Board Members on detail of policing policy and practice, the Board's Committee structure, which should permit a more targeted oversight of the activities of the PSNI, the presentation of the Board's Annual Report, and the level of 'leaks' of sensitive information from the Policing Board (although the Committee recognised that there had been no recent leaks). Specifically, the Committee said that:

'The importance of maintaining the confidentiality of sensitive information provided by the PSNI to the Board cannot be overestimated... Sensitive information provided to the Board in the course of its work must never be divulged to third parties. Such gross breaches of trust are entirely unacceptable and must not be repeated if the reputation of the Board is to be maintained.'

The report invited the Secretary of State to consider whether, in the light of past breaches, the present arrangements were sufficient or whether maintaining strict confidentiality about all information received by the Board should be a formal condition of appointment. In his evidence to the Committee, the Policing Board Chairman had stated that the overall position in terms of responsibility had improved.

NIAC pointed to significant overlap between the functions of CSPs and DPPs, which, it said, had led to duplication of work and wasted resources; the Government needed to give further consideration to the scope for rationalisation. The Committee also criticised the cost of the process for recruiting DPP members and establishing the Partnerships.

The publication of the Committee's report provoked some criticism from certain Board Members, particularly with regard to the reference to leaks and the criticism of the Committee structure.

The Policing Board and the NIO submitted written responses separately (published together on 12 October 2005). The response from the Policing Board pointed to enhanced contact between the Board and the Ombudsman, a series of briefings for Board Members on specific policing practices, and the revised Committee structure decided upon by the Board itself. The Board strongly endorsed NIAC recommendations in relation to CSPs and DPPs and presented the case to NIO Ministers for reform, as described in the following chapter.

In winter 2004/05 the Policing Board considered a first draft of a self-assessment of the Board's performance against the APA self-assessment framework for Police Authorities. At the Chairman's suggestion, the Policing Board decided to commission an external, independent assessment of its role and work over the previous four years. The assessment was conducted by a Panel of five persons, chaired by Sir Keith Povey, the former Her Majesty's Chief Inspector of Constabulary. (The other four members were Graham Gordon, former clerk and solicitor to the Cheshire Police Authority; Rotha Johnston, a Northern Ireland businesswoman; Professor James Mackey, former Professor of Theology in Edinburgh; and Dr Maurice Manning, President of the Irish Human Rights Commission.)

The terms of reference tasked the Panel with assessing the performance and effectiveness of the Policing Board and identifying the key learning experiences in the following three areas:

' • *first, the extent to which the Board has fulfilled the Patten vision of its role;*

• *second, the impact the Board has had within the new policy arrangements; and*

• *third, the statutory framework within which the Board operates and the extent to which it has fulfilled its statutory responsibilities.'*

Panel members conducted a wide range of interviews and their report was published on 7 December 2005. The Panel focused on five key areas – a) leadership and strategic planning, b) performance management,

c) community engagement, d) corporate governance and structures, and e) human rights. Within each, the Panel sought to identify not just the major achievements of the Board but also those key strategic areas where the Board would benefit by concentrating their efforts in the short to medium term.

Overall, the Panel found that the Board was well organised and led, and that its Members and officers were highly committed to the task of securing the best possible policing arrangements for Northern Ireland. Further, it noted that:

'Whilst the report does identify important areas for further development, the substantial achievements of the Board during its first four years should not be underestimated... The very survival of the Board in a political climate not envisaged by Patten has been a major achievement in itself.'

Under the heading of leadership and strategic planning, the Panel heard a wide range of public opinion to the effect that not only had the Board survived in a political situation that made survival very difficult, but it had also been able to provide effective leadership in the development of policing in Northern Ireland. The Board, particularly through its Committees, had given strong leadership to assist the PSNI in the development of policy and strategy in a range of areas, including human resources, training, information technology, estates, finance, and human rights. However, the Panel warned that Board Members must resist the temptation to become overly involved in the implementation of policy – 'micro-management' – as this was the responsibility of the Chief Constable.

The Panel also believed that it was timely for the Board to take a clear lead in setting the policing agenda by identifying those key interests and major concerns about policing, particularly within the most hard-to-reach communities. Another criticism was that the Board had failed to sell itself sufficiently as a corporate entity – for example, in its critical role of holding the Chief Constable to account publicly – and that it should do still more to engage with challenging communities and representative non-governmental organisations.

The Panel shared the view of NIAC that the Board and the Police Ombudsman should work more closely together, and recommended that the Board develop a formal process, to be implemented in a

gradual manner designed to address any perceived failures of management within the PSNI. (This largely referred to the Board's strategic
oversight of complaints against the police in the 'Regulation 20'
reports by the Ombudsman.)

The Panel were impressed by the work of the Board in setting the
Service-wide agenda for policing and establishing targets for the PSNI;
they noted that the performance of the police against those targets
was scrutinised, with senior police officers subject to robust questioning by Members. In relation to community engagement, the Panel
felt that establishing all the DPPs was a considerable achievement,
although there were opportunities for the Board to provide clearer
direction and guidance to DPPs in a number of important areas,
including induction and training, and links with the Board.

The Panel also noted that the approach of the Board to creating a
human rights-compliant Service had been professional and systematic, and it was significant both that the experience of the Board was
regularly used by the Council of Europe in devising its human rights-
based policy on policing and that, for many external police forces,
Northern Ireland had now become a model to be followed.

The Policing Board accepted all 16 recommendations and identified
a further eight areas for improvement, including research, the Board's
relationship with the NIO, and recognition of its role in the tripartite
policing arrangements. The Board took forward a programme of action
in each of the 24 areas. In particular, it developed an action plan to
identify gaps in its understanding of community needs and created
a community engagement sub-group; developed a formal process for
addressing perceived failures of management in the PSNI; published
a new training plan for DPP members in December 2005; conducted
a training needs analysis and put in place enhanced training and
induction arrangements for Board members; reviewed the Board's
approach to openness, outreach, and public involvement; and reviewed
contact with external bodies in relation to human rights. The action
programme was kept under review by the Board, with progress reports
forthcoming on the implementation of recommendations in summer
2006 and summer 2007.

The Policing Board agreed that a Best Value review of how the
Policing Board held the Chief Constable and the PSNI to account
would be carried out during 2006/07. The purpose of the review was

to consider the key processes in relation to how the Board discharged its legislative functions in holding the Chief Constable and the PSNI to account and to make recommendations to secure continuous improvement having regard to a combination of economy, efficiency, and effectiveness.

Accordingly the management consultants KPMG were contracted to conduct a review entitled 'Holding the Chief Constable to Account'. The review adopted the Home Office procedure for Best Value methodology and the APA self-assessment framework of evidence. It focused on three specific areas – leadership and strategic planning, performance management, and community engagement. It included a stakeholder survey and an assessment of public perception and comparator organisations.

The summary was favourable:

'Overall the Policing Board has made great strides in driving and shaping the policing agenda in Northern Ireland and in holding the Chief Constable to account since the introduction of the legislation in 2000. When weaknesses have been identified in the current structure, the Board has acted to change many of the processes or activities.'

The report also applauded the work performed for the Board by independent assessors. The report noted, from the Omnibus Survey conducted in October 2006, that 84% of respondents had heard of the Policing Board and that 40% considered that the Board was holding the Chief Constable publicly to account either well or very well, with only 10% thinking it was done poorly or very poorly. However, on the question of how well or poorly respondents thought the Board did on consulting with the public on policing issues, only a quarter of respondents said well, while as many said poorly.

The key recommendations from the review included the following: targets within the Policing Plan should be more robust and measurable, the Board should develop mechanisms and frameworks to engage the public effectively, the Board and the PSNI should work together to deliver the continuous improvement programme; more time should be set aside for questioning the Chief Constable at Board meetings; and there should be compulsory training for all Board members in confidence building. In addition, the results from the Omnibus and

DPP surveys should be used to create a baseline and the Board should consider the role that the DPPs played in their community engagement strategy, with the emphasis being on greater inclusion.

In conclusion, the Best Value review determined that the Board was effective in clearly holding the Chief Constable to account, although there was some scope for improvement in relation to planning processes and the questioning of the Chief Constable. Consequently, a number of suggestions were put to the Board by officials for changes to the arrangements.

In February 2010 the Policing Board commissioned an independent continuous improvement assessment of its role and work. The devolution of policing and justice two months later (following the inter-party Agreement at Hillsborough on 5 February that year) was seen as an opportunity for reassessing and refocusing on future priorities. The assessment benchmarked against other police authorities, based on the then national assessment criteria:

' • *setting strategic direction*

• *scrutinising performance outcomes*

• *achieving results in community engagement and partnership*

• *ensuring value for money*.'

Recognition was given to the unique context within which the Policing Board had operated over the previous 10 years and the particular challenges for the Board in the future. A detailed report was presented to the Board in November 2010 and published in early 2011. The report concluded that the Board had, within its governance capacity, dealt with some difficult policing issues and had a good record of success in complex political and social circumstances. The resilience, fortitude, determination, and commitment of members and officials over this period were seen as admirable.

There were a number of areas for improvement. While the report commended the work to identify a new vision for the Board, it criticised the absence of a long-term strategy capturing the challenges that lay ahead and the potential risk from other bodies in the political and governance arena in Northern Ireland. Moreover, while the report noted the development of an engagement and consultation strategy, it recommended a review of current consultation methods and operating procedures in relation to DPPs. It felt that the (NIO-led) consultation on merging DPPs and CSPs presented an opportunity that the Board should take, which was interesting given that the Board had itself advocated just such a consultation!

6.9 In Conclusion

This chapter vividly demonstrates the Policing Board's dynamic evolution in both adapting to external events and developing through following up on a range of organisational reviews. It kept its internal structure, its planning, and its communications arrangements under regular review and sought to obtain the views of third parties on improvements.

The importance of the two-way relationship between the Northern Ireland Policing Board and the APA should not be overlooked. From the inception of the Board the Chairman saw both the opportunity to learn from the APA and also the potential to influence it.

As we show throughout this book, in a number of areas the Northern Ireland body moved significantly earlier than the APA in introducing new measures in key areas such as human rights and the assessment of senior police officers' performance. To quote an example noted in this chapter: by 2004 the APA had developed a self-assessment framework for Police Authorities. HMIC had correspondingly developed a framework of evidence and was offering to undertake inspections of Police Authorities in England, Wales and Northern Ireland. The first inspection of a Police Authority was being undertaken in North Yorkshire at the end of 2004. In December 2004 the Policing Board's Corporate Policy Committee considered whether to ask HMIC to conduct a similar inspection. In the event the Board decided to tailor the approach with a review led by Sir Keith Povey which also included other experts to ensure that the particular characteristics of the Northern Ireland context were taken into account.

A second point worth noting is that the contribution made by the Policing Board's Committees, although not usually attracting a high media profile, increased over time. This was partly a function of the Members of each Committee gaining greater knowledge of the particular subject and ownership of the issues, but it also reflected the value that could be added by the input and drive from the individual Chairs. Moreover, a Committee might be materially aided through working in tandem with a source of special expertise such as, for example, the Human Rights Advisers.

References

Code of Practice on Reports and Inquiries, issued by the Secretary of State, 2004

Building Communities, Beating Crime, Government White Paper for England and Wales on Police Reform, November 2004

The Functions of the Northern Ireland Policing Board, Northern Ireland Affairs Committee, 2005a (HC 108), HMSO, London

The Life and Times of the First Northern Ireland Policing Board, Northern Ireland Policing Board, 2006

Best Value Review of Holding the Chief Constable to Account, as at 31 March 2007, Final Report by KPMG for the Policing Board, July 2007

Irish News, 2 October 2007

Appendix 6.A

The Policing Board's Evolving Committee Structure

An initial review of the Policing Board's Committee structure was undertaken early in 2003, reflecting the developing role of the Policing Board. Some changes took effect in June 2003 with a sharper focus on human resources. The changes sought also to reduce the overlap between individual Committees and the timing commitment required of members.

In June 2004 the annual election of Chairman and Vice-Chairman of Committees took place. At that time the chairs were as follows: Community Involvement – Denis Bradley; Human Resources – Pauline McCabe; Finance and General Purposes – Sammy Wilson; Human Rights and Professional Standards – Eddie McGrady; Audit and Best Value – Fred Cobain; Press and Public Relations – Tom Kelly.

By June 2005 the size and frequency of meetings of the individual Committees had developed as follows:

- Audit and Risk Management (6 members – 6 meetings per annum)
- Corporate Policy (9 members – 11 meetings pa)
- Community Involvement (10 members – 10 meetings pa)
- Finance and General Purposes (6 members – 6 meetings pa)
- Human Resources (7 members – 11 meetings pa)
- Human Rights and Professional Standards (7 members – 5 meetings pa)

This entailed a total for all members of 411 meetings, with an average of 21/22 Committee attendances per member each year.

The Corporate Policy Committee consisted of:

- the Chairman of the Board (Chair)
- Vice-Chairman of the Board (Vice-Chair)

- Chairs of all the other Committees (five)
- two floating Independent Members (appointed for 12 months)

The Corporate Policy Committee had a number of roles:

- coordination of Board and PSNI strategies and policies
- oversee development of the Annual Policing Plan
- oversee HMIC, Oversight Commissioner reports
- appointment/discipline of senior officers
- oversee the Policing Board's research strategy
- oversee Policing Board compliance with legislation such as equality, human rights
- review/update Policing Board Committee structure, standing orders etc
- monitor Policing Board communications strategy
- oversee staffing of the Board – structure, composition, and senior appointments
- strategic issues not under the remit of any other Committee

Major issues dealt with by this Committee included:

- development of the Annual Policing Plans
- appointment of the Chief Constable, Deputy Chief Constable, and four Assistant Chief Constables
- review of chief officer structure and remuneration
- introduction of appraisal system for the Chief Constable
- development of Policing Board Corporate Plans
- review of Policing Board organisation and structure
- development of the Board's communications strategy

The Committee met monthly and could meet more frequently. It provided a valuable forum on occasions for dealing with major contentious issues prior to consideration by the full Board. All Committees were represented on what was regarded as the 'senior' Committee of the Board.

A further revised Committee structure was introduced in 2005/06:

- Audit and Risk Management (6 members – 4 meetings pa)
- Corporate Policy, Planning and Finance (10 members – 10 meetings pa)
- Community and Human Rights (9 members – 10 meetings pa)
- Human Resources (9 members – 10 meetings pa)
- Resources and Improvement (9 members – 10 meetings pa)

(This structure was seen as more streamlined, to match more effectively with the PSNI structure and to have fewer Committees, though Committee meetings would be held more frequently and with a larger membership.)

The Policing Board also kept under review the criteria used to measure the performance of Policing Board Committees. An internal audit review of corporate governance and risk assurance (Committee structure) carried out in August 2005 included a recommendation on measuring the performance of Committees. The initial proposals included delivery of the corporate and business plan objectives for each Committee, but, following Board discussion, it was agreed that each Committee would also be assessed on its role in the delivery of major strategies for policing.

A meeting of the Corporate Policy, Planning and Performance Committee in June 2008 noted that the performance of Committees during 2007/08 had been very positive, with the achievement of 93% of the Policing Board's business plan targets and an effective role for Committees in the delivery of major strategies for policing. (However, lower than average attendance at two of the Committees was a matter to be addressed the following year.)

The Policing Board again discussed the arrangements for Committees at its meeting in October 2008. It agreed to a further reduction in the frequency of meetings, although it endorsed two public engagement meetings in a year. (The report noted that there were increasing demands on the time of Board members both through the additional interaction with DPPs and the requirements of attendance at the Assembly.) The Board also considered a series of recommendations in a recent Internal Audit report of Committee structures; one related to the delegation of additional authority to Committees.

In June 2009 a sub-Committee of the Corporate Policy, Planning and Finance Committee was set up to consider the further restructuring of Committees. The aims were to maximise members' contributions, ensure alignment with the Board's strategic priorities, and enhance the ability to hold the Chief Constable to account, including reviewing the public meeting arrangements. Preparation for the devolution of policing and justice was also another major driver, as Policing Board members were concerned that the duties of the Board might be taken on by other organisations if the Board did not reassess its focus and how it did its work.

The sub-Committee formulated a proposal for a revised Committee structure: Corporate Policy, External Relations, Resources, Continuous Improvement and Audit, and Resources (which brought together finance, human resources, equipment, and the PSNI estate).

CHAPTER SEVEN

Police Emblem and Flag

7.1 The Independent Commission's Recommendations and Government Legislation

In any disciplined organisation changes to the name and the emblems associated with the organisation are likely to be among the most challenging. This was particularly true in the Northern Ireland context, given that for most of the majority Unionist community the Royal Ulster Constabulary (RUC) title and the harp and crown emblem symbolised continuity and indeed sacrifice, while for many in the minority Nationalist community it was that very association with the Crown that constituted a chill factor both in terms of overt dealings with the police and recruitment into it. As the Report of the Independent Commission On Policing For Northern Ireland (the Independent Commission) put it:

'The problem is that the name of the RUC, and to some extent the uniform too, have become politicised – one community effectively claiming ownership of the name of "our" police force, and the other community taking the position that the name is symbolic of a relationship between the police and unionism and the British state. The argument about symbols is not an argument about policing, but an argument about the constitution.'

'In our judgement that new beginning cannot be achieved unless the reality that part of the community feels unable to identify with the present name and symbols associated with the police is addressed.' (Paragraphs 17.4 and 17.6)

We have set out, in Chapter 3 above, how the highly charged debate about the name of the police and how the Independent Commission's proposition that the RUC should not be disbanded was largely resolved during the passage of the legislation. Nevertheless, nervousness remained among Nationalist representatives about the actual term that would be used to refer to the new police service after the transition. This was heightened by claims from elements within the Ulster Unionist Party (UUP) who asserted that the 'long title' contained in section 1 of the 2000 Act would still be widely used. Following Weston Park, the Updated Implementation Plan stated (at page 59) that:

'The Government has made it clear, however, that the new name, the Police Service of Northern Ireland, will be used for all operational and working purposes, including whenever and in whatever circumstances the police interface with the public. It will also be used when there is a need to refer to the police service for contractual purposes.

The Government is aware that concern has been expressed that the legislation could possibly result in the name not being used in the manner outlined above. It will, as with all aspects of the legislation, keep this under review and will be willing to return to it if it proves necessary. The use of the new title will be monitored by the Oversight Commissioner.'

Thus, the nomenclature issue was effectively removed from the purview of the Policing Board. However, the same did not apply to the highly sensitive issue of the emblem and the flag for the new police service. It was widely expected in certain quarters that the debate about these matters, if left to locally elected representatives, would dissolve into a divisive and sterile argument about where parties stood in relation to the constitutional question. It was hugely to the credit of the newly established Policing Board that a positive result was achieved in a very short period of time with a very high degree of consensus. The story deserves to be fully told.

The Independent Commission's Report recommended that:

'The Northern Ireland Police Service adopt a new badge and symbols which are entirely free from any association with either the British or Irish states (we note that the Assembly was able to adopt a crest acceptable to all parties).' (Paragraph 17.6)

The precedent of the Assembly crest was not a very close one. While it is true that there was no pre-existing consensus on what a new motif for the Assembly should be, there was no previous crest, as it was in itself a new body and therefore there was little scope for argument about either its retention or its replacement. In the event, the Assembly came up with what some regarded as a low common denominator – flax flowers – based on a traditional agricultural practice in Northern Ireland.

Moreover, the Independent Commission's Report (which was published in the autumn of 1999) did not fully bring out the extent of the disagreement between the Unionist and Nationalist parties in relation to the flying of the Union flag over Government buildings. This issue was to bedevil political development in 2000, with a complete lack of agreement among the parties represented on the Executive, leading ultimately to regulations imposed by the Secretary of State for Northern Ireland in November of that year stipulating the precise dates on which the Union flag could be flown on Government buildings. It provided a further demonstration of the huge sensitivities relating to symbols of cultural and constitutional allegiance.

The provisions in the Police (Northern Ireland) Act 2000 relating to the emblems and flags are contained at section 54. They provided that the Secretary of State may make Regulations in essence a) prescribing the design of an emblem for the police and b) prescribing the design of a flag for the police, and regulating the flying of that flag on land or buildings used by the police. Before making any such Regulations the Secretary of State was required to consult the Northern Ireland Policing Board (the Policing Board or the Board), the Chief Constable, the Police Association, and any other person or body appearing to him to have an interest in the matter. This arrangement effectively allowed one of two outcomes – either the Secretary of State could bless, in Regulations, a solution that had already been reached by another body (which could only be the Policing Board), or the Secretary of State would himself have to prescribe in the Regulations what the outcome should be if the Policing Board were unable to arrive at an agreed solution.

As early as a debate in the House of Lords on 8 November 2000, the Government Minister Lord Falconer had stated:

'*Rather than confronting the shadow Board with a single piece of paper, my Right Honourable Friend will discuss a range of ideas with it, consistent with the objective of securing cross-community support for the new service. It will be open to the Board to endorse these ideas or to come forward with alternative proposals.*

If the Board is able to reach a consensus on an emblem and a flag based on it that is capable of commanding wide support in the new police service and is also acceptable to the Chief Constable, my Right Honourable Friend cannot conceive of circumstances in which he would wish to take a contrary view. That is the simple scenario which, as I say, is not impossible.

However, matters may not be simple. Therefore, in the absence of a consensus and in the light of comments received, my Right Honourable Friend will need to decide what proposals to lay before Parliament. He has already made it clear that he does not accept that the new symbols must, as a matter of principle, be free of all association with both traditions. Equally, it would be entirely counter-productive to seek to prescribe symbols which have a high probability of being objectionable to one part of the community or another.'

Two points of interest arise from this speech. First, it refers to the earlier statement by Peter Mandelson, as Secretary of State, in which he sought to provide some reassurance to Unionists by stating his personal view – ostensibly contrary to the terms of the Patten recommendation – that he did not accept that the new symbols must, as a matter of principle, be free of all association with both traditions. As was to be demonstrated, although his remarks provoked consternation among some Nationalists at the time, they were prescient. Second, it shows that as early as November 2000 – precisely one year before the Board was established – the Government anticipated acting as indeed they did in the autumn of 2001.

The Government's Updated Implementation Plan, published in August 2001, again sought to tread warily in this sensitive field. It made clear that a new badge would be introduced, that the Policing Board would be consulted on the design, and that a new police service flag (based on the new badge) would be introduced. It continued (also at page 59):

'The Government is fully aware of the sensitivity in this area. That is why the Secretary of State has made clear that he wants to obtain a genuine cross-community consensus if he possibly can.

During the passage of the legislation, Government Ministers stressed that

they would be looking to the Policing Board to provide views on this matter.
The Secretary of State could not conceive of rejecting the Board's proposals if
genuine cross-community consensus emerges. Otherwise he would not impose
an outcome either on the emblem or the flying flags which would deter recruit-
ment or be objectionable to a substantial part of the community.

... The Government will consult the Board and other consultees in October
2001.'

The commitment in the penultimate sentence above might have
proved challenging had the Secretary of State had to impose an
outcome in the absence of a cross-community consensus. The deadline
in the final sentence brought out the second challenge for the Policing
Board in this area: that is, that there was a very short period in which
the newly formed Board could discuss and seek to reach agreement on
this issue if the deadline of providing a new badge and flag wherever
they were needed for the changeover to the retitled police service at
the beginning of April 2002 was to be met. A good deal of preparatory
work had already been carried out within the RUC in relation to the
Patten recommendation that a new, more practical style of uniform
should be provided. Research had been conducted, and indeed new
styles of uniform had been proposed. However, to demonstrate in a
very tangible way the change from the RUC to the Police Service of
Northern Ireland (the Police Service or the PSNI), not only the new
uniform but also the new badge and flag were required.

Given the time taken in establishing the Policing Board, as noted
in Chapters 3 and 4, Government Ministers had prudently taken the
precaution of commissioning some preparatory work on a design for a
new emblem.

The work undertaken by the Northern Ireland Office (NIO) had
perforce to be done on a confidential basis. One Belfast design firm
that had already done work for the Department was invited to draw up
some illustrative proposals in autumn 2001.

Following the establishment of the Policing Board, the Minister
of State responsible for Security, Jane Kennedy, wrote to the Policing
Board Chairman on 19 November 2001. (This followed an unsuccessful request by the UUP seeking to head the Government off from
proceeding on the basis that it had set out, one year previously, in the
House of Lords debate.)

The Minister's letter explained that, '*in order to assist the consul-tation process*', the Government had provided possible designs of the emblem or badge. These draft designs, which were intended to assist the Board in their consideration of the matter, were attached to the draft '*Police (Northern Ireland) Act 2000 – Emblems and Flags Regulations*'. The letter drew attention to the Government's intention to have the new emblem, badges of rank, and police service flag ready by the spring for the new recruits. Taking account of the procurement period that would be required, the Government needed to make the Regulations in January 2002 at the latest. This required comments from consultees in less than a month's time, by 14 December.

On the same date the Northern Ireland Office issued a press release opening the consultation on the draft Regulations and publicising seven alternative emblems (prepared by the Department's chosen design company) along with the draft badges of rank. An explanation of the designs accompanied the press release. A number of different approaches were adopted for the emblem, two drawing on the flax flower motif, two with crosses, and three largely neutral designs with the new wording making the main visual impact. Each design was set on a background of a star which would form the shape of the badge. The badges of rank replaced the traditional crown and pips, as used by other United Kingdom police services, with more neutral motifs including symbolic oak leaves.

It is fair to say that the initial reaction from the public to the publi-cation of these potential designs ranged from lukewarm to strongly critical. Lord Kilclooney (UUP), then a *Political Member* of the Policing Board, told the BBC on 19 November 2001 that in his view:

'*The Secretary of State has pre-empted us and I think he has now made it impos-sible for the Board to reach any agreement on this subject.*'

As he saw it, none of the design ideas were acceptable and all ran contrary to the Belfast Agreement. Ian Paisley Jnr (Democratic Unionist Party (DUP)), also a *Political Member*, told the BBC that all the designs were meaningless. He added:

'*We have very good symbols as it exists – we have the harp, the Crown and indeed the shamrock. But all those things are now considered not acceptable*

and we have the complete ruination of anything British or anything which links
the police service to the British connection.'

Gerry Kelly, the Sinn Féin North Belfast MLA, was quoted by the BBC
as saying that the Patten Report was very clear and unambiguous on
the issue. He criticised the British Government for not dealing with
the issue the previous year, when it had published the legislation: he
was reported as saying '*despite the unnecessary delay around this issue, it*
should now do so'.

The *Belfast Telegraph* newspaper ran a public competition for
alternative designs.

7.2   The Solution Reached by the Policing Board

The Chairman of the newly established Policing Board had been alerted
to the issue, but was very conscious that the time for consideration
and consultation was very short. In many ways, what the Government
was asking the Board to do was unreasonable. On the other hand, it
may be that that very perception assisted the Board in achieving the
impossible.

On 19 November 2001 the Chairman issued a press statement
headed '*New badge and emblems for the police service of Northern Ireland*'.
He noted that Board Members would have an opportunity to discuss
the issues at a meeting later that week. The statement concluded by
restating what he had said at the first *Public Session* of the Board:

'*As we commence our work we will have the ability to shape our future and the*
future of policing in Northern Ireland. We recognise and we accept our respon-
sibilities. We are also realistic about the challenging and the sometimes difficult
issues and decisions that we will consider and have to make. We will consider
each issue carefully in a balanced way; decision-making will benefit from the
diversity of our members, who each have an enormous contribution to make to
shaping the future of policing in Northern Ireland. We must self-consciously, as
a Board, take ownership of the policing agenda.'

The Chairman's comments certainly applied to these issues.
An ad hoc Committee of the Policing Board was created at a meeting

of the Board on 20 November 2001 to make recommendations to the Board about the Emblems and Flags Regulations. The Committee should bring back any agreed recommendations to the Board, but if it did not reach agreement or was unlikely to do so within the specified deadline then the Chair of the Committee was to advise the Chairman of the Board. Various scenarios were taken into account, such as whether an extension of the deadline would be required. It was also agreed that Board officials would write to the PSNI to clarify what planning permission, if any, had been sought to change name signs from RUC to PSNI at stations and other buildings throughout the police estate.

The ad hoc Committee was chaired by Pauline McCabe (an *Independent Member*); the other members were Viscount Brookeborough (an *Independent Member*), Fred Cobain (UUP), Tom Kelly (an *Independent Member*), Eddie McGrady (Social Democratic and Labour Party (SDLP)), and Sammy Wilson (DUP). The selection of the individual Members of the Committee, both as Board Members with influence among their colleagues and in representing a broad range of opinion, was itself important in achieving a successful outcome.

The ad hoc Committee met on 30 November. They focused on what they wanted the corporate image to communicate, what images/ graphics might achieve this, and what was good/not good in meeting all of the different needs they wanted to consider. With the assistance of Tom Kelly, arrangements had been made for representatives of three nominated public relations agencies to join part of the Committee's discussion on 30 November and to be briefed regarding the design requirements with all Members still present.

Less than two weeks later, on 12 December, the ad hoc Committee presented to the full Policing Board a full set of proposals. At its heart was the new emblem which, in the terms put to the Board:

'*Explores the notion of inclusiveness and parity with the simple stylistic representation of a variety of symbols that reflect our diversity, our aspirations and our desire to mutually respect and protect difference through policing. The sunburst surrounding the roundel represents a new beginning or new dawn for the new Police Service. The shape is echoed in the central star that provides six areas between its rays for a series of symbols – all of equal prominence. These symbols include: an olive branch; a torch; a harp; the scales of justice;*

a shamrock leaf; and a crown. The centrepiece houses the Cross of St Patrick which places all six symbols in the context of Northern Ireland. The simplistic rendering of these symbols in a neutral format of things that unite not divide reflects an inclusive society where all our values, common interests and differences are recognised, celebrated and protected.'

At the Board meeting, on behalf of the Committee, Pauline McCabe outlined the rationale behind the design and explained that some final artwork was required to polish the design, which had been produced to meet a tight deadline. When the Board Chairman sought the views of Members a number stated that, while the design was not their preferred option, it was an acceptable compromise. It was noted that the Chief Constable, on behalf of the police, was content with the Board's Committee's recommendations. With agreement on some fine-tuning of the detailed artwork, the Board agreed unanimously to recommend the emblem to the Secretary of State.

In addition, Pauline McCabe advised that the Committee also recommended that the PSNI uniform buttons be black with a raised St Patrick's Cross, and that the designs of the badges of rank forwarded by the Secretary of State were acceptable and should be adopted, although the superintendents' badge should be the central six-pointed star and St Patrick's Cross from the main emblem. These proposals were also agreed by the Board. It was agreed that a press release should be issued. The central wording of the release reflected the terms put to the Board above. In addition, the Board Chairman expressed gratitude to everyone who had sent their designs to the Board and to the *Belfast Telegraph*, *Irish News* and *Derry Journal* for their cooperation in encouraging public input.

Later that same evening a short press release was issued by the Secretary of State, Dr John Reid, welcoming the decision of the Policing Board. He noted that the work done in reaching a cross-community consensus on a new design boded well for the future of policing in Northern Ireland. When he wrote subsequently to the Board Chairman, the Secretary of State said that:

'Many people doubted it could be done, but this is an example to us all of what can be accomplished when everybody works together to come to a mutually acceptable position.'

Dr Reid added that he aimed to lay Regulations early in January so that the new uniform, with the new emblem, would be ready for the recruits when they moved on to other duties in the spring (having finished their training).

The Government indeed moved quickly, for its part. On 9 January 2002 Jane Kennedy laid the draft Police Emblems and Flags (Northern Ireland) Regulations 2002 before Parliament. In a press release she said that she was delighted to confirm that the new badge would be the one on which the Policing Board reached unanimous agreement in December. On 21 January the Regulations were debated at Westminster. The PSNI had confirmed to the Board in early January that this Service would meet the 5 April target date for introduction of the new uniform badge.

On 26 March 2002, along with the Policing Board, at a well-attended preview event held in the Europa Hotel the PSNI formally launched the new emblem which would be worn by all police officers from 5 April. The keynote speakers were Professor Rea and Assistant Chief Constable Alan McQuillan. The Board Chairman recalled that:

'Presented with an impossible timescale and what to some seemed like an insoluble problem, my fellow Board members showed great maturity and ingenuity and after lengthy consideration agreed a design proposal, which is respectful of diversity, inclusiveness and parity. We believe we have created an emblem which all communities in Northern Ireland, including everyone in the policing service, can claim is their own.'

He continued:

'It is also important to recognise the vast amount of work and effort being put in to establish a new beginning in policing. We are part of an overall drive where fundamental changes are being made to policing structures to ensure we have in place a service which is effective and efficient and fulfils the aim of policing with the community. This is a long-term process but we can all be proud of the successes to date, certainly not just of the Board but of all the other significant developments including the continued success of the recruitment drive, of which a further campaign has been recently launched.

The Policing Board is the foundation stone for police accountability and we have pledged our support and commitment to meeting all our responsibilities in driving that process forward. Of course we have had, and probably will have a few more hiccups. But that certainly makes life challenging, if not interesting and enjoyable – I can assure you of that! We are beginning to tackle the real issues at the heart of policing here and look to the future with great confidence in the pursuit of an effective and efficient police service to tackle all policing issues. It is this overall pursuit which makes days like today even more signif-icant. What we see before us today is not simply a new style of uniform but a symbol of a fresh start, a new beginning and of us working together with the police and others to create real community policing which we all need and deserve.'

In his remarks Alan McQuillan observed that while the new uniform would perhaps be one of the most visible changes in the face of policing, the last two years had already seen a huge programme of fundamental change in the police service. He highlighted, in addition to the estab-lishment of the Policing Board, new systems of accountability through both the Board and the Police Ombudsman, and the implementation of the most comprehensive programme of work on human rights in any police force in the United Kingdom – a programme designed to put respect for the protection of human rights at the very centre of all aspects of the service.

He noted that none of the changes had been easy and that tran-sitions were always difficult times. Moreover, there were also the continuing problems of terrorism and disorder that had been so apparent over the preceding 12 months. However, he emphasised that the new trainees would be joining their colleagues in working ever harder to provide the best possible policing service to the community.

The new flag was formally presented by the Chairman on behalf of the Policing Board to the PSNI at the graduation ceremony for the first police trainees held on 5 April 2002 at the Police Training College at Garnerville. As the press release issued by the Policing Board that day stated:

'It will be particularly gratifying for the Board to attend the celebrations today and to see the new emblem being displayed on both the new uniforms and on the flag.'

7.3   In Conclusion

There is no doubt that the approach of the Policing Board was highly successful. In an extraordinarily short time, and in the public gaze, consensus was reached on an issue that had the potential to create delay and division. As the Chairman noted in his public comments, Board Members displayed remarkable imagination and maturity to come up with a solution that was acceptable not just to the Board but also to the Police Service. Moreover, the design has stood the test of time and has been unchallenged for over ten years.

As noted already, the Members of the ad hoc Committee had credibility with their colleagues and were seen as representative of the range of political viewpoints on the Board. The chosen design was not strictly compliant with the Independent Commission's recommendation, which had favoured symbols that were entirely free from any association with either the British or Irish States, but rather it reflected elements of both traditions in Northern Ireland.

It is doubtful if, in the climate of bureaucratic caution and risk aversion that appears so prevalent in Northern Ireland today, the fast-track approach adopted by the Policing Board which proved so successful (or indeed the preliminary work by the NIO) would have been allowed. The regulations now surrounding procurement that prevent consultancy contracts being awarded other than after a prolonged public competition do constrain the ability of organisations to get things done in a common-sense and pragmatic fashion – for which they can subsequently be held to account should there be considered to be any inappropriate action.

References

BBC News, Northern Ireland, 19.30 GMT on Monday 19 November 2001

CHAPTER EIGHT

Policing at District Level/
Policing with the Community

8.1 The Independent Commission Report and District Policing Partnerships

In its Chapter 6, which also contained the proposals for what was to become the Northern Ireland Policing Board, the Report of The Independent Commission On Policing For Northern Ireland (the Independent Commission) introduced the concept of what it called District Policing Partnership Boards (DPPBs, although in practice the title was later shortened to DPPs). The Report set out that, while the Policing Board would be the central institution of democratic accountability,

'An important theme of this Report is that policing should be decentralised, and that there should be constant dialogue at local levels between the police and the community.' (Paragraph 6.25)

The report recommended that

'Each District Council should establish a District Policing Partnership Board as a committee of the Council, with a majority elected Membership, the remaining independent Members to be selected by the Council with the agreement of the Policing Board.' (Paragraph 6.26)

Taken as a whole, each DPP was to be broadly representative of the district in terms of religion, gender, age, and cultural background. Given the size of the Belfast District Council area, the Belfast DPP should have four geographical sub-groups. Importantly, all the DPPs should be coterminous with a police district.

The functions of the body would be *'advisory, explanatory and consul-tative'*. They should *'represent the consumer, voice the concerns of citizens and monitor the performance of the police in their districts'*. The police District Commander should present a report monthly and answer questions. While the DPPs should not have comparable accountability powers to the Policing Board, their views should be taken fully into account by the police and the Policing Board in the formulation of Policing Plans and strategies at the central level.

The Independent Commission's Report recommended that the administration costs of the DPP should attract a 75% grant from the Policing Board, with the remaining 25% to be funded by the District Council. It also recommended that District Councils should have the power to contribute an amount up to three pence in the pound towards the policing of their district; moreover, it recommended a lower tier body as well, in that local communities should be encour-aged to develop consultative forums on lines that suited them and the neighbourhood policing manager.

In Chapter 7 the Report set out the Independent Commission's proposal for what they called *'policing with the community'*. In partic-ular, the Report recommended that *'Policing with the community should be the core function of the police service and the core function of every police station'* (Paragraph 7.9).

The Report laid stress on the role of dedicated neighbourhood policing teams, with probationary police officers undertaking the operational phases of their training, doing team policing in the community, and providing for continuity of team members serving in a neighbourhood. It also recommended that, where practicable, policing teams should patrol on foot. Neighbourhood policing teams should be empowered to determine their own local priorities and set their own objectives within the overall Annual Policing Plan and in consultation with community representatives.

The Report also emphasised that *'an integral element of successful community policing is problem-solving'*. It recommended that the police should conduct crime pattern and complaint pattern analysis to provide an information-led, problem-solving approach to policing, and that *'All police officers be instructed in problem-solving techniques and encouraged to address the causes of problems as well as the consequences'* (Paragraph 7.16).

The Independent Commission recognised the scale of the challenge, and that it was a very different type of policing from the reactive, security-focused policing to which most police officers in Northern Ireland had been accustomed. Policing with the community called for new structures, new management practices, and new training, all addressed in subsequent chapters in their Report. However, the prize was great:

'If successfully implemented, community partnership policing will lead to a police service that is both more widely accepted by the community and more effective in securing the safety of the community.' (Paragraph 7.19)

8.2   The Legislation in Relation to District Policing Partnerships

In formulating the legislation that became the Police (Northern Ireland) Act 2000, the British Government introduced several deviations from the recommendations in relation to the DPPs, in part to soften the impact for Unionists. Given the comparatively stark electoral arithmetic in the four geographical areas that made up Belfast, there were concerns about the extent to which some of the Belfast sub-groups might adopt a somewhat one-sided approach to policing. Separately, members of the Ulster Unionist Party (UUP) made strong representations against the recommendation that District Councils should have the ability to contribute funds to the DPPs.

Importantly, the Government took the view that the overall responsibility for appointments to the new bodies should be vested in the Northern Ireland Policing Board (Policing Board or the Board) rather than District Councils. These changes were spelled out in the Patten Report Implementation Plan. The Secretary of State would issue a Code of Practice on the appointment of *Independent Members* to DPPs, while the Policing Board were to issue a Code of Practice on the exercise of DPP functions.

Under section 16 of the Police (Northern Ireland) Act 2000, the role of the DPPs was to:

- provide views to the District Commander on any matter concerning policing in the district

- monitor the performance of the police in carrying out the local Policing Plan

- obtain the views of the public about matters concerning policing of the district

- obtain the cooperation of the public with the police in preventing crime

- act as a general forum for discussion and consultation on matters affecting the policing of the district

Section 25 of the Police (Northern Ireland) Act 2000 required the views of DPPs to be taken into account by the Policing Board in formulating policing plans and strategies, and by the District Commander before issuing a local Policing Plan (section 22). Section 17 required DPPs to submit an annual report simultaneously to both the District Council and the Policing Board, though they could also make other reports on policing at any time. In addition, the legislation provided specifically that *'Each district, other than Belfast, shall be a police district'*.

In relation to the Independent Commission Report's recommendations on policing with the community, there was a comparatively modest provision at Section 32 (5) of the 2000 Act requiring that *'Police officers shall, so far as practicable, carry out their functions in cooperation with, and with the aim of securing the support of, the local community.'*

As we have seen elsewhere, the Nationalist parties in Northern Ireland pressed for changes in the original legislation in a number of areas, including issues to do with both community policing and DPPs. The Social Democratic and Labour Party (SDLP) in particular represented that there was a need to state more explicitly in the legislation the Independent Commission Report recommendation that *'Policing with the community should be the core function of the police service and the core function of every police station.'*

Accordingly, an amendment was introduced in the Police (Northern Ireland) Act 2003 entitled *'Core policing principles'*, as follows:

(1) Police officers shall carry out their functions with the aim –

   (a) of securing the support of the local community, and

   (b) of acting in cooperation with the local community.

*(2) In carrying out their functions, police officers shall be guided by the code of
ethics under Section 52'.*

A related amendment to the 2000 Act required the Policing Board to
monitor policing with the community (and to report on it in its annual
report). This development highlighted the importance attached to
policing with the community for police officers in Northern Ireland,
as against their counterparts in the rest of the United Kingdom, and
indeed the Republic of Ireland.

Various changes were also made in 2003 to the original provisions
relating to DPPs – at the request of the Policing Board, the Board was
placed under a statutory duty to ensure that each DPP was so far as
practicable reflective of the local community (as the Independent
Commission Report had recommended).

When the British Government published in November 2002
what was then the Police Bill, it also published additional clauses
that the Government stated would be included dependent on 'acts
of completion' by the IRA (which included a full sign-up to policing)
and the restoration of the Northern Ireland Assembly. Two sets of
amendments related to the Membership of DPPs and the Belfast sub-
groups. The first set introduced a declaration against terrorism, with
provision to establish whether a DPP Member had acted in breach
of the terms of a declaration. It also limited the extent of the original ban on individuals who had previously received a sentence of
imprisonment.

Subject to these 'acts of completion', the changes virtually made
the Belfast sub-groups DPPs in their own right. Each sub-group would
now have 11 Members – six Councillors (all Members of the Belfast
DPP) and five *Independent Members*.

8.3   The Creation of Police Districts

District Commanders were appointed for each of the 26 District
Command Units (DCUs) in April 2002, before the DPPs were created.
The Independent Commission Report Recommendation 78 was that:

'District commanders should be required regularly to account to their senior

officers for the patterns of crime and police activity in their district and to
explain how they propose to address their district's problems.'

Thus the Report had <u>not</u> recommended that District Commanders be
accountable to the DPPs in the same way that the Chief Constable was
accountable to the Policing Board.

Police Service of Northern Ireland (the Police Service or the
PSNI) senior management proposed twice yearly meetings between
the Regional Assistant Chief Constable and each individual District
Commander. The format of the meetings included a presentation by the
District Commander on performance against the objectives, performance indicators and targets in the Annual Policing Plan, the patterns
of crime, the management of police activity and resources, standards
of leadership, and the promotion of the current change programme. As
part of the accountability process the Acting Chief Constable invited
Policing Board Members to take part in these meetings to see at
first-hand how District Commanders were performing against the
Policing Plan.

PSNI District Commanders and their teams were trained in
advance of the creation of DPPs, as the PSNI Change Manager told
the Policing Board's Community Affairs Committee in December
2002. The training reflected key themes, including policing with the
community, working in partnerships and problem-solving, and the
local Policing Plan. Under the legislation the District Commander was
responsible for issuing the local Policing Plan, although, before doing
so, he was required to consult the DPP and to take account of any
views expressed.

By the end of 2004/05 the District Commander accountability
meetings had developed. By then the National Intelligence Model
(NIM) had been introduced and a more sophisticated system of performance monitoring established, including a traffic light assessment
covering a wide range of performance indicators. This had become an
effective mechanism for the Policing Board and the DPP to measure
delivery at district level.

In 2004 the Chief Constable asked the Police Service to examine
the possibility of grouping or clustering the command teams and
functions within DCUs with a view to improving effectiveness and
efficiency and better facilitating the implementation of the NIM.

The Policing Board were reassured that this would not take away from the existing coterminosity between local commands and local Councils.

One key element in the success of any DPP proved to be the relationship between it and the PSNI District Commander, which depended a good deal on the approach and interpersonal skills of the latter. Even given training and encouragement to adopt a more outgoing approach to the DPP and its public meetings, not every Commander was able to develop an optimal relationship.

8.4   The Establishment of District Policing Partnerships

The creation of the DPPs was a major challenge for the Policing Board comparatively early in its existence. Their successful setting up represented another huge step forward. It was a very major appointment exercise and involved also 26 District Councils. The process was risky at that stage in Northern Ireland's political development, in that it was essential to obtain sufficient candidates across the various categories, especially Nationalism. The then lack of support for the process from Sinn Féin, allied to the dangers of threats and physical attacks from dissident republicans, meant that in some areas of Northern Ireland coming forward to serve on DPPs required considerable personal courage and commitment.

The selection process began in September 2002 – some months later than originally anticipated – with the launch of the recruitment campaign, accompanied by widespread media advertising and a fact sheet on DPPs produced by the Policing Board, with a series of public information evenings throughout Northern Ireland. (PricewaterhouseCoopers were selected as recruitment consultants after an open competition to manage the process on behalf of the Policing Board; the cost of the contract for the recruitment process was about £500,000.) The competition closed on 18 October 2002.

Prospective Independent Members who met the initial selection criteria were first interviewed by their local District Council. A representative Policing Board selection panel was then established to consider each Council's list of potentially appointable candidates and to appoint Independent Members to the individual DPP. (The process conducted by the District Councils whittled the initial number of applicants down by about half.)

The exercise culminated in an announcement on 4 March 2003 in which the Policing Board published the names of 207 people appointed to serve as Independent Members on 25 of the 26 DPPs. Over 1,500 people had applied. Of the 207, 61% were women. The age of Independent Members ranged from 22 to 75 years old. They came from all walks of life, according to the Policing Board's announcement: *'From dinner ladies to teachers, company directors to tax inspectors, students to community workers, hairdressers and farmers to retired civil servants'*. Roman Catholics numbered 108 and non-Roman Catholics 99, thus ensuring a representative make-up for each DPP, following the appointment of 241 Elected (i.e., Political) Members. To demonstrate compliance with the statutory requirement the Policing Board published the full community and gender background for each DPP, alongside similar breakdowns in the 2001 Census.

All the Independent Members were appointed until the date of the next local government election, which was scheduled for May 2005. Of the 26 DPPs, 14 had the maximum 19 Members (10 Political and nine Independent, five had 17 Members, and seven had the minimum membership of 15 Members.

Of the 241 Political Members, the political representation was as follows: Alliance – nine; Democratic Unionist Party (DUP) – 69; Independent Unionists – two; Independent Councillors – 12; Progressive Unionist Party (PUP) – one; SDLP – 68; UUP – 80. Sinn Féin declined to appoint Councillors to DPPs or to take part in the appointment process.

The Policing Board's selection panels considered the make-up of each District Council area, taking into account, for example, the age, gender, religious background, disability, and sexual orientation of candidates. The Northern Ireland Office (NIO) Code of Practice stated that:

'The Board's panel has a particular responsibility to ensure that candidates are appointable, and that those selected are representative of the community in the Council area; in doing so, the Board's panel will wish to reflect on the composition of the Council Members appointed to the DPP.' (Section 3.3(e) paragraph 6)

In their approach, the Policing Board's panels used the information they had about the Elected Members appointed to the DPP and compared that to the community profile as defined by the 2001 Census. That enabled the Board to identify the gaps in the community profile that should be filled by Independent Members to ensure that the DPP was representative of the community.

The Policing Board's selection panels included *Political* and *Independent Members* of the Board, as well as independent selection panel members and four impartial assessors accredited by the Office of the Commissioner for Public Appointments (OCPA). The impartial assessors made a presentation to the Community Affairs Committee on 13 February 2003. Their task was to monitor the total selection process for adherence to the police legislation, the NIO Code of Practice, Policing Board policies, and OCPA best practice. They emphasised that the exercise was not just a large and complex process but a *'ground-breaking'* one as well. The Board Committee decided that the report of the impartial assessors should be published.

John Keanie, one of the impartial assessors, said that

'Given the size, complexity and political context of the exercise, the impartial assessors were genuinely impressed by the cooperation shown by all local Councils and the commitment shown by the Board in ensuring that the DPPs are as inclusive and as representative of the community as could be made.'

The full report by the impartial assessors contained a number of recommendations including the prior preparation of rules relating to late applications, the training of members of District Council interview panels, and arrangements for non-attendees at interview. As the report noted:

'Ultimately, success depended on the response of the public. The efforts on this particular process generally were well rewarded ... Overall, the results of the Northern Ireland – wide recruitment process were impressive, enabling the formation of DPPs in which men and women from a representative range of backgrounds will be able to contribute to policing in their respective communities. The impartial assessors are satisfied that the design, documentation, implementation and recording of the process to recruit independent Members of DPPs has been fair, robust, open and transparent and guided by

the principles and methods stipulated and recommended in the OCPA and NIO Codes.'

The first meeting of many of the newly instituted DPPs took place in April 2003, with Fermanagh being the first to hold a meeting in public.

There was a delay in setting up the DPP in Dungannon and South Tyrone as the Policing Board selection panel concluded that the initial appointments process had not attracted a representative cross section of the community from which the Board could make appointments: that is, there were not enough Nationalists. The panel's conclusion was endorsed by a majority of the full Board on 6 February 2003. The competition was extended in that location by the Council after discussion with the Policing Board up to 21 March 2003.

The steps towards setting up the 26th DPP took time. In October 2003 the Council decided at a special meeting not to appoint a panel from the existing DPP Members to take part in interviews to select Independent Members. A news release was issued on behalf of the UUP on 7 October 2003 in which Ken Maginnis, described as the Chairman of the Dungannon and South Tyrone DPP, called on the Policing Board Chairman and Vice-Chairman to resign. He claimed that the process adopted by the Policing Board had 'undermined the Borough Council's practice of *'responsibility sharing'* in favour of a system designed solely to *'pander to Sinn Féin's unwillingness to honour its democratic obligations'*. In response, the Policing Board wrote to the Council outlining the steps which the Board would expect to be followed if the NIO and the Board were required to set up the DPP, in line with the contingent provisions in the 2000 Act. Subsequently the Secretary of State, Paul Murphy, wrote on 2 February 2004 to the Mayor of Dungannon and South Tyrone directing that the Council proceed to nominate to the Board the names of those persons who were suitable for appointment to the DPP from among those candidates who had applied under the supplementary competition for Independent Members and additional to those nominated following the original competition. By June 2004 the Policing Board noted that the Council had agreed to proceed with the establishment of a DPP and that officials would reactivate the appointment process. The Dungannon and South Tyrone DPP was finally functioning by February 2005.

The establishment of the DPPs was a major step forward in developing real community policing across Northern Ireland. It was also an important and integral part of the new policing arrangements envisaged by the Independent Commission.

8.5 The Roll-out of DPPs

The Policing Board had published its Code of Practice on the functions and responsibilities of DPPs in September 2002. The Code tackled as the first priority how DPPs should operate to gain the cooperation of a wide cross section of the public with the police in preventing crime. It required the DPP within 12 months to produce a report setting out the strategy for this, identifying specific outcomes in terms of crime prevention, accompanied by annual targets supported by budgets and resource allocation. The DPP should review the strategy annually, consulting with the District Commander as part of the review. It was required to seek to coordinate its work with other relevant community safety organisations in the district.

The Code dealt with procedural issues relating to public meetings – a minimum of six per year, and the requirement on the District Commander to present a report to them. Once every six months the DPP was to ask the District Commander to present a report on the policing of the district to a public meeting. The DPP was to ask the police questions that had been forwarded by members of the public and was required to ensure that marginalised or hard-to-reach groups within the District were informed. Information should be made available for public scrutiny unless there were legal reasons or it was in the public interest to hold it back. Reports of each public meeting would be made available not just to the police and the District Council but also to members of the public.

The DPP should submit to the District Council a general report on the exercise of its functions during the year, copying it to the Policing Board. Every two years each DPP should undertake a community survey throughout the District Council area to identify the views of the public concerning the policing of the District. Information generated through this exercise should be used to identify the key issues that the public wished to see addressed, which the DPP should then prioritise. In turn the DPP should invite the District Commander to use the report when developing the local Policing Plan.

Detailed proposals were put to the Policing Board's Corporate Policy Committee in early March for the DPPs' roll-out under the following headings: launch, training and development, communication, interface between Policing Board and DPPs, surveys and planning, staff and resources.

Two seminars to launch DPPs were held in Derry/Londonderry on 15 March 2003 and in Belfast on 19 March 2003. Independent and Political Members of the DPPs attended. The Policing Board Chairman opened the conferences, with the Vice-Chairman closing both. Others who addressed the conference included the Chief Constable, the Acting Deputy Chief Constable Chris Albiston, Ivan Topping from the University of Ulster, Peter Smith QC and Members of the Policing Board. These seminars were important opportunities to generate publicity for the formation of DPPs and to give information to the newly appointed Members.

The training was to begin on 24 March 2003 and be completed within a five-week period; it was delivered on behalf of the Policing Board by PricewaterhouseCoopers. Additional programmes were provided for DPP Chairmen and Vice-Chairmen and DPP managers. The DPP Members' two-day induction programmes, which were completed by the end of April 2003, included exploring critical issues relevant to the success of the DPP, establishing the framework within which the Members of the DPP would work together, defining the relationship of the DPP to other key players, and agreeing short-term goals and longer-term measures of success. Members of the Policing Board were encouraged to join the training sessions.

The Policing Board monitored the training; in October 2003 a Board paper noted concerns about the initial training and the communications between the Board and the DPPs. It was agreed that a meeting should be convened with DPP Chairmen, the Policing Board Chairman and Vice-Chairman, and relevant officials. The roll-out programme also identified the development of effective communications between the Policing Board and the DPPs as important in terms of, for example, the way in which individual reports from DPPs would be processed, with the key points brought to the attention of Members of the Policing Board. A scheme of performance indicators was developed against which to monitor the effectiveness of the DPPs, with targets for each of the statutory objectives. Results of public opinion surveys were one important performance indicator. At its March 2003 meeting the Board's Community Affairs Committee approved a questionnaire to be used by DPPs to survey local communities.

Ministerial approval was obtained for additional funding of £2.87m for the running of DPPs in 2003/04.

In June 2003 the Policing Board issued a survey to 60,000 households across Northern Ireland as a DPP public consultation survey. Responses were received from 16,800 households – a 28% return (59% of the responses were completed by Protestant respondents and 31% by Catholic respondents; the remainder stated a different religion or none). The survey included a number of core questions covering attitudes to policing priorities, police resourcing, satisfaction with the police, and information on DPPs. In addition, some DPPs chose to add local questions which covered a range of issues, including drug and alcohol abuse and satisfaction with PSNI response times. The core questions were as follows:

- *What do you feel are currently the biggest problems in your District Council?*
- *Which activities do you think the PSNI in your District Council should be concentrating most resources on?*
- *Overall, how satisfied are you with policing in your District Council?*
- *Overall, how satisfied are you with policing in Northern Ireland as a whole?*
- *How satisfied are you with levels of beat patrols in your District Council?*
- *How satisfied are you with levels of police vehicle patrols in your District Council?*
- *Have you heard of District Policing Partnerships?*
- *Do you know who the Members of your local DPP are?*
- *Do you know how to contact your local DPP?*

The most frequent responses to the first question were domestic burglary, underage drinking, speeding, young people causing a nuisance, vandalism, and attacks on the elderly. The activities upon which individuals thought the police should concentrate most resources were beat/foot patrolling (by some margin the largest percentage), investigating crime, prompt response to emergencies, crime prevention, and vehicle patrolling. Public satisfaction was lowest for foot patrolling, with just 10% of respondents satisfied or very satisfied. Fifty-nine per cent of the public were aware of DPPs, though only 16% were aware of the Members of their local DPP, with slightly fewer knowing how to contact their local DPP. The results were broken down by District Council area. The following year's survey included questions regarding how confident the public were that their local DPP was helping to address local policing problems and whether respondents were prepared to contact their local DPP regarding local policing.

This survey was in addition to the two existing Northern Ireland-wide surveys: the Community Attitudes survey, published each May, and the Omnibus survey, undertaken twice yearly. The Community Attitudes survey of 2003 asked, in addition, which issue should receive most attention across Northern Ireland. Interestingly, the answer to this question was markedly different, with the highest priority in both communities seen as paramilitary activity.

The 2004 Community Attitudes survey found that 59% of people were confident that DPPs would address local policing issues and that 60% of people would contact their local DPP. In October 2004 the results of the second DPP public consultation survey were published. This survey recorded an upward trend regarding satisfaction levels with local policing; by now 67% of all respondents had heard of DPPs.

In November 2003, at a *Public Session* of the Policing Board, the Chief Constable was asked to comment on the level of public participation in DPP meetings. He stated that there was more public interest in DPPs in Northern Ireland than in many places in England, although the organisation was still developing and public interest was likely to vary from location to location.

On 4 February 2004 the Policing Board Chairman hosted a conference in Templepatrick for the Chairpersons, their representatives, and managers of DPPs. There was general agreement that both DPPs and the PSNI needed to build a closer relationship to allow for support and constructive criticism where necessary. Increasing numbers were attending DPP meetings, including, for example, sixth-form students. The Policing Board noted that many DPPs were moving towards opening up their meetings to enable greater participation by the wider public in term of allowing questions from the floor.

In spring 2004 the Policing Board published the anniversary edition of a quarterly magazine dedicated to DPP Members – *DPP News*. The autumn 2004 edition provided a snapshot of initiatives undertaken by DPPs. These included an approach to all eight Armagh post-primary schools in a meeting to be held in the town; a postal survey and focus groups on crime and policing in the Whitehead area conducted by the Carrickfergus DPP; the hosting of a second regional conference by Limavady DPP; the creation by Antrim DPP of an award for Antrim community police officer of the year; a newsletter to all 33,000 house-holds in Ards Borough; a breakfast meeting to engage with youth hosted by Newtownabbey DPP; and a themed public meeting on roads policing organised by Omagh DPP.

On 13 September 2004 the second DPP Chairmen's Forum was held. The Policing Board Chairman arranged for a speech to be given by the then Northern Ireland Lord Chief Justice, Sir Brian Kerr, as gaining an understanding of the wider criminal justice system was valuable for DPP Members. The Policing Board Chairman then said about DPPs:

'Their determination and resilience, often in the face of adversity, has provided a strong foundation for the way ahead for policing with the community in Northern Ireland.'

On 4 November 2004, when the Policing Board were meeting in Armagh, the Chairman announced the launch of the new DPP website, set up by the Board as a dedicated resource for DPP Members. Each DPP had its own page, with links to the local Policing Plan, dates of meetings and events, and so on.

In 2004 the Policing Board launched a 'light touch' review of the work of the DPPs chaired by the Board's Chief Executive. A survey was sent to all DPP Members, DPP Managers, District Council Chief Executives, and PSNI District Commanders seeking their views on a number of issues. (While 51% of Independent Members responded to the survey, only 28% of Political Members did.) The purpose was to review how DPPs had operated in their first year and to identify areas that could be improved to ensure a more effective and efficient service both by and to the DPPs. The review group included representatives from the Board and the NIO, DPP Managers, District Council Chief Executives, and DCU Commanders.

The final report to the Policing Board in March 2005 made clear that the dedication and commitment of all involved had contributed to the success of DPPs. Key findings included: there was a need for guidance in the DPP Code of Practice as to how the DPP should gain the cooperation of the public with the police in preventing crime; there was concern about duplication between DPPs and Community Safety Partnerships (CSPs; see below), Community Police Liaison Committees, and the police neighbourhood beat forums; the need to improve the ways the DPPs monitored police performance to enhance the input into the local Policing Plan process; the need to improve communications between the DPPs and the Policing Board; and the need for additional training for DPP Members. Thirty recommendations and proposed actions were set out in the report.

The key findings were set out in the *DPP News*. The spring 2005 edition demonstrated its importance as a vehicle for communicating with DPP Members and Managers as well as also including items on the first new-style Annual Policing Plan 2005–2008, the launch by the Board of its first Human Rights report, a summary of the latest policing legislation, the publication by the Board of its own new Corporate Plan, the PSNI's revised human resources planning strategy, the appointment of a number of new Chairs and Vice Chairs to DPPs, joint initiatives on tackling hate crime, and the launch of the Dungannon and South Tyrone DPP.

8.6   Personal Security Challenges To District Policing Partnerships

Given the state of the peace and political processes in Northern Ireland at that time it was always likely that security would pose challenges for individuals and the wider system. It did not take long for this to be demonstrated. The first meeting of the Omagh DPP on 21 May 2003 had to be abandoned owing to noisy protests by some members of the public. The Corporate Policy Committee of the Policing Board considered the issue the following day, noting that the protests appeared to have been led by Sinn Féin and fearing that this approach could be replicated at other DPP meetings. The Policing Board Chairman and Vice-Chairman briefed the media about the Board's reaction and the Chairman wrote to the Omagh DPP Chairman to express the Policing Board's support, which was explicitly shown when the Board chose Omagh as the location for its first *Private* and *Public Sessions* away from its Belfast headquarters, held early in 2004.

In July 2003 there were attacks on Members of the Strabane DPP, with continuing attacks and intimidation over subsequent months (amounting to over a dozen incidents in all). Also in July the police advised that names and addresses of Belfast and Castlereagh DPP Members might have fallen into the hands of dissident republicans through unauthorised access to individuals' medical records held at the Royal Victoria Hospital in Belfast. In correspondence with those expressing concern about the security of DPP Members, the Policing Board Chairman noted that:

'What we are seeing is an indication of how effective the DPPs are considered to be. If someone or some organisation is against bringing about a new beginning in policing then they will try to "strike" at those who are clearly making this new beginning a reality.'

In a very public demonstration of support for DPPs, together with the Policing Board Chairman, two Members of DPPs met with President Bush and other senior representatives of the American administration in Washington on St Patrick's Day 2004. President Bush specifically referred to their commitment to democratic policing in his speech in the White House.

Following threats to DPP Members in Newry and the postpone-ment of a DPP meeting in Forkhill in May 2004, the Policing Board funded a survey of every household in the Forkhill electoral ward in the Newry and Mourne District Council area. There had also been challenges for the Belfast DPP sub-groups in holding their meetings in the community. There had been protests at meetings in both East and West Belfast, together with a hostile environment. As a practical measure, the DPP agreed to continue sub-group meetings in the City Hall.

In all, there were 56 separate incidents of threatened or actual violence recorded towards DPP Members during the first two and a half years of their existence. Just a tiny handful of Independent Members left office before their term was complete.

At the DPP Chairmen's forum on 28 September 2005 – less than a week after a vicious physical attack on Denis Bradley, the Board's Vice-Chairman and Chairman of its Community Engagement Committee – the Board Chairman said:

'DPPs were born and still exist in a period of political uncertainty. Already diffi-cult and challenging circumstances were intensified by threats of violence and intimidation against DPP Members. However, resilience shone through and thanks to the commitment and dedication of those who sit on the Partnerships and those who work with them, DPPs are working across Northern Ireland to achieve Patten's vision of bringing policing closer to the community it serves. It is the Board's belief that DPPs have made, and will continue to make, a signifi-cant difference to policing in our communities. Through their efforts to monitor local policing and consult with the public, DPPs are making a positive impact on the delivery of policing services... DPPs' success to date is also evident in their influence on policing priorities, both at a local and regional level ... Patten recommended that policing with the community should be the core function of the police service, and it is up to DPPs to engage the public and monitor local policing to ensure that this vision becomes a reality.'

Again, speaking in November of that year, the Policing Board Chairman told a reception for DPP Members that:

'The people of Northern Ireland will judge DPPs according to their own experi-ences of crime in their community. ... DPPs, more than any other body, must strive to make our streets and neighbourhoods safer, and build the relationships with the police officers who are also part and parcel of that street and neigh-bourhood. And they will need to acknowledge that the timescale is not infinite. People and police need to know that things are getting better, even if slowly. There must be successes to absorb the defeats.'

On 4 May 2005 the Policing Board Chairman held a meeting with hard-to-reach groups promoting involvement in DPPs. This 'outreach' continued in the run-up to reconstitution; for example, in October 2005 the Policing Board arranged a workshop primarily for DPPs entitled 'Engaging communities, tackling crime, and accepting responsibility'. The Board brought to the attention of DPP Members the work that the Policing Board and the Police Ombudsman jointly commissioned from the Institute for Conflict Research in 2005 focusing on attitudes and experiences of individuals from the minority ethnic and lesbian, gay, bisexual and transgender (LGBT) communities in relation to the new policing arrangements.

In the DPP News of autumn 2005 the Policing Board Vice-Chairman reflected on the achievements of the first term of DPPs. He noted that DPPs had been born and still existed in a period of political uncertainty. The already challenging circumstances were intensified by threats of violence and intimidation against DPP Members. However, resilience had shone through and much had been achieved. During the first term, in his view, DPPs had been reasonably successful in consulting with the public to identify policing priorities, working with the police to incorporate these in local Policing Plans, and monitoring police performance against those Plans. However, he concluded that engagement with the public had been less successful. Gaining the cooperation of the public with the police in preventing crime was a tremendous task by anyone's standards, particularly in an environment where widespread support for the police was lacking. He stressed that DPPs must ensure that policing with the community remained at the heart of policing in Northern Ireland.

At the Public Session of the Policing Board on 7 April 2005 the Chief Constable drew attention to the reduction in crime:

'I am absolutely clear you do not achieve a 10% crime reduction year-on-year across all bands and that has been achieved by my officers, it is down 20% in two years, without increasing community support. We cannot rightly claim it as a policing success, part of it is, without doubt a police success, but it is a success around working in partnership. I think it reflects growing confidence in policing across the communities, including those that historically did not trust us, and there is no doubt that at a local level, using DPPs and other groups, it has been important.'

8.7   Reconstitution of the District Policing Partnerships in 2005 and their Work

Prior to the scheduled reconstitution of DPPs in 2005, the NIO introduced the District Policing Partnerships (Northern Ireland) Order 2005. The main purpose was to extend temporarily the length of time that current DPP Members could hold office until new Members were appointed and the successor DPP fully established. The Order came into effect on 1 April 2005.

In May 2005 the Policing Board published for consultation a revised Code of Practice on the exercise of functions and responsibilities of DPPs. This put into effect some of the recommendations in the Board's review of DPPs.

The closing date for receipt of applications from candidates for appointment as Independent Members was 31 May 2005.

On 2 December 2005 the 215 Independent Members of DPPs were announced; these included 133 sitting Members and 82 new Members. Of the appointments, 56% were from the Roman Catholic community and 60% were female, while 13% stated that they had a disability, 2% were from ethnic minorities, and 1% were lesbian/gay/bisexual. Once again, the process was overseen by three impartial assessors accredited by OCPA. (One additional measure was the appointment of an accredited OCPA Member to deal with complaints for any candidate unable to have their complaint resolved by the Policing Board.)

The representation of Political Members of DPPs was as follows: Alliance – 11, DUP – 98, Independents – 9, PUP – 1, SDLP – 56, and UUP – 64. Sinn Féin again declined to appoint Councillors to DPPs or to take part in the appointment process.

The report of the impartial assessors was presented to the Policing Board in January 2006. The assessors again concluded that the process had been fair and robust and had complied with the NIO Code of Practice, but their report did contain recommendations, of which one was that there should be more developed performance appraisal for Independent Members of DPPs. In future appointments appraisal results should be used to decide on eligibility for inclusion in the pool of candidates.

Prior to the reconstitution of the Policing Board in spring 2006, the

Chief Constable responded to the Chairman's remarks about DPPs at the Policing Board's final public meeting on 1 March 2006. He then said:

'You also, quite rightly, highlighted the role of DPPs and I think that is a very important part of the structure, again now seen as best practice in the latest Government White Paper on Police Reform in the United Kingdom because they drive that accountability level down to my District Commanders. I am grateful again for the interest of Members in those District Policing Partnerships and visiting, supporting and indeed sustaining them.'

This was reinforced by remarks he made later. At a meeting of the Policing Board in December 2007 the Chief Constable said that he had absolutely no intention of interfering with the DPP structure even if he could. He added:

'I think it is one of the centres of excellence in Northern Ireland. It is a system of accountability which is looked upon with some jealousy by colleagues from across the water, it works.'

At the *Public Session* of the Policing Board held the previous month the Chief Constable noted that it did take a lot of resource, with DPPs, CSPs, and various methods of oversight. Then Assistant Chief Constable Judith Gillespie pointed to a recent DPP meeting held in Crossmaglen as a good example of positive public engagement – members of the public, for the first time in that community, had the opportunity to hear police give an account of how they dealt with anti-social behaviour and local crime problems in their District.

In June 2006 the Policing Board discussed ways in which it might provide additional support for and two-way communication with DPPs. The Board Members agreed in September 2006 to a proposal for each Board Member to support a particular DPP, to assist in which a monthly briefing paper detailing the issues in each DPP would be provided to the Members.

During 2006 DPPs had a particular focus on themed meetings covering matters such as 'young people in the community', part time police officers, police call management, respecting diversity and addressing hate crime, drugs, alcohol and the impact of anti-social behaviour, domestic violence, crimes against the elderly, the impact of speeding and nuisance motoring, and robbery.

Another positive development was the announcement by the Policing Board Chairman on 5 March 2007 of over £250,000 from the International Fund for Ireland for the development of a programme to facilitate engagement between DPPs, local communities, and the police. This initiative had been submitted by the Policing Board the previous year. The money was used by the Board to create opportunities for community representatives to work with DPP Members and the Police Service to identify difficult issues, such as sectarianism and hate crime, and develop solutions. It encompassed additional training for DPPs moving beyond the monitoring role into the critical area of community engagement by means of building the capacity of the DPPs. Given that the annual training budget for DPPs was £55,000 at that stage, this represented a major fillip.

8.8   The Review of Public Administration

In June 2002, the Northern Ireland Executive initiated a Review of Public Administration (RPA), the most significant item of which was a planned reduction in the number of District Councils from 26, which would be accompanied by an increase in their powers in areas such as community planning. It was initially envisaged that the exercise would be completed within just a few years, with the Council boundaries changing in 2009. This clearly had major implications for the structure of the PSNI, in particular the alignment between DCUs, District Councils, and DPPs. The continuing uncertainty over the implementation of the RPA – in terms of both its scale and its timing – was to pose challenges for the Policing Board, the PSNI, and DPPs.

The PSNI decided to reduce the number of District Commands prior to RPA implementation. At the *Public Session* of the Policing Board on 6 September 2006 Alex Attwood (SDLP) asked the Chief Constable about the process for recruiting the police officers to head the new merged 'super' District Command areas that the PSNI was proposing. Sir Hugh Orde replied that, in terms of size, the new districts would be similar to an average District Command elsewhere in the United Kingdom.

The Policing Board were aware of concerns among DPP Members about the implications of the RPA; on 12 September 2006 the Policing Board held a dedicated briefing on the implications of the RPA for DPPs while, at the DPP Chairmen's forum that same month, the then Board Vice-Chairman Barry Gilligan spoke on the subject.

On 28 September 2006 the Oversight Commissioner published a thematic report on devolution. This contained a section on the RPA, which, it said, *represented an opportunity for rationalising the increase in the organisation's efficient use of these resources thereby allowing a greater police presence and visibility in the community*. While the report advised on the need to ensure that all parties rose to the challenge, it warned about guarding against *hard-won partnerships and a dutiful focus on local concerns* being lost.

The Policing Board considered the issues, both in Committee and in plenary. For example, an information paper was brought to the Board in October 2006 and a visit was arranged by the Chairman and Vice-Chairman, with two other Members, to the Strathclyde Police Service. This visit took in community planning at the local level and information about relationships between the police and the community.

It was agreed that a group representing the party political representatives on the Policing Board should be drawn together to discuss the future arrangements for DPPs. Board officials prepared a consultation paper which was to be issued to aid consultation with DPPs and other interested parties. It included the fundamental premise that, while the out-workings of the RPA would result in significant changes, it was the Policing Board's view that the impact of the RPA, particularly the introduction of community planning, provided an opportunity to move closer to the model of DPPs originally envisaged by the Independent Commission on Policing, of an inclusive partnership responsible for a wide range of duties.

In March 2007 the Policing Board considered a report on the findings of the consultation exercise. Responses to the models outlined in the paper indicated an overwhelming support for a fully integrated DPP/CSP within a community planning framework. On 28 March 2007 the Policing Board submitted its consultation paper on the responses to the NIO Minister.

The PSNI set up a new project known as CORE (Corporate Opportunity for Resilience and Efficiency) to plan for the restructuring of the PSNI in accordance with the RPA. Its planning assumption was that there would be a basic structure of eight new DCUs. Assistant Chief Constable Roy Toner made a presentation to the Policing Board on the CORE project in November 2006. The basic structure for each new DCU was envisaged as a Chief Superintendent, two Superintendents, one business manager, and a personnel manager. A number of forces in Great Britain had been visited to examine best practice. The new District senior management teams were to be in place by 1 April 2007 and the Chief Superintendents to command the eight DCUs were announced prior to that date. The Policing Board arranged a special briefing for the DPPs to provide an update on the implementation programme. (The CORE project also included establishing a corporate vision for PSNI headquarters and workforce modernisation.)

The Policing Board continued to monitor progress. Its Corporate Policy, Planning and Performance Committee was given a further presentation on the CORE project by Assistant Chief Constable Toner in November 2007. This Committee agreed the following month that the Board should write to the Chief Constable seeking his commitment to the development of a protocol that would clarify the relationships between and roles and responsibilities of DPPs and Commanders of Police Areas and Districts. The Board were also concerned that there should be clarity in the terminology. The Chief Constable gave an assurance that, having taken legal advice, and provided a designated officer was in a position of responsibility in the 'small' districts (Area Commands), the bigger District Commands could be developed to assume operational responsibility. Thus the existing DCUs could be grouped before the legislation was formally amended, providing that each District still had a designated District Commander to liaise with the DPP.

In April 2008 the then Minister of the Environment wrote to the Policing Board Chairman about the rationalisation of the 26 District Councils to create 11 new Councils. The letter recognised the Independent Commission's recommendation ensuring coterminosity between the council structure and the local policing command structure, and the Policing Board were invited to submit views on how that could best be achieved in the new structure. At the *Public Session* of the Policing Board in September 2008 the Chief Constable reaffirmed that he believed that an eight-district structure for the PSNI was appropriate, and he would not intend moving to an 11-Area basis as then proposed under the RPA.

The RPA is to be implemented in spring 2015.

8.9   The 2007 Reconstitution of District Policing Partnerships

Discussions between the Northern Ireland political parties and the British and Irish Governments took place at St Andrews in October 2006. Given the matters of support for policing and the future devolution of policing and justice, policing was central to the negotiations. The British Government swiftly enacted the Northern Ireland (St Andrews Agreement) Act 2006. When the Bill was introduced in Parliament the Policing Board issued a release on 22 November 2006 regretting the implications for some DPP Members and stating the belief that:

'Reconstitution should have been on as minimal a basis as possible to ensure full community and political representation on each DPP rather than in effect to require the full reconstitution of most DPPs.'

Schedules 8 and 9 to the Northern Ireland (St Andrews Agreement) Act 2006 provided for the reconstitution of DPPs outside the trigger of the local government election. The 2006 Act also gave effect to the provisions of Schedule 1 to the Police (Northern Ireland) Act 2003, which dealt with the development of the four Belfast sub-groups, introduced a declaration against terrorism for Independent Members of DPPs, and amended the provisions for the disqualification from being a Member of a DPP. At its commencement date, 4 September 2007, the Policing Board were required within 15 days to ascertain whether each DPP met the 'political condition' laid down in the Act, and to report to the Secretary of State accordingly. Paragraph 20(2)(6) of Schedule 8 stated that:

'The political condition is met in relation to a DPP if the Political Members of the DPP reflect, so far as is practicable, the balance of the parties prevailing among the Members of the Council on the commencement date.'

In determining the 'political condition' of each DPP, the Policing
Board concluded that 23 DPPs did not meet the requirement and were
therefore reconstituted in line with the Northern Ireland (St Andrews
Agreement) Act 2006. (The three DPPs that did meet the political
condition and accordingly were not reconstituted were Ballymena,
Banbridge, and Coleraine.)

The process of selecting Independent Members began in October
2007, with advertisements placed the following month. Political nominations to Belfast DPP and the sub-groups were made from October
2007. New Political Members took up office by 6 December. Just the
night before, Strabane District Council filled only three of the five Sinn
Féin posts (other Councillors of that party being unwilling or unable
to take up the posts to which they were entitled under the d'Hondt
system), with the remaining two offered to DUP Councillors. Sinn Féin
West Tyrone MP Pat Doherty was reported by the media to have said
that he was disappointed: *Sinn Féin is fully committed to engaging with
all of the policing structures*.

The Policing Board announced all the Independent Member
appointments on 1 April 2008. Commenting, the Policing Board
Chairman said:

*'This completion of the DPP reconstitution process marks another milestone in
policing history and delivers on the agreements reached in respect of policing
at St Andrews. Through the Political and Independent Membership, DPPs are
now fully representative of the local communities they serve. ... We are now in
a new era for policing in Northern Ireland with support for policing from right
across the political spectrum. The wide range of applicants from all sections
of our community reflects the desire to achieve a policing service which is fully
responsive to the community it serves.'*

The Policing Board were required to fill 211 vacant Independent
Member positions on the 23 DPPs and four Belfast sub-groups. Of
those appointed 89 had previously served, while 122 were new.
Exactly 50% of the Independent Members were from the Roman
Catholic community, and 61% were female. (This compared with 43%
of Political Members perceived to be from the Roman Catholic community and just 21% of Political Members being female.)

Taking account of the Belfast City Council nominations of Political

Members and the profile of the areas in the four sub-groups, the Policing Board had to appoint five Roman Catholic Independent Members to the West Belfast sub-group and five non-Roman Catholic Members to the East Belfast sub-group.

8.10   Policing with the Community

From the Policing Board's beginning, policing with the community was a topic of continuing and developing importance. Even before the Policing Board came into existence, initially the Royal Ulster Constabulary and then the PSNI addressed the Independent Commission's recommendation in relation to policing with the community and community safety. A draft policy entitled 'Policing with the Community in Northern Ireland' was prepared by the Police Service in spring 2001. The purpose was 'to set in place a policy which promotes policing with the community as a core function of all policing activity'.

The document noted that at the consultation stage of the review by the Independent Commission there had been many submissions calling for more 'community policing'. However, this term meant different things to different people, and the Patten Report adopted the term 'policing with the community' as this encapsulated more clearly

'What most people want to see – the police participating in the community and responding to the needs of that community, and the community participating in its own policing and supporting the police.' (Paragraph 7.2)

The document set out that transformation of the policy into operational practice was to be the subject of an implementation plan which had to take account of issues such as human rights, training, information technology, managing public expectations, and the prevailing security situation. Realisation of the policy would also be dependent on the commitment of police officers throughout the organisation that it was the core function of all policing activity, adequate allocation of resources, and 'the acceptance, commitment and support of the many communities across Northern Ireland for this style of policing and for the police'. So, from the beginning, there was recognition that it was a two-way issue.

The key elements of policing in the community were stated as being:

- *Partnership*, envisaging consultation with communities, including the engagement of consultative forums
- *Problem-solving*, defined as *'the process of studying crime and disorder issues, usually in geographically defined areas, so that responses can be identified and implemented to address the causes of those issues'*
- *Empowerment*, emphasising the importance of creating joint ownership among members of the community and the police to address crime and community safety, with a management style empowering officers to tackle issues raised locally
- *Accountability*, understood as the natural corollary of working with the community – if a police officer is tackling a locally identified problem in partnership with the community, the officer should be held to account for what is or is not done
- *Service delivery*, reflecting the concept that the police exist to serve the community – policing should be community-centred and it should also be effective and efficient in addressing problems

Problem-solving was seen as a core function of Community Beat officers, although all staff in a DCU would have a role in supporting and implementing problem-solving initiatives. The document recognised that a structure which supported policing with the community had to be decentralised. It recognised that, while the initial transition to community policing might be made within a few months, *'institutionalising the approach to the degree that it informs all police activities usually takes much longer'*.

On 14 February 2002 Assistant Chief Constable Sam Kinkaid, together with Acting Assistant Chief Constable Colin Burrows, gave a presentation to the Board's newly established Community Affairs Committee on *'Policing with the Community in Northern Ireland'*. They explained that the constraints included a potential lack of resources (for example, owing to the take-up of the severance programme) and the challenges of public disorder and security (in 2001 there had been 673 recorded injuries to regular officers). The risks included raising expectations and the potential lack of engagement by partners, including community involvement. They reported that training on community and race relations was included as a core theme in the PSNI's Training, Education and Development strategy but noted that, while the core standards for policing with the community would be the same for all areas of Northern Ireland, the actual style of policing might have to be adapted to suit a particular area.

On 1 May 2002 Acting Chief Constable Kinkaid submitted the draft implementation plan. He invited the Policing Board to read the draft and provide their views and comments. The importance of the plan, and the work it represented, he wrote, 'cannot be overstated'.

The plan was created in response to the recommendations in the Independent Commission's Report (Recommendations 33 and 44 to 49) and also the second report of the Office of the Oversight Commissioner, dated September 2001, which had set out a series of relevant performance indicators. The organisational model included, as per Patten Recommendation 45, a neighbourhood policing team reporting to a Sector Inspector within each DCU. The plan emphasised that there was 'much more to successful policing with the community than the creation of neighbourhood policing teams', looking ahead to, for example, the future relationship between the DCUs and the DPPs. It stressed that policing with the community depended upon community support – this must extend to assistance in helping the police to move to responding to needs rather than responding to demand.

DCU Commanders were required to have established neighbourhood policing teams by autumn 2002.

In October 2002 and again in April 2003 PSNI briefings were provided to the Policing Board's Community Affairs Committee, presaging a quarterly reporting pattern. Assistant Chief Constable Duncan McCausland reported on specific performance indicators in relation to the number of neighbourhood policing teams, community beat officers, consultative forums, and problem-solving initiatives. At that stage there were 105 neighbourhood policing teams with 690 community beat officers and 548 consultative forums. (It is interesting to note that this was an early reference to the introduction of 'neighbourhood policing teams'.)

Annual Community Policing awards were developed by the PSNI in partnership with the Policing Board. They were instituted in 2004 to recognise and honour the endeavour and commitment of officers and staff. By 2006, the local District Commanders in partnership with DPPs made the nominations; members of the public were also able to make recommendations in the Community Police Officer of the Year category.

On 19 April 2005 a policing with the community conference was held in Belfast. This was partly to mark the creation of a 'policing with the community' fund that would make up to £1m per year available to DCUs for local community initiatives for the following three years. The fund's purpose was to encourage a visible commitment to an enhanced policing with the community ethos in partnership with other interested groups. Individual projects were required to provide at least 20% matched funding against the total project cost from other partners. The conference also rolled out a menu for use in performance reviews of DCU Commanders and their staff at all ranks, against the four headings of service delivery, problem-solving and partnerships, empowerment, and accountability.

In May 2005 the then Leicestershire Chief Constable Matt Baggott addressed an Association of Chief Police Officers (ACPO) conference on *'professionalising the business of neighbourhood policing'*. He stressed that ACPO were at one on the future of neighbourhood policing – *'it is what we stand for'*. He said it also demonstrated the importance of mainstreaming neighbourhood policing, the essential role of the NIM in determining both BCU structures and tactics, and the importance of clarifying accountabilities and expected outcomes. Neighbourhood policing was about

'Confidence that the police understand the issues that matter to people, and are dealing with them. Confidence in policing is essential. It provides the legitimacy and public support needed to act in preventing crime and bringing offenders to justice.'

In September 2005 the Policing Board's Community Involvement Committee considered a paper on a monitoring framework to assist the Board in its assessment of the PSNI's work in policing with the community. The paper proposed a two-part monitoring process the first stage of which was analysing the strategic and policy documents relating to policing with the community and assessing their capacity to deliver the key recommendation in the Patten Report. The second stage was to monitor the operational implementation of that strategy and review what was happening in practice.

The Policing Board promoted policing with the community in other ways too. For example, in March 2006 the Policing Board, in partnership with the PSNI and the Community Safety Unit of the NIO, organised a Neighbourhood Watch briefing for representatives from the then more than 100 accredited schemes established across Northern Ireland. DPPs in particular had supported the establishment of Neighbourhood Watch schemes and drawn on them both to identify the policing concerns of local residents and to ensure they were addressed. In July 2006 a meeting of the Corporate Policy, Planning and Performance Committee approved research into the views and experiences of individuals involved in Neighbourhood Watch schemes.

In October 2006 the Policing Board were briefed by the PSNI on the Policing With The Community Branch in the Criminal Justice Department of the PSNI. A steering group had been set up in November 2004 on a cross-functional basis to identify progress in the programme of work to embed policing with the community. The Deputy Chief Constable was the policing with the community Champion. The steering group had promoted a number of items in the previous months, including a partnership conference, a recruitment pilot, knowledge-sharing workshops, and the submission of performance indicators.

This PSNI report to the Policing Board concluded that moderate or substantial progress had been made in five of the eight key areas – partnerships, recruitment, training, knowledge sharing, and the use of the new Challenge Fund, but was critical of progress in three – the NIM, performance and accountability, and call handling. The priority was to design an improved model of neighbourhood policing by spring 2007. This would include capturing neighbourhood issues in the NIM, role profiling neighbourhood officers, and identifying individual officers, while integrating performance indicators into existing performance management systems.

Reflecting the importance it attached to this area, in spring 2007 the Policing Board approved a proposal to appoint an adviser to the Board who would be specifically responsible for oversight arrangements regarding policing with the community. Mr Bob Lunney, a senior Canadian police officer who had been a Member of the Oversight Commissioner's team for some years, met Members of the Board to discuss the project.

In the *Public Session* of the Policing Board in May 2007 the Deputy Chief Constable Paul Leighton responded to a question on neighbourhood policing. He stressed that:

'We originally started talking about front-line policing and now we have come to a stage where policing with the community is for absolutely everyone. We are desperately trying to get that into everyone's head, be they a headquarters officer, a District Command Unit based officer or a front-line response neighbourhood police officer, a CID officer or whatever they may be, so policing with the community is at the forefront of everyone's mind and should actually be the focus on what we are trying to do.'

Numerically, the Policing Board were told that just over one-third of the 4,379 officers deployed in the eight Districts were now engaged in response policing and in neighbourhood policing teams.

In August 2007 Assistant Chief Constable Drew Harris briefed the Board's Community Engagement Committee on neighbourhood policing. He emphasised that its purpose was to deliver the right people at the right places in the right numbers in order to create neighbourhoods that were safe and felt safe. The public would be given access to local policing services through a named point of contact. Twenty-five specific recommendations had been formulated to promote the delivery of neighbourhood policing. These included:

- the identification of *geographic neighbourhoods* within each DCU
- the development of a *neighbourhood profile*
- an identifiable officer for each *neighbourhood* with the sergeant or senior Constable leading each *neighbourhood team*
- each DCU developing a *community engagement strategy*
- a *neighbourhood consultation forum* in keeping with the Partners and Community Together model to be established within each neighbourhood
- the involvement of partners in the *neighbourhood consultative forum* established

- *neighbourhood officers* normally working at least 80% of their duty hours on *neighbourhood policing duties*

At the *Public Session* of the Policing Board held the following month the Chairman of the Community Engagement Committee, Alex Maskey, said that ACC Harris and his team had made a fulsome report and had had quite a considerable engagement with the Members of the Committee. '*Members were, for the most part, quite satisfied with the response they were given and certainly the commitment which was expressed by the top team*'. He went on to stress the centrality for all police officers of policing with the community and pressed the Chief Constable to endorse that, which indeed he did. ACC Harris added that the 25 recommendations which were now being implemented across the Police Service had been developed through the CORE procedures. That process would take 18 months to 2 years to complete. He noted that, whereas Police Community Support Officers (PCSOs) were an integral part of neighbourhood policing teams in England and Wales, there were none as yet in Northern Ireland, although the PSNI's full time neighbourhood officers were supplemented with 900 Police Officers Part Time.

Mr Lunney reported to the Board's Community Engagement Committee in October 2007 with proposals for developing a monitoring framework, noting that it was due to the unique circumstances in Northern Ireland that such a framework would work. It was important to ensure that monitoring was embedded in the annual Policing Plan. Members discussed the need to ensure the integration of neighbourhood and response policing and their measurement. Concern was expressed about the scope for a gap between policy and actual practice. At their subsequent meeting in January 2008 it was noted that the PSNI accepted Mr Lunney's report and that they would work on developing a range of performance indicators to enable the implementation of policing with the community to be measured.

The practical working out of policing with the community was largely delivered by the PSNI through neighbourhood policing. Responding to a question from the Policing Board in December 2007, the Chief Constable referred to neighbourhood policing workshops that had been run in each of the eight District units during June and July of that year, the establishment of a neighbourhood policing project governance board, a neighbourhood policing project plan, and now a neighbourhood policing project implementation board. The neighbourhood policing framework was being rolled out in all Districts and would:

'enable the public to identify and engage with the local officer (ACCESS), have influence (INFLUENCE) over agreeing neighbourhood level priorities to be actioned, become involved in collaborative problem-solving solutions (INTERVENTIONS), and get feedback (ANSWERS) on the result of police, partner and public problem-solving initiatives.'

The interest taken by the Board was not restricted to formal briefings and public meetings; for example, in September 2007 the Chairman and Vice-Chairman met the Member of Parliament for North Belfast together with two representatives of the Upper North Belfast Community Police Liaison Committee who wished to make represen-tations concerning the reported lack of visible policing and a reduction in the number of community police officers, together with the relo-cation of neighbourhood officers within the District. The discussion led to a further meeting to be arranged by the Chair of the Policing Board's Community Engagement Committee and a question to be put to the Chief Constable at the next Policing Board meeting.

The Policing Board Chairman noted at the Board meeting on 4 December 2008 that in the latest Omnibus Survey 86% of respondents had confidence in the police's ability to provide a day-to-day policing service for everyone in Northern Ireland – an increase of 3% over the previous figure. In addition, 63% had heard of the concept of neigh-bourhood/community policing.

The DPPs were asked to report to the Policing Board on their assess-ment of the implementation of the neighbourhood policing framework over the period April to September 2008. DPPs noted some concerns in relation to the level of abstraction (i.e., official absence from duty) for neighbourhood officers. The Assistant Chief Constable provided an assurance to the Board on 5 February 2009 that all the targets of 80% had been met and achieved (i.e., neighbourhood officers were not being removed from providing that service within any of the 176 defined neighbourhoods across Northern Ireland for more than 20% of the time).

In November 2008 the Vice-Chairman of the Policing Board asked the Chief Constable what measures had been introduced, relating both to culture and to operational delivery, to ensure that policing with the community was the core policing activity of the PSNI's Tactical Support Groups (TSGs) and the Crime Operations Department. The response referred to the restructuring of TSGs to support Districts, and local Policing Plans, which were moving the culture of TSGs away from reactive towards proactive, preventative policing. The NIM business process now included neighbourhood policing. Uses of the TSG included, for example, operating 'Get Home Safe' to reduce assaults and night-time disorder in Belfast and Bangor and anti-social behaviour patrols in South and East Belfast.

In March 2009 a report was published on policing with the community following a joint inspection by the Criminal Justice Inspection Northern Ireland (CJINI) and Her Majesty's Inspectorate of Constabulary (HMIC). There were four key criteria – the relevant Patten recommendations, the five principles of community policing (service delivery, partnership, problem-solving, empowerment, and accountability), progress of the neighbourhood policing programme, and progress against the HMIC baseline inspection of 2006. The report noted substantial progress of neighbourhood policing since 2006 and in implementing the policing with the community recommendations of the Patten Report. Inspectors found many instances of excellent partnership work being pursued and sustained locally by the dedication of neighbourhood policing officers and community partners, often under difficult conditions. There were tangible policing with the community goals in the Policing Board's Policing Plan. However, work remained to fully embed policing with the community as the core function of the Police Service and the core function of every police station, and the PSNI's policing with the community strategy needed to be updated. Better call management was also required.

The Policing Board's Community Engagement Committee pressed the PSNI to update its strategy to a tight deadline. The Committee Chairman sat on the steering committee for the new strategy and other Board Members were on the challenge panel.

At the *Public Session* of the Board on 2 April 2009 the PSNI advised the Board that they would be introducing accredited training for neighbourhood officers from September that year. However, the Chief

Constable added a cautionary note – Constable Stephen Carroll, who had been murdered in Lurgan, was delivering neighbourhood policing at the time. He was a TSG officer responding to a call from the community. Local communities wanted ordinary policing, but

'What is incredible is that our men and women out there delivering that level of policing are prepared to do it. My role is to make sure they feel adequately protected, but the bottom line is, policing is a risk business. My officers recognise that and they still go out and do it and I think that is the most powerful message we can send, and they will not step back.'

8.11   Community Engagement

In January 2008 the Policing Board launched a consultation process on its Community Engagement Strategy, which had been developed in 2006. The Policing Board had responsibility under Section 3(3)e of the Police (Northern Ireland) Act 2000 to *'make arrangements for obtaining the cooperation of the public with the police in the prevention of crime'*. To fulfil its responsibility, the Policing Board set as a key objective in its 2005–2008 Corporate Plan the development of a strategy to encourage public confidence in policing, including the development of the community engagement strategy.

The aim was to raise public awareness of the work of the Policing Board, increase public confidence in its work and in the PSNI, and create a platform on which the DPPs could develop more detailed local responses. A working group with Members from the Board's Community Engagement Committee was set up.

The Policing Board's Annual Report for 2007/08 summarised progress, which included establishing terms of reference and action plans for a number of reference groups, commissioning scoping work from the Northern Ireland Youth Forum on effective ways to engage young people, and a range of high-profile events with the business community and the minority ethnic communities. The Board established sector reference groups for disability, LGBT, older people, young people, minority ethnic communities, and women. In this context, the Board also recognised other communities traditionally disengaged from policing, such as people living in Loyalist and Republican areas.

This exercise gathered views on how the Board's framework for effective community engagement could be further developed. The Policing Board defined its approach as:

'To support and enable all communities in Northern Ireland to meaningfully participate in shaping the police service they use and thereby contribute to a reduction in crime, enhanced confidence in policing, and an improved quality of life.'

One of the questions posed in a consultation document was *'How best can the Board and DPPs work together to further develop effective community engagement?'* Another was whether there were other communities that the Board should include. There were a number of consultative events with key stakeholders, including DPPs and the wider community, which included the holding of two round-table discussions on community engagement.

The PSNI were asked by Board Members in June 2008 what definition of community engagement they used. The response was that there was no one single definition, but it involved consultation, community capacity building, and empowerment. It had to be tailored to the needs of the relevant community. *Independent Member* David Rose noted that the Board had come across a range of different definitions from different police forces across the United Kingdom. The PSNI undertook to work with the Board on a common definition.

In September 2008 the Chairman of the Community Engagement Committee reported to the Board that the Committee had approved a revised community engagement strategy and brought it to the Board for approval. Board Members were also encouraged to make local 'seeing is believing' visits in support and to monitor the implementation of the recommendation that each District should develop its own community engagement strategy.

On 18 September 2008 the Policing Board held what was described as its first *'public engagement meeting'* in the King's Hall in Belfast, at which the revised community engagement strategy was launched. In addition to presentations by the Board Chairman, the Vice-Chairman, and the Chief Constable, the Chairman of the Board's Community Engagement Committee, Alex Maskey, also spoke on the Board's refreshed approach to community engagement. The emphasis was on the work that the Board was doing to help build public confidence, secure safer communities, and respond to local communities. A summary report of the issues was circulated to DPPs for information. Further community engagement public meetings were subsequently held in Londonderry and elsewhere.

8.12   The Relationship between District Policing Partnerships and Community Safety Partnerships, and the Replacement of Both by Policing and Community Safety Partnerships (PCSPs)

One of the issues that engaged the Policing Board for 10 years before resolution was the relationship between DPPs and CSPs. It was one of the two issues on which the Policing Board fundamentally disagreed with the position of the NIO (the other being the Department's structural approach to organised crime).

The Independent Commission had envisaged that the DPPs would be involved with the policing of their Districts in a wide sense, entailing engagement with agencies other than the PSNI with a view to resolving wider community safety issues. However, in 2002 the NIO created CSPs following the introduction of the British Government's Crime Reduction Strategy in November 1999 for England and Wales and a recommendation in the separate Criminal Justice Review published in March 2000. Local CSPs were established in each District under the Justice (Northern Ireland) Act 2002, initially on a voluntary basis, as a structure that brought together all of the statutory organisations, including those dealing with health, education, social services, probation, and the police. A total of £2.5m per year was made available for CSPs across Northern Ireland.

The Policing Board consistently expressed concern to NIO Ministers and officials about this development, as it foresaw scope for confusion and duplication between DPPs and CSPs, stultification of the DPPs, and additional burdens on police and District Council resources. On 3 July 2002 the Board unanimously adopted a resolution that DPPs should be the sole mechanism for delivering policing with the community and that community safety functions should be subsumed into the DPP.

However, this was rejected by the NIO at Ministerial level, as was a joint approach by the Board and the PSNI to the NIO the following year.

Over succeeding years, various external reviews reached conclusions closer to the Board's position. These included. the Northern Ireland Affairs Committee at Westminster in October 2005, the Preparation for Government Committee of the Northern Ireland Assembly in September 2006, and the Criminal Justice Inspection Northern Ireland in November 2006.

In 2006/07 the Board initiated a public consultation which indicated overwhelming support for an integrated model. Although in late 2007 the NIO Policing and Security Minister, Paul Goggins, announced a review of the current arrangements in the context of the work on the RPA, no material changes resulted. Finally, on 11 March 2010, less than a month before the devolution of policing and justice, Paul Goggins issued a long-awaited consultation paper seeking views on 'the best way to deliver the functions of CSPs and DPPs in the future through single partnerships'.

On 10 April 2010 responsibility for policing and justice was devolved to the Northern Ireland Executive. A month later the Minister of Justice, David Ford, met the Policing Board and made clear his intention to legislate for a single partnership as soon as practicable. The Justice Act (Northern Ireland) 2011, passed by the Northern Ireland Assembly, created Policing and Community Safety Partnerships (PCSPs), which brought together the functions and responsibilities previously undertaken by the DPPs and the CSPs. A PCSP was established for each District Council, with four in Belfast. Their main roles were to

- consult and engage
- identify the particular issues relevant to the District and prepare plans for how they could be tackled
- monitor the performance of the police and achievement against targets in the local policing plan and the delivery of their own partnership plan
- deliver a reduction in crime and enhance community safety in their District

Their Membership consisted of eight to 10 Political Members nominated by the District Council, seven to nine Independent Members appointed by the Policing Board, and at least four representatives of designated organisations which the PCSP would have selected because of their local contribution. Each PCSP would have a Policing Committee consisting of Political and Independent Members. After public consultation, and appointment processes first for Political and then for Independent Members, the PCSPs duly got underway in summer 2012.

8.13   Developments in Great Britain

In a speech on 19 February 2008 the Policing Board Chairman said that DPPs had been widely showcased and in recent years had hosted visitors from across the world, including from Canada, Pakistan, and Israel. It is curious that, while the Policing Board played an active role in the Association of Police Authorities (APA), and while PSNI senior management was similarly involved in ACPO, in terms of central government in Whitehall, there was for many years little evidence of willingness to learn from the Northern Ireland experience of policing with the community.

In July 2008 the Home Office issued a consultative document entitled *'From the neighbourhood to the national: policing our communities together'*. This consultative paper was informed by the work of Louise Casey's review *'Engaging communities in fighting crime'*, in which she identified the top 10 policing approaches that the public wanted to see. These included elements such as a service that takes action, a visible uniformed police presence, named contacts, continuity in the local police team, and good engagement with the community. As part of the measures to meet expectations the Home Office developed a two-page Policing Pledge which was being implemented by each police service in England and Wales by the end of 2008. The 10 points in the Policing Pledge were very similar to many of the issues identified in the Northern Ireland policing with the community and the community engagement process over the previous years, including identification of dedicated neighbourhood policing teams, effective call handling, regular public meetings, and providing monthly updates on progress.

In May 2009 the Home Office published a document entitled *'Support Framework – Delivering Safer and Confident Communities'*. It noted that a wide range of partners was involved with the core authorities on each Crime and Disorder Reduction Partnership (CDRP). It quoted the *'Review of Policing'* carried out by Sir Ronnie Flanagan and published in early 2008 which stated that *'Policing is far too important to be left to the police alone'*. CDRPs were part of a new performance framework with four main elements:

- National Public Service Agreements measured through the National Indicator Set
- the Local Area Agreement
- the Comprehensive Area Assessment
- the Place Based Survey

Each CDRP was required to prepare an annual strategic assessment, produce a partnership plan, undertake community consultation and engagement on crime and disorder issues, and share information. While there was no direct linkage between the Crime and Disorder Committee and the local Police Authority, the paper stipulated that it was vital that local authorities' community safety scrutiny complemented the specific statutory role of Police Authorities to hold the police to account.

A Home Office paper entitled *'A Year in Neighbourhood Policing'* was published in 2009. In the foreword the Prime Minister, Gordon Brown, noted that April 2009 marked the first full year in which neighbourhood policing had been available throughout England and Wales. On 1 March 2010 a document entitled *'Safe and Confident Neighbourhoods Strategy: Steps in Neighbourhood Policing'* was published. This bore the hallmark of many organisations – the APA, ACPO, the National Policing Improvement Authority, the Welsh Assembly, the Ministry of Justice, the Home Office, the Attorney General's Office, and the Department for Communities and Local Government. The Ministerial Foreword stated that over 13,500 officers and 16,000 PCSOs were committed to tackling crime and anti-social behaviour. While referring to the Policing Pledge, it removed all nationally set targets in relation to policing except one – improving public confidence.

This document was the launch of Total Place, described as 'enabling more efficient and effective partnership working by increasing local freedoms and flexibilities'. Among the steps involved were the promotion of neighbourhood partnerships and an expectation of a wide range of agencies forging strong links with their neighbourhood policing team. The document noted that it was some six years after the initial launch of neighbourhood policing teams. At the local level, 80% of areas in England had targets set out in the Local Area Agreement relating to confidence or perceptions of anti-social behaviour. The document also stated that Forces could be held to account by individuals or communities if they felt they were not adequately addressing crime and anti-social behaviour concerns.

Yet, for all these central initiatives promoting engagement with the local community, there were some sceptical voices. For example, in an article in *The Guardian* newspaper on 2 April 2012, a former Deputy Assistant Commissioner at the Metropolitan Police wrote that '*In any liberal democracy, policing must be by consent, and you lose that consent immediately if you alienate the community and treat them as the enemy*'. He felt that the traditional service ethos had been sacrificed on the altar of management efficiency over the previous 15 years and said that officers were nowadays trained to see the public as a threat, and that preventative patrolling had been abandoned. The article went on to suggest that '*People too often accept what they are told by police leaders and politicians, and seldom demand policing be accountable at all times and at every level of interaction*'.

8.14   In Conclusion

In Northern Ireland it remains to be seen how the integrated PCSPs will work. Reorganisation of local government in 2015 will pose a further challenge at a time when the new bodies will not long have bedded in. However, following the story of the previous 10 years, it is hard to do other than breathe a huge sigh of relief at the effective amalgamation of DPPs and CSPs. The purity of the Patten model in relation to DPPs did not sit easily with the recommendations for community safety in the Criminal Justice Review, and it would be easy to argue that a mistake was made in the creation of two separate bodies. While there were distinctions between an element of policing accountability on the one hand and the wider promotion of community safety across a range of organisations on the other, undoubtedly it did lead to confusion, duplication, and additional expense. Yet it can be argued that the clarity of the DPPs' focus on policing was helpful in respect of getting them established, developing their relationship with the Policing Board, and, indeed – notwithstanding the very real threats and attacks on Members during the initial years of their existence – providing a local entity for community engagement and critical policing issues that helped in the development of Sinn Féin's attitudes towards support for policing and the police. That element of local consent, allied to demonstrable efforts by the PSNI to develop both policing with the community and neighbourhood policing teams, was a critical success factor.

Institutionalising policing with the community was, as the Independent Commission and indeed the top management of the PSNI saw, a major challenge, especially given the continuing security threat in significant parts of Northern Ireland. There were always two sides of this coin – establishing structures and instilling in officers a readiness to engage with the community on the one hand and the preparedness of the community to engage with the police on the other. The PSNI were among the first police services in the United Kingdom to implement meaningful neighbourhood policing teams.

The Policing Board also sought to give a lead from the beginning in establishing a Committee dedicated to community affairs/involvement and sustaining the pressure on the PSNI in the implementation of their policing with the community strategy. As we have seen in regard to DPPs, community engagement was perhaps harder and slower to get established.

The effectiveness of particular DPPs varied, depending on the input of the key players and especially the relationship between the PSNI District Commander and the DPP chair. It also appears to have been the case that rural DPPs made better headway than urban ones, or at least the Belfast DPP. This was in part due to there being issues in Belfast that did not apply elsewhere, with the functional split between the city-wide DPP and the four sub-groups. In addition, the ever-present political rivalries in Belfast may have hindered the development of a DPP system that performed consistently effectively.

The terms of reference of the DPPs did not, as we have seen, include the same specific accountability function as those of the Policing Board. The accountability of each individual PSNI District Commander was to his or her Assistant Chief Constable, not to the DPP. That said, the DPPs were set up to monitor the performance of the police in their District, and this would inevitably involve probing and challenging the senior PSNI representatives at their public meetings. There was, perhaps inevitably, a degree of confusion about this. For example, Hugh Orde, when he was Chief Constable, would refer publicly to the DPPs' accountability role. It may be argued, especially now that DPPs have morphed into PCSPs, that this ambiguity was not unhelpful. It could be seen as another instance of that 'constructive ambiguity' that has so often been an outcome of political negotiations in Northern Ireland and which has generally been helpful in taking forward both the *peace* and the *political processes*.

In terms of their specific functions, the DPPs did come to play an effective part in providing bottom-up input to the Annual Policing Plan. Moreover, as we show in Chapter 14, DPPs had a key role in establishing the views of the local community in relation to the potential closure of individual police stations. In addition, the process for extensive annual surveys involving both the Policing Board and the DPPs ensured that both they and the police had regular, good-quality information on which to base their plans and policies.

Finally, it must be recognised that the lead given by the Policing Board to establish the DPPs initially and then take forward their reconstitution on several occasions was a great success. It was the first such Northern Ireland-wide appointment exercise undertaken by a body other than central government, and was conducted under the spotlight on its political legitimacy and its compliance with the legislative and OCPA requirements.

References

Shaping the Future Together, a response from the Police Authority for Northern Ireland to the Report of the Independent Commission on Policing, Police Authority

Creating a safer Northern Ireland through Partnership, a consultative document, Northern Ireland Office, March 2003

Ulster Unionist Party press release, 7 October 2003

Building Communities, Beating Crime, Government White Paper for England and Wales on Police Reform, November 2004

Daily Ireland, 21 September 2005

The Review of Policing, by HMCIC Sir Ronnie Flanagan, 7 February 2008

From the neighbourhood to the national: policing our communities together, published by the Home Office, 17 July 2008.

A Year in Neighbourhood Policing, published by the Home Office, 2009

Support Framework – Delivering Safer and Confident Communities, published by the Home Office, May 2009

Safe and Confident Neighbourhoods Strategy: Steps in Neighbourhood Policing, 1 March 2010

The Guardian, 2 April 2012

CHAPTER NINE

The Principle of Consent and Affirmative Action

9.1   The Principle of Consent

One of the most controversial sections in the Report Of The Independent Commission On Policing For Northern Ireland (the Independent Commission) was Chapter 14, entitled 'Composition of the Police Service'. In the view of the authors, the Commission's recommendations in this area were to prove integral to the new Service's acceptance across the whole community, and indeed to the positive evolution of the political process.

However, as this chapter highlights, for the two main Unionist parties the Report's recommendations in regard to the <u>composition</u> of the Service were the most objectionable – both in theory and in practice. The elected representatives of both the Ulster Unionist Party (UUP) and the Democratic Unionist Party (DUP) consistently opposed their implementation from the introduction of the legislation in 2000 to the conclusion of the special measures when the compositional target had been reached in 2011. It was also an issue that created much constituency correspondence. Notwithstanding their strong objections, the representatives of both parties were prepared to work within the Government's framework on the Policing Board. For their part, the Nationalist parties were adamant that the recommendations be implemented in full.

The opening sentence of the chapter in the Independent Commission's Report grounded the analysis in the terms of the Belfast Agreement itself:

'The parties to the Agreement believe it is essential that the police service should be 'representative of the society it polices'. The Royal Ulster Constabulary

(RUC) is not representative. Only about 8% of its officers are Roman Catholics, while more than 40% population of Northern Ireland is Roman Catholic... Only 12.6% of its officers are women. ... The RUC is widely seen as overwhelmingly Protestant and male.

We take the view that ... real community policing is impossible if the composition of the police service bears little relationship to the composition of the community as a whole. The MacPherson report on the investigation of the murder of Stephen Lawrence in London made a similar point.'

The Independent Commission made some other important points: representativeness was a matter affecting the effectiveness and efficiency of policing, not just a matter of fairness; nor was it a matter of having Catholic police officers to police Catholic people – communities as a whole should see themselves as having a stake in the police service as a whole. If that was achieved there would be a better cooperative partnership between community and police and therefore more effective policing.

The authors believe this analysis is just as relevant in the context of the composition of, say, the Metropolitan Police Service today, and its relationship with the community that it serves.

The Independent Commission's Report also noted that the underrepresentation of women was a problem for police services everywhere (though, by some yardsticks, Northern Ireland was not doing badly – for example, 37% of the first Royal Ulster Constabulary (RUC) recruit intake of 1999 was female).

However, the Independent Commission concluded that it was right to make detailed proposals only for recruitment and composition targets in relation to the Catholic – Protestant imbalance (Paragraph 14.9).

The Commission's Report had dealt, in Chapter 13, with the size of the police service for Northern Ireland. The Commission noted that

'The Royal Ulster Constabulary (RUC) currently has 13,000 officers – a regular force of 8,500, a Full Time Reserve of 2,900 and a Part Time Reserve of 1,300 – and some 3,000 (full time equivalent) civilians. For a population of 1.675m this is a large police service. A comparable geographical area with a comparable population elsewhere in the United Kingdom would, according to the Home Office model, have a police service of about 4,300 officers and 1,700 civilians.' (Paragraph 13.1)

The Commission went on to state that *'the security situation since the Agreement, although greatly improved, has by no means yet come to resemble the situation faced by other police services in the United Kingdom'* and *'Public order policing remains a large demand on police resources.'* Accordingly, the Commission recommended that

'Provided the peace process does not collapse and the security situation does not deteriorate significantly from the situation pertaining at present, the approximate size of the police service over the next 10 years should be 7,500 full time officers.' (Paragraph 13.9)

It went on to stress that this was *'approximate'* – it could not be a precise science and the Chief Constable should have some discretion as to the precise numbers and ranks of officers and civilians who should be employed within the budget at his disposal. This was to prove highly relevant in the ensuing debates on the Policing Board about the future of the Full Time Reserve (FTR), as this chapter brings out.

The Independent Commission worked with consultants on a model for the establishment (or complement) of the police over the ten-year period. This model covered the downsizing of the police service, especially over an initial three-year period (by the end of which the number of regular officers would have reduced to 7,100), and a change in the composition by means of a new recruitment strategy over the full 10 years. This was based on three particular elements – the introduction of a generous early retirement or severance package offered to regular officers and full time reservists aged 50 or above (with management able to decline to allow an individual officer early retirement if his or her particular skills needed to be retained), the FTR being phased out over three years, and recruitment being increased to 370 new officers per year.

The Report identified that, on the basis of this model, the proportion of Catholic officers would more than double within four years to between 17% and 19%, reaching 30% in year 10. In addition, it recommended a target of some 1,000 new reserve police officers being recruited from Nationalist areas to constitute a total strength of 2,500 locally based part timers. Together, there could be a total Roman Catholic representation within the police service of some 40% within 10 years.

The Independent Commission expressed the view that the same principle of a balanced and representative workforce should also apply to the civilian staff, but did not make specific recommendations in relation to their recruitment.

Chapter 15 of the Independent Commission's Report dealt with Recruitment. There were two key recommendations:

' • *We recommend that all candidates for the police service should continue to be required to reach a specified standard of merit in the selection procedure. Candidates reaching this standard should then enter a pool from which the required number of recruits can be drawn.*' (Paragraph 15.9)

' • *We recommend that an equal number of Protestants and Catholics should be drawn from the pool of qualified candidates.*' (Paragraph 15.10)

In addition, the Report contained a number of other recommendations:

- the police should contract out the recruitment of both police officers and civilians
- there should be lay involvement, including community representatives, on recruitment panels
- lateral entry of experienced officers from other police services should be encouraged
- the Gaelic Athletic Association should repeal its Rule 21 which prohibited members of the police in Northern Ireland from being members of the Association
- young people should not be automatically disqualified for relatively minor criminal offences

The Report also made clear, however, that '*we emphatically do not suggest that people with serious criminal or terrorist backgrounds should be considered for police service ...*'

The Report recognised the key to making the police service representative of the communities – '*indeed the key to the successful implementation of nearly everything in this Report*' (authors' underlining) – was that the leaders of communities should now actively encourage their young people to apply to join the police service:

'*We therefore recommend that all community leaders, including political party leaders and local councillors, bishops and priests, schoolteachers and sports authorities, should take steps to remove all discouragements to members of their communities applying to join the police and make it a priority to encourage them to apply.*' (Paragraph 15.2)

9.2   Affirmative Action

The British Government accepted that the future size of the police service should be 7,500 full time regular officers in the circumstances envisaged by the Independent Commission. This would leave Northern Ireland with more full time regular officers per head of population than anywhere else in the United Kingdom, recognising the particular policing requirements. In the Updated Implementation Plan published in August 2001 it stated '*in an enabling security environment, downsizing to 7,500 full time regular officers will take place over a three-year period beginning in the second half of the 2000–2001 financial year*'. It added that, '*subject to the security situation*', the FTR would be phased out.

The provisions in the Police Bill when it was introduced in Parliament relating to what quickly became known as 50:50 recruitment were to prove highly controversial. Section 44 of the Police (Northern Ireland) Act 2000, when enacted, provided for the Secretary of State to prescribe in regulations the arrangements to be made by the Chief Constable, or an agency appointed by him, in relation to the recruitment of persons for appointment as police trainees. Before making such regulations the Secretary of State was required to consult the Policing Board, the Chief Constable, the Equality Commission for Northern Ireland, and the Police Association. Critically, under section 44(5), the regulations were also to '*include provision for the selection of qualified applicants to form a pool of applicants for the purposes of section 46 (1)*'. This sub-section provided that:

'*(1) in making appointments under section 39 on any occasion, the Chief Constable shall appoint from the pool of qualified applicants formed for that purpose by virtue of section 44(5) an even number of persons of whom –*

(a) one half shall be persons who are treated as Roman Catholic; and

(b) one half shall be persons who are not so treated.'

In addition, the legislation also provided (in section 47) that the *'temporary provisions'* made by the Secretary of State in relation to 50:50 recruitment would last for only up to three years, although they might then be extended for one or more further periods of three years, the Secretary of State having consulted with the Policing Board, among others. Such reviews would take account of progress towards a police service representative of the Northern Ireland community. On a contingent basis, there was also provision for the Secretary of State, by Order, to amend the 50:50 quota if there were insufficient numbers of one community to meet recruitment requirements, although in practice this was never required.

The British Government was obliged to get a special exemption or derogation from European Directive 2000/78/EC on employment equality to allow for these exceptional recruitment arrangements. Article 15 (1) of the Directive provides:

'1. *In order to tackle the under-representation of one of the major religious communities in the police service of Northern Ireland, differences in treatment regarding recruitment into that service, including its support staff, shall not constitute discrimination insofar as those differences in treatment are expressly authorised by national legislation.'*

The 50:50 rule was also exempted from Northern Ireland fair employment legislation as a temporary measure.

The special recruitment provisions in the legislation also applied to recruitment competitions for police civilian support staff (at section 44(7)) where six or more posts were involved. Section 48 of the Act required the Policing Board to make and revise action plans for monitoring the number of women in the police and increasing the number if they were under-represented. The Chief Constable was responsible for managing the severance process, with enabling provisions contained in section 49.

Section 3(3)(c) required the Policing Board to:

'*Keep itself informed as to* ...

    (iv) trends and patterns in recruitment to the police and the police support staff;

(v) the extent to which the membership of the police and the police support staff is representative of the community in Northern Ireland.'

The Police (Recruitment) (Northern Ireland) Regulations 2001 made under the 2000 Act required the Policing Board to appoint Independent Community Observers who served for three years in a voluntary capacity, attending elements of the recruitment process for police trainees and civilian support staff.

9.3   50:50 Recruitment to the Police Service of Northern Ireland and the Role of the Policing Board

Even without the politically controversial element, it was clear from the beginning that human resources in general, and recruitment in particular, would be major issues requiring the Policing Board's close attention. Perhaps inevitably, the issues obliged Board Members not just to address strategic matters but to delve into detailed application. As we shall see, this was an area where what might be termed 'creative tension' between the Policing Board and senior members of the Police Service of Northern Ireland (the Police Service or the PSNI) was an important factor in achieving the outcome. It was also an area where strongly held views of *Political Members* of the Board were often divergent and sometimes directly opposed.

A presentation on the recruitment and selection of police trainees was arranged for the Policing Board on 12 December 2001 by the Police Service's senior Human Resources managers and a representative from Consensia. (The contract to provide an independent recruitment agency had been awarded in January 2001 to the Consensia Partnership, led by Deloitte & Touche.)

The first recruitment campaign – Competition One – had been launched on 23 February 2001, with the pool of qualified candidates finalised by September that year. There had been a strong response, with 7,843 applicants for 264 places. Of those who applied, 60% were Protestant, 35% Roman Catholic and 40% female. In the final pool of qualified candidates (usually known as the *'merit pool'*), 165 were Roman Catholics and 428 non-Roman Catholics. The assessment of the

Police Oversight Commissioner was that '*the recruitment programme is well-designed, aggressive and meets contemporary policing standards*'.

The second recruitment campaign – Competition Two – had just kicked off, with 4,928 application forms returned, including 530 applications from addresses in the Republic of Ireland and 127 in Great Britain, and a slightly higher proportion of Roman Catholics.

Board Members were advised that the new trainees were drawn on a 50:50 basis from the merit pool in any one competition, until such time as it was no longer possible to do so on a 50:50 basis, at which point the trainees would then start to be drawn from the following competition. Applicants who were not selected from the residual merit pool were obliged to reapply to join the PSNI in a subsequent recruitment campaign.

The Policing Board noted that the cost of Competition One was £4m, that there was no appeal mechanism for unsuccessful candidates, and that advice had been received from the Northern Ireland Equality Commission that each competition must be regarded as separate.

The Policing Board continued to monitor recruitment closely. There was a second presentation by PSNI and Consensia staff in March 2002, together with a presentation on the voluntary early retirement/severance programme. The Secretary of State had announced the voluntary severance programme on 24 July 2000, and it had been finalised three months later. In effect, the age of a serving officer together with the length of his or her service was added together and converted to a points score; a points threshold was then set for each year to determine those who might be eligible to leave. The scheme provided officers with a lump sum, a pension enhancement, a payment in lieu of pension, and outplacement support. It was managed by the PSNI Voluntary Severance Support Unit.

A total of 483 officers had left the Service under the terms of the voluntary severance programme by 31 March 2001, with a further 824 scheduled to leave in 2001/02; in year three of the programme 686 were anticipated to leave. This would be in addition to the 'normal' departure of officers during the year for reasons including ill-health and resignation, then at around 175 regular officers and 150 officers in the FTR. It was also noted that sickness absence was then running at 17.9%, which equated to around 1,000 officers a day. It was recognised in the presentation that the severance programme would entail a loss of expertise in some specialisms.

At its meeting on 6 March 2002 the Policing Board considered a paper that had been prepared by its own staff at the request of the Board's Personnel and General Purposes Committee on manpower levels in the PSNI, setting out the probable short-term impact of recruitment, wastage, and severance on the number of officers available to the Chief Constable. The paper noted that the staffing of the PSNI at 1 February 2002 was 7,011 regular officers, 2,207 officers in the FTR and 1,018 officers in the Part Time Reserve (PTR). The paper also pointed out that no final decision on severance beyond 2002/03 or on the date for standing down the FTR had been taken.

The recruitment programme was geared to bring in 540 trainee officers a year – compared to the 370 included in the Patten model – this being the maximum number of students that the Police College at Garnerville could deal with at any one time. In the first calendar year 534 police trainees were appointed.

It was agreed that the Chief Constable should be asked to develop for the Board's May 2002 meeting a manpower strategy illustrating how the manpower requirements of the PSNI would be met. The approach was to be holistic, including severance, the future of the FTR, part time officer recruitment, civilianisation of posts, management of sickness, and wastage from all sections of the Service. The PSNI response, which took the form of the Human Resources Planning Strategy, is set out in the section below.

The Policing Board also sought information on the geographical and socio-economic background of applicants to the PSNI and on information given to unsuccessful candidates. Another of the issues raised by the Policing Board was the considerably higher proportion of female candidates who had failed certain of the physical competence tests in the first two recruitment competitions; the Board were told that a review was being carried out by Sheffield University.

In October 2002 the Policing Board's Corporate Policy Committee considered the issue of the lack of specialist skills within the PSNI in certain areas, in particular the shortage of experienced detectives, and the time that it took to train new detectives. The Committee considered a draft letter to the Secretary of State proposing amending legislation to enable detectives from Great Britain and – in due course

– the Garda Síochána, at constable level, to transfer to the PSNI permanently, without being subject to sections 39 and 46 of the Police (Northern Ireland) Act 2000.

On 12 December 2002 the Northern Ireland Office (NIO) Minister responsible for Security, Jane Kennedy, replied to the Policing Board Chairman regarding the requirement for PSNI applicants who had met the merit standard but had been rejected owing to their community background to undertake the entire recruitment competition afresh. The Minister stated that she had sought the views of both the PSNI and the Equality Commission, who had both pointed up significant practical difficulties were candidates in the merit pool to be carried forward from one competition to the next. Evidence suggested that candidates who repeated the recruitment process tended to improve their score and thus their chance of selection. Furthermore, the current arrangements allowed Consensia and the PSNI to modify the recruitment process, if it was shown to be justified, each time the competition was run.

Tensions continued in relation to the 50:50 recruitment process. For example, early in 2003 Board Member Sammy Wilson (DUP) issued a press release stating that

'The latest figures for recruitment to the Police Service show once again the discriminatory and ineffective nature of the 50/50 recruitment role for recruiting new police officers. Out of 748 people who passed the latest recruit-ment exercise only 180 were Roman Catholics, less than 25%... the lowest percentage to date and shows that despite all the efforts being made, rules being changed and the discrimination being exercised, the 50/50 requirement is a failed policy.

... The irony is that while IRA/Sinn Féin are doing their best to stop people joining the police, the Government is dreaming up all kinds of incentives to get IRA/Sinn Féin to join the Police Board.

... It is clear that the 50/50 requirement first proposed by the Ulster Unionist Party (UUP) is a failed policy.'

There was an issue in relation to the number of student police trainees joining the Police College at Garnerville in the early months of 2003. The Police Service advised the Board in early February 2003 that by the end of Competition Three the number of trainees had fallen below that originally anticipated and, as a consequence, the final intakes had been split into two groups of 32, although there were potentially 300 further trainees becoming available from Competition Four. This was followed up with a letter from the Chief Constable on 14 February 2003 in which he noted that:

'The recruitment of trainees is a success. The level of applications from Roman Catholics has been consistent across the four competitions conducted under the new arrangements and exceeded all expectations.'

He added in the letter that it was expected that the number brought in during the full year would still be 540 trainees, resulting in the number of regular police officers reaching 7,500 by April 2004. The next month he advised that the recruitment process had been improved, within the remit of the legislation, by the introduction of an exemption at the initial selection test stage and revision of the physical competence assessment.

The Policing Board were advised in May 2003 of an appeal using the judicial review process on behalf of Mark Parsons, a 19-year-old, whose application to join the PSNI was rejected even though Roman Catholics with a lower score had been accepted. Parsons' lawyer argued that section 46(1) of the Police (Northern Ireland) Act 2000 was incompatible with Article 9 of the European Convention on Human Rights guaranteeing the right to freedom of thought, conscience, and religion. However, the Northern Ireland Court of Appeal held that the 50:50 rule was not incompatible with the Human Rights Act 1998.

On 10 March 2003 the Policing Board Chairman wrote to the Secretary of State stating that the Board had very carefully addressed the shortage of detectives and the case for recruiting constables from other police services in special circumstances (lateral entry). The letter recommended that a draft clause should be brought forward as an amendment to the existing legislation. The policy noted that, while police officers at any level above constable could permanently transfer between individual police services within the United Kingdom, the operation of the 50:50 rule prevented this at constable level. The Board made a proposal that would allow for the Chief Constable to submit a request to the Board setting out in considerable detail the case for setting aside the 50:50 rule. In order to activate this exceptional route, the unanimous support of every Board Member would have to be secured.

The Board's proposal was incorporated as a special lateral entry route in section 47A of the Police (Northern Ireland) Act 2000 (as amended by section 23 of the Police (Northern Ireland) Act 2003), entitled 'appointment of constables with special policing skills'. The amendment placed the Policing Board in the driving seat on whether the Chief Constable should be authorised to appoint as constables in the PSNI a specified number of persons with a particular policing skill, setting aside the 50:50 rule, provided it was satisfied that the need for such persons could not be met through the normal 50:50 recruitment process.

In the event, one request was made by the Chief Constable in summer 2003 on the new basis, to enable the appointment of 65 detective constables. This was approved unanimously by the Policing Board at its meeting on 2 July 2003 and an advertisement accordingly appeared in the Police Review the following month.

After consideration by the Policing Board's Lateral Entry Sub-group, agreement was reached with the PSNI at the Board meeting on 2 July 2003 on an appropriate policy in regard to training accreditation for police officers who had received previous training outside the PSNI; the Secretary of State was then asked to make the necessary amendments to the draft Police Trainee Regulations.

On 21 September 2003 Jane Kennedy, the NIO Minister, wrote to the Chairman of the Policing Board announcing a review of the effectiveness of the 50:50 recruitment process, which had been legislatively commenced on 30 March 2001, as provided for under the Police (Northern Ireland) Act 2000. Views were sought from the Board by 19 December 2003. Prior to this, the Policing Board had made preparations for their role in the consultation process, as required under the statute. Its Corporate Policy Committee had agreed in June 2003 that a letter should go to the Equality Commission, the Northern Ireland Human Rights Commission, the European Commission, the European Court, and the NIO seeking their views on the 50:50 recruitment process arrangements.

The Minister's letter was considered at the Board's October 2003 Corporate Policy Committee meeting. That Committee concluded that, while there were differing perspectives on the principle of 50:50, a draft response should be prepared; further, it would be helpful, in formulating that response, if the PSNI were invited to make a presentation to the Policing Board on the operation of the 50:50 arrangements and their perspective on renewal of them.

Consequently, at the Board's November 2003 meeting the PSNI Senior Director of Human Resources advised the Board that the PSNI were content that a reasonably efficient methodology of operating the system was now in place, that 50:50 was not restricting the flow of applicants to the Service, and that the operation of the 50:50 recruitment process was on target to achieve the 30% Roman Catholic proportion by 2010/11, the end of the ten-year period. By September 2003 the proportion of regular police officers who were Roman Catholic had risen from 8.23% two years previously to 13.30%.

Board Members had further discussions about the response to the NIO Minister. Following those, the Chairman wrote on 4 December 2003 to NIO Minister Jane Kennedy recording that:

'Despite the fact that we have debated this issue at length it has not, given the Political Membership of the Board, been possible to give you a corporate Board response.

Rather we have decided to leave it to the political parties [with representatives on the Board] to make the written submissions to Government and to the Independent Members to do likewise if they so wish.'

On 17 December 2003 five *Independent Members* of the Policing Board, including the Chairman and Vice-Chairman, wrote further to Jane Kennedy. They recorded as their starting position that all Board Members would share the view that it was regrettable that there was a need to have the 50:50 arrangements. They then stated that a more representative service could not be achieved other than through the current legislative arrangements. The letter went on that the authors noted the evidence supplied by the PSNI that the 50:50 arrangements had not restricted the flow of applicants to the Service and that the Chief Constable had not deemed it necessary to utilise the 'set aside' arrangements which were provided for in the 2000 Police Act. Moreover, the special arrangements put in place in the 2003 Act for special appointments should an operational difficulty at constable level arise had been activated only once. On the other hand, they recognised the frustration felt by applicants who applied several times to join the PSNI and stated that they would be happy to explore how carry-over would improve the efficiency of the process. They also acknowledged the significant costs associated with the operation of 50:50 and their willingness to explore any improvements that would enhance effectiveness and efficiency. In respect of civilian support staff, the letter stated that the goal of delivering more officers to operational duties (and creating more civilian staff vacancies) had the unanimous support of Board Members. Board Members agreed that more large-volume civilian recruitment competitions were necessary if substantial compositional change was to be effected.

On 12 February 2004 Jane Kennedy laid in Parliament the Police (Northern Ireland) Act 2000 (Renewal of Temporary Provisions) Order 2004 to renew the 50:50 recruitment provisions for a further three years. In the accompanying press release she said:

'It is clear that the 50:50 recruitment provisions are bringing real results in improving the representativeness of the Police Service. However, I understand that many people find it very hard to accept the principle of 50:50 recruitment, particularly those who have not been appointed to the police because of it. The Government does not want to continue the practice for any longer than necessary, but we believe that, for the moment, it remains essential to bring to an end the historic imbalance in the representativeness of the police.'

In an interview with Gemma Murray in the *News Letter* published on 17 June 2004 the Policing Board Chairman was quoted as saying:

'I know the 50:50 rule causes great concern in the Protestant/Unionist community, but there is a prize for us to win.

We want to police every part of the community, have recruits from every part of the community and for them to be able to live in the areas from whence they came. That is the goal – the 50:50 is a necessary evil for us to achieve that.

That is the formal position of this Board although I have Members of this Board who do not agree. That is life. But the prize is there to be won.'

At the *Public Session* of the Policing Board held in Armagh on 4 November 2004, the PSNI Director of Human Resources gave a presentation on the composition of the PSNI. The number of Roman

Catholics in the PSNI had increased from 600 to almost 1,200 in the space of a very few years. The proportion of Roman Catholics applying in each recruitment campaign was consistently between 35% and 38%. He also noted that in October 2004 the PSNI had launched their Gender Action Plan. Over the same period the number of female police officers had risen from around 900 to 1,350. The changes introduced following the external study had worked well and there was no longer the dropout that had previously been seen among female candidates, although he emphasised that the standard of fitness for all officers entering the PSNI was probably one of the highest for any UK police service.

Policing Board Members noted that the degree of change in the composition of the civilian support staff was not so marked and pressed for it to be fully addressed as part of the revised Human Resources Strategy. In response, it was noted that there had not been the same degree of turnover of civilian staff, with a consequently much lower proportion of vacancies into which to recruit. Nevertheless, there had been a five or six percentage point increase in Roman Catholic representation in the civilian staff over the same period of time; moreover, the PSNI civilian recruitment agents were at that time working on 40 live competitions.

In response to a further question about the 50:50 recruitment process the Director stated that, while the PSNI had not been looking at information about the class background of applicants, this was something it had started to look at with the recruitment agency. The challenge of attracting recruits from *'lower social economic groupings'* was endemic to all police services.

Another Policing Board Member asked what could be said to members of the Protestant community who had applied unsuccessfully on two, three, or, in some instances, four occasions. Their lack of success was discouraging a great deal of people within the majority community, he asserted. In response, it was pointed out that applicants who qualified for the merit pool from both sides of the community were consistently being turned down, given the consistent level of successful applications as against the annual *'quota'* of 540 trainees that could be taken into the Police College. Another Policing Board Member pointed to the remark in the Police Oversight Commissioner's report that *'other police services would be envious both of the numbers applying and the quality of the applicants who are accepted into the PSNI'.*

In the autumn of 2005 the Chief Constable said after a *Public Session* of the Policing Board in Ballymena that:

'People want to be protected by police officers who operate with the highest integrity. That does exclude people who have serious criminal convictions. We are no different from any other police service in that regard, and I am at one with the Chairman.'

At the same time, the Policing Board Chairman was quoted as saying: *'This Board will not allow progress that has been made on policing to slip – nor to become a football for the purposes of political expediency.'* These comments came against the background of speculation that ex-IRA men with criminal records could be recruited to serve as community officers at a time when Sinn Féin had endorsed the PSNI. The Board Chairman was also quoted as informing the meeting that the Independent Commission's position that people with serious criminal or terrorist backgrounds should not be considered remained the majority Board viewpoint.

The October 2005 Policing Board meeting agreed that the recommendation in the Patten Report in relation to the criminal records of prospective applicants was entirely appropriate and that no further discussion on this matter was required at that stage.

Addressing the Social Democratic and Labour Party (SDLP) annual party conference in November 2005, the Policing Board Vice-Chairman Denis Bradley asserted that the 50:50 rule would have to go eventually if Northern Ireland were to have a proper human rights culture. A leader article in the *Sunday Life* newspaper stated that:

'Quotas of any sort sit ill with the increasingly multi-cultural nature of Northern Ireland society. The roadmap to all our futures extends far beyond the ghettos we call unionism and nationalism. Denis Bradley should be lauded for reminding all of us of this transparent truth.'

On 4 September 2006 the NIO Minister responsible for security wrote to the Policing Board Chairman advising the Board that the temporary provisions which gave effect to the 50:50 recruitment arrangements would be due to expire on 28 March 2007 unless renewed. The Government was again carrying out a consultation exercise, and the views of the Board were invited.

A paper at that time noted that, since 2004/05, the annual intake to the Police College had reduced from 540 to 440. (This change had been made commensurate with the maintenance of a complement of 7,500, the continuance of the early severance scheme and the achievement of the composition target in line with the Patten model.) The proportion of Roman Catholic officers in the PSNI had risen to 20.28% at 20 August 2006, while in police support staff Roman Catholics had risen to 19.15%.

The Board's Human Resources Committee considered the Minister's letter at its meeting in October 2006. That Committee agreed that the Board should be encouraged to agree a corporate response to the consultation, bearing in mind the impact of the 50:50 rule, although Members did accept that this might be unrealistic. The full Board in turn considered its response on 1 November 2006. It was agreed that, as the *Political Members* of the Board had differing views on the renewal of the temporary provisions, individual political parties should respond separately, while – as before – *Independent Members* should be offered the opportunity to sign a letter to the Secretary of State.

On 30 November 2006 a letter signed by the Chairman, the Vice-Chairman, and six other Policing Board *Independent Members* was sent to the Minister. It stated that the undersigned Members supported the need for the 50:50 arrangements to continue until the 30% Roman Catholic representation had been achieved in 2010/11. They welcomed the introduction of legislation scheduled for 2007 which would reduce the costs of recruitment exercises by requiring the PSNI to vet medically only the successful candidates rather than all candidates in the merit pool, as had been the process prior to that point. They also would encourage the development of quotas or targets for ethnic minority representation in the PSNI.

The Order to renew the temporary provisions in the Police (Northern Ireland) Act 2000 for a further three years was laid in Parliament on 29 January 2007.

Also in January 2007, following inaccurate information about recruitment and retention of Roman Catholic PSNI officers in press articles which quoted the British Irish Rights Watch, the Policing Board Chairman wrote to that organisation's Director pointing out that of the 2,420 student officers who had been appointed since 2001, a total of 70 had resigned or been dismissed, of whom 53 were from the Roman Catholic community.

In February 2007 the PSNI published a full equality impact assessment on the process of recruitment. This consultative document contained a vast amount of material, including details on the changes to the selection process following individual recruitment campaigns and differential application rates between the campaigns by categories (e.g., marital status and sexual orientation as well as community background).

The following response of the Policing Board to the PSNI was agreed by the Members at the 2 May 2007 Board meeting:

'The Board considers that the recruitment of regular officers has been one of the significant successes of the change management programme since its introduction in 2001. The recruitment process has continued to deliver the target number of student officers into the PSNI and has continued to attract an increasing number of applicants every year, with the total number of applicants throughout the 12 campaigns at 73,000...

Members regard the recruitment process as robust and standardised and believe that the independent community observers who were appointed by the Board to observe the recruitment process, have contributed to the fairness and independence of the recruitment and selection process.'

The Chief Constable set out for the Board the details of the initiatives taken by the PSNI in an attempt to attract members of ethnic minority communities; these included specialist magazines carrying the profile of an officer from an ethnic minority background, recruitment stands at ethnic minority festivals in Northern Ireland, round-table talks with senior members from various ethnic minority communities, and a DVD on police trainees that was then in production.

In autumn 2006 the Board had raised again the shortfall of detectives. Assistant Chief Constable Peter Sheridan explained in response that there were a number of factors at work in addition to the early severance programme; for example, officers wishing to move to Crime Operations now had to complete a national examination, for which there was a 40% failure rate, followed by a six-week training programme and then a further year as trainee investigators. Representations were made to the NIO and the provision to recruit experienced detectives outside Northern Ireland was renewed in legislation early in 2007. A campaign was duly launched to target the labour market for these posts in Great Britain and the Republic of Ireland. (On this occasion the PSNI recruited only 13 detective constables from other police forces.)

At the *Public Session* of the Policing Board held in Bangor on 4 October 2007 the Chief Constable noted that the most recent recruitment campaign for new officers had seen a significant increase in the number of applicants from the Roman Catholic tradition, at 44%. A Sinn Féin member of the Policing Board expressed concern that the proportion of Roman Catholics at senior ranks in the PSNI was expected to fall in the coming period and pressed for some kind of affirmative action. The Chief Constable responded that every appointment for senior rank was advertised nationally and across the island of Ireland. He made the point also that the proportions at senior level, for women officers as well, was a function of the past – there was going to be a gap before a more representative sample at senior rank was seen. He stressed that for the police service in general, '*the more representative you are, the more likely you are to be effective*'. The Director of Human Resources added that, for the latest Chief Superintendent competition, the PSNI had made direct approaches to the Garda Síochána to encourage individual officers at Superintendent rank to apply, although so far without success.

In the summer of 2008 the Policing Board were asked to submit their views to the NIO on the Draft Police Trainee (Amendment) Regulations (Northern Ireland) 2008. This was required in part following changes to the classification of offences which were deemed in the previous Regulations to be unsuitable for the purposes of a police trainee. The NIO proposed to deal with the list of offences in a similar way to the practice in England and Wales, through providing the Chief Constable with discretion as to which matters would be taken into account in deciding the suitability of a person for appointment. The previous position would obtain, in that anyone who had had passed on them a sentence of imprisonment or detention would automatically be ruled out, but the Chief Constable could set the criteria in relation to the type of cautions and disqualifications which might make a person unsuitable for appointment. The majority of the Policing Board were content to advise the NIO that this discretion should be granted the Chief Constable on the understanding it would be exercised in consultation with the Board, though the Sinn Féin representatives recorded their opposition to this resolution.

At the Policing Board meeting in July 2008 the Chief Constable was probed on steps being taken to improve the under-representation in police trainees from working class areas. The Chief Constable responded that he too was concerned about this. Clever advertising campaigns were not necessarily successful compared with, say, face-to-face contact. Consensia were conscious of the concerns that had been raised by himself and the Policing Board in this regard. Of all applicants, 10% were from the 20% most deprived areas in Northern Ireland.

On 1 October 2008 the NIO Security Minister announced that all civil servants seconded to the PSNI would become direct recruits, thereby ending the long history of secondment arrangements within the Northern Ireland Civil Service (NICS). This change was in line with the Patten Report. The Chief Constable noted that over 94% of the affected staff had chosen to remain with the Police Service. The Board Chairman expressed his pleasure that so many members of staff had chosen to continue their careers with the PSNI and welcomed them as official employees of the Policing Board. (Since January of that year staff had been given the choice to remain with the PSNI as direct recruits or seek a return to the NICS – just 68 had returned to the NICS.)

In January 2009 the Policing Board again met with the relevant Assistant Chief Constable to discuss the continuing shortfall of detectives. The Board were asked to approve the extension of recruitment of uniform officers to include the role of Trainee Intelligence Officers for the Crime Operations Department, as had previously been agreed for Trainee Investigators. The new officers would spend one year in training, following their initial two-year probation in Districts, before being signed out as Intelligence Officers. On 17 February 2009 the Policing Board Chairman wrote to the Chief Constable advising him that the Policing Board had approved this recommendation. However, as this was a novel approach to solving what was clearly a difficult problem, the Policing Board requested a dedicated briefing on the training programme. Her Majesty's Inspectorate of Constabulary (HMIC) would monitor the new arrangements.

In a press release issued on 31 March 2009 the NIO Minister, Paul Goggins, noted that the St Andrews Agreement had made it clear that the temporary 50:50 recruitment arrangements to the PSNI would lapse when the Government's target of 30% Catholic officers had been achieved.

At the *Public Session* of the Policing Board meeting on 2 April 2009 the Chairman noted that there were then 31 officers within the PSNI from an ethnic minority background. The percentage of female officers had almost doubled, from 12% to 23.43%, while the Roman Catholic representation had risen from 8% to 26%. Fourteen recruitment campaigns had by now been held and continued to attract a high number of applicants. The fifteenth recruitment campaign would particularly seek to target applicants from the top 20% of deprived areas in Northern Ireland, those living West of the river Bann, and black and ethnic minority applicants.

In 2010 the Government renewed the temporary 50:50 recruitment provisions for one final year to 28 March 2011 to ensure the target 30% Catholic composition was reached. Over the nine years to 2010, since the first recruitment campaign in 2001, the PSNI had received over 115,000 applications in 16 recruitment campaigns; approximately 37% of applicants indicated their religious background as Roman Catholic, with approximately 33% of applicants being female and 2% being from an ethnic minority background. In the same nine-year period, almost 4,000 new police trainees had been appointed.

In 2013 recruitment to the PSNI was recommenced, no longer on a 50:50 basis. Of the just on 7,500 initial candidates, 30.6% were Roman Catholic.

9.4   The Full Time Reserve

The future – or rather the running down – of the Full Time Reserve (FTR) was both a significant operational issue for the Chief Constable and a major bone of political contention for the Policing Board.

The Independent Commission had said in its Report (in

Recommendation 103) that: '*The future police service should not include a Full Time Reserve.*' The Report noted that the FTR was a direct result of the security situation of the previous 30 years, with officers engaged on three-year contracts to support the regular police force in security-related policing work. Over the years its members had become an integral part of the RUC, carrying out the same duties and bearing the same risks as their regular colleagues. The Report noted that the RUC's own Fundamental Review in 1996 proposed that, in the event of a sustained improvement in the security situation, the FTR should be disbanded. The Report added that this was in no way a judgement on the calibre and commitment of the reservists, and it envisaged that there should be an opportunity for them to apply for the regular service.

At the time of the Independent Commission's Report there were 2,900 FTR officers. The Updated Implementation Plan published in August 2001 noted that the strength of the FTR had already reduced by around 800 and there had been no recruitment for three years – '*the reduction has in effect begun*'. The next step would be the notification of the non-renewal of contract, which would happen subsequent to the first recruits to the PSNI completing their training in 2002, when the prevailing security situation and policing requirements would be reviewed; the Government had accepted the recommendation that the phasing out should happen over a three-year period.

The future of the FTR was a matter of debate among politicians in the period leading up to the launch of the PSNI Human Resources Strategy on 3 October 2002. For example, an article by Chris Thornton in the *Belfast Telegraph* the day before asserted that Unionist Members were expected to declare victory in their fight to save the FTR at a time when they were threatening to resign from the Policing Board. On the other hand:

'*[Social And Democratic Labour Party] Members – wary of giving Sinn Féin opportunities to criticise their policing involvement – are already emphasising that the [FTR] question was part of an overall package designed to get more officers on the street.*'

Policing Board Member Joe Byrne (SDLP) was quoted as saying that, while some people were flagging up the Reserve '*as being the most important issue*', he saw it as part of the strategy for the PSNI for the short and medium term.

The PSNI Human Resources Strategy included a commitment that there would be redeployment of the FTR to security-related duties, although the subsequent Oversight Commissioner's report noted that this had not fully occurred. In line with the Strategy, FTR contracts had been renewed with a common end date of 31 March 2005. The Strategy stated that, subject to a review of the prevailing security environment and the continued success of the recruitment campaign for PSNI Regular Officers, arrangements would be made to phase out the remaining officers over an 18-month period thereafter. The NIO would resume discussions with the Police Federation about the FTR with the aim of reaching an agreed severance package available from April 2005.

Following the announcement, Jeffrey Donaldson (DUP) was quoted in the *Belfast Telegraph* as saying '*yesterday's decision represents a step in the right direction, but we are pressing for the retention of the [FTR] on a permanent basis*'. Sinn Féin, on the other hand, were quoted in the same newspaper as saying in a submission to the Government on policing reform that disbandment of the FTR was long overdue and should start '*forthwith*'. The then Police Federation Chairman, Irwin Montgomery, called for confirmation that the position of the FTR was guaranteed '*for the foreseeable future*'. An article in the *Belfast Telegraph* on 10 October 2002 noted that in some areas the FTR as a percentage of the total of uniformed police was quite high; for example, in West Belfast it was 44%.

By 12 December 2003 FTR numbers had reduced to 1,659. Sir Dan Crompton noted that there were still sizeable numbers in mainstream policing roles and that the issue had been made critical by the slow progress in building up the PTR. The British Government's Spending Review 2004 projected significant efficiency savings through the rundown of the FTR after April 2005.

The Policing Board Chairman issued a press release on 18 June 2004 noting that the Chief Constable was scheduled to review the security situation formally in the late summer or early autumn of 2004. The release added that a specific goal of the Human Resources Strategy was to create some certainty around timescales so that FTR officers could start to make plans for the future.

The *Belfast Telegraph* carried an article on 19 June 2004 quoting Policing Board Member Ian Paisley Jnr (DUP) that a more effective and efficient police service would be created if the manpower issue was addressed in a way that utilised the 1,600 FTR officers. In a further article on 28 June 2004 Mr Paisley was quoted as saying that the phasing out of the FTR would have '*catastrophic consequences*' for emergency policing. The article added his belief that the reason the FTR was being slashed was to '*satisfy the unrealistic and plainly sectarian demands of Patten*'. In a press release issued on 30 June 2004 fellow DUP Board Member Sammy Wilson also urged the retention of the FTR. However, in a press release issued by Sinn Féin on 7 September 2004 Sinn Féin spokesperson on policing Gerry Kelly said that the removal of the FTR was a clear demand of Patten and a demand which must be met.

On 9 September 2004 the Chief Constable gave a presentation to a special meeting of the Policing Board on the future of the FTR. Beginning his remarks, he said:

'*This decision has been one of the most challenging and difficult I have had to make over the past two years. It is made against a backdrop of decreasing crime and an improving security situation.*'

He added that the decision which he and his Senior Management Team had made together and which he was there to communicate to the Board would give rise to much comment and debate. He was aware that all the Northern Ireland political parties had a view on the issue, and he had had meetings with most of them. He recognised that this decision would play in the political world, but he emphasised that it was not a political decision, but a policing one. It was an operational decision that took the current security situation fully into account and he accepted responsibility for it.

The conclusion was that, of the existing 1,487 FTR officers, the PSNI should retain 680 officers on the basis of a three-year contract to be issued from 1 April 2005; the remaining officers would be released in a phased manner across an 18-month period from the termination of their contracts. Negotiations were in hand with the Police Federation on the basis of selection for severance. The Chief Constable added that, by the end of 2004, the target size for the PSNI of 7,500 regular officers would be reached.

Each Policing Board Member was given an opportunity to question the Chief Constable in more detail. He stressed that the decision had been reached on an operational basis following a security review and had not been influenced by political considerations or by Government. He recognised that, since some serving officers and the Police Federation would not be satisfied with the outcome of the decision, managing it internally would be as difficult as managing it externally.

After the Chief Constable had left the meeting a Board motion was proposed expressing concern at the loss of 800 FTR police officers, but it was lost by seven votes to eight.

Following the announcement the Policing Board closely monitored implementation, including the arrangements for retraining FTR members before they left the service, with regular presentations from the independent validator. At the *Public Session* of the Policing Board on 7 April 2005 the Chief Constable was probed on how many FTR officers had 'lost their jobs' since his statement. He noted that the figure of 7,500 officers to police Northern Ireland was no longer a matter for debate. He added that '*the Board has kindly allowed me to keep a substantial number of the FTR to deal with specific issues in relation to security*'.

In May 2005 the Policing Board's Human Resources Committee had received a presentation from the Police Rehabilitation and Retraining Trust on the retraining for FTR officers and phasing-out plans; this followed a presentation at the end of April from the Chief Constable, the Deputy Director of Personnel, and other PSNI colleagues.

Policing Board Members were notified prior to a Special Board meeting on 21 September 2007 that the Chief Constable had been conducting a review of the remaining complement of FTR officers. The Board Chairman noted that much had changed since the Chief Constable's announcement on 9 September 2004. This included both policing and political developments, including the restoration of devolution. He noted that the last report by Sir Dan Crompton, as independent validator for the Board, had recorded a high degree of satisfaction among FTR officers regarding the severance and retraining package.

The Chief Constable then announced his decision on the future of the FTR. In summary, it was to reduce the requirement for FTR officers from 680 to 381, though this would not have an immediate impact as no FTR officer currently in post was scheduled to leave prior to 31 March 2008. The Chief Constable and his Senior Management Team had concluded that there remained a need to retain a FTR complement to secure the police estate and to provide protection and security in the external police environment. Again, the Chief Constable stressed in his remarks that it was a policing decision based firmly on operational policing and security considerations – *while it may give rise to political debate – that is a matter for others*.

In the ensuing discussion, Policing Board Members raised a number of points. These included the programme of police station closures and provision of security at stations, the communications strategy for informing Members of the FTR, and future funding.

The FTR ceased to be operational after 31 March 2011.

9.5   Recruitment of Part Time Officers

The recruitment of part time officers was to prove – perhaps surprisingly – one of the more tricky areas in which to deliver change. While the issue did not engender as much cross-party political controversy on the Board, there were debates about the extent to which recruitment could be facilitated in areas that would promote a higher proportion of Roman Catholic applicants. Developments such as the introduction of Police Community Support Officers (PCSOs) in England and Wales pointed to a move away from the model in the Independent Commission's Report, while financial constraints became an increasingly influential factor. The Policing Board were involved in all the discussions, though rarely in direct drive.

The Independent Commission had recommended (Recommendation 104) that:

There should be an enlarged Part Time Reserve of up to 2,500 officers, the additional recruits to come from those areas in which there are currently very few reservists or none at all. (Paragraph 12.18)

The Updated Implementation Plan published in August 2001 noted that legislative provision for PTR officers had been included in the Police (Northern Ireland) Act 2000. Regulations made under the

Act covered recruitment to the PTR, but additional regulations were required covering terms and conditions. The priority had been recruitment of regular officers, and, although the aim was to start the process for the PTR as soon as practicable, it took place later than intended.

On 24 January 2003 the Policing Board welcomed the launch of a pilot scheme for the recruitment of PTR officers for the PSNI. The first phase concentrated on recruitment in four districts – Newtownabbey, Lisburn, Banbridge, and Coleraine – although it was scheduled to be extended across Northern Ireland over the following three years, with 1,500 new PTR positions being created as part of the PSNI Human Resources Strategy. Substantial work had been done by the PSNI and the Policing Board to make sure that the role of these officers was community-focused. Applicants had to demonstrate that they had a local knowledge of and connection with the policing area they wished to work in. The Chairman of the Board noted that, together with the nearly finalised establishment of the District Policing Partnerships (DPPs), the roll-out of this scheme marked a further milestone in achieving the goal of real community policing for the whole community.

The Policing Board were advised on 5 June 2003 that the Community Involvement Committee would consider the issue of the name to be given to the new PTR. (Later that year the term 'Police Officers Part Time', or POPT, was coined to describe all part time police officers in the PSNI.) The Board also agreed that at least two of the areas for the next recruitment of POPT should be in District Command Units (DCUs) where the majority of the community had a perceived Roman Catholic community background. (Moyle and Down Districts were suggested.)

A Sub-group of the Policing Board was then set up to address outstanding issues in relation to the recruitment of the PTR in early summer 2003. The Policing Board Chairman wrote to the Chief Constable on 27 June 2003 expressing concerns about the need for both strategic planning in this area and a short delivery plan for their recruitment. Members of the Sub-group subsequently met representatives of the PSNI and the NIO on 1 August 2003.

It was reported on behalf of the Sub-group to the Board's Corporate Policy Committee on 16 October 2003 that, taking account of all the legal advice received, Members were of the view that no further PTR appointments should take place in any DCUs until the entire process had been reviewed and a detailed report produced. On 17 October 2003 a press release issued in the name of the Policing Board Vice-Chairman said that the new PTR officers to be appointed from the four pilot recruitment schemes would have an important part to play in delivering local community policing. However, before moving forward, the overall success of the campaign needed to be evaluated: *'the purpose of running pilot schemes was to ensure that any lessons to be learned from the process could be learned'*. Some 170 vacancies had been identified across the four districts. (The evaluation revealed that just 12% of those finally appointed had been Roman Catholics, although nearly 50% of applicants had been female.)

The Chief Constable reported to the *Public Session* of the Policing Board on 3 March 2004 that later that week the PSNI would be attesting the first new PTR officers in the four pilot districts. At a later meeting of the Policing Board the Deputy Chief Constable advised that existing PTR officers were being retrained during 2004/05 to update their skill base and make them more suitable for the role which the Independent Commission envisaged.

In June 2005 Members of the Policing Board were briefed by representatives from West Yorkshire and Sussex police on their experience of part time policing, in particular the role of PCSOs. A Sub-group on POPT was set up in autumn 2005, comprising Members of the Policing Board, the Deputy Chief Constable, and other PSNI and NIO representatives.

At the *Public Session* of the December 2005 Board meeting both Sam Foster (UUP) and Pauline McCabe stressed the need to give a higher priority to resolution of the outstanding issues in relation to developing the PTR cadre.

Meeting on 2 February 2006, the Policing Board agreed in principle to the recruitment of PCSOs in Northern Ireland. This was subject to no variation between the vetting criteria for recruitment as PCSOs and those for the recruitment of regular officers, and confirmation of both the proposed terms of employment of PCSOs and the draft legislation. In addition, four new areas of recruitment in respect of PTR officers should be rolled out. A paper prepared for discussion by the Board emphasised that the PSNI's preferred route was for PCSOs rather than further PTR officers, although the PSNI recognised that a good deal more work was needed to make the PCSO option a reality. A Tripartite Working Group consisting of representatives of the NIO, the PSNI, and the Policing Board was established to implement the introduction of PCSOs.

At a briefing for the Policing Board's Human Resources Committee in September 2006 Consensia reported that the percentage of applications from Roman Catholics in the DCU areas where a second phase of PTR recruitment had been undertaken was 34%. The five Districts chosen were Ballymoney, Foyle, Moyle, Newry and Mourne, and South Belfast. The Board were advised on 5 July 2007 that 113 officers were recruited in this exercise.

Four briefings on PCSOs were held by the Policing Board, in Coleraine, Cookstown, Armagh, and Templepatrick, on two consecutive days in mid-November 2006. They included contributions from Lancashire and Merseyside Constabularies, as well as the PSNI and the Board. In his opening remarks the Policing Board Chairman said that the events were the first stage in the consultation process which would allow for the introduction of PCSOs with limited policing powers. While precise numbers had yet to be finalised, there was a working assumption that 400 PCSOs would be recruited across Northern Ireland. It was envisaged that the first deployments would take place in spring 2008.

In December 2006 the NIO began consultation on the draft Policing (Miscellaneous Provisions) (Northern Ireland) Order 2007 which provided for the introduction of PCSOs. The Order was introduced into Parliament on 5 February 2007.

It was anticipated in March 2007, at a meeting of the Policing Board, that the recruitment campaign for PCSOs would start in May 2007. However, delays were introduced. At the Board meeting on 6 December 2007 Assistant Chief Constable Drew Harris advised that the recruitment process had not begun; this could only really be decided upon when the Government's Comprehensive Spending Review 2007 was complete and the resources available to the PSNI were known. Four months later, in April 2008, he told the Board that, working within the constraints of the Comprehensive Spending Review, the PSNI had been unable to take forward the introduction of PCSOs.

In response to a question from a Policing Board Member in May 2008, the Chief Constable assured the Board that the PSNI would

continue to keep a watching brief on current and all future developments of PCSOs in England and Wales. The future judgement on the
introduction of PCSOs within the PSNI would be dependent not only
upon budget constraints but also upon their effectiveness in other UK
police services.

Another issue which the Board addressed was whether there should
be some form of recognition or gratuity for the PTR service. Ian Paisley
Jnr (DUP) put outline proposals to the Policing Board Chairman late
in 2004 designed to ensure that PTR officers qualified for a medal and
that a 'duty payment' be made in recognition of the level of service
they had given. There was subsequently a presentation to the Board's
Corporate Policy Committee in May 2005 by an elected representative
(himself a former member of the PTR) proposing a gratuity payment
for PTR service. At that time the Chief Constable had said that he was
happy to give the matter further consideration if the Policing Board
Committee could provide information on how this might work. Then,
at the Board *Public Session* on 5 October 2005, the Chief Constable
responded to a question from a Board Member that although it was
with regret, he did not feel able to support the payment of a gratuity
to PTR officers. He felt that it would be divisive and outside the
existing reward and recognition schemes available to PSNI employees,
including the PTR.

At the Board meeting of 3 November 2005 it was resolved by a
majority that the Board supported some form of financial recognition
for PTR officers and that the issue be referred to the NIO for consideration. A letter was sent by the Chairman to the then Secretary of State,
Peter Hain. However, his response was that successive NIO Ministers
had considered the possibility of further financial recognition and had
decided against it, and he agreed with that decision.

The Chief Constable was again pressed on this subject by Policing
Board Members in autumn 2007. He said that any initiative to recognise PTR officers' contribution was a matter for the Secretary of State
rather than the Chief Constable.

On 8 November 2010 the Minister of Justice, David Ford, released
the details of a ring-fenced gratuity scheme for former members of the
PTR. This had been agreed in principle in the run-up to the devolution
of policing and justice earlier that year.

9.6   The Northern Ireland Policing Board and the Police Service of Northern Ireland's Human Resources Strategy

One of the issues that exercised the Policing Board during its first year was getting the Police Service to bring all the various human resources issues together in a single document. The Board sought confidence that the Police Service had both a coherent strategy and a realistic delivery plan.

On 4 July 2002 the Policing Board Chairman wrote to the Acting Chief Constable, Colin Cramphorn, emphasising that the Board saw it as imperative that human resources issues were dealt with in the immediate future – '*the Board considers, as an absolute priority, the need to address comprehensively the problems*'.

In October 2002, after a good deal of proactive work by the Board's Committee leading on Human Resources, which was chaired by Pauline McCabe, the Policing Board approved the first PSNI Human Resources Strategy. In the executive summary, the PSNI Human Resources Strategy made clear that:

'*The purpose of this plan is to have more police officers delivering policing through the District Command structure. The strategy will ensure that resources are allocated to meet operational policing priorities and the achievement of the Policing Plan objectives. By doing so, there will be delivery of Patten recommendations most obviously around recruitment, compositional change, development of responsibilities to local management and a reduction in the size of Headquarters.*'

The PSNI Human Resources Strategy was comprehensive, covering restructuring and redeployment, recruitment, severance, sickness absence, security deployments, the FTR and PTR, civilianisation, secondments, specialist skills, and staff retention. One key target was to ensure that there were 5,400 officers in District Command Units by March 2004, an increase of over 10% on the position in autumn 2002, with a reduction in those employed on static security. Chief Officers and District Commanders were to look for posts that could be civilianised, releasing officers for operational duties. The Strategy concluded with a 41-point action plan, together with individual responsibilities for delivery, over the following three-year period.

Following completion of the first PSNI Human Resources Strategy, Sir Dan Crompton was appointed by the Policing Board in the role of independent observer or validator of progress on implementation. The Policing Board's press release of 3 October 2002 stated that the monitor appointed to track progress would be *'reporting to the Chief Constable'*. He undertook to produce detailed progress reports on implementation every four months, alongside a report from the PSNI Human Resources Department. His first report was considered by the Policing Board's Personnel and General Purposes Committee in March 2003. Sir Dan was clear that the task was far from easy, but *'delivery by the PSNI and the Policing Board would represent one of the most significant achievements in modern police history'*. In his reports he stressed the need for acceleration in *'actual people redeployed'*.

During 2003 another issue that exercised the Policing Board, and was a subject that the Nationalist parties were keen to nail down, was a new tenure of post policy which had been recommended by the Independent Commission. The Board were clear that it needed to be part of the overall Human Resources Strategy.

The Policing Board had set up a Working Group, chaired by Pauline McCabe, which had discussions with the PSNI on a tenure of post policy document. In line with HMIC guidance, every policing role was defined within one of three classifications – core policing, core specialist policing, and specialist policing. Certain posts were classed as specialist posts with a fixed period of tenure of five years, while flexible tenure of post would apply to core specialist posts, allowing for a two-year extension. The policy was approved on a majority basis at the Policing Board meeting on 1 October 2003. By October 2006 a presentation to the Board's Human Resources Committee noted that 88% of police officers had less than five years' tenure in their current post, while 97% had less than seven continuous years in their current specialist area.

In autumn 2004 Sir Dan Crompton provided an 'end of term' report on the PSNI's (first) 2002 Human Resources Strategy for the Policing Board's Human Resources Committee. He concluded that the PSNI was heading in the right direction: reducing sickness rates, the organisation of the Crime Operations Department, radical changes in the Criminal Justice Unit, a developing performance culture, performance reviews with local Commanders, improved crime reduction results, the boost to civilianisation, and the targeting of bureaucracy were distinct pluses. On the other hand, rigorous action was still needed around 'restrictive duties' and identifying police posts in administrative roles which could be subject to operational deployment.

The PSNI presented its (second) costed Human Resources Planning Strategy for 2005/08 to the Policing Board at a special meeting on 16 December 2004. There were 22 actions in the delivery plan. This second Strategy included a commitment to adopt the national frontline policing measure as a key indicator of improvements in effectiveness and efficiency – this was projected to increase from 57% in 2004/05 to 72% in 2007/08. The document noted that, since the adoption of the original Strategy in 2002, more than 350 posts had already been civilianised.

In 2006 the NIO commissioned HMIC to carry out a value for money establishment review of the PSNI to consider staffing after 2010/11. This followed negotiations with the Treasury in Whitehall and was to feed into the Government's Comprehensive Spending Review 2007. The Policing Board's Corporate Policy, Planning and Performance Committee was briefed by NIO officials and HMIC representatives on 17 January 2007. Assuming that normalisation continued, the report recommended that the future establishment of the PSNI should be 6,028 full time equivalent police officers, 932 police officers part time, and 3,091 police staff, including 400 PCSOs. HMIC proposed that, before any final decision, a further review should be carried out in late 2009. The Policing Board issued a release on 17 January 2007 confirming that it had received a report from the NIO outlining recommendations for the future staffing of the PSNI, but it would seek the Chief Constable's assessment before responding to the NIO. They would also wish to hear the views of the Police Staff Associations and trade unions. The Board would come to its own view on the report and would seek to ensure that there were sufficient resources to ensure an effective and efficient police service in Northern Ireland.

As we have seen, one of the issues that exercised the Policing Board regularly was increasing the proportion of police officers on front-line duty. The Board were given an analysis of the comparison in July 2009 between the PSNI and its five most nearly equivalent police forces in England and Wales. The Board were reminded that the Chief Constable had given his commitment to releasing 600 officers back to front-line duties within six months. Members of the Board also visited the Greater Manchester Police and the Merseyside Constabulary to make the comparison for themselves. The July 2009 statistics showed that 12% of officers in the PSNI were in operational support or organisational support roles. The project to deliver the Chief Constable's commitment targeted around 250 extra officers in neighbourhood policing teams and around 300 extra officers in response roles.

9.7   Diversity and Gender

On 17 November 2001 rule 21 of the Gaelic Athletic Association (the GAA) was abolished. This stated that:

'Members of the British armed forces or police shall not be eligible for Membership of the Association. A member of the Association participating in dances, or similar entertainment, promoted by or under the patronage of such bodies, shall incur suspension of at least three months.'

The PSNI set up a GAA Club in 2002 and, on 30 October 2002, for the first time, members of the PSNI played the Garda Síochána at Gaelic Football for the McCarthy Cup, named after Inspector Thomas McCarthy, a member of the Royal Irish Constabulary who had been one of the founding Members of the GAA in 1884. (Four years later, Members of the Royal Irish Constabulary (RIC) had been banned from GAA sports.)

Under section 48(1) of the Police (Northern Ireland) Act 2000, the Policing Board were required to make, and from time to time revise, *'a plan (its "action plan") for monitoring the number of women in the police and the police support staff, and ... if they are under-represented for increasing the number'*. Under Section 48(2) the Chief Constable was required, if asked by the Policing Board, to prepare and submit a draft plan.

The Policing Board and the PSNI set up a Working Group. On 19 October 2004 the PSNI launched its first-ever Gender Action Plan, entitled *'Dismantling Barriers to Reflect the Community We Serve'*. It addressed emerging issues relating to recruitment, work/life balance, retention, and deployment in respect of female officers and staff. The aim was to ensure a workforce that represented the community and reflected its diversity. The Working Group also examined issues relating to promotion, specialist postings, development opportunities, and cultural issues impacting upon the implementation of the plan.

At that time the overall proportion of female officers in the PSNI had risen to 17%, compared with just under 12% before the Independent Commission's Report. The Gender Action Plan noted that if current female recruitment trends continued, representation would rise to approximately 26% by 2010.

Within the PSNI a group chaired by the then Assistant Chief Constable Criminal Justice (Judith Gillespie) was set up to oversee the implementation of the Gender Action Plan. Progress was also monitored by the Policing Board. At the *Public Session* of the Policing Board meeting of 2 June 2005 Judith Gillespie noted that a Strategic Programme Board, on which Denis Bradley and Suneil Sharma had been invited to represent the Policing Board, would meet for the first time on 6 July.

At the Board's *Public Session* in November 2006, held in Newcastle, the Director of Human Resources PSNI, Joe Stewart, followed up the Chief Constable's initial response that 11% of the 623 posts at Inspector or above were held by women. In his view, this was the outworking of a decision taken in the early 1980s not to employ female officers. Female officers with potential for advancement to the rank of Superintendent were now being posted where they would get broader experience.

At the meeting of the Policing Board's Human Resources Committee in November 2006 a presentation was made by the PSNI Diversity Manager on delivery of the Diversity Strategy and the Gender Action Plan, on the recommendations from the PSNI's Cultural Audit, the LGBT Report, and the Black and Minority Ethnic (BME) Report.

In February 2007 Policing Board Members were provided with details of the new PSNI Diversity Strategy entitled 'Policing a Shared Future', which covered equality, diversity, addressing the legacy of the conflict, and promoting good relations. There were 35 action areas to deliver outcomes in four programmes of work. A joint Diversity Workshop was held between Members of the Policing Board and the PSNI on 1 March 2007.

The Board's Human Resources Committee agreed in November 2007 that a benchmarking exercise with other UK police services should be carried out in relation to the gender breakdown of officers, and that the Gender Action Plan should be toughened up with specific timescales. A revised Gender Action Plan came to the Policing Board on 7 February 2008. It was reported that the original Gender Action Plan had generated worldwide interest. It was noted that the proportion of women at Chief Inspector level had risen from 8% to 19.7%.

The revised Gender Action Plan was jointly launched by the Policing Board Chairman and the Chief Constable on 7 April 2008, during a conference for the recently formed Women's Police Association at Templepatrick in County Antrim. In his remarks, the Board Chairman stressed that '*the PSNI's efforts to secure a more representative police service in terms of gender was vital to building public confidence in the Service*'. He added that the Policing Board's Human Resources Committee would monitor progress closely and give every support to the full delivery of this plan.

In April 2008 Members of the Policing Board met the PSNI Ethnic Minority Police Association (EMPA). Issues raised included concerns about the promotion process relating to equality and diversity issues, a zero tolerance approach for breaches of the Code of Ethics in respect of equality and diversity, and the reporting of racist incidents, language and behaviour. The EMPA said that they would welcome the appointment of a diversity champion for the Policing Board to help encourage a climate where everyone could challenge inappropriate behaviour within the organisation, reinforcing the principles of dignity and respect.

9.8   In Conclusion

This chapter began with the following statement: 'One of the most controversial sections of the Report of the Independent Commission ... was Chapter 14, entitled *Composition Of The Police Service*'. In fact, the Report in its totality was controversial. The SDLP endorsed it. The DUP didn't accept it full stop, and the UUP – apart from its leader at time of publication, David Trimble, to whom it was anathema –was perhaps a little more positive. The principal bone of contention appeared to relate to the Independent Commission's Recommendations on the composition of the police service.

The Unionist parties found the then imbalance in the RUC as down fundamentally to the threats from the Provisional Irish Republican Army (PIRA) to RUC officers and their families and almost all of the Unionist *Political Members* on the Policing Board objected to the 50: 50 recruitment rule. On the Policing Board – as is evident in Section 9.3 above – it became a deeply divisive issue, with the *Independent Members* delivering the majority vote. Likewise, the disbandment of the FTR, which was largely Protestant, engaged in mostly a security role, and had borne the heat of the night throughout the Troubles, was to be a bitter pill for the Unionist Members to swallow; here, again, the *Independent Members* held the ring. In respect of the PTR progress faltered for a similar basic reason and in the end, for that and other reasons, came to a halt. To their credit, Unionist *Political Members* did not walk away from the Board.

Changing the composition of the PSNI through the mechanism of early severance and the application of the 50:50 rule was undoubtedly critical not just to its acceptance across the whole community in Northern Ireland but also to the positive evolution of the political process.

Individuals living in predominantly Republican areas in particular should be commended for their courage in coming forward – and indeed continuing – to serve the community, despite considerable evidence of threats and intimidation, especially in the earlier years of the transformation programme. On the other side of the community, there were undoubtedly frustrations for significant numbers of Protestant applicants, some of whom went through the recruitment process on several occasions. However, in a point that was not always appreciated by representatives of that community, the great majority of unsuccessful non-Roman Catholic applicants were rejected not because of the 50:50 rule, but simply because the number of applicants to join the PSNI across Northern Ireland was so high.

The severance programme was the single most costly element in the entire Independent Commission implementation exercise, at a total additional sum to the taxpayer of over half a billion pounds. But that programme and the application of the 50:50 rule did enable the PSNI to achieve the target of 30% of the uniformed officers being from the Roman Catholic community by 2010/11 and paved the way for consent – arguably the most significant objective of the Independent Commission.

In that regard, the experience in Northern Ireland is a beacon for what can be achieved elsewhere. In England and Wales the non-white British population had grown to 9.1m in 2009, yet the proportion of non-white police officers was vastly less than that in the population as a whole. Moreover, a report compiled by the former Chief Constable of Thames Valley, Peter Neyroud, on behalf of the Home Secretary, Theresa May, concluded, according to *The Guardian*'s account of the report's publication in April 2011, that the police remain dominated by an '*overwhelming white male culture*' and there was a perception that it still operated on '*jobs for the boys*' principles. The report stated that greater representation of women and black and minority ethnic groups at all ranks would make the most difference to the culture of police forces. However, an equality assessment for the review cited estimates that it would take 24 years at the current rate of progress to get to even 35% female representation in the three most senior ranks, while it would be 11 years before there were 7% of black and minority ethnic officers in the senior ranks, with a further seven and a half years to achieve that across the whole of the police service.

An article in *The Times* of 21 January 2013 headed 'New Generation of Senior Police On Course To Be "Stubbornly White"' noted that no force had had a black or ethnic minority Chief Constable for almost three years and there were only five permanent female Chief Constables among the 43 forces in England and Wales. The Association's President was quoted as saying that '*the issue of diversity was not high on the agenda for police chiefs*'. He could have contrasted the position in Northern Ireland.

In November 2013 the Independent Police Commission chaired by former Metropolitan Police Commissioner Lord Stevens, which had been set up by the Opposition Labour Party, noted in their report: '*Having the police reflect the society they serve is also one key part of securing public consent.*' While arguing the need for greater diversity in the workforce the Commission concluded:

'*While there is little enthusiasm for radical action such as the 50/50 policy introduced in Northern Ireland to increase the number of Catholic officers joining the Police Service of Northern Ireland, there are sufficient, as yet, unused powers within the current legislation to hasten equality of deployment and promotion within the service.'*

The authors of this book, while not as familiar with the relevant legislation in England and Wales, would not necessarily concur. It is a fact that the composition of the PSNI has changed within a ten-year period to a far greater degree than that of any British police service.

However, the case for some form of affirmative action in England and Wales is gathering momentum. In January 2014 Chief Constable Alex Marshall, head of the new College of Policing, was reported as saying that affirmative action might be necessary to make the police more representative of the communities they serve (*The Observer*, 19 January 2014). During the previous week *The Guardian* had reported the shadow Home Secretary Ms Yvette Cooper as saying that a Labour Government would place a legal requirement on police forces to actively recruit black and minority ethnic officers and would consult on changing the law to 'New York-style affirmative action' in their recruitment policies.

It is also interesting to reflect briefly on the wider principle of affirmative action. An article in *The Economist* of 27 April 2013 noted that *'such rules, once in place, are almost impossible to get rid of'*. On balance, the magazine concluded that affirmative action replaces old injustices with new ones, dividing society rather than uniting it. Against that background, the Northern Ireland experience was unusual in that the anticipated time limit was adhered to, having had the desired effect. 50:50 was certainly a cause of division between the communities, but perhaps less than it might have been had there not been the previous history of fair employment legislation in Northern Ireland, which was designed to reduce some of the former inequalities.

The United States Supreme Court delivered a judgment in June 2013 on affirmative action in the context of selection for university places. It ruled that schools must prove *'there are no race-neutral alternatives'* to achieving diversity on campus. Time will tell how substantive a step this represents in rowing back, but already a number of States have voted to ban affirmative action in university selection procedures.

More recently, the events of August 2014 in Ferguson, Missouri appear to bring into sharp focus once more consent issues stemming from the composition of a police force that does not reflect that of the local community. Media reports stated that all but three of Ferguson's 53-strong police were white, while more than two-thirds of the suburb's population were black.

Finally, it should be added that this chapter has not sought to include every aspect of the Policing Board's activities that might be encompassed under the heading of human resources. Rather, the aim has been to bring out those aspects particular to the Northern Ireland context. Thus topics with which the Policing Board were regularly concerned and monitored closely, including PSNI training and its comprehensive Training, Education and Development strategy, levels of PSNI sick absence, and police pay awards, have not been dealt with at any length. The issues of secondments and lateral entry between the PSNI and the Garda Síochána are dealt with in Chapter 19.

It is also worth recording that in March 2014 the Northern Ireland Assembly's Public Accounts Committee released a report examining the use of agency staff by the PSNI, which had cost a total of £106m since 2004. The report highlighted a number of concerns about the procurement and questioned whether the PSNI could ensure that value for money had been achieved. While the Committee acknowledged there were concerns over equality issues arising from the PSNI's employment of its former officers, it did agree that there were sound operational reasons for employing temporary staff in the PSNI. In the associated press release dated 26 March 2014 the Committee's chairperson said:

'The implementation of Patten and the introduction of a radical new structure for policing over the last ten years represented an enormous challenge. The Committee does not underestimate the difficulties faced by the PSNI but we must also ensure that the use of agency staff must be well managed and appropriate.'

At its meeting on 3 April 2014 the Policing Board questioned the Chief Constable over the use of agency staff. The current Board Chair, Anne Connolly, was quoted as saying that:

'Board members welcome the report and whilst some steps have been taken by both the Board and the PSNI to make sure that governance arrangements *in this area have been improved, there are 10 recommendations with the PAC report which require oversight to ensure full implementation. The Department of Justice will be making a formal response to the PAC report. The Board will be responsible for overseeing the implementation of recommendations to make sure appropriate action is taken to address the matters raised in the report.'*

References

Chris Thornton, *Belfast Telegraph*, 2 October 2002

'*400 Protestants discriminated against in latest police recruitment*', a statement issued by DUP Policing Board member, Councillor Sammy Wilson MLA prior to the Policing Board meeting on 6 February 2003

Gemma Murray, *News Letter*, 17 June 2004

Belfast Telegraph, 19 June 2004

The Gender Action Plan – Dismantling Barriers to Reflect the Community We Serve, PSNI and the Policing Board, 19 October 2004

'Ex-terrorists ruled out of playing part in policing', *Belfast Telegraph*, 1 September 2005

'Thugs won't get into my force', *News Letter*, 2 September 2005

'Brave words from Bradley', *Sunday Life*, 13 November 2005

'Greater diversity would transform attitudes', *Guardian*, 6 April 2011

'Garda to open ranks to PSNI officers', *Irish Times*, 14 March 2012

'New generation of senior police on course to be stubbornly white', *The Times*, 21 January 2013

The Guardian, 16 January 2014

The Observer, 19 January 2014

CHAPTER TEN

Human Rights

'*The people of Northern Ireland have the right to expect you to work with effectiveness, efficiency, fairness, impartiality, and integrity; just as you have the right to a workplace free of any form of harassment or unfair discrimination ... effective policing means protecting human rights.*' Professor Desmond Rea, Chairman of the Northern Ireland Policing Board.

10.1   Introduction

At its core, the area of human rights is about expectations; the legitimate and proportionate expectations of the individual, of each other, and, most of all, of the State. In the context of policing the interplay of expectation runs in several directions: between the State – of which the police are an arm – and the citizen, but also between the relevant policing bodies and the officers and staff they employ. Often overlooked, this last dynamic area of human rights is placed at the centre of Professor Rea's address to the police officers of Northern Ireland and it is of central importance to understanding what follows in this chapter – and why the role of human rights is more than just a chapter in the story of the development of policing in Northern Ireland.

There are many dates that resonate deeply within the various communities of Northern Ireland. The chronology of the Troubles is staked with waypoints representing the high and low contours on what has been a momentous journey.

The previous chapters have considered the many key events,

decisions, publications, and people without which the progress that once seemed beyond reach could never have been achieved. However, of all the developments in that chronology the publication of the human rights monitoring framework by the Northern Ireland Policing Board was possibly one of the most significant indicators of just how far the communities and those who served them had come – and the direction in which those who came after would need to continue.

The Report of The Independent Commission On Policing For Northern Ireland (the Independent Commission) was absolutely key in setting human rights at the heart of policing in Northern Ireland.

In tracking the establishment of a human rights approach to policing in Northern Ireland and its practical implications for communities and the police themselves it is critical to follow the developments over the period 2000–2005. It was during 2000–2003 that many of the seminal developments in human rights and policing in Northern Ireland really began to take shape, with the publication of many key strategic schemes and documents and the making of key appointments. From 2003 to 2004 the practical effect of these changes was beginning to be seen by the communities who relied on the police as well as the police themselves, and by 2005 it was clear that these things were capable of being sustained, allowing the first review and audit processes to identify the outcomes that all this investment of energy, effort, and emotion had produced.

In order to understand these developments and the specific issues in the context of Northern Ireland, it is necessary first to be clear about the place occupied by human rights in policing generically – and *vice versa*.

10.2   Human Rights and Policing

The Universal Declaration of Human Rights adopted by the United Nations General Assembly on 10 December 1948 states that:

'Everyone shall be subject only to such limitations as are determined by law solely for the purpose of securing due recognition and respect for the rights and freedoms of others and of meeting the just requirements of morality, public order and the general welfare in a democratic society.' (Article 29, paragraph 2)

This extract alone demonstrates the essential position that human rights occupies within policing across many jurisdictions, both in the United Kingdom and beyond. However, the specific position and importance of human rights in policing within the United Kingdom goes further, building on that post-war foundation. Enacted some 50 years later, the British Government's Human Rights Act 1998 was also a key piece of legislation affecting policing in Northern Ireland. Contrary to popular reporting, the Act – which applies to England, Wales and Scotland too – did not 'introduce' human rights into policing or wider society; rather, it gave further effect to rights and freedoms set out in the Convention for the Protection of Human Rights and Fundamental Freedoms, otherwise known as the European Convention on Human Rights (ECHR).

Many, if not all, police forces in the UK now have relatively well-embedded human rights strategies, with all key policies being certified as 'compliant' and staff training in the relevant principles being *de rigueur*. It is therefore easy to look back from here, from a position of familiarity and general compliance, and miss the importance of what took place in Northern Ireland a decade ago. Over and above the generic challenges facing every policing service in establishing human rights as a fundamental feature of our constitutional landscape, the challenges in Northern Ireland were labyrinthine. The achievement in establishing a proper place for, and the proper role of, human rights within policing in Northern Ireland becomes clear only once the specific cadences applicable to policing in Northern Ireland are understood and the vernacular heard. Many of those peculiarly local issues are discernable from the official records of the time and it is those documents that form the basis of this chapter.

10.3   Human Rights and the Policing of Northern Ireland

'The problems faced by the police service in Northern Ireland are in a sense unique to a divided society, with its own history and culture... How can the police ensure that their practices recognise and uphold the human dignity and the rights of individual citizens while providing them with effective protection from wrongdoing? How should human rights standards and obligations be reflected

in the delivery of policing on the streets?' (Independent Commission's Report, paragraph 1.5, page 3)

As we have seen already, the Independent Commission's Report high-lighted many key issues facing policing reform in Northern Ireland but focused keenly on the particular impact of policing on the Human Rights Act 1998. One of the strengths of the Report was its practical tone and in Chapter 4 it highlighted the impact of the Act – and, by extension, the articles and protocols of the Convention – on policing, including pre-trial procedures, custody of people after arrest, covert policing, and emergency planning.

While human rights and policing have presented many challenges across all Member States of the European Council, several things made the Northern Ireland arrangements unique. Many of these issues, arising principally within the Patten Report, have been considered in earlier chapters but can be summarised here as including:

- Context: the Report found that *'organised terrorism and peculiar threats to public order have limited what the police in Northern Ireland could do'*. In particular, the traditional parades organised and executed on an annual basis in various parts of Northern Ireland represented a level of complexity in community policing that was difficult to compre-hend for most other policing bodies in the United Kingdom. Then there is the jurisdiction and presence of the military which, while substantially attenuating during the period, nevertheless remained a significant and unique feature of the policing landscape for many of the years covered by this chapter.

- Constitution: the Patten Report highlighted (in paragraph 1.15) that the structural question of the Police Authority for Northern Ireland had been particularly difficult because of the *'truncated nature of local democracy'* and the *'political imperative understandably accorded to secu-rity issues'*. The report went on to say in the same paragraph that the Police Authority had been obliged to operate as a *'surrogate'* for an accountability mechanism, recognising that the lack of any demo-cratic basis had reduced its credibility, a situation further weakened by the refusal of most Nationalist politicians to identify themselves with it. Among its recommendations the Patten Report proposed (in paragraph 6.10) the creation of a new Policing Board with clear responsibilities, including activity going beyond mere supervision of the police and extending into co-ordination of other agencies' efforts stretching across education, environment, economic development, housing and health, youth services, probation, and appropriate non-governmental organisations, all of which contributed to the context in which any meaningful reform had to take place and therefore, according to the report, were needed in the constitution of the Policing Board.

- Composition: the Independent Commission's Report noted that

  'Real community policing is impossible if the composition of the police service bears little relationship to the composition of the community.' (Paragraph 1.18)

As we have noted in the previous chapter, while this observation has minatory undertones for all policing bodies across the United Kingdom, the composition of the police in Northern Ireland was another peculiar product of the area's history and culture. Citing evidence received from the Equal Opportunities Commission, the Independent Commission's Report recorded that it was not enough simply to have a few recruits from another gender or religious background and that:

'As long as they [the minority representation in the police] are less than 15 per cent they will never be able to have a substantial influence on the culture.'

Tellingly, the very first recommendations of the Independent Commission were about human rights in policing. They included:

a. a comprehensive programme of action to focus policing in Northern Ireland on a human rights-based approach;

b. a new oath to be sworn by new and existing constables expressly including a pledge to uphold human rights;

c. a new Code of Ethics, integrating the ECHR into police practice;

d. a training programme to include both the principles of human rights and also their practical implications for policing, and an appraisal of individuals' performance against that awareness and respect;

e. the appointment of a suitably experienced lawyer to advise the police on human rights compliance;

f. the performance of the police service as a whole in respect of human rights should be monitored closely by the Policing Board.

Some of the analysis in the Report is also worth noting. The members of the Independent Commission were very clear about the fundamental importance of human rights:

'It is a central proposition of this report that the fundamental purpose of policing should be, in the words of the Agreement, the protection and vindication of the human rights of all …

We cannot emphasise too strongly that human rights are not an impediment to effective policing but, on the contrary, vital to its achievement.' (Paragraphs 4.1 and 4.3).

The Report noted that in the Independent Commission's contacts with the Royal Ulster Constabulary (RUC) they had found the Force broadly aware of these issues, but at a very early stage of considering how to address them and then mainly in the context of the specific implications for policing of the Human Rights Act 1998. Specifically, human rights training in the RUC lagged behind that in other police organisations with which the Commission had been in contact.

10.4   The Legislation and the Updated Implementation Plan

The Police (Northern Ireland) Act 2000 included a number of references to human rights. In the passage on the general functions of the Northern Ireland Policing Board (Policing Board or the Board) section 3(3)(b)(ii) required the Board to monitor the performance of the police in complying with the Human Rights Act 1998, while section 57(2)(a)(ii) required the Policing Board to include an assessment of the police in complying with the Human Rights Act 1998 in the Board's annual report.

Section 52 provided for the Policing Board to issue a Code of Ethics for the purpose of laying down standards of conduct and practice for police officers and making police officers aware of the rights and obligations arising out of the Convention rights (within the meaning of the Human Rights Act 1998). A draft of the Code was to be submitted by the Chief Constable to the Board for it to consider and adopt with such amendments as it might determine. Before issuing the Code the Board was required to consult a number of bodies, including the Secretary of State, the Police Ombudsman, the Northern Ireland Human Rights Commission, the Police Association (which was made up of the police representative bodies), and the Equality Commission for Northern Ireland. Once issued, the Chief Constable was required to ensure that all officers had read and understood the code and that a record was accordingly kept. In turn, under section 3(3)(d) the Policing Board was required to assess the effectiveness of the Code of Ethics issued under section 52. Moreover, by virtue of section 32(4), in carrying out their functions all police officers were to be guided by the Code of Ethics.

Section 38 of the Police (Northern Ireland) Act 2000 contained the wording of the declaration to be made on attestation as a constable – that is, the new oath. This too was a new departure for police services in these islands, and contained explicit reference to human rights:

'I hereby do solemnly and sincerely and truly declare and affirm that I will faithfully discharge the duties of the office of constable, with fairness, integrity, diligence and impartiality, upholding fundamental human rights and according equal respect to all individuals and their traditions and beliefs; and that while I continue to hold the said office I will to the best of my skill and knowledge discharge all the duties thereof according to law.'

In addition to the general duties arising from the European Convention and the provisions of the Police (Northern Ireland) Act 2000, the Northern Ireland Act 1998 required public authorities (including the police) to have due regard to the need to promote equality of opportunity between people of different religious beliefs, political opinions, racial groups, age, marital status, sexual orientation, and gender, people with and without disability and people with and without dependants (in section 75). The Act also required public authorities to have regard to the desirability of promoting good relations between people of different religious beliefs, political opinions and racial groups.

Section 75 of the 1998 Act therefore added an important Northern Ireland vernacular to the legal elements embedding the ideology of human rights and fundamental freedoms into everyday dynamics.

The Updated Implementation Plan published by the Northern Ireland Office (NIO) in August 2001 contained some important – albeit ambitious – commitments in relation to the human rights recommendations in the Independent Commission's Report. In relation to recommendation 1, for a programme of action, this was to be published by January 2002. As part of the exercise to highlight the application of human rights to policing the Chief Constable, Sir Ronnie Flanagan, had arranged a major conference to be held in October 2001 on 'human rights and policing'. The new police oath was to be brought to the attention of existing officers from September 2001 onwards, and would be taken by all new entrants. The aim was for the Chief Constable to present the draft Code of Ethics to the Policing Board in October 2001. The Service's Training and Education strategy, which would form part of the Policing Board's policing plan, would include training in the fundamental principles and standards of human rights and the practical implications for policing. The draft strategy was to be ready for consideration by the Policing Board in October 2001. A new appraisal system for police officers was to be introduced by April 2002. The post for the Police Service's human rights lawyer had been advertised on 31 May 2001.

10.5   The Practical Application

On 27 February 2002 a meeting was held between senior Members of the Northern Ireland Policing Board and the Northern Ireland Human Rights Commission. The following day, the Policing Board Chairman wrote to the Chief Commissioner. The Commission had formulated a memorandum of understanding (based on one which the Commission had agreed with the Equality Commission) which they wished to put before the Policing Board, with a proposal for a meeting every four months, and the Chairman undertook to put this before the Policing Board. One of the items discussed by the Board with the Commission was the Training, Education and Development strategy for the Police Service of Northern Ireland (the Police Service or the PSNI), which included human rights training. This had been considered by the Policing Board's Personnel and General Purposes Committee at its meeting on 22 February 2002 and was to be referred to the full Board shortly thereafter. The Chairman confirmed that the Code of Ethics was one of the first issues that the Policing Board had dealt with, having considered it in depth in November 2001. It was then formally presented to the Policing Board in the New Year and issued by the Policing Board as a draft for consultation, with a closing date of 1 April 2002.

Also on 27 February 2002 the Policing Board Chairman and Vice-Chairman met the chair and members of the Northern Ireland Equality Commission. They covered issues such as the recruitment policy for the PSNI, gender imbalance and minority ethnic groups, and the Service's equal opportunities policy.

On 18 April 2002 Assistant Chief Constable Sam Kinkaid gave a presentation to the Policing Board's Corporate Policy Committee on the human rights programme of action. He noted that this would include an annual assessment of the Code of Ethics, human rights training, the appraisal system, the Service's transparency policy, and the introduction of a neutral working environment. It would also include an assessment of the police use of force and conflict resolution, the introduction of service level agreements between Special Branch and District Command Units (DCUs), compliance with section 75 of the Northern Ireland Act 1998, and the use of both Terrorism Act and stop and search powers. There would be consultation with both statutory and non-statutory bodies active in this field. He flagged up that it could involve some hard truths in applying human rights, including tensions with other public bodies and NGOs, and discourage risk-taking, as well as raising additional resource implications.

Importantly, a draft of the PSNI's comprehensive human rights programme of action was formally presented to the April 2002 meeting of the Policing Board's Corporate Policy Committee. At that stage the PSNI were still consulting – internally and externally – on the programme, which was not expected to be finalised until late June of that year. The programme adopted the Council of Europe approach to enable the PSNI to strive to be a 'human rights champion'.

To see the practical application of the statutory obligations we need to go to June 2002. In a consultation paper circulated that month, the

Board reached out to 166 groups and organisations and to 150 community and police liaison groups. The initial consultation period was extended to allow time for a fuller response, during which time the Board Members made personal contact with 41 of the smaller groups to offer help in framing and submitting their response. The principal purpose of the initial consultation was to find out if people thought the Policing Board had identified all of its policies, which of those needed equality impact assessments, and how they should be prioritised. The Board also wanted to know how it could promote equality or good relations more effectively, whether people agreed with the factors being proposed for prioritisation, and whether there were policies that could be grouped together to make impact assessment more meaningful.

By way of response to its initial consultation exercise, the Policing Board had received 23 replies representing a disappointing response rate of less than 7%, although it recognised that those responses were very detailed. As part of their consultation process the Board asked consultees about the approach it had taken and determined that the design and delivery of the policing plan survey needed improvement, as did its procurement policy. In March 2003 the Policing Board sent out a second stage consultation, recognising that respondents had identified the key issues as being social need, effects of policies on people's daily lives, and their effect on social, economic, and human rights.

In seeking views on the design and delivery of the consultation paper itself the Policing Board's second survey 'made it very clear that sending out a document and expecting responses can no longer be considered to be effective consultation'. As a result the Board planned to work with individuals and groups in each of the section 75 categories and draft a new consultation policy.

By 2003 the Policing Board had come a considerable way when compared to the internal consultation with the PSNI only a year earlier, when considering the Programme of Action. In the official document collating the responses from internal consultees and external partners there is an explanatory comment at the conclusion of the PSNI section by an acting Inspector, which says:

'No department has actually declined to undertake any of the proposed action. Neither have they overtly accepted them.'

This response, thus described, is surprisingly lack-lustre in the context of one of the Independent Commission's key recommendations. In that document the officer goes on to offer a perceptive explanation for the paucity of their colleagues' responses to the consultation:

'... I am compelled to say, that the lack of understanding displayed either reflects that those concerned did not give the attention it deserves or the lack of appreciation of human rights that still exists'. (Source: Review of the Consultation Process for the Programme of Action – Patten Recommendation 1 – C370/19 – 10 April 2002 Human Rights Project Team Knockagoney)

How far this explanation – or even the need for one – was shared by the chief officer team at the time is unclear, but in a subsequent presentation by Assistant Chief Constable Sam Kinkaid on 18 April 2002 the slide on consultation bears simply one word: 'excellent'.

10.6   Leading Change

As with all historical reconstructions, the indicators of success are relatively easy to see when viewed under the benign light of hindsight. Success in the area of human rights for policing in Northern Ireland was ultimately achieved but what were the key ingredients for that success and how visible were they at the time? From the documentary evidence it seems that those ingredients probably included the right blend of political will, recognition of the consequences and risk attending any alternative, and the stake that communities and key individuals had invested in the programme of reform. Bringing these elements together and harnessing them called for leadership and strategy: the right people, in the right places, at the right time, doing the right things. The approach of the Policing Board Chairman and Board Members and the Chief Constable Hugh Orde supplied the leadership without which the potential would not have been realised.

However, the professional leadership of another individual was to be the key determinant of success. That individual's appointment came at the start of the seminal year of 2003, on 14 January.

Looking back, it would be difficult to overstate the impact of the appointment of Keir Starmer QC (subsequently the Director of Public

Prosecutions in England and Wales, and later Sir Keir) as Human Rights Adviser to the Policing Board. A highly accomplished barrister from England and an early pioneer of human rights matters across the United Kingdom, Mr Starmer was to be critical in establishing and embedding human rights within the police reform programme for Northern Ireland. In this work he was ably assisted by Jane Gordon, who was appointed some months later.

The successive Chairmen of the Policing Board's relevant Human Rights Committee, in particular Eddie McGrady MP MLA (Social Democratic and Labour Party (SDLP)) and Basil McCrea MLA (Ulster Unionist Party (UUP)), and their respective Vice-Chairs, also played important roles.

At its meeting in May 2002 the majority of the Policing Board's Corporate Policy Committee had concluded that there were insufficient 'in-house' skills available to the Policing Board to carry out the requirement to assess the PSNI's compliance, and that it would be appropriate to seek expertise in the human rights field externally. In the Oversight Commissioner's second report he had included four performance indicators in relation to the Policing Board's monitoring role. Policing Board officials identified seven areas in which evidence would be sought:

a. the promotion of human rights as a basic value within the Service,

b. a human rights-based approach to staff,

c. human rights as a core theme for all training,

d. a human rights-based approach to management practice,

e. the promotion of human rights in all operational documents and in operational policing,

f. a structure which embraces the promotion of human rights as a core element of policing

g. a comprehensive regime for holding the Service to account.

The Policing Board noted at its meeting on 4 September 2002 that the Corporate Policy Committee had agreed that approaches should be made to five named individuals to ascertain their interest in serving as the Human Rights Adviser to the Policing Board. Following interviews in January 2003, the Policing Board appointed Keir Starmer

QC on a consultancy basis subject to regular review; he took up his appointment on 27 February. Consistent with recommendation 6 of the Patten Report, the Board appointed Mr Starmer to advise it on how to meet its principal legislative requirements and to develop a programme for monitoring PSNI compliance with human rights obligations.

The role included consultation with key stakeholders, which Mr Starmer promised early in his tenure, setting out his plans to consult with all key groups, including the Police Ombudsman, the Parades Commission, the Police Federation of Northern Ireland, the Human Rights Commission, the Oversight Commissioner, and the PSNI command team, in his inaugural report, which he provided at the Policing Board meeting on 3 April 2003.

In that initial report Mr Starmer outlined his strategic plan, his approach, and methodology. The development of the human rights monitoring programme would include the definition of meaningful measures of compliance, the development of an outline programme for agreement with the Board, a screening outline programme with section 75 implications, consultation on the programme, and collection and analysis of data. Performance monitoring would start with the Code of Ethics. Mr Starmer put forward three broad principles for the Board to endorse:

a. that it was the PSNI's performance as a whole which was being monitored, i.e. success as well as failure;

b. that the process of monitoring should be dynamic and one in which the PSNI considered there was a positive dialogue between it and the Board which recognised and addressed problems as they arose;

c. that the process of monitoring should not be retrospective.

The clear intention of the Board was to keep the focus firmly to the fore rather than reviewing the past. This approach represented a sensitive strategy, although one which seems now to have been borne out by subsequent progress.

The appointment of Keir Starmer was supplemented and strengthened by the appointment, on 3 July 2003, of Jane Gordon, a former litigator and judicial assistant to the Lord Chief Justice of England and Wales. However, their appointments – at the time and subsequently

– were not universally welcomed. For example, at a meeting of the Board's Corporate Policy Committee on 16 October and then of the full Board on 6 November 2003 the appointments were reviewed and approved, although Ian Paisley Jnr (Democratic Unionist Party (DUP)) recorded a strong objection at the Committee to their continuation.

Assistant Chief Constable Sam Kinkaid gave a presentation to the Policing Board's Corporate Policy Committee on 24 July 2003 on progress in implementing the shared values and human rights programme. While the majority had been implemented or subsumed, there was one outstanding matter to be finalised – the programme of action on the human rights-based approach to policing. Mr Kinkaid explained that the PSNI were awaiting proposals from the Board's Human Rights Adviser on the monitoring plan before finalising it.

10.7   Ethics, equality and professional standards

Some two weeks before Mr Starmer's appointment had come another milestone: the publication by the Policing Board of the Code of Ethics for the PSNI. The Code had been finalised after wide consultation with organisations concerned with human rights and policing.

The Code was another early item of business for the Policing Board. Assistant Chief Constable Sam Kinkaid presented an initial draft of the proposed Code of Ethics to the 21 November 2001 Policing Board meeting, following which on, 31 December 2001, the Chief Constable formally submitted a revised draft for the Board's consideration. Following the Board meeting in January 2002 the draft Code was issued by the Policing Board for wide-ranging consultation. The Board's Corporate Policy Committee considered the responses to the consultation in May 2002 and by October of that year the final draft of the Code had been forwarded to the PSNI for internal consultation prior to its finalisation and launch.

This Code of Ethics, which was launched on 13 February 2003 and came into force one month later, was to set the tone and direction of human rights and policing in Northern Ireland. It is from the Chairman's foreword to the Code that the remarks at the opening of this chapter are taken. The Code spelled out for the first time in clear terms what were acceptable and unacceptable behaviours and made police officers aware of the rights and obligations coming from the ECHR. It also included the new oath. Police officers believed to be in breach of the Code could be the subject of complaints to the Police Ombudsman or internal disciplinary investigation. On the other hand, as the Chairman spelled out, when police officers carried out their duties in accordance with the Code they had the right to expect the full support of the community.

The Code was the first of its kind in the UK and Republic of Ireland, at a time when most police organisations had separate ethical statements and discipline regulations. The PSNI Code of Ethics was unique in that it combined both. Comprising ten articles and covering everything from professional duty to equality and integrity, the Code reflected the two-way relationship essential to policing by consent. The fundamental premise of the Code was that communities are entitled to expect that their human rights will be protected and upheld by their police and, in return, the police are entitled to expect the support of their communities when carrying out their duties. The Code also reflected the internal and external focus as set out in the Chairman's foreword – namely, that all officers and staff are entitled to a working environment free of prejudice and unfair discrimination.

At publication it was stressed that the vast majority of PSNI officers already carried out their work to a standard which would fully satisfy the requirements of the Code. The Code would help officers make difficult judgements on a daily basis in providing an effective policing service.

The PSNI reported to the Policing Board in July 2003 that the training programme in respect of the Code of Ethics was almost complete.

This internal focus on entitlement to respect and equal treatment and a reminder that 'police officers have human rights too' was very apparent in the PSNI conference (of that name) held in Belfast on 15 September 2003 on behalf of the European Platform for Policing and Human Rights. In the context of Northern Ireland the ability not only to aspire to but to demonstrate that such a workplace had been created mattered deeply, not least because the Policing Board's strategic ambitions for attracting, establishing, and retaining a representative workforce were at the centre of the Independent Commission's reform programme.

Another key event was the publication by the Policing Board of a draft equality scheme, approved by the Equality Commission on 12 February 2003. The complex statutory framework knitting the various duties of public bodies together included the Police (Northern Ireland) Act 2000. This required the Board to monitor the performance of the police in complying with the Human Rights Act 1998. In doing so the Board was also required under the legislation to have regard to the need to co-ordinate activities with those of other statutory authorities and to co-operate with them.

Further points along the way included the issuing by the Chief Constable of the General Order entitled 'Transparency Policy' in June 2003, signalling a commitment to openness by the PSNI's leadership and setting out a framework for Freedom of Information. Another General Order, 'The Terrorism Act 2000 – Human Rights and Monitoring Issues', went on to require all stop and search forms, along with records of 'stop and account' situations, to be completed and submitted in a manner that ensured the consistent application of human rights considerations and fair monitoring.

10.8   The Board's Human Rights Monitoring Framework

On 15 December 2003 the Policing Board's Human Rights Monitoring Framework was formally launched. (A presentation on the document had previously been given to a meeting of the Board's Human Rights and Professional Standards Committee, to which all Board Members were invited, on 3 October 2003.) Setting out 12 different aspects of policing from a human rights perspective, the Monitoring Framework formed the strategic foundation for ensuring human rights compliance in the PSNI for the coming years. The specific categories were as follows:

- The PSNI Programme of Action – oversight arrangements and performance indicators for the Oversight Commissioner
- Training – the integration of human rights into all training programmes, evaluation of the human rights toolkit, random checks of training sessions, external observation mechanisms, e.g. from the Learning Advisory Council

- *Policy* – Integration of human rights considerations into all policies, overall compliance with the 1998 Act, random selection for audit areas
- *Police Operations* – providing for the independent observation of planning meetings and public order audits; records of all stops and searches
- *Code of Ethics* – adherence by all police officers, including evaluation and audit
- *Complaints, Discipline and Civil Actions* raising human rights issues
- *Public Order* – a review of all policy documents, operational planning, and implementation in relation to four parades in 2003 in selected areas – and the agreed attendance at parades for human rights observers
- *Use of Force* – making provision for all Regulation 20 reports to be reviewed, joint training events with military planned, the review of the use of force training materials and training observations
- *Covert Policing* – MoUs (memoranda of understanding) were developed to allow human rights advisers access to planning and training materials and to examine the mechanisms in place for ensuring that all PSNI officers complied with the requirements of the Regulation of Investigatory Powers Act 2000
- *Victims' Rights* – training and also a victims' conference attended by human rights advisers.
- *Treatment of Suspects* – provided for meetings with the Independent Commissioner for Detained Terrorist Suspects and plans for an independent custody visitors scheme
- *Human Rights Awareness* among PSNI officers – a human rights questionnaire had been issued and the results analysed; the new Annual Performance Review included an appraisal of human rights awareness.

The Monitoring Framework also contained an appendix setting out how human rights were engaged by policing activity in practical terms and where the Code of Ethics fitted in, cross-referencing its provisions with the Human Rights Framework throughout. It also set out the role of other statutory bodies responsible for aspects of human rights compliance in Northern Ireland, identifying 13 separate bodies or units.

In launching the framework the Policing Board Chairman observed that the final report by Tom Constantine as the Police Oversight Commissioner, which had been published the previous week, had noted that the PSNI and the Policing Board had introduced a human rights-based approach to policing. The accompanying press release described the Monitoring Framework fairly as a 'comprehensive and robust framework'. The Policing Board Chairman said:

'Achieving and ensuring human rights standards in everyday policing is a critical factor in securing community confidence in the delivery of the policing service, and the Board is committed to meeting its responsibilities in achieving this.'

In 2004 the momentum was maintained on a broad front. By early 2004 the first human rights questionnaire had been drafted with the full support of all the relevant staff associations. The meeting of the Human Rights and Professional Standards Committee of the Board on 13 February 2004 also noted that the PSNI General Order on a neutral working environment had been issued and that a further audit of compliance with the Order in police stations across Northern Ireland was being considered.

Finally, on 10 September 2004, the PSNI's Human Rights Programme of Action was published. It was divided into seven sections dealing with basic values, staff, training, management practice, operational policing, structure, and accountability. In each section initiatives that had been completed and those that were ongoing were set out. In his foreword the Chief Constable noted that some of the processes introduced by the PSNI were 'innovations in policing', including attestation (the oath), the Code of Ethics, the appointment of the PSNI human rights legal adviser, and initiatives such as annual human rights conferences. By definition, this document was significantly different to the original draft Programme of Action that had been distributed on a consultative basis in January 2002. Many of the actions and aspirations identified in the earlier document had already been put into effect.

By the end of the year the value of the Board's Human Rights Advisers' roles, together with the contributions of the post-holders, had been demonstrated to the satisfaction of the Board, who extended their contracts at the meeting of the Corporate Policy Committee on 16 December 2004. Both were to be called upon again in the following year to compile another key report into serious public disorder.

10.9   Public Order and Human Rights

There are few better examples of how human rights and fundamental freedoms in a mature society have to be balanced by its police than where one group of individuals wishes to take part in a public expression of views which another group finds deeply provocative. Individuals who want to take part in public parades clearly have human rights, including the right to freedom of expression (ECHR Article 10) and the right to free assembly (Article 11), along with the right to expect the police to protect their peaceful exercise of those rights (see, for example, *Platform Artze fur das Leben v Austria* [1988] EHRR 204). At the same time, those who oppose the parades in the areas where they live also have rights, including the right to protest peacefully and the right to peaceful enjoyment of their private lives (Article 8). Similarly, those people are also entitled to expect the protection of the police. Importantly, the police officers and soldiers involved in those operations also have human rights, including the right to be protected by the State from the risk of injury and death (Article 2).

One of the unique features of policing and human rights in Northern Ireland as identified by the Independent Commission's Report was the historical and highly emblematic practice of individuals exercising their right to pass symbolically through areas populated by others who were viscerally opposed to their doing so. These events brought the various and competing human rights expectations of the groups referred to above into direct conflict. Balancing them required clear regulation not only by law but also by clear policies adopted by the police.

The operation of the relevant activities, the legal framework, and the applicable policies were all areas for monitoring by the Northern Ireland Policing Board. With the new arrangements and the Monitoring Framework in place, the Board was able to go into 2004 with an eye on the policing calendar – and one of the key areas selected for scrutiny and monitoring by the Board as part of its statutory duty was the Ardoyne Parade, in Belfast, to take place on 12 July 2004.

As a result of what were described as 'very serious concerns raised by a number of individuals and groups' and represented to the Board by Alex Attwood (SDLP), the Chairman decided to ask the Board's Human Rights Advisers to produce an in-depth report on the policing that summer of the 12 July Parades passing the Ardoyne area. (The Human Rights Advisers were already monitoring the parade.)

As the following chapter deals holistically with civil unrest and public order policing, the Human Rights Advisers' reports specifically on this parade and subsequent ones, together with their conclusions, are set out there.

10.10   The First Human Rights Annual Report, March 2005

The launch of the first Human Rights Annual Report on behalf of the Policing Board took place in 2005. (Keir Starmer and Jane Gordon had initially presented that draft report to the Policing Board on 14 December 2004.) Unveiled on 7 March, the report was formally launched in the presence of the Chief Constable and the Board, MLAs, District Policing Partnerships, Independent Custody Visitors, the Oversight Commissioner, the Northern Ireland Council for Ethnic Minorities, and representatives from UNESCO.

Opening the event, the Policing Board Chairman said

'The publication of this report is the first of its kind within UK policing ... Ensuring human rights standards in everyday policing is an essential require-ment for effective, efficient and impartial policing ...

It is clear that since the publication of the Code of Ethics significant progress has been made and the PSNI are committed to putting human rights at the heart of everything the Service does.'

The Chairman also noted that the Oversight Commissioner, in his last report, had said that in drawing best practice from other police services *'the actions taken by the PSNI now constitute a model of best practice that other police services might emulate'*. The report provided a detailed assessment of the integration and application of human rights by the PSNI across each of the 12 areas contained in the original Monitoring Framework. It contained a large number of recommendations for the PSNI and the Policing Board to take forward and was to be used by the Board as a benchmark for moving forward on the human rights agenda, as the Chairman of the Board's Human Rights and Professional Standards Committee, Mr Eddie McGrady (SDLP), stated.

It may be instructive to summarise this first, 270-page, human rights report. In their introduction the two authors noted that no similar duty to monitor police performance had been placed on any other police oversight body anywhere else in the United Kingdom. The report was, accordingly, very much the first of its kind. They stressed that they had not been refused access to any officer or to any incident or event that they had wanted to observe, nor to any documentation they had asked to inspect – '*such an open, transparent approach to policing is unprecedented*'. The authors concluded that '*in our view it (the PSNI) has done more than any police service anywhere else in the UK to achieve human rights compliance*'.

In relation to the PSNI programme of action (published on 10 September 2004), the authors noted that the initiatives '*probably go well beyond any policing initiatives in Europe*'. They pointed out, however, that, owing to the lapse of time, the document should be seen more as a report on the implementation of the original programme of action rather than a separate programme of action as such itself. They recommended that the PSNI should set clear targets and timelines on an annual basis to tackle the issues identified by the Policing Board as important to the ongoing task of achieving a human rights-compliant police service in Northern Ireland.

In relation to training, the authors shared some of the concerns voiced by the Human Rights Commission in their evaluation of the Course for All, a '*bold venture*' which had been delivered to all existing members of the PSNI, both police and civilian, between November 2002 and the end of April 2003. They recommended that external evaluation of the delivery of PSNI training should continue.

With respect to policy, the authors noted that no less than 841 General Orders were available on the PSNI intranet. Since 2000 it had been the duty of policy writers to ensure that any new or amended policy was human rights-compatible. The authors had audited policies in 12 randomly selected subject areas, though they noted that many of these were due to be reviewed under the PSNI's General Order on Policy, Procedure and Guidance, which had been issued in June 2004.

Mr Starmer and Ms Gordon had observed the planning and execution of three live operations in 2004 – the policing operations for the 1 July Short Strand parade, the 4 July Drumcree parade, and the 12 July Ardoyne parades – and the final stages of a covert surveillance operation. They particularly focused on the arrangements for building in human rights legal advice. They were particularly impressed by the operational briefing to officers before they were deployed on surveillance duties.

The report noted that the Code of Ethics was *'unique as a police disciplinary Code based entirely on human rights principles'*. However, the authors had concerns, from their interaction with police officers in focus groups that they set up to gauge human rights awareness in the PSNI, regarding how far officers were fully familiar with the Code.

In terms of complaints against police officers from members of the public, it was noted that the proportion of allegations in respect of the use of force was steadily reducing, while the percentage alleging failure of duty was increasing; *'the vast majority of complaints and allegations do not result in adverse findings'*. It was also noted that a total of 174 files had been submitted to the Director of Public Prosecutions in the period April 2003 to March 2004, although in 164 of these cases it was recommended by the Director that no further action be taken. Separately, some 400 complaints had been informally resolved.

In monitoring the performance of the PSNI in complying with the Human Rights Act, the Policing Board had undertaken to review all PSNI policies relating to public order. The authors were impressed by the PSNI General Order on Protest Activity in Public as being *'clear and comprehensive'*. They found that the level of PSNI community consultation in respect of the Drumcree parade was impressive, as was the de-escalation operation following the event.

The PSNI guidance for the use of water cannon and CS incapacitant spray (covered more fully in the next chapter) was found to be clear and comprehensive, although the authors were concerned that the PSNI were not routinely monitoring records of all incidents involving the use of force.

In respect of covert policing, the authors read four reports following inspections by the Chief Surveillance Commissioner's team of inspectors over the previous two years. While the pattern that emerged was mixed, the work then being done by the PSNI in respect of policies, procedures, and mechanisms recently adopted was judged to provide a very sound platform for the future. As the Chief Surveillance Commissioner had observed, the adoption by the PSNI of a manual for the management of covert human intelligence sources and procedures for the dissemination of intelligence and handling of confidential information supplied by members of the public should result not only in even higher standards of compliance with the requirements of the Regulation of Investigatory Powers Act 2000 but – the authors added – with the Human Rights Act.

In relation to victims' rights, the report noted that the PSNI had established a number of specialist units and appointed a number of specialist officers to support victims of crime. Generally, it was found that the PSNI had included in many of its core policies reference to the treatment of victims and the PSNI's responsibilities to victims, though the Service had not to date developed a comprehensive policy on the treatment of victims.

On the treatment of suspects, the authors reviewed the reports of other statutory bodies charged with responsibility in this area, including the reports of the Policing Board's custody visiting teams – community volunteers who made unannounced visits to police custody suites. The report noted with satisfaction that the Policing Board's custody visiting scheme ensured PSNI compliance with the Human Rights Act in relation to the treatment of detained persons.

The 12th chapter addressed human rights awareness in the PSNI, drawing on the human rights questionnaire which the authors had devised and issued as a joint initiative between the PSNI and the Policing Board to a large sample of all PSNI officers, including those in the Full Time Reserve and the Part Time Reserve. According to the questionnaire 78% of police officers considered that human rights issues cropped up in their work most days, while 90% considered that the training they had received in human rights had assisted them. In some areas, the proportion of correct answers was impressive (including on issues such as the rights of members of the public to protest and march, the criteria for arresting individuals, and those in relation to protection of life) although in one or two areas, such as the criteria for the use of lethal force and access to a lawyer, the proportion was less good.

The report noted that further aspects of the PSNI's work would be scrutinised during the following year, including the areas of privacy, data protection, and DPPs, as well as notifiable memberships.

On 10 June 2005 the Board's Human Rights and Professional Standards Committee approved a detailed workplan arising from the Human Rights Annual Report, the main focus of which was future areas of monitoring activity, sensitive areas, 'quick reaction work', and oversight of workplan. It recommended the recruitment of a legally qualified person to undertake analytical work on the 60 recommendations in the Annual Report.

10.11   Subsequent Developments

On 29 September 2005, in line with its own programme, the Policing Board arranged a workshop on human rights monitoring and the role of District Policing Partnerships (DPPs). Other human rights stakeholders also attended.

In December 2005 the PSNI published an updated human rights programme of action which contained a response to each of the recommendations for the PSNI set out in the Human Rights Annual Report published earlier that year.

Other programmes of action looking further down the road were considered and approved. In the 2006/2007 PSNI Programme of Action the Chief Constable felt emboldened enough to claim that *'Human rights underpin all aspects of good policing – my officers know this and practise it.'*

At the *Public Session* of the Policing Board on 3 May 2006 (its first in public after reconstitution), the Deputy Chief Constable was probed on the fatal shooting by the PSNI on 16 April 2006 of Stephen Colwell at a police checkpoint in Ballynahinch. He explained that the information he could provide was limited as the incident was under investigation by the Police Ombudsman. In his question, Alex Attwood (SDLP) noted the significant reductions in the use of police force in recent years, a consequence of new approaches by the PSNI and the accountability structures. The Deputy Chief Constable noted that in the previous 14 months weapons had been drawn by police officers 112 times but had been used on only eight occasions. Most of the incidents involved the firing of warning shots into the air; the Deputy reminded Members of the occasion in September 2005 where a chimpanzee had escaped at Belfast Zoo and warning shots had been fired! He assured the Board that lessons were learned from each shooting incident.

On 14 June 2006 Mr Starmer and Ms Gordon presented the second Human Rights Annual Report to the Policing Board's Community and Human Rights Committee. It again set out their monitoring activity, observations, and conclusions in respect of the 12 originally identified areas, together with privacy and data protection and policing with the community. At the Committee's subsequent meeting in August they advised that, out of the 111 recommendations in their first Human Rights Annual Report, 68 had been implemented in full, 17 in part, and some 22 were outstanding. The second Annual Report, itself containing 45 recommendations, was published on 5 September 2006. At the *Public Session* of the Policing Board on the following day the Chief Constable was asked by the Vice-Chairman, Barry Gilligan, how he was going to ensure that those recommendations would be implemented.

On 14 December 2006 Assistant Chief Constable Drew Harris gave a presentation to the Board's Community and Human Rights Committee on the PSNI programme of action that had been published the previous week. This contained the Service's response to each of the 45 recommendations in the second Human Rights Annual Report.

A new issue raised by the Policing Board with the Chief Constable originally in the summer of 2006 was the legal position in relation to the retention of DNA and Article 16 of the United Nations Convention on the Rights of Children. Concern had been expressed by the Northern Ireland Commissioner for Children and Young People about the practice of retaining DNA from young people who had never been charged with or convicted of a crime. This was a matter on which the PSNI liaised closely with their counterparts in Great Britain, in particular over the detailed ACPO good practice manual. In Northern Ireland the PSNI policy provided the District Commander where the offence incident gave rise to the taking of fingerprints or sample with discretion to decide whether or not the DNA sample or the fingerprints should be retained or destroyed.

The latter issue was discussed on a number of occasions at Policing Board Committees and in plenary in late 2006 and spring 2007. The Board's Human Rights Advisers provided guidance on the issue in general, and in particular on the approach adopted in Scotland, which was different to that in the rest of the UK and was being challenged at the European Court. The Policing Board did not find it easy to reach a definitive collective position on the issue.

At the *Public Session* of the Policing Board on 2 May 2007 the Deputy Chief Constable was asked to indicate how many young people's DNA had been retained. The answer was that some 3,333 young persons were recorded on the police database, of whom approximately 1,200 had not received a formal sanction. He added that when the Northern Ireland database had been joined to the national database the previous year there had been 133 identifications made against crime scenes in England and Wales.

The Policing Board was also involved in the consultation exercise launched by the Home Office ahead of the proposed Counter Terrorism Bill 2007. Its views were sought by the Association of Police Authorities (APA) and the Board in turn sought the views of the PSNI Chief Constable. A written response was received from the Chief Constable dated 17 July 2007; at the Policing Board meeting on 6 September that year Sinn Féin Board Members stated that they could not support all of the views expressed by the Chief Constable in his response.

In August 2007 Keir Starmer and Jane Gordon presented their third Annual Report to the Board's Human Rights and Professional Standards Committee. This document contained 15 chapters, the additional items being children and young people.

In November 2007 Mr Starmer advised the Policing Board Chairman that he felt it was time for him to move on. The following month the Committee considered a paper in discussion with their Human Rights Advisers on a review of the Board's human rights monitoring strategy. This review addressed a number of factors, including the sustainability of the current level of scrutiny and the need to develop a longer-term strategy, as well as the continued avail-ability (and costs) of Human Rights Advisers. It was agreed to adopt a revised approach, concentrating on auditing mechanics of human rights compliance within the Annual Report and a proposal for the production of an annual thematic report focusing on specific subject areas. (In addition, individual ad hoc reports could be produced.) This approach would allow for more direct contact with stakeholders in the specific areas.

In September 2006 the Policing Board, in line with section 52(1) of the Police (Northern Ireland) Act 2000, had established a joint Policing Board/PSNI working group, including their respective Human Rights Advisers, and launched a wide-ranging consultation exercise on revisions to the original Code of Ethics. PSNI officers were extensively consulted in the first two months of 2007. On the basis of comments received a revised draft was sent out for further consultation on 23 March 2007. Finally, a revised version of the Code of Ethics was launched on 6 February 2008, having been signed off by the Policing Board in December 2007.

In his remarks at the launch, the Policing Board Chairman noted that the Code had been *'one of the success stories in advancing the human rights agenda within the PSNI, as envisaged by The Independent Commission On Policing For Northern Ireland'.* The revised Code represented *'a model of best practice for police services across these islands and further afield'.* The Chairman of the Board's Human Rights and Professional Standards Committee, Basil McCrea (UUP), said:

'The revised Code includes updated guidance across a range of areas, including the gathering, retention and use of information by police officers, notification by officers of civil or criminal action against them, and the acceptance of gifts or gratuity.'

The statement by the Police Ombudsman on her investigation into the circumstances surrounding the death of Raymond McCord Junior and related matters was published on 22 January 2007 (the Operation Ballast Report). It contained 20 recommendations, the last of which required the Policing Board to establish a mechanism to review the PSNI response to the recommendations in the Operation Ballast Report within six months and at appropriate intervals thereafter. The Policing Board met on 24 January 2007 to discuss the Operation Ballast Report. The Board accepted its responsibility for overseeing the implementation of the recommendations and agreed that its Human

Rights Advisers should examine, validate, and report on their implementation. An interim report was delivered to the Policing Board in 19 July 2007, with a further report brought before the Board's Human Rights and Professional Standards Committee on 16 January 2008, following which a press release was issued in the name of the Committee Chairman, Basil McCrea (UUP). The release noted that, of the 17 recommendations relating to the PSNI, 10 had been implemented in full and six were progressing satisfactorily. The 6 March 2008 meeting of the Policing Board resolved that the report should be published.

On 21 May 2008 the Policing Board announced the first human rights thematic inquiry, into the effectiveness of the PSNI's approach to tackling domestic violence against women. Basil McCrea, as Chairman of the Board's Committee, said:

'Through these human rights thematic enquiries, the Board hopes to highlight issues of public concern, promote debate and raise awareness of important human rights issues.'

The press release noted that in the previous year the PSNI had responded to over 23,000 domestic incidents and that 9,283 crimes with a domestic motivation were recorded.

In August 2008 the Equality and Human Rights Commission that had been established by the Equality Act 2006 undertook an inquiry to find out how human rights worked in Britain. Evidence was taken from the Policing Board Chairman, accompanied by Hugh Orde and Keir Starmer, at a meeting in London with the chair of the inquiry on 24 October 2008.

On 21 October 2008 the fourth Human Rights Annual Report was launched. In his opening remarks the Policing Board Chairman noted that the responsibility for ensuring that a police service complied with the Human Rights Act had recently been extended to Police Authorities in England and Wales. The APA issued guidance in January 2009 on human rights and commissioned training to support police authorities in implementing the guidance and their new legal duty. (It was an example of good practice in Northern Ireland leading the way in Great Britain and elsewhere.)

The press release for the launch of the fourth Annual Report noted that, of the 149 recommendations made by the Policing Board since the first Report in 2005, 135 had been implemented in full, 11 had been withdrawn and just three were outstanding.

With effect from 1 December 2008, following an analysis of the options for the further provision of human rights advice and a subsequent interview, Alyson Kilpatrick was appointed for a one-year term as the Policing Board's Human Rights Adviser. (A competitive selection process was to be taken forward in 2009.)

On 15 December 2010 Jane Gordon co-chaired an event celebrating the first 10 years of the Human Rights Act. In an article for the event she used police oversight in Northern Ireland as a case study. She stated that:

'The Policing Board's human rights Monitoring Framework represents the most comprehensive monitoring of human rights compliance of a police service that has ever taken place. This novel accountability mechanism has made a significant contribution to police reform in Northern Ireland. It is fair to say that the PSNI has done more than any other police force in the United Kingdom to achieve human rights compliance. The Human Rights Annual Reports have demonstrated the PSNI's commitment to the monitoring enterprise and have assisted in breaking down the traditional closed culture of policing. They have fostered a positive human rights dialogue between the PSNI and the Policing Board. The process has also had a much wider social impact through its contribution to the increased support for the PSNI among the people of Northern Ireland.'

She also noted that the APA guidance for police authorities was modelled on the Northern Ireland Monitoring Framework.

The way in which the Policing Board sought to achieve a dynamic presentation of its engagement on human rights issues with the wider community is shown in the following example. On 26 January 2011 the Policing Board launched the Human Rights and Professional Standards Committee's thematic review on policing with children and young people. This area had been identified by the Committee as a key priority. Publication followed work by the Committee with the youth charity Public Achievement over a number of months to develop a social media strategy for promoting the human rights work of the Policing Board, and for seeking the input and views of a wider range of individuals on key issues regarding the policing of communities. Public Achievement had built and would run a multi-media social networking website known as 'faircop' and campaign to promote dialogue and debate on such issues. The charity had set up groups on Facebook and feeds on Twitter and had experimented with text-based campaigns. The launch was streamed live on the faircop website and Policing Board Members and officials provided content and commentary for the website as well as media content such as video interviews.

As a summary of the impact of the human rights monitoring framework and the annual reports, Table 10.1 shows that from 2005 to 2011 a total of 220 recommendations was made in the successive Human Rights Annual Reports, of which 192 were implemented in full, 27 were withdrawn or replaced and one was outstanding.

Table 10.1   Human Rights Annual Report Recommendations 2005–11

	Implemented	Withdrawn	Outstanding	Total
2005	56	4	0	60
2006	42	3	0	45
2007	38	6	0	44
2008	20	10	0	30
2009	17	3	0	20
2010	4	1	0	5
2011	15	0	1	16
Total	**192**	**27**	**1**	**220**

10.12   Registration of Notifiable Memberships

The registration of notifiable memberships by PSNI officers was to prove another challenging issue for the Board over a number of years.

The Independent Commission were clear that police officers, like everyone else, were entitled to their private views and to join legal organisations that reflected those views. The key issue, however, was 'whether membership of such organisations affects officers' ability *to discharge their duties effectively and impartially'*. The Commission concluded that, while the problem was largely one of perception, it was unhealthy and incompatible with the openness and transparency advocated elsewhere throughout their Report.

Therefore, the Independent Commission's recommendation 126 was that:

'All officers – those now in service as well as all future recruits – should be obliged to register their interests and associations. The register should be held both by the Police Service and by the Police Ombudsman.'

Section 51 of the Police (Northern Ireland) Act 2000 provided for the Chief Constable to give guidance to police officers in connection with what it termed *'notifiable memberships'*. Before doing so, he was obliged to consult the Policing Board and others. The Act obliged the Chief Constable to require each police officer to inform him of any notifiable membership which that officer believed he had, or, if he believed he had no notifiable memberships, of that belief. The issue had proved controversial during the passage of the Act and the Government had removed the proposed list of organisations from the final legislation, substituting instead what came to be known as *'a subjective belief test'*.

In August 2002 Assistant Chief Constable Sam Kinkaid brought to the Policing Board a consultative document in relation to the registration of notifiable memberships. As he rightly put it, *'the issue is clearly one that requires thorough but sensitive consideration'*. The document was considered by the Policing Board Corporate Policy Committee on 18 September 2002. In his response the Chairman noted that a few Members were opposed to the need for either a register or guidance on notifiable interests, but the majority of Members appreciated that the legislation had placed requirements on the Chief Constable and were keen to offer their views on a way forward.

The views expressed by the Board at this stage were that while the PSNI could fulfil its statutory obligations without producing a list of organisations that needed to be registered, the Board would advocate the Chief Constable giving guidance, including a suggested list.

It was not until 5 August 2003 that the PSNI finally announced its policy on the issue. In his accompanying release the Chairman of the Policing Board stated that this announcement should be viewed as a further measure for building confidence in policing in Northern Ireland. He noted that the PSNI had stressed that the register was *'not a comment on the legitimacy or propriety of any organisation, it was about negating public perceptions about membership of certain organisations'*. He added that officers must have complete confidence that information disclosed to meet the requirements of the register would not be used inappropriately or improperly. The Policing Board's monitoring responsibility for the Code of Ethics included compliance with the register of notifiable memberships.

Officers were required to notify the Chief Constable if they were members of the following organisations:

- The Ancient Order of Hibernians
- The Apprentice Boys of Derry Association
- Grand Lodge of Freemasons of Ireland
- The Independent Orange Order
- The Knights of St Columbanus
- Loyal Orange Institution (including the Women's Orange Order)
- The Royal Black Institution
- Any organisation proclaiming/holding views on race, ethnicity or national identity which may be perceived to be in conflict with section 32 of the Police (Northern Ireland) Act 2000 and section 75 of the Northern Ireland Act 1998.

The PSNI announcement was discussed at the September 2003 Policing Board and Corporate Policy Committee meetings, following which the Chairman invited Assistant Chief Constable Kinkaid to discuss issues arising from the register, including the list of organisations and the process for finalising the guidance on the register. (There was a perception in some quarters that the register or list was weighted against Protestant/Loyalist organisations.) The Policing Board noted that the Chief Constable had said that the list would be reviewed annually. Assistant Chief Constable Kinkaid briefed the Board's Corporate Policy Committee the following month. He explained that the register of organisations could not simply be amended, but that it was scheduled to be reviewed in July 2004 and the Board was included in the consultees.

On 1 April 2004 the Chief Constable issued 'notes for guidance' for all police officers on the registration of notifiable memberships in line with the legislative requirement in the Police (Northern Ireland) Act 2000. The Policing Board was advised that the process of collating information regarding individual officers' notifiable memberships would begin on 19 April 2004.

However, on 9 June 2004 leave to apply for a judicial review was granted to three police officers and the Grand Lodge of Freemasons of Ireland; the basis of their application was their perception that section 51 of the 2000 Act was incompatible with various Articles of the ECHR. Following legal advice, the Chief Constable suspended the process of registration on 29 June 2004.

At the *Public Session* of the Policing Board held on 7 July 2004 the Chief Constable and his Deputy were probed by Eddie McGrady (SDLP) on the position. The Chief Constable explained that the legal advice he had received was that the notes for guidance were not lawful. He was determined to get a system that had the confidence of the community, as well as the confidence of his officers.

On 11 November 2004 the judicial review was conditionally withdrawn. It was agreed that those officers who had already submitted a notification form under the original process were given the option of 'opting in', whereby the Chief Constable was requested to take account of their form and they were thereby deemed to have registered. Those who had already submitted a notification form, but who did not wish to 'opt in', would be required to register again in accordance with section 51(5), their original forms having been destroyed. The third category of those who had not yet registered would be required to do so. The original notes for guidance issued by the Chief Constable were withdrawn.

The NIO was formally asked by the Chief Constable to amend the legislation, removing the subjective element of the test at section 51(5). The Policing Board wrote to support this. However, NIO Ministers stated that they preferred to consider the outcome of the second registration process before making a definite commitment to amend the Act. Following publication of revised guidance and a further PSNI General Order on 11 April 2005, a new registration process began the following week and was completed on 31 March 2006.

The Policing Board was notified in November 2005 that by that

time 94% of officers had registered, in line with the guidance. The
Policing Board was further advised by the PSNI in March 2007 that a
total of 606 officers then serving in the PSNI had indicated that they
held a notifiable membership.

At the meeting of the Policing Board on 5 July 2007 the Chief
Constable was asked about the outcome of the subsequent consultation on the inclusion of the Gaelic Athletic Association (GAA) and
Opus Dei in the list of organisations requiring registration. It was
noted that the PSNI were still consulting with various groups and
would bring the matter forward later in the year. Policing Board
Member Jeffrey Donaldson (DUP) observed that the Chief Constable
had been presented with a request signed by all ten Unionist Members
of the House of Commons asking that both organisations should be
included. In his response the Chief Constable noted that this was
a very difficult, emotive subject. Board Member Trevor Ringland
dissented, noting that the GAA were making massive changes.

10.13   An Independent Assessment of
the Board's Human Rights Function

Another – independent – angle on the Policing Board's human rights
work came from the Independent Assessment of the Northern Ireland
Policing Board conducted in 2005. The panel that conducted this
review was chaired by Sir Keith Povey, a former Her Majesty's Chief
Inspector of Constabulary (as described in Chapter 6). It was the view
of the Panel, as set out in the report published in December 2005, that:

*'in the period since the publication of the Patten Report and the establishment
of the Northern Ireland Policing Board, great progress has been made towards
the creation of a police service which is not just human rights compliant but
which has a positive and structured approach to the creation of a dynamic
human rights regime.'*

The Panel considered this achievement all the more meritorious given
the initial difficulties; these included the fact that many in the Police
Service were dubious about the value, and there was hesitancy on the
part of some Board Members too. However, as the Panel observed:

'A more significant difficulty, however, was the absence of any obvious role models to follow. For example, only one of the 52 police authorities in the United Kingdom – Thames Valley – has appointed a Human Rights Adviser and no European police force has as yet devised a comprehensive human rights-based approach to policing. As a result, the Board found itself left to its own devices in seeking to create new human rights compliant structures and to implement in full the findings of Patten in this regard. Against this background, the success so far of the Board in instilling a human rights-based approach to the implementation and monitoring of the new policing arrangements in Northern Ireland is commendable.'

The Panel identified as key elements in the Board's approach: the publication *'Monitoring PSNI Compliance with the Human Rights Act'* and the subsequent Programme of Action, which was published in 2004; the institutionalising of the recommended Oath; the appointment of high-level Human Rights Advisers; the publication and acceptance of a Code of Ethics which integrated the ECHR into policing practice; the incorporation of human rights training into all police training curricula, and the provision for an annual human rights appraisal of police practice. The Panel also found wide agreement on the value of the contribution made by Keir Starmer QC and Jane Gordon, which had added an extra layer of credibility to the overall process.

The Panel concluded that:

'The net result is that the experience of the Board is regularly used by the Council of Europe in devising its human rights-based policy on policing and for many external police forces Northern Ireland has now become a model to be followed.'

The Panel set out some areas for future consideration. It stressed the importance of human rights and cultural awareness training across the police training curricula and emphasised the need for Members of the Board and DPPs to have education and training in the human rights-based approach. It encouraged the Policing Board to engage more fully with other human rights bodies.

10.14   In Conclusion

In reviewing historical developments and their contemporary relevance some years later there is always a risk of post hoc rationalisation. However, there is no gainsaying that the progress made by the Policing Board in its pursuit of the Independent Commission plan for improvement was heavily – if not principally – reliant on a fundamental understanding and embedding of the human rights considerations. This required conspicuous leadership, professional guidance, and personal stamina of the highest order.

There is a view that '*the police are accountable to the law and the law alone*'. This narrow constitutional view of the police and their place in society emanates from a case presided over by Lord Denning (*R v Metropolitan Police Commissioner, ex p Blackburn* [1968] 2 QB 118; 2 All E.R., 319), which has been routinely misquoted ever since. The judgment had been specifically singled out as inaccurate by the Patten Report (at paragraph 1.14). The quotation from Denning's judgment is that a police officer '*is not a servant of anyone, save of the law itself*', particularly in the context of human rights considerations. The Independent Commission had strongly agreed with the opposite view, expressed by another denizen of constitutional matters, Lord Scarman: that the police <u>are the servants of their community</u>. That surely is and must be what the PSNI is about, and the Policing Board should strive to be the guarantor.

As a postscript, we have noted the growing debate, primarily among members of the British Conservative Party, about the British Government's commitment to the European Court of Human Rights and indeed the ECHR. In *The Times*' account on 21 July of the Ministerial reshuffle in summer 2014 the British Attorney-General, Dominic Grieve, was quoted as saying that it was possible that '*he had been dismissed for advising Mr Cameron not to pull Britain out of the European Convention on Human Rights*'.

This chapter has flagged up the centrality of human rights for the new beginning to policing in Northern Ireland, and indeed the extent to which police services in Britain subsequently followed suit. It is too early to tell what the implications for policing of any change to the current position may be, although the British parties' election platforms may provide some guidance.

References

The Universal Declaration of Human Rights, adopted by the United Nations General Assembly, 10 December 1948

The European Convention on Human Rights

The Brixton Disorders – Report of an Inquiry, The Rt. Hon. The Lord Scarman, HMSO, London, 1981

An Evaluation of Human Rights Training for Student Officers in the Police Service of Northern Ireland, Northern Ireland Human Rights Commission, Belfast, 2002

Equality Implications of the Policing Board's Policies – Second stage consultation paper, Policing Board, March 2003

NIPB 'Monitoring PSNI Compliance with the Human Rights Act 1998', Policing Board 15 December 2003

A Report on the Policing of the Ardoyne Parades 12 July 2004, Policing Board

Report on the Policing of the Ardoyne and Whiterock Parades 2005, Policing Board

Gordon, Jane, 'A developing human rights culture in the UK? Case studies of policing', *European Human Rights Law Review* 6, December 2010

NI Policing Board, Human Rights Annual Report 2012, p. 158

Tory Minister 'was sacked after taking a stand on EU', *The Times*, 21 July 2014

CHAPTER ELEVEN

Civil Unrest and Public Order Policing

Part One: Civil Unrest and Parades

11.1 The Context and Parades Issues

Problems of public order arising from demonstrations, processions, parades, and open air public meetings are, of course, not new: they have been around for at least 200 years. In the early 19th century such public demonstrations probably claimed common law protection but the absence of a policing service meant that disorder was met by the military, as in the period 1812 to 1819, as Robert Poole records. A hundred years later the existence of policing had not made public order more secure. Two World Wars in the 20th century brought a greater focus on human rights and the European Convention on Human Rights (ECHR) provided a guide even though it was not part of United Kingdom domestic legislation until 2000.

Public order issues in Ireland have been imbued with issues of Nationalism and Unionism, land and a whole range of social issues. After 1922, public order issues became the responsibility of two Governments – the Irish Government in Dublin and the Northern Ireland Government in Belfast. The former had to defend its authority in a civil war; the latter had to deal with the overflow of the civil war and the hostility of a significant minority that preferred a united Ireland to partition. Emergency Powers remained on the statute book, north and south, throughout the 20th century. The outbreak of public disorder in Northern Ireland from 1969 required extraordinary measures, including the suspension of local political institutions, the introduction of the military in support of the police, and the use of emergency legislation.

The inner city riots in England in 1981 also produced new public order legislation, the Public Order Act 1986. In Northern Ireland too, following extensive Unionist protests after the Anglo-Irish Agreement in 1985, the Public Order (NI) Order 1987 introduced significant new police powers over parades and protests. The paramilitary ceasefires in 1994 seemed to deflect attention to communal differences and issues of identity, so that parades and protests attained a higher profile. Very serious disorder developed after the annual Orange church parade to Drumcree Parish Church on Sunday 7 July 1996, affecting many parts of Northern Ireland. An independent review of parades and marches was set up by the Secretary of State, Sir Patrick Mayhew, in August 1996, under the chairmanship of Dr Peter North QC, Vice-Chancellor at Oxford University, assisted by two prominent local clergymen – Father Oliver Crilly and Very Reverend John Dunlop.

The January 1997 report of that Independent Review (the North Report) began with these words – *'we all have a problem'*. It said that there was an importance attached to parades which needed careful and sensitive analysis, although it acknowledged that in the previous year there had been over 3,000 marches or parades across Northern Ireland and *'all but a tiny minority passed off peacefully'*. The parades issue was a microcosm of the political problems of Northern Ireland, and was not new. The issue had the capacity to polarise both local communities and wider society – a society which the Review Team considered lacking in tolerance and sensitivity to the perceptions of other groups within it. *'It engages in individuals levels of personal emotion and commitment to wider groupings within society that are reached by few other issues'*, the report's Foreword acknowledged. The report noted that policing public disorder surrounding marches could require vast public expenditure.

The Review Team noted that the police were widely perceived, under the Public Order (NI) Order 1987, to be responsible for both making the decision about a particular parade and then enforcing it. (That legislation permitted the Royal Ulster Constabulary (RUC) to impose conditions or for the Secretary of State to ban a parade on information from the Chief Constable.) In contentious parades the police could find themselves caught between the disputing parties.

The Review Team's analysis showed that parading was much more prevalent among Protestant organisations than Catholic, and the latter were more political (Nationalist) than religious. The report analysed the various strands of the problem, including the human rights framework, public attitudes, and the legislative framework. Residents groups formed to oppose Orange parades had succeeded in delaying and preventing parades. The legislative framework appeared to reward those threatening violence, actual or potential through massed numbers. The report brought out that there were competing rights of individuals and groups (neither of which were absolute) to be addressed; moreover, the exercise of those rights brought with it certain responsibilities. The report highlighted the commonly held views that it was not right for the police to make and then enforce the decision, and there was a role for an independent body of either an advisory or decision-making nature. The Review Team's proposals presented a way of managing marches and proposed new law to provide the framework.

The North Report, published at the end of January 1997, proposed the creation of an independent Parades Commission comprising a Chairperson and four Members. The Commission would have an education function, promote mediation in contentious parades, keep under review a proposed Code of Conduct for parades and protesters, and arrange for the monitoring of contentious parades. Crucially, the North Report recommended that it should be the new Parades Commission, rather than the RUC, that should have the role in respect of the small number of contentious parades in considering,

'if mediation fails, ... what conditions might be imposed in respect of individual parades where such conditions are merited under the statutory criteria, and, after consultation, issuing determinations'.

In recognition of the 'principle of the operational independence of the Chief Constable', the North Report recommended that if the Chief Constable judged exceptionally that the Commission's determination had to be reviewed, he could give evidence of concern about that determination to the Secretary of State and a revised determination could be issued after consultation with the Parades Commission and the Police Authority. The police should retain their existing powers to intervene on public order grounds if there was a serious threat to public order. The report also recommended that notice of parades to the police be extended from 7 to 21 days to allow for discussion and mediation. It also recommended that the impact of a parade on relationships within the community be added to the conditions set out in the Public Order (NI) Order 1987 Article 4(1). It recommended that a new offence be created to penalise individuals who, through force of numbers or threat of disorder, deliberately contravened a Commission determination.

The North Report recommended greater transparency, with the lead being taken by the Parades Commission, which would prepare guidelines to be used in considering whether to impose conditions on a parade. The report said that breaches of the Code of Conduct (also to be drawn up by the Commission), by participants or protestors, could then be considered at a subsequent application.

The Public Order (Amendment) (NI) Order 1997 began the process of legislative change. A new Parades Commission was appointed by the Secretary of State in March 1997, in advance of the legislation, with (Sir) Alastair Graham as Chairperson and four other Members. This, initially, was to operate on an advisory rather than a decision-making basis.

What became the Public Processions (NI) Act 1998 was introduced by the Labour Government late in 1997. It provided the legal basis for the Parades Commission, its Members were appointed by the Secretary of State, and the Commission now had the full decision-making responsibility for parades and setting down conditions for them. The effect was to manage parades and marches through a system of prior notification, conditions, and named individual organisers; it also included penalties for non-compliance. Enforcement of any conditions was the responsibility of the Police Service of Northern Ireland (the Police Service or the PSNI).

The Bill was amended significantly during passage through the House of Lords. The power of the Secretary of State to ban parades was limited to risk of 'serious public disorder' and 'serious damage to property' from the original lower threshold. In the House of Commons debates on 18 December 1997 the Northern Ireland Office (NIO) Minister, Adam Ingram, stated that 'The Bill is to ensure that no RUC Chief Constable is boxed into that position again'. He said that the Parades Commission was first to seek accommodation over parades and that the use of determinations was the last resort; long-standing routes would be recognised.

However, Unionist MPs in the Commons were not reassured by changes made in the Lords. Rev. Dr Ian Paisley (Democratic Unionist

Party (DUP)) claimed that the Bill was too focused on the cultural expression of one community and that it should 'assist the rule of law and discourage those seeking to break it'. David Trimble (Ulster Unionist Party (UUP)) described the Bill as 'the most serious and substantial assault on the civil rights of the people of Northern Ireland this century'. In summing up, Adam Ingram said the aim was 'to ensure that parades never again become the focus for sectarian bitterness'.

The Minister's hopes were not immediately fulfilled and protests and stand-offs over local parades continued. The talks leading to the Belfast Agreement 1998 left the issue of the future of the RUC to an Independent Commission. Irrespective of the outcome of policing reform, issues to do with parading remained. While the police no longer made the decision about parades and related protests, they had to give advice on the impact of a parade and to give effect to any determination by the Parades Commission which had the force of law.

A review of the Parades Commission and the Public Processions (NI) Act 1998 was conducted in 2001/02 by Sir George Quigley for the Secretary of State and reported in September 2002. His report contained 34 recommendations and proposed alternative structures to the Parades Commission – a Parades Facilitation Agency and a Rights Panel.

The Parades Commission rejected the proposals because it considered that the Act was working well at that moment and required a more sustained period before review. It argued that it was 'not the time to change it for something more revolutionary ...'. It cited statistics showing that only a small proportion of parades, 7%, were contentious, and 74.5% of those had no restrictions imposed. The Northern Ireland Affairs Committee (NIAC) Report on the Parades Commission and Public Processions (NI) Act 1998 also rejected the Quigley proposals. 'Replacing it [the Parades Commission] with new organisational arrangements ... could entail considerable disruption and place at risk the progress towards a peaceful marching season.'

After the reinstatement of devolution in 2007 a further attempt was made to tackle the parading issue, with Paddy Ashdown being appointed to chair a review. In October 2007 Members of the Northern Ireland Policing Board (the Policing Board or Board) met the Review Panel, bringing out the Policing Board's role in relation to monitoring PSNI compliance with the Human Rights Act in policing operations and the Board's interest in promoting better dialogue with community groups. In 2008 the Panel produced an Interim Consultative Report of the Strategic Review of Parading. The report referred to 'an immense gulf in understanding of the culture and traditions of each community'. It recommended a separation in the mediation and adjudication func-tions, with a new Adjudication Panel appointed by the Office of the First Minister and the deputy First Minister. Despite a welcome by the Northern Ireland Executive, the proposals were rejected by the Orange Order.

In June 2010 the First Minister and the deputy First Minister launched a consultation on the draft Code of Conduct relating to the Public Assemblies, Parades and Protests Bill (Northern Ireland). Fresh proposals in a joint initiative were rejected by the Orange Order in July of that year.

Late in 2013 changes to the parades legislation were again discussed by the panel of the Parties in talks chaired by Dr Richard Haass, although no agreement was reached at that time.

11.2   The European Convention on Human Rights Framework

The rights to peaceful assembly and the freedom of expression are enshrined in the ECHR Articles 10 and 11. The signatory govern-ments have the obligation to protect and promote those rights; in addition, there is a requirement that 'no unnecessary restrictions' be placed on 'people's rights to peaceful protest'. Rights cannot be absolute for the protesters – those protested against, police, journalists, and bystanders also have rights to be considered. The Article protects the participants and organisers of peaceful assemblies from interference by the State in their activities. That interference also applies to the use of 'unreasonable indirect restrictions'. Article 11.2 states that:

'No restrictions shall be placed on the exercise of these rights other than such as are prescribed by law and are necessary in a democratic society in the inter-ests of national security or public safety, for the prevention of disorder or crime, for the protection of health or morals or for the protection of the rights and freedoms of others...'.

Freedom of assembly includes participation in private and public meetings, processions, mass actions, demonstrations, pickets, and rallies. It does not include participation in violent protests but does include a sit down on a public road even though it disrupts traffic. Courts determine whether a protest is peaceful and the intention of the organisers is the key factor.

Any interference with freedom of assembly must be *'prescribed by law'* and be *'necessary in a democratic society'* – the burden is on the State to provide *'convincing and compelling reasons to justify an interference with this right'* and show that the interference was proportionate to the aim pursued.

Restrictions may be a ban, or involve the proposed place or agreeing to one place but not another. Such decisions must be based on Article 11 and be an acceptable assessment of relevant facts. The Court has ruled that freedom of assembly is so important that it cannot be restricted in any way so long as the person does not commit any reprehensible act. Where authorities fear disruption to public order, a certain degree of tolerance should be shown where demonstrators did not engage in acts of violence. The Joint House of Lords/House of Commons report in 2008/09 interpreted this to mean *'the police should be exceptionally slow to prevent or interfere with a peaceful demonstration simply because of the violent actions of a minority'*.

A Panel of Experts on Freedom of Assembly of the Office for Democratic Institutions and Human Rights and the Organisation for Security and Cooperation in Europe produced Guidelines on Freedom of Peaceful Assembly:

'1. *Respect the regulations in force: a high threshold is needed before a public assembly will unreasonably infringe the rights and freedoms of others.*

2. *Where prior notice is required, disbanding a peaceful assembly, without any illegal conduct, amounts to a disproportionate restriction on freedom of assembly.'*

11.3   The Policing Board and the Policing of Parades

As we saw in the last chapter, the Independent Commission Report Recommendation 1 placed human rights and community policing at the heart of what became the PSNI. The Police (Northern Ireland) Act 2000 required the Policing Board to monitor the PSNI's compliance with the Human Rights Act 1998. This legal requirement clearly brought the Policing Board into play through the human rights dimension in addition to the statutory duty of the Policing Board to hold the Chief Constable to account.

It can thus be seen that, for the Policing Board, the issue of parades and civic unrest associated with contentious parades was bound to be a significant concern.

Chapter 10 set out in full the approach taken by the Policing Board towards complying with its human rights duty. Put briefly, the Board decided that the monitoring process should be guided by three principles:

- the performance of the PSNI as a whole should be monitored
- the process was envisaged as dynamic, with problems addressed as they arose through dialogue between the PSNI and Policing Board
- the process would not be retrospective

After the appointment of two independent Human Rights Advisers a framework document on monitoring was published by the Policing Board in December 2003. It set out 12 areas of policing – training, policy, operations, complaints discipline and civil actions, adherence to PSNI code of ethics, public order, use of force, covert policing, victims' rights, and treatment of suspects. It can be seen immediately that several of these areas of policing bore on parades, civil unrest, and, indeed, the tactics and technology used by the PSNI in dealing with public order.

The monitoring results were published by the Policing Board in its Annual Report on Human Rights. In addition, the Advisers were asked on behalf of the Board to monitor and report on a number of contentious parades. Their reports were also published by the Board.

In the Annual Human Rights Report 2004–5 the Advisers reviewed PSNI documentation relating to public order (for example, General

Orders on the Code of Practice framework for strategy and planning public events; protest activity on public thoroughfares; relations with the Parades Commission; and the use of tactical advisers). They also reviewed the paperwork relating to several 2003 parades. They attended the planning meetings for the same parades in 2004, with the addition of the Whiterock parade. In 2004 they attended the Ardoyne, Drumcree, and Short Strand parades and observed both on the ground and from the PSNI control rooms. They spoke to PSNI officers with responsibility for planning and controlling parades and had unrestricted access to documents and materials. They also attended the PSNI debriefing meeting on the summer parades held on 6 September 2004.

As noted in the last chapter, the Human Rights Advisers also agreed to undertake a special report on the policing of the Ardoyne parade on 12 July 2004. The Parades Commission determination that placed restrictions on a section of roadway at Ardoyne was interpreted as banning parade supporters from that section of the road. However, a judicial review of the determination was sought and on 9 July 2004 the review was denied by Mr Justice Weatherup (in the Matter of an Application by 'JNR1'). But in stating that the Parades Commission determination applied only to the parade and organisers and not followers – as distinct from participants – PSNI planning was seriously affected. Returning parade supporters were subject only to the general powers of the police over breach of the peace, which concerned individuals and not groups. It resulted in a delicate situation on a contested section of road which was resolved by holding parade supporters back for eight minutes until the parade had completed the restricted section of road. Parade supporters were then permitted to rejoin the bands and Orangemen. However, there was considerable violence; at one stage two military road blocks at the top of the Crumlin Road failed and there was the danger of clashes between rival groups.

On 15 July 2004, in a press release on behalf of the Policing Board, the Chairman called on the Chief Constable to provide a full report on the policing of that year's parades to the Board's September meeting. The release noted that 'once again, in North Belfast, the police were placed in a "no win" situation and I fully endorse the view that the police cannot be held responsible for the fallout from the parading issue'. In a reflection of the political pressures that arose from parading issues, one Social

Democratic and Labour Party (SDLP) Belfast City Councillor mooted SDLP resignations from the Policing Board as a protest against PSNI's handling of the march past the Ardoyne shop fronts, although the Policing Board Member and former SDLP Vice-Chairman Tom Kelly was quoted in *The Sunday Business Post* on 18 July as saying the remarks were '*regrettable in both tone and content*'. To what end would resignations be helpful, he added?

In the *Public Session* of the Policing Board held on 2 September 2004 the Chief Constable, together with Assistant Chief Constables McCausland and Sheridan, gave a full account of the PSNI's handling of contentious parades that summer. He stressed that they had sought throughout to uphold the rights of people to march as long as they did so peacefully within the law and the Parades Commission's determinations, and, in addition, they had sought to uphold the rights of those who wished to protest against marches and parades peacefully and legally. That was a difficult balance, but he thought that the PSNI had done their honest best. In a comprehensive question and answer session the issues raised included those relating to human rights, police planning and reactions, and the interpretation of the Parades Commission's determinations.

The Human Rights Advisers' recommendations arising from the Ardoyne parade 2004 were significant. They included a review of protocols for effective communication between the PSNI and the Parades Commission. The Advisers were satisfied that the policing operation had been '*carefully planned and executed*' and, as a whole, complied with the requirements of the Human Rights Act, but there were some areas of criticism. They advised a review of PSNI General Orders on public order. The report's authors also felt that it would have been 'preferable' if the police had taken further legal advice between 9 and 12 July '*even though it would not have affected the decisions made by those responsible for policing the parades*'. While it could be argued that the italicised part of this recommendation rendered it largely academic, that would be to miss the point – namely that a key part of changing attitudes and culture in the area of human rights involves establishing processes and inculcating approaches that are grounded in the law.

On 4 November 2004 Jane Gordon presented to the *Public Session* of the Policing Board an overview of the Human Rights Advisers' report on the Ardoyne (which was then published). At the same session, the Chief Constable was then invited to respond. He noted that no other Police Service in the United Kingdom would have allowed such unrestricted access to third parties in such situations. The chairman of the Policing Board's Human Rights and Professional Standards Committee, Eddie McGrady (SDLP), said that the Committee had endorsed the recommendations in the Advisers' report.

The second Annual Report on Human Rights compliance followed the progress of implementing the recommendations made in the first report. Recommendation 35, requiring the review and revision of PSNI General Orders on Public Order, was not completed, but was promised for 2006. The legal gap exposed by the Weatherup decision in July 2004 had been remedied by the Public Processions (Amendment) (NI) Order 2005 on 14 May 2005. The Parades Commission, now headed by Roger Poole and reconstituted, was given power to impose conditions on *any person supporting a parade* (section 8(1)); it also gave the Commission power to impose conditions on *protest meetings* associated with a parade (section 9A).

In 2005 Mr Starmer and Ms Gordon were asked by the Policing Board to conduct a review of the policing of two further significant parades: the parade that passed through Ardoyne on 12 July that year and the Whiterock parade that should have been held on 25 June but which was postponed, finally taking place on 10 September 2005. The Ardoyne parade was punctuated by serious violence which led to 105 police officers and at least eight members of the public being injured and the explosion of several blast and petrol bombs. Water cannon were deployed and 21 Attenuating Energy Projectiles (AEPs – see later in this chapter) were discharged. Serious disorder attended the Whiterock parade and the report estimated that 150 live rounds were fired at police, their vehicles, and their military colleagues.

A special briefing on parades was provided by the Chief Constable for members of the Policing Board on 3 August 2005. At the Board's *Public Session* on 1 September the Chief Constable was questioned by Sammy Wilson (DUP) on the apparent delay in approval for the firing of baton rounds by a police officer. The Chief Constable said that he and his senior managers had reviewed the procedures for granting authorisation to deploy and fire AEPs – Northern Ireland was the only part of the United Kingdom where blast bombs were thrown in public order situations. In addition to the normal review by the

Police Ombudsman, an investigation was carried out by the Northern Ireland Health and Safety Executive, as well as by an internal PSNI review panel (although the Health and Safety Executive's report was not completed until 2008, when its existence and some of its contents became matters of controversy.)

On 29 September 2005 Members of the Policing Board met Members of the Parades Commission at the former's premises.

The Human Rights Advisers' report on the 2005 Ardoyne and Whiterock parades was published on 15 December 2005. It contained analysis of whether

- the policing of these parades complied with the requirements of the Human Rights Act 1998
- the determinations of the Parades Commission were properly policed
- overall, the use of force by the PSNI was justified

In his introductory remarks at the launch, the Policing Board Chairman noted that the violence at Ardoyne and ensuing from the Whiterock parade was the worst witnessed on the streets in recent years. It was important that the Policing Board monitor whether or not the PSNI carried out their duties in a human rights-compliant way and tell the public their findings: *'this is what public accountability is all about'*.

The Policing Board's press release on the day of the launch summarised the position of the report's authors:

'In respect of each parade we are satisfied that the policing operation was carefully planned and executed; that the human rights implications of all the key decisions were considered at every stage; and that the use of force overall complied with the requirement of the Human Rights Act 1998. ... The human rights of the rioters and their supporters, protesters, residents, police officers and the military were taken into account at all stages of the planning process and the Senior Command responsible for both operations reacted to the changing circumstances of the operations as events unfolded with care and diligence.'

The extent of monitoring activity and, indeed, intrusive scrutiny conducted on behalf of the Policing Board is clear throughout this second report. Written in a readable style and presented in an accessible, non-technical way, this report works through the context of the human rights framework, explaining the police policies and their relevance to the two parades under consideration. It then proceeds carefully through the chronology of the parades themselves, picking out the proposed routes, the determinations of the Parades Commission, and the submissions of the proposed protest meetings. The authors attended the strategic command meetings, tactical meetings, and planning meetings. They made recommendations on the importance of recording tactical advice (and occasions where it was departed from).

It is worth noting that very fine measures were applied to police activities taking place in a highly pressurised and fast-moving situation. Very little time, for example, separated the throwing of missiles at the police and their subsequent response by water cannon, while the consideration by police commanders of whether methods of response other than AEP rounds were available was undertaken while those officers came under fire from blast bombs thrown from rooftops.

The marching season in 2006 was characterised by significantly less public disorder. In briefing the Policing Board, the Chief Constable praised stewarding, and the Policing Board's Human Rights Advisers commended the extensive community consultation carried out by senior PSNI officers. It was also the first time for many years that the parades had passed without the assistance of the military in controlling potential public disorder.

The fourth Annual Report on Human Rights commended the reintroduction of public order training after a lapse in 2007. It reported serious discussions with the Parades Commission over its definition of parade marshals and stewards arising from the Whiterock parade in 2007, when the PSNI was concerned at the slow speed of response to requests. It proposed that specific parades at Whiterock Road and Ardoyne would not be monitored to the same extent in 2009 but it was conditional on continued successful compliance with human rights requirements. The report also included new information from the PSNI, namely the number of prosecutions for breaches of public order legislation by police district. It stated that there were 11 cases in urban areas and 25 involving 39 defendants in rural areas.

At the meeting of the Policing Board on 5 June 2008, in the

run-up to that year's Whiterock parade, the Chief Constable was again probed on the lines of communication with the Parades Commission to ensure expeditious clarification of determinations, particularly around contentious parades. The PSNI team advised the Board that there had been a number of discussions at the most senior level with the Commission on this point.

It was not only the Orders' parades and protests that could prove contentious. On 2 November 2008 a parade was organised in Belfast by the Ministry of Defence to mark the homecoming of soldiers in the Royal Irish Regiment and the Territorial Army who had served in Iraq and Afghanistan. The Parades Commission also gave permission for a 500-strong Sinn Féin protest against the parade. Representatives of dissident republicans announced that they were planning to go ahead with illegal parades and other demonstrations. Tension arose in the run-up to the day, with Prime Minister Gordon Brown appealing for calm in Parliamentary exchanges (as quoted in Northern Ireland newspapers on 30 October 2008). The occasion called for the deployment of around 1,000 police officers, at a cost approaching half a million pounds. Again, the Chief Constable, together with Assistant Chief Constable Alistair Finlay, was questioned on operational matters after the event by the Policing Board at its meeting on 6 November.

As regards public order, the fifth Annual Report said that the Advisers had attended the planning meetings ahead of the 2009 marching season. It noted the serious violence at Ardoyne on 13 July and at Mountpottinger on 31 August that year, although this was beyond its reporting period. It reported that the PSNI now supplied the Policing Board with statistics on the use of force on a six-monthly basis and in electronic format. The report noted that the PSNI would put into force an alcohol seizure strategy in the summer of 2009 to remove alcohol as a factor in disturbances at parades and protests.

At the meeting of the Policing Board on 7 May 2009, the last one chaired by Sir Desmond Rea and the first after the election of Sir Hugh Orde as the next President of the Association of Chief Police Officers (ACPO), both referred in their remarks to the importance of the forthcoming marching season and the huge amounts of preparatory and community consultation work ongoing.

The sixth Annual Report commented on the extensive training programme and that it would occur every two years. Police parade planning and execution were monitored in a North Belfast parade where extensive violence occurred and the report signed it off as complying with the Human Rights Act. It cited favourable comments on the Northern Ireland experience in a Report by Her Majesty's Inspector of Constabulary (HMIC) entitled 'Adapting to Protest' as having lessons for Britain. The report commented that earlier criticism of the slow response on the production of information and statistics by the PSNI had been addressed.

The seventh Annual Report on Human Rights followed the pattern of its predecessor. The PSNI had to report to the Policing Board every six months instances where force was used and the context of the use of force. There were two categories: first, where force was used, and injuries and damage to property occurred; and, second, the use of AEPs. Twelve such instances were reported in 2011.

The summer of 2011 was troubled, including Short Strand in East Belfast on 20–22 June, when water cannon and 130 AEPs were fired; the 1 July Somme commemoration clashes between about 200 persons at the interface; disorder on 9 July in Ballyclare after PSNI officers removed flags; and disorder in Carrickfergus on 10 July. There were three trouble spots in Belfast on 11–12 July, all bonfire-related. On 12 July there was disorder at the Ardoyne shop fronts. There were disturbances over several nights in Portadown from 11 to 16 July and there was also trouble in Armagh and Ballymena on the evening of 12 July. The Human Rights Adviser was available throughout and also in the command room for the Ardoyne disorder.

The eighth Annual Report on Human Rights (published in 2012) made 12 new recommendations, with one carried over from the previous year. It set out the extent of PSNI Human Rights training and noted that the Policing Board's Committee received public order briefings throughout the year. The Human Rights Adviser was present throughout the 12 July 2012 parades and the 28–29 September 2012 Ulster Covenant parades. She reported that the policing of the events was well planned, human rights standards were applied, and the PSNI decision-making process was within a strict framework. There were disturbances at Ardoyne on 12–13 July 2012, when 200–250 persons attacked the police, and there were minor disturbances in Portadown and Craigavon. There were also disturbances at Carlisle Circus from 2 to 4 September that year. The Ulster Covenant parade of 30,000 on 29

September had no major incidents, although there were some claims of breaches of Parades Commission determinations.

After the violence of 2011 it was decided that the Human Rights Adviser would conduct a thematic review of public order policing from February 2013.

11.4   The Position on Parades and Protests in Great Britain and the Read-Across from Northern Ireland

The joint report of the House of Lords and House of Commons Joint Committee on Human Rights (2009) entitled 'Demonstrating Respect for Rights? A Human Rights Approach to Policing Protest' provided a good summary of the legal position in Great Britain at that time. Public order in Great Britain was governed by the Public Order Act 1986, which covered the policing of processions and protests whether moving or static. Protest marches must give advance notice, except where the march is a customary local event, a funeral procession, or a spontaneous protest that turned into a march. Under Section 11 police may impose conditions before a march or during it, if it is believed necessary to prevent serious public disorder, serious damage to property or the life of the community, or if the march is intended to intimidate others. Failure to provide advance notice or to comply with conditions is an offence. There is no general requirement to give notice of a public assembly or static protest to the police, but police can impose similar conditions to those on marches (Section 14). The Act also sets out a series of offences related to protest and behaviour of a threatening, abusive, and insulting nature.

'Demonstrating Respect for Rights? A Human Rights Approach to Policing Protest' expressed some general concerns about the impact of public order policing on human rights:

- First, where legislation was overboard or excessively vague, police officers were left with wide discretion over the line between what was lawful and unlawful.

- Second, increasing legislative limitations on protests produced over-lapping powers and made law less predictable. For example, only some of the legislation causing concern had been introduced for specific public order situations. The Serious Organised Crime Act (2005) criminalised public order offences at designated sites, including Parliament, nuclear sites, and military facilities. Police could use 'stop and search' powers under the Police and Criminal Evidence Act 1984 (PACE). However, the Terrorism Act 2000 (Section 44) also permitted search of persons and vehicles in a 'designated area', though this was not intended for general public order use. Other legislation, such as the Protection from Harassment Act 1997 and Anti-Social Behaviour Orders, could be applied to public order situations. The police also had the power of arrest for breach of the peace under the common law.

- Third, the courts were reluctant to provide clear limits by interpreting legislation in the light of the Human Rights Act 1998, Section 3. It was the view of the Joint House of Lords/House of Commons Joint Committee that human rights law made clear that the balance should always fall in favour of those seeking to assert their right to protest unless there was strong evidence for interfering with their right. Inconvenience or disruption were not sufficient reasons for preventing a protest taking place, though there might be good reasons to reroute it or place other conditions on it. Given the value of the right to protest, a certain amount of inconvenience or disruption needed to be tolerated.

The House of Lords/House of Commons Joint Committee had taken evidence that an understanding of human rights was now part of everyday police work and that the police viewed it as helping rather than hindering effective policing. The Committee took a number of lessons specifically from the Northern Ireland experience:

- First, the PSNI employed a dedicated human rights lawyer to advise all officers
- Second, human rights were explicitly referred to in PSNI policy
- Third, the PSNI Code of Ethics was based on ECHR and other international instruments, and violations of the Code might constitute a disciplinary offence
- Finally, leadership must be fully committed to implementing human rights within the PSNI

The Joint Committee considered that monitoring compliance was important. It recognised the Northern Ireland model of active compliance through annual human rights compliance reports. Through dialogue and prior notification of parades, police could aim to have no surprises at the event.

The style of policing had changed, with many more police now tending to be deployed. Policing in Britain at major protests was criticised for the use of 'kettling', or holding protesters for long periods. In Northern Ireland numbers of police at parades had also increased but it was noted that the PSNI approach to uniform and equipment was designed to reduce tension. The style was to have normal uniformed officers up front, with back-up in riot gear out of sight but in the vicinity. This has been described by Michael Hamilton and Neil Jarman, as quoted in the Joint Committee's report, as *a shift from escalated force to negotiated management models of protest policing*. The report recommended that this approach be used, where appropriate, in England and Wales *to support peaceful protest and uphold the right to peaceful assembly*.

Part Two: Policing Public Disorder and Individual Situations of Violence

11.5 The Independent Commission's Recommendations and the Research Programme

The following section of this chapter deals largely with the introduction of less lethal equipment for use by the PSNI (and indeed the police throughout these islands) in responding to threats of violence and violent situations, whether they arise at an individual level or in a public disorder context. This was another issue which was inevitably contentious for the Policing Board, with sensitivities heightened as a result of fatalities and injuries, predominantly among Nationalists, caused by plastic baton rounds (PBRs) in public disorder during the Troubles.

The Independent Commission On Policing For Northern Ireland (the Independent Commission) addressed the issue of public order policing directly. It noted in Chapter 9 of its Report that:

'A major and controversial feature of policing in Northern Ireland has been public order policing ... The problem remains one of the greatest challenges in the policing of Northern Ireland, particularly during the so-called marching season ... It presents the unwelcome spectacle of police in riot gear and armoured vehicles, and involves the use of a controversial weapon – plastic baton rounds (PBRs).'

Members of the Independent Commission made clear in their Report that they would like to see the use of PBRs discontinued as soon as possible. However, they recognised that they did not wish to see a situation in which the police would have no choice but to resort to live rounds sooner than would be the case were PBRs available. Members of the Commission were impressed by the efforts and commitment to developing non-lethal alternatives in the United States, particularly at the Institute for Non-Lethal Defence Technologies at Pennsylvania State University and the National Institute of Justice. Chapter 9 of the Report also referred to the advantages of using personal protection CS spray (as then issued to most police officers in Great Britain) and the potential use of water cannon (which the RUC had borrowed from their Belgian colleagues in 1999).

The Independent Commission made three recommendations in this particular area:

'An immediate and substantial investment should be made in a research programme to find an acceptable, effective and less potentially lethal alternative to the PBR.' (Recommendation 69)

The police should be equipped with a broader range of public order equipment than the RUC currently possess, so that a commander has a number of options at his or her disposal which might reduce reliance on, or defer resort to, the PBR.' (Recommendation 70)

The use of PBRs should be subject to the same procedures for deployment, use and reporting as apply in the rest of the United Kingdom ... Use of PBRs should in the first instance require the authorisation of the district commander. This should be justified in a report to the Policing Board, which should be copied to the Police Ombudsman.' (Recommendation 71)

Recommendation 73 was that the Policing Board *'should actively monitor police performance in public order situations, and if necessary seek reports from the Chief Constable and follow up those reports if they wish'*.

In the Updated Implementation Plan published in August 2001 the British Government stated that the Government was fully committed to these Recommendations (69 and 70). It had launched a research programme in July 2000. The Plan also committed to making arrangements, as soon as the Policing Board was in place, to ensure close cooperation between it and the project board for the research programme. It noted further that the Policing Board was among the bodies to be consulted (under section 53 of the Police (Northern Ireland) Act 2000) before the Secretary of State issued guidance on the use of equipment for maintaining or restoring public order.

In summer 2000 the Secretary of State for Northern Ireland established a United Kingdom-wide Steering Group on Alternatives to the Baton Round to lead a research project aimed at:

'*Establishing whether a less potentially lethal alternative to the baton round is available, and*

Reviewing the public order equipment which is presently available or could be developed in order to expand the range of tactical options available to operational commanders'.

The Steering Group comprised representatives from Her Majesty's Inspectorate of Constabulary (HMIC), the Home Office, the Association of Chief Police Officers (ACPO), the Ministry of Defence, the Police Authority for Northern Ireland, the Police Scientific Development Branch of the Home Office, and the RUC, and was chaired by the NIO.

Terms of reference were drawn up based on the above objectives, containing four sequential phases. The work of the Steering Group continued for a number of years, with the NIO in the chair, before the lead was passed to ACPO. The Group's achievements, especially as expressed in its successive published reports, is a story worth fully telling in its own right, but that is for another day.

It is important to note that the work of the Steering Group was not just about less lethal equipment – its programme also took in and promoted alternative models for policing conflict management, including the human rights context. Another element, which continues to this day, was the internationalising of the approach, following the lead given in the Independent Commission report. Northern Ireland law enforcement leaders, with GB colleagues and Pennsylvania State University, established the International Law Enforcement Forum (ILEF) for Minimal Force Options, which continues to be a valuable tool for research and dissemination of good policing practice for many police services overseas as well.

The rest of this chapter focuses primarily on the Policing Board's deliberations in relation to the policing of public disorder and individual violence, and in particular the equipment with which the PSNI were to be provided for such situations.

On 4 April 2002 there was an initial presentation to the Policing Board on the work of the NIO-led Steering Group covering the research programme itself and the importance of alternative policing approaches towards the management of conflict that would be consistent with the key themes of human rights-based policing and policing with the community.

In line with Recommendation 73 of the Independent Commission Report, from 13 May 2002 the PSNI provided the Policing Board with early reports of situations involving the discharge of baton rounds and public disorder incidents. These reports enabled the Board to monitor police performance in public disorder situations and were provided within 24 hours of the incident. At the meeting in December 2002 Board Members were invited to visit the PSNI Sprucefield site to observe training given to PSNI officers using baton rounds.

Issues relating to public order and the police response to violent situations were not confined to Northern Ireland or the United Kingdom. In November 2002 the Irish Minister for Justice, Mr Michael McDowell, announced that, at the request of the Garda Commissioner, he had authorised the introduction of three additional technologies for use where it was necessary to avoid firearms – the beanbag shot, a pepper spray device, and a ferret pepper spray shot.

The International Law Enforcement Forum met for the first time in October 2002 at Pennsylvania State University. This two-day conference looked at three key cross-cutting themes: a) the gaps in critical areas such as capability and medical evaluation; b) how better to share information; and c) the scope for developing common standards. The conference also noted the work of the Human Effects Advisory Panel set up through the Applied Research Laboratory at Pennsylvania State University, which had, in the previous year, published a report entitled 'Crowd behaviour, crowd control and the use of non-lethal weapons'. Drawing on this research, the Steering Group noted the lack of guidance for the PSNI in enabling further understanding of how best to ensure that crowd control was not incompatible with community policing. It suggested that this might be an area which would repay further scrutiny, perhaps prompted by the Policing Board.

A second international conference on less lethal technologies was held on 21 November 2002 in London, attended by 150 invited delegates, including representatives from almost every police force in the United Kingdom, the relevant ACPO policy portfolio holders, and representatives from the Policing Board. Speakers at the conference included the Policing Board Vice-Chairman Denis Bradley and the Northern Ireland Police Ombudsman.

11.6   The Introduction of Water Cannon and CS Incapacitant Spray in Northern Ireland and Other Consideration of Alternatives to the Plastic Baton Round

In July 2002 the Chairman of the Policing Board welcomed the announcement by the NIO Minister of the procurement of six vehicle-mounted water cannon by the PSNI in July 2002. He said:

'The Policing Board fully supported the proposal by the Acting Chief Constable to purchase the water cannon and I am pleased that approval has now been given to proceed.

We recently saw the successful deployment of water cannon to deal with public order situations in Belfast and Drumcree. Whilst we understand water cannon are not effective in all situations, we believe it is a positive first step.'

The Chairman added:

'Clearly, the Policing Board would much prefer to be in a position where the police did not have to resort to the use of public order equipment. However, the recent serious violence and disorder which has been witnessed in Belfast and other parts of the Province has reinforced the need for police to have equipment available to them for dealing with such incidents.

Protecting and ensuring the safety of police officers and innocent members of the public in disorder situations is a difficult task. There is a duty of care to do so and the Policing Board is committed to this. The Policing Board has a responsibility to monitor police performance in public order situations and there are stringent guidelines in place for police use of public order equipment.

It is essential that the public has confidence in how the police deal with public order situations. Ultimately though, it is the responsibility of protesters and the whole community to help prevent such instances of disorder occurring.'

In April 2003 the PSNI guidelines for the use of water cannon were copied to all members of the Policing Board. A year later the publication of the medical assessment of the use of water cannon and full ACPO guidance allowed the PSNI to make operational use of their newly acquired water cannons.

On 31 December 2002 the Chief Constable sent to the Policing Board Chairman a business case which had also been submitted to the

NIO for the funding of the introduction of CS incapacitant spray to provide PSNI officers with another option when dealing with violent confrontation. He noted that the Police Ombudsman had at a recent seminar raised the question of why the PSNI was not equipped with CS spray when other police forces in Great Britain were. The business case concluded that CS spray would help fill the 'capability gap' between the use of the baton and the use of PBRs.

A presentation was given to the Policing Board's Corporate Policy Committee meeting on 23 January 2003. It was stressed that the CS incapacitant spray was not intended for large-scale public order use, nor as an alternative to baton rounds. Its use might, however, be appropriate in violent incidents such as pub fights where officers might use it to defend themselves or others or to effect arrest. The Committee noted that, under paragraph 9 of the *Conditions of Grant to the Chief Constable*, he was required to notify the Policing Board of any expenditure that was deemed to be novel or contentious and, in his letter of 31 December 2002, the Chief Constable had done so. The Committee agreed that it was content with the Chief Constable's proposal and that the Board should be asked to confirm the Committee's recommendation.

At its meeting on 6 February 2003 the Policing Board confirmed the Committee's endorsement.

In March 2003 the Police Ombudsman completed a research report on a study of complaints involving the use of batons (at that time either wooden truncheons or the longer riot batons) by the police in Northern Ireland between November 2000 and March 2002. This highlighted that '*by October 1998 all but three of the 43 forces in England and Wales had introduced CS spray, with a consequent diminution in baton use*'. The same report noted that police officers in Northern Ireland were as much as six times more likely to be assaulted than their colleagues in Great Britain. The report concluded that the Ombudsman welcomed the approach from the Chief Constable to request from the NIO the supply of funds to equip officers with CS spray.

Under the provisions of section 55(4) of the Police (Northern Ireland) Act 1998 and Regulation 20 of the Royal Ulster Constabulary (Complaints etc.) Regulations 2000, the Police Ombudsman produced reports on every discharge of a baton round by the PSNI, which were submitted to the Policing Board. In the vast majority of cases the

Ombudsman's report concluded that '*taking into account all the circum-stances and evidence in this case, it would appear that the use of force was proportionate, within legislation and guidelines necessary to prevent serious injury and in accordance with instructions and training*'.

On 8 April 2003 the Northern Ireland Human Rights Commission (NIHRC) published a report on PBRs. On the following day the NIO Security Minister, Jane Kennedy, issued a statement emphasising that:

'*The Government is very aware of the sensitivities surrounding the use of baton rounds. Our objective is that not a single baton round would need to be fired in public disorder by the police, or the Army acting in support ... With the avail-ability of water cannon this summer, the progressive equipping of police officers with personal incapacitance sprays and the implementation of the community policing programme, the need for baton rounds will be further reduced. The aim would be that the need for baton rounds should be reduced to the point of deployment current in Britain.*

The Chief Constable and the Policing Board have a duty of care for police officers ... On the basis that an acceptable and effective and less lethal alterna-tive is available, the baton round would no longer be used after the end of 2003. In the event that that has not been achieved, the Government would report on the progress of the fourth phase of the research programme and review the options for less lethal alternatives, consulting widely with a range of interested parties including the Chief Constable and the Policing Board.

In close consultation with the Board the Government will progress the urgent developmental work that has been commissioned by the research programme set up to take forward Patten recommendations 69 and 70.'

In May 2003 the Policing Board Chairman received a joint letter from the Directors of the Northern Ireland Children's Law Centre and Save the Children urging the Policing Board to press for a definitive time-table to be attached to the research on an alternative to the baton round, and recommending that the police were instructed not to use them in any circumstances where children and young people were present. In his response the Policing Board Chairman referred to Jane Kennedy's statement of 9 April 2003 and pointed out that, as the use of baton rounds was an operational issue, the Policing Board was not in a position to give instructions to the Chief Constable in respect of how baton rounds were deployed, although the Board could, of course, hold him to account, and in that context received reports from the Ombudsman on the circumstances surrounding each discharge of a round.

On 22 May 2003 the Policing Board's Corporate Policy Committee (to which all Board members were invited) was given a presentation by the Chairman of the Steering Group on Alternatives to Baton Rounds, accompanied by the Independent Assessor of Complaints against the Military.

In June 2003 the Policing Board Chairman responded in a letter to the NIHRC's Chief Commissioner concerning a report on baton rounds which had been prepared on behalf of the Commission. He noted that only one recommendation was specifically directed to the Policing Board:

'We recommend that the Policing Board investigates why the numbers of people arrested in public order incidents are so low and makes appropriate recommendations aimed at redressing this situation and reducing reliance on baton rounds.'

The Chairman's letter noted that this had been raised with the Chief Constable at the Policing Board's *Public Session* in May 2003. Points made in response included that police officers were subject to a far higher degree of violence at public order situations in Northern Ireland than were officers in Great Britain, increased use was being made of CCTV and other techniques to arrest people after the event, and in public order situations priority was placed on Article 2 of the ECHR and that this guided the policing response, primarily towards disengagement of the rioting factions and attempts to place a buffer between them.

However, even topics as serious as public order could occasionally provide amusement. At the *Public Session* of the Policing Board meeting on 2 July 2003 the Chief Constable was asked a question by Ian Paisley Jnr (DUP) about the forthcoming parading season which he prefaced with reference to 1690. Hugh Orde observed that while he had not yet been asked to reinvestigate the Battle of the Boyne, no doubt it would come in the near future.

Assistant Chief Constable Sam Kinkaid noted that the issues surrounding the 2003 parade in the village of Dunloy in North Antrim were an example of how the community's failure to reach an agree-ment on a local parade massively reduced the ability of local police to carry out other tasks – the very tasks that the Policing Board had set them in terms of policing plans. The cost of policing any individual parade could often be exacerbated if the particular organisation chose not to give the PSNI an indication that they would abide by the Parades Commission determination. He added that there was no policing solu-tion to the parades in Dunloy – there could only be a community solution, for which there were successful precedents elsewhere.

In October 2003 the Policing Board issued in the Chairman's name a press release commending the positive and constructive approach taken by the police and community representatives in helping to ensure a peaceful 'Twelfth' and summer period. The Chairman concluded that:

'Whilst the police alone are not responsible for solving all the problems within our communities, through partnership working with the community, real progress can be made.'

At the request of the Policing Board, Dr Neil Jarman had been commissioned in 2003 to carry out research in regard to the dynamics of crowds and public disorder. In January 2004 Dr Jarman briefed the Policing Board on his research, which had been conducted mainly in North Belfast, and presented his report.

The research was intended to address a number of questions, including: What is the make-up of the crowd? Are crowds organised in any way? What causes a peaceful crowd to turn into a disorderly one and what roles do police actions play in precipitating disorder? When and where do riots occur? and What makes the disorder stop? The research was also interested in the number of broader questions about the potential for the control of crowds and reduction of crowd violence, including:

a. What can the police do to reduce the potential for violence and disorder?

b. What improvements could be made in the policing of potential disorderly situations?

c. What is the scope and potential for community-based organisations to reduce the potential for disorder?'

The report noted that the relatively peaceful summer of 2003 was due to a variety of actions and approaches involving a wide range of organisations working at a number of different levels. For example, community networks had mobilised to respond to potential disorder at interfaces; protests over parades were well stewarded; the parades themselves were well marshalled and largely well ordered; and a diverse range of monitoring groups improved communication between the key parties. Crucially,

'The PSNI also played their part in continuing their revisions to their approaches to the management of public order. There was a greater willingness to work in partnership with community-based groups and to share strategies for event management; there was a more sensitive deployment of police officers and vehicles on the ground; and a greater willingness to stand back and let partner groups intervene at potential flashpoint incidents.'

The report noted that, in striving to manage conflict without resort to force, the PSNI had integrated their approach to policing disorder with their community policing strategy by empowering District Commanders and public order commanders on the ground to take a problem-solving approach to potential conflict situations.

The Northern Ireland Police Ombudsman undertook, from 6 August 2004, at the request of the Chief Constable, to investigate every use of CS spray up to the end of that year under the provisions of section 55(4) of the Police (Northern Ireland) Act 1998. A copy of her report on every individual case was supplied to the Policing Board.

The Ombudsman also produced a composite report published in January 2006, which recorded 60 CS spray incidents between 1 July 2004 and 31 December 2004. More than two-thirds of all incidents took place between midnight and 6 a.m., many at the weekend, with half arising in response to public disorder situations. In just under three-quarters of the incidents self-defence was at least one of the reasons given for the spray's use. An arrest was made following the spray's use in 44 incidents. The Police Ombudsman concluded that there was little doubt that the introduction of CS spray had been of benefit in situations that perhaps in the past would have required the officer to draw a firearm or a baton. The use of CS spray as a crowd dispersal tool was inappropriate, she noted, owing to the high possibility of cross-contamination, although its use might be justified where an officer found themselves confronted with a violent person in a public disorder situation. Overall, the report concluded that:

'Despite its relatively recent introduction in Northern Ireland the findings of this report indicate that, with a few exceptions, the use of CS spray has been justified and proportionate given the circumstances prevailing at the time.'

The Chief Constable was regularly probed at Board meetings on individual and overall usage of the spray. He reported to the Chairman in June 2006 that it had been agreed that all PSNI student officers would have to obtain a competence standard in all aspects of Personal Safety Programme training, including CS spray training, in an assessed process.

11.7   The Introduction of the Attenuating Energy Projectile (AEP)

On 26 January 2005 the Chief Constable sent a letter to the Policing Board Chairman referring to the work of the Steering Group on Alternatives to the Baton Round and advising the Board that, following its research programme, a new, safer projectile – the Attenuating Energy Projectile (AEP) – was intended for use by all UK police services as a replacement for the current L21A1 baton round. Subject to further consultation with the Policing Board, and in line with the Government's commitment that the new projectile would be ready for full operational use in summer 2005, the Chief Constable set out his proposed training programme.

A presentation on the AEP was given to the Policing Board at a special meeting on 24 March 2005. The following motion was adopted by a substantial majority of members:

'At its meeting tonight the Board took full cognisance of all the representations made to it. The Board decided to accept the Chief Constable's recommendation in respect of the adoption of the less lethal alternative to the plastic baton round (the Attenuating Energy Projectile), subject to him fully demonstrating that he had consulted with relevant bodies, including the Children's Commissioner.'

In June 2005 the Policing Board subsequently accepted, again by a substantial majority, the Chief Constable's recommendation to introduce the AEP. At the Board's *Public Session* on 2 June the Chief Constable made clear that the new round (the AEP) was a baton round, that it was safer, and that it was less likely to hurt or to commit fatal injury if it was fired. He pointed out that, at that stage, the PSNI had not fired a baton round anywhere in Northern Ireland for nearly three years. Speaking in the same session, the Policing Board Vice-Chairman, Denis Bradley, recalled that some very close friends of his had been injured or killed by baton rounds in their old form or by the rubber bullet that had preceded them. He stressed that it was important that the research should continue, and paid tribute to the foresight of the Patten Commission in this recommendation. Alan McFarland (UUP) stressed that the Policing Board had a duty of care to protect police officers, and that it was logical that the Board should select this less lethal alternative.

The Policing Board were advised that AEPs were not to be used as an indiscriminate means of crowd control or disposal – they were intended to be used against specific individuals to stop them causing serious physical harm to themselves or others. The rules for the issue and use of the equipment were very restrictive. Every specially trained officer issued with AEPs was accompanied by another officer responsible for keeping a record of the circumstances in which they were fired. The guidance stated that the AEP had not been designed for use as a crowd control technology, but was intended as a less lethal option 'in situations where officers are faced with individual aggressors whether such aggressors are acting on their own or as part of a group'. If it was used in a public order situation this must be against clearly identified individuals presenting a threat that must be countered and when other tactical options available were considered inappropriate in the circumstances.

The fifth report of the Steering Group noted that on 21 June 2005 the new AEP had been made operationally available across the United Kingdom, as a safer replacement for the L21A1 baton round. The report set out the very different performance of the AEP, in particular the way in which it attenuated its energy by reducing peak forces, extended the duration of impact, and spread the area of contact. The AEP maintained the accuracy characteristics introduced by the previous round and launch platform and improved sight, which reduced the risk of an inadvertent strike to a vulnerable part of the body. Importantly, medical evaluation had concluded that the risk of serious and life-threatening injury to the head from the AEP would be less than that from the L21A1.

In addition, the report noted that the select number of officers equipped with the new projectile had to demonstrate – and regularly redemonstrate – that they were aware of law, policy, and human rights issues, and could meet high levels of target accuracy and stringent training requirements. The command protocols, training, equipment, and operational guidance being used by the PSNI were in line with those being used in the rest of the UK, and were now recognised as a world-leading model of best practice. The report emphasised that in Northern Ireland the Police Ombudsman would investigate any operational discharge of the AEP before reporting findings to the Policing Board (while, in Great Britain, firings were reported to ACPO).

The first 22 AEPs were fired on 12 July 2005 in the Ardoyne area, and a further 11 were fired on 4 August in Woodvale. A further 486 were fired on 11 and 12 September.

On 16 September 2005 the Policing Board's Human Rights and Professional Standards Committee considered a PSNI General Order setting out guidance for officers on the issue, deployment, and use of AEPs in situations of serious public disorder.

At a meeting on 6 November 2006 Members of the Community and Human Rights Committee of the Policing Board met assembled representatives of relevant bodies for discussion on the use of AEPs where children were involved. (While the PSNI and ACPO guidelines made clear that '*every effort should be made to ensure that children are not put at risk by the firing of an AEP; this is particularly relevant in public order situations where children may be amongst a crowd and be placed in danger should an AEP miss its intended target*', the Northern Ireland Children and Young Persons Commissioner continued to press for a ban on the use of AEPs against children.)

In July 2007 the Policing Board Chairman wrote on behalf of the Human Rights and Professional Standards Committee to the Children's Commissioner for England, inviting his views on the issue. At the Policing Board meeting on 6 September 2007 the Chief Constable was questioned by Sinn Féin Policing Board Members on the point, following a further meeting that had been held with the Northern Ireland Commissioner for Children and Young People. The Chief Constable stated that his concerns were the same as the Commissioner's, but stressed that there had been no deployment of AEPs between September 2005 and the incident that autumn at the Kilcooley estate in Bangor.

The Policing Board continued to monitor the use of AEPs and review the Ombudsman's reports. For example, at its meeting on 8 March 2012 the Board's Human Rights and Professional Standards Committee questioned Assistant Chief Constable Alistair Finlay about the use of AEPs in Northern Ireland (where some 350 had been fired in 2011) and the comparative approach taken by police services in Great Britain in dealing with public disorder. Among other matters, the PSNI were asked to provide information on the latest position regarding the alternatives to AEPs.

11.8   The Introduction of the Taser in Northern Ireland

On 31 January 2006 the PSNI presented to the Policing Board a case for the limited introduction of the Taser through the purchase of 12 Taser units for use on a pilot basis by specialist firearms officers. A key issue discussed was the lack of consultation in Northern Ireland prior to that point. Previously, in March 2005, following extensive trials and medical testing, the Home Secretary had agreed that the Chief Officers of all police forces in England and Wales could make Taser available for authorised firearms officers.

The Policing Board initially consulted a range of organisations, both statutory and voluntary, in spring 2006 and, as a result, requested that the Chief Constable carry out an equality screening exercise and instructed the Board's Human Rights Advisers to consider the human rights implications of introducing Taser. In June 2006 the Board's Human Rights and Professional Standards Committee met the Chief Constable and – while the Board accepted that the introduction of Taser was an operational matter for the Chief Constable – probed him on how he planned to take on board the advice provided by the Board's Human Rights Advisers, the section 75 equality process followed by the PSNI, and the 'capability gap' that had been identified by the

PSNI as the requirement for the introduction of this new equipment. The Northern Ireland Equality Commission recommended that a full equality impact assessment on the introduction of Taser be carried out by the PSNI.

A presentation was made to the Policing Board's Human Rights and Professional Standards Committee on 14 June 2007 on the proposal to introduce the Taser by the Chief Constable and colleagues. Following this meeting the Board Chairman wrote to the Chief Constable setting out the approach that the Policing Board would adopt, including seeking further advice from its own Human Rights Advisers, attending the meeting between the PSNI and the Equality Commission, and placing as much information as possible in the public domain. A full press release was issued after the meeting, together with a copy of the Human Rights Advisers' report to the Policing Board on the introduction of the Taser. It stated that the Committee 'noted the Chief Constable's comments that the introduction of Taser is his responsibility, his desire to be guided and informed by all the human rights considerations, and that the Policing Board was the best place to have the debate and discussion'.

Also in June 2007, the Policing Board's Human Rights Advisers met representatives of ACPO together with the PSNI.

The Chief Constable assured the Policing Board at its meeting on 5 July 2007 that no action would be taken until the PSNI had given a further presentation to the Board's Human Rights and Professional Standards Committee.

On 7 August 2007 the Chief Constable informed the Chairman of the Policing Board that the PSNI Senior Command Team had decided to commence a six-month operational pilot of the Taser in tandem with completion of the equality impact assessment that the PSNI was conducting.

There was a further meeting with the Human Rights and Professional Standards Committee on 12 September 2007, and the Committee sought further information from the PSNI and the Board's Human Rights Advisers before making a recommendation to the Board. On the following day a Policing Board Member, Martina Anderson (Sinn Féin), was interviewed on BBC Radio Foyle setting out her concerns and those of her party. On the same day the Assistant Chief Constable Operational Support wrote to the Equality Commission stating that the PSNI would now conduct a full equality impact assessment on the introduction of Taser as a less lethal option for use by specialist and authorised firearms officers only. The letter advised that the Chief Constable and his senior command team had concluded that an operational pilot of 12 Taser units should commence while this assessment was being completed, although, with the time required for procurement and training, it would be some months before Taser would be operationally available for deployment. The letter noted that the Garda Síochána had been given authorisation to purchase and use Tasers from 3 April 2007.

The Policing Board then discussed the introduction of Taser by the PSNI at its meeting on 4 October 2007, having had an update from its Human Rights Advisers. It was passed by a majority on a without prejudice basis subject to various conditions, which included further discussions between the PSNI, the Policing Board, and the Equality Commission; the ultimate decision being for the Board informed by the results of the PSNI equality impact assessment, with no deployment prior to the completion of that assessment; that the Board's Human Rights Advisers would be consulted and satisfied with regard to the proper legal test for the use of the Taser; the identification of the 'capability gap'; and the policy guidance and training regarding the use of the equipment by PSNI officers. Both the Sinn Féin and SDLP Members on the Board recorded their opposition to any introduction of Taser by the PSNI.

Prior to the Policing Board meeting on 6 December 2007 Board Members were provided with legal opinions from two Counsel on the respective roles of the Board and the Chief Constable, primarily in relation to their respective responsibilities for deciding whether to equip the PSNI with the Taser and for purchasing the equipment. The advice that had been furnished by the Counsel to the Northern Ireland Children and Young Persons Commissioner suggested that the purchase of Taser might well be a decision for the Policing Board, whereas that provided to the Board by Senior Crown Counsel for Northern Ireland took the view that it was for the Chief Constable. A Notice of Motion was submitted to the Board at that meeting from Martina Anderson (Sinn Féin) to the effect that the Board should seek new independent legal advice regarding their statutory obligations under Section 6 of the Police (Northern Ireland) Act 2000. In a show of hands, following discussion, the Motion was lost.

At the *Public Session* of the Policing Board on 6 December 2007, responding to opening remarks by the Chairman, the Chief Constable provided detailed opening comments in relation to Taser. He added that it was a subject that had certainly gripped the Board's imagination and, to a lesser extent, that of the public. He told the Board that on 16 November 2007 he had written to the Secretary of State for Northern Ireland seeking approval to purchase a small number of Taser units (as he was required to, as Taser was a prohibited weapon). When permission was granted he intended to buy 12 Taser units for deployment by the PSNI Specialist Firearms Unit and a small number of training staff. He would not, however, deploy any Taser until he was satisfied on a number of other conditions which the Board had touched on. These included procedures and guidance for use of Taser, compliance with human rights advice, and completion of a two-day course that included human rights and scenario-based training. He stressed that Taser would be deployed in limited circumstances during a pilot phase, to be used only by officers from the Specialist Operations Branch attending at pre-planned events.

The Chief Constable added that there was by this time a wealth of information within the United Kingdom in terms of the deployment and use of Taser (it having been on issue to police services in Great Britain since 2003), and the conditions under which they would be operating in Northern Ireland were '*far more stringent than any other police force in the world*'. Moreover, any PSNI use of Taser would be looked at by the Police Ombudsman certainly during the pilot period, if not longer.

The Chief Constable said that, as the head of the PSNI, he was personally vulnerable about putting an officer in a situation where he or she could probably have used less lethal options than a firearm but had no choice but to use a more lethal option because he had denied them the use of Taser. The PSNI had conducted a comprehensive equality screening exercise on the proposed use of Taser as a less lethal option which had involved writing to 56 different organisations. Following further consultation with the Equality Commission he had taken the decision to undertake a full equality impact assessment on this issue, thus further protracting proceedings.

The Chief Constable then sought to illustrate the 'capability gap', in which the Taser was not available to the police, with real-life examples.

One was a call to the police to deal with a man in possession of a large knife who had already stabbed five people – on that occasion a police officer disarmed the man using his baton, albeit at considerable risk. A second incident followed a 999 call concerning an attack on a house by five men, two of whom were armed with handguns. Police drew their firearms, shouted warnings, fired a warning shot, deployed CS spray unsuccessfully, and were able to arrest only some of the suspects, with the remainder escaping. Taser would have incapacitated an individual more fully than the spray had.

The Chief Constable added that the accountability and oversight arrangements in Northern Ireland would ensure that Taser was used as an option of last resort rather than, as in other places, perhaps as an option of first resort. These included the medical tests that had been undertaken independently, the ACPO Manual of Guidance on Police Use of Firearms, the authority levels for use, the accountability structure under Northern Ireland legislation, accountability under human rights, independent post-incident investigation, and the additional accountability provided by the Policing Board.

The Chief Constable then responded to a number of questions from Policing Board Members. One concern expressed related to the death of Mr De Menezes in London on 22 July 2005: it was noted that human error and system error could have far-reaching consequences. The Chief Constable stressed that the approach taken to the use and deployment of Taser in the United States was *'fundamentally different'* to how the PSNI were going to deploy Taser. He also noted that, had he ignored the advice of other agencies who were expressing concerns about the introduction of the Taser in Northern Ireland, he would have implemented it 18 months previously.

In his concluding remarks in this *Public Session*, the Policing Board Chairman restated that the Board had not reached a view on the use of Taser. It would do so as and when the equality impact assessment was complete, but it recognised that the Chief Constable had made his decision in terms of his operational responsibility.

Operational Procedures and Guidance for the use of Taser were approved at the Chief Constable's Forum on 17 December 2007. All uses of Taser were to be referred to the Police Ombudsman. The training for PSNI officers began in January 2008, and Members of the Board were invited to attend and view it. Deployment began on 25 January 2008.

The Policing Board's Human Rights Advisers updated the Board on 7 February 2008, reporting that they had signed off both the agreement and the legal test for the use of Taser and the capability gap, although there remained concerns in respect of training. Further questions were put to the Chief Constable at that meeting about the deployment of Taser. Certain Board Members commented that the approach being taken by the Chief Constable on the issue was undermining confidence in policing in certain sections of the community.

On 9 April 2008 the Policing Board's Human Rights and Professional Standards Committee met the Northern Ireland Equality Commission chair; the discussion covered the PSNI Taser equality impact assessment then in process. The consultation period ended on 11 April 2008, later than originally reported to the Board.

A Taser was used for the first time by the Garda Síochána (prior to any usage by the PSNI) in early April 2008, during an arrest in Limerick city.

A draft version of the completed equality impact assessment was made available on a confidential basis to the Policing Board on 11 June 2008. The assessment concluded that the introduction of Taser would have differential impact on certain groups. It also referred to alternative courses of action and potential options to mitigate the adverse impact identified if the decision was made to introduce Taser.

The Chief Constable briefed members of the Board's Corporate Policy, Planning and Performance Committee on 19 June, and further discussions were held with the Human Rights and Professional Standards Committee on 27 August.

On 16 August 2008 a Taser was used for the first time in Northern Ireland, in Derry/Londonderry, as officers responded to a man holding his children hostage in the family home.

At the Policing Board meeting on 4 September 2008 the Chief Constable pointed out that the PSNI was the only police service in the United Kingdom that was running a very limited pilot in the use of Taser – all others were able to deploy it more extensively.

The Policing Board Chairman announced in the *Public Session* on 2 October 2008 that at that morning's Board meeting Members had carried the following motion by a majority vote:

'*This Board supports in principle the Chief Constable's decision to permanently issue Taser to Special Operations Branch and to Armed Response Vehicles, subject to completion in respect of the latter, of a satisfactory pilot.'*

The Board Chairman noted for the record that Sinn Féin and one *Independent Member* had recorded their opposition to the motion. The decision had been reached on the back of substantial work that had been completed over many months, ensuring that human rights and legal safeguards had been put in place. (The Human Rights Adviser, Jane Gordon, had advised the Board prior to the meeting that the outstanding concerns in relation to training had been met.)

A number of questions were put to the Chief Constable at this *Public Session*. Ian Paisley Jnr (DUP) observed that the Policing Board were probably *'the most informed police authority in the United Kingdom now on Taser'*. The Chief Constable noted that the evidence showed that, regrettably, Taser had to be routinely deployed against people in heightened situations of tension, quite possibly around domestic violence or mental health issues.

At the *Public Session* of the Board in the following month the Chief Constable reported that he had, after careful consideration of the findings arising from the equality impact assessment, taken the decision to issue Taser on a permanent basis to officers in Armed Response Vehicles (ARV) as well as to those in the Specialist Operations Branch. This followed a suggestion from the Board that the issue to those in ARV should be on a pilot basis, and he was happy to agree to that. ARV officers would undergo exactly the same training on Taser as their Specialist Operations Branch colleagues, and the pilot would run for six months, following which the Chief Constable would report back to the Board.

There was a subsequent challenge by way of an application for judicial review to the decision of the Chief Constable and the Policing Board to introduce the Taser. The application for interim relief prohibiting use of Taser pending the outcome of the judicial review was dismissed. In a judgement given in January 2011 the Lord Chief Justice, Declan Morgan, upheld the conclusions reached by the Chief Constable and the Policing Board and dismissed the application.

11.9   In Conclusion

As was noted at the beginning of this chapter, problems of civil unrest and public disorder are not recent phenomena. However, policing in Northern Ireland has been especially prone to such challenges, particularly in regard to the annual cycle of parades and – in a small minority of cases – associated protests which involve keeping the peace between protagonists. These by their very nature require rather different policing approaches to those that have been the norm in Great Britain during, for example, protests against the Government on some specific issue.

At one level, this chapter is about the parading issue, potential public disorder, and types of equipment introduced for PSNI use in responding to individual or collective violence. But that would be to miss the fundamental point that, particularly in as small and as divided a society as that of Northern Ireland, the approach taken to the policing of such protests and disorder is vastly important. It is critical not just to the outcome of any given disorder situation but for the wider perceptions of sections of the community and the consequent ramifications for confidence in the PSNI, the Policing Board, and the wider processes.

In Northern Ireland the police's actions in any violent situation, whether public disorder or at the individual level, are scrutinised to a far greater degree than in probably any other jurisdiction. The information provided to the Policing Board, especially the comprehensive assessments of their expert Human Rights Advisers, who had unique access to PSNI planning and operations, and the reports of the Police Ombudsman, enabled the Board to hold the Chief Constable directly to account and provide the public with an informed commentary in this important area.

The two Independent Commission recommendations relating to a less lethal alternative to PBRs led to a major research programme initiated in Northern Ireland that had important international collaborative elements (especially in North America) and, along the way, directly influenced the ACPO policy and guidance on public order policing. But that exercise again demonstrated some of the key differences between the policing of public disorder in Northern Ireland and Great Britain. In Belfast, in particular, very often the PSNI are obliged to interpose themselves to maintain a physical distance between two opposing factions, usually showing great restraint when sometimes faced with attacks by petrol and blast bombs, before resorting, when human rights considerations have duly been considered, to the use of public order equipment such as water cannon or AEPs. On the other hand, in London in particular very often the police approach to dealing with threatened disorder is to maintain close physical contact with those who are creating the threat.

One senses, however, that the nature of the challenge posed in Great Britain is changing, as may be the police and the police authorities' response. In spring 2013 the Mayor of London announced that he would be ordering three water cannon for use by the Metropolitan Police. In January 2014 it was reported that ACPO were to ask the Home Secretary to authorise the use of water cannon by any police force in England and Wales to deal with anticipated street protests. Reportedly Chief Constables had also been asked to discuss water cannon with their Police and Crime Commissioners.

References

The Independent Review of Parades and Marches, HMSO, 1997

House of Commons debate 303 (18 December 1997) c.494

General Order 44/2000 – Code of Practice framework for strategy and planning public events; General Order 15/2003 Protest activity on public thoroughfares; General Order 43/2000 relations with the Parades Commission; General Order 12/2004 Use of Tactical Advisers

Crowd behaviour, crowd control and the use of non-lethal weapons, a report published by the Human Effects Advisory Panel of the Applied Research Laboratory at Pennsylvania State University, January 2001

A Research Programme into Alternative Policing Approaches towards the Management of Conflict, Successive Reports of the Steering Group on Alternatives to the Baton Round, with the first published in April 2001

Review of the Parades Commission and Public Processions (NI) Act 1998, Sir George Quigley, 2002

House of Commons Sir George Quigley, Review of the Parades Commission and the Public Processions (NI) Act 1998, Belfast, 2002 NI Affairs Committee, The Parades Commission and Public Processions (NI) Act 1998, HC 172–11, January 2005, Ev 85

Jarman, Neil, *Nothing Happened? A Review of Public Order during the Summer of 2003*

'SDLP Resignation call was "reckless"', *The Sunday Business Post*, 18 July 2004

A Report on the Policing of the Ardoyne Parades, 12 July 2004, Policing Board, 2004

Chief Concerns: Police Management of Mass Demonstrations – identifying issues and successful approaches, published by the US Police Executive Research Forum, 2005

Report on the Policing of the Ardoyne Parades 12 July 2005 and the Whiterock Parade 10 September 2005, Policing Board, 2005

The Parades and Public Processions (NI) Act 1998, House of Commons, Northern Ireland Affairs Committee, 2005

Plastic bullets: a Human Rights perspective, a report produced for British Irish Rights Watch, September 2005

Poole, Robert, 'By the Law or the Sword: Peterloo Revisited', in *History* 91, Issue 302, 2006, pp. 254–76

Demonstrating Respect for Rights? A Human Rights Approach to Policing Protest, House of Lords/House of Commons Joint Committee on Human Rights, March 2009

Adapting to Protest, Nurturing the British Model of Policing, HMIC, 2009

Article by Alan Travis in *The Guardian*, 22 January 2014

CHAPTER TWELVE

Personality Matters

12.1 Sir Ronnie Flanagan

If the words Royal Ulster Constabulary (RUC) ran in anyone's blood-stream, it would have been in Ronnie Flanagan's. How was it that someone who joined the Force in 1970, and who served in some especially challenging roles that called for the utmost commitment to the organisation, became such an effective leader of the change process following the publication of the Report of The Independent Commission On Policing For Northern Ireland?

Sir Ronnie, as he is now, having been knighted in 1998, spent his early years in uniformed and CID disciplines. Promoted to Inspector in 1976, he was transferred to Londonderry and later Strabane, where he experienced Border policing. He also served for a period in the Personnel Department. In 1982 he was appointed to Special Branch and the following year, on promotion to Chief Inspector, he was responsible for the selection, training, and operational control of specialist uniformed anti-terrorist units. After a spell as Superintendent, based in Armagh, and following his subsequent promotion to Chief Superintendent in 1990, he was appointed to the Police Staff College at Bramshill as Police Director of the Senior Command Course, which prepares officers for the Chief Officer rank.

Returning to the RUC in Northern Ireland in 1992, on appointment as Assistant Chief Constable (ACC) he headed the Operations Department. In August 1994 he was appointed Head of Special Branch, the following year becoming Acting Deputy Chief Constable. He was formally appointed Deputy Chief Constable (DCC) in February 1996, taking over Operations in April of that year. It was during 1996 that he led the Fundamental Review of the structure and organisation of the RUC that recommended significant changes, many of which were incorporated into the Independent Commission's Report. On 4 November 1996, aged 46, he took up office as Chief Constable, following Sir Hugh Annesley's retirement. He served in that capacity until 31 March 2002, when he was appointed Her Majesty's Inspector of Constabulary of the London and the East Region. He became Her Majesty's Chief Inspector of Constabulary in 2005. (In July 2010 Sir Ronnie succeeded Lord Condon as the head of the International Cricket Conference's Anti-Corruption and Security Unit.)

In his role as the last RUC and then the first Police Service of Northern Ireland (the Police Service or the PSNI) Chief Constable, Sir Ronnie Flanagan undoubtedly established the future direction of policing in Northern Ireland; subsequently, in his work with the Inspectorate, he did much to help shape the form of policing in Great Britain.

Ronnie Flanagan attracted a much greater degree of personal and professional loyalty among his RUC colleagues than most senior managers ever achieve. His officers knew both that he spoke with the strength of first-hand experience and that his commitment to supporting them was exceptional. Against this background, he was very well placed to lead the change process from the front, both within the RUC and the wider police family and also across the community. Ronnie Flanagan almost always exhibited also a shrewd understanding of the political picture in Northern Ireland, and had considerable communication skills.

An explanation is thus required for the fact that his departure from office at the helm of the new PSNI came earlier than anticipated and in circumstances that were at best unfortunate. The Police Ombudsman's investigation into the 1998 Omagh bombing, which was published early in 2002, undoubtedly played a significant part.

Sir Ronnie had given no prior indication of his planning to stand down as Chief Constable (certainly not to the Chairman of the newly established Policing Board) before the news appeared in the media on 2 November 2001 indicating that he intended to leave the following year. The Belfast Telegraph reported that, while he was 'absolutely committed' to the policing service changes, he planned to leave once the first contingent of officers graduated and started duty with the new service the following spring.

Naturally, the Chief Constable's position was an important item on the agenda for the very first meeting of the Northern Ireland Policing Board (the Policing Board or the Board) on 7 November 2001. He indicated then to the Board that he would shortly advise them of his intention to resign. It was noted that he was obliged to provide three months' notice, but undertook to keep his departure date flexible to facilitate the Board. On 30 November 2001 the Chief Constable wrote formally to the Board Chairman stating his intention to retire and to leave the service in three months' time. The press statement issued in the name of the Policing Board Chairman, also on 30 November, stated that *'Professor Rea has expressed regret at Sir Ronnie's decision'*. The release included confirmation of receipt of the letter from the Chief Constable which was described as coming after *'he had previously reported his intention verbally to the Board as its inaugural meeting earlier this month'*. On the same date the then Secretary of State, Dr John Reid, paid public tribute to Sir Ronnie Flanagan, adding that *'his tremendous qualities of courage and leadership have helped to ensure the successful implementation of major police reform'*.

Informally, Sir Ronnie had indicated to the Policing Board at one point that he was willing to continue to serve until a successor was appointed by them. At the third meeting of the Board, on 12 December 2001, the Chairman reminded Members of the Chief Constable's indication that he would be willing to serve until the Board appointed a successor. There was continuing media speculation on the precise date for his departure into early 2002, with some press reports referring to September, as journalists appreciated that the process to select his successor was unlikely to be practically completed before the summer at the earliest. On 21 February 2002, following a confidential discussion at the sixth meeting of the Policing Board, the Chairman wrote to Sir Ronnie advising him that, having considered all relevant matters, the Board had decided to invite him to remain in post until 31 March 2002, and the Board desired him to use his authority and leadership to ensure full implementation of the Policing Board's recommendations on the Omagh bombing. This timing ensured that, while there would inevitably be a delay in making a substantive appointment of his successor, from his perspective Sir Ronnie's departure would be appropriately recognised.

The Board Chairman recalls telephoning Ronnie Flanagan, as soon as practical after the business had been discussed, to advise him of the Board's decision on this matter, only to be told by the Chief Constable that another Board Member had already told him the outcome of the discussion about half an hour earlier. (This was not the first or last time that the Chairman had to deal with such issues.)

It is worth recording that several of the key elements in the procedural relationship between the Chief Constable and the Policing Board were established in the Board's first dealings with Sir Ronnie Flanagan. This included arrangements for the Chief Constable to have at least a half-hour *Private Session* with Members of the Board prior to the one hour's *Public Session*, and both the written and verbal reports provided by the Chief Constable (and his senior staff) for each monthly meeting. It was agreed from the beginning that the Chief Constable's report would include a section on the progress of the Change Management Programme and a more detailed presentation on one or more particular aspects of that Programme.

The authors of this book asked Sir Ronnie for his recollections of the 1995–96 Fundamental Review and his attitude toward the recommendations of the Independent Commission. He noted that the then Chief Constable of the RUC, Sir Hugh Annesley, had given him a brief in 1995:

'To examine our approach to policing and make recommendations as to how our approach to policing should change, if the "ceasefires" were to hold and if we were then truly to be in an increasingly improving security environment. In fairness to Hugh it was then left to me to define how I would approach this. And thus was born a concept of a Fundamental Review because I wanted it to be a fundamental review of every aspect of activity in which we were engaged ... I arranged, for example, that I would spend night after night, in open forum meetings, throughout the Province.'

He created an 'Operational Inspectorate' from various ranks and parts of the Service against which to test the practicability of the ideas being put forward.

'The results – the ideas – the innovations were truly inspiring. Of course so too were the anxieties, the fears, and the concerns very real and I had to deal with these honestly and "head on". My commitment to them was if they convinced *me these things would not work operationally, that would be the end of it. And lo and behold these people, whom some might have called the dinosaurs – the red necks – the old "this is the way it always has been" people – became the most innovative, the most progressive group of all. Operationally they were brilliant. How they now also proved their openness to change – their dedication to policing and to public service.'*

By the end the exercise had produced almost 200 recommendations, representing a programme of real change. These were 'mapped' against three different security scenarios in terms of how the recommendations could and should be implemented. (They were broadly the same scenarios identified in the Independent Commission's Report.) With the resumption of Provisional Irish Republican Army attacks during 1996 and into 1997, little was done by way of implementation or even publication of the Review findings, Sir Ronnie recalled. He added:

'In the first week of the Patten Commission's existence I handed everything to them, to do with it what they wished. They could ignore it, adapt it or adopt it. In fact the now Lord Patten and some of his Commissioners have been quoted as saying the bulk of their recommendations actually came from our Fundamental Review ... when it ultimately came to implementation of the Independent Commission's Report, I continued with the series of open forums.'

He stressed the importance of communicating effectively – and in two directions – with the Service during this critical period. He put in place other means of communication, including in-Service magazines, videos, and a hotline to counteract the inevitable rumours:

'I truly believe these processes allowed the organisation to embrace the changes. The processes meant that so much of the change was their own.'

The authors asked Sir Ronnie for his views on some of the most sensitive recommendations made by the Independent Commission. He recalled:

'On the question of the title and the crest – let nobody be in any doubt that they meant as much to me as they meant to anyone. But as an organisation (the R.U.C. George Cross) which was no stranger to absorbing pain on behalf

*of others, if these symbols – very dear though they were to us – were actually
"a chill factor" preventing young Catholic men and women coming forward to
join our outstanding organisation in numbers that we had never ever been
able to achieve in the past, then the pain involved in any change to our title
and the crest would be worth enduring for the great gain of attracting many,
many more Catholic colleagues. This was what I truly felt and what I said over
and over again in the media; in my open forum meetings and in communication
news-sheets and videos distributed throughout the organisation.'*

12.2   Colin Cramphorn and the Policing Board's Selection
of the Next Chief Constable

Mr Colin Cramphorn started his police career in Surrey. He was
appointed DCC to Sir Ronnie Flanagan in 1998, when he first came to
Northern Ireland, and served until his appointment as Chief Constable
of West Yorkshire in November 2002. Sadly Mr Cramphorn died from
cancer, at only 50 years old, in December 2006, having tackled some
notable challenges in his new post, and being obliged to retire from
the Service in the autumn of that year. (He was awarded the CBE
posthumously, having accepted the nomination before his death.) Mr
Cramphorn and Sir Ronnie formed a somewhat different double act to
the norm for the division of duties between the two top posts in the
RUC; as DCC, Cramphorn focused particularly on administrative and
financial matters rather than operations.

Mr Cramphorn was able to provide valuable continuity in the
top echelons of the police service in Northern Ireland following Sir
Ronnie's departure on 31 March 2002 until the appointment and
bedding in of his successor, Hugh Orde. It was also the case that there
were two senior RUC ACCs preparing to retire in the first six months
of 2002.

DCC Cramphorn sought to establish ground rules relating to interaction between Board Members and the PSNI in early April 2002.
There had been a number of occasions, and issues, on which *Political
Members* of the Board had attended meetings with the previous Chief
Constable or his chief officers as part of a political party delegation
to discuss specific policing matters. It was clear that – politically –
this was a situation that was likely to recur fairly frequently. One

(unrealistic) option would have been for Board Members to refrain from participating in party delegations on a self-denying basis, while the other, suggested by the Deputy, was that, if they took part, they should notify all the other parties represented on the Board so they could request a similar meeting. He anticipated that this would have the effect of reducing the frequency of such meetings on the assumption that the other parties would then demand equal access. In practice, however, and from the time of Hugh Orde's taking up office, there was not such a stark alternative. Individual parties might, and continued to, include *Political Members* of the Board in their delegations, but by the nature of Northern Ireland such meetings were almost invariably publicised – that was usually, after all, the reason why a political party chose to seek such a meeting – and it was not the case that each of the political parties represented on the Board would seek a meeting at the same time or indeed on the same issue.

DCC Cramphorn was in post in June 2002, at the time of the launch of the Annual Report of the Police Service of Northern Ireland (the Police Service or the PSNI) which accounted for the transition to the PSNI. He spoke then in terms of the Police Service having taken all the pain of the new beginning for policing, but not yet seeing any of the gain, which was the rationale for that new beginning being embraced. This he attributed quite largely to the non-delivery by civic society of the role envisaged for its representatives in the Independent Commission's Report; in other words, not all elected representatives were yet expressing support for the police.

At the end of that summer, following a difficult period of policing interface tensions and public disorder during 2002, DCC Cramphorn took pains to bring to the Board's attention his concerns that the operational capability of the new Police Service was being overstretched by a combination of factors. He pointed to the demands of countering increasing levels of terrorist activity and in particular to the investigative burden in respect of major crime enquiries at a time when large numbers of experienced Detectives of all ranks had by now left the Police Service under the agreed early severance terms. This was, in his view, inevitably impacting on the new Police Service's ability to develop policing with the community.

Other matters that called for early finalisation by the Policing Board – even without Sir Ronnie's announcement of his departure from the most senior post – were the arrangements to be put in place by the Board for filling within the PSNI all future chief officer vacancies – that is, ACC, DCC, and Chief Constable. This was a matter on which the Policing Board recognised that they required guidance from Her Majesty's Inspectorate of Constabulary (HMIC); it was, for most Members of the Board, their first exposure to the professional advisory role provided by the Inspectorate.

Prior to advertising for the vacancy, the newly established Policing Board had to decide the criteria for eligibility. An issue had previously arisen in relation to appointments to ACC in the PSNI in March 2001 as to whether senior officers in the Garda Síochána would be eligible for consideration. The Board had to decide if it was going to continue the approach adopted then in the time of the Police Authority that all candidates having passed the Extended Interview must have attended the Strategic Command Course at Bramshill, the Police College for England and Wales. In its December 2001 meeting, just one month after its formation, the Board decided that, in future, while passing an acceptable Extended Interview would be essential, attendance at this course would be desirable but not essential for ACC posts. This potentially opened the door for applicants from the Garda Síochána, who would not have attended the Bramshill course, though any successful candidate would be required to do so once in post. (Note: it was only after spending considerable time organising an acceptable Extended Interview that the Chairman discovered that the Garda Síochána did not advertise its senior posts; in fairness, they were not clamouring for reciprocity.) However, the Board concluded that it would not change the requirement to have completed the Strategic Command Course in respect of candidates for the Chief Constable position.

The basic requirements for the Chief Constable position were these: applicants must have at least two years' experience at Chief Officer level in a police service with a substantial complement of officers; in addition, candidates must have successfully completed either the Strategic Command Course, the Senior Command Course, or the Strategic Leadership Development Programme, including successful completion of the Extended Interview Process for entrance to these courses or a course deemed by HMIC to be of equivalent standing. The decision on the equivalence of a course was to be made by the Board's Selection Panel. The appointment would be for a fixed term of not

less than four years. The first two duties set out in the job description were working with the Policing Board to implement policing with
the community, and implementing the Programme of Change arising
from the Recommendations of the Independent Commission's Report.
The final two duties referred to the anticipated '*extreme pressures of the
post*' and the requirement to work with the Police Ombudsman and
the Oversight Commissioner.

The post of Chief Constable of the PSNI was advertised on 15
March 2002, with a closing date of 10 April. The Scottish Police College
at Tulliallan provided guidance on aspects of the recruitment process,
including some training for the Board Members on the selection
panel. The Northern Ireland Labour Relations Agency also vetted the
procedures and were satisfied. The process included a number of new
procedures designed to increase confidence in the whole process with
a view to recruiting the best possible candidates for both the Chief
Constable and the ACC posts.

There were three candidates to be interviewed for the post of
Chief Constable – two from within the PSNI, ACCs Alan McQuillan
and Chris Albiston, and Deputy Assistant Commissioner Hugh Orde
from the Metropolitan Police Service. Her Majesty's Inspector of
Constabulary with responsibility for Northern Ireland, Dan Crompton
(later Sir Dan), sat in on the interviews and provided professional
advice, but the decision was taken by the panel set up by the Policing
Board. The process was – as so often in Northern Ireland – widely
reported in the media. The panel consisted of the Board Chairman and
Vice-Chairman, *Political Members* Joe Byrne (Social Democratic and
Labour Party (SDLP)), Fred Cobain (Ulster Unionist Party (UUP)), and
Sammy Wilson (Democratic Unionist Party) and *Independent Members*
Barry Gilligan, Pauline McCabe, and Suneil Sharma. The press
reported that the process included a prior psychometric session at an
assessment centre, followed by an initial presentation and then a one-
hour question-and-answer session. The Policing Board had initially
scheduled a press conference to announce the successful candidate at
6 p.m. on 29 May 2002, but there was considerable discussion among
the panel members as to the respective merits of each candidate.
According to the *Irish Times*, the announcement was further delayed as
the Secretary of State, John Reid, whose consent was required under
the legislation, was uncontactable in transit from Northern Ireland to

London. At 9 p.m., according to the newspaper, it was announced to the assembled journalists that Hugh Orde had been selected, though the two Unionist members of the panel were not then present at the press conference. There was speculation in the press that they had queried Mr Orde's relative youth for the position.

It is reasonable to surmise that there was a difference of approach between the Nationalist and Unionist *Political Members* – the former were hoping to appoint someone from outside Northern Ireland who would not be seen as associated with the RUC, while the latter were keener to have an appointee from within the organisation. Hugh Orde's role in relation to taking forward the Stevens III investigation could also have been a factor in influencing the perception of his potential approach in future.

Separately there were inappropriate leaks to the media relating to the appointment process. That lack of professionalism placed the Board Chairman in a difficult position and, having taken legal advice and with Board backing, he personally met both PSNI candidates individually to apologise on the Board's behalf. Both were gracious in response, privately and publicly. A press release was issued by the Board on 21 June 2002 apologising for the breach of confidentiality.

Mr Hugh Orde took up his post as PSNI Chief Constable on 1 September 2002.

It is right to record here that on 26 January 2007, during an election campaign, the SDLP placed an advertisement in the *Irish News*. In fact, this advertisement was a fuller version of one that had originally been published in an earlier election campaign in November 2002 in which the SDLP had sought to take credit, through its position on the Policing Board, for the ending of the RUC, Ronnie Flanagan, British symbols, and Special Branch. However, the advertisement of January 2007 caused a controversy that lasted somewhat longer. It stated that:

'Against the wishes of Tony Blair and John Reid, we made sure that the Policing Board showed Ronnie Flanagan the door. Against the wishes of Tony Blair and John Reid, we ensured that the Policing Board appointed Hugh Orde – and not a policeman from the old RUC order.'

Following discussion by the Policing Board the Chairman wrote to the SDLP leader, Mark Durkan, on 30 January 2007 asking him to reconsider, publicly withdraw the comments, and apologise to all those involved in the process. The Chairman and then Vice-Chairman, Barry Gilligan, met Mr Durkan on 11 February. This followed an appearance by Mr Durkan on the BBC's *Inside Politics* programme the previous day, in which he had set out the position more fully. He began the interview on the programme by saying the advertisement was a wide-ranging one rebutting a number of specific allegations made by Sinn Féin. He restated his belief that he himself and his party had come under pressure from the quoted politicians in favour of an internal appointment; however, he said that the pressure had been resisted and the party had defended an independent merit-based process. He stressed that the party's representatives on the Policing Board had played their proper, professional role in relation to the panel and the selection of Hugh Orde.

At the time both the unsuccessful candidates indicated publicly that they were considering legal action in respect of the advertisement. The Policing Board conducted a review and concluded that there had been due process in relation to the appointment.

Interestingly, the controversy also brought out in public the role of the Policing Board Chairman in the February 2002 Board meeting, when it had been his casting vote, after the Board tied 9:9, that granted the month's extension in office beyond his three-month statutory notice, to the outgoing Chief Constable Sir Ronnie Flanagan.

12.3   Sir Hugh Orde

Mr Hugh Orde had joined the Metropolitan Police, aged 18, in March 1977. He remained in that Force until his appointment as the PSNI Chief Constable. His early career focused on uniformed territorial policing and included being fast tracked to Inspector. At Superintendent rank he had Support Group (including public order policing) and Divisional uniform command roles. Promoted to Detective Chief Superintendent in September 1994, he took on responsibility for serious and organised crime investigation in south-west London for nearly three years until he attended the Strategic Command Course at the Bramshill Police Staff College. For nine months after that he led the Force level 'Community Safety and Partnership Unit', which included involvement in the Force's response to the Stephen Lawrence inquiry and developing the diversity strategy, before he was appointed as Commander in the south-west London area. In this role he had particular responsibility in Operation Trident for tackling violent drug- and gun-related violence within the black community and for liaising with local representatives. A five-month period acting as Deputy Assistant Commissioner in that team preceded his appointment to the substantive rank and a full time role in relation to historic and highly sensitive investigations in Northern Ireland, usually known as the Stevens III Inquiry, from December 1999; this involved investigations into allegations of collusion between members of the British Security Forces and Loyalist paramilitaries. (He also had some experience on the international front, for example in advising the South African authorities and as a member of the committee of experts at Strasbourg developing a code of police ethics for the Council of Europe.)

Perhaps better even than was seen at the time of Mr Hugh Orde's appointment, these varied experiences, albeit most of them within one very large police force, equipped him well to deal with the task that awaited him in Northern Ireland. Mr Orde had an unusual balance of a down-to-earth approach allied to well-grounded policing skills, and the sophistication required to develop and deliver policing reform in the political atmosphere of Northern Ireland. He understood from the beginning the critical need to engage constructively with the Policing Board in relation to the policing changes. He was also committed to a policy of positive engagement with communities and of admitting frankly when mistakes were inevitably made.

Mr Hugh Orde was very clear from the beginning on the scale of the task, being fond of describing driving the implementation of the Independent Commission's Recommendations and bringing the Service with him while simultaneously meeting the demands of day-to-day policing as being akin to trying to change the engines on an aeroplane while it was flying across the Atlantic. In policing terms, these issues entailed focusing on both the present and the future; they would have been challenging enough for the most experienced senior officer, but Mr Orde additionally had to face a third huge challenge unique to Northern Ireland – the legacy of the past. In structural terms, the creation of the Historical Enquiries Team (HET) to reinvestigate unsolved murders between 1968 and 1998 was largely, and in

terms of the particular shape it took solely, down to him. On top of
all that was the need, found in no other senior policing post in these
islands, to manage the politics – again in three dimensions – of the
past, the present, and the future.

It would have required the wisdom of Solomon for any one individual to have 'called' the politics correctly every time. Moreover, issues
that are raised in the political domain in Northern Ireland can quite
often have personal undertones. During his early months, perhaps
partly as a function of the perceived manner of his appointment, the
new Chief Constable may have felt that he was subject to a degree of
criticism from some Unionist representatives. It is also understandable if he felt that there were individuals within the ranks of the PSNI
who would have preferred a different, local leader, quite apart from the
resistance to radical change and those associated with it that is likely
to be found in some parts of any large organisation. And, of course,
media accounts, perhaps in certain newspapers that have political
alignments, may in Northern Ireland, as elsewhere, choose to quote
certain remarks selectively without recording the full context.

One of Chief Constable Orde's strengths was his willingness to say
things as he saw them. From time to time this could make for a bumpy
ride and land him in controversy. For example, when on a visit with
Sir John Stevens to America in January 2003, still comparatively early
into his appointment, in an address to the National Committee on
American Foreign Policy he was reported to have expressed criticism
of disloyalty among senior officers and a perception that there were
those who wanted him to fail. In a very comprehensive speech setting
out the huge reform task that lay ahead, as well as the progress already
made, he did observe – accurately – that '*there are people who want the
process to fail*'. At the same time, again and rightly, he took the opportunity to press Sinn Féin to take up Membership of the Policing Board,
denying that that was a political statement and pointing, for example,
to the benefits in the recruitment of members of the Catholic/
Nationalist/Republican communities that would follow.

As a result of the reporting, while the Chief Constable was still in
America, the Policing Board Chairman was obliged to issue a release
making clear that it would not be right to prejudge the discussion
Board Members would have with him at the following Board meeting,
which would no doubt include close questioning on the content of his

New York speech. On his return, one Policing Board Member asked in the *Public Session* how many and which of his senior colleagues wished him to fail. The Chief Constable gave a full reply, correcting certain misreporting, but stressing that he believed it was right to describe accurately the range of contacts that he had had with officers within his organisation.

Some other parts of Chief Constable Orde's speech on that occasion are worth quoting. He said that the question he had been asked on most of the days since taking up post was '*why on earth did you go for that job?*' He continued:

'*With my previous experience in Northern Ireland, I could see the beginnings of a new organisation led by the Independent Commission's reforms. I think taking those forward is probably the ultimate challenge in European policing today with a huge prize attached to it. ... I refuse to accept things just because they have always been done that way. I do not accept the phrase "it won't work over here" so frequently used in the context of policing in Northern Ireland and I don't accept the phrase "we're different". We are not most of the time in policing terms. I am very open to new ideas and relationships, not only with yourselves, but with those who have previously been seen as the critics of police, a huge issue in Northern Ireland, moving my people on to engage with those who still do not trust. Personally I believe it is vital to engage with those players and people who are not traditionally seen as friends of the Police Service.*'

Chief Constable Orde's approach was always inclusive, and he fully recognised the role of the Policing Board. For example, at a special internal conference on crime operations in June 2003, which the Chief Constable had set up, he invited the Board Chairman and Vice-Chairman to attend. The discussion moved into the sensitive territory of the future structure of Special Branch and Crime Branch; at this point one of his senior officers drew attention to the presence of those outside the PSNI. Orde's response was simply '*that's the way it's going to be*' – it was typical of his style.

However, in another important regard Chief Constable Orde was similar to his predecessors. He made clear that he was not prepared to put his officers at significant risk as the Service continued to push the boundaries of policing communities where there remained an active terrorist threat. For example, when asked a question about progress towards normalisation, he told a *Public Session* of the Policing Board in June 2006 that

'*I have not made, or given, and will not give any instruction to a District Commander on how he or she patrols. It is their judgement working with their officers and their communities supported by very sophisticated intelligence, so we know what the risks are.*'

He was consistent in his approach towards delegation and devolution within the PSNI. While he considered, almost certainly correctly, that 26 District Command Units were far too many, he made clear that his:

'*commitment was to let my District Commanders decide on their priorities and build on the Policing Board's priorities in consultation with local communities. That is what we have got. There is no central control in a way of how we enforce the law at local level because that is not a way of running this sort of organisation. The headline "Chief Constable loses control" would not be helpful, but the point is we have given control to those who are best placed to make the decisions to protect their communities.*'

One year later, in April 2004, Belfast hosted the 21st International Association of Chiefs of Police (IACP) European Policing Conference. The choice of location was a recognition of the progress made in policing reform in Northern Ireland, the international credibility of the Chief Constable, and no doubt the IACP contacts with the Oversight Commissioner and members of his team. It was a very valuable occasion to showcase what had been achieved thus far in Northern Ireland policing. The conference was closed by Chief Constable Orde and Joseph Polisar, the then IACP President.

The international dimension did take up a good deal of Chief Constable Orde's time. This included not only his own attendance at, for example, FBI courses, but also at more political venues such as the White House and the House of Representatives. He also represented the PSNI at events in Australia, Dubai, and Iraq, the last of which he visited with other Chief Constables to assess the policing situation. Nationally, he was regularly in England as Director of the Police National Assessment Centre and was involved in presentations and discussions about the far-reaching policing reforms being made in

Northern Ireland and how they might be extended to Great Britain, as well as being required to participate in discussions related to the *political* and *peace processes* in Number 10 Downing Street and elsewhere. The Irish dimension, including attendance at a range of fixtures including the All-Ireland football final and GAA matches, was also important.

In 2005 Hugh Orde was knighted.

In 2004, at the initiative of the Policing Board and its Chairman, new arrangements were introduced for performance and development review and performance-related pay objectives for the Chief Constable. In this Northern Ireland led the way, as a year later somewhat similar arrangements were put in place in England and Wales. In liaison with HMIC, this provided for a key role in the appraisal to be made by the Policing Board Chairman in consultation with the Vice-Chairman, which at the end of the year the former brought to the Board's Corporate Policy Committee. Each year's prospective objectives, performance indicators and targets were set and signed up to by the Board Chairman, HMIC, and the Chief Constable. This process provided the Policing Board, through its Chairman, with a very clear role in setting the personal and professional objectives for the Chief Constable in the context of the planning process. For example, it provided the Board with a ready-made vehicle for ensuring that the agreed recommendations in the important Crompton, Blakey, and Stevens reports arising from the Omagh bombing were taken forward. The Chief Constable's objectives also recognised explicitly the importance of working in partnership with external bodies, not just in Northern Ireland. In addition, as the system developed, in part following additional guidance at a national level, the Policing Board Chairman ensured that the Vice-Chairman and the Chairman of each of the Board's committees also had the opportunity to provide input to the assessment. From 2006 the Chief Officer Bonus Scheme was introduced nationally for all Chief Officer ranks, superseding the original arrangements for the Chief Constable.

As Chief Constable Orde made plain on a number of occasions, the PSNI was (and remains) surely the most inspected police service in the world. As is noted in Chapter 17, below, such inspections and oversight undoubtedly place significant resource demands on the organisation under review, and can also skew its performance objectives. The Chief

Constable raised his concerns with the Policing Board and, early in 2006, the Board Chairman chaired a meeting of all the main agencies which then inspected the PSNI, including the National Audit Office, HMIC, the Northern Ireland Office, the Office of the Oversight Commissioner, and the Criminal Justice Inspector Northern Ireland. The meeting culminated in agreement that the Board would coordinate a three-year rolling inspection programme in consultation with the inspection bodies.

On Sunday 1 October 2006 the third National Police Memorial Day service was held at the Waterfront Hall, Belfast – the first time it had been held in Northern Ireland. The purpose of the service was to remember all police officers who have been killed or died while on duty in 175 years of policing across the United Kingdom. More than 2,000 people attended. However, a furore erupted when it emerged that Sir Hugh was participating in a charity half-marathon – the Great North Run – elsewhere at the time. This was when it also came out that his relationship with his wife had broken down. Inevitably in Northern Ireland, there were calls for his departure on moral grounds. The Policing Board Chairman discreetly contacted all the Board Members, who were unanimous in their view that the issue did not affect the individual's fitness to continue doing the policing job.

In February 2007 two articles by newspaper columnists appeared in the *Belfast Telegraph* further commenting on Sir Hugh's personal affairs and raising questions as to whether public funds might have been used inappropriately. In March Sir Hugh asked the independent Chairman of the PSNI Audit Committee to review his diary and expenses over the previous three years and to provide a report to him and to the Chairman of the Policing Board. The review was to identify whether there had been any instances of expenditure of a personal nature being paid for by the PSNI without subsequent refunds being made by the Chief Constable within a reasonable timescale of the expenditure being incurred. While certain elected representatives sought to make political capital out of this, the review, which was carried out by Deloitte, fully exonerated the Chief Constable.

In May 2007 the Policing Board were advised that the Secretary of State, then Peter Hain, had approved the extension of Chief Constable Orde's contract, as the Board had recommended, for up to three years from the conclusion of his then contract on 31 August 2007.

In July 2007 the Chief Constable travelled to Whiterock in West Belfast, where he was publicly photographed shaking Gerry Adams, the Leader of Sinn Féin, by the hand at a meeting with community representatives to discuss a local feud.

In September of that year Sir Hugh gave an extended interview to the BBC, elements of which are worth repeating. He illustrated the progress that had been made by recounting that only two weeks previously he had accompanied local police officers to a District Policing Partnership meeting in Crossmaglen at which around 30 members of the public were present. (He added that that was probably about 25 people more than he would have got at an equivalent public meeting in West London 10 years previously.) He noted that when he had first came to Northern Ireland that would not have been seen as achievable.

He reiterated that 'the Independent Commission's Recommendations are not rocket science'. The Independent Commission's Report provided a good blueprint for policing, much of which could apply in most places in the world, while 50:50, District Policing Partnerships, perhaps, and the Policing Board were bespoke to Northern Ireland. He added that the Oversight Commissioner had probably facilitated the change being made as quickly as it had, although, that said, he would personally have liked to move more quickly. He stressed that no Secretary of State had ever tried to influence him from an operational perspective – they had, however, had to deal with the consequences!

Reflecting on the search in Stormont (see Chapter 15) which had taken place barely a month after his appointment, he said that he had no regrets from a policing point of view that a search had taken place. That said, he had specifically made a statement to say that the police could have conducted the search in a different way which he believed could have taken the heat out of the situation.

Referring to the Policing Board, Sir Hugh said:

'It shouldn't be and never was a cosy relationship. The moment you get comfortable with your police authority or Policing Board … that's a bad day for policing. There has to be a healthy tension, we have to feel obliged to account to them. We have to be able to go there when they want … I've been here five years, I think that in that total time, I've missed two public meetings of the Policing Board, that's how seriously I take it.'

When he was asked how annoyed he had been that, on the day he was appointed, one of the Members of the Policing Board had said that the selection process should have been nullified, with none of those candidates being appointed, Sir Hugh reflected philosophically that it had not annoyed him:

'I actually didn't realise until one of your people, one of the journalists in the room, asked me how I felt given some parties had chosen not to be at the press conference. If you can't cope with that, you shouldn't be Chief frankly. I mean I didn't come here to make friends and win people over in that sense, I came to deliver policing and all I would ask is that people judge us on our performance.'

In relation to performance, he said that he was pleased with the level of crime reduction and the progress in clear-up rates, while recognising that both had further to go. He took the opportunity to renew his criticism of the then criminal justice arrangements, including the fact that there was standard 50% remission of sentences, and the ever-increasing role for police officers in the management of dangerous offenders post-sentence. (This was another topic, particularly when he appeared to suggest in a speech in North America that Northern Ireland judges gave over-lenient sentences, which had got him into hot water with some in Northern Ireland.)

Commenting on the debate three years previously on the future of the Full Time Reserve (see Chapter 9), he said *'the decision was probably the most cathartic day of my career to date'*. There had been anger and resentment – a feeling that he and his Deputy had let people down – but it had been a professional judgement at the time and one he stood by. In relation to recruitment, he reflected that, when he had been in the Metropolitan Police Force, they were getting better and better at recruiting people from minority communities, but they had not been good at retaining them. That could damage the organisation more than recruiting in the first place. Retaining Roman Catholics within the PSNI had not been a problem, he added.

In spring 2008 Sir Hugh was awarded the international Leadership Award from the United States Police Executive Research Forum (PERF). This award is given to an officer who has shown outstanding leadership and vision, and Sir Hugh was the first police chief outside the US who had been honoured in this way. This event again testified to the significance for Northern Ireland of the US links. The letter of award from Chuck Wexler (the PERF Executive Director) gave Sir Hugh praise for leading:

'The Northern Ireland police through what must be the most comprehensive programme of change that any police department in a modern democracy has undergone … It is no exaggeration to say that the police reform process actually led the political reconciliation process in Northern Ireland.'

Reflecting his growing reputation outside Northern Ireland, Sir Hugh was interviewed by *The Guardian* at the end of May 2008. He was quoted as saying that he could not think of one terror campaign in history which had ended without negotiation and that Britain's leaders had to be prepared to *'think the unthinkable'*. He also called for the number of police forces in England or Wales to be cut from 43 to just 9 to fight terrorism more effectively.

The fluctuating threat from dissident republicans is dealt with in Chapter 16. It is, however, worth noting here that Hugh Orde did not shrink from seeking additional support for the PSNI where he felt it was justified. In March 2009 he requested a detachment of the Special Reconnaissance Regiment to supply communications expertise that the PSNI did not have. He stressed this was support of a purely technical nature and that he was *'not doing anything any other Chief Constable would not do'*, according to a newspaper article of 7 March (see References). While Martin McGuinness of Sinn Féin criticised the move, Board Member Basil McCrea, then of the UUP, said that it was an operational matter over which the Board had no remit and that Sir Hugh should have all available resources to this end. The debate proved transient, probably helped by the Chief Constable's transparent approach.

In early summer 2009 Sir Hugh Orde was elected by his peers as President of the Association of Chief Police Officers (ACPO). His departure was announced at the beginning of May. Given the circumstances surrounding the announcement of his appointment, it was interesting to note the tribute paid to him by Ian Paisley Jnr and other Unionist Members of the Board at the first *Public Session* on 7 May following the news of his departure.

1 September 2009 was Sir Hugh Orde's last day in office as Chief Constable of the PSNI. He had been in the post for seven hugely

demanding years; as he said informally to one of the authors at the time of his departure, it was a long time to sustain the role. However, he had demonstrated resilience in spades! (Sir Hugh was re-elected ACPO President in 2013.)

By the time Sir Hugh left the PSNI the composition of the uniformed chief officers was completely different from that in existence when he took up the post. For most of his term, Paul Leighton had provided very valuable continuity as DCC. Paul had returned to Northern Ireland on 31 March 2003; he had previously served as ACC in Northumbria, although he had begun his policing career with the RUC in 1980. (He had been promoted to Superintendent in the RUC in 1994 and had then been seconded to HMIC for some 18 months.) As DCC, he was responsible for internal discipline, progressing the new Police College, and working closely with the Chief Constable in providing overall direction to the PSNI. He was an excellent foil to Sir Hugh, with his thoughtful and measured approach, and drew on extensive knowledge of the RUC and his colleagues in providing unstinting support. He retired from the PSNI at the end of May 2009, being succeeded as DCC by Judith Gillespie. It was, of course, the Policing Board that made the chief officer selection in every case at Assistant, Deputy and Chief Constable levels. In that sense, both the Board and Sir Hugh 'owned' this top team. After all the change of the first couple of years of the Board's existence, the chief officer team was remarkably stable for the following five years or more.

12.4   Matt Baggott

Mr Matt Baggott was selected by the Policing Board to succeed Sir Hugh Orde in September 2009. He had previously been Chief Constable of Leicestershire since December 2002. He spent the first 20 years of his police career with the Metropolitan Police Force. In 1998 he was promoted to ACC in the West Midlands Service, where his responsibilities included diversity and criminal justice; within ACPO he also oversaw national policies on hate crime and local strategic partnerships, before being promoted to DCC in November 2001. He was Vice-President of ACPO from 2004 to 2007 and took a lead in promoting neighbourhood policing.

Matt Baggott also worked with Sir Ronnie Flanagan on the National Review of Policing commissioned by the Home Secretary in 2007. The report was published in February 2008, some months after an interim report. It contained 33 Recommendations that helped set the course for policing change. The first concerned the relative accountabilities for performance and productivity – no doubt reflecting some of the Northern Ireland experience in the key area of accountability. One key Recommendation concerned the roll out of the '*Simple Speedy Summary Justice*' initiative, including integrated prosecution teams, while a group focused on developing effective neighbourhood policing.

In a private discussion with the authors, Chief Constable Baggott provided some personal insights into his approach to policing. In his view policing is about protecting the vulnerable and sustaining the quality of life of the community being policed, and should be inspirational, as well as personal, professional, and protective.

In terms of how policing should be conducted, he emphasised first that public confidence was critical – without that, a police service had no mandate and it would not obtain support from the community across the full spectrum of its work, ranging from minor local issues to the most serious. A single incident mishandled could have a major ripple effect, undermining confidence.

Second, policing had to be evidence-based, with the right resources in the right place doing the right thing. This required a corporate approach based on in-depth analysis of vulnerable areas so that police officers were deployed to deal with the things that mattered. Without standards, policing was artisan, not scientific.

Third, accountability was vital. Policing was conducted today in an age of far greater scrutiny, not least given the size of the policing budget. It was right to have effective performance measures that enabled those to whom a police service was accountable to drill into the expenditure. That said, he believed it was not helpful to have targets for everything – that led to over-regulation.

Fourth, policing had to be businesslike. Managers of a police service had to manage a reducing budget to deliver better outcomes, and he saw that ability as one of the strengths in his application for the PSNI post. The modern skills demanded of policing were about technology, negotiating ability, and understanding that accountability was ever-present. These were very different skills to those traditionally required of police officers and senior ranks in previous years. It was essential to be able to scan the future and its changing demands and plan accordingly, especially where business transformation was required. The challenges that police services faced were ever-changing – those today included cyber-crime and people-trafficking. Traditionally some police chiefs had not been so good at this. It was helpful to think of public confidence as a share price that could go up and down, and he noted that the most recent assessment of public confidence in the PSNI had risen to its highest level yet of 87%.

Chief Constable Baggott paid tribute to the scope of the Independent Commission's Report and the remarkable achievements of the Policing Board, politicians, and his predecessor. He singled out the importance of the 50:50 provision and the role that this had played in creating confidence across the community, and the completion of the policing developments. The working through of the Independent Commission's Report as a whole had transformed the workforce into a high calibre organisation remarkably fast. The approach had included some pragmatism – for example, the use of temporary staff (i.e. the re-recruitment for a period of officers who had taken early retirement) which had later been criticised, but without which such progress would not have been achievable. The changes that had flowed from the Independent Commission had improved the quality of policing and the scrutiny of policing, and had facilitated the devolution of policing and justice. Without in any way diminishing the contribution of those who had served previously, the 'refresh' to the skills of the organisation from the early severance programme and the associated recruitment drive had undoubtedly played a role in giving the PSNI the modern capability that it now possessed. Chief Constable Baggott also paid warm tribute to the calibre of the senior management within the PSNI.

Chief Constable Baggott, as had Sir Hugh Orde, criticised the continuing level of over-regulation, as evidenced, for example, in conflicting reports from the various regulatory bodies. He noted that the PSNI was a truly modern police service, yet it was ironic that the direct experience of some of those in regulatory organisations was of policing in Northern Ireland in earlier times. This issue also manifested itself in the comparative number of external reviews and reports – he had experienced more inspections in six months in the PSNI than he had during his seven years as the Chief Constable of Leicestershire. There was an important distinction to be made between accountability based on outcomes, which was entirely proper, and excessive regulation, which could get in the way of delivering results and developing the organisation further. He cited a particular example: as a result of one recommendation in one external report, in 2009, the PSNI had created no less than 57,000 files in connection with work with children at an additional cost of millions of pounds – a burden that did not apply to any other police service in these islands, and which had taken several years to work through.

He acknowledged that there was a case for targets, but stated that in general they were appropriate only where police service managers had direct control. Such targets included issues such as reduction in incivility complaints, such as in an area such as follow-up contacts with victims of crime. Caution was required, as targets could provide perverse incentives; for example, currently the numbers of reports of previous sexual abuse had risen significantly whereas the logic of a target-setting regime would be to reduce such reports.

The matter of targets was one that was in debate between himself and the Policing Board. Given the Policing Board's role in terms of accountability and target-setting, he wished to have the opportunity for more in-depth discussions on the comparative merits of a range of targets. It was important in his view that credit should be given for demonstrable PSNI successes, which included the best performance outcomes for many years.

Picking up the points he had made about business management, he took the view that it was important that any accountability body should in principle have the expertise and the structures to scrutinise that essential element of the business. He stated that this was an undoubted strength of the Policing Board – the combination of the input from the *Independent Members* alongside the elected representatives. Each provided a balance to the other.

Chief Constable Baggott emphasised that in the policing context it was important to see human rights not as an abstract philosophy but as a decision-making model. The tests of necessity, proportionality, and reasonableness were a great template. This approach had provided the practical guide to handling the flags issue that had arisen in late 2012 and early 2013. It was important to note that the PSNI's approach to this issue had been endorsed by both the United Nations and the Northern Ireland Human Rights Commissioner. While there were those at the time who had been arguing for earlier intervention, he pointed to the fact that some 300 individuals had been brought before the courts subsequently. He was aware of the dangers to police officers and mindful of the need to balance his obligations to them. In terms of the outcome, he noted that no member of the public had been seriously hurt and no significant damage had been done to property in the city centre in what had been a volatile situation.

As Chief Constable of the PSNI, Chief Constable Baggott stated that he was very conscious of the potential ramifications of misuse of force, not just for perceptions of policing in Northern Ireland, but for the wider *peace process*. Issues such as this were particularly emotive in Northern Ireland, and he understood that politicians would often seek to reflect the views of the community that they represented. He observed that one of the distinctive factors about the role as head of the police service in Northern Ireland was the call upon the Chief Constable to meet elected and community representatives on specific issues. (There was also, inevitably, a pressure on Northern Ireland politicians to comment on and get involved with operational policing matters in a way that was not usually the case in Great Britain.)

He noted that the Strategic Review of the PSNI that had been conducted in 2009 had been valuable in challenging ineffective practice. This had provided a basis for a further significant leap towards transferring police officers to the front line through managed services. Business management had provided a means to reduce costs and meet an efficiency target of savings of £130m to be achieved over four years. At the same time, the PSNI had significantly increased its counter-terrorism and public order capability in both technical and human resource terms.

Chief Constable Baggott paid tribute to his predecessor's initiative in setting up the HET, which is covered more fully in Chapter 20. Given the pervasive influence of the past in Northern Ireland, it had been a very imaginative move to balance the Article 2 human rights dimension with the unique politics. That said, there were now major issues of demand and resourcing. Given the role of the HET, it was essential that they had access to the latest policing investigative and forensic skills. This inevitably entailed major demands on the resources of the PSNI's own Major Investigation Teams. Such demands, in turn, conflicted with those stemming from current policing issues such as people-trafficking, international drug-dealing, and the terrorism threat, and indeed individual high priorities such as policing the G8 conference in Loch Erne in June 2013. He referred to the challenging report from HMIC in the summer of 2013, which was critical of the HET's investigations of Army killings.

Since the devolution of policing and criminal justice in 2010 one of the challenges of handling the interaction of politics and business management related to the source of funding for the PSNI. Chief Constable Baggott noted that the funding for the Service's counter-terrorism role came from the Treasury in London and this required a separate negotiation to that concerning the funding of the majority of the PSNI's work.

He suggested that there might be value in reviewing one aspect of the Policing Board's role. The Board did not have precepting powers (that is, the ability to raise a contribution towards the local police service through the domestic rates or other revenue-raising capability). In his experience, in England and Wales (where the power lay with local authorities), this had been a valuable tool, and one that had provided a basis for valuable discussions about local policing and its cost. The Policing Board was very much an accountability mechanism; noting, as had the first Policing Board Chairman, that the policing legislation in Northern Ireland contained no explicit requirement on the Board to support the PSNI, Mr Baggott considered that such an enhancement to its role could constitute an important positive development. It could also counterbalance the inevitable pressure on those Policing Board Members who were elected representatives to seek to get involved in operational policing matters.

Chief Constable Baggott stressed that the relationship between the PSNI and the Garda Síochána was excellent. The two Services cooperated on a partnership basis in both strategic and practical matters.

It was announced on 22 January 2014 that Mr Baggott would not seek an extension in post beyond September 2014.

12.5 George Hamilton

On 29 May 2014, following interviews of three candidates, including Assistant Commissioners from the Garda Síochána and London's Metropolitan Police, the Policing Board chair, Anne Connolly, announced that PSNI ACC George Hamilton would succeed Mr Baggott.

George Hamilton joined the RUC in August 1985, serving in a variety of operational roles. In 1994, on promotion to Inspector, he was seconded to serve in England. From 2002 to 2007 he worked in CID, first as a Detective Chief Inspector and then Detective Superintendent. In 2007, as Chief Superintendent, he was selected as District Commander for South and East Belfast. Two years later he was appointed ACC for Crime and Public Protection in the Strathclyde Police. In December 2011 he returned to the PSNI when he was appointed ACC Criminal Justice, where he instigated a change programme that resulted in the creation of the Service Improvement Department. In June 2013 he was appointed as ACC Rural Region.

He took up his new post on 30 June 2014.

In his remarks to his first meeting of the Policing Board after his appointment, Chief Constable Hamilton stressed that he had joined the police service to keep people safe. Keeping all members of society in Northern Ireland safe would be his top priority. He recognised that how the police delivered safety was vital to increasing confidence in the PSNI – *'While keeping people safe is what we do, policing with the community is how we do it'*, he added.

The Chief Constable also stated that public confidence could not be had without accountability – *'effective accountability must work hand in hand with leadership and responsibility'*. He therefore welcomed the opportunity for the PSNI's Senior Executive Team to engage with the Policing Board and for local Commanders to attend local Policing and Community Safety Partnerships. He concluded *'by reiterating my desire to work in partnership with and be held to account by the Policing Board'*.

12.6   In Conclusion

The period covered by this book has seen four very different Chief Constables at the helm of the PSNI. In any disciplined organisation the personality of the man or woman at the top has a significant influence on its strategic direction. The post of Chief Constable of formerly the RUC and now the PSNI has been and remains undoubtedly one of the most testing in these islands, and indeed internationally. It demands resilience and a sense of perspective.

Each of the four leaders described in this chapter has brought a different balance of character, experience, and communication skills. Each has served their time as Chief Constable in an evolving context, as the *political* and *peace processes* in Northern Ireland have twisted and turned. Those processes have required a further skill set not always found in or associated with operational leaders – a sound political nous. Moreover, Northern Ireland has been unique in having a Policing Board (still finding its feet during part of Sir Ronnie Flanagan's tenure), during Sir Hugh Orde's accession and tenure and latterly with Chief Constable Matt Baggott. The relationship that all three established with the Board and its Members was critical not just in moving the Police Service forward but also in improving policing for the benefit of the whole community.

Sir Ronnie Flanagan played a particularly valuable role at the time of transition. He understood both his own officers and the politics of the situation. He had himself advocated, in the prior Fundamental Review of the RUC, many of the changes set out in the Independent Commission's Report. Without his leadership at that time the intro-duction of the comprehensive reforms set out in the Independent Commission's Report would have been a greater challenge.

Sir Hugh Orde came from a very different policing background, but by the time of his appointment he had already had useful experience of Northern Ireland and its troubled past. While there were inevi-tably many challenges and distractions during his seven-year tenure, he retained a clear focus on implementation of the Independent Commission's Recommendations, especially in key areas such as human rights and district policing. His very public recognition of the accountability role of the Policing Board was both striking and consistent.

Chief Constable Matt Baggott took up post at a time when the agenda was no longer so clearly set by the Independent Commission's Report. He brought first-hand knowledge of neighbourhood and community policing and an appreciation of contemporary business methods that, again, were right for the time and have certainly served the community well.

George Hamilton is the first PSNI officer to be appointed by the Policing Board as the Service's Chief Constable. He brings deep operational knowledge of policing in Northern Ireland, together with experience of policing in neighbouring jurisdictions.

References

Belfast Telegraph, 2 November 2001
Irish Times, 30 May 2002
The Guardian, 30 May 2008
Daily Mirror, Saturday 7 March 2009

CHAPTER THIRTEEN

Police Performance

13.1 Introduction: The Planning Process

A central theme of The Report of The Independent Commission On Policing For Northern Ireland (the Independent Commission) was the accountability framework in which the new police service would operate and the respective roles and responsibilities of the Secretary of State, the Policing Board, and the Chief Constable. Holding the Chief Constable to account was seen as the primary statutory function of the Northern Ireland Policing Board (the Policing Board or Board). The accountability model envisaged by the Independent Commission had the Secretary of State determining long-term objectives and priorities, the Policing Board setting medium-term (3–5 year) objectives, and the Police Service of Northern Ireland (the Police Service or the PSNI)) developing short-term tactical plans to deliver the objectives.

The direction for policing would be formalised in an Annual Policing Plan and the Policing Board would be responsible for monitoring performance against the Plan. The Independent Commission envisaged the Policing Board having an interest in crime trends, public satisfaction with the service provided by the police, and internal workforce issues such as recruitment patterns, equal opportunity performance, and training and development. The Annual Policing Plan is therefore key to establishing priorities, associated performance indicators, and targets for the PSNI. While the legislation makes clear that it is for the Chief Constable to prepare the initial draft, it is the Policing Board's Policing Plan and the Chief Constable's draft can be amended as the Policing Board sees fit.

13.2   Reviewing the Evidence

'Outward Facing Aspects Of Performance'

This chapter will draw on published data to review performance against Policing Plan objectives and will address the limitations of the data in making judgements about the effectiveness of the PSNI. Finally, we will propose some principles to develop performance measurement in future Policing Plans which address some of the limitations associated with current practice.

A wide range of quantitative and qualitative data has been collected over the past 10 years with which to measure the performance of the PSNI against targets set in Policing Plans. Sources include crime statistics routinely collected by the PSNI itself, surveys on perceptions of crime and anti-social behaviour and confidence and satisfaction with the police (commissioned mainly by the Board and the PSNI), reports from inspections by Her Majesty's Inspectorate of Constabulary (HMIC) and the Criminal Justice Inspection Northern Ireland, the annual National Audit Office (NAO), and, subsequent to devolution to the Northern Ireland Assembly of responsibility for policing and justice, the Northern Ireland Audit Office (NIAO). Administrative data are also generated within the PSNI on human resources and finance issues. In addition to the outward facing aspects of performance e.g. crime rates, detections and public confidence, Annual Policing Plans also include indicators which are more internally focused such as the processing of case-work and internal indicators related to workforce issues. This chapter will focus principally on the former although for completeness some key efficiency indicators are addressed in Appendix 13.A.

Trends in Recorded Crime 2001–02 to 2011–12

Statistics on recorded crime are collected and published by the PSNI. The systems used to record crime change over time and this may artificially inflate or deflate the recorded crime statistics. For example, the Integrated Crime Information System (ICIS) replaced a paper-based system of data collection from 1 April 2001 and is believed to have resulted in more low-level crime being captured. ICIS was replaced in April 2007 by the Northern Ireland 'Niche' record management system, which was specifically designed to record and manage 'occurrences'. In addition, the Northern Ireland Crime Survey provides evidence that a considerable volume of crime is not reported to the police, and the proportion not reported is different for different types of crime. For example, in 2010–11 the Northern Ireland Crime Survey demonstrated that, for comparable crimes experienced by victims, only around 44% were reported to the police. Furthermore, while the England and Wales Crime Surveys estimate that there are around 78,000 rapes in an average year, only about 15,670 per year were recorded by the police, of which some 3,850 were classed as detected, leading to court proceedings (*The Times*, 11 January 2013). Recorded crime, therefore, cannot be taken as a reliable measure of the volume of crime in any year.

Policing Plans have tended to focus on different types of crime throughout the life of the Policing Board and the following analysis is therefore restricted to those crime categories which have featured most consistently in Policing Plans over the years.

The number of recorded offences in 2001–02, at 139,786, followed successive significant increases in previous years. While the target set by the Board for 2002–03 was '*to reduce the rate of increase in overall crime*', Table 13.1 shows a further increase of 2% to a new peak of 142,496 recorded crimes in that year. No target for recorded crime was included in the 2003–04 or 2004–05 Policing Plans but a target was reintroduced in 2005–06 (to continue to reduce the number of recorded crimes) and in subsequent years, with either specified percentage reductions or absolute levels (e.g., fewer than 100,000 crimes by 2010–11). While Table 13.1 shows a sustained reduction in recorded crime over the 10-year window, recorded crime still remained above 100,000 in 2010–11. (However, the figures published for 2012–13 show a further drop in recorded crime of 2.9%, bringing the total down to 100,389 (*Belfast Telegraph*, 10 May 2013).) The recorded crime rate per 100,000 of the population in Northern Ireland (2010–11) stood at 5,838, which compares with a rate of 7,572 in England and Wales (Department of Justice Digest August 2012) The reduction in recorded crime in Northern Ireland from 2002–03 to 2011–12 was 26.3%.

Table 13.1   Trends in Police Recorded Crime in Northern Ireland 2001–02 to 2011–12

	2001–02	2002–03	2003–04	2004–05	2005–06	2006–07	2007–08	2008–09	2009–10	2010–11	2011–12
All recorded crimes (000s)	139.8	142.5	127.9	118.1	123.2	122.1	108.5	110.1	109.1	105.0	103.4
Violence against the person	30,038	32,653	32,951	32,814	34,717	35,623	32,986	33,039	33,380	33,033	33,979
Domestic burglary	9,071	10,122	8,943	7,302	7,255	6,831	6,712	7,350	7,269	7,081	6,650
Theft from a vehicle	6,584	7,140	7,506	5,371	4,404	3,994	3,395	3,823	4,018	3,350	3,126
Theft of a vehicle	11,635	8,410	5,369	4,451	3,708	3,367	3,242	2,769	2,743	2,469	2,066
Total vehicle crime	18,219	15,550	12,875	9,822	8,112	7,361	6,637	6,592	6,761	5,819	5,192
Criminal damage	39,967	36,577	32,406	31,433	34,800	36,322	30,893	28,428	26,445	24,996	23,255

Trends in Violence against the Person

Violence against the person includes offences against the person (both with and without injury), sexual offences, and robberies. Recorded crimes in this category increased by more than a quarter between 2001–02 and 2006–07, from 30,038 to 35,623, before settling around 33,000 in subsequent years. A target of reducing the number of violent crimes by 2% in 2006–07 was therefore not achieved, as the number of crimes recorded increased by 2.6%. However, a similar target for a reduction in violent crimes in 2007–08 was comfortably exceeded; the number of such crimes recorded remained relatively stable over the following three years.

Trends in Domestic Burglary

The Policing Board retained a focus on domestic burglary in every Policing Plan between 2002–03 and 2011–12. Concern with domestic burglary was also a recurring theme in consultation with District Policing Partnerships (DPPs) on policing priorities. Targets in most Annual Policing Plans were specified in terms of percentage decreases from a base year of between 2% and 5% with a specific target of fewer than 6,000 burglaries recorded being set in the 2008–11 Policing Plan, to be achieved by end of 2010–11.

While there has been a general downward trend in domestic burglary from just over 10,000 in 2002–03 to 6,650 in 2011–12, the number of recorded domestic burglaries fluctuated from year to year so that Board targets were not consistently met. However, most recent figures, which represent a drop of 34%, are the lowest recorded during the life time of the PSNI.

Trends in Vehicle Crime

The handling of vehicle crime in successive Policing Plans illustrates how performance indicators and targets are revised and reconstituted. Vehicle crime, specifically theft from a vehicle or unauthorised taking of a motor vehicle, featured in Policing Plans between 2002–03 and 2006–07 but not subsequently. Furthermore, while the 2002–03 Policing Plan differentiated between the two categories of vehicle crime, in the following three years, reflecting the Secretary of State's objective to reduce vehicle crime by 10% based on 2001–02 out-turn, the two categories were combined into a single indicator of vehicle crime.

As Table 13.1 demonstrates, there has been a significant and sustained reduction in vehicle thefts over the past 10 years. The reduction of thefts from a vehicle since 2003–04, after successive increases in the previous three years, has also been marked, with the result that targets set for the PSNI in Policing Plans between 2003–04 and 2006–07 were achieved and surpassed.

While vehicle crime no longer featured in Policing Plans after 2006–07, it was not totally removed from public concern. A new offence of aggravated vehicle taking was introduced in 2004 and between 224 and 250 such offences have been recorded over the past three years. These offences, which usually include violence directed towards the car driver and occupants, tend to come in spates and generate intense media interest and public concern.

Trends in Criminal Damage

Criminal damage is an amalgam of various crimes against property and vehicles, including arson. It is a relatively high-volume category of crime, with recorded offences reaching almost 40,000 in 2001–02, fluctuating between 30,000 and 36,000 until 2008–09, and then steadily declining to 23,255 in 2011–12. This represents a reduction of some 42% compared with 2001–02. Targets in relation to reductions in recorded incidents of criminal damage were introduced in the 2007–08 Policing Plan, prompted in part by concerns arising from DPPs, and included in Policing Plans for the following two years. The targets set were achieved and exceeded.

Trends in Race, Homophobic and Sectarian Hate Crime

A review of Policing Plans shows that the Policing Board took an early interest in hate crime, and the 2004–05 Policing Plan contained the following target: *'To monitor the number of incidents of a racist or homophobic nature and to continue to work towards establishing an accurate baseline of racist and homophobic crimes.'* The PSNI applies to all hate crime the definition for racially motivated incidents recommended by the Stephen Lawrence inquiry: '*Any incident which is perceived to be racist by the victim or any other person.*' Not all incidents recorded as having a hate motivation will result in the recording of a crime (User Guide to Police Recorded Crime Statistics, PSNI August 2012). The Policing Plan for 2005–06 had a target to monitor racist and homophobic crimes/incidents and to establish a baseline for the number of religious and sectarian motivated incidents/crimes and incidents/crimes against people with a disability; in addition, the 2005–06 Policing Plan set targets to increase the clearance rates for religious and sectarian motivated crimes and crimes against people with disabilities.

Later Policing Plans (with the exception of 2008–09) focused on improving the clearance rates (not always quantified) for racist, homophobic and sectarian crime, although no target rate was set in respect of homophobic crime in 2006–07. The numbers of recorded crimes with a hate motivation are shown in Table 13.2.

Crimes with a sectarian motivation account for by far the highest proportion of hate motivated crimes, with between 1,000 and 1,500 recorded between 2002–03 and 2009–10; while the numbers dropped below 1,000 in the following two years, they continue to account for more than half of hate motivated crimes. From a peak of 861 recorded racist motivated crimes in 2006–07 there has been a general downward trend in incidents recorded in subsequent years. Homophobic motivated crimes have fluctuated between 112 and 157 between 2004–05 and 2011–12, without any clear trends emerging, while religious/faith motivated crime has declined significantly, from a high of 120 in 2006–07 to as few as 6 in 2011–12.

Trends in Anti-social Behaviour

The 2006–07 Policing Plan identified anti-social behaviour as an emerging area of concern in Northern Ireland. Anti-social behaviour is a collective term for a range of behaviours which adversely affect the quality of life in local neighbourhoods. Anti-social behaviour features prominently and consistently in local community consultations as an issue which the PSNI and other agencies are expected to address. The first substantive target in respect of anti-social behaviour appears in the 2008–09 Policing Plan, and was to reduce the number of anti-social

Table 13.2   Hate Crimes 2004/05 to 2011/12

	2004–05	2005–06	2006–07	2007–08	2008–09	2009–10	2010–11	2011–12
Racially motivated	634	746	861	757	771	712	531	458
Homophobic motivated	151	148	117	114	134	112	157	120
Sectarian motivated	1470	1217	1056	1017	1264	995	885	
Religion/faith motivated	78	120	62	35	15	17	6	

Table 13.3   Recorded Incidents of Anti-social Behaviour 2006–07 to 2011–12

	2006–07	2007–08	2008–09	2009–10	2010–11	2011–12
Anti-social behaviour	100,365	97,548	85,171	80,813	76,947	64,184

behaviour incidents by 15% by 31 March 2011 from the level recorded in the 2006–07 financial year (100,365). The target was significantly surpassed, with a reduction to 78,686 (21%) recorded anti-social behaviour incidents by March 2011 (see Table 13.3). A further sharp drop followed, with 64,184 incidents of anti-social behaviour recorded in 2011–12.

Serious and Organised Crime

The Policing Board, in its first Policing Plan (2002–2005), identified the increasing threat of illegal drugs and organised crime as trends which were expected to influence the future policing environment. Initial targets were framed in terms of increasing the value of illicit drugs seized within Northern Ireland and *'to maintain the number of persons charged/summonsed for supply offences under the Misuse of Drugs Act as a proportion of all those arrested'*. These targets were repeated in the 2003–04 and 2004–05 Policing Plans but were replaced in the 2005–06 Policing Plan with a target of increasing the quantity of Drugs Seized based on 2004–05 performance (defined as monetary value). In 2007–08 and subsequent Policing Plans the focus switched to performance indicators reflecting PSNI success in frustrating, dismantling or disrupting Organised Crime Gangs.

Police performance on these various indicators is shown in Table 13.4, which demonstrates annual increases in drug seizures from 1,781 in 2002–03 to 2,767 in 2005–06, and a 10 percentage point increase in the number charged or summonsed as a proportion of all those arrested for all Drug Offences. The number of drugs seizures increased steeply again from 2007–08, doubling over the 10-year period. In addition (Table 13.5), there was a significant increase in the number of organised crime gangs frustrated, disrupted, or dismantled between 2006–07 and 2011–12.

Road Safety

Road traffic fatalities and serious casualties featured in Policing Plans from 2006–07 to 2011–12 with a general target of reducing the number of people killed or seriously injured year on year in Northern Ireland using 2005–06 data as a baseline. The data (Table 13.6)

Table 13.4   Policing Activity in Relation to Illegal Drugs

	2002–03	2003–04	2004–05	2005–06	2006–07	2007–08	2008–09	2009–10	2010–11	2011–12
All arrests	1295	1574	1356	1440	1726	1896	2014	2250	2435	2534
Charged or summonsed as a % of all arrests	15.4	19.3	22.4	20.2	25.6	*	*	*	*	*
No. of drug seizures	1781	2347	2402	2767	2590	2968	3198	3319	3564	
Value of seizures (£m)	11.1	15.1	9.5	5.5	22.5	7.1	23.3	9.0	9.0	13.2

*Data on charges/summons as % of arrests no longer published.

Table 13.5   Policing Activity in Relation to Organised Crime 2006–07 to 2011–12

	2006–07	2007–08	2008–09	2009–10	2010–11	2011–12
Organised gangs						
Frustrated	6	29	41	70	40	36
Disrupted	4	25	17	25	61	71
Dismantled	2	4	5	7	37	23

present an encouraging picture of progressive reductions in collisions and adult and child fatalities and casualties over the entire 2002–2011 period, although with some fluctuation from year to year. Road deaths in 2011 were 60% of the 2002 level and are now at their lowest level since records began.

The decline in deaths and serious injury on the road is also evident in neighbouring jurisdictions; England and Wales shows a decline in road deaths from an average of 2,816 (2005–2009) to 1,901 in 2011, a reduction of 32%, while the decline in road deaths in Scotland between 2002 and 2011 has been 38%; and in the Republic of Ireland there were 190 fewer deaths in 2011 than in 2002, a reduction of 50%. The PSNI attribute the lower road casualty rate to engineering (both vehicle and roads), education, and enforcement respectively.

Table 13.6   Road Fatalities and Serious Injuries in Northern Ireland 2002–2012

	Collisions	All killed	All seriously injured	Children killed	Children seriously injured	England and Wales all killed	Scotland all killed	Republic of Ireland all killed
2002	6,784	150	1,526	13	181		302	376
2003	6,049	150	1,288	15	156		336	335
2004	5,633	147	1,183	11	140	3,221	308	374
2005	4,947	135	1,073	15	114	3,201	286	396
2006	5,628	126	1,211	9	143	3,172	314	365
2007	5,990	113	1,097	5	101	2,946	281	338
2008	6,223	107	990	7	94	2,538	270	279
2009	6,251	115	1,035	4	116	2,222	216	238
2010	5,666	55	892	2	93	1,850	208	212
2011	5,594	59	825	2	91	1,901	186	186

13.3 Detection Rates

The Policing Board have viewed clearing crime as a basic measure of police performance and have included targets for detection or clearance rates in successive Policing Plans. However, the specific performance indicators employed and how targets are expressed have changed significantly over time, reflecting the changing priorities of the Board. So, in 2003–04, the focus was on detection rates for violent crime, while in the following year an additional series of performance indicators was introduced focusing, inter alia, on motoring offences and illegal drugs. The terrain changed again in 2005–06 to include clearance rates for all crimes, crimes of domestic violence and hate crimes, while, in subsequent years, detections for motoring offences were dropped as new performance indicators and new targets emerged around organised crime.

Despite its popularity as a measure of police effectiveness, the limitations of detection rates are well recognised, in that the denominator can vary independently of the actual volume of crime owing to changing patterns of reporting and recording crime (M. Maguire in Maguire, Morgan and Reiner, *The Oxford Handbook of Criminology*). Furthermore, rates are also affected by the policy approach to detection taken in particular police forces. *The Times* (5 September 2013) reported that the Greater Manchester Police (GMP) actively pursues only about 40% of all reported crimes while the Metropolitan Police 'screen out' around 50% of crimes where the absence of investigative leads, whether forensic, witness, or technical, mean that the investment of resources would be unlikely to result in the perpetrators being detected. In the case of GMP, of the 161,000 crime reports in 2012–2013, about 100,000 were therefore not being actively investigated. Finally, the well-publicised examples of detection rates being manipulated by police officers in Kent in order to meet crime detection targets (*The Times*, 15 November 2012) demonstrate the need for caution in using comparative crime detection rates as a reliable measure of police effectiveness.

The PSNI publication '*Trends in Police Recorded Crime in Northern Ireland*' (July 2012) reports on trends in detection rates between 1998–99 and 2011–12. The data need to be interpreted with caution in the light of a number of administrative and procedural changes over the period, including the introduction of the ICIS within the PSNI for recording crime . This change is considered to have contributed to a 7% drop in detection rates between 2000–01 and 2001–02. In addition, the higher evidential standard required following the establishment of the Public Prosecution Service in 2006 was believed to be responsible for a fall in the overall detection rate from 30.6% in 2005–06 to 23.6% in 2006–07. Furthermore, from April 2007, as a result of the introduction of new rules governing the non-sanction disposals,[1] these can no longer be claimed as detections, which reduced the overall detection rates further, from 23.6% to 20.5% in 2007–08. Finally, the introduction of Discretionary Disposals (see Appendix 13.A.3) for more minor offences in 2011–2012, which are not a recognised Home Office detection method, is estimated by PSNI statisticians to have reduced detection rates by around 3% in that year.

Of the range of detection related performance indicators featuring in Policing Plans from 2003–04 to 2011–12, a number appeared over several years and are worthy of review. These include detection rates for all crimes; domestic burglary; violence against the person; offences against vehicles; criminal damage; hate crimes and drugs offences.

Table 13.7 illustrates the change in detection rates for these offences over the period 2002–03 to 2011–12.

Targets were set for detection rates for all recorded crime for 2005–06 through to 2011–12 (with the exception of 2010–11 when no specific target was included in the Policing Plan). Initial targets related to both sanction and non-sanction detections but, as a result of a Home Office decision not to include non-sanction detections from 2007–08, the data in this and subsequent years relate only to sanction detections. (Non-sanction detections accounted for between 10% and 13% of all detections between 2002–03 and 2005–06). PSNI Statisticians recommend that sanction disposals are used for year-on-year comparisons, as they are less subject to administrative changes. As noted above, the introduction of Discretionary Disposals for minor offences in 2011–12 is likely to have a negative impact on the detection rates for that and subsequent years.

---

[1] Sanction detections occur when the offender receives some formal sanction, such as being charged or summonsed, cautioned or having an offence taken into consideration at court. Non-sanction detections occur when an offence is cleared but where there is no further action.

Table 13.7   Sanction Detection Rates 2002–03 to 2011–12

	2002–03	2003–04	2004–05	2005–06	2006–07	2007–08	2008–09	2009–10	2010–11	2011–12
All Offences	13.0	14.5	15.8	17.4	19.6	20.5	23.0	25.8	27.3	26.3
Domestic Burglary	7.0	8.5	10.4	8.3	10.3	10.0	9.9	10.0	9.7	12.0
Violence Against the Person		20.6	21.7	23.8	26.7					
(including Sexual Offences and Robbery)	22.4	54.1	51.1	53.9	33.2	28.6	32.1	36.0	39.2	36.2
Vehicle Crime	5.7	7.9	8.7	10.0	11.3	11.9	12.9	13.3	15.4	17.2
Criminal Damage	6.3	7.1	7.2	7.5	9.0	9.7	10.7	12.3	12.9	13.3

Sanction detection rates increased consistently year-on-year for 'All offences' from 2002–03 to 2011–12 (Table 13.7), with the rate in the most recent year around twice as high as in 2002–03 and comparable to the total sanction and non-sanction detection rates in 2003–04 and 2004–05. Detections for domestic burglary have hovered around 10% over the past five years. A target of increasing the detection rate for violent crime (defined as violence against the person, sexual offences and robbery) featured in Policing Plans between 2003–04 and 2006–07. The target of a 55% clearance rate for 2003–04 and 2005–06 was not achieved; there was, furthermore, a marked dip in detection rates to just 33% in 2006–07, the last year in which this performance measure was included in Policing Plans. However, detection rates for offences of violence against the person, excluding sexual offences and robbery, have shown a significant increase between 2002–03 and 2011–12, while detections for both vehicle crime and criminal damage have also risen markedly.

Policing Plans have included performance indicators in relation to detection rates for hate motivated crimes since 2005–06. The objective has been to increase detection rates for racist, sectarian and homophobic crimes. However, as Table 13.8 shows, it is difficult to discern any clear patterns from the data. Sanction detection rates for racist motivated crimes have fluctuated between 11% and 16.8%, with a trend towards improved performance over the past three years, while clearance rates for homophobic crimes fell mainly in the 15% to 20% range, with some decline in evidence between 2008–09 and 2011–12. With the exception of 2007–08, the targets set in the Policing Plan for increased detection rates for homophobic crime were not achieved. Sanction detection rates for sectarian hate crimes have been typically between 14% and 17%.

13.4   Benchmarking Performance with Other Jurisdictions

Benchmarking with a Caution...

In addition to reviewing performance over time, it is also useful to benchmark PSNI performance against neighbouring jurisdictions in Great Britain and the Republic of Ireland and with other forces

Table 13.8   Detection Rates for Hate Crimes 2004–05 to 2011–12

	2004–05	2005–06	2006–07	2007–08	2008–09	2009–10	2010–11	2011–12
Crimes which have:								
Racist motivation								
Sanction detection[1] rates	11.0	13.1	11.7	11.4	12.5	16.2	13.4	16.8
All detections	15.9	20.5	13.4	11.4	12.5	16.2	13.4	16.8
Homophobic motivation								
Sanction detection rates	13.2	20.3	15.4	15.8	21.6	18.8	17.5	15.0
All Detections	22.5	32.4	23.1	15.8	21.6	18.8	17.5	15.0
Sectarian motivation								
Sanction detection rates		11.1	14.4	14.4	15.2	16.9	28.8	16.8
All detections	14.4	14.4	16.4	14.4	15.2	16.9	28.8	16.8
Religious motivation								
Sanction detection rates		9	6.7	16.1	11.4	6.7	0.0	16.7
All detections		17.9	7.5	16.1	11.4	6.7	0.0	16.7

[1] Sanction detections occur when the offender receives some formal sanction such as being charged or summonsed, cautioned or having an offence taken into consideration at court.

operating in comparable circumstances. (An example of benchmarking the PSNI with 'Most Similar Forces' in England by Her Majesty's Inspector of Constabulary is reported in this chapter below). However, the severe terrorist threat and the unique public order situation in Northern Ireland, together with differences in legislation, classification, and recording practice, mean that all such comparisons have to be interpreted with caution.

Benchmarking Recorded Crime

Table 13.9 shows that there have been significant reductions in recorded crime in Northern Ireland, England and Wales, and Scotland over the past decade. Decreases have been observed in most categories of recorded crime in these jurisdictions, with the exception of drugs offences, which have almost doubled in Northern Ireland and increased by 60% in England and Wales. Crimes of Violence Against The Person in Northern Ireland and the equivalent in the Republic of Ireland have shown an increase of 4% and 29% respectively, compared with reductions of 12% in England and Wales and 20% in Scotland.

Table 13.9   Changes (%) in Recorded Crime 2002/03 to 2011/12 Northern Ireland, England and Wales, Scotland, and Republic of Ireland 2003–2010

	Northern Ireland	England and Wales	Scotland[1]	Republic of Ireland[2]
All recorded crime	−27.4	−33	−24.8	
Domestic Burglary	−34.3	−54	−38.4	−1.5
Violence Against the Person	+4.0	−12	−20.1	+29
Offences Against Vehicles	−71.2	−60	−69.7	−12.5
Criminal Damage	−36.4	−52	−22.9	+14.3
Drugs Offences	+96.5	+60	−14.1	+112

[1] Excludes 'offences'

[2] The Republic of Ireland does not publish totals

There have been marked drops in domestic burglary, offences against vehicles and criminal damage in Northern Ireland, England and Wales, and Scotland. Changes in the Republic of Ireland have been more modest, with only vehicle crime showing a marked reduction.

The evidence of a reduction in recorded crime is supported by victimisation survey data from crime surveys which calculate the risk of members of the population becoming victims of particular types of crime. The *Digest of Information on the Northern Ireland Criminal Justice System*, Spring 2012, published by the Department of Justice, reports that 12.6% of all households and their adult occupants included in the 2010–11 Northern Ireland Crime Survey were victims of at least one of the crimes included in the survey, the lowest level since the survey was introduced in 1998. The risk of victimisation in Northern Ireland is significantly lower than in England and Wales and Scotland, where the comparable rates respectively were 21.5% and 17.8%. In terms of specific crimes, victimisation rates for domestic burglary were 2.6% in England and Wales, 1.1% in Scotland, and 2.2% in Northern Ireland, while rates for vehicle related theft were 5.4% and 2.5% in England and Wales and Northern Ireland respectively and 2% in Scotland. Finally, 6.1% of households in England and Wales reported being victims of vandalism, compared to 3.7% in Northern Ireland, while Scotland recorded a rate of 7.2%.

There are competing explanations for the observed reductions in crime over the past decade, particularly as criminologists might have predicted increasing levels of crime in a period of recession. Farrell et al. 2008 argue that car crime and burglary are 'debut crimes' and that technological advances which make cars more difficult to steal and homes more secure not only reduce car theft and domestic burglary but may also result in fewer young people embarking on a criminal career. Farrell notes that although in 1996 77% of cars did not have an immobiliser and 60% did not have central locking the respective percentages had reduced to 22% and 12% by 2006. The link between household security and the risk of domestic burglary has been demon-strated by an analysis of data from the British Crime Survey 2009–10 which found that households with 'less than basic' household security measures were six times more likely to have been victims of burglary (5.8%) than households with 'basic' security (0.9%) and ten times more likely than 'households' with 'enhanced' security (0.6%).

Table 13.10   Detection Rates (%) Northern Ireland (2002–03 and 2011–12), England and Wales 2011–12, Scotland 2011–12 and Republic of Ireland 2010

	Northern Ireland 2002–03	Northern Ireland 2011–12	England and Wales 2011–12	Scotland 2011–12	Republic of Ireland 2010
All offences	13.0	26.3	27.1	49	
Domestic Burglary	7.5	12.0	13.0	24	25.5
Violence Against the Person	22.4	36.2	43.5	37	63.2
Offences Against Vehicles	5.7	17.2	10.7	28	15.4
Criminal Damage	6.3	13.3	13.5	25	23.0
Drugs Offences	66.0	76.8	92.3	99	98.6

Benchmarking Detection Rates

Detection rates for all offences in Northern Ireland and England and Wales are similar, although significantly lower than in Scotland (Table 13.10) (though the latter are not directly comparable, principally owing to differences in legislation and classification). Detection rates in Northern Ireland for domestic burglary are also similar to those in England and Wales but only half the rate recorded for Scotland and the Republic of Ireland. While the detection rate for violent crime in Northern Ireland remains lower than in England and Wales and significantly lower than in Scotland or the Republic of Ireland, in contrast the PSNI's detection rates for vehicle related offences are much higher than in England and Wales and more comparable to rates recorded in the other jurisdictions. Detection rates for some categories of offences, such as drug offences, can be influenced by police decisions on enforcement, which results in apparently high detection rates, although there are still notable differences between the four jurisdictions, with detection rates ranging from 77% in the Northern Ireland to 99% in Scotland.

13.5   Public Satisfaction with the Performance of the Police

Overall Levels of Satisfaction as Assessed by Household Surveys

The Policing Board draws on the following two household survey instruments to fulfil its responsibilities under section 3(3)(d) of the Police (Northern Ireland) Act 2000 'to assess the level of public satisfaction with the performance of the police and of District Policing Partnerships (DPPs)':

- the Northern Ireland Omnibus Survey
- the Northern Ireland Crime Survey

The Northern Ireland Omnibus Survey is designed to provide a snapshot of the behaviour, lifestyle, and views of a representative sample of the population of Northern Ireland. The survey results also contribute to the Board's assessment of performance in meeting targets set in the Policing Plan. While the detail of the questions asked has changed throughout the life of the Survey, the content has been sufficiently consistent to draw conclusions about the satisfaction of the Northern Ireland public with various aspects of policing. The Omnibus Survey has normally run twice annually (Spring and Autumn), which provides a useful barometer for in-year changes in public attitudes. However, this is also a limitation in that the results cannot be annualised and may be influenced by high-profile public order events around the time of the survey fieldwork.

The Northern Ireland Crime Survey complements the Omnibus Survey but runs continuously throughout the year and is thus not subject to random events which can affect public attitudes positively or negatively at a point in time. The Northern Ireland Crime Survey reports on a range of criminal justice issues, including victimisation, and also provides an estimate of public confidence in policing and police accountability arrangements (the latter referring to the Policing Board and the Office of the Police Ombudsman for Northern Ireland (OPONI)) using data aggregated from a number of related questions. The estimate is weighted so that the policing questions account for two-thirds of the estimate and the Policing Board and OPONI for one-sixth each. Confidence in policing was a Public Service Agreement performance target in the 2004 Spending Review, with a target to increase the level from a baseline of 73% in 2003–04 (Omnibus Survey estimate) by 3 percentage points by 2007–08. The 2007 Comprehensive Spending Review included a similar performance measure under the 'Making Communities Safer' Public Service Agreement with a target of 79% by 2010, a target which was retained by the Minister of Justice when responsibility for policing and justice was devolved to the Northern Ireland Assembly. The overall confidence rating, following a step increase of 6 percentage points between 2003–04 and 2007–08, remained at around that level over the subsequent three Northern Ireland Crime Surveys, rising to 81% in 2011–12. Key policing measures contributing to the overall confidence measures also demonstrated a similar step change between the 2003–04 baseline and 2007–08. Following some random fluctuation over the next three years, all three measures showed a significant uplift in 2011–12.

As noted above, the then Secretary of State also looked for a 'progressively narrowing of the gap in confidence between the two main communities in Northern Ireland' and the Northern Ireland Crime Survey provides evidence for the extent to which this aim has been achieved. Table 13.11 demonstrates how overall confidence has moved both for the two main identities and also for different age-groups between 2003–04 and 2011–2012. The results from the Northern Ireland Crime Survey show that the overall confidence rating improved for both identities and across the three age groups. While the 'gap in confidence between the two main communities' has closed from 10 percentage points in 2003–04 to between 5 and 6 percentage points, there has been no corresponding convergence in the confidence rating for different age groups: younger people (16–29) continue to express lower levels of confidence than those aged 30–59 years, typically by 4–5 percentage points, while people over 60 years report the highest levels of confidence, rising to 85% in 2011–12.

Table 13.11   Confidence in Policing In Northern Ireland By Religion and Age, 2003-04 to 2010-11[1]

	2003–04[2]	2005	2006–07	2007–08	2008–09	2009–10	2010–11	2011–12
All adults	73	76	75	79	79	79	78	81
Religion								
Catholic	67	70	70	76	76	76	75	78
Protestant	77	79	78	82	82	81	81	83
Age								
16–29		71	72	75	74	77	73	76
30–59		76	74	79	79	79	78	80
60+		79	80	84	84	82	83	85

[1] Results exclude 'Don't knows' and 'Refusals'

[2] The three questions on the police were not included in the 2003–04 Northern Ireland Crime Survey. In turn, these have been sourced from Northern Ireland Statistical and Research Agency's April 2004 NI Omnibus Survey

Table 13.12   Perceptions of Local Policing from the Northern Ireland Crime Survey 2006–07 to 2011–12

	2007–08	2008–09	2009–10	2010–11	2011–12
Confidence in Local Policing[1]	60	60	59	61	66
Engagement	42	41	40	38	40

[1] Percentage who 'Strongly Agree/Tend to Agree' that 'Taking everything into account, I have confidence in the police in this area'

Confidence in Local Policing in Northern Ireland

The Northern Ireland Crime Survey from 2007–08 also reports on *'Confidence in local policing in Northern Ireland'* (see Table 13.12). Performance on this measure was relatively stable between 2007–08 and 2010–11, with around 60% of respondents expressing 'A lot' or 'Some' confidence in local policing, followed by a significant increase to 65.5% in 2011–12. Comparative estimates from the British Crime Survey for 2009–10 provide an estimate of confidence in local policing of 69% for England and Wales.

Respondents were also asked about their confidence in local police and other agencies to work together to tackle anti-social behaviour and other crime issues. A composite measure referred to as *'Engagement'* addresses two issues:

- whether people's views are sought about anti-social behaviour and crime issues that matter in this area
- whether local police and other agencies are dealing with anti-social behaviour and crime issues that matter in this area.

The engagement measure is the average of the two scores. The proportion of respondents who 'Agreed' or 'Agreed Strongly' with these propositions fell by four percentage points between 2007–08 and 2010–11 (from 42% either Agreeing or Strongly Agreeing to 38%) before rising to 40% in 2011–12. This compares with a rate of 49.7% in the British Crime Survey for 2010–11 on a comparable measure (Digest of Information on the Northern Ireland Criminal Justice System Spring 2012). The difference in the two jurisdictions was particularly marked in terms of the proportion of respondents agreeing that local police and other agencies are dealing with anti-social behaviour and other crime issues with 38% so agreeing in Northern Ireland compared to 52% in England and Wales.

Critics of population surveys argue that surveys such as the Northern Ireland Crime Survey fail to uncover pockets of disaffection, particularly in deprived areas of Northern Ireland and in Loyalist and Republican communities. In addition, as Dr John Topping (University of Ulster) noted in his address to the PSNI/NIPB 'Change and Challenge' conference in November 2011, an overall Northern Ireland level analysis can mask significant variations within and between subsets of the population. Topping further argues that insufficient attention has been paid to the process of confidence building as a much wider issue than can be adequately captured in population surveys. This critique emphasises the importance of a more broadly based approach to understanding the drivers of confidence, including the role of civil society structures, and of quantitative methods being complemented by focused qualitative research designed to explore the underlying dynamics of confidence.

Perceptions of Crime and Personal Safety

Finally, the Northern Ireland Crime Survey measures respondents' perception of crime and their own personal safety. This is an important indicator in that public perceptions are frequently at variance with more reliable measures of crime volumes such as officially recorded crime or estimates derived from self-reporting. The Northern Ireland Crime Survey uses three measures to assess perceptions:

- perceptions about crime and personal safety
- perceptions of risk of victimisation
- the effect of crime on quality of life

Comparing the Northern Ireland Crime Survey results for 2003–04 with those for 2011–12 (see Table 13.13 below) shows that the proportion of respondents who are 'Highly worried' about three common

Table 13.13   Perceptions of Crime and Personal Safety

(a) Percentage of respondents 'highly worried' about three crime categories

Crime category	Northern Ireland Crime Survey 2003–04	Northern Ireland Crime Survey 2011–12	Crime Survey England and Wales 2011–12
Violent crime	24	19	14
Burglary	21	15	11
Car crime	20	12	10

(b) Percentage of respondents who think they will be victims of crimes in the coming year

Crime category	Northern Ireland Crime Survey 2006–07	Northern Ireland Crime Survey 2011–12	Crime Survey England and Wales 2011–12
Risk of violent crime	15	9	12
Risk of burglary	18	15	13
Risk of car crime	26	14	18

(c) Percentage who felt fear of crime had an impact on their quality of life

Impact	Northern Ireland Crime Survey 2003–04	Northern Ireland Crime Survey 2011–12	Crime Survey England and Wales 2011–12
Minimal	57	67	70
Moderate	36	27	25
Great effect	6	5	5

crimes has declined significantly over this period. Almost 15% respondents were 'Highly worried' about being the victim of burglary in 2011–12 compared to 1 in 4 in 2003–04. There was a 5 percentage point reduction in respect of worries about violent crime, while the reduction for car theft was 8 percentage points.

Most respondents thought it unlikely that they would fall victim to those crimes in the coming year, with just 9% believing that they might be the victim of a violent crime, while 14% and 15% respectively thought that they might be the victim of burglary or car crime. while these rates are lower than those reported in the 2006–07 Northern Ireland Crime Survey, they are considerably higher than the objective risk of succumbing to these crimes. Northern Ireland respondents perceived themselves to be less at risk than respondents in England and Wales of being victims of car crime or violent crime but at a higher risk of experiencing a burglary.

Finally, there has been a statistically significant increase in the proportion of Northern Ireland respondents who felt that the fear of crime had minimal impact on their quality of life. In addition, those claiming that the fear of crime had a moderate effect on their lives reduced from 36% in 2003–04 to 27% in 2011–12. The results for Northern Ireland are comparable with those for England and Wales, where 70% of respondents claimed that their lives are minimally affected by the fear of crime while 25% stated that it has a moderate effect.

13.8   Her Majesty's Inspector of Constabulary (HMIC) Best Value Studies

Section 28 in Part V of the Police Act (Northern Ireland) 2000 requires the Policing Board to '*make arrangements to secure continuous improvement in the way in which its functions, and those of the Chief Constable, are exercised, having regard to a combination of economy, efficiency and effectiveness*'. In addition to the administrative and survey data generated by the PSNI and the Policing Board, the HMIC is required under the provisions of the Act to carry out an annual inspection of the PSNI. In some cases inspections have been conducted with other statutory bodies, such as the NAO. While the HMIC is independent of both the Policing Board and the PSNI, in practice there is consultation with both bodies to ensure that Northern Ireland's policing priorities are appropriately reflected in the Inspection Programme. Successive inspections have focused on a range of areas of PSNI activity and have made recommendations the implementation of which have been reviewed by HMIC and monitored by the Policing Board.

In response to significant policy shifts, including the Government's modernisation agenda for the public sector, the National Policing Plan, and the HMIC Police Performance Assessment Framework, HMIC introduced a Baseline Assessment approach in the 2003 Inspection (reported in 2004). The Baseline Assessment was intended to provide a strategic overview of police forces/service and in particular to identify strengths and areas for improvement. The Inspection reviewed three broad areas – Operational Performance; Leadership and Corporate Governance and Partnership and Community Engagement. Key features of the Baseline Assessment were:

- *assessment was structured around frameworks of issues/core questions, with descriptions of good performance;*

- *more use was made of self-assessment and the views of other regulators and partners; and*

- *a tailored programme of inspection activity for each police force, driven by the assessment but integrated with each Force's strategic development plan.*

(HMIC Baseline Assessment of the PSNI April 2004)

The 2005 Inspection moved to a 'Domain' approach which had been developed in the context of HMIC experience in England and Wales. A further development was the identification of most similar forces among police authorities in England. While the unique public order and security situation limited the value of benchmarking with police forces in Great Britain, a number of general conclusions can be drawn from this work:

- Northern Ireland has comparatively lower levels of most categories of recorded crime than most similar forces

- levels of satisfaction with the police as assessed by the British Crime Survey in England and Wales and the Northern Ireland Crime Survey tend to be higher here, although England and Wales respondents expressed greater satisfaction levels with local police than is found in Northern Ireland

- detection rates have been historically lower in Northern Ireland, although the gap has narrowed considerably in recent years

HMIC have also carried out a wide range of thematic inspections, including reviews of Performance Management, Roads Policing and Transport, the Role of the Board In Holding The PSNI To Account (undertaken by KPMG), Protecting Vulnerable People (also undertaken by KPMG), the Use of Firearms, and the Capacity Of The PSNI To Respond To Serious and Organised Crime.

13.9   Performance

In Summary

An overview of crime statistics and other administrative and survey data relating to policing in Northern Ireland paints a picture of a range of changes over the past ten years which reflect the ambitions of the Independent Commission On Policing For Northern Ireland.

Significant downward trends in all offences recorded by the police, domestic burglaries, car crime, and criminal damage are consistent with trends elsewhere in the United Kingdom, while detection rates, a frequently used if somewhat limited measure of police performance, have in general trended upwards. While there has been some convergence with detection rates in England and Wales, the picture is not consistent across all categories of crime. Comparisons with performance in Scotland and the Republic of Ireland are more problematic because of the different systems of criminal justice in these jurisdictions. The PSNI have also recorded major successes in the area of serious and organised crime through the frustration, disruption, and dismantling of criminal gangs. Finally, the number of people killed or seriously injured on the roads has improved dramatically over the past 10 years, with 91 fewer road deaths in 2011 than in 2002 and 634 fewer seriously injured. Child road fatalities also declined from 13 deaths in 2002 to just two in 2011, with serious injuries down by a half.

There has also been an increase in public confidence in the police and associated arrangements, with 81% expressing confidence in 2010–11 compared with 73% in 2003–04. Furthermore, the *'confidence gap'* as between the two largest identities narrowed significantly over the same period. (However, as noted above, relying solely on social surveys on their own to measure confidence is unlikely to provide a sufficiently comprehensive assessment of public confidence in the police.) The lower prevalence of crime as measured both by crimes recorded by the police and through self-report surveys was reflected in the public's perception of crime and its impact on their lives. The proportion of the survey respondents who were 'Highly worried' about three high volume crime categories – burglary, violent crime, and car crime – has declined; people perceive themselves as being at a lower risk of being the victim of one of these crimes; and an increasing number of respondents reported that fear of crime had no more than a minimal impact on their quality of life. Significantly, however, the public are much less satisfied with the performance of the PSNI and other agencies in dealing effectively with anti-social behaviour.

The PSNI are required to have in place a programme of continuous improvement, and a review of the efficiency issues which the Policing Board selected for inclusion in Policing Plans demonstrated improvements in case-processing targets (although recent reports from the Criminal Justice Inspectorate suggest there is still some way to go in what is a wider issue for criminal justice agencies); improvements in sick absence for both uniformed and civilian staff; the transfer of in excess of 600 officers from back office to frontline duties; and officers on operational duties spending a greater proportion of their shift away from their station as a result of increased deployment of modern communications technology.

Finally, a Criminal Justice Inspection Northern Ireland report published in 2011 on Customer Service concluded that customer service was taken seriously by PSNI senior management, driven by the Chief Constable's strategic intent for the organisation to deliver *'personal, professional, protective policing'*. The commitment was underpinned by a number of projects to enhance public confidence under the Policing with the Community initiative using the Confidence Route Map[2] which was developed to assist police forces in England and Wales to deliver against their Public Service Agreement public confidence target. However, the Criminal Justice Inspection noted that, at the time of the Inspection, *'personal, professional, protective'* policing

---

[2] The Confidence Route Map sets out five linked themes of public confidence, which are: (a) to tackle anti-social behaviour; (b) to drive effective partnerships; (c) to deliver a high-quality local service; (d) to develop an empowered, engaged, confident team; and (e) to work with, and for, the public.

was not fully and consistently understood at local level and made a number of recommendations to ensure more effective implementation of the strategy.

Interpreting PSNI Performance

Establishing and interpreting performance measures for any public sector organisation poses particular challenges, and measuring the performance of the police service is no exception. The challenges include the complexity of the policing environment, identifying relevant and appropriate performance indicators and associated targets and isolating the unique contribution of policing to achieving the targets. Policing is conducted in the context of rapid demographic, social, economic, technological, and political change, which can have significant implications for the services required from all the criminal justice agencies.

The scale and range of responsibilities discharged by the PSNI make it very difficult to capture performance in a manageable number of numerical targets. Any suite of performance measures will therefore result from a process of selection of those aspects of the Police Service on which the spotlight will fall. This makes the process of selection itself worthy of examination.

For the PSNI that process includes the long-term policing objectives formerly set by the Northern Ireland Secretary of State and currently by the Minister of Justice. The Secretary of State's initial objectives were expressed in terms of working in partnership with others to reduce the incidence of crime, including organised crime, and to diminish the fear of crime, upholding and maintaining the rule of law and building and maintaining confidence in the police service and police accountability arrangements, and increasing Catholic representation in the police. In February 2012 the Minister of Justice outlined five long-term objectives for policing over the next 10 years which emphasised:

- the protection and vindication of human rights
- policing with the community such as to provide '*an effective, accessible and accountable policing presence*' which would increase public confidence in the police

- effective partnerships with the statutory, voluntary, and private partners
- the role of policing in building a more inclusive and cohesive society
- to be demonstrably independent, answerable to the community through the Northern Ireland Policing Board and the Policing and Community Safety Partnerships, which have succeeded District Policing Partnerships

The Policing Board also takes account of the views of the Policing and Community Safety Partnerships and the public on policing priorities. These feed into consultations with the PSNI through annual strategic planning workshops from which performance indicators and targets for the Policing Plan emerge. The strength of the collaborative approach to setting targets for the PSNI is that annual Policing Plans reflect the priorities of the Minister, the Board, the PSNI, and the public and are sensitive to the changing policing landscape. However, this is often at the expense of consistency, with the result that performance indicators change from year to year as new priorities emerge. The terminology in which performance indicators and targets are couched is also subject to periodic change and refinement, which complicates the interpretation of trends.

A review of Part 2 of the Policing Plans between 2002–03 and 2011–12 reveals the evolution of the 'packaging' of performance indicators over the life of the Policing Board. (While Policing Plans are published as three-year Plans, in practice the focus is usually on Year 1, and performance indicators and targets rarely span the full three years.) As the 2009–12 Policing Plan notes, performance indicators may be removed from the Plan when they are no longer considered strategic or relevant policing priorities, or where recent performance is such that the Board does not see the need for continued scrutiny in that year. Indeed, in some cases crime (e.g. car crime) continued on a downward trajectory after being removed from the Plan as a performance indicator. The terminology used to describe performance indicators and targets has evolved over time, which also contributes to the difficulty of building up trend data. This is illustrated in Appendix 13.B, which lists the performance indicator descriptors used in three recent Policing Plans.

In reports published in September 2013 and May 2014 the NIAO was critical of the lack of precise targets in Policing Plans, which the Comptroller and Auditor General considered diminished the effectiveness of the Policing Board's scrutiny of police performance. In addition, the NIAO report commented on the difficulty of discerning trends in performance as a result of the lack of year to year continuity in the measures which are used.

Not all performance indicators lend themselves to SMART (Specific, Measurable, Achievable, Realistic, Time-bounded) targets and this is reflected in a range of approaches being adopted throughout Plans. The use of milestone targets is not uncommon and where numerical targets are employed, the NIAO report comments that they are frequently in the form of 'to increase X' or 'to decrease Y' without the specific extent of change being quantified. Policing outcomes are of course affected by a range of factors, with the most important often being outside the control of the police. Furthermore, it is rarely possible to draw a simple cause and effect link between actions or initiatives taken by the police and the specific performance indicator they are expected to influence. It follows that any attribution of changes in performance (positive or negative) to the action taken by the police is problematic.

A relevant example is car crime where there has been a sharp decline both in vehicle theft and in theft from vehicles over the past 10 years. This decline is evident throughout the United Kingdom and the Republic of Ireland despite the fact that car ownership has increased. Clearly the main factor in the decline has been 'target hardening' – the technological advances in car security and improved surveillance in car parks rather than directly attributable to police action. That is not to ignore the advocacy role the police will have exercised in promoting car security both to manufacturers and the public. There is also an argument that reductions in car thefts have contributed to the observed decrease in Domestic Burglaries which are often dependent on the perpetrator being mobile. The reduction in recorded crimes of domestic burglary, an offence with a low rate of detection, has similarly been in part due to enhanced household security, including the installation of burglar alarms and the provision of crime prevention advice on basic security measures. In addition, it is probable that a policy of closely monitoring repetitive offenders deployed in many police forces can have an impact on more than one category of crime. Demographic change may also have a part to play in explaining a lowering in recorded crime over the past decade with a decline in the size of the young adult age group which has the highest risk of offending.

It is evident from the above observations that changes in most of the performance indicators and targets in Policing Plans cannot in themselves provide a reliable assessment of the performance of the PSNI. This is frequently acknowledged by Senior Officers who note the multiple factors outside the control of the police which contribute to criminal or anti-social behaviour. In addition, much of the work of the police in areas such as policing with the community or surveillance may produce only medium to long-term benefits and are not amenable to short-term measurement.

Alternative Approaches to Performance Management

Reiner in *The Politics of the Police* (2000) notes that police work is more complex, contradictory, and, indeed, confused than current theories of policing allow and comments that '*the police operate not mainly as crime-fighters or law enforcers but rather as providers of a range of services to members of the public, the variety of which beggars description*'. An Activity Based Costing exercise undertaken by HMIC to predict manpower needs demonstrated the significant time spent by the PSNI on non-crime incidents. The study estimated that around 60% of police time was allocated to reducing or investigating crime with the remaining 40% spent on providing assistance with non-crime incidents, attending at road traffic incidents, providing public reassurance and policing special events.

This illustrates the challenge of finding appropriate performance indicators and targets against which to assess the performance of the police. The situation in Northern Ireland is undoubtedly exacerbated by the challenging environment in which policing services are frequently delivered.

Notwithstanding these additional constraints, the current arrangements for assessing the PSNI's performance are confounded by the lack of consistent application of performance indicators and targets over a sustained period. While Policing Plans are published as three-year documents, in practice the focus has tended to be on agreeing performance indicators and targets for the initial year. These have changed, sometimes significantly, from year to year. An alternative approach would be to link a three- or four-year Corporate Plan to the relevant Budget or Spending Review with a core of key performance indicators linked to and monitored over the period of the corporate plan.

Annual Policing Plans would continue to be produced and would retain a focus on the small number of objectives and key performance indicators linked to both the Corporate Plan and the budget. The policing objectives and associated performance indicators would, as envisaged by the Independent Commission, be informed by the Minister of Justice's long term objectives for policing, the Board's priorities and the evidence emerging from Police and Community Safety Partnerships. There would, of course, be scope to respond to new pressures within the life of the Corporate Plan, but these would not displace the key priorities unless there was a strong case for them to do so.

A further difficulty with current arrangements is the absence of a model which explicitly links activities to performance measures and targets. The requirement for organisations, both statutory and voluntary, which deliver public services to demonstrate that they do so effectively and efficiently has led to the development of an array of models of performance management and measurement. These have developed out of a recognition of the need to set performance in a framework and in the wider social, economic, political, and environmental context in which services are delivered. Not all models are equally applicable to all situations but there are two generic performance frameworks which may have relevance to measurement performance in the PSNI. The first is the *Outcome Based Accountability* framework developed by Mark Friedman (Friedman 2005); the second is the Logic Model, which is a widely used evaluation tool one variant of which is described in the Canadian Government's *'Supporting Effective Evaluations – a Guide to Developing Performance Strategies'* publication (www.tbs-sct.gc.ca).

Friedman's *Outcome Based Accountability* framework distinguishes between two levels of accountability – Population accountability, which is concerned with high level population outcomes and indicators such as improvements in child health and making communities safer; and Performance accountability, which focuses on the delivery of services or programmes, such as improvements in literacy and reducing reoffending. Performance measures, therefore, become the means of assessing progress towards the desired population outcomes.

(A fuller description of the *Outcome Based Accountability* framework is outlined in Appendix 13.C.)

An alternative framework for performance management is provided by the Logic Model, which is informed by the Theory of Change. The Theory of Change is described as:

'*A set of assumptions, risks, and external factors that describes how and why the programme is intended to work. This theory connects a programme's activities with its goals. It is inherent in the programme design and is often based on knowledge and experience of the programme, research, evaluations of best practices and lessons learned.*'

(www.tbs-sct.gc.ca; also see Appendix 13.D).

13.9   In Conclusion

Policing in Northern Ireland has changed radically as a result of the reforms arising from the Report of The Independent Commission On Policing For Northern Ireland. The policing environment continues to be particularly challenging and the aspirations for implementing community policing across Northern Ireland as envisaged by the Independent Commission and promoted by the Policing Board and the Chief Constable in successive Policing Plans remain to be realised. While the available evidence demonstrates many positive developments since the establishment of the PSNI in 2001, systematically assessing the performance of the Police Service is complicated by a lack of consistency in the annual performance indicators and targets set in Policing Plans. This is the inevitable result of the Policing Plan attempting to reflect the priorities of a range of stakeholders and the frequently short-term nature of targets. As in most public services, there are few unambiguous measures of performance which can comprehensively account for the unique contribution which the Police Service makes. Policing takes place in a social, economic, and political context which can exert a greater influence on crime, criminality, and anti-social behaviour than the activities of the Police or the wider criminal justice system. However, there is value in scrutinising trend data and benchmarking with comparable organisations, as demonstrated by the HMIC investigations, and there are clearly areas where a more consistent application of performance measurement would be beneficial. The monitoring of confidence has rightly occupied a central place in discussions about PSNI performance and the annual population surveys have been a staple part of this process. The limitations of aggregate data are increasingly recognised and an early imperative would be the introduction of more sophisticated analytical techniques to better understand and evaluate the dynamics of this key dimension of policing. Some models are proposed which would provide a more robust basis for identifying performance indicators and targets and which, if applied over a sustained period and linked with Comprehensive Spending Reviews, would provide a more systematic approach to assessing police performance.

References

Anti-social Behaviour Statistics www.psni.police.uk/directory/updates_statistics/updates_anti-social_behaviour_statistics.htm

'Province's crime rate now at 15-year low', *Belfast Telegraph*, 10 May 2013

Best Value Studies www.nipolicingboard.org.uk/index/publications/content-bvr.htm

Case Processing Criminal Justice Inspectorate www.cjini.org/The inspections/Inspection-Reports/

Consumer Survey Criminal Justice Inspectorate www.cjini.org/Theinspections/Inspection-Reports/

Crime in England and Wales www.statistics.gov.uk

Crime in England and Wales 2009/10 Findings from the British Crime Survey and police recorded crime

Flatley, John, Kershaw, Chris, Smith, Kevin, Chaplin, Rupert and Moon, Debbie (eds), *Digest of Information on the Northern Ireland Criminal Justice System* (Spring 2012) www.dojni.gov.uk

Friedman, Mark, *Outcome Based Accountability (Trying Hard is Not Good Enough)*, Trafford Publishing, 2005

Garda Recorded Crime Statistics www.garda.ie/

Long Term Policing Objectives February 2012 www.dojni.gov.uk/index/media-centre

Maguire, Mike, Rod Morgan and Robert Reiner (eds) *The Oxford Handbook of Criminology*, 5th edition, Oxford University Press, 2012

Northern Ireland Audit Office, *Review of Continuous Improvements in Policing*, September 2013

Northern Ireland Audit Office, *Continuous Improvements in Policing Arrangements*, May 2014

Northern Ireland Crime Survey www.dojni.gov.uk/index/statistics... northern-ireland-crime-survey-s-r.htm

Northern Ireland Omnibus Survey www.nipolicingboard.org.uk/index/publications/omnibus-surveys.htm

Northern Ireland Policing Board Annual Reports and Accounts www.nipolicingboard.org.uk/index/publications/annual-rports.htm

Policing Board's submission of September 2004 to the Northern Ireland Affairs Committee

Policing Plans: The Northern Ireland Policing Board and the Police Service of Northern Ireland www.nipolicingboard.org.uk/index/publications/policing-plans.htm

Recorded Crime in Scotland Annual Reports www.scotland.gov.uk/stats

Reiner, Robert, *The Politics of the Police*, Oxford University Press, Oxford, 2000

Road Traffic Statistics www.psni.police.uk/directory/updates_road_traffic_statistics.htm

Scottish Crime and Justice Survey www.scotland.gov.uk/publications/

Supporting Effective Evaluations – a Guide to Developing Performance Strategies (www.tbs-sct.gc.ca).

Farrell, Graham, Tilley, Nick, Tseloni, Andromachi and Mailley, Jen, *The Crime Drop and the Security Hypothesis*, British Society of Criminology Newsletter, No. 62, Winter 2008

'Five police held over "false crime statistics"', *The Times*, 15 November 2012

'Scale of rape revealed in national crime survey', *The Times*, 11 January 2013

'Sixty per cent of crimes are not investigated, admits police chief', *The Times*, 5 September 2013

Trends in Domestic Abuse and Hate Motivation Statistics 2004–05 PSNI July 2012 www.psni.police.uk/directory/updates_domestic_and_hate_motivation_statistics.htm

Trends in Police Recorded Crime in Northern Ireland 1998/99 to 2011/12, Annual Bulletin published by the PSNI, 5 July 2012

User Guide to Recorded Crime Statistics in Northern Ireland (PSNI August 2012) www.psni.police.uk/directory/updates_statistics/updates_crime_statistics.htm

Appendix 13.A: Inward-facing (Efficiency) Indicators

13.A.1   Case Processing

The time taken to process cases within the criminal justice system has been the subject of two reports by the Criminal Justice Inspection Northern Ireland (2006 and 2010). As the police are a significant link in the chain it is not surprising that the Policing Board have set targets and monitored PSNI performance in terms of case processing. As Table 13.14 shows, performance has improved significantly from when monitoring was first introduced and administrative time limits were achieved in respect of custody cases between 2006–07 and 2009–10, the last year when such targets were set, and for bail cases from 2007–08 to 2009–10. Additional targets were set for processing indictable and summary cases between 2007–08 and 2009–10, with mixed outcomes. While targets for indictable cases were not met over this three-year window, summary cases were processed within administrative time limits in two of the three years. The most recent Criminal Justice Inspection Northern Ireland report (June 2010) found that case processing in Northern Ireland continues to be significantly slower than in England and Wales.

13.A.2   Efficient Use of Police and Civilian Staff

Policing Plans from 2004–05 have included performance indicators and targets to track overtime and sick absences and more recently to monitor the time spent by patrol officers away from the station. A new target was introduced in 2011–12 to reflect the requirement to move police officers from back office posts to frontline duties. The performance indicators and targets have evolved over time, which means that tracking performance is not straightforward. For example, the 2004–05 Policing Plan introduced a three-year overtime reduction strategy, while the 2006–07 Plan set a target of reducing the amount

Table 13.14 Case Processing within Administrative Time Limits

	2003–04	2004–05	2005–06	2006–07	2007–08[5]	2008–09	2009–10
Custody cases[1]	55.7	73.8	79.8	92.5	93.7	85.5	85.7
Bail cases[2]	64.6	77.5	85.2	94.1	95.3	89.8	88.2
Indictable[3]					74.8	59.3	67.4
Summary[4]					64.2	50.7	67

Administrative time limits were as follows:

[1] Custody cases – to process 85% of cases in 90 days

[2] Bail cases – to process 85% of cases in 110 day

[3] Indictable cases – to process 75% of cases within administrative time limits

[4] Summary cases – to process 60% Of cases within administrative time limits

[5] Target increased in respect of Custody and Bail cases to more than 87% processed within 90 days and 110 days respectively

of overtime worked by 20% by 31 March 2007 (compared with the 2001–02 baseline), a target which the Annual Report and Accounts for 2006–07 show was achieved.

A target of reducing the average number of days lost through sickness to 12.5 days for police officers and 13 days for civilian staff was set for 2005–06, a target which was met for police officers (11.65 days) but missed for civilian staff, who lost an average of 14.92 days through sickness (see Table 13.15). The downward pressure on sick absence continued in subsequent Policing Plans, with absence levels of 8.19 days for police staff and 9.21 days for civilian staff recorded in the Annual Report and Accounts for 2009–10 against targets in each case of five days for each group.

Table 13.15   Targets and Actual Performance for Police and Civilian Staff Absence 2005–06 to 2010–11

	2005–06	2006–07	2007–08	2008–09	2009–10
Police staff	11.65 (12.5)	11.35 (12)	11.2 (10)	8.86 (7)	8.19 (5)
Civilian staff	14.92 (13)	12.64 (12)	11.0 (10.0)	9.07 (7)	9.21 (5)

The Board's objectives to increase the number of police officers on frontline duties and the time spent by beat officers away from the station featured in more recent Policing Plans. In the 2010–11 Policing Plan a target of increasing by 600 the number of police officers assigned to neighbourhood and response policing roles was achieved and marginally exceeded (611). Similarly, targets for increasing the percentage of time spent in operational duties outside stations by 6% in 2010–11 and 5% in 2011–12 were met and exceeded.

13.A.3   Resolution of Cases by Police Discretion

Finally, the option of discretionary disposals was introduced in 2011–12 so that comparatively minor offences might be deal with informally, rather than through the formal criminal justice process. A discretionary disposal can be used where the offender and the victim agree on a suitable form of reparation, such as an apology, and results in the offence being dealt with promptly with a minimum of bureaucracy. The popularity of this form of disposal is reflected in the 5,698 cases resolved through police discretion in 2011–12 (against a Policing Plan target of 3,000).

Appendix 13.B: Examples of Performance Indicator Terminology Employed in 2009–10, 2010–11, and 2011–12 Policing Plans

2009–10

- In partnership with the community and other agencies, to make communities and neighbourhoods safe and feel safe.
- To continue to build, broaden, and sustain confidence in the police.
- To ensure that policing with the community is at the core of delivery of the policing service.
- To improve efficiency and effectiveness.

2010–11

- Service Excellence
- Tackling Serious Harm
- Personal Policing (Dealing with local concerns)

2011–12

- Personal Policing (Dealing with local concerns)
- Professional Policing (Delivering an excellent service)
- Protective Policing (Tackling serious harm)

Appendix 13.C: Friedman's Outcomes-based Accountability Model

Friedman lists seven population accountability questions that provide a check list which links the outcomes or quality of life conditions which it is aimed to achieve and a small number of indicators relevant to each outcome through to the actions which will be taken to deliver the outcomes. The service key population accountability questions are:

- What are the quality of life outcomes which we want for the children, adults, and families who live in our community? (Outcomes)
- What would these conditions look like if we could see them? How can we measure these conditions? (Indicators) How are we doing on the most important of these measures?
- Who are the partners that have a role to play in doing better?
- What works to do better, including no-cost and low cost ideas?
- What do we propose to do?

Performance Accountability, on the other hand, focuses on two key dimensions – *effort* and *effect*. There is a parallel set of questions in respect of performance accountability questions which begins by identifying customers or clients, determines the conditions which it is intended to target and the associated measures, clarifies relevant partners, and specifies what services will be delivered in pursuit of the objectives, drawing on evidence-based research. Performance accountability focuses on:

- How much are we doing?
- How well are we doing it?
- Is anyone better off?

While these are the critical performance questions, they will not capture all the relevant performance information and Friedman advocates that the data are supplemented by reference to accomplishments, positive activities not included in the above, and anecdotes, which are the stories behind the statistics and show how the service has or has not benefited the user.

Service Performance measures can be represented schematically as below:

	QUANTITY	QUALITY	
INPUT (EFFORT)	How much did we do?	How well did we do it?	Efficiency Measures
OUTPUT (EFFECT)	Is anyone better off?		Effectiveness Measures
	Number	Percentage	

Performance can then be considered in a number of dimensions: first, performance compared to previous history; secondly, comparisons with most similar peer organisations, taking account of any special factors; and, thirdly, comparison against national or international standards. Performance measures have a dual role – their primary function is to assess the effectiveness of the services being delivered but, in addition, they feed into population indicators, although the extent to which they will affect these indicators is largely dependent on the scale of the programme and wider environmental factors which may either facilitate or restrict change in the indicator.

Appendix 13.D: The Logic Model

The Logic Model, which attempts to make causal links between inputs, activities, outputs, and outcomes (the 'results chain'), has wide application to public and third-sector organisations and has been incorporated into a comprehensive evaluation strategy by the Canadian Government.

Inputs will include human and financial resources, equipment, and physical facilities, while activities are what the organisation actually does, and constitute the 'how' of a programme. Outputs are the direct products or services generated by the organisation – what the organisation does – and will normally be tangible and readily measurable: for example, training sessions completed or number of people trained. Outcomes are the differences which result from the programme outputs; they demonstrate the 'why' of the programme and are also referred to as the impacts or results.

The Canadian model describes outcomes at three levels – those which are immediate and directly attributable to the programme's outputs; those which are intermediate and can be expected logically to flow from the immediate outcomes; and, finally, ultimate outcomes, which can be expected to occur when a number of intermediate outcomes have been achieved. Clearly, measurement and attribution tend to become more complex for intermediate and ultimate outcomes.

A practical application of the Logic Model in the form of an Outcomes Map for Crime and Safety has been constructed by the Social Return on Investment network in partnership with New Philanthropy Capital, which could provide a Performance Management Framework for consideration by the Policing Board and the PSNI.

CHAPTER FOURTEEN

The PSNI Estate Strategy, Including the Police College

14.1 Introduction

One of the issues that came to have more salience for the Northern Ireland Policing Board (the Policing Board or Board) than was perhaps anticipated by The Independent Commission On Policing For Northern Ireland (the Independent Commission) was the development of an estate strategy by the PSNI and the handling of proposals for the closure of individual police stations. What was to have a bearing on the latter was, of course, the presence of *Political Members* on both the Policing Board and the District Policing Partnerships (DPPs) which led, perhaps inevitably in some cases, to a tension between rational grounds for decision-making and a weather eye on re-election. An issue that was particularly resonant for Nationalists, relating to the closure of the former police holding centres, was largely resolved before the Policing Board came into existence. The scope for the future development of the physical estate in terms, for example, of new or replacement police stations was of course related to and dependent on the outcome of the annual or later biennial expenditure rounds between the Northern Ireland Office (NIO) and Her Majesty's (HM) Treasury.

Three specific Independent Commission Recommendations – numbers 52, 53, and 54, which related to police stations. (During the Troubles police stations in most parts of Northern Ireland, except those where the risk of attack was minimal, had taken on the appearance of fortifications, including – after a number of fatal attacks – protection against home-made mortars.) Chapter 8 in the Independent Commission's Report, which contained the following Recommendations, was entitled '*Policing in a Peaceful Society*':

'52. Police stations built from now on should have, so far as possible, the appearance of ordinary buildings; they should have low perimeter walls, and be clearly visible from the street; but they should have security features which may be activated or reinforced as necessary.

53. Existing police stations should – subject to the security situation in their areas and to health and safety considerations – be progressively made less forbidding in appearance, more accessible to public callers and more congenial for those working in them. The public reception areas inside police stations should be made more welcoming, and civilian receptionists could replace police officers.

54. District police commanders should have discretion to decide in consultation with their local community how best to balance their resources between static posts and mobile patrols.'

The Independent Commission's Report recognised that there were still some areas where change would, for the time being, be constrained by the security threat to community policing. The section on police stations began: 'if a police service is to be an integral part of the community, it must be accessible to the public'. The Report also noted that the Independent Commission had received several submissions suggesting that there should be more small police stations and neighbourhood police 'shops' or kiosks, as in Japan. It noted that there were different views and different experiences relating to whether or not this helped bring police and community together. On balance, however, the Independent Commission came down in favour of, say, weekly 'surgeries' in premises which might be leased or borrowed from other community agencies.

Separately, in Chapter 10, 'Management and Personnel', the Independent Commission's Report contained a brief section on the police estate. The Independent Commission referred to a highly critical report produced by the Audit Commission in March 1999 on the police estate in England and Wales. Criticisms included many buildings being in the wrong place to support police operations, many being out-dated and unable to cope with modern technology, sites being underused, and a backlog of maintenance work. The Independent Commission identified similar problems in Northern Ireland. They concluded that neither the police – nor the Police Authority, which had had responsibility for the estate until 1999 – had a strategy for the management of the estate, which consisted of 190 sites. They noted that the Fundamental Review of the Royal Ulster Constabulary (RUC) in 1996 had envisaged a substantial cut in the establishment of the police and the elimination of 14 sub-divisional headquarters, but there had been no assessment of the scope for disposing of parts of the estate. Accordingly, the Independent Commission's Report recommended that:

'*The police should commission a comprehensive audit of the whole estate, to include outside experts, and develop a strategy for achieving an effective and efficient estate to meet the objectives for policing as outlined in this report.*' (Paragraph 10.28)

The Independent Commission's Report also recommended, in Chapter 16, '*Training, Education and Development*', that the existing Police College at Garnerville should be replaced with a new purpose-built police college:

'*The Northern-Ireland police should have a new purpose-built police college and the funding for it should be found in the <u>next public spending round</u>.*' (Paragraph 16.6; authors' underlining; Recommendation 131)

Clearly the future of individual police stations and indeed the wider estate strategy was not something that would be encompassed in legislation. On the other hand, it was important that the Bill that implemented the Independent Commission's Recommendations provided clarity on the respective responsibilities of the PSNI and the Policing Board (and indeed DPPs) in this area. The Police (Northern Ireland) Act 2000 provided in sections 6 and 7 respectively that the Board might provide and maintain buildings and equipment for police purposes and acquire, hold, and dispose of land for police purposes. However, section 6 of the 2000 Act also stated that, in regard to the provision and maintenance of buildings and equipment, '*the powers of the Board under this section shall be exercised, on behalf of and in the name of the Board, by the Chief Constable*'.

Within the first few months of the Policing Board's existence the practical application of these provisions, allied to the approach that felt 'appropriate' to the PSNI's senior management and the Policing

Board, came into question. However, it was not until the summer of 2004 that legal advice was sought by the Policing Board. That advice was clear that, in essence, decisions as to whether a police station be closed or remain open were operational decisions for the Chief Constable. Moreover, the fact that the power to acquire, hold, and dispose of land remained with the Policing Board did not enable the Board to countermand a decision of the Chief Constable to close a particular police station.

The British Government's Updated Implementation Plan, published in August 2001, included a commitment in regard to the recommendation on the estate strategy that 'a comprehensive strategy for the development of the police estate is being taken forward and will cover the scope for rationalisation'. The Government and the Chief Constable similarly committed to implementing the Independent Commission's Recommendations 52 and 53, with implementation dependent on the security situation; the issues were to be addressed through the development of the estate strategy. The Government also stated that it was 'committed to funding the implementation of the programme of change'.

The Independent Commission's Recommendation in relation to the new police college – Recommendation 131 – was 'accepted in principle'. The Plan noted the need to involve the forthcoming Policing Board and to resolve whether the option of a public/private partnership model was appropriate. The target date for completion of the full business case was December 2002.

14.2   The Involvement of the Policing Board

In practice, the issue of the potential closure of individual police stations came up in the exchanges between PSNI senior management and the Policing Board prior to the development of the police estate strategy. (Indeed, even before the creation of the Policing Board a paper had been presented by the Police Service to the Police Authority on station closures in September 2001.)

At the Policing Board's meeting in March 2002 – the last he was to attend – Sir Ronnie Flanagan said that:

'We do have to rationalise our estate [but] ... nothing will be done of course *without the full consultation of the Board and the Board's very strong involvement before we even contemplate closing a station.'*

In the same month, the Policing Board's Finance and Resources Committee endorsed the Police Service's (Estate) Strategy Review, though that endorsement did not include a station closure strategy, which was to be subject to specific discussion between the Chief Constable and the Board.

At the *Public Session* of the Policing Board's meeting in April 2002 Acting Chief Constable Colin Cramphorn spoke at some length of the tensions between the advantage of rationalising the police estate and wider consultation when he said:

'Progress on the consultation regarding station closures ... The consultation exercise was concluded at the weekend just past ... [On] 25 stations that had previously been notified... There is a good deal of public disquiet about the issue and the majority of those stations are not supported for closure as a result of the consultation exercise. However, there are other stations that we now need to review ... There is a specific recommendation in the Independent Commission's Report – Recommendation 54 – saying the district commander should have the discretion to decide in consultation with their local communities how best to balance resources between static posts and mobile patrols. So we have to be aware, all of us, that we do not actually cross a line regarding that particular Recommendation.'

At the *Public Session* of the following month's Board meeting Mr Cramphorn said:

'The vast majority of the stations that we consulted with members of the public about have not, in the end, been recommended to you for closure. There are three stations that ... we would like to press ahead with closure on now, these three being Springfield Road (Belfast), Castlehill (Dungannon), and Corry Square (Newry).'

In June the Policing Board agreed that the PSNI should be asked to provide an economic appraisal on the three proposed closures, and that *'A final decision on the Acting Chief Constable's recommendation would be made following the consideration of the appraisal.'*

In July 2002 the Policing Board noted a paper presenting information on the business case in respect of the proposed closure of these three stations. After discussion, the Policing Board agreed to advise the Acting Chief Constable that the Board supported his recommendation to close Springfield Road station, but decisions on the other two should be deferred pending a more comprehensive business case. In addition, the Acting Chief Constable was to be advised that a more detailed business case was similarly required in respect of any further proposed closures and that the Policing Board would wish to discuss the future closures with the Chief Constable, probably in public session.

In the event, that October the Policing Board agreed to support the PSNI recommendation to close the other two stations, with three *Political Members* recording their opposition to that decision.

Decisions were taken on further individual station closures through to spring 2004, with, if the case was clear-cut, a comparatively short rationale provided by the PSNI.

However, the proposed closure of Andersonstown police station in West Belfast was symbolically as well as practically an important one. The West Belfast District Commander had put the case for closure at a public meeting of the West Belfast sub-group of the Belfast DPP in June 2003. Following discussion in the Belfast DPP in September of that year the DPP expressed its opposition to the proposed closure of Andersonstown station on the grounds that such a move would be likely to be interpreted as the police withdrawing from, rather than attempting to become more involved with, the local community. There was also some discussion as to the respective roles of the District Commander and the DPP in relation to taking forward the consultation with the local communities that both parties agreed was appropriate. The DPP was of the view that the PSNI rather than it should be expected to consult on operational issues, though the DPP agreed that a letter should be sent to the Policing Board seeking clarification.

With effect from 1 February 2004, the opening hours of Andersonstown police station were reduced by the District Commander from 24 hours per day seven days a week to 12 hours per day. (A survey had found that there was just a handful of callers each day, only two of whom on average reported an incident.) A community survey was carried out by February; 16% of households responded, with 43% of those both in favour of closure and opposed to it and the remaining 14% offering no opinion. Similarly, of the local businesses within the station area, the numbers for and against closure were equally split. Representatives of political parties in the Andersonstown area supported the proposed closure.

A presentation was made by the relevant Assistant Chief Constable and District Commander to the Board's Corporate Policy Committee in May 2004. The Committee concluded that the Vice-Chairman should contact the Belfast DPP and the West Belfast sub-group to ascertain their views in more detail and that the matter should then come before the next Policing Board meeting. The Board were in turn apprised of the contacts that had taken place at the local level in 2003 and the DPP members were given the opportunity to comment direct to the Policing Board on the proposed closure.

The issue was fully discussed at the Policing Board in June 2004. While there was a proposal that the Policing Board should reject the proposition to close the police station it was agreed that the Vice-Chairman should hold discussions and report further. The Policing Board Chairman also wrote to the DPP Chairman, seeking clarification of the information to be provided by the PSNI.

Following the discussion in the Policing Board's July meeting the Chief Executive wrote to the Deputy Chief Constable (DCC) in July 2004 advising him that:

'The Board would wish to put in place a general framework for the consideration of proposals for station closures ... A framework should be set within the context of an overall estate strategy and might include two main elements – process and criteria.'

'Process' would include how local consultation had been undertaken, how the PSNI rated its recommendation, and how the recommendation was considered by the Board. 'Criteria' could include an operational assessment, public usage, operating costs, capital expenditure, and security issues. (It was against the background of the need to reach a decision on the proposed closure of Andersonstown police station that the Policing Board sought legal advice on the respective responsibilities of the Board and the PSNI.)

At the September meeting of the Board's Corporate Policy Committee it was recognised that the proposed closure and disposal of police stations could be at times a difficult issue for *Political Members* of the Policing Board and that thought should be given by the Board to a different approach: one idea considered was to debate proposed closures at the full Board and then remit the final decision to a sub-group comprising a number of *Independent Members*, but in the event this idea was not adopted.

Considerable work on the preparation of a '*station closure template*' was put in by Policing Board officials and PSNI officers. This document provided a detailed assessment in relation to any individual station that might be considered for closure by the Policing Board. The community consultation process was seen as the first stage. In October 2004 officials pointed out to the Corporate Policy Committee that there was at that time a requirement for the PSNI to advise the Policing Board that the community consultation phase had commenced. Indeed, there were cases throughout the Policing Board's first years when the Board felt that local district commanders had 'jumped the gun' in initiating the process. This issue was seen as particularly important by *Political Members* of the Policing Board. The Committee was advised that the template would form part of the PSNI's estate strategy document which was then expected to come forward in December 2004. Again, at this time, the Committee deferred consideration of the closure of Andersonstown and three rural stations pending submission of a completed framework for each by the PSNI. A subsequent letter from the Policing Board's Chief Executive to the DCC made the point strongly that it would be much easier for everyone if the proposed closure of individual stations were to be considered in the context of a coherent, long-term estate strategy.

The first substantive use of the station closure template was in relation to the proposed closure of Andersonstown police station. This came forward together with the results of the PSNI survey of local residents. The issue was initially discussed by the Policing Board's Corporate Policy Committee. That Committee recommended that the Board should accept the PSNI proposal to close and dispose of the station. The issue finally came before the whole Board at its meeting on 1 December 2004. The Policing Board Membership was almost split on this matter, but, with one Member abstaining, the recommendation of the Corporate Policy Committee accepting the PSNI's proposal for closure was carried by seven votes to six.

14.3   The PSNI Estate Strategy of 2005

The first fully comprehensive PSNI estate strategy was not finalised until April 2005, significantly later than should have been the case, which inevitably led to some of the tensions over the proposed closure of individual police stations described above. However, one benefit of the delay was that the scope of the document clearly reflected a level of detail in terms of audit and analysis that would not have been available earlier.

The estate strategy also took account of the full range of recommendations in the Independent Commission's Report, including those relating to the closure of the three holding centres (Recommendation 62) and the introduction of video recording into all PACE (Police and Criminal Evidence) custody suites (Recommendation 63). In addition, the document took note of other recommendations of the Independent Commission that impacted on the estate strategy, including Recommendations 44, 45, and 46 referring to policing in the community. The estate strategy noted that improved local policing strategies would allow reviews of the viability of individual stations focused on delivering enhanced policing plans at local level using alternative methodologies, such as mobile police stations and shared multi-agency facilities. Recommendation 97, relating to a slimmer structure at police headquarters and reflecting the shift of focus towards community policing and the delegation of responsibility to District Commanders, also had implications for the future estate.

The estate strategy began with a vision statement, namely to develop estate services that complemented and enhanced operational policing strategies based on using police resources, staff, equipment, and buildings in the most effective and efficient manner. It noted the assessment that had already taken place and the commitment to increase expenditure on the estate over the following five-year period by investing over £200m (of which more than half would be new capital, as opposed to maintenance and minor works). Developments that had taken place included new District Command Unit (DCU) headquarters at Coleraine (completed in 2003) and Magherafelt (2004) and a new sector station at Moira, alongside major refurbishments at Antrim Road in Belfast, Enniskillen, Newtownards, Ballycastle, Portadown, and Strand Road in Londonderry. The three new stations had each been designed in compliance with Independent Commission Recommendation 52. In addition, substantial maintenance or upgrade works were planned at a further 30 PSNI stations during the 2005/06 financial year, and 40 projects were being progressed in softening the appearance of police stations, making them more accessible and user-friendly.

The estate strategy recognised that, notwithstanding some progress made since the publication of the Independent Commission's Report, the PSNI estate remained disproportionately larger and older than those of comparable police services in Great Britain, with a considerable number of under-utilised stations. It emphasised that a key part of the strategy was to:

'*support the delivery of local community-based policing plans, an inherent part of which is full community consultation, including DPPs, leading to the review of specific stations based on alternative and flexible community policing plans ...*

Local Commanders will prepare plans in relation to potential closures of stations in which all aspects of community consultation, and development of alternative policing strategies are considered in detail, examples of which are the use of shop fronts, other non-police property such as community facilities or mobile police vehicles. These plans will be submitted to the ... Policing Board for consideration, review and endorsement prior to any action being taken at local level to close a station.

... The PSNI recognises that a communication and information-sharing strategy addressing concerns of local communities is absolutely essential to providing reassurance where reviews of stations are being progressed.'

At the time of the estate strategy the police estate consisted of 135 police stations, 11 headquarters locations, 39 hilltop/portal sites, and six training/administration sites. Just 57 of the police stations were open 24 hours a day, with 71 having limited opening hours, and seven stations being kept on a 'lock and leave' basis. Just on half of all the stations were more than 50 years old.

It had been recognised that the current police estate, including as it did 29 DCU structures, had too many facilities requiring too much maintenance to be sustainable in the medium term. Benchmarking against other UK police services underlined both the disproportionate size of the PSNI estate and the absence of limited opening stations in other services. In addition, an earlier closure list, consisting of 25 stations, had been developed in 2001 and endorsed by the Police Authority, prior to the establishment of the Policing Board. The strategy recognised that, '*due to the sensitivities of the issues surrounding the closure of stations*', progress in implementing the closure list had been slow, with only six station closures actioned by this time. The strategy underlined that a new process should be developed between the PSNI and the Policing Board in relation to future station closures in an attempt both to generate momentum within the programme and to smooth the path to Policing Board endorsement of a proposed closure. The strategy included the template that had been agreed between the Policing Board and the PSNI in late 2004.

The estate strategy noted that the current major works programme had originally been proposed by the former RUC Buildings Branch, as amended to reflect the DCU structure and subject to reassessment by Chief Officers in a 2002 estate strategy exercise. A further assessment had taken place in 2003, with the endorsement of a rationalised custody structure consisting of four custody 'super suites' and 13 designated PACE suites. The first of those super suites, at Antrim, had been completed in 2003. Less progress had been made in taking forward a review of the headquarters establishment following an initial review in 2000 and then a revisiting of the plans in relation to the headquarters buildings in 2003. A security procedures audit of the PSNI in 2002 (see Chapter 15) had contained a number of recommendations that had specific implications for the estate. Implementation of those recommendations, the strategy noted, included the relocation of sensitive functions to more secure accommodation and required a substantial number of work projects.

Estate audits, expedited at the beginning of 2004, had identified a significant number of police stations which might be under-utilised within a DCU structure based on community policing plans. A major police estate conference with DCU Commanders was held in September 2004. This recognised the requirement to retain a police presence in local communities in the event of the closure of an under-utilised station.

The document acknowledged the criticisms in reports of the Oversight Commissioner in relation to progress on implementing the estate strategy. (For example, in the last report that he wrote as Oversight Commissioner, in December 2003, Tom Constantine highlighted the absence of an overall estate strategy, internal inconsistencies in the PSNI approach, slow progress in improving the appearance of police stations, the impact this was having on the development of community policing, the lack of a clear funding stream from the Government, and even the occasional use on a strictly temporary basis of Gough Barracks.)

The inter-relationship between the continuing *political process* and policing was demonstrated in the Joint Declaration by the British and Irish Governments of April 2003. In '*Annex 1 Security Normalisation*' it was stated in Clause 7 that:

'*By the end of 2003 in an enabling environment, we would have achieved [inter alia] the initiation of a full review of the police estate, carried out by the Chief Constable, covering the options for redevelopment of each site as a police only community police station, de-fortification and closure, and of the nature of policing operation to achieve a rationalisation and normalisation reflecting the policing needs of 1.7 m people. In preparing proposals, the Chief Constable will take account of the views of his District Commanders and their respective local communities, before submitting his recommendations to the Policing Board.*'

Clause 9 stated that – in the same politically significant phrase – '*in a continuing enabling environment*' by April 2005 '*there would have been further implementation of the review of the police estate, as determined by the Policing Board*'. The pace of security '*normalisation*' or, as others would put it, '*demilitarisation*' would inevitably impact on the size, location, and nature of the police estate.

Nor was the NIO without involvement. The Chairman of the Policing Board chaired a regular tripartite estate steering committee including NIO officials along with the DCC.

A further uncertainty was introduced by the stop–go progress of the Review of Public Administration. At the time of the completion of the 2005 estate strategy, while the PSNI had proposed a reduced DCU structure it was yet to be the subject of full consultation and endorsement. Moreover, the issues relating to the phasing out of the Full Time Reserve (as well as the recruitment of a variety of part time and, in theory, police community support officers) added to the potential complexity.

Finally, the estate strategy also noted that, notwithstanding the strength of the overall approach or indeed individual business cases, the outcome of the biennial financial settlements between the NIO and the Treasury could inevitably impact on the pace of implementation.

The PSNI estate strategy was considered by the Policing Board initially in the first month of 2005, when the DCC also set out the strategy publicly for the Northern Ireland media. The Board sought certain clarification and additional information on benchmarking with other police services. Members of the Board were concerned that public confidence should be maintained and that there should be no reduction in the availability of police to the community. In principle the Board endorsed the strategy. At the Board's *Public Session* on 7 April 2005 *Political Member* Alex Attwood (Social Democratic and Labour Party (SDLP)) asked how many police stations the PSNI were recommending should be reviewed in the next five years, including the initiation of the consultation. The DCC responded that a total of 61 stations were identified to be reviewed over the following five years, with half of the reviews scheduled to commence within the next 12 months. He also confirmed that the PSNI were trialling some mobile police stations.

Writing to the Policing Board Chairman in June 2005, at the end of the process, the Chief Constable stressed that:

'It is the responsibility of DCU Commanders to examine their individual estate needs, instigate consultation with the communities they serve, recommend closures where appropriate and examine innovative policing alternatives. And, it will be Commanders who will make final decisions on closures.'

He also stressed that the effective management of communications was vital to the success of the estate strategy, reflecting as it did its whole 'bottom up' approach.

14.4   The Closure of the Former Holding Centres

In Chapter 8, 'Policing In A Peaceful Society', the Independent Commission's Report dealt with the issue of the three police holding centres at Castlereagh, Gough Barracks (Armagh), and Strand Road (Londonderry), which had been used for the questioning of persons detained under the emergency legislation. The report noted that several submissions had called for their closure and that the then Commissioner for Holding Centres, Sir Louis Blom-Cooper, had advised the Commission that there was no longer a case for holding such persons in separate centres from those held under PACE (the Police and Criminal Evidence (Northern Ireland) Order 1998). The Independent Commission's Recommendation 62 was that:

'The three holding centres at Castlereagh, Gough Barracks and Strand Road should be closed forthwith and all suspects should in future be detained in custody suites based in police stations.'

There were two related recommendations, namely that 'video recording should be introduced into the PACE custody suites' (Recommendation 63) and that 'responsibility for inspecting all custody and interrogation suites should rest with the Policing Board, and Lay Visitors should be empowered not only to inspect conditions of detention (as [then] occurred) but also to observe interviews on camera subject to the consent of the detainee (as was [then] the case for cell visits)'(Recommendation 64).

Northern Ireland had been progressive in the introduction of audio and video recording of interviews into holding centres, which had occurred on 1 January 1999.

Following the publication of the Independent Commission's Report the closure of the holding centres was regularly urged by the SDLP in discussions with the British Government on policing. In the event, Castlereagh holding centre closed on 31 December 1999 and Strand Road holding centre closed on 1 October 2000. Progress on implementation of the Independent Commission's Recommendation 62 was further discussed at Weston Park in July 2001 and the subsequent text published by the NIO and the Department of Foreign Affairs stated the British Government's commitment to publishing a revised Implementation Plan which would set out in greater detail the plans for implementing, among other matters, the closure of Gough holding centre. The Updated Implementation Plan published in August 2001 stated that '*the Government and the Chief Constable have accepted that the holding centre at Gough Barracks should close as soon as is practicable*'. It further specified in relation to timescale that the third holding centre would close in September of that year. Alternative temporary arrangements were made to hold all suspects in a custody suite based in Lisburn police station, while '*the next step will be to provide long-term facilities, built for the purpose, at Antrim Police Station – these are scheduled to be available in late 2002.*'

14.5   Taking Forward the PSNI Estate Strategy

The PSNI estate strategy was signed off by the Policing Board in May 2005. At the end of June specific proposals came forward to the Policing Board concerning the future of 17 individual police stations, all of which were within the Rural Region, eight being in Fermanagh. Detailed proposals were also put to the Board concerning the process by which the public would be consulted in relation to reviewing the requirements for individual stations. The initial approach would be made by the District Commander to the DPP, including his or her plans for consulting the public as part of this review and any alternative local Policing Plans. Following the consultation, the DPP would arrange a themed meeting in public to consider the review of the station, though it was accepted that this might not be feasible in every area, in which case alternative arrangements should be made. The role of the Policing Board would be at the end of the process in terms of either formally accepting or rejecting the assessment contained within the station closure template and notifying the PSNI of their decision.

In the discussion at the Policing Board's June 2005 meeting concern was raised, particularly by elected representatives from Fermanagh. On the other hand, the Chief Constable pointed out that Fermanagh had a population of only 57,000, yet it had 13 police stations. The PSNI were determined to deliver a more effective service using police officers outside, rather than inside, stations. He went on to stress, however, that no station would be closed without proper consultation, and he recognised that it was always an emotive issue. The Policing

Board decided to endorse the Chief Constable's recommendation to close nine stations outside Fermanagh, with further consideration for those in Fermanagh, including the opportunity to explain the strategy further to the Fermanagh DPP and the wider community and fully outline the alternative policing arrangements to be put in place.

The issue of Fermanagh police station closures was further discussed by the Policing Board on 1 September 2005. Prior to that meeting the Assistant Chief Constable Rural had notified the Board that, after discussion with the District Commander and taking account of the expressed views of the community, the DPP, and the Policing Board, he wished to withdraw the recommendation regarding the closure of two of the eight stations. The Fermanagh DPP had held a themed meeting in public on 17 August. The Policing Board Chairman advised the DPP chair that he would be willing to give an extension to the DPP for further consideration, but that the Policing Board were determined to reach a definitive position on the issue at their meeting on 1 September. Following discussion at the Board on 1 September, the Policing Board agreed to endorse the recommendation to close six stations, although the *Political Members* representing the Democratic Unionist Party (DUP) and the Ulster Unionist Party (UUP) wished it to be formally recorded that they demurred from the decision to close any stations. The DCC advised the Board's *Public Session* on that date about a range of alternative policing plans, including the use of district council property, health, family, and community centres, secondary schools, housing executive premises, and mobile police stations.

On 1 August 2005 the then Secretary of State, Peter Hain, published plans for the normalisation of the security profile across Northern Ireland. (This followed an IRA statement on 28 July.) While the majority of the statement referred to the closure of military bases in Northern Ireland, it also included reference to further de-fortification of police stations and further implementation of the police estate review as determined by the Policing Board.

In October 2005 the PSNI delivered two joint briefings with the Policing Board to DPPs to inform DPPs about the revised PSNI estate strategy.

Closure proposals in respect of individual police stations continued both to cause controversy and to be very carefully considered. One such example was Middletown in County Armagh. The station review framework was initially considered by the Policing Board's Finance and General Purposes Committee, which was not satisfied that a convincing case for closure had been made, in part evidenced by the cross-community opposition to closure. Following further exchanges with the PSNI, the DPP, and local community representatives, which included the former setting out detailed arrangements for the provision of policing activity in the Middletown area, the Policing Board resolved in February 2006 to endorse the Chief Constable's recommendation to close Middletown police station.

Another example concerned the closure of Coalisland police station, which came before the Policing Board initially in the summer of 2006. Again the Policing Board ensured that the PSNI presented a detailed plan for delivering a community policing service to the area in the wake of the station closure. The plan addressed short-, medium-, and long-term arrangements. The Board endorsed the recommendation to close and demolish the police station subject to satisfaction with the plan.

In the same period the Policing Board gave careful consideration to the proposed closure of Rosemount police station in Derry/Londonderry. This had been included in the 2005 estate strategy, and consultation, including advertisements in local newspapers, had taken place over a three-month period from October 2005. Most respondents took the view that the existing station should be closed. The view of the DPP, following a public meeting in January 2006, was that the station should close and that the site should be given over to community use, which should include the provision of a police surgery type facility. The Policing Board agreed in December 2006 to endorse the Chief Constable's closure proposal. The Board was sensitive to local initiatives to promote community usage of closed police stations. In 2007 the Board considered the planned closure of the Crumlin station and proposals from a local community group to provide for development of the community centre to include police accommodation.

More generally, the Policing Board continue to monitor implementation of the estate strategy. A mid-year review presentation was made by the PSNI Director of Finance and Support Services to the Resources and Improvement Committee of the Policing Board in September 2006 which was in turn reported to the full Board.

There were also wider reviews that fed into the Policing Board's approach. The National Audit Office (NAO) published the report of its value for money study on the PSNI estate on 19 December 2006. The report favoured a more defined and shorter period of time associated with police station reviews leading to potential closures and faster disposal thereafter. The report also recommended an enhancement of the benchmarking process, focusing on space utilisation and customer satisfaction.

At the Board's *Public Session* in February 2007 the Policing Board followed up with the Chief Constable and the Assistant Chief Constable on developments in Fermanagh, after the closure of six stations there. The PSNI recommitted to preparing service level agreements that would be subject to discussions with local Community Police Liaison Committees. In addition, it was reported that the new mobile police station had been proving a very effective resource, with 33 beat patrols from it since its launch in November 2006. Later that year the Assistant Chief Constable reported plans for three more mobile police stations for delivery in the autumn, alongside an internal evaluation of their effectiveness to identify good practice and share it across the PSNI.

In 2008 the PSNI updated the estate strategy. It followed broadly the same approach as the 2005 strategy, though it took account of the audit by the NAO. The strategy included as a core element over £200m in support of community policing plans, new-build police stations, maintenance upgrade projects, softening and energy conservation schemes. The revised strategy reflected the introduction of the eight DCU structure. Twenty-six potential station reviews were identified following a second Independent Commission-compliant audit of the entire police estate. The strategy noted that there were to be four custody super suites at Musgrave Street (Belfast), Antrim, Craigavon, and Waterside (Londonderry). The 12 designated PACE suites would be at Lisburn, Bangor, Downpatrick, Ardmore, Dungannon, Enniskillen, Omagh, Strabane, Coleraine, Limavady, Ballymena, and Cookstown, but a further review of the proposed custody structure had recently been commenced. There had been a review of the headquarters estate in 2006, and a further review, known as CORE, was currently in train.

The initial draft of the revised estate strategy was dated April 2008 and was first discussed by the Policing Board at its meeting on 5 June.

Reflecting the sensitivity of station closures, the press release issued in the Policing Board Chairman's name that day was headlined '*no decisions on station closures until estate strategy approved*'. It stated that the Board had agreed that day that no decisions around individual stations would be taken prior to full Board discussion and approval of the revised estate strategy, which was expected to be in September/October 2008. The release continued:

'*Board members want to assure local communities that in considering proposals brought forward by the PSNI, the Board will take fully into account the views of DPPs and local people. The Board is sensitive to the debate this issue generates and the need to provide community assurance that where station closure is being proposed, the police will bring forward realistic alternative policing arrangements for the area which will ensure that the policing service delivered does not become less effective.*'

The draft estate strategy was then remitted to the Board's Resources and Improvement Committee for detailed consideration. The Committee required the PSNI to give further consideration to the plan for station reviews, the impact of District Council and DCU coterminosity and the Government policy on the retention of surplus sale receipts before resubmitting the revised document.

A question by a Board Member in October 2008 established that of the 135 police stations that had been open and accessible to the public in 2003, there were now only 84.

In December 2008 the Assistant Chief Constable Rural brought forward station closure templates for a further 16 stations. In a number of these cases the individual police station had effectively been closed for a considerable period. (In others, as, for example, Greyabbey, the police station was being opened up specially twice a week for a total of four hours; in the first nine months of 2007 just four people called at the station during the advertised opening hours.)

In November 2008 the Policing Board Chairman proposed that a special Policing Board meeting should be arranged in January 2009 to consider the updated police estate strategy. Following consultation with Board Members it was decided to postpone the meeting for one month, reflecting various concerns, including the late presentation of the revised strategy. However, in the meantime a proposal came forward for the closure and disposal of Dromara station. Concern was voiced at the Policing Board meeting on 5 February 2009; the Chief Constable stated that from his perspective budget constraints meant that it was a high priority to avoid continuing to spend significant sums of money on redundant buildings. Certain Board Members, for their part, stressed the importance of completing the consultation process before decisions were finalised, while others recognised the value of swift decisions. The scheduled special meeting for later in February 2009 was then postponed again to allow further consideration of this and related issues. Subsequently the PSNI proposed that the meeting be rearranged for the autumn of 2009; it was scheduled for 6 August, with the finalisation of the updated estate strategy being put back accordingly.

14.6   The 'Police College' at Desertcreat

As noted above, Recommendation 131 of the Independent Commission on Policing was that: '*The Northern Ireland police should have a new purpose-built police College and the funding for it should be found in the next public spending round*' (Paragraph 16.6).

The Independent Commission was highly critical in its report on the Police Training Centre at Garnerville in East Belfast, noting that it was inferior to the Garda Síochána's training centre at Templemore. The Commission saw an advantage in having the College located away from other police facilities, ideally in an area convenient for links to be established with a University.

The British Government's Updated Implementation Plan, published in August 2001, accepted the Recommendation in principle, referring to '*funding arrangements and an agreed specification of requirements*' and noting that an options appraisal was being undertaken, including the scope for a Public/Private Partnership (also known as a Private Finance Initiative) arrangement. While '*decisions [were] awaiting appointment of [the] Policing Board*', the target date for completion of the full business case was December 2002.

Sadly, for a variety of reasons, including major issues in relation to both the funding arrangements and the specification of requirements, it was to be almost 10 more years before the revised business case was finally accepted, let alone the new College built. This was long after the major intake of new recruits into the PSNI and the substantial retraining of existing staff had taken place.

The Northern Ireland Policing Board were directly involved in at least one crucial decision in relation to the new College – its location. However, the Board were thereafter less able to influence either the direction or the pace of events.

Initially, some progress was made between the RUC and the former Police Authority in preparing and assessing the options appraisal for a new College. However, further work was deferred pending the establishment of the new Policing Board.

From its creation in 2000 the Chairman of the Project Board responsible for taking forward the new Police College was the DCC, initially Colin Cramphorn. Even before the Policing Board came into existence, DCC Cramphorn was flagging up his concerns about the funding for the College.

The Policing Board Chairman met DCC Cramphorn on 27 November 2001 to discuss the College project. He also visited the Scottish Police Training College at Tulliallan in early January with the Interim Chief Executive of the Board and wrote to the NIO Minister seeking an urgent meeting of the Police Buildings Steering Committee, which he was then invited to chair. Discussions were also held with the two Northern Ireland Universities, and a visit made to Templemore.

On 2 May 2002 it was announced that the British Government had agreed with the Northern Ireland administration that the Maze site was to be transferred to the latter at no charge.

At the Policing Board meeting on 3 July 2002 the Chairman reminded Members of the pressing need for the provision of the new College. (The outline business case for the College could not be taken forward, at least to the full business case stage, until the Policing Board had addressed the issue of site provision.) The Policing Board noted that the Board Chairman, Acting Chief Constable Cramphorn, and the Chief Constable Designate agreed that the site at the Maze (occupied by the former prison and an Army base), which was becoming available, fulfilled all the requirements of the key criteria. The Board unanimously agreed that the Chairman should contact the Northern Ireland Secretary of State Dr John Reid, First Minister David Trimble (UUP, Leader), and deputy First Minister Mark Durkan (SDLP, Leader) to indicate the Board's interest in the Maze site as a location for the College.

The Chairman met Secretary of State Dr John Reid and put the proposal to him; he said he would back the proposal if the Board had the support of the First Minister and the deputy First Minister, but added that he wouldn't be giving the site away and at the same time giving the Board the money to buy it. The Chairman next met the deputy First Minister and gained the impression that the latter would like the site to be in the Derry/Londonderry area; he neverthe-less agreed to consider the proposal. Later that month the Policing Board Chairman recorded that in a telephone conversation with the First Minister the latter had said that the Policing Board's proposal 'did not fit with the Northern Ireland Executive's plans for the Maze site and that we [the Policing Board] couldn't afford it'. Two of the then UUP Political Members of the Policing Board, Messrs Fred Cobain and Alan McFarland, sought but failed to persuade the First Minister to change his mind. The Board was subsequently advised in writing that the First Minister and the Deputy First Minister were of the view that the Maze might not be available within the Board's timescale (if at all).

The Policing Board set up a Working Group to take forward the provi-sion of the College, chaired by Barry Gilligan, who also represented the Board on the Project Board chaired by the DCC. (The other Working Group Board Members were Joe Byrne (SDLP), Sam Foster (UUP), and Ian Paisley Jnr (DUP)). In late December 2002 the PSNI submitted the outline business case to the Policing Board. This noted that under a privately financed option the estimated future annual charge would be of the order of £6m, nearly six times the then current annual expendi-ture on the training estate. (The initial estimated capital construction cost, excluding the price of the land, was just on £75m.)

On 29 January 2003 the Chief Constable advertised for a suitable site, inviting expressions of interest for the provision of an 80- to 90-acre site within a 30-mile radius of Belfast, though the radius was subsequently increased to 45 miles.

At the Public Session of the Policing Board on 6 February 2003 the Chief Constable and Assistant Chief Constable Roy Toner gave a pres-entation on training, including the College. Chief Constable Hugh Orde began by confessing to a degree of frustration that the project had not been moved further forward. ACC Toner set out the requirements as seen by the PSNI at that time, which included the capacity to train up to 450 new recruits each year, specialist training facilities, provision for driver and purpose-built public order training, and 11 ranges for firearms. He added that it was anticipated that the construction contract should be awarded in early 2005, with a completion date of 2007. The Policing Board unanimously agreed that the outline business case should be formally submitted to the NIO with the Board's full endorsement.

At the beginning of March 2003 an invitation to tender was issued to all the valid expressions of interest that had been received. The process was for the PSNI to put forward recommendations after evaluation to the Project Board, which would in turn be discussed by the Policing Board's College Working Group, which would make a final recommendation to the Policing Board for the decision on the preferred location. However, a case was made that the 45-mile limitation would exclude, for example, Derry/Londonderry and Fermanagh. It was agreed by the Project Board that a fresh tendering process should be run.

In a letter dated 24 September 2003 the Policing Board was notified by the NIO that the Treasury had stated that they were content with the outline business case, provided the annual cost was absorbed within the existing baseline. At this stage it was still envisaged that a Public/Private Partnership (PPP) route would be preferred, with the public sector comparator costs being £137m.

At the Policing Board meeting on 19 February 2004 the DCC and the Project Board Members made a presentation on the College, concluding with a unanimous recommendation that the new site should be at Desertcreat, near Cookstown. The Policing Board endorsed the selection of Desertcreat and looked to the NIO to provide the additional revenue costs. Following the public announcement of the chosen site Members of the Policing Board led a number of community information events in the area. At this time completion of what was seen as a state-of-the-art college, drawing on best practice from around the world, was anticipated in spring 2008.

At the Policing Board meeting on 3 November 2005 there was a further presentation which brought forward a revised outline business case, including a number of changes to the project and an increase in the overall cost to around £131m. Costing issues associated with the PPP approach still favoured by the Treasury were discussed. Following the meeting the Policing Board Chairman wrote to the NIO Security Minister affirming the Board's position. However, following the then Spending Review, it became apparent by early 2006 that there remained a significant gap in funding for the proposed College, with the NIO having secured only up to £90m capital expenditure. Reflecting the Policing Board's concerns, the Chairman wrote in March of that year to the Prime Minister requesting a meeting to discuss the funding package. The letter stressed the linkage between investment in the new College and increasing confidence in the PSNI.

At the same time the preference for a PPP approach over a traditional capital build was coming into question.

At the *Public Session* of the Policing Board meeting on 1 June 2006 the Chairman reiterated that the PSNI and the Board were committed to providing a world-class police training facility. The Chairman stated that the Board had now made two formal requests for a meeting with the Prime Minister, reflecting the importance they attached to this issue, and that they would be meeting Paul Goggins, the NIO Security Minister, shortly in support of this request. The Chief Constable indicated his support for the Chairman's comments. The Policing Board Chairman and Vice-Chairman, together with three *Political Members*, met Mr Goggins on 20 June 2006 and the Minister explained that he was looking at a range of options, including the scope for cooperation with other emergency agencies, to help find a way forward.

At the *Public Session* of the Policing Board meeting on 5 October 2006 Alex Attwood (SDLP) asked if it might help if the Irish Government were to contribute financially to the funding of the College. Later that month the Board Chairman wrote to the Secretary of State suggesting that possibilities for joint funding with the Irish could be explored at Ministerial level, and that the financial needs should be considered as part of the discussions on a funding package arising from the St Andrews Agreement. In his reply the Secretary of State, Peter Hain, stated that the possibility had been raised with the Irish. It was agreed by the Board that the Chairman should make an informal approach to Irish Ministers as well. In the event the Chairman was advised by the Secretary General of the Department of Justice, Equality and Law Reform that the Irish Government did not intend making a capital contribution although, when the new College opened, further discussion on cooperation between the two police services in respect of training could take place.

On 19 February 2007 Security Minister Paul Goggins wrote to the Board Chairman advising him of the imminent announcement by the Secretary of State of the intention to proceed on the basis of combining Police, Prison Service, and Fire and Rescue training in a shared facility at the Desertcreat site. This would remove uncertainty over the College and 'ensure that we maintain momentum to bring it to a speedy conclusion', assuming a favourable outcome at the forthcoming Comprehensive Spending Review. Costs were to be kept within the gross £90m funding envelope, and the governance and project management arrangements would accordingly be amended to include the Northern Ireland Fire and Rescue and Prison Services. There would inevitably be a need to prepare a revised business case.

In response to a question from Board *Political Member* Tom Buchanan (DUP) on 27 June 2007 the Chief Constable replied that a two-year construction programme should commence in summer 2009. At the *Public Session* of the Board on 3 April 2008 *Political Member* Ian Paisley Jnr expressed his view that 'I no longer believe there is going to be a College at Desertcreat'. He went on to say that the 'non-capital issue' was something that should concern the Board.

On 11 July 2008 the Policing Board Chairman wrote to the Ministers for Finance and Personnel and for Health, Social Services and Public Safety urging that the business case from the Department of Health, Social Services and Public Safety in respect of the Fire and Rescue Service element of the College be processed as expeditiously as possible. On 7 August 2008 the Minister for Health, Social Services and Public Safety, Michael McGimpsey, advised the Chairman that formal approvals were now in place and a joint business case would be prepared with the NIO.

In spring 2010 the Policing Board was advised by the Desertcreat Programme Manager that completion of the College was now targeted for 2013. Design development had progressed towards a full planning application and the business case had been submitted to the funding departments in December 2009. It was envisaged that advertisements for contractors could be placed in summer 2010. Nevertheless, it was not until July 2012 that the full planning application was submitted for the joint college. Approval in late 2013 for the business case, though not yet the full and final business case, allowed discussions to begin with the preferred construction consortium, which had been chosen in December. Construction was then expected to begin on what was now called the Northern Ireland Community Safety College later in 2014. However, the Community Safety College Programme Board announced on 2 April 2014 that it had discontinued the current stage of the preferred bidder process, as the consortium had 'unfortunately been unable to demonstrate that they can offer an affordable and compliant bid'. The Programme Board undertook at that point to re-evaluate the options.

14.7   In Conclusion

There are few issues that that can provoke greater local interest in the community than the proposed closure of a local police station. Where the local community becomes vigorous in expressing its views this, in turn, puts pressure on the locally elected representatives to be seen to be making a robust case against closure. It certainly proved to be an important issue for the credibility of individual DPPs and it was important that the District Commander should properly be seen to be seeking their views in any consultation prior to consideration for closure. It was another area where the balance of *Political* and *Independent Members* on the Policing Board allowed that body, albeit in some cases after protracted consideration, to reach a consensus on decisions to be taken and progress made, while nevertheless permitting elected members to be seen to have argued their case on behalf of 'their' constituency.

This issue also brought into play the long-standing debate as to how a community is best policed. Often community representatives will, reflecting the views of individuals as shown in the annual DPP survey, for example, press for the maximum beat patrols on foot. Such a facility can be associated in the public's mind with a local police station. On the other hand, especially in Northern Ireland, with the heightened security threat, every police station that is kept open ties up additional resources in safeguarding the building and those based there. With the closure of individual local police stations, despite the limited introduction of bicycle patrols, there was inevitably an increased usage of vehicles, at least to transport police officers from what was then the nearest station to the particular locale being policed.

It is interesting to observe that similar issues have been addressed in more recent times by the Garda Síochána. It was announced in the *Irish Times* of 12 December 2011 that a total of 39 stations were to close or had already been closed, with 31 of these to be closed during 2012. It was then announced in spring 2012 that the Minister for Justice had asked the Garda Commissioner to drop a second list of locations that could be closed, with the issue being addressed in the Garda's policing plan for 2013. The President of the Association of Garda Sergeants and Inspectors was critical of the Minister's approach. However, the Minister was reported in the *Irish Times* of 3 April 2012 to have asked: *'Can anyone plausibly argue that we absolutely need 703 Garda stations in such a small country?'*

Much has been written elsewhere about the stop–start progress on the new Police College. It is probably the biggest single failure in implementation of the Independent Commission recommendations. Certainly the planning has dragged on for far too long, with the result, not least, that the vast majority of the new recruits to the PSNI have all been trained in the inadequate facilities at Garnerville. And when (or perhaps, in the light of developments in spring 2014, it should rather be 'if') the College is finally built at Desertcreat, only time will tell whether the traditional bricks and mortar model of police colleges has become outmoded. However, there should be advantages for all three organisations (the PSNI, the Northern Ireland Prison Service and the Northern Ireland Fire and Rescue Service) in the Northern Ireland Community Safety College as now proposed.

It is perhaps possible to attribute – in part – some responsibility for a few of the delays along the way, such as the changes to the original decision over the distance from police headquarters in Belfast, to the Policing Board, but, as shown above, the Board was consistently robust in both promoting the College and pressing at all levels of the British Government and the devolved administration (and even the Irish Government as well) to get on with it. More substantive delay factors have been the ambition of the original plans as compared with the funding that was actually available, the complexity of the Northern Ireland system in processing business cases, and the actual cost estimates.

References

The Estate Strategy of the Police Service of Northern Ireland, National Audit
   Office, HC 101, December 2006
Irish Times, 12 December 2011
Irish Times, 3 April 2012

CHAPTER FIFTEEN

Individual Incidents and Cases that Impacted on the Policing Board

15.1 Introduction

In any assessment of the Northern Ireland Policing Board (the Policing Board or Board) due account must be taken of incidents and events that occurred during the period under review. In addition, some issues arose from incidents that had happened in the years before the Board's formation.

While some of these incidents and cases occurred as a consequence of the particular circumstances then obtaining in Northern Ireland, none of the specifics were predictable and some posed major challenges for the Policing Board. This was not just in terms of the Board's role in holding the Chief Constable to account but also in regard to both its internal dynamics and its ability to respect the confidentiality of information provided to Members from the Police Service of Northern Ireland (the Police Service or the PSNI) or other security sources. A further dimension was the impact that major incidents had on the relationship between political parties and on both the *political* and *peace processes*. As this chapter shows, such challenges cropped up pretty much from the Board's very beginning. When one considers the frequency and salience of the incidents it is the more remarkable that the Policing Board not only held together as an entity but also showed leadership in handling matters of wide public concern of a kind that would rarely, if ever, be required of police authorities in other jurisdictions.

This chapter highlights some of the incidents and individual cases, while bringing out the Policing Board's response. It can do so only on a selective basis, however, as otherwise the account would be disproportionately long. However, it should not be concluded that the Board did not give equally serious consideration to other cases that are not mentioned in the following paragraphs.

Some of the matters cited were the result of organised crime, while others were individual or random criminal acts.

15.2   Individual Incidents

15.2.1   The Castlereagh Break-in

On Sunday 17 March 2002 (St Patrick's Day) there was a break-in, strictly an 'aggravated burglary', into the Special Branch office in the police station at Castlereagh in East Belfast. The incident was to pose a major challenge for the Policing Board at an early stage in its development. Significantly, it provided a further avenue for the Board to press for reforms to Special Branch and other changes in line with the Recommendations in the Report of The Independent Commission On Policing For Northern Ireland (the Independent Commission).

It was apparent from the moment the news broke that the incident would have major repercussions. The fourth meeting of the Policing Board's Corporate Policy Committee was due to be held on 20 March 2002. The then Chief Constable, Sir Ronnie Flanagan, together with Detective Chief Superintendent Phil Wright, briefed those present on the situation and the police action to date. The Chief Constable made clear that he viewed the incident as extremely serious and that a criminal investigation was ongoing. The matter had also been referred to the Police Ombudsman's office under section 55 of the Police (Northern Ireland) Act 1998. A review of security had been instantly directed.

A press statement issued by the Policing Board after that meeting on 20 March 2002 quoted the Board Chairman as saying:

'The Policing Board has been kept fully informed since this incident occurred. This is a very serious incident and we are concerned about all the implications of what happened at Castlereagh on Sunday night.

The Chief Constable has today updated us on the steps he is taking to ensure this matter is fully investigated. The Board has also been briefed on the remit of the Ombudsman and the role of the independent investigator to be appointed by the Secretary of State.

We are satisfied that these measures will assure the wider public that positive action is being taken to get to the bottom of this serious breach in security and ensure that all possible ramifications are fully assessed and dealt with.

The full facts of the incident are still being put together but the Chief Constable has been asked to provide regular updates to the Board on progress in all aspects of the investigation.

When this has been completed, the Board will objectively assess the facts and take whatever action it considers necessary to meet its responsibilities and ensuring the openness, accountability, effectiveness and efficiency of the Police Service.

Members of the Board want to satisfy themselves that effective mechanisms will be put in place to ensure this never happens again and most importantly, that any lessons learned are fully acted on.'

On the same day, 20 March 2002, the Secretary of State for Northern Ireland, Dr John Reid, announced that he had asked Sir John Chilcot (a former Northern Ireland Office (NIO) Permanent Secretary) to conduct a review into issues arising from the break-in at Castlereagh. Sir John's terms of reference were to establish

' • *How an unauthorised access was gained to a Special Branch Office;*

• *the extent of any damage caused to national security;*

• *the adequacy of action subsequently taken to mitigate any such damage and to prevent unauthorised access there and in similar buildings elsewhere in Northern Ireland;*

• *any wider lessons to be learned; and*

• *to make recommendations.'*

Sir John Chilcot was to be assisted by Mr Colin Smith, a former Her Majesty's Inspector of Constabulary. Sir John's review was to proceed in parallel with the criminal investigation. The announcement added that '*in the nature of the exercise, it is unlikely that this report can be placed in the public domain*'.

On the morning of 22 March 2002 the Policing Board Vice-Chairman, Denis Bradley, was interviewed on the BBC Radio *Good Morning Ulster* programme. Mr Bradley began by stating that in his opinion Sir John Chilcot would not be seen as wholly independent, given his previous involvement in Northern Ireland, asserting that he had been 'at least partially responsible for MI5 at a time when the peace process was trying to kick off'. He then said, in response to a question, that this was:

'going to give a field day to two groups of people, those who complain that [the Independent Commission] is a total disaster and those that complain that [its Recommendations] aren't exactly implemented. In other words, those who say that [the Independent Commission] has brought about all our problems on the one hand, and those, like Sinn Féin, who say that [its Recommendations] haven't been implemented. Now the truth of the matter is that we are on a journey which is going to bring us hopefully, and I think we've made great strides in this, into a new policing arena in which there's going to be policing for all of the community. A police that is not paramilitarised, police that has moved out of a war situation into civilian and civilised policing made accountable, open and transparent to the public. That's what we are about and I think we have made great strides.'

Mr Bradley added that the Policing Board had not been consulted about the appointment of Sir John Chilcot and that their views had been made known to John Reid.

At the Policing Board meeting's *Private Session* on 4 April 2002 the Chairman informed Members that he had met with Sir John Chilcot and Mr Colin Smith the previous week. Members decided to ask Acting Chief Constable Colin Cramphorn for further information about the lines of inquiry being carried out, as there were public confidence issues associated with the incident. They also discussed the need for legal advice about the extent to which the Policing Board might reasonably have access to Sir John Chilcot's review and recommendations. The Chairman advised Members that the matters would be considered further by the Corporate Policy Committee.

One issue for the Board was the feeling of some Members that the first and part of the third bullet point in the terms of reference for the Chilcot inquiry were more to do with the physical security of premises owned by the Policing Board than with national security; in other words those points should come under the Board's rather than the Secretary of State's jurisdiction.

On 19 April 2002 BBC Radio Ulster News announced that:

'*Detectives here have found IRA intelligence files which included a list of senior members of the Conservative Party. The information was found in police searches which followed the Castlereagh break-in. The files are also said to have details on Army bases in Britain and security sources say they believe the IRA's intelligence-gathering operation had been recently updated.*'

In response to a question Acting Chief Constable Colin Cramphorn said in an interview on the lunchtime programme that it was no secret that the PSNI had carried out a number of actions which had taken them into the Republican community. It was certainly a line, and a major line, of enquiry, although of course there were other lines of enquiry as well.

On the same day Mr Conor Murphy of Sinn Féin said in a BBC Radio *Talkback* interview that '*Republicans have been very upfront, very open and said quite clearly that this is absolutely nothing to do with them.*' The security commentator Brian Rowan said on the same programme that the initial assessment had been that it was some sort of inside job, but '*then, you know, the assessment changed to something even more unthinkable, people suggesting that this was the IRA, aided by an insider*'. He added that the detectives carrying out the investigation were still keen to talk to a former chef at the Castlereagh complex, who had since gone to live in America and '*who was in the building on the day of the robbery, even though he no longer worked there*'. Brian Rowan also said in the interview that the police had carried out a number of searches in Belfast and Derry/Londonderry after the break-in, and in those searches they had found '*what they believe is IRA intelligence-gathering information*'.

At the meeting of the Policing Board on 2 May 2002 the Chairman advised Members that Sir John Chilcot had said that he would inform the Secretary of State that the Policing Board wished to be informed about his report. The Chairman had also asked the Secretary of State to speak to Members on the issue of national security at a dinner with the Policing Board on 21 May 2002. On the specific point as to whether the Policing Board had a legal right to see the Chilcot report on completion, the legal advice was clear that it had not. The decision on whether or not to release part or all of the report would be a matter for the Secretary of State.

The Policing Board agreed at its 2 May 2002 meeting that the Board should seek a report into security procedures currently operational at police stations or police buildings in Northern Ireland. Subsequently, the Board's Chief Executive wrote to the Acting Chief Constable requesting a report covering the steps that the PSNI had taken to review the security of police stations and establishments following the Castlereagh break-in, together with the results of such reviews and the action taken or planned to rectify any weaknesses identified.

On 22 June 2002 the Guardian newspaper carried a report which stated that:

'Senior security service and British police sources now believe that the extraordinary break-in at the Castlereagh complex in East Belfast was an "inside job", undertaken by renegade special branch officers, possibly with the help of agents working for an undercover army unit.'

The article went on to say that in the weeks after the raid security services had pointed the finger at Republican paramilitaries and that *'Republicans were outraged when police and soldiers swooped on 12 homes and business premises in Belfast and Derry, arresting six people, including the former IRA hunger striker Raymond McCartney and Bobby Storey whom security sources claim is the IRA's head of intelligence.'* It added that none had been charged in connection with the raid, but police were seeking, however, to extradite a named person, a chef who formerly worked at Castlereagh, from the United States. The article inferred that there was a difference in approach between the PSNI investigation, led by Phil Wright, which was *'still focusing on republican involvement'*, and that of British security sources, who *'have had a change of heart'*.

On 1 July 2002 the Acting Chief Constable wrote in reply to the Policing Board's Chief Executive. He stated that the first priority had been to have an immediate review of all Special Branch accommodation at certain locations, and a number of recommendations had been made in respect of each. A further audit was taking place in other locations. On 3 July 2002 the Policing Board Chairman wrote to the Secretary of State after it had come to the attention of the Board at its meeting on that day that Sir John Chilcot had delivered an interim report on the national security issues of Castlereagh. He requested copies of the interim report for the Board, redacted as necessary.

Following a meeting with the Board Chairman the Secretary of State wrote in response on 18 July 2002. He began by stating that he had confirmed in Parliament the previous week that he had received a work-in-progress report from Sir John Chilcot and expected to receive the full report later that year. The (interim) report focused on the stage reached in their work and set out areas of further study, rather than drawing conclusions at this stage. Accordingly, the Secretary of State did not propose to make the report more widely available. That said, it highlighted serious concerns over aspects of security arrangements at Castlereagh and over the adequacy of remedial steps taken since the break-in. The Secretary of State would be writing to the Acting Chief Constable to draw those to his attention. This letter was placed before the Policing Board's Corporate Policy Committee at its next meeting on 22 August 2002 and thereafter was circulated to all Board Members.

At the Policing Board meeting of 3 October 2002 Hugh Orde, who had taken up post as Chief Constable the previous month, updated Members about the investigation into the break-in at Castlereagh. The Assistant Chief Constable (ACC) Operations informed Members that he would head a major review into the security of PSNI stations.

On 22 October 2002 the Policing Board Chairman and Vice-Chairman met Sir John Chilcot and Mr Colin Smith. A number of key points were recorded, including the work of the PSNI criminal investigation, the review of security police premises that had been commissioned by the former Chief Constable Sir Ronnie Flanagan, and that Sir John's report relating to wider lessons learned had not yet been completed. It was agreed there would be further contact, with an invitation extended to Sir John to attend a future Policing Board meeting, should the Secretary of State be agreeable.

At the Policing Board *Private Session* on 6 November 2002 the Chief Constable provided an update on the review into security. On 19 November 2002 the Policing Board Chairman wrote to Sir John Chilcot, specifically inviting him to address the Policing Board on issues regarding security of police premises, which clearly fell within the remit of the Policing Board. He suggested that the meeting might take place with the Corporate Policy Committee of the Board, which was due to meet on 17 December 2002. In the event, Sir John advised the Policing Board Chairman that that date would not be practicable as he had yet to complete his report to the Secretary of State. The Committee decided that the Chairman should write to the Secretary of State seeking his permission for Sir John to meet Policing Board Members, and the Chairman did so on 19 December 2002.

On 19 February 2003 the new Secretary of State, Paul Murphy, replied to the Chairman's letter, in conclusion agreeing that in taking forward its responsibilities in this area it would be helpful for the Policing Board to discuss with Sir John his views on physical security. He would leave the arrangements to Sir John.

At the meeting of the Policing Board on 3 April 2003 Members noted that the NIO had advised that Sir John's report was not yet completed. The ACC Operations updated the Board on the progress in implementing the recommendations from the PSNI security review.

On 9 July 2003 Sir John Chilcot and Mr Colin Smith met the Policing Board Chairman and Vice-Chairman. The main focus of the meeting was the security of police premises, and Sir John and Colin Smith said that they were content with the progress that had been made in taking forward physical security. It was recognised that there was a balance to be struck when deciding the level of security to be implemented, taking account of the high cost of implementation. It was agreed there was a continuing role for the Policing Board in ensuring that progress was maintained. Sir John stated that he had yet to complete his report but hoped to do so shortly.

On 15 July 2003 the Secretary of State advised the Board Chairman that he had now received the full report. Given the subject matter he did not intend making the report public, but he shared a copy of the statement that he had made in Parliament that day. On one matter, the Secretary of State said:

'There has, over the months, been a significant degree of speculation about who might have been involved in this incident, including allegations of collusion. I can confirm that the review did not uncover any evidence whatsoever that Members of Government agencies were in any way involved in this incident, although the police investigation is continuing. The review was also able to provide a satisfactory assurance about the quality of the police investigation, confirming the conclusions of a separate review of the professional quality and standard of the investigation, carried out by the Metropolitan Police Service last year at the request of the PSNI ...

The report came to certain conclusions about how the incident might have occurred and made recommendations about how to avoid any similar incidents *happening in the future. I am sure that the House will recognise that I am constrained by the wider aspects and implications of national security from going into any details on these matters.'*

On 24 July 2003 the Policing Board's Corporate Policy Committee noted developments. On 6 August 2003 the Policing Board's Acting Chief Executive wrote to the Chief Constable stating that Board Members would like a greater understanding of what recommendations were made following the break-in, the progress made in implementing them, and the cost. He noted that Sir John had suggested that this was an area where the Policing Board could usefully undertake a monitoring role. On 13 October 2003 the Chief Constable provided the Policing Board with a synopsis of the 40 recommendations that had been made with regard to security improvements within PSNI as a result of the external audit of existing security procedures, together with a summary of progress on implementation for each.

At the Policing Board *Public Session* on 3 December 2003 Sam Foster (Ulster Unionist Party (UUP)) asked about progress with the police investigation. The ACC advised the Board that the file was still with the Director of Public Prosecutions. The Policing Board continued to keep implementation of the recommendations under review. For example, at the Policing Board's *Public Session* on 12 May 2004 a summary update was provided by the PSNI Director of Finance and Support Services.

15.2.2   The Search at Stormont

At approximately 8:30 a.m. on the morning of 4 October 2002 the PSNI arrived at Stormont Parliament Buildings in a large convoy of Land Rovers to conduct a search of the Sinn Féin offices on the second floor of the building. This operation followed the search of a property in West Belfast which had recovered significant numbers of documents including sensitive targeting information. The following factual account of the search at Stormont is taken from the subsequent public statement by the Police Ombudsman Nuala O'Loan, following her investigation into complaints about it:

'The PSNI officers were met by security and administrative staff from

Parliament Buildings who refused entry to the offices until a suitable search warrant had been produced. Once the search warrant had arrived, four officers were admitted to one of the Sinn Féin offices in order to conduct the search which lasted some 50 minutes; one Sinn Féin member was permitted to watch the search which involved two teams. The search teams, which at the maximum during a changeover period had 25 officers present, were mostly wearing public order uniforms consisting of blue overalls and peaked caps. Both the highly visible nature of the operation, which was extensively filmed and later shown on television news, and the fact that the search was carried out in Sinn Féin offices within a government building, made it highly controversial. In particular, there was widespread condemnation in the immediate aftermath of the search of the size of the PSNI team and their public order uniforms.'

In a press statement issued later that day the Chairman of the Policing Board stated:

'It is the job of the Policing Board to hold the PSNI to account for their actions not to direct or authorise specific operations. Clearly criminal investigation and resulting search operations, such as has happened today, are operational matters – such operations are not and should not be authorised in advance by this Board. However, I believe that the Board will raise this matter with the Chief Constable at its next meeting. There has been speculation in the press reporting of this morning's operation that the police may have been heavy-handed in their approach – obviously if any complaints arise from this operation they will be dealt with by the Police Ombudsman.'

In an interview on 7 October 2002 on Sky News Chief Constable Hugh Orde was asked *'Are you happy with the way Friday's raid happened?'* He replied: *'I am not happy ... We could have done the raid in a more sensitive and appropriate style, though that is easy to say with the benefit of hindsight.'* He added that he had met the Speaker of the Northern Ireland Assembly to express his disappointment to him. On the other hand he added that the need to search that office was clear in his mind as an investigator. The PSNI were focusing on a major crime investigation, and serious charges had been brought. The search was not the issue – it was the style in which it had been conducted. He emphasised that no one had put him under any political pressure whatsoever in relation to it – it was a police investigation.

On the following day, 8 October 2002, the Policing Board Chairman welcomed the Chief Constable's apology relating to the search operation:

'It takes true professionalism and real strength of character to admit when mistakes are made and to do so publicly. The Chief Constable has stated that while the raid at Stormont was necessary it could have been done in a more sensitive and appropriate style – I welcome his openness and honesty. Clearly the Board will want to question Mr Orde more fully about the way this raid was carried out and will do so at the earliest opportunity available. It is after all the job of the Board to hold the PSNI to account through the Chief Constable for its actions.

But the Board's role is to look at the policing aspects of this issue not the political – the Board will want to keep politics out of policing, and ensure an effective and efficient service is maintained.'

On 10 October 2002 the Chief Constable and colleagues met the Policing Board's Community Affairs Committee at the invitation of the Board's Chairman. The Chairman of the latter Committee, Vice-Chairman of the Board Denis Bradley, explained that Members of each political party on the Board had been consulted before the invitation had been issued. The Chief Constable said that he welcomed the opportunity to meet Board Members to discuss the events of 4 October. He advised that he been aware that the search operation was taking place at Stormont but had not been briefed on the specific tactics for it. The search had been carried out using approved Home Office guidelines and had been conducted according to those rules. The Chief Constable said that training would be reviewed to include 'critical incident training'.

Dixon and O'Kane tell the next part of the story succinctly:

'The head of Sinn Féin's Northern Ireland Assembly administration, Denis Donaldson [along with three other Republicans] were arrested. As a result of the raid both the Democratic Unionist Party (DUP) and Ulster Unionist Party (UUP) Ministers threatened to resign unless Sinn Féin was expelled from government (the UUP had announced a month earlier that that its members would resign in January 2003 if the IRA failed to demonstrate it had left violence behind for good). On 14 October 2002 the British Government suspended the Assembly.' (p. 103)

At the meeting of the Policing Board on 5 December 2002 the Chairman informed Members that he had received a letter of complaint (dated 1 December) from former Chief Superintendent W.J. (Bill) Lowry. The Chairman and Vice-Chairman stressed the need for the Board to deal with the matter in a responsible, impartial, and confidential manner, particularly in view of media speculation. It was agreed that a press release be issued indicating that the complaint had been received and that legal advice was being taken. On 9 December 2002 Ulster Television asserted in a story that a *'major internal row erupted after Ian Paisley Jnr (DUP) alleged [Policing Board] Members were misled over Chief Superintendent Bill Lowry's early retirement from the force'*. The *'Special Branch chief stood down last month just weeks after he led the raids on Parliament Buildings and the arrest of four Republicans'*, the report added. On the same day a Policing Board release confirmed that the Chairman had received a letter of complaint in respect of Chief Superintendent Lowry's grievance from Ian Paisley Jnr and that he would be responding to him in due course.

The legal advice that the Policing Board received was discussed at a special meeting of the Board held on 11 December 2002. A press release issued confirmed that *'as a result of the advice and that discussion, the Board has agreed to forward the complaint to the Police Ombudsman, Nuala O'Loan, for her attention'*. In turn, the Police Ombudsman issued a release on 15 December stating that, as the matter was not a public complaint (to which section 52 of the Police (Northern Ireland) Act 1998 refers), she could not accept it as such, but she had informed the Policing Board that she would investigate the matter if referral was made either under section 55(1) of the Act or under Regulation 7 of the RUC (Conduct) (Senior Officers) Regulations 2000. Further legal advice was taken on behalf of the Board and the Corporate Policy Committee met on 17 December, following which it was agreed to write to Mr Lowry to advise him that the Board had decided to make preliminary enquiries in relation to the allegations in his letter of 1 December 2002 and to clarify a number of issues raised in it. Following a further exchange of correspondence with the Policing Board Mr Lowry gave an interview to the *Daily Telegraph* which was published on 13 January 2003. In the interview Mr Lowry asserted that

'[He] was forced out of his job to appease Sinn Féin after the raid at their offices

at Stormont last year ... I was the fall guy for the raid. I was given as a gift to Sinn Féin to make the talks work.'

He added that MI5 had contacted the PSNI Chief Constable and said that he, Mr Lowry, *'had to go because they wouldn't work with him any more'*.

On 15 January 2003 the Chief Constable wrote to the Policing Board Chairman outlining a brief factual version of events in relation to the incident. He stressed that he had made his decision without the benefit of any external influence, and that Mr Lowry had not been forced to retire. On 22 January 2003 reports appeared in various Northern Ireland newspapers to the effect that the Police Ombudsman was set to probe Mr Lowry's allegations. On the following day the Policing Board's Corporate Policy Committee met and decided, as set out in a press release issued on behalf of the Policing Board, that in the light of the preliminary enquiries made by the Board no proceeding should be taken under the RUC Regulations 2000, but that in view of the allegation that the Chief Constable may have acted improperly, influenced by external considerations, it was desirable that in the public interest the Police Ombudsman should investigate the matter under section 55 of the Police (Northern Ireland) Act 1998. The Policing Board Chairman stated on behalf of the Board in the release that:

'Since its creation, the [Policing Board's Corporate Policy] Committee has shown by its record that it is willing to deal thoroughly with all issues that have come before it and reporting its actions publicly when it has been in a position to do so ... It is important that the matter is investigated in a manner that is open and transparent. The Committee considers the allegations contained in Mr Lowry's complaint of outside influence to be of a public interest and to ensure justice for all concerned warrants a full investigation by the Police Ombudsman.'

The Board Chairman wrote accordingly to the Police Ombudsman (and also the Chief Constable and Mr Lowry) on 24 January 2003.

All Policing Board Members were invited to a special meeting of the Board's Corporate Policy Committee on 9 July 2003, at which the Police Ombudsman was to present a report of her investigation into the allegations against the Chief Constable by Mr Lowry. In her

presentation the Police Ombudsman emphasised the highly confidential nature of the report. Board Members were advised that five
complaints against the Chief Constable had been identified; in respect
of each of those complaints, none were found to be substantiated. The
Police Ombudsman recommended no disciplinary action.

At the Policing Board meeting's *Public Session* on 3 March 2004,
in response to a question from Vice-Chairman Denis Bradley, and
following a preliminary appearance in court on 5 February that year,
ACC Kinkaid gave details of the charges against three individuals who
had been returned for trial – Denis Donaldson, Ciaran Kearney, and
William MacKessy. They were each indicted on accounts of possessing
information of a kind likely to be of use to terrorists.

On 1 August 2004 the Police Ombudsman published a statement
following her investigations into complaints about the PSNI search of
the Sinn Féin offices in Stormont on 4 October 2002. The statement
began:

*'The Police Ombudsman said she has found no evidence to substantiate allega-
tions that the searches were "politically motivated" but has also said the scale
and manner of the police operation was totally disproportionate.'*

In her statement she said that she had received six complaints relating
to the police search, which included allegations that the search had
been politically motivated, that the police had alerted the media prior
to the search, and that it had itself been excessive. A further allegation was made that people were not permitted to enter the room to
be searched prior to the search, and that police officers had assaulted
two people during the search. In the course of her investigation 35
people had been interviewed, including police officers, Assembly and
Parliament Building staff, Sinn Féin representatives, and the Justice
of the Peace who signed the warrant to allow the search to take place.
PSNI intelligence files, 'control logs', and other documentation were
examined, as were broadcast and security videos.

The Police Ombudsman said that she had found no evidence to
suggest that the search was politically motivated, or that it was
designed to damage Sinn Féin and the *peace process*. The search of an
office was part of the normal police process following the search of a
home in circumstances such as this. She concluded specifically that:

'On the basis of the intelligence available, I can say that the Detective Chief Superintendent's decision to seek a warrant authorising a search of a specific desk in the Sinn Féin offices was reasonable, proportionate and legal.'

However, no proper consideration was given by police to the fact that they were searching the buildings of a legislative assembly and this was a significant failing. Moreover, there was no necessity for the presence at Stormont of the large number of officers who attended. She welcomed the Chief Constable's early decision to apologise for the heavy-handed nature of this operation – 'he was right to do so'.

In addition, the Ombudsman upheld the right of the police officers to preserve the integrity of the search scene pending the arrival of the search warrant and noted that there was insufficient evidence to warrant disciplinary actions against any officer.

Subsequently, on 9 December 2005 the Policing Board Chairman advised Members of the withdrawal of the charges against all three individuals, following consideration by the Director of Public Prosecutions. The Chairman also advised Members that, together with the Vice-Chairman and a representative from each the political parties represented on the Board, he would be meeting the Chief Constable and the Deputy Chief Constable (DCC) for an update.

In an article in the *Sunday Times* dated 11 December 2005 the journalist Liam Clarke wrote that:

'The collapse of the Stormont "spy ring" prosecutions last Thursday followed a decision by the security forces to protect the identity of a civilian informant who gave RUC Special Branch access to IRA intelligence records. Last week, however, the prosecution decided to give no evidence when they learned that they would have to divulge details of the informant as well as a range of bugging and surveillance operations that were run against IRA suspects over a three-month period.'

In an interview on the BBC *Good Morning Ulster* programme on 20 December 2005 the Chief Constable described in some detail the documents that had been recovered from the property in West Belfast on 4 October 2002. He said that much of the material was

'Sensitive targeting information against politicians, civil servants, members of

the police service, and members of the prison service, but also a large number of
documents relating for example to discussions between the Prime Minister and
the President of the United States.'

He also referred to records of discussions between Governments and
Northern Ireland parties, and documents that had been taken from
the Parades Commission also being recovered from the property
in West Belfast. Following that, the limited search in one office in
Stormont had resulted in two disks being taken from there in relation
to the same investigation. In response, the interviewer, Wendy Austin,
pointed out that the search had in the end resulted in the suspension
of the Executive. She asked if the information had come from Denis
Donaldson, *'who tells us now that he was a spy?'* The Chief Constable
responded that it was not the search that brought Stormont down, but
the activity of people stealing documents from Government offices
that the PSNI had recovered in West Belfast that brought Stormont
down. He went on to state that there was case law that said very
clearly that you must not confirm or deny that any person is or is not
an informant. He added that he had pushed seriously for a prosecution because he thought the best way of airing the subject would have
been through a court of law where everyone could have stood back,
looked at the evidence, and formed a view in their own minds on
what went on. However, the Director of Public Prosecutions had made
what he said was the right decision for wider public interest issues.
The Chief Constable also stressed that every time the PSNI recruited
an informant they were subject to the Regulation of Investigatory
Powers Act 2000, which constrained how they recruited and used
informants, and was subject to oversight. The PSNI complied with
the law very, very strictly.

The interview with the Chief Constable followed a news release
issued by the Secretary of State, Peter Hain, the previous day, 19
December 2005. He stated:

'The fact is that there was a paramilitary intelligence-gathering operation
at Stormont. The fact is that a huge number of stolen documents were recov-
ered from a house in West Belfast. The fact is that these documents – many of
them classified as Secret and Confidential – related not only to the work of the
NIO, but to contacts between the British and Irish Governments and with the

American administration. The fact is that as a result over 1000 people had to be warned and it cost some £35m to ensure their safety.'

A special meeting of the Board's Corporate Policy Committee was convened on 20 December 2005 to discuss the matter and consider whether any recommendations should be made to the Policing Board. The Board Chairman reported on meetings that he and the Vice-Chairman had had with the Secretary of State, the Chief Constable, and the Police Ombudsman in recent times. Members discussed the case itself, its impact on public confidence in the PSNI, and the role of the Policing Board as it related to the case.

The lines used with the media after that meeting noted that in the *Public Sessions* of Policing Board meetings presentations had been delivered on the new structures, policies, processes, and practices in place for Crime Operations and the management of intelligence and that, perhaps for the first time in United Kingdom policing, the Policing Board was briefed on the stringent requirements to be met for the management of informants – all on the public record.

Denis Donaldson was shot dead at his remote County Donegal home early in April 2006. On the back of the Report by Judge Smithwick published in Dublin in December 2013 into the murders of two senior Royal Ulster Constabulary (RUC) officers in South Armagh on 20 March 1989, Jim Cusack, in the *Sunday Independent* of 8 December 2013, commented: *'no group claimed his killing but, according to usual reliable sources, his killers were members of the Tyrone Provisional IRA ...'.*

15.2.3   Sean Brown's Murder

Sean Brown, a prominent member of the local Gaelic Athletic Association club, had been abducted and murdered near Bellaghy on 12 May 1997. The RUC had considered this a sectarian attack and a full-scale murder investigation was launched, but the police had not charged anyone at the time. Some years subsequently, following a complaint from solicitors acting on behalf of the widow of Mr Brown in January 2001, the Police Ombudsman undertook an investigation into the original police investigation under section 55 of the Police (Northern Ireland) Act 1998. The Ombudsman's report was published on 19 January 2004. It contained three recommendations: a full independent review into the murder; the review to be linked to two other murders in which the same weapon was used; and that compensation should be paid to the Brown family. Other issues were identified in the report, including the following: an assessment that the investigation by the RUC had been incomplete and inadequate; there had been a failure of leadership and management of the RUC inquiry; dissemination of information from Special Branch had been poor; and critical documents including the investigation policy file had gone missing after the Ombudsman was called in; however, there was no evidence of police collusion in the murder. The report concluded that the investigation into the murder of Mr Brown had not been properly carried out, and that *no earnest effort was made to identify the persons who murdered Mr Sean Brown*.

The Ombudsman's report recommended that there should be a full independent review of the inquiry into the murder, which would identify and assess all evidential opportunities. However, in the same paragraph (16.1) the Ombudsman recorded that: *the Chief Constable has now informed the Police Ombudsman that he intends there will be a full reinvestigation of the murder which obviates the need for a review*.

In a statement issued on the day of publication Martin McGuinness, then Mid-Ulster MP, said that the report was *a damning indictment of collusion and cover-up*. He said there was an onus on Chief Constable Hugh Orde to state publicly if the individuals involved in the original investigation were still members of his force and to explain how files went missing from barracks where only his officers had access to them.

In a letter to the Policing Board Chairman dated 23 January 2004, solicitors acting on behalf of Mrs Brown asserted that a full reinvestigation of the murder by the PSNI would not be consistent with their client's right pursuant to Article 2 of the European Convention on Human Rights. The letter asked whether the Policing Board proposed to recommend or direct that a police force other than the PSNI should have carriage of any new full reinvestigation.

At the Board's meeting in *Public Session* on 5 February 2004 Members considered the Ombudsman's report. The DCC Paul Leighton was questioned about the Ombudsman's recommendations. Alex Attwood (Social Democratic and Labour Party (SDLP)) asked that, while the police might enhance the investigation in a number of regards that might indeed help build confidence, was it not better to adopt the recommendation (for a full independent review). The DCC said that *'our minds are still open as to what method of reinvestigation we will opt for'*. The PSNI were committed to a reinvestigation; they accepted that there were failings in the original investigation; and they would try to proceed as expeditiously as possible in order to provide both justice and confidence. Ian Paisley Jnr (Democratic Unionist Party (DUP)) noted that the family of Mr Brown and their legal team had made it very clear publicly and in writing to the Policing Board that they really were not interested in the police or the Chief Constable having anything further to do with this case. He added *'I think that is very sad, but nonetheless that is their right to have that position.'* He added that:

'It is maybe best for the police and for the authorities to stand back and to allow the family and their legal team to try and get their independent inquiry from the Government, as other organisations and as other people have done in the past. Would there be any merit in you considering that aspect of it or is it that you feel the police have a duty on this particular matter?'

Mr Leighton said in reply that he felt the police had a duty to investigate all crimes and investigate them properly, and that he thought it was their duty to do their best to remedy the situation. He added that the PSNI were still trying to make contact with the family through solicitors and that they were still waiting for formal responses, so he could not definitely answer the question that day. *Independent Member* Barry Gilligan asked about the disappearance of police documents. Mr Leighton said that the *occurrence book*, which was one of the missing documents, had been recovered but he accepted that the disappearance of the *policy log* was a much more serious matter, which they were continuing to investigate. Immediate measures had been put in train to ensure that there could be no repetition.

Political Member Sammy Wilson (DUP) noted that there had been many unsolved cases and many cases which people across Northern Ireland over the previous 30 years felt might have been dealt with in a better way, including the longstanding murders of former police officers. He felt there might be a need for criteria on which cases were going to be dealt with, rather than an appearance that, if one shouted loud enough, one would get an independent inquiry. He asked the DCC what historical cases they had, where they were really policing the past rather than the present, and what kind of resources this tied up. Mr Leighton said that there were nearly 1,900 unsolved murders in Northern Ireland. The PSNI were committed to try to ensure equity, but they must work firstly on cases where there were leads that they could follow. Where there was no evidential trail their duty was to try to communicate with the family as soon as possible, and, in all of these cases, the family must be remembered as paramount.

The Policing Board subsequently considered the correspondence from the solicitors; having taken legal advice, the Board asked the solicitors for clarification as to how the proposed course of action by the Chief Constable would violate their client's Article 2 rights.

On 12 May 2004 the Chief Constable outlined to the Policing Board the progress made by the PSNI and the family of Mr Brown in deciding the way in which the murder of Mr Brown would be reinvestigated. In the event, it was carried out by the PSNI.

In January 2010 the inquest into the murder of Sean Brown was informed that '*a police review of the murder could take as long as two years; it is a complex case*'. The murder was being re-examined by the Historical Enquiries Team.

15.2.4   The Northern Bank Robbery

On 20 December 2004 a major robbery took place at the premises of the Northern Bank in Belfast. Over £26m was stolen. Two families were kidnapped and threatened with death if they did not cooperate with the criminals concerned. In the case of one of the families, the gang, masquerading as police officers, tricked their way into the house by claiming that a family member had been killed in a car accident; once inside they donned masks, produced guns, and threatened the family. One of the hostages was later taken to an isolated forest where her car was burned and she was abandoned in the snow. At the suggestion of the PSNI the Northern Bank subsequently withdrew their current banknotes from circulation and replaced them with notes of a different design.

The next set meeting for the Policing Board was in early February. There were calls from Policing Board Members such as Ian Paisley Jnr (DUP) for an emergency meeting prior to Christmas. The Policing Board Chairman was quoted as saying:

'Our role is to hold the Chief Constable to account for the delivery of effective and efficient policing, so we will be looking to him in due course to talk us through the police's actions in this case. However, it is important that the PSNI are given the space to conduct their investigation unhindered by speculation or interference. The detectives involved need to be left at this time to do their job.'

Furthermore, in an article on 2 January 2005 the *Sunday Life* newspaper reported that the Policing Board Chairman had rejected demands from DUP *Political Members* both for a special meeting of the Policing Board in the following week and to summon the Chief Constable to probe police failures over the robbery. In a statement issued by Sammy Wilson on 3 January 2005 he welcomed what he described as:

'The climb down by the Chairman of the Policing Board who has relented to the DUP call for a special meeting ... The reluctance of the Chairman of the Board ... to call such a meeting is astonishing. Equally astonishing is the backing which he was given by Independent and other Political Members. ... There must be no holding back by the Chief Constable for fear of the political consequences. If PIRA was involved then the public has a right to know and it is up to politicians to decide what the political consequences for PIRA/Sinn Féin are ... The meeting with the [PSNI] on 20th January 2005 will give an opportunity to seek answers to these questions but the public have a right to ask why it is that such a meeting cannot take place until a month after the crime.'

On 6 January 2005 a press release was issued by the Policing Board announcing that the Chairman and Vice-Chairman would meet the Chief Constable and ACC Sam Kinkaid on the following day for a briefing on progress with the investigation into the Northern Bank robbery. Commenting ahead of those discussions, the Chairman said:

'Naturally, public interest in progress with the investigation is high, but equally, PSNI need to be given time and space to conduct their investigation – they need to focus on their lines of enquiry, and to see that any prosecutions that follow are not prejudiced. ... The role of the Policing Board is to hold the Chief Constable to account. As such, I have been briefed on developments by PSNI since the [Northern Bank Robbery] took place, and tomorrow's meeting with the Vice-Chairman and myself is just the latest briefing. The Chief Constable *will attend a further meeting of the Board's Corporate Policy Committee on January 20, to which all Board Members have been invited for this item, to brief them, and to take their questions ... In the meantime, the Policing Board will continue to monitor the situation closely.'*

In this release the Chairman, on behalf of the Policing Board, sought to strike a balance in tone in relation to the PSNI between support-iveness (thus adding to reassurance) and accountability (thus avoiding hostages to fortune and reinforcing the Board's independence).

On 7 January 2005 the Chief Constable Hugh Orde indicated that in his professional opinion responsibility for the Northern Bank robbery should be attributed to the Provisional IRA (PIRA).

The issue was of such significance that on 11 January 2005 the Secretary of State, Paul Murphy, made a statement in the House of Commons. He began by recalling that:

'As the House will be aware a major robbery took place at the Northern Bank in Belfast just before Christmas. At the end of last week the Chief Constable of Northern Ireland indicated that in his professional opinion responsibility for that robbery should be attributed to the PIRA. He also made the point that quite apart from the massive scale of this robbery – over £26m – it was in no sense a victimless crime. I have no doubt that the Chief Constable's opinion is well-founded. ... The PSNI thought initially that five groups could have been responsible for the robbery. Only when a great deal of evidence had been sifted did the Chief Constable make his statement.

Since the Chief Constable's statement, there has been much comment about the impact of these developments on the political process in Northern Ireland. I cannot hide my own judgement that the impact is deeply damaging.'

The Secretary of State went on to refer to the proposals that had been put forward by the British and Irish Governments for a comprehen-sive agreement which had been published earlier in December 2004, which represented a series of statements that would have been made; they included a statement to the effect that paramilitary activity by the PIRA would cease immediately and definitively. He regretted that this progress had been put in jeopardy and that he could not forecast with certainty when it would prove possible to re-establish an inclu-sive power-sharing Executive. He added that, as the Prime Minister had said repeatedly, it was entirely reasonable for Unionists to with-hold their cooperation until certain tests had been met.

A scheduled meeting of the Corporate Policy Committee of the Policing Board, to which all Board Members were invited, took place on 20 January 2005. The Chief Constable and ACC Kinkaid provided a confidential briefing on the Northern Bank robbery investigation, and all those present gave an assurance that the content of the briefing would remain confidential.

Following this *Private Session* with Policing Board Members, the *Irish Times* reported on the following day that *'the DUP and the SDLP say they are convinced that top-level republicans were behind last month £26.5 m [Northern Bank] robbery in Belfast'.* The paper quoted *Political Member* Alex Attwood (SDLP) as saying *'on the basis of what he [the Chief Constable] confirmed to the Board today, I... have no doubt his attribution in relation to this matter was correct.'* *Political Member* Sammy Wilson (DUP) was quoted as saying *'the one thing that was clear from the briefing given was that this would not have been done by people who were low-level operatives'.* The Board Chairman was quoted as saying that the briefing had gone into significant detail about the status of the investigation and that Members would leave the meeting much more informed: *'they would very much adopt the position that the PSNI should have the space to get on with the investigation'.*

In Ireland, the *Sunday Independent* newspaper of 30 January 2005 contained an article by Jim Cusack in which he expressed his opinion that:

'The reason for this limited return to war was that the PIRA/Sinn Féin leadership was facing a break in the ranks from hardliners who had come to believe that Adams and McGuinness were preparing to dump them in return for ministerial Mercs and perks at Stormont.'

He reported that the Garda Commissioner, Noel Conroy, had delivered *'a frank – and chilling – report to the Taoiseach'.*

At the *Public Session* of the Policing Board meeting on 3 February 2005 the Chairman noted that this was the first public meeting since the 'heist' on the Northern Bank which had exposed the PSNI to a high degree of press, public, and political scrutiny. As a public service, it was right and proper that the Police Service should be open to scrutiny in all aspects of its work and should be, through the Policing Board, publicly accountable. The Board was also responsible for supporting the PSNI towards the ends of effective and efficient policing, as well as for holding the Chief Constable to account for the delivery of those ends. The Chairman went on to say that the Policing Board had been instrumental in overseeing the changes that had taken place in the PSNI Crime Operations Department, which had formed part of a major restructuring arising from the recommendations of three major reports on crime investigation and intelligence sharing – Blakey, Crompton, and Stevens. The implementation of the recommendations of those reports was aimed at ensuring the procedures, processes, and practices now adopted by the PSNI met the highest UK standards in all aspects of crime investigation and intelligence gathering. He added that the successes of the Crime Operations Department had been significant; many thwarted crimes, for tactical reasons, never made the news agenda. The Board would continue to monitor progress but past experience would therefore suggest that the PSNI had the leadership, detective expertise, and officers necessary to handle the Northern Bank robbery investigation, complex as it was.

At the 3 February 2005 *Public Session* the Chief Constable updated Members on the progress of the investigation into the robbery. He said that over 1,400 actions had been taken, including 320 statements, 902 documents, and over 1,100 exhibits. It was the biggest inquiry currently underway in Northern Ireland. He made clear that he stood by his previous statement as to whom he believed was responsible for the raid, viz. the PIRA.

On 10 February 2005 the NIO published the latest report by the Independent Monitoring Commission (IMC) into paramilitary activity. In a written statement in Parliament the Secretary of State, Paul Murphy, said:

'*The IMC report concludes that the Northern Bank robbery was planned and undertaken by the PIRA. The Commission also concludes that PIRA was responsible for a number of other robberies which are listed in the report. The IMC concludes that Sinn Féin must bear its share of responsibility for the incidents mentioned in the report.*'

At the Board meeting's *Public Session* on 2 March 2005 the Chief

Constable said that the enquiries into the Northern Bank robbery continued. The PSNI had been working very closely with the Garda Síochána in relation to the substantial recovery of cash they had made. He added that the level of engagement between the two police services had been so substantial that it had gone as far as agreeing to joint forensic strategies. The Board continued to obtain regular updates from the Chief Constable on the progress of the Northern Bank robbery investigation: for example, in the Policing Board *Public Sessions* on 2 June 2005 and 7 December 2005 the DCC went into some detail about the nature of the search at Casement Park in West Belfast. He stressed that a full community impact assessment had been conducted during the planning of the operation, and the fewest possible resources were committed commensurate with the task. The use of four Land Rovers, one unmarked van, and one unmarked car represented a significant reduction in the resources that could reasonably have been expected to be committed 12 months previously. He pointed out that, by that date, 13 persons had been arrested in connection with the robbery, 22 searches had been conducted, and over 5,000 actions had been raised.

On 19 February 2014 the *Belfast Telegraph* reported that in a Cork court hearing Timothy Cunningham had admitted two counts of money laundering arising out of the Northern Bank robbery. The paper added that he was the only person convicted over the 2004 robbery.

15.2.5 The Murder of Robert McCartney

Messrs McKitterick and McVea tell us that on 30 January 2005 *'a crisis arose with the killing of Robert McCartney, beaten and stabbed to death at [Magennis's Bar, a public house in central Belfast] used by members of the PIRA and Sinn Féin'* (2012, p. 359) and where it was known that he had been seen by a considerable number of people. There was a belief that the PIRA used its influence to either discourage or even intimidate individuals from coming forward with information and had removed forensic evidence from the scene that would assist the PSNI in taking forward their investigations. Dixon and O'Kane saw this as reducing the chances of a DUP–Sinn Féin deal; they commented:

'[This] was very damaging for republicans as the McCartney's family were

Sinn Féin supporters ... McCartney's sisters and partner waged a high profile campaign for justice which increased the pressure on Sinn Féin. In a clear snub to [the latter,] no members of the party were invited to the White House on St. Patrick's Day in 2005 but the McCartney family had a brief meeting with President Bush.' (p. 106)

They added that

'the PIRA and Sinn Féin suspended and expelled a number of their members in the aftermath of the McCartney murder ... [and that in April 2005] Gerry Adams publicly called for the PIRA to fully embrace and accept democratic means as Sinn Féin launched it Westminster election campaign.'

At the *Public Session* of the Policing Board on 2 March 2005 the Chief Constable said:

'We want to build a case, we need the community to build a case, the family have a right to have that case built. 70 people were in that public house when a man was there who was then shortly after murdered and we need those people to come forward to tell us what happened. We need the people who witnessed the event to come forward and tell us what happened. In my judgement, that is the way we solve this case. The reality is, as it is well known, post event the scene was cleared, tapes were stolen, intimidation was put into place. What we are trying to do is to dismantle that, we are working very closely with the family, we are utterly committed to doing whatever we can to solve this crime which is why I do mention, whilst our preferred option is obviously they come and speak to us, if people feel more confident in the first instance as a stage before they come to us, speaking to other people, that is best practice. It is best practice in the rest of the United Kingdom, it is what we have done in the Sean Brown case, this is no different.'

At the Policing Board's *Public Sessions* on 2 June and 1 September 2005 the Chief Constable was asked for a progress report on the investigation into the murder. *Political Member* Alex Attwood (SDLP) asked in June how many people had provided statements to the Police Ombudsman in relation to the investigation, either in person or through a solicitor, and how many had attended for interview by the police and had exercised their right to silence at interview, as there was public discussion about those questions. The ACC stated that 10 persons had provided statements through the office of the Police Ombudsman, all of which were signed statements in a format presentable to the courts. By then 13 suspects had been arrested by police and interviewed in connection with serious offences arising out of the investigation of the murder of Robert McCartney and the attempted murder of Brendan Devine. All the arrested persons up to then had exercised their right to silence. The police were looking at over 80 hours of CCTV footage and 151 witness statements had been received, a small number of those by the Police Ombudsman. He added that:

'We still keep to the same line that we have said that members of the PIRA were involved in the murder of Robert McCartney but we do not believe that it was sanctioned by that organisation. Various statements and press announcements made since that date would, I believe, support the assessments of the PSNI.'

The Policing Board meeting on 4 October 2007 followed a meeting between the PSNI and Sinn Féin in relation to the investigation of the murder of Robert McCartney. Board Member Dolores Kelly (SDLP) asked the Chief Constable what response the police had had from Sinn Féin. ACC Peter Sheridan said he was constrained in what he could say, but he did confirm that:

'[the] senior investigating officer did have a number of working meetings with representatives of Sinn Féin at their request. At the last meeting, Sinn Féin members agreed to look at encouraging members of their party and witnesses to come forward. I can say that as of this date, no new witnesses have come forward.'

Mr Terence Davison from Belfast was subsequently charged with the murder of Robert McCartney. On 27 June 2008 the Daily Telegraph reported that Mr Davison had been cleared of the murder at Belfast Crown Court. Two other men were also cleared of charges of affray on the night of the killing. In his judgment Lord Justice Gillen wrote:

'The law is not a feather for every wind that blows and the need to ensure that defendants are only found guilty if there is proof beyond a reasonable doubt cannot be sacrificed to genuine and justifiable public concern that miscreants *should be brought to justice ... I have no doubt that the investigation into this crime will continue.'*

15.2.6 The Murder of Thomas Devlin

At the Policing Board meeting in Ballymena on 1 September 2005 the Chairman referred to murders and a number of other very serious incidents which were to be totally abhorred; he specifically cited the murder in the previous month of the 15-year-old North Belfast schoolboy Thomas Devlin. The PSNI were probed at the *Public Session* on particular incidents and on knife crime in general. The ACC noted that the murder was a dreadful event which had brought tremendous distress to his family, the wider community in North Belfast, and many people in the room who were themselves parents. He added that more than three-quarters of knife murders were committed by offenders who had a known relationship with their victims.

It was to be several years before those responsible for the death of Thomas Devlin were brought to justice, but the Policing Board continued to take a close interest. At the *Public Session* of the Board in September 2006 the ACC noted that the PSNI, along with the family of Thomas Devlin, had launched a media appeal at the time of the anniversary to encourage witnesses to come forward. In addition, the senior detective investigating the murder put on record his thanks to people in the Mount Vernon area of North Belfast for the cooperation and assistance that the investigation team had received. He added that the PSNI had arrested 12 people, over 1,000 witness statements had been recorded, 2,500 actions around the murder had been completed, 37 flats and houses had been searched, and 775 exhibits had been seized. It was still a very live investigation. A further update was sought on 1 November 2006 and then, again, at the *Public Session* of the Board exactly a year later, the Chairman noted that Board Members had asked to be updated on the position of the investigation into the Devlin murder. The DCC reported that there had been several arrests in the case, and one person had by then been charged.

Subsequently Gary Taylor and Nigel Brown were convicted of the murder of Thomas Devlin; their appeals against conviction were dismissed in November 2012.

15.2.7   The Murder of Harry Holland

In September 2007 65-year-old grocer Harry Holland was murdered in West Belfast, stabbed by a teenager as he attempted to stop the theft of his delivery van. A 15-year-old girl appeared at Belfast Youth Court later that week charged in connection with the fatal stabbing. Harry Holland was described in the *Irish Times* of 21 September 2007 as a *'veteran Republican ... his family connected by friendship and activism of various kinds to Gerry Adams among others'*. In the aftermath of the killing of Harry Holland, Mr Adams led a delegation to the nearest police station.

The Harry Holland murder was an issue for the Policing Board. In media interviews the Chairman welcomed the response to police appeals for information and the subsequent charges. He pointed to the opportunities for local people to have their say on policing through District Policing Partnerships (DPPs), while stressing that anti-social behaviour at all levels was a problem not just for Belfast but also for major cities and towns across the United Kingdom and Ireland, and required a response that took a broader look at society and not just policing and its response to anti-social behaviour. He pointed to the remarks of Geraldine McAteer that *'the best tribute paid by society is to work together to ensure this does not happen again'*. He said that the Chairman of the Board's Community Engagement Committee, Alex Maskey, would be facilitating a round-table meeting with local church leaders and others to consider community concerns.

At the Policing Board meeting's *Public Session* on 1 November 2007 the DCC noted that there had been a number of significant incidents in Northern Ireland since he had last met the Policing Board, including the murder of Harry Holland, although *'it was due to cooperation of the public and good police work that we now have several people charged with that murder'*.

At a meeting of the West Belfast DPP sub-group in November 2007 a member of the public expressed concern to the Chief Superintendent representing the PSNI about the police response times to 999 calls, referring specifically to the murder of Mr Holland and the circumstances of his death. The sub-group Chairman undertook to raise the issue with the Chairman of the Policing Board's Community Engagement Committee.

On 14 March 2008 Frank McGreevy was murdered in West Belfast. On 12 May 2008 the NIO Minister responsible for security, Paul Goggins, announced an initiative to tackle crime and anti-social behaviour in West Belfast. There was to be a new partnership called the West Belfast Community Safety Forum. The Forum would draw its membership from statutory agencies, non-statutory organisations, community groups, and political representatives. The Minister wished to involve the West Belfast DPP sub-group. This approach was based on the lessons of other partnerships, including the Upper Springfield Safer Neighbourhood Forum. This initiative raised a number of issues for the Policing Board, including the governance arrangements relating to the position of the West Belfast DPP sub-group and its relationship with the Belfast Community Safety Partnership, as well as the Policing Board's role itself. In the event, after pressure on the NIO from the Policing Board, Members of the DPP sub-group sat on the Forum and regular briefings were given both to the sub-group and to the Belfast DPP.

In the *Public Session* of the Board meeting in May 2009 the Chief Constable noted that a man had pleaded guilty to the murder of Harry Holland. That, together with two others being charged with lesser offences, followed a major and successful police investigation. Sir Hugh concluded that those successes, along with the resolution of a number of other crimes, were a vindication of the decisions taken in relation to the establishment of the Crime Operations Group six to seven years previously.

15.2.8   The Murder of Michael McIlveen

On 7 May 2006 Michael McIlveen, a 15-year-old boy, was brutally assaulted in Ballymena and died in hospital the following day. The attack was widely perceived to have been sectarian in motivation. On 9 May the Policing Board issued a release condemning the murder and calling for community support. The Chairman joined with police and community leaders in calling for calm and in reducing sectarian tension. In its briefing, the Policing Board reinforced the PSNI position that the police alone could not solve sectarian crime – this was a social and community issue. The murder was widely condemned;

for example, the Taoiseach Bertie Ahern described it as a *'shocking reminder of the evils of sectarianism'*.

At the Board meeting in early May 2008 an ACC was asked about sectarian and racist attacks in Ballymena, with concerns being expressed by a *Political Member* that there was a rising number of incidents and that it was only a matter of time before there was another murder such as that of Michael McIlveen. The PSNI response showed that, while the level of reports was broadly consistent, crime in Ballymena and the surrounding district had reduced and that that Police District had the highest detection rate across the PSNI.

On 3 March 2009 seven people were convicted in relation to the murder of Michael McIlveen, of whom four received life sentences. Concern was raised by the family as to the length of the tariff set by the judge as the minimum period in prison before which those convicted could be eligible for consideration for parole. Sir Hugh Orde advised the Policing Board that he would be writing to the Director of Public Prosecutions to seek an assessment as to whether the matter should be raised with the Attorney General in relation to a review of the sentence length in some of those cases.

15.2.9   Michael Stone

On 24 November 2006 Michael Stone – a notorious loyalist gunman – attempted to force entry to Stormont Parliament Buildings while armed with various devices. The sitting of the Northern Ireland Assembly that was taking place in the building had to be suspended. The Speaker of the Assembly, Eileen Bell, wrote to the Chief Constable on 29 November, with a copy to the Policing Board Chairman, expressing concern about the security of Parliament Buildings.

At the Policing Board meeting on 7 December 2006 the Chief Constable was asked to brief Members on the security arrangements agreed between the PSNI and the Speaker's Office of the Northern Ireland Assembly for Parliament Buildings and wider security at the Stormont estate. On 7 February 2007 the PSNI reported to the Policing Board that the Assembly had commissioned a review of security arrangements at Parliament Buildings, the results of which were awaited.

15.2.10 Paul Quinn

In October 2007 the body of Paul Quinn from Cullyhanna was found in a burnt-out barn in County Louth, across the border from South Armagh. According to the *Belfast Telegraph*,

'[21 year old Mr] Quinn was lured to a farm near Oram, Co Monaghan, where a dozen masked men wearing black military style clothing lay in wait. He was beaten with iron bars and nail studded cudgels. Every major bone in his body was broken. Eighteen people arrested after the killing were released without charge.'

Following their son's murder his parents campaigned for his killers to be brought to justice; his family blamed the PIRA for his killing, although this was denied by Republicans.

In response to a question at the *Public Session* of the Policing Board meeting on 1 November 2007 the DCC said of the murder '*we are cooperating with the Garda Síochána very actively on that*', although naturally he could make no operational assessment. In response, *Political Member* Jeffrey Donaldson (DUP) commented that

'It [the murder] has major political consequences, never mind the criminal investigation. ... We have names being bandied about all over the place of who may or may not have been involved in the murder.'

The ACC added that there were

'House-to-house enquiries going on in South Armagh with a Garda officer and a PSNI officer in homes right across the border where no police officer, either on the Garda side or on our side, has been refused entry.'

As to arrests, he said that the PSNI would have to be led by where the Garda wanted to go on that. Both he and the DCC made clear that they did not wish to prejudice the Garda investigation in any way.

On 5 August 2013 it was announced that Gardaí investigating the murder of Paul Quinn had the previous day arrested a man in Co Louth. He and other individuals who had also been questioned were released without charge.

15.2.11 The Events of March 2009 and Subsequently

On 9 March 2009 Constable Stephen Carroll was murdered by dissident republicans in an ambush in Craigavon. The Continuity IRA claimed responsibility. This followed two days after the murders of Sappers Mark Quinsey and Patrick Azimkar at Massereene Barracks in Antrim, for which the Real IRA claimed responsibility. At the first Policing Board meeting after those events, on 2 April, a minute's silence was held at the start of proceedings in their memory.

Two years later, on 2 April 2011, Constable Ronan Kerr died when a device exploded under his car outside Omagh. Dissident republicans were again believed to be responsible. The BBC correspondent Mark Simpson commented at the time that 'a murder designed to divide people has actually brought them closer together' (BBC News, 6 April 2011).

In March 2012 Brendan McConville and John Paul Wotton were convicted for their part in the murder of Constable Carroll. In October 2013 judgment was reserved in the case of the two men's appeal against the conviction.

In 2009 Colin Duffy and Brendan Shivers were charged with the murder of the soldiers. In January 2012 Mr Duffy was acquitted of involvement but Mr Shivers was convicted. However, in January 2013 his conviction was overturned on appeal. A May 2013 retrial found Mr Shivers not guilty.

15.3   In Conclusion

It is remarkable, looking back, to note the scale and range of the external events that impacted on the Policing Board. Several of the incidents raised issues about the extent of support for the police in different parts of the community. The Board, through its Chairman and Vice-Chairman, led calls for full cross-community support for PSNI and for policing. The Board also took pains to demonstrate the public accountability of the Chief Constable for police operations through, for example, the use of reports and probing questions in *Public Sessions* of Policing Board meetings. Moreover, could any other police authority in the United Kingdom or the Department of Justice in the Republic of Ireland have had to deal with such a range of high-profile incidents and murders? Add to that question another challenge unique to Northern Ireland: ... which entailed the handling of issues that could have materially impacted on the *Political* as well as the *Peace Processes*?

The following chapter continues the theme of how two external bodies impacted on the Board and how it sought to fulfil its statutory responsibility in challenging areas.

References

BBC NI Radio *Good Morning Ulster*, 22 March 2002

BBC NI Radio news, 19 April 2002

BBC NI Radio *Talkback*, 19 April 2002

Dixon, Paul and O'Kane, Eamon, *Northern Ireland Since 1969*, Pearson Education, Harlow, 2011

McKitterick, David and McVea, David, *Making Sense Of The Troubles – A History Of The Northern Ireland Conflict*, Viking, London, 2012.

The Guardian, 22 June 2002

UTV, 9 December 2002

Sunday Life, 2 January 2005

'Sinn Féin wanted a Special Branch scalp', *Daily Telegraph*, 13 January 2003

Irish Times, 21 January 2005

Sunday Independent, 30 January 2005

Sunday Times, 11 December 2005

BBC NI Radio *Good Morning Ulster*, 20 December 2005

Daily Telegraph, 27 June 2008

BBC News, 6 April 2011

Belfast Telegraph, 5 August 2013

Sunday Independent, 8 December 2013

Belfast Telegraph, 19 February 2014

CHAPTER SIXTEEN

Organised Crime and the Independent Monitoring Commission

16.1 Introduction

One of the important policing issues with which the Northern Ireland Policing Board (the Policing Board or Board) had to grapple was organised crime. The Report of the Independent Commission On Policing In Northern Ireland (the Independent Commission) had not dealt overtly with the particular nature of organised crime in Northern Ireland and how it might specifically be combatted, as opposed to other types, such as volume crime. As a result of the Province's troubled past, the complexion of organised crime in Northern Ireland has been rather different from that in the rest of the United Kingdom; such crime was not conducted in Northern Ireland so much by geographical or indeed ethnic gangs, but by groupings with paramilitary affiliations.

Moreover, as Section 16.2 highlights, a further structural challenge was posed for the Policing Board in that the British Government had set up an Organised Crime Task Force (OCTF) a year <u>before</u> the Policing Board was created, and the Northern Ireland Office (NIO), which was responsible for chairing the OCTF, declined to give the Policing Board a seat on the Task Force. Policing Board Members collectively and continuously considered that this reduced their role and capacity in an important area of policing.

Section 16.3 deals with the Independent Monitoring Commission (IMC), which was set up in 2003 by the British and Irish Governments. While that section seeks to highlight the interaction between the IMC and the Policing Board it also brings out through the lens of the IMC's reports both the policing and indeed political salience of organised crime in Northern Ireland and also the extent to which it was a paramilitary legacy issue.

The IMC reports were a critical source of information for the public on the security agencies' (North and South) assessments of the extent to which the various paramilitary groups were involved in violence, including the growing threat from dissident republicans.

16.2   The Organised Crime Task Force

16.2.1   The Organised Crime Task Force: Its Origins

On 25 September 2000 – a year before the Policing Board was created – the Secretary of State announced a new multi-agency approach to tackling organised crime in Northern Ireland. The OCTF was established to provide the strategic direction for this. In March 2001 the OCTF published the first-ever Organised Crime Threat Assessment for Northern Ireland and, alongside it, a strategy for confronting the threat to society from organised crime. The strategy set a number of strategic priorities which included reducing extortion, intimidation, and blackmail; disrupting the supply of illegal drugs; tackling fuel, alcohol, and tobacco smuggling; targeting money-laundering activities; and developing a methodology for prioritising organised crime criminals in Northern Ireland for concerted action by the relevant agencies. By January 2003 the OCTF comprised the following organisations: the NIO, the Police Service of Northern Ireland (the Police Service or the PSNI), HM Customs and Excise, the National Criminal Intelligence Service (NCIS), the Home Office, the Inland Revenue, and other Government agencies.

The March 2001 organised crime threat assessment identified some 78 groups within Northern Ireland, comprising 400 individuals, which met the NCIS's definition of organised crime. Just over half of those groups had either current or historic links to Republican or Loyalist paramilitary groups. As the following year's organised crime threat assessment put it, 'the legacy of terrorism is a significant influence'.

The land border with the Republic of Ireland, with associated issues such as fuel smuggling, created a further difference from the organised crime threat assessment in Great Britain. There were clear links between certain crime categories, such as money-laundering and drug offences. It was noted that the PSNI seized more counterfeit products in 2001/02 than all other United Kingdom police services collectively; armed robbery, particularly against cash-in-transit targets, was also more widespread in Northern Ireland.

There was recognition from the beginning that the OCTF needed wider community support if organised crime was to be tackled effectively. As the first OCTF chair, the then NIO Security Minister Jane Kennedy, put it at an OCTF Awareness evening in Armagh in 2002:

'Organised crime requires a long-term resource-intensive commitment but there can be no hiding place for these people who are exploiting our communities. Everyone has a part to play in creating a safer society.'

In June 2003 the NIO and its partners arranged for Belfast to host a major conference on organised crime – the first such on this topic to be held in the United Kingdom. Policing Board Members were invited to attend.

In 2003 the Proceeds of Crime Act 2002 provided for the creation of the Assets Recovery Agency (ARA). This was a national body, with the Director appointed by the Home Secretary, while an Assistant Director was appointed by the central Director to exercise the ARA functions in Northern Ireland. These included the provision of advice and assistance to the Secretary of State on relevant issues. The first Northern Ireland Assistant Director was the former PSNI Assistant Chief Constable (ACC) Alan McQuillan. Once established, the ARA became a member of the OCTF.

In March 2002 the Secretary of State had invited Professor Ronald Goldstock (the former head of the New York State Organised Crime Task Force) to report on how international experience might be brought to bear on tackling organised crime in Northern Ireland, and the extent to which it was hindering the transition to normal civic society. He reported to the NIO in January 2004, and his report was subsequently published in July 2004, together with the Government's responses to his recommendations. He noted that paramilitary organisations in Northern Ireland were structured so as to protect the hierarchy of the organisation from direct involvement in criminal activity, thus insulating them from traditional techniques of law enforcement. He stressed the importance of improving cross-community support.

In January 2003 the Policing Board Chairman, together with the Vice-Chairman and three other Board Members, met Minister Jane Kennedy to discuss the work of the OCTF and the relationship with the Policing Board. The Minister sought the assistance of the Board in ensuring delivery by the PSNI of their part of the organised crime strategy, including the setting of objectives which would be monitored by the Board, with reports from the Chief Constable, and their role in helping to gain wider community support for the campaign to tackle organised crime. On 5 March 2003 NIO officials provided a presentation to the Board about the OCTF. One of the issues probed was the respective roles of the Policing Board and the Task Force in determining policing priorities. At the *Public Session* of the same meeting the Northern Ireland Assistant Director of the ARA gave a presentation to the Board on the ARA's work.

At the Policing Board meeting in July 2003 the Chief Constable was asked to give an assessment of the extent to which paramilitary groups were involved in organised crime. It was noted that the OCTF had by then identified over 110 groups involving over 700 people involved in organised crime; of these, some 80% had some sort of paramilitary connection. The Chief Constable advised that linking into the National Intelligence Model would improve police performance in this area and that the District Policing Partnerships (DPPs) would also drive improved performance at District Council level.

Following the June 2003 conference and this discussion with the Chief Constable, the Policing Board Chairman wrote to Minister Jane Kennedy to advise that the Policing Board believed that it should have a greater involvement in this area. Looking forward to the devolution of law and order issues to a local administration, it was argued that the Policing Board should be seen to be included among those who had ownership of the campaign against organised crime. He suggested a meeting with the Minister in the autumn.

At the *Public Session* of the Policing Board meeting on 4 September 2003 the Chief Constable, together with PSNI colleagues in the Police Service's Serious and Organised Crime Squad, made a presentation on serious and organised crime. The briefing included intellectual property crime and extortion. It was noted that, at that time, one in every three CDs sold in Northern Ireland was counterfeit. The OCTF threat assessment for 2003 recorded that the PSNI had seized £6.7m worth of counterfeit goods, though this represented only some 5% of the total market. A total of 200 people had been prosecuted for counterfeiting offences; in this area 93% of the groups involved had paramilitary connections. Extortion, it was explained, was traced directly to terrorism; many local criminals derived their status and influence from current or historic paramilitary links. Reference was made to the report in July 2002 of the Northern Ireland Affairs Committee (NIAC) which had taken evidence on the extent of violence and intimidation in Northern Ireland. It was estimated that as little as 10% of extortion was reported to the police. It was particularly rife in the construction industry. Extortion was, in the view of the PSNI, a cornerstone of paramilitary fundraising activity for groups from both sides of the community. In the previous year the PSNI had run 25 proactive investigations into extortion, with 11 people so far being arrested and charged with extortion-related offences. In response to questions, the Chief Constable added that the Loyalist paramilitary groups continued to be particularly active in relation to drugs.

On 11 November 2003 the Policing Board Chairman and Vice-Chairman met Minister Jane Kennedy for a further discussion on the Board's involvement in the work of the OCTF. Subsequently the Minister wrote, setting out a number of outcomes to assist the Policing Board in being better informed about this work; these included quarterly meetings between the Board Chairman, the Vice-Chairman, and senior NIO officials and annual briefings by the Minister to the Policing Board (to be held following the launch of the annual OCTF threat assessment).

At the following Board meeting Members emphasised the need to ensure that the policing of organised crime was treated as a high priority and that the Board should be fully briefed on developments.

ACC Sam Kinkaid, together with Alan McQuillan, briefed the Policing Board's *Public Session* on 3 March 2004. Mr Kinkaid spoke about money-laundering and the steps taken to build up the PSNI Financial Intelligence Unit. Mr McQuillan stressed the partnership relationship between the ARA and the PSNI. *Political Member* William Hay (Democratic Unionist Party (DUP)) commented: '*First of all we would all say that the Assets Recovery Agency has been a success story in such a short time, there is no doubt about that.*'

Questions from Policing Board Members probed whether the ARA had sufficient resources for its task. It was proposed by the Policing Board that a representative from the Criminal Assets Bureau in Dublin, which had a good reputation for effectiveness, should speak to the Board, but the invitation was declined.

On 10 February 2004 Minister Jane Kennedy wrote to advise the Policing Board of the creation of what became known as the Serious Organised Crime Agency (SOCA) in an announcement by the Home Secretary the day before. She explained that, while SOCA would have a UK-wide remit, its creation would not affect the current arrangements in Northern Ireland, recognising the distinctive features of organised crime in Northern Ireland. In March 2004 the Home Secretary published a document entitled '*One Step Ahead, a 21st Century Strategy to Defeat Organised Crime*'. This White Paper set out how the British Government intended to enhance the efforts against organised crime, including the role of SOCA. The document stressed that change at national level would not lead to success unless the national law enforcement effort was effectively joined up with police forces and other enforcement agencies at local level and on the borders.

At the *Public Session* of the Board's meeting in October 2004 the Chief Constable reported that armed robberies in Northern Ireland had reduced by 24%, largely as a result of the PSNI's armed robbery investigation teams. He was questioned about a reported £2m heist at Gallaher's (a tobacco factory in Ballymena, County Antrim), in response to which ACC Kinkaid advised the Board that all paramilitary groups from both sides of the community in the previous six months had been involved in serious robberies in Northern Ireland.

Later in October 2004 the then NIO Minister responsible for security briefed the Policing Board. That session included a discussion on the Goldstock report.

That year the NIO published a Research and Statistical Bulletin entitled '*Views on Organised Crime in Northern Ireland: Findings from the April 2004 Northern Ireland Omnibus Survey*'. Of those surveyed, 97% thought that there was a problem with organised crime in Northern Ireland and 75% thought that paramilitary organisations were mainly responsible for committing offences related to organised crime.

On 24 February 2005 the NIO Minister wrote seeking the views of the Policing Board in an NIO-led review of the OCTF.

On 7 April 2005 Policing Board Members were briefed by the

Chairman on the meeting that he and the Vice-Chairman had had on the previous day with NIO officials on the work of the OCTF. They had taken the opportunity again to lobby for the Policing Board to have a more formal role on the OCTF, in relation to which they detected a fresh willingness to look at the issue. This was not exclusively one-way traffic; the Chairman in turn advised the NIO officials on the productive meeting held on 24 March 2005 that he had hosted between the PSNI and representatives of some of the financial institutions and the recognition at that meeting that, while the police had a role to play, individual companies had a significant contribution to make in keeping themselves, their assets, and their staff safe. He proposed that the Board should receive briefings from the PSNI and the ARA.

In the following week the Policing Board Chairman wrote to the NIO Minister, restating the view that Policing Board Members should be afforded a seat on the OCTF. They did not see this as incompatible with the Board's role in being responsible for independent oversight of the PSNI. Indeed, the letter argued that this was complementary to the vision in the Independent Commission's Report that the Policing Board would go beyond supervision of the police itself, extending to 'the contributions that people and organisations other than the police can make towards public safety'.

At the Board's *Public Session* on 2 June 2005 the Chief Constable reported that two persons had been arrested in relation to an attempted robbery of £1.2m from Securicor and were currently in custody awaiting trial. It was noted separately that in 2004/05 28 organised crime gangs had been disrupted or dismantled and 126 arrests had been made.

16.2.2 The Organised Crime Task Force: Its Stakeholder Group

The Policing Board Chairman advised Members of the Corporate Policy Committee at its meeting in September 2005 that, following the review of the OCTF, the NIO Security Minister had invited the Policing Board to nominate two Members to sit on the Stakeholder Group of the OCTF. The Stakeholder Group, chaired by the NIO Minister, was to meet twice a year to advise and monitor progress in achieving cross-cutting objectives to combat organised crime in Northern Ireland, and to support the law enforcement agencies in carrying out their statutory duties by creating a climate, both politically and presentationally, to enhance their effectiveness. The Stakeholder Group would comprise one representative from each of the law enforcement agencies. This invitation was said to recognise the Board's statutory obligation under Section 3 of the Police (Northern Ireland) Act 2000 to make arrangements for obtaining the co-operation of the public with the police in the prevention of crime.

The Chairman and the Vice-Chairman subsequently met the Minister and requested that the level of representation be further reviewed. A further letter from the Minister in October 2005 to the Policing Board Chairman clarified that the Stakeholder Group was in essence an expanded version of the previous OCTF meeting, and that the other structures under the OCTF umbrella (working groups in which Ministers were not involved) supported the Stakeholder Group.

On 13 December 2005 Shaun Woodward, the then NIO Security Minister, wrote to the Policing Board Chairman informing him of the final agreed outcomes of the review of the OCTF. The organisation was restructured into a Ministerially-chaired Stakeholder Group (the public face of the OCTF), a smaller strategy group of senior representatives from the law enforcement agencies, and eight work streams progressed by expert groups. The Stakeholder Group also included, in addition to the two seats for the Policing Board, the Northern Ireland Chamber of Commerce and Industry, the Federation for Small Businesses, and the Confederation of British Industry.

A public issue arose over an apparent difference between the PSNI and the NIO in the context of the *Private Session* briefing of the Policing Board on organised crime by NIO Security Minister Shaun Woodward in his capacity as OCTF Chairman on 17 January 2006 (which did not remain private for long). The perception of the Policing Board was that the PSNI and the other agencies advised that all paramilitary groups were still involved in organised crime. This appeared to be at odds with the position of the Minister, who emphasised that his point was that the British Government believed that the Provisional IRA (PIRA) leadership intended to take that organisation in a different direction. (The Minister later stated in an interview that this was meeting with the PIRA leadership's strategic intent as that organisation had stated it on 28 July 2005.) In a subsequent exchange the Minister acknowledged that there were complex assessments to be made in distinguishing between criminality by individual PIRA members for their own gain and criminality carried out by PIRA members which was authorised by the organisation. It was the job of the IMC to comment on such difficult issues and the next regular report of the IMC was due very shortly. He stressed that there was no dichotomy between himself as chair of the OCTF and the PSNI. Given the public interest which had arisen following the Board briefing, he put his letter into the public domain, having discussed the contents with the Chief Constable, who was content with this approach. In his response, which was also published, the Policing Board Chairman asserted that Members remained of the view that a dichotomy had been evident.

An article in the *Belfast Telegraph* on 18 January 2006 reported that the Secretary of State, Peter Hain, was believed to be 'deeply angry' after details of the private briefings to the Board by NIO Security Minister Shaun Woodward and ACC Sam Kinkaid were leaked. On the same day a statement was issued by the Policing Board Chairman *'following a breach in confidentiality on a briefing in respect of the role and work of the Organised Crime Task Force'*. This statement included the following passage:

'By definition private and confidential briefings are based on trust. If the initial breach of confidentiality in respect of yesterday's briefing emanated from a Member of this Board, I have no doubt that the vast majority of Board Members will be disappointed to say the least. This breach, regardless of where it emanated, has damaged that trust and that is a matter of regret.'

The first meeting of the newly formed Stakeholder Group took place on 7 February 2006. The Director General (Designate) of SOCA also attended. The Policing Board Chairman made a number of points on behalf of the Board in relation to organised crime and the PSNI's approach. The Board Vice-Chairman spoke of the importance of understanding cultural issues in order to change perceptions, and urged greater consultation with local businesses and communities. In the press release issued after the meeting Secretary of State Shaun Woodward said that the Policing Board *'brings a vital dimension to the effectiveness of the Task Force'*.

In May 2006 the Policing Board Chairman wrote to the Clerk of

NIAC, as he had to the NIO, setting out the Policing Board's views on the unsatisfactory level of its representation on the OCTF and asking the Committee to consider the Board's comments during its inquiry into organised crime in Northern Ireland. The Committee reported on 5 July 2006. The Committee concluded that the fear created by the hold of paramilitaries on communities had a negative impact on the reporting of organised crime, and that a perception existed in Northern Ireland that those perpetrating these crimes were *'getting off lightly'* because the crimes were seen as *'victimless'*. They shared the concern of the IMC about the potential for the process of paramilitary transition to create instability that was open to exploitation by criminals with paramilitary backgrounds engaged in organised crime. They also expressed particular concern about the extent of extortion, especially in the building industry. The report added that *'Ministers should be in no doubt that their political efforts could be completely undermined by another Northern Bank robbery'*. It commended the measures taken by the PSNI in tackling the major area of organised crime in Northern Ireland, but also recognised that the success of the police would be limited so long as Sinn Féin withheld its support for, and recognition of, the legitimacy of the PSNI.

On 1 June 2006 the Policing Board sponsored a seminar on organised crime in Armagh. Later that month the annual OCTF Report and Organised Crime Threat Assessment was published. During the previous year over £30m of assets had been restrained and £10m of counterfeit goods and almost £10m of drugs had been seized. For the first time, the NIO Security Minister, as chair of the OCTF, had invited representatives of the Policing Board to attend the launch of the Report, and to talk to the media about the dangers and harms of organised crime. The Policing Board issued a press release stressing that organised crime was an area of great concern to the Board, and that it had set specific targets for PSNI in tackling organised crime in the Policing Plan for 2006–2009. The release also emphasised the role that DPPs had in engaging with local people to raise awareness and gain their cooperation in preventing organised crime, thereby making communities safer for everyone.

In July 2006 NIO officials wrote to invite the Policing Board to accept an additional seat on the Stakeholder Group (with two of the Board's nominees being *Independent Members*). In addition to the

Chairman and Vice-Chairman, Alex Attwood (SDLP) and Ian Paisley Jnr (DUP) served in rotation. On 18 July 2006 NIO officials briefed the Policing Board on the work of the OCTF Operational Strategy Group. The role of the Strategy Group was to establish a shared understanding of the nature of organised crime in Northern Ireland, to identify barriers to tackling the problem, and to develop strategies to overcome them. In the discussion Members of the Policing Board addressed how the Board could add value to the work of the Stakeholder Group and other OCTF activities, the public attribution of responsibility for organised criminal activities to illegal paramilitary groups, the merit of further legislation to combat organised crime, the establishment of SOCA, the NIAC report on organised crime, and the future involvement of the security services in the work of the Group.

At the *Public Session* of the Policing Board's meeting on 6 September 2006 the Chief Constable reported on police investigations into two so-called '*tiger kidnappings*' in September 2004 and April 2005 which had resulted in nearly £500,000 being stolen in Downpatrick and £1.3m being stolen in Belfast. (These crimes involved usually one or more members of the family of a businessperson or, say, a bank employee being held securely by a criminal gang while the principal was obliged to source money (usually cash) from their place of business.) Sir Hugh Orde advised the Board that a major police operation had led to three people being arrested and charged with kidnap, possession of firearms with intent to cause fear and violence, and armed robbery.

On 12 October 2006 the Policing Board supported a special information event hosted by the Derry/Londonderry and Strabane DPPs to raise awareness of the fight against organised crime among the community, business, and retail sectors. The briefing was chaired by the Policing Board Vice-Chairman, Barry Gilligan, with a keynote speech by Alan McQuillan of the ARA. The associated press release stressed that organised crime was an area of great concern to the Policing Board. This event, together with a similar one organised by Armagh DPP, was an excellent example of how '*DPPs and other agencies are working in partnership to engage with key stakeholders in order to raise awareness of this important issue and gain their co-operation in preventing organised crime for the benefit of everyone in their communities*'.

On 19 October 2006 representatives from SOCA gave a presentation to the Policing Board's Corporate Policy, Planning and Performance Committee. Discussion included an exploration of SOCA's priorities and ways in which the organisation would develop its relationship with the PSNI.

In December 2006 the Policing Board's Corporate Policy, Planning and Performance Committee discussed the Board's role and its participation in the Organised Crime Stakeholder Group. Concerns were expressed that the Policing Board's future role could become diminished given developments including the proposed transfer of responsibility for national security, the establishment of SOCA, and the increasing membership of the Stakeholder Group. It was suggested that this combination could lead to the main responsibilities of the Policing Board being reduced to holding the Chief Constable to account primarily for volume crime.

On 11 January 2007 the Home Office announced that the Government intended to bring forward proposals to merge the ARA with SOCA by April 2008. (Subsequently the Serious Crime Bill received Royal Assent on 31 October 2007.) On the same day the Secretary of State for Northern Ireland, Peter Hain, wrote to the Policing Board Chairman stating that he had gained assurances from the Home Office that there would be no diminution in the resources available for the work of freezing, seizing, and recovering the assets of those engaged in criminal activity in Northern Ireland. The merger was in no way a reflection on the excellent job the ARA had done and the ARA team would transfer to SOCA.

The Policing Board Chairman reported to the Policing Board meeting on 7 February 2007 that he had written to the NIO Minister emphasising the grave concerns expressed by the Corporate Policy, Planning and Performance Committee at its January 2007 meeting about the merger. In particular, he had noted the success of the ARA in Northern Ireland, the higher profile it enjoyed in this part of the United Kingdom, the clear message sent by the ARA in the past to the perpetrators of organised crime that there were no hiding places, and the concern that SOCA would not work with the same vigour as the ARA in disabling the perpetrators operating at all levels of organised crime in Northern Ireland, if there were more appealing prospects to be pursued in Great Britain. The Policing Board issued a press release along these lines the following day.

The Chief Constable was pressed on the same issue at the Board meeting's *Public Session* on 7 February 2007. He said that the ARA had been hugely successful in Northern Ireland for a number of reasons, including the seamless transfer of information from the PSNI. He stressed that community impact was as important as monetary value and that it was important to operate against people who might be below the normal threshold in terms of value because of the impact they had on communities. ACC Peter Sheridan added that the Home Office had given assurances that resources that would currently be in Northern Ireland for assets recovery would remain for proceeds of crime work. Mr Hay (DUP) commented that it was regrettable that on such an important issue neither the Chief Constable nor the Policing Board had been consulted.

In his written response the NIO Security Minister passed on the Home Secretary's assurance that there would be no reduction in resources for the work and that Northern Ireland priorities would be taken into account, so that local priority targets would not be subject to the monetary threshold limit that might apply elsewhere.

On 21 June 2007 a meeting of the Policing Board's Corporate Policy, Planning and Performance Committee was briefed by the NIO Security Minister, Paul Goggins, and representatives from the ARA, HMRC, SOCA, PSNI, and NIO. This provided Board Members with an opportunity to raise their concerns about the planned merger of the ARA and SOCA, problems of immigration and human trafficking, further legislation to combat organised crime, illegal dumping of waste, and fuel smuggling.

At the meeting of the Policing Board on 1 November 2007 ACC Peter Sheridan answered a number of questions on progress in tackling cross-border smuggling. He reported that in 2005/06 16 fuel-laundering plants had been disrupted and one million litres of fuel and just under 1,000 vehicles had been seized. At the previous week's Organised Crime conference in Dublin colleagues from law enforcement agencies in Northern Ireland and the Irish Republic had met and drawn up a level of agreed targets for the forthcoming year.

In June 2008 the Policing Board published a comprehensive report that it had commissioned from KPMG the previous October into crimes against businesses in Northern Ireland. (This formed part of the Board's statistical and research strategy 2006–2010.) The objective was to understand better the nature of business crime, how it affected the local business community, and how it could best be tackled. In the accompanying press release the Policing Board stressed that business crime ranged from shoplifting and counterfeiting to extortion and armed robbery. The research showed that 30% of those businesses which had responded across Northern Ireland had been the victim of crime in the previous 12 months. The report provided 14 recommendations, nine of which were designed to assist the police in dealing with business crime, including measures to be taken to encourage businesses to report all crimes to the police. The Policing Board undertook to continue to work in partnership with the police against the criminals and to monitor the implementation of the PSNI's business crime strategy (to be published later that year) and the report's recommendations so that business crime was effectively tackled.

The Regional Director of SOCA and other representatives briefed the Policing Board's Corporate Policy, Planning and Performance Committee on 19 June 2008 on the work of the Agency and its particular role in Northern Ireland and future plans. It was agreed that it would provide statistical information to the Board in respect of its success in disrupting serious and organised crime in Northern Ireland, and that regular meetings should be held between the Board and SOCA representatives.

At the meeting of the Policing Board on 3 July 2008 ACC Judith Gillespie reported on the widespread operation that had led to 77 arrests in relation to the cultivation of cannabis in Northern Ireland. She stated that all of those arrested were Chinese, Vietnamese, or south-east Asian nationals. Many of them had been brought to Northern Ireland by organised criminals as illegal immigrants, and were in fact victims of organised crime. The Chief Constable stressed that these were not individuals from within Northern Ireland's own Chinese community. At the subsequent meeting of the OCTF Stakeholder Group in September 2008 the Policing Board Vice-Chairman proposed that the Policing Board's Community Engagement Committee could provide a valuable avenue in communications with the Chinese community within Northern Ireland.

In August 2008 the Policing Board Chairman wrote to the NIO concerning the transfer of responsibility for civil recovery in Northern

Ireland to the Public Prosecution Service (PPS). The NIO Minister stressed in his reply that SOCA would continue to have some responsibility for civil recovery in Northern Ireland following the merger with the ARA, but he was confident that the extension of civil recovery powers to the PPS would strengthen rather than diminish the effectiveness of the work of the OCTF and its partner agencies in recovering the proceeds of crime.

On 15 January 2009 the Policing Board's Corporate Policy, Planning and Performance Committee was given a confidential briefing by Her Majesty's Inspectorate of Constabulary on its recent inspection of serious, major and organised crime in Northern Ireland, adopting the grading criteria that had been agreed with the Association of Chief Police Officers. HMIC reported that, overall, the arrangements in Northern Ireland met, and often exceeded, the standards, although it had identified a number of areas for improvement. Policing Board Members again took the opportunity to explore both the arrangements for the recovery of criminal assets following the transfer of powers from the ARA to SOCA and the scope to improve working relations between the Irish Criminal Assets Bureau and the agencies responsible for Northern Ireland.

Following this meeting the Policing Board Chairman had a further exchange with the NIO Security Minister, seeking assurance that the PPS had the resources to ensure no diminution in the effectiveness of asset recovery.

At the Policing Board meeting on 5 February 2009 ACC Drew Harris responded to a question about progress in respect of recent tiger kidnappings. He stated that, while there had been a number of these offences over the Christmas period, the numbers had been reducing in recent years. The crime remained a high priority for the PSNI, which was working in partnership with the OCTF and industry – in particular the Business Advisory Forum – to prevent such crimes. Since 2004, when Crime Operations took responsibility for tiger kidnappings, there had been a total of 55 such incidents, including failed attempts. From those incidents, 42 people had been charged, 10 had been convicted, and a further 25 cases were still pending.

The OCTF arrangements continued after the devolution of policing and justice in April 2010. For example, on 4 July 2012 Justice Minister David Ford published the OCTF Annual Report in which he emphasised that 33 potential victims of human trafficking had been rescued, 30 fuel-laundering plants dismantled, and £13m of illegal drugs seized.

In 2010 the Home Secretary announced that SOCA would be replaced by a new National Crime Agency (NCA) with wider powers, including immigration and border control in addition to combatting organised crime.

The NCA became operational in October 2013. However, prior to that, both Sinn Féin and the SDLP made clear that they had concerns at the NCA's lack of accountability to devolved institutions, in particular the Northern Ireland Policing Board. Chief Constable Matt Baggott was reported in the *Belfast Telegraph* of 27 June 2013 as saying that '*Lives would be put at risk by curtailing the powers of the NCA.*' The same article reported that Sinn Féin and the SDLP '*blocked moves to give the Agency powers to carry out policing operations and recruit agents*'.

16.3   The Independent Monitoring Commission

16.3.1   To Monitor and Report...

The British and Irish Governments announced in the Joint Declaration of 1 May 2003 and in a supplementary paper entitled '*Agreement Between the British And Irish Governments: Monitoring and Compliance*' that they would establish a body to monitor and report on paramilitary activity and security normalisation. The leadership of the Ulster Unionist Party (UUP), under David Trimble (later Lord Trimble), was influential in persuading the two Governments of the case for such a body. In September 2003 the Governments published an International Agreement setting out the aims, functions, and constitution of the Independent Monitoring Commission (IMC). This Agreement was implemented in January 2004, following legislation in both Parliaments.

There were four IMC Commissioners – John Alderdice (later Lord Alderdice,) a former Northern Ireland Assembly Speaker; Joe Brosnan, former Secretary General of the Department of Justice in Dublin; John Grieve, former Deputy Assistant Commissioner in the Metropolitan Police; and Dick Kerr, former Deputy Director of the US

Central Intelligence Agency. The IMC produced a total of 26 reports, either at six-monthly intervals or specifically at the joint request of the two Governments.

The Commission had three main functions:

- to report on the continuing activities of paramilitary groups,
- to report on security normalisation in Northern Ireland, and
- to consider claims by parties in the Northern Ireland Assembly that Ministers or other parties are not committed to non-violence and exclusively peaceful and democratic means or are not conducting themselves in accordance with the Pledge of office.

Particularly in respect of the first of those three functions, the work of the IMC was of considerable interest to the Policing Board, and some of its reports were to have a bearing on the Board's deliberations. It is important to note, however, that the IMC was a comparatively late feature in the *peace* and *political processes* architecture, being established some years after the future course of policing development had been set.

This section of this chapter highlights the interaction between the Commission and the Policing Board, and also points up the salience of organised crime in the Commission's reports. It is also important to note that the IMC reports were a critical source of public information on the security agencies' assessments of the extent to which the various paramilitary groups were involved in violence, including the growing threat from dissident republicans.

16.3.2 The Independent Monitoring Commission: Its Role

According to Article 3 of the International Agreement, the IMC was to carry out its functions with a view to promoting the transition to a peaceful society and stable and inclusive devolved Government in Northern Ireland. Article 4 provided that

'In relation to the remaining threat from paramilitary groups, the Commission shall:

(a) monitor any continuing activity by paramilitary groups including:

   i.   *attacks on the security forces, murders, sectarian attacks, involvement in riots, and other criminal offences;*

   ii. *training, targeting, intelligence gathering, acquisition or development of arms weapons and other preparations for terrorist campaigns;*

   iii. *punishment beatings and attacks and exiling;*

(b) assess:

   i. *whether the leaderships of such organisations are directing such incidents or seeking to prevent them; and*

   ii. *trends in security incidents.'*

Under Article 7 the IMC was empowered to recommend any remedial action considered necessary.

The first report of the IMC was published on 20 April 2004. Prior to this the IMC issued a statement on 9 March 2004 to clarify the way it was going about its work. The statement stressed that activities committed by paramilitary groups of a *'criminal'* as opposed to a *'terrorist'* nature were equally within its remit, whatever it was or wherever it had taken place. The first report included a number of guiding principles determined by the IMC Commissioners, the last of which was that:

'It is not acceptable for any political party, and in particular for the leadership, to express commitment to democratic politics and the rule of law if they do not live up to those statements and do all in their power to ensure that those they are in a position to influence do the same.'

The Commissioners also stated that they had set themselves the following challenge:

'To contribute in whatever way we can to the ending of the violence, other criminality, and exertion of pressure by or on behalf of paramilitary groups, and to help the people of Northern Ireland live their lives untroubled by paramilitary activity.'

The Commissioners had meetings with, and took evidence from, a wide range of groups and individuals. Prior to their first report they met with the Policing Board Chairman. The Commissioners noted in their first report:

'We have heard many times, including from bereaved families and others who have experienced the suffering caused by paramilitary violence, of the increasing stranglehold that these groups have over some communities.'

They stated that the first report would focus mainly on the use of violence by paramilitary groups, while subsequent reports would deal with the connections between these groups and organised crime, and with their sources of funding. The report then provided a brief description of the main paramilitary groups. It noted that the number of deaths attributable to paramilitary groups had declined sharply from the figure of 55 in 1998, and had not since exceeded 18 in any one year. However, those same years had 'seen a marked increase in total paramilitary violence short of murder by both republican and loyalist groups'. The report pointed out that while the number of murders, attacks on security forces, and bombings by paramilitaries had sharply decreased the level of other paramilitary violence continued to be considerably higher than before the Belfast Agreement; this, the authors stressed, demonstrated the importance of moving the debate on from one about ceasefires and breaches of ceasefires to one about the totality of illegal paramilitary activities.

The first report briefly covered the incident on 20 February 2004 in which four masked men entered a bar called Kelly's Cellars in Bank Street, Belfast, dressed in white forensic suits, balaclavas, and surgical gloves. They severely beat a Mr Robert Tohill before dragging him to the vehicle in which they had arrived, and departing with him. The vehicle was intercepted by a PSNI patrol and four men were subsequently charged with causing grievous bodily harm, unlawful imprisonment, and the possession of items likely to be of use to terrorists. (On 24 February 2004 the British and Irish Governments had issued a statement in which they explained the serious impact of this incident on the ongoing discussions with the Northern Ireland political parties.) The IMC report stressed that Article 13 of the International Agreement required the IMC to do nothing which would either prejudice a legal case or place anybody's safety at risk and this constrained them in what they might say. Nevertheless, the concluding sentence of that chapter in the report was as follows: '*We do, however, believe that this material, taken as a whole, indicates that the operation was one planned and undertaken by the Provisional IRA.*'

The first report then went on to consider the leadership of paramilitary groups. The Commissioners concluded that '*some members, including some senior members of Sinn Féin are also members, including, in some cases, senior members of PIRA*'. They recognised that there might not have been a PIRA ceasefire in the first place without influence from the leadership of Sinn Féin, but Sinn Féin must bear its responsibility for the continuation by the PIRA of illegal paramilitary activity and must recognise the implications of being in this position. Similarly, while recognising the role of the Progressive Unionist Party (PUP) and others in exerting a positive influence in achieving the Loyalist ceasefires, they believed the PUP had not sufficiently discharged its responsibility to exert all possible influence to prevent illegal activities on the part of the Ulster Volunteer Force. Accordingly, the Commissioners concluded that, had the Northern Ireland Assembly then been functioning, they would have recommended in respect of Sinn Féin and the PUP measures up to and possibly including exclusion from office. All politicians and others in prominent roles must exert every possible influence to bring about a cessation of paramilitary activity.

In his statement to the House of Commons on 20 April 2004 the NIO Secretary of State said that both Governments accepted the Commission's conclusions and recommendations. On 28 April he announced that he had removed the entitlement to financial assistance from Sinn Féin and the PUP for a period of one year.

At the first meeting of the Policing Board held following publication of the IMC's first report, the Chief Constable was asked a number of questions about it. He emphasised the wide consultation that the IMC had engaged in when preparing their report and advised in broad terms that he did not disagree with its overall content.

The IMC's second report was published on 20 July 2004 under Article 5 of the International Agreement. This Article required the Commission to monitor whether, in the light of its assessment of the paramilitary threat and the British Government's obligation to ensure the safety and security of the community, the commitments the British Government had made in its published programme of security normalisation were being fulfilled to the agreed timescale. The

IMC had been asked by the British Government to prepare a report which included the demolition of towers and observation posts and the withdrawal of troops from police stations in Northern Ireland.

In its chapter on the context, the IMC's second report noted the recommendations in the Independent Commission's Report relating in particular to the police in Northern Ireland assuming a more normal profile, including the reduction in the role of the Army and police stations assuming a more normal appearance. The report also noted (at paragraph 2.9) that there were many others deeply involved in pursuing and measuring change in law enforcement and criminal justice generally, including the Policing Board, DPPs, the Police Ombudsman, and the Office of the Oversight Commissioner. Contentious issues such as the PSNI's Full Time Reserve, Holding Centres, and the reduction in the number of police stations were being addressed. The report took as its baseline the position in December 1999 when the British Government had published its Security Strategy paper against which the IMC was asked to measure changes.

The second report addressed the question of what was normal law enforcement, noting that at that time law enforcement in Northern Ireland was far from normal, both in terms of the task faced and the response to it. Then, in 2004, the number of troops in Northern Ireland remained some three times higher than the Joint Declaration had envisaged would be the case in normal circumstances. The basic question addressed in this second report was: '*What measures beyond the normal are justified by the security threat, which we know is subject to change?*'

The second report noted that from 1999 to May 2004 the monthly average of military personnel based in Northern Ireland had reduced from 14,892 to 12,658, the lowest number since 1970. The Joint Declaration had envisaged a staged withdrawal of troops in an '*enabling environment*', with Army support for the police being reduced to a residual level, providing specialised Ordnance disposal and support for public order as described in the Independent Commission's Report. With the British Army at '*Garrison strength*' there would be just 5,000 personnel in Northern Ireland.

While some significant changes by way of reduction in abnormal security arrangements had already taken place, the Commissioners concluded that, while the enabling environment had not been fully realised, that did not mean that acts of normalisation consistent with the prevailing assessment of the security threat could not be proceeded with. They noted that:

'Normalisation of security arrangements is contingent upon, and has to be measured against the prevailing assessment of the security threat. The level of community support the police enjoy is also a vital factor.'

They added that, as envisaged in the Belfast Agreement and the Joint Declaration, the logical outcome of an enabling environment and all those changes would be the devolution of policing and justice to Northern Ireland institutions.

The IMC's second report was considered by the Policing Board's Corporate Policy Committee.

The IMC's third report was published on 4 November 2004. The report stressed that the paramilitary phenomenon in Northern Ireland was a complex one. The question for the Commissioners was:

'Whether over the period covered by this report, a paramilitary group has been engaged in any form of violent or other criminal activity, is preparing for it, or remains in a state of readiness to resume it.'

The third report concluded, in respect of the PIRA, that there was no fundamental change in the capacity of the organisation or its maintenance of a state of preparedness, but the Commissioners also found no evidence of activity that might presage a return to a paramilitary campaign. During the period it had reduced shootings and assaults, and towards the end of the period it appeared to have suspended action against those it believed to be behaving anti-socially while still monitoring what people were doing. The Commissioners believed that it was responsible for a major theft of goods in Dunmurry in May 2004 and was engaged in significant amounts of smuggling.

The report noted that non-terrorist organised crime by paramilitaries represented a major continuing legacy of the campaign of terrorism. It cited evidence from the OCTF and made a number of recommendations about its work. This report also looked at community restorative justice. The Commissioners stated that they had received evidence, which they found convincing, that community restorative justice could under the right conditions help offer alternatives to paramilitary violence and intimidation.

On 10 February 2005 the IMC submitted a report specifically on the robbery at the headquarters of the Northern Bank in Belfast on 20 December 2004. The report stated:

'*We have carefully scrutinised all the material of different kinds that has become available to us since the robbery, which leads us to conclude firmly that it was planned and undertaken by the PIRA.*' (paragraph 7)

Noting that this incident was one of a series of crimes involving violence or the threat of violence which the report said enabled the PIRA to gain very significant resources in recent months, it added that:

'*In our view Sinn Féin must bear its share of responsibility for all the incidents ... Sinn Féin cannot be regarded as committed to non-violence and exclusively peaceful and democratic means so long as its links to PIRA remain as they are and PIRA continues to be engaged in violence or other crime.*'

It concluded that the leadership and rank and file of Sinn Féin needed to make the choice between continued association with and support for PIRA criminality and the path of an exclusively democratic political party.

On 20 April 2005 the Policing Board Chairman had a meeting with representatives from the IMC. On the following day the Policing Board's Corporate Policy Committee discussed the effect that organised crime was having on the community in Northern Ireland, and agreed that consideration should be given to organising a workshop to discuss issues around it.

The fifth report of the IMC published on 24 May 2005 concluded that '*PIRA remains a highly active organisation*'. The report contained a specific chapter on the murder of Robert McCartney in central Belfast on 30 January 2005. It stated the belief of the Commissioners that members of PIRA were involved in the murder, although they did not believe that the central PIRA leadership had sanctioned it in advance. The report also contained a chapter on the activities of prisoners released under the Belfast Agreement. In a section on the role of the political parties the report made clear that they should all '*play a full and constructive role in the participative organs of the criminal justice system such as the Policing Board and the District Policing Partnerships'.*

At the *Public Session* of the Policing Board on 2 June 2005 held in Derry/Londonderry, Ian Paisley Jnr (DUP) asked the Chief Constable to comment, particularly on reported reoffending rates by prisoners released under the Belfast Agreement. The Chief Constable noted that the IMC report had stated that 14% of former paramilitary prisoners from all groups had been charged and convicted or had prosecutions pending in the period from release up to September 2004, with Loyalist paramilitaries having the highest percentages.

On 12 October 2005 a meeting open to all Policing Board Members was held with the IMC Commissioners. In a wide-ranging discussion it was noted that the IMC report was a useful source of information on PSNI activity and therefore in holding the Chief Constable to account.

The seventh report of the IMC, published on 19 October 2005, followed the PIRA statement of 28 July 2005 and the decommissioning of weapons reported by the Independent International Commission on Decommissioning (IICD) on 26 September that year. The seventh report concluded that, while the statement was potentially very significant, it was too early to be drawing firm conclusions about possible overall changes in behaviour. The seventh report also noted that the number of paramilitary murders in the six months from 1 March 2005 to 31 August 2005 was the largest since the corresponding six-month period in 2003; all were attributable to the Ulster Volunteer Force (UVF) or the Ulster Defence Association (UDA) and arose from the UVF/Loyalist Volunteer Force (LVF) feud on which the IMC had reported in its sixth report in September 2005. The report concluded that, because of the level of paramilitary involvement, organised crime was the biggest long-term threat to the rule of law in Northern Ireland.

On 15 December 2005 Board Members met the IMC to discuss elements within the PSNI's estate strategy that impacted on normalisation. This followed an NIO statement on 1 August 2005 which set out the British Government's plans for normalisation. It detailed a number of steps that would be taken within finite periods, assuming that an 'enabling environment' was created and maintained. These plans included items such as the further defortification of police stations and the continuation of the review of the police estate and subsequent implementation. (It will be remembered that the PSNI's estate strategy had been approved by the Policing Board in May 2005.)

The IMC's eighth report, produced at the request of the two Governments in February 2006, stated that:

'We believe that changes are taking place amongst paramilitary groups on both the Loyalist and Republican sides – indeed there is a dynamic of change which is likely to encompass associated political parties and other political groupings, although it is patchy in its occurrence and impact ... There seems to be a growing awareness within groups on both sides that violence and crime – even if they had been considered an acceptable option in the past – do not now offer a way forward which is either right or likely to bear political fruit in the longer term.'

The eighth report stated that the Commissioners were of the firm view that the present PIRA leadership had taken the strategic decision to end the armed campaign and pursue the political course which it had publicly articulated, though they added that the position was not entirely straightforward.

In response to a question from Ian Paisley Jnr at the *Public Session* of the Policing Board on 1 March 2006 the Chief Constable reassured the Board that every scrap of information which was relevant to paramilitary activity would be given to the IMC in a fully analysed way that they could build into an overall picture. He confirmed that there was no intelligence whatsoever to suggest that the PIRA were doing anything other than their declared public intent in terms of (not) going back to any sort of terrorist campaign.

The ninth report of the IMC, published on 8 March 2006, was the first on the published security normalisation programme. The IMC concluded that the measures required by the programme at that stage were entirely proportionate, though they noted that the situation could change very fast.

The IMC's tenth report followed quickly afterwards, on 26 April 2006. The tenth report stated that:

'The PIRA leadership has committed itself to following a peaceful path. It is working to bring the whole organisation fully along with it and has expended considerable effort to refocus the movement in support of its objective. ... In the *last three months, this process has involved the further dismantling of PIRA as a military structure.'*

The report added that the PIRA continued to seek to stop criminal activity by its members and prevent them from engaging in it. However, it noted that progress with regards to other paramilitary groups remained *'extremely uneven'*. Dissident republicans remained determinedly committed to terrorism and deeply engaged in other crime, though they were not always capable of fulfilling their paramilitary ambitions and had recently been foiled by successful police operations.

A further meeting was held between Members of the Policing Board and the IMC on 26 September 2006. A range of matters was discussed, including increased acceptance of the policing in communities where previously such acceptance had been low, normalisation of police buildings and single officer patrolling, organised crime, and community-based restorative justice.

Earlier that month the eleventh report of the IMC was published, specifically dealing with security normalisation. This report contained a full chapter on the police estate. It noted that, under the terms of the security normalisation programme, in the first period up to March 2006 the review of the police estate should continue *'with action as agreed by the Policing Board following consultation with District Commanders and local communities'* and that the review was to include *'work to de-fortify some 24 police stations'*. In the second 12-month period to March 2007 there was to be *'further de-fortification of police stations'*.

The eleventh report recognised that action on the review of the police estate was a matter for the Policing Board and the PSNI rather than for the British Government, and also that a number of the components flowed directly from the Independent Commission's Report. The IMC report also referred to the June 2006 assessment of the Police Oversight Commissioner on this subject. In his report the Oversight Commissioner had regretted the extent to which fortified buildings remained, both because of how they struck the public and because working conditions within them were often substandard. He concluded that much more remained to be done.

The IMC Commissioners noted that the Policing Board had

conducted a formal examination of the estate strategy in February 2006 and planned a further one that autumn; that the programme of work to defortify existing police buildings continued with funding, and that 55 schemes were scheduled for implementation. Given the involvement of the Policing Board, the IMC concluded that the requirements in the normalisation programme in relation to the police estate had been met.

The same report also included an assessment of the *progressive development, and extension, of varying patrol patterns*' by the PSNI. This element of the programme had been due to start on 1 April 2006. Again, the IMC report noted that the Oversight Commissioner had concluded in his June 2006 report that the recommendation on foot patrolling had been implemented. For its part, the IMC noted an increase in single officer patrolling during 2006.

In the IMC's twelfth report, published on 4 October 2006, the Commissioners noted that the situation had been transformed from what it had been three years previously, particularly in regard to the PIRA. In paragraph 2.21 the report said:

'It remains our view that the leadership has accepted the need for engagement in policing and wishes to achieve it. The leadership has given public indications to this effect and efforts have been made to secure membership support. While many accept the pragmatic need to make the change, the matter remains controversial for some in the movement.'

At the *Public Session* of the Policing Board on 5 October 2006 the Board Chairman asked the Chief Constable if he shared the assessment of the IMC that the leadership of the PIRA did not consider a return to terrorism as in any way a viable option and that it continued to direct its members not to engage in criminal activity. Sir Hugh Orde confirmed that he concurred broadly with the whole report. Other Policing Board Members also probed on the contents of the report relating to the PIRA and to the extent to which the UVF and UDA were continuing to engage in criminal activity. *Political Member* Ian Paisley Jnr (DUP) asked the Chief Constable what it would mean for PSNI senior command having Republicans actively supporting the police. Sir Hugh said that he had been '*boringly consistent on this – Sinn Féin need to join the Policing Board – nothing else is good enough in my judgement*'.

They needed to engage fully with the processes of the Policing Board and to hold him to account through processes which in his judgement were 'pretty effective'.

The IMC's thirteenth report of the IMC was published on 30 January 2007. As the Commissioners noted, the decision taken by the Sinn Féin Ard Fheis on 28 January, just two days before, to support policing and criminal justice was 'a very major development' and achieved through the commitment and efforts of the Sinn Féin leadership. The report stated: 'The directions from the PIRA leadership to members remained clear and consistent; terrorism and violence have been abandoned.'

The thirteenth report noted (in paragraph 2.19) that opposing opinions on the issue of policing had become more widely expressed within the Republican movement in the months covered by the report and significant leadership effort was made to maintain the momentum of the strategy. It noted also that the expression of differences of opinion was of itself a healthy part of the democratic process where those disagreements had been articulated by political rather than violent means. In addition to two recently formed groupings with Republican paramilitary credentials, the IMC had noted a further one that had emerged focusing particularly on the issue of policing. The report noted that the leadership had engaged in dialogue with this grouping, as it had with the movement generally in advance of the Ard Fheis.

In a written Ministerial Statement in the House of Commons on 30 January 2007 the Secretary of State, Peter Hain, said that the Government believed that this thirteenth report removed 'the final, major impediment to the restoration of stable and lasting devolution in Northern Ireland'. (The timing of this report was at the request of the British and Irish Governments, following the St Andrews Agreement of 13 October 2006.)

On 12 March 2007 the Policing Board Chairman and Vice-Chairman met members of the IMC. This was the day on which the IMC launched its fourteenth report, which focused primarily on the process of normalisation, including the police estate. The overall assessment of the IMC was that the process of normalisation was on or indeed slightly ahead of target. They believed that the requirements of the normalisation programme in respect of the police estate had been met, although they indicated that there might be value in undertaking a fundamental review of the current strategic approach to the police estate.

The IMC's sixteenth report, published in September 2007, again noted that the implementation of the security normalisation programme was inevitably dependent on other factors; examples cited were the replanning of the District Command Units ahead of the Review of Public Administration and the report of the National Audit Office on the estate strategy of the PSNI, published in December 2006. However, it also observed that the Policing Board had kept the review of the police estate and its implementation under continuing formal and informal review. It concluded that the pace of defortification needed to be increased (as had the Police Oversight Commissioner in his last report, published in May 2007).

In their seventeenth report, published on 7 November 2007, the IMC Commissioners stated that following Sinn Féin's entry into the Northern Ireland Executive, they had decided that they no longer needed to give an analysis of the PIRA's activities at the same length as they had in the past. The report noted that during that summer's parading season, the organisation had urged cooperation with the police. Moreover, some people whom the PIRA had previously exiled had been able to return to Northern Ireland.

The IMC's eighteenth report, published on 1 May 2008, included an assessment of the murder of Paul Quinn on 20 October 2007. The Commissioners wrote that they thought that the attack was planned and carried out by local people and that it arose from local disputes; that among those involved were people who had in various ways been associated with the PIRA at a local level; but that the killing was clearly contrary to the instructions and strategy of the leadership of the PIRA. They did not attribute the killing to the PIRA. That report stated clearly that both the Continuity IRA and the Real IRA had sought to enhance their organisations' capacity during the period under review.

At the *Public Session* of the Policing Board on 5 June 2008, the Chairman referred to the IMC's eighteenth report, noting the stark warning it had contained on the dissident threat. He added that while dissident republicans had been responsible for three attacks on police officers the shooting of an officer in Carrickfergus was attributed to Loyalists. He emphasised that there was no logical reason for weapons to be retained (by paramilitary organisations) – it could only be assumed, as highlighted in the IMC report, that they were being kept purely for criminal and organised crime purposes. As the Secretary of State had stated, the *'decommissioning train was leaving the station'*.

The IMC's nineteenth report, published in September 2008, was undertaken at the request of the two Governments, which had sought a fuller assessment of the completion of the transformation of the PIRA. The Commissioners stated that:

'Under PIRA's own rules the Army Council was the body that directed its military campaign. Now that that campaign is well and truly over, the Army Council by deliberate choice is no longer operational or functional.'

They concluded that the PIRA did not present a threat to peace or to democratic politics.

The IMC's twentieth report was published on 10 November 2008. The Commissioners commented that progress to date on Loyalist decommissioning had been disappointing. They concluded that the devolution of justice and policing would provide an entirely fresh opportunity for a strategic approach to the integration of law enforcement with other domestic policy and to the operation of the whole criminal justice system. They looked forward to such devolution.

The next three reports were published at six-monthly intervals, although the IMC did choose to publish a twenty-fourth report in September 2010 specifically on the murder of Bobby Moffett in Belfast on 28 May 2010. The Commissioners concluded that the murder was committed by members of the UVF acting as such, and that they had sanction at central leadership level. The report noted that the murder represented a serious backward step after a period when all the paramilitary groups other than the dissident republicans had moved decisively away from violence. It contrasted this action with the statement issued by the UVF in May 2007 in which the organisation had said that it would renounce violence and transform itself from a military into a civilian organisation.

The IMC's twenty-fifth report was published on 4 November 2010. The Commissioners noted that:

'Our examination of the activities of the various dissident groups shows that they continued to pose a substantial and potentially lethal threat, particularly

against members of the security forces, and so far as Great Britain is concerned the Government raised the threat level from moderate to substantial ... the high level of dissident activity would undoubtedly have led to many more deaths, injuries and destruction had it not been for the law enforcement and security agencies North and South and their ever closer cross-border cooperation.'

At publication it was announced that the two Governments had asked the IMC to prepare one more final report on their work, following which they would bring the IMC arrangements to an end. Its last report was published on 14 March 2011 and the IMC completed its work on 31 March of that year.

16.4   In Conclusion

It is striking how far the NIO, in its leadership of the OCTF structures and related activities, chose not to include the Policing Board. From the inception of the arrangements in 2000 through to 2005/06 there was no Policing Board representation. Even as late as July 2008, when a cross-border fuel fraud enforcement group was created, the Policing Board was advised only by means of a press release. While Ministers were punctilious in carrying out their commitment to brief the Policing Board annually, this was seen primarily as a listening exercise for the Board Members.

Peter Smith QC, when invited in a private capacity to comment on the relationship between the Policing Board and the OCTF, noted that the Independent Commission, in its deliberations in 1999, had been concerned as to the consequences of the Policing Board becoming involved, even by merely being consulted, in police decision-making. If the Policing Board were to be viewed as becoming complicit in any particular decision it would be more difficult, if not impossible, to hold the Chief Constable effectively to account for it afterwards.

A further issue related to the nature of the discussion at the OCTF. Again, the Independent Commission had foreseen difficulties arising from confidential advance briefings of the Chairman or another representative of the Policing Board; how could participation in a body such as the OCTF inform the work of the whole Board if the Chairman or other representative could not repeat to the Board what had been discussed? (It is worth noting that this did happen, however, in the intelligence area, where the Policing Board Chairman and Vice-Chairman were trusted to meet with the ACC responsible for Crime Operations.)

There came to be an understandable nervousness in the Policing Board against the background of a number of other developments, including the transfer of lead responsibility for national security, the integration of the ARA within SOCA, and the prospect of the devolution of policing and justice, that all contributed to a feeling that the Board's role, or at least its ability to influence the direction of policing within Northern Ireland, either was being or would be diminished in regard to organised crime. As has been demonstrated, in Northern Ireland organised crime was a comparatively greater issue to be tackled than in Great Britain. Although largely a legacy of the Troubles and what some have described as the 'paramilitary transition', this was also a factor of Northern Ireland being the only part of the United Kingdom to have a land border, and the differential taxation arrangements in the two parts of Ireland.

It is interesting to note that in a press release relating to the findings from the 2009/10 Northern Ireland Crime Survey published by the Department of Justice on 3 December 2010, as many as 66% of all respondents felt that organised crime overall generated a minimal level of harm in the local area. The effects of the OCTF were perhaps more successful in harnessing multi-agency law enforcement cooperation within Northern Ireland than in changing the fundamental perception of the majority of the community that organised crime was largely 'victimless'. Again, had the Policing Board been more directly involved in the work from the beginning, its level of community representation and contact with DPPs and other representative groups could well have been a valuable asset.

In an article on 10 August 2013 the *Economist* concluded that the nature of organised crime, at least in Great Britain, had changed significantly in the past decades. Whereas from the 1950s to the 1970s it had tended to be local, with a focus on hard cash, there had then been a period in which drugs had been more profitable than extortion or robbery. In turn, with greater globalisation, the current focus was more on less tangible vehicles such as international money-laundering, though drugs and people-trafficking still remained potentially lucrative sources of revenue and exploitation for cross-border organised criminals.

Northern Ireland, as so often, exhibits some of these developments, but also has its own patterns of organised criminality. Certainly, the links to paramilitary organisations, both present and past, provide one local characteristic not found elsewhere.

The IMC was independent of both Governments and of the Policing Board. It did fulfil a useful function for the Board Members in terms of providing them with a commentary, informed through access to the security agencies, on developments bearing directly or indirectly on policing. Moreover, in its assessments in relation to the threat from paramilitaries and the progress of security normalisation, especially in regard to the police estate, the IMC was a an important alternative source of information for the Northern Ireland public.

References

One Step Ahead, a 21st Century Strategy to Defeat Organised Crime, Command 6167, Home Office, March 2004.

Views on Organised Crime in Northern Ireland: Findings from the April 2004 Northern Ireland Omnibus Survey, NIO

Sunday Times, 11 December 2005

BBC Radio, *Good Morning Ulster*, 20 December 2005

Belfast Telegraph, 18 January 2006

Public Attitudes towards Crime and Recovery of Assets by the Assets Recovery Agency in Northern Ireland: Findings from the July 2005 Northern Ireland Omnibus Survey, NIO, 7 March 2006

Belfast Telegraph, 27 June 2013

'Farewell to the Heist', *The Economist*, 10 August 2013

CHAPTER SEVENTEEN

The Police Oversight Commissioner

17.1   A Particular Form of Oversight...

At one level the story of the Police Oversight Commissioner is simply told. The role was recommended in the Report of The Independent Commission On Policing For Northern Ireland (the Independent Commission): it was provided for by the British Government in legislation; and an American law enforcement expert was selected, who in turn appointed a supporting team of experienced North American police officers to assist him to produce and publish triannual reports reviewing progress in implementing each of the Independent Commission's 175 recommendations. The Commissioner's mantle passed after three and a half years from Tom Constantine to his chief of staff, Al Hutchinson, who continued in office until the production of the 19th and final report in May 2007 – an extension by the British Government of the originally envisaged term at the request of Nationalist representatives. Responsibility for monitoring the 35 recommendations then judged partially or wholly outstanding was principally passed to the Northern Ireland Policing Board (the Policing Board or Board).

However, such a summary would grossly underestimate the importance of the work of the Oversight Commissioner, the dynamic impact of his reports on the policing reform programme, and the wider contribution to the continuing *peace* and *political processes*. Moreover, the role was without precedent, and – despite being discharged successfully in the main – is not, to the best of the authors' knowledge, an approach that has been adopted elsewhere. It is worth assessing, therefore, not just what this particular form of oversight achieved in Northern Ireland but also how far it might be exportable to other situations.

17.2   The Oversight Commissioner:
A Mechanism to Oversee Change

The very last chapter in the Independent Commission's Report contained four recommendations designed to create:

'A mechanism ... to oversee the changes required of all those involved in the development of the new policing arrangements, and to assure the community that all aspects of our report are being implemented and being seen to be implemented.' (Paragraph 19.3)

The recommendations proposed that an eminent person, from a country other than the United Kingdom or Ireland, be appointed as an Oversight Commissioner, with perhaps two colleagues and a small staff in Northern Ireland. This person would review progress three or four times a year. The Commissioner would – importantly – provide more than the stocktaking function, as 'the review process would provide an important impetus to the process of transformation'. Thus the Report recommended that various bodies should provide the Commissioner with regular reports on progress achieved and account for any failures to achieve the objectives. The Commissioner would report publicly on the progress achieved, together with observations on the extent to which any failures or delays were the responsibility of the policing institutions themselves or due to matters beyond their control. Finally, the Report recommended that the Commissioner should be appointed for a term of five years, and, while it left open the notion that there might be a further appointment beyond that time depending on progress made, the Independent Commission expressed the hope that at that point, or soon afterwards, it would be possible to have responsibility for policing in Northern Ireland vested entirely with the people of Northern Ireland, where it belonged.

The British Government moved fast to implement these recommendations. The Police (Northern Ireland) Act 2000 contained provisions (at sections 67 and 68) for a Commissioner. This included a stipulation that the office of Commissioner should cease on 31 May 2003 unless the period was extended, as it might be for up to three years at a time. The Commissioner was to make at least three periodic reports in each year, and in addition he might at any time make a report to the Secretary of State on matters arising in the course of his performance of his general function. Schedule 4 to the Act set out the more detailed arrangements providing for the appointment of the Commissioner; his terms of reference, which were to be set by the Secretary of State for Northern Ireland and which would '*in particular describe the changes in policing in Northern Ireland the implementation of which it is the general function of the Commissioner to oversee*'; and his ability to appoint staff with the approval of the Secretary of State for Northern Ireland.

The Government did not wait for the completion of the legislation in November 2000 before appointing the Oversight Commissioner. As has been noted, there was no specific requirement in the Independent Commission's Report that the Commissioner should have operational policing experience. The British Government did consider a range of possible backgrounds for the appropriate '*eminent person*' from outside these islands; as with other roles in Northern Ireland, for example, someone with a judicial or diplomatic background might have had suitable credentials. On 29 May 2000 the then Secretary of State for Northern Ireland, Peter Mandelson, appointed Tom Constantine, who had just retired as the head of the United States Drug Enforcement Administration. Prior to that, for some eight years, he had been head of the New York State Police, having first joined that organisation as a trooper.

Some interesting perspective is gained from Tom Constantine's chapter in '*Policing the Narrow Ground*', published in 2010. He pays tribute to the Independent Commission's Report, which he compares in quality to the gold standard of the 1967 President's Commission Report in the United States, '*The Challenge Of Crime in A Free Society*'. In his public remarks Tom Constantine was clear from the beginning about the scale of the policing reform programme. In the same book he says:

'*Nowhere in the modern history of policing in a democratic society has a reform programme of such magnitude and scope been attempted. When all of the reports had been written and all the oversight implemented, it was always the police that were required to carry out the recommendations. The changes would have been difficult enough in any environment, but the emotional impact of changing names, symbols and uniforms can never be underestimated.*'

Mr Constantine laid stress on establishing standards of integrity, fairness, and professionalism for his office. He believed that it was vital for the Commissioner to have both the confidence of the public and credibility with the policing community. In recruiting his support team he sought to choose, in the words of Noah Webster, *'men of virtue'*. They included Professor David Bayley, a specialist in international policing and criminal justice at the University at Albany, State University of New York; three senior former or serving members of the Royal Canadian Mounted Police (Bob Lunney, Roy Berlinquette, and Al Hutchinson, who was to be Tom Constantine's Chief of Staff), and Charles Reynolds, Gil Kleinknecht, and Robert Warshaw, each of whom had been career law enforcement individuals in the United States; Charles Reynolds was also a former President of the International Association of Chiefs of Police (IACP). Each was assigned a specific subject area of the Independent Commission's Report.

17.3   The Oversight Commissioner: His Methodology

The Commissioner's first report was published in January 2001. The very first sentence stated that: *'The proposed revisions for the policing services in Northern Ireland are the most complex and dramatic changes ever attempted in modern history.'* That report provided the first indication of how the Oversight Commissioner would go about his task in terms of methodology. Later in the same report (p. 7) he wrote:

'The magnitude of the proposed revisions and the impact on the task of the oversight process is clearer when the details become apparent. Each of these hundreds of recommendations and subsets of the recommendations will produce numerous policy papers, manual changes, training curricula and course outlines. The cumulative impact of these documents may easily be in the thousands. In order for the oversight process to be effective, each of these documents will need to be reviewed in order to ensure compliance with the agreed-upon performance indicators. It is expected that there will be numerous performance indicators for each of the hundreds of recommendations. All of these will be part of the evaluation process.'

The key elements in the approach were as follows:

a. an inventory (conducted by the Commissioner and his team) of all the proposed initiatives, including receipt of *implementation plans and schedules*

b. *performance goals* for each *implementation programme*

c. *performance indicators* identified for each *recommendation,* both quantitative and qualitative

d. the collection of *baseline information* against which to measure progress

e. *progress reporting schedules*

f. frequent *interviews* of key personnel along with *observation of activities* on the ground

g. discussion by the Commissioner and his staff both in Northern Ireland and North America about the *level of achievement* of the implementation of each *recommendation*

h. *regular reporting of progress*, probably three times a year

Mr Constantine had also set store, from his earliest visit, on obtaining the professional peer review input from the IACP. He asked the then President of the IACP to establish a 'Blue Ribbon' panel of incumbent senior police executives to assist the Commissioner to ensure that his reports represented best available practices in policing.

The Oversight Commissioner's second report was published on 19 September 2001. That report laid down a total of 772 performance indicators in respect of the 175 recommendations in the Independent Commission's Report. For this purpose, individual recommendations that were clearly linked would be grouped together with a combined total of performance indicators; for example, 17 performance indicators in all were identified in respect of recommendations 71, 73, and 74 – police performance in public order situations. Usually the first performance indicator against any individual recommendation was the assignment of responsibility to a specific name and position for the implementation of that recommendation. The Commissioner sought to establish performance indicators that he regarded as, for the most part, '*best practices*' that would normally be in place.

Publication of this suite of performance indicators in the second report followed the issuance of the Updated Implementation Plan by the British Government (which followed the multi-party talks at Weston Park), the draft report having been held in abeyance for several months until then by the Commissioner.

17.4   The Oversight Commissioner:
His Reports

The third report was published not long afterwards, in December 2001. It was based on the first substantive oversight review against the performance indicators, which had been conducted from 10 to 20 September 2001. The individual policing organisations were required to produce evidence of administrative compliance against the individual Independent Commission's recommendations through reference to the specified performance indicators. The objective of the Commissioner was to establish a benchmark of exactly where the institutions and agencies were in the change process as at 1 October 2001, so that subsequent reviews could measure progress against an established reference point. (Tom Constantine and several senior members of his team were in Northern Ireland when the heinous attacks in America on 11 September 2001 occurred, bringing a brand and indeed a scale of terrorism to America that it had never experienced before.)

In his third report the Commissioner also indicated plans for future on-site reviews in December, April, and September of the following year. In this report the Commissioner established the precedent of beginning each report with '*the Commissioner's overview*'; he noted: '*The overall impression of the Oversight Team is that the Police Service and the other relevant institutions have made an excellent start in fulfilling this very difficult task*' (p. 10).

In the third report – the first substantive implementation report – the Commissioner stated that in some areas there were inevitably limitations on the progress to report, given that the Policing Board had been set up only at the beginning of November 2001. He also adopted an approach, sustained to the end of the oversight process, of identifying separately '*progress and accomplishments*' and '*areas of concern*'. In the former category the Commissioner cited '*leadership*' as a prerequisite – '*in order for change to occur, it requires commitment from the top*'. He went on to say that '*in our opinion the Chief Constable has demonstrated such commitment*'. He was also complimentary about the Police Service of Northern Ireland's (the Police Service or the PSNI) Change Team, recognising that the Police Service, '*like most institutions in the public and private sector[,] is traditionally challenged by change*'. The report also laid stress on the role of the police District Commanders, appointed in April 2001, as a critical element in the success of the new policing strategy. It noted the results of the first round of recruitment and selection to the new PSNI. Finally, it lauded the appointment of '*a dedicated and talented group of individuals*' to the Policing Board.

However, the Commissioner was plain-speaking in a number of '*areas of concern*' that he identified. The first criticism was in relation to the lack of written policies, directives, and orders that were available to evidence administrative compliance with a large number of the recommendations. A second generic area arose from contacts had by the Commissioner and his other expert colleagues with rank-and-file officers and first-line supervisors in Northern Ireland. Many recognised the need for change but expressed their concern about the implications for their own safety and the ability to deliver services to the community in a professional manner. They flagged up that the entire community must support the police service as they embarked on this historic change.

Other specific '*areas of concern*' in the third report included training, education and development and documentary evidence of administrative progress on issues involving Special Branch.

Next, setting the precedent that would be followed until the introduction of thematic reports several years later, the rest of the third report then dealt with the Independent Commission's recommendations, chapter by chapter. Again, '*progress and accomplishments*', on the one hand, and '*areas of concern*', on the other hand, were identified in each. An individual comment was then recorded in respect of compliance against each of the 175 recommendations. Demonstrating that pressure was not only on the Police Service to deliver, the Commissioner was also critical of the Police Ombudsman for not responding on the issue of coordinating information systems with respect to complaints and police discipline between her office and the Police Service.

The Commissioner's fourth report appeared in April 2002, although it was based on the visit by the Commissioner and his team the previous December, with the deadline for the submission of written material falling on 7 January 2002. In both the Introduction and the Commissioner's Overview he referred to five bodies as cooperating in the oversight process and in demonstrating progress in many areas – the PSNI, the Policing Board, the Northern Ireland Office (NIO), the Police Ombudsman's Office, and the General Officer Commanding the Army. He also paid tribute in this report to Sir Ronnie Flanagan, who had announced his retirement towards the end of the previous year. Tom Constantine reiterated that, while the scope and magnitude of the change might require seven to 10 years to fully complete, most of the more critical recommendations could be completed in a much shorter period of time. He continued: 'As the oversight reviews have progressed, it has become increasingly obvious that the actual implementation of change has stretched the resources of the agencies responsible.'

The section on 'progress and accomplishments' in the fourth report began with a very genuine tribute to the Policing Board, including its Chairman and Vice-Chairman and Members. It highlighted the crafting of a solution to the contentious issue of badges and symbols, adding that the Board had demonstrated a sense of professionalism and strength of purpose in being able to craft other skilful solutions. The second area singled out for praise was the PSNI's recruitment programme and the graduation of the first class of new officers on 5 April 2002. Others included progress by the police in the planning and policy development of a Policing with the Community strategy. Somewhat contrary to the Commissioner's normal retrospective practice, the fourth report looked forward to the first formal policing conference to be held between the Garda Síochána and the PSNI in April 2002.

The first 'area of concern' that the Commissioner highlighted in his fourth report related to the adequacy of police resources to implement the required changes while simultaneously providing adequate police protection to the citizens of Northern Ireland. While stating that it was not the role of the Oversight Commissioner to advise on the optimum size of the police service for Northern Ireland, the report expressed concern about both the lack of progress towards civilianisation and the implementation of the Part Time Reserve, and the extensive amount of sick leave. The report noted lack of progress in some areas of the human rights programme and the issue of Special Branch reorganisation. It also noted that in January 2002 the Chief Constable issued an internal conceptual policy paper that described a limited amalgamation of the command level structure, describing the Special Branch under one single command along with the realignment of support units to the responsibility of Crime Branch. However, the Commissioner stated that the police plan provided did not appear to meet the intent of the Independent Commission's recommendations to bring the resources of Special Branch together with Crime Branch.

On a separate point, the fourth report flagged up the importance of the Policing Board approving the PSNI Training, Education and Development Strategy, and its implementation thereafter. Significantly, this report brought out for the first time a leitmotiv in virtually all subsequent reports – the lack of significant progress on the launch of a new Police College. The report made clear in the '*future direction*' section that the next oversight process would focus on these '*areas of concern*'.

The shape and pattern of the Commissioner's successive reports had now been established. His fifth report was published in September 2002, following a two-day session at the IACP's headquarters in Virginia in July 2002, involving the then Commissioners of the Royal Canadian Mounted Police (RCMP) and the Boston, Massachusetts Police Department, among others. Interestingly, in his Introduction he sought to explain the 'time lag' of three to four months in the Commission's reporting process. He made clear that many of the institutions were continuing to make progress on the recommendations during this period, but the progress achieved would not be included in the immediate report.

The Oversight Commissioner was also very clear that he was to report on progress in policing reform, not on wider political matters. Nevertheless, his Introduction to the September 2002 report did flag up an issue that

'*Should be of concern to anyone who desires a safe community where children can be raised free from violent crime or the threat of violence. The increasing rates of violent crime directed at individual citizens and group violence directed at the police officers, as these try to preserve peace, can threaten the entire*

*concept of police reform and particularly of policing with the community. ...
The changes recommended by the Independent Commission, and supported in
the Implementation Plan and legislation, require a substantial amount of risk
taking on the part of the Police Service and of the entire community. If major
changes are to be brought about, the police and others involved will need the
entire community's support.'*

'Areas of progress' cited in the Oversight Commissioner's fifth report
were the production by the Policing Board of the first Policing Plan
in March 2002, including the Plan for Change component, which
committed the Policing Board and the Police Service to implementing policing with the community as the principal service delivery
philosophy of the new policing service. The report also noted the introduction of the new Police Emblem and Flags Regulations (Northern
Ireland) 2002, along with the introduction of new uniforms on 5
April 2002 and the Inter-governmental Policing Agreement signed
by representatives of the British and Irish Governments on 29 April
2002.

In the fifth report *'areas of concern'* were the delay in the establishment of District Policing Partnerships (DPPs) and the lack of further
devolution of responsibility to PSNI District Commanders. The lack of
civilianisation, the management of sick leave absence, and the bringing
of the resources of Special Branch together with Crime Branch were
continuing concerns. The report reiterated the issue, particularly sensitive for Nationalists, of the need for Special Branch to provide timely
and accurate information to Crime Branch, though the report also
explicitly recognised the need for governments to have sophisticated
and adequately staffed counter-terrorism units, *'especially in a world
where terrorism has become such a major threat'.* The report criticised
the PSNI for not producing the requested documentation in this area,
pointing to other reviews and investigations involving Special Branch
which could alter the manner in which the PSNI implemented changes.
The report made clear the Commissioner's view that a revised implementation plan for Special Branch should not be in conflict with any
of the then current external reviews, thus enabling the Team to fulfil
their oversight responsibilities without interfering with any of these
reviews. This section of the Commissioner's Overview concluded by
setting out a robust expectation that *'the Police Service will address the*

need for a revised Implementation Plan in an expeditious fashion'. Finally, further criticism of the progress towards the new training regime and the lack of development of the new Police College was made.

The Oversight Commissioner's sixth report was published in December 2002. The Introduction made clear that this report was intended to represent the total experience of the oversight process since the autumn of 2001, rather than focusing more narrowly on individual recommendations. It also brought out that as part of their regular inspections the Oversight Commissioner and his team conducted a range of meetings with elected and appointed government officials, major political parties, leading members of the clergy, and a number of non-governmental organisations, including senior officers and hundreds of rank-and-file members of the PSNI. For the first time the report presented in tabular form an assessment of the implementation status of each individual recommendation, ranging from completion through to minimal progress. The Introduction stated on behalf of the Oversight team:

'In our opinion, both the Policing Board and the Police Ombudsman have excelled at fulfilling their intended roles, and should continue to receive the support of the Government, the police and the public.'

It also noted that the Police Service and the Policing Board (and the former Police Authority) had made *'excellent strides in fulfilling the object of attracting high-quality young people who are representative of the entire community of Northern Ireland and in getting them to consider a career in policing'.* This sixth report, like others, paid tribute to the calibre of the new recruits and indeed the skills with which they graduated from the initial training programme, notwithstanding the fact that not all community leaders were taking steps to remove all discouragement to members of their communities from applying to join the police, and there were indeed, in some cases, reports of intimidation. On the other hand, the Commissioner's Overview was critical of the training programme for existing officers, noting that, as of 30 September 2002, the 'Course for All' curriculum had not been provided.

In the sixth report the most sensitive issue dealt with in the Commissioner's Overview, in the section on *'areas of concern'*, related again to the amalgamation of Special Branch and Crime Branch. The report recognised that there had been a number of external reviews involving Special Branch, and paid tribute to the professionalism of the Policing Board in dealing with the issues raised by Her Majesty's Inspectorate of Constabulary, which, if the recommendations were implemented, the Commissioner believed would satisfy the intentions of the Independent Commission. However, he expressed concern that the Stevens inquiry would not now be completed until the spring of 2003. If there was no implementation of a new plan until spring 2003 the Commissioner's review of a revised plan could not take place until the autumn of that year at the earliest, whereas the present term of the Commissioner was scheduled to conclude on 31 May 2003.

The sixth report flagged up, in the Commissioner's Overview, two other issues that were also long-lasting. The first concerned the comparatively slow progress made in implementing the PSNI Estate Strategy Review. The second, again, concerned the size of the Police Service, with emphasis on the role of the Full Time Reserve.

The Oversight Commission's seventh and eighth reports, in May and September 2003 respectively, reverted to the traditional approach of reporting on progress against each individual recommendation. The seventh report highlighted the continuing and indeed worsening trend of organised crime. The Introduction noted that:

'The recognition by the Policing Board of the danger inherent in the growing influence of these violent criminal gangs on the entire society of Northern Ireland will be important in addressing this problem.'

The Commissioner's Overview stated in turn that:

'The support of the entire community for the Policing Board will be critical to the long-term safety and security of the citizens of Northern Ireland.'

The Oversight Commissioner's eighth report took account of the establishment of the DPPs operationally in April 2003, but, given the time lag, could say nothing about their accomplishments. With regard to the amalgamation of Special Branch and Crime Branch, the Commissioner noted that a new organisational structure had been publicly announced in July 2003, but that he had not been provided with any final approved plan.

The ninth report, published in December 2003, was Commissioner Constantine's last. He wrote that he had advised the Secretary of State a year previously that the concept of a permanent Oversight Commissioner would not, in his opinion, be in the best interests of the citizens of Northern Ireland, but that he recommended the oversight position be extended for at least one year. He himself accepted the Secretary of State's request to extend his initial period of appointment for six months but made clear that, after that, he wished to spend more time with his family in America.

This ninth report was again of a more summary nature. In the Introduction the Commissioner assessed the overall position as 'general and substantial progress':

'When the reforms are considered collectively ... it is clear that policing in Northern Ireland is moving steadily in the direction intended by the Independent Commission [On Policing For Northern Ireland].'

By this stage, in addition to previous accomplishments, the Commissioner pointed to a timetable and plan for phasing out the Full Time Reserve and steps to enlarge the Part Time Reserve; the establishment of community policing as a core function; and improved methods of public order policing. He recognised that the pace of progress would be impacted by factors beyond the control of the policing institutions – the first being the need for predictable and adequate financial support, the second being the intimidation of persons involved in policing. While still a potential area for concern, the Commissioner referred positively to the detailed plan produced by the Police Service on 14 November 2003 for the implementation of reforms designed to meet the Independent Commission's recommendations relating to Special Branch. Commissioner Constantine reiterated what he saw as the inexcusable failure to progress the new police training college.

In his concluding remarks Commissioner Constantine paid tribute to both Chief Constables with whom he had dealt during his time as Oversight Commissioner, and their leadership skills, as they faced the unprecedented challenge of reforms in the policing of Northern Ireland. He stated that, during his tenure,

'*I have witnessed progress in the implementation of the [Independent Commission's] recommendations at a pace which I would not have thought possible in such a relatively short time.*'

In the Introduction to his first report, the tenth Oversight Commissioner's report, published in April 2004, Al Hutchinson stressed that the fundamental approach to oversight would not change during his tenure, which was now scheduled to end in May 2005. However, in addition to normal reporting, he announced that he would also provide a series of in-depth thematic reports on those areas deemed crucial to sustainable success in the modern policing organisation. The first was to focus on training. He also noted that '*the level of overall community support envisioned by the Independent Commission as necessary for real change to occur has unfortunately not yet been provided.*' He too referred to the threats, intimidation, and attacks against individuals who chose to involve themselves in policing, whether by serving in the PSNI or on the Policing Board or DPPs.

This report was the first to refer to the introduction by the PSNI of the National Intelligence Model. It picked up the start of the debate about the number of District Command Units, although – sticking with the purity of the Independent Commission's Report – the new Commissioner noted that the recommendation had favoured the engagement of local communities ahead of efficiency. It also pointed to the fact that, in relation to personnel exchanges with the Garda Síochána, enabling regulations in the Republic of Ireland had not yet been completed, which was an impediment to fulfilling the intent of the Independent Commission.

Challenges in the Oversight Commissioner's eleventh report, published in September 2004, included those arising from the experience of the DPPs. In particular, the report noted that while the primary efforts of the Policing Board and the Police Service focused on reducing crime and improving crime clearance rates, local community interests tended to reflect concerns based on quality-of-life issues, including noise complaints, vandalism, and under-age drinking. It would be important for District Commanders to balance these competing perspectives and for the Policing Board to integrate bottom-up desires for changes in policing with the top-down strategic objectives.

The eleventh report referred to the decision announced to phase

out the Full Time Reserve beginning in April 2005, subject to a security review by the Chief Constable, which was due in September 2004.
The Commissioner was critical of the uncertainty this was causing,
and the operational implications; his Overview referred to the decision announced by the Chief Constable on 9 September 2004, but
which was not substantively covered in this report. Again, the report
was critical of the fact that after five years no actual results had been
delivered in relation the recommendation for exchanges of personnel
between the Garda Síochána and the PSNI.

The Oversight Commissioner's twelfth report, published in
December 2004, included the thematic report on policing with the
community. The report noted that there were many definitions of ways
of looking at policing with the community. One approach described
three inter-related elements, or levels of change, at the heart of any
successful policing with the community strategy: organisational,
tactical, and external. These were reflected in many ways in the PSNI's
own policy. This analysis – covered in more detail in the chapter above
on policing with the community – was interesting in its own right as
an area where the Oversight Commissioner and his team had to strike
out on their own in determining their approach to the assessment. The
overall conclusion was that policing with the community had generally been a success in many areas of Northern Ireland, although it was
important that the momentum of the initiative should be sustained.

The Commissioner's overview noted 'positive progress' in achieving
all of the changes in relation to Special Branch recommended by the
Independent Commission and other reviews. The first 'area of concern'
was the extent to which behavioural changes and outcomes were being
achieved in relation to the changes in human rights training and
development structures in place. Again, the absence of a comprehensive estate strategy was criticised.

The Oversight Commissioner's thirteenth report, produced in
June 2005, provided a further tabular update on the implementation
progress of each individual recommendation, as an addition to the
standard narrative account. This showed steady progress in implementation, building on the results in the first such assessment. Overall,
the Commissioner assessed 114 of the 175 recommendations to be
deemed implemented.

The Commissioner began his Overview by recording that his term had been extended by the British Government until 31 May 2007. Accordingly, for completed recommendations he would move to annual updates only, with two of the three reports each year focused on thematic issues – the first of these being on human rights and accountability (rescheduled from May 2005) and the second an update of the previous training thematic review. The Overview paid tribute to progress in relation to accountability as follows: '*The leadership of the Policing Board, Chairman Sir Desmond Rea and Vice-Chair Denis Bradley, and their committees has been key to achieving these results.*'

In the same report the Commissioner noted that the Government had announced that the Security Service and not the police would have primacy for national security in 2007, although no details had yet been vouchsafed. (He added that when details became available they would be examined to assess their impact on the Independent Commission's recommendations.) In relation to '*areas of concern*', the Commissioner noted that there was scope for '*role confusion*' and effort overlap among the plethora of community and other groups involved in supporting policing and justice; he referred to the DPPs, Community Safety Partnerships, Community Police Liaison Committees, and a host of other groups, amounting in all to over 500 bodies that the police interacted with and which could be in competition for its time and resources.

The Oversight Commissioner's fourteenth report, published in September 2005, was solely focused on human rights and accountability. Publication followed a brief period that month of violent public order disturbances in many parts of Belfast. The Commissioner noted that those unfortunate events served to highlight the crucial role that accountability structures would play in the future policing of Northern Ireland. He went further, adding

'*Let me be blunt: politics has failed policing in Northern Ireland ... The current democratic deficit creates the risk of either undermining or stagnating efforts to create a widely accepted, human rights-based, accountable policing service.*'

In the section in the report on human rights the Commissioner noted that the kind of human rights-based policing envisioned by the Independent Commission might not be delivered under any circumstance if there was insufficiently broad support in the community.

The report noted the importance in this area not only of the role of the Policing Board in holding the Chief Constable to account but also that of the Human Rights and Professional Standards Committee of the Board in promoting human rights and ethical standards within the Police Service and monitoring delivery. In the section on accountability the Commissioner flagged up as remaining issues the devolution of policing powers, operational responsibility, and the intimidation of members of DPPs.

The fifteenth report of the Oversight Commissioner, published in December 2005, again focused on training. The report concluded that the training regime had moved forward significantly and was moving in the right direction, although the journey was by no means complete. In the sixteenth report, published in June 2006, the Commissioner noted that, while he did not expect that all of the remaining recommendations would be fully implemented by the following year, the permanent institutions of governance and accountability, in particular the Policing Board and the Ombudsman, had demonstrated their ability to satisfactorily fulfil their mandates.

The Oversight Commissioner's seventeenth report, published in September 2006, focused on devolution in policing. In his Introduction the Commissioner again regretted the obstacles to achieving the accepted and representative policing service envisioned by the Independent Commission for reasons which he described as essentially political and societal in nature; the collective political failure and its resulting vacuum had a clear impact on the success of further policing reforms and on the well-being of all communities in Northern Ireland. The thematic report concluded that, with the exception of the devolution of policing powers to the Northern Ireland Assembly, the devolution of authority and decision-making had generally been accomplished as intended. It attributed this largely to the successful stewardship of the Policing Board and the keen scrutiny of the Ombudsman, while giving significant credit to the PSNI itself.

The Oversight Commissioner's eighteenth report, published in December 2006, identified the 46 recommendations and 103 associated performance indicators that then required completion by the various stakeholders, principally the PSNI.

The final report of the Oversight Commissioner was published in May 2007. Al Hutchinson, as the outgoing Oversight Commissioner, set out to produce a comprehensive document that would stand alone in reflecting the progress made in implementation of all the 175 recommendations of the Independent Commission. The document accordingly has particular value as a summary of the entire process. The timing was especially appropriate as, earlier that year, the Northern Ireland Assembly had resumed its role, with a new Executive led by the Rev Ian Paisley as the First Minister and Martin McGuinness as the deputy First Minister. It was also clear in May 2007 that the political process was going to be completed in relation to policing, with the advent of Sinn Féin representatives on the Policing Board following that party's endorsement of the policing process. In another positive development the Government announced in 2007 a commitment to funding the new Police College in the Cookstown area, at Desertcreat, in an innovative partnership with the Northern Ireland Fire and Rescue and Prison Services.

The final report identified 35 remaining recommendations to be monitored by the Policing Board and the Northern Ireland Office. This represented 80% completion of all the Independent Commission's recommendations, with commendable progress in a further 16%, while just 3.5% were disappointing and 1.8% were not implemented at all. A number of areas of concern were flagged up, mostly familiar themes from earlier reports, including human rights training, but also the implementation of the new appraisal system introduced in April 2007. He said that it was important that qualitative indicators were identified to reflect the concerns of the community over issues such as the fear of crime, victimisation, and public safety. Implementation of both the estate and information technology strategies was a slow process, as were exchanges with the Garda Síochána, civilianisation, and increasing levels of Roman Catholic representation among the PSNI's civilian workforce. The Commissioner also flagged up the transfer of national security responsibilities from the Police Service to the Security Service, noting that experience in other jurisdictions was a good indicator that eventual difficulties would occur in the overlap areas of policing and national security. He opined that it would be important for the Policing Board, from the perspective of the accountability of policing in Northern Ireland, to monitor the area of overlap for any emerging difficulties; while the Policing Board did not have oversight of national security matters, it would be important that they took up their responsibility to the boundary of their remit.

The Commissioner included, in this report, a final section on future challenges. He described this as being, in a sense, '*a reality check against undue expectations.*' He set out his comments under four headings – community engagement; sustainability and capacity; a choice: policing the past or policing the future; and accountability.

The Commissioner stressed first the need for meaningful results and outcomes to flow from community engagement between the PSNI and the multifarious community groups – '*talking shops do not benefit anyone*'. Looking ahead to the anticipated changes in the Review of Public Administration, he stressed the governance role of the Policing Board in providing the appropriate leadership and strategic vision for the right balance of community engagement, for all groups in Northern Ireland.

Second, in respect of sustainability and capacity, he flagged up the need for continuing human and financial resources. The Commissioner noted that:

'*The reality of the future is that the current level of resources is not sustainable and will not be available at levels that currently exist ... This resource shortfall will not match the expectations of the residents of Northern Ireland ... But it will be important that the Policing Board have the governance capacity to deal with it through ensuring a more efficient and effective use of resources by the Police Service.*'

The third challenge related to the issues arising from the past. The Commissioner noted that people wanted different and often conflicting things:

'*Truth, justice, retribution, an opaque wall shielding the past, or simply the end of the financial drain from reliving the past. What is clear to me is that it is an issue hindering the forward progress of policing.*'

The Commissioner said that he had not previously publicly discussed this issue, simply because it was so emotive and almost defied rational discussion. It was his belief, however, that Northern Ireland society somehow had to find the proper architecture to deal with the past, and learn from it; otherwise the issues of the past would establish a barrier in the road towards re-establishing the trust necessary for the full achievement of the new beginning to policing in Northern Ireland.

In the section on accountability the Commissioner also flagged up his concern about the extent to which the Police Ombudsman was expending so many resources on determining accountability for past policing issues. But his second concern was in relation to the dual role of the Policing Board – it was providing governance for the police that required both a *'positive "nurturing role" (acquiring and distributing resources, promoting public trust in the police, supporting, and rewarding) and a parental "tough love" role – in other words, "accountability".'* While to date the Policing Board had handled these roles appropriately and without difficulty, it would face two future challenges. The first would stem from the issue of finite resources, while the second was the need to *'operate at a distance'* and avoid the trap of police accountability bodies elsewhere being 'captured' by the police whom they governed, with a consequent reduction in their ability to hold the police to account.

17.5   The Oversight Commissioner: His Relationship with the Policing Board

The relationship with the Oversight Commissioner was an important one for the Policing Board, not least in part to ensure a positive assessment of the role of the Board in the Commissioner's regular reports, as a means of creating public confidence and credibility in that organisation. In process terms, it can be simply described. On each visit to Northern Ireland by the Commissioner he would meet the Chairman and Vice-Chairman of the Policing Board shortly prior to publication of his report. In addition, about annually, the Oversight Commissioner would have a meeting with the full Membership of the Board. This first occurred on 2 May 2002. It was perhaps helpful for the Commissioner to be reminded that some Members of the Board did not accept all the recommendations of the Independent Commission; there was also scope for discussion of the effect of the then prevailing security environment on the implementation of the Independent Commission's recommendations. Board Members sought to have advance copies of the Oversight Commissioner's report prior to publication, as the *Political Members* wished to be in a position to respond to media enquiries concerning its content.

As has been demonstrated already in this chapter, the Oversight Commissioner was consistently positive in his remarks about the Policing Board. Nowhere in the 19 reports is there an explicit criticism of the Board's performance or any of its decisions. At most, the Commissioner might flag up the importance of the role that the Board could play in ensuring implementation of particular Independent Commission recommendations – interestingly, the Commissioner did not reflect in any of his reports the lack of consensus among certain Board Members in relation to some of the Commission's 175 recommendations.

The seventh report of the Oversight Commissioner, published in May 2003, was in some respects a particularly significant one, not only because it was followed by an extensive press release issued on the behalf of the Policing Board, establishing a precedent that was regularly followed, but also because the Chief Constable was asked by the Board to provide a plan and timetable for addressing the *'areas of concern'* regarding PSNI that had been highlighted in the Commissioner's report. A document was published by the PSNI in September 2003, responding to the Commissioner's following report, entitled *'Progress in Action'*. With a Foreword from the Chief Constable, it welcomed the positive recognition of achievements and provided a specific Police Service response to each of the individual comments in the *'areas of concern'*. This was a valuable opportunity for the PSNI to set out the approach towards restructuring Crime Branch, including the amalgamation with Special Branch, and a diagrammatic breakdown of the six individual departments within the Branch. The Foreword provided the opportunity for the Chief Constable to refer to the time lag between each of the Commissioner's inspections and the subsequent report, and to illustrate progress in the intervening months.

Commenting on the final report produced by Commissioner Constantine in December 2003 – the ninth report – the Policing Board Chairman chose in his press release to express a challenge in relation to Sinn Féin's position on policing:

'Like the Oversight Commissioner, the Policing Board recognises the contribution of all those involved in policing here who he says "have courageously accepted the obligations of citizenship", it is time others did the same.'

The Commissioner's fourteenth report, the thematic review on human rights and accountability, did flag up the position of the Policing Board, noting that, in the Independent Commission's estimation, that organisation came with its own democratic credentials, which would ensure that neither the Government nor the Police Service would be in a position to easily disregard its views. In particular, the Policing Board had the power to compel reports and initiate inquiries as necessary, thereby exercising significant authority over the Police Service. The Commissioner referred to the report that had then recently been carried out by the Parliamentary Northern Ireland Affairs Committee into the functions of the Policing Board. He observed that the Committee had noted that *'information leaks by some Board members had led to a certain loss of confidence in the Board on the part of the Police Service and the Ombudsman'*, but also that the Policing Board had developed a constructive relationship with the Police Service under difficult circumstances. The Commissioner also repeated the commendation by the Committee on the Board's efforts to engage with the public, in particular to make accountability meetings more accessible to the public.

In turn, the Policing Board followed up the Commissioner's fifteenth report on training with a reaffirmation of the Board's determination that the Government should fund the £134m cost of the new Police College then estimated.

Both the Commissioner and the Policing Board had been considering, nearly a year before the actual ending of the Oversight Commissioner role, the part that the Board might play in overseeing completion of the outstanding Independent Commission's recommendations after May 2007. The Board followed this up by requesting the Chief Constable to provide an update in relation to the recommendations judged outstanding early in 2007.

In May 2007 the Policing Board considered a paper on the oversight of the outstanding Independent Commission's recommendations. The Board sought to achieve, in the arrangements it made, sustainable, credible, and independent oversight. Consideration was given to the

extent to which individual Board Members could play a direct monitoring role.

In the event, the Board agreed that individual outstanding
Independent Commission's recommendations should be taken to
the relevant Board Committee for prioritisation and consideration
as to how they wished to monitor them. (In practice, about half the
recommendations were directly monitored by a Board Committee,
with the rest being covered by outside experts or agencies.) In addition, a composite paper should be prepared with a view to publishing a
progress report on implementation annually, beginning in May 2008.
To facilitate this the Policing Board agreed in December 2007 that
it should appoint the last Oversight Commissioner's Chief of Staff,
Mark Reber, as a specialist resource to review the 32 outstanding
Independent Commission's recommendations for which the Board had
assumed responsibility in May 2007. In taking this forward, Board
Members were provided with an update paper in January 2008 on the
status of each of the outstanding recommendations.

In June 2008 Mark Reber presented to the Policing Board an
updated status report. His conclusion was that just under a third of
the Independent Commission's recommendations judged outstanding
one year before could now be considered implemented. The PSNI was
asked for comment, following which the Board determined to publish
the report.

17.6   The Significance of this Oversight Model
for Other (Policing) Situations

In September 2003 Al Hutchinson completed a thoughtful academic
assessment of 'Independent Oversight: a mechanism of effective governance assurance for the policing reforms in Northern Ireland', on which he
has kindly allowed the authors to draw.

His thesis confirmed that, at least at that time, there were no
similar independent mechanisms overseeing policing reform elsewhere in the world. The Northern Ireland model offered a unique
glimpse of an evolving approach to policing governance, although he
recognised that his assessment could not be comprehensive until the
completion of the work of the Oversight Commissioner.

Hutchinson's study began by looking at the development of govern-ance models and, while noting the multi-layered approach proposed in the Independent Commission's Report, went on to consider the various forms of accountability. An essay by Janet Chan noted that account-ability, in the context of policing, is a term that has two competing meanings. It can be seen as control over the police or, alternatively, as the requirement on the police to give accounts or explanations of conduct. She adopts this definition:

'Being answerable to audiences for performing up to certain prescribed stand-ards, thereby fulfilling obligations, duties, expectations and other charges ... When people are accountable, they can be made to explain and justify their conduct, and their behaviour can be scrutinised, judged and sanctioned by audiences.'

However, as Kersten noted, *'there is no consensus in criminology about the efficiency of external and/or internal mechanisms for controlling the police'*. Chan observed that there could be unintended consequences of introducing accountability mechanisms and external *'watchdog'* agen-cies, one of which she identified as *'colonisation'*, which she described as the domination of the accountability process by external agencies to the detriment of organisational efficiency and effectiveness.

Hutchinson referred to the emphasis placed on accountability by the Independent Commission:

'Accountability should run through the bloodstream of the whole body of the police service and it is at least as much a matter of the culture and ethos of the service as it is of the institutional mechanisms.'

He noted that the terms of reference issued by the Northern Ireland Secretary of State for the Oversight Commissioner contained a section that explicitly excluded accountability <u>to</u> the Oversight Commissioner by the Secretary of State, the police, and the Policing Board.

Hutchinson went on to note that there is even less consensus on the definition of oversight. While in England and Wales statutory bodies such as Police Authorities used *'oversight'* to describe an oversight role, it was more in the sense of a function, relating inwardly more to performance management and accountability. Internationally, there was more reference to civilian oversight of policing, often used in the context of attempts to control what are seen as undesirable behaviours in the police – examples include independent investigation, police investigation with civilian review or appeal to civilian authority, and investigation by external commissions and policing bodies. One commentator referred to the *'capture theory'* to explain poor oversight performance, where the oversight loses objectivity and is 'captured' by the interests of the organisation being overseen.

The difference with the independent oversight recommended by the Independent Commission, noted Hutchinson, is that it had:

'"A finite objective (to measure change against agreed recommendations), for a finite period and without direct governance or accountability responsibility". In other words, it is a normative – behavioural mechanism with its power coming from public reporting to Parliament.'

As Tom Constantine observed (some seven years later) in his chapter in *Policing the Narrow Ground*, the Independent Commission's Report *'did not include any specific measures to monitor progress in relation to its 175 recommendations'*. Constantine continued:

'In reality, the authorities of the Oversight Commissioner are limited. The Commissioner cannot promote, demote or provide financial incentives; all he can do is publish a report outlining the progress or lack of progress that occurs on implementing the Patten recommendations.'

However, he added:

'I originally seriously underestimated the impact of the public release of the oversight reports and the subsequent media analysis of the results. It became apparent almost immediately that the individuals and agencies saw the findings of the Oversight Commissioner as a professional report card, and they expended a great deal of effort to try to have a positive review from the Oversight Commissioner.'

Hutchinson cites Arie Halachmi as pointing out that there can be pathologies and dysfunction in the application of performance measurement, and that it needs to be context relevant:

'The political context of performance measurement influences, if not determines, the instrumental value of performance reports to managers, policymakers, the public at large and professional employees in public agencies, and their clients.'

Halachmi also observes that, while the justification for the introduction of performance measurement is often to assure accountability, it does result in a loss of capacity in that it moves resources from *'production to overhead'*. He adds that performance measures can limit progress and learning if managers are unwilling to change from the course they are being measured against.

Mike Bolton offers a practitioner's view of some successful measurement criteria: measures should measure key success factors; offer views from different perspectives; reflect concerns of all stakeholders; be both qualitative and quantitative; and be unobtrusive, not disrupting primary tasks.

As Hutchinson rightly concludes, the Independent Commission envisaged that independent oversight would not only measure progress but also facilitate change, even though the oversight arrangements would have no direct accountability or governance role. It is interesting, however, that the original Independent Commission's Report did not explicitly refer in the rationale for the oversight process to the important objective of ensuring public confidence in the change process.

For the purposes of his study Hutchinson set about generating data in the Northern Ireland context through multi-level semi-structured interviews and sampling. The institutions that he approached included the PSNI, the Policing Board, the Ombudsman, the Northern Ireland Office, and the Office of the Oversight Commissioner. Within the PSNI a range of responses was obtained from officers on the ground through to the Chief Constable. A range of secondary data was available in, for example, public reports and surveys of public opinion relating, for instance, to changes in public confidence in policing over time.

In terms of the key findings, he recorded that respondents saw the primary purpose of the Oversight Commissioner as ensuring the implementation of the Independent Commission's recommendations. Some respondents recognised a secondary, normative purpose, such as providing reassurance to the public. In relation to the question of impact respondents had a variety of observations, identifying oversight as an influencer, enabler, and lever of change. Those in senior leadership or management positions with direct responsibilities for achieving change referred to the assistance that they had had from the oversight process, not least in persuading either their own staff or other stakeholders, as a lever to push people. This applied not just to the PSNI but also to other policing bodies charged with accountability or governance functions. However, Hutchinson distinguished between the top leaders (i.e. the ones with most autonomy) and senior operational managers (those with comparatively less power), with the latter perceiving a greater degree of impact in the oversight process.

All respondents agreed that there had been a significant resource cost as a consequence of oversight, with some negative aspects; one respondent also said that, from the leadership point of view, it could disrupt the governance of policing. Interestingly, some operational managers also felt that the process impacted on priorities, having the potential to skew them, although this particular danger did not seem to have been identified. (This was a concern identified by Robert Reiner.) Respondents did recommend a reduction in the number of performance indicators, with more consultation on the oversight methodology and process, as well as concerns in relation to this functionality – that is, the cost to society and to the organisations of multiple layers of governance and accountability.

It was important that the attributes felt to be associated by respondents with the Oversight Commissioner and his team included integrity, independence, credibility, and objectivity.

Respondents were asked specifically if they felt that the independent oversight mechanism could be applicable to other public sectors such as education or health. On balance, the responses were positive in terms of increasing the public accountability of the public sector, although the expense was a potential concern.

Al Hutchinson noted in his commentary the importance of context. Thus, for example, there were several developments in the last few months of 2001 that together had a major impact – the creation of the Policing Board, the Ombudsman's report on the Omagh bombing, and the commencement of the oversight process. All of these had the effect of 'unfreezing' the previous position. One aspect was that they brought home areas of a comparative lack of progress in the change process. Hutchinson stressed the valuable role of the independent oversight mechanism as an influencer, an enabler, and a lever of change. He concluded that, while the lack of direct impact was a function of the legally prescribed role, it was the lack of direct involvement in governance and accountability that led to the increased effectiveness of this oversight mechanism. This was because the lines of legally prescribed governance and accountability were relatively clear, the leaders had a clear sense of their roles and accountabilities, and the role of oversight was relatively non-threatening to organisational or personal interests. Adequate resourcing for the mechanism and a fixed term to ensure independence were also seen as critical success factors.

A different perspective is provided by another member of the original oversight team – Professor David Bayley, writing in 2008, after Sinn Féin's endorsement of the policing arrangements. His article examined the relevance of the reform experience in Northern Ireland to other countries emerging from conflict where policing was critical to peace and stability. It specified four challenges that Northern Ireland faced that were common to other post-conflict societies, but also suggested four other factors that made reform possible in Northern Ireland that might not occur in similar situations elsewhere. Bayley concluded that Northern Ireland showed that meaningful police reform could occur despite years of bitter conflict, but that certain conditions might be necessary for it. Importantly, he noted that:

'The world has also learned that reconstructing and reforming police after conflict is not easy. Failure is more common than success. There is one case, however, where reform after prolonged conflict has been notably successful. That is Northern Ireland. It is generally agreed that the police of Northern Ireland have undergone a substantial transformation since the Good Friday Agreement of 1998, particularly with respect to its commitment to human rights, external accountability and responsiveness to the community.'

In terms of the similar factors, Bayley cites

a. the length and bitterness of the conflict;

b. the fact that issues of both sovereignty and religion were involved;

c. the need for peacemakers to transform the police from one preoccupied with protecting the government and itself to a force dedicated and deployed to protect individuals regardless of their community affiliation; and

d. that police reform also had to confront the mutation of armed political partisans into criminal gangs.

Bayley went on to assess the importance of the Independent Commission:

'[it is,] in my judgement, the most insightful, thorough and well-reasoned plan for the development of a democratic police force that has ever been done. Its principles applied not only to police emerging from conflict, but to police at any stage of development who aspire to act in ways that conform to and are supportive of democracy.'

Bayley commended the PSNI for rarely complaining even informally about the unprecedented regime of accountability, apart from understandable concern about the amount of work entailed in responding to the varied overseers.

He identified four advantages in Northern Ireland that many post-conflict situations would not have:

a. an agreement between the contending parties that violence would stop and power be shared in a new government

b. the people of Northern Ireland shared democratic habits of mind and an appreciation of the rule of law

c. Northern Ireland had a well-developed capacity to govern, with a well-educated population, and the police service was itself well-organised with expert and well-trained officers

d. Northern Ireland was rich in its 'civil society', with many active community groups, an attentive media, and an organised bar; the police themselves cooperated routinely in international policing activities

In conclusion, Bayley was optimistic about the likelihood that police reform would last in Northern Ireland, but pessimistic about the prospects in other post-conflict situations lacking the four characteristics that he identified.

17.7   In Conclusion

The oversight process in Northern Ireland did not come cheaply. The total cost of the arrangements for the Oversight Commissioner and his Office over the seven-year period, which included a Chief of Staff and supporting team permanently based in Northern Ireland, was of the order of just under £10m. This, of course, does not take account of the additional – unquantified – costs incurred by policing and other organisations in servicing and responding to the oversight process. It does not seem that the members of the Independent Commission had in mind quite as extensive a process as emerged; some, for example, would have had in mind a small team headed by a single judicial figure. That did perhaps reflect, however, a possible element of naivety about the scale and extent of the reform programme, especially for the police service that the Commission were recommending and hence the level of associated oversight required.

It should also be noted that the creation of the role of the Northern Ireland Justice Oversight Commissioner was clearly a direct by-product of the policing oversight role recommended by the Independent Commission. The post was announced in December 2002 and was filled by Lord Clyde, an eminent Scottish judge. Even though the original Criminal Justice Review, published in 2000, had not specifically recommended an oversight function, the consultation process following publication of that Review had demonstrated substantial support for one. There was also cross-party support in the Northern Ireland Assembly for the appointment of a Commissioner with a remit to oversee the implementation of the reform of the criminal justice system. While the oversight process was broadly similar, Lord Clyde established a much smaller supporting team and did not draw up such detailed performance indicators. He also made clear from the beginning that he would not serve beyond his initial three-year term of office, and accordingly the Justice oversight function was terminated at that point.

The authors had the opportunity to talk to Al Hutchinson early in 2012, shortly before he concluded his period as the Northern Ireland Police Ombudsman – the post to which he was appointed following his term as Oversight Commissioner. Hutchinson endorsed Professor's Bayley's view that the Northern Ireland oversight mechanism provided a framework rather than a prescriptive model, and that the approach adopted must fit the local context. He reflected that he had agreed, with some reluctance, to the extension of the five-year term of the police Oversight Commissioner. While he appreciated the political justification, he felt that the oversight process was inevitably delivering diminishing returns after that length of time. The process had been 'refreshed' with the adoption of the thematic report approach, but there was a danger that, towards the end, the Oversight Commissioner had, in effect, become part of the established furniture, with a reduced impact. Hutchinson was also aware of the danger of being 'captured' by the police; for example, the Oversight Commissioner declined invitations from the PSNI to sit on working parties or attend internal meetings on specific issues. That would have risked both compromising the accountability relationship and losing something of the healthy tension that arguably is a prerequisite for success in any oversight mechanism.

One of the strengths of the oversight process was the approach adopted first by Commissioner Constantine and then by his successor. The perception of independence and integrity was important. It was also important that – at a time when there were no direct contacts or communications between Sinn Féin and the PSNI – the Oversight Commissioner could develop and sustain regular contacts with that political party. It was another means of assisting Sinn Féin to gain a more comprehensive – and triangulated – understanding of the multifarious issues to do with policing. This also paved the way for an invitation to Al Hutchinson to address the Sinn Féin Ard Fheis in Dublin prior to that party's formal decision to endorse the policing institutions in Northern Ireland.

There is no doubt that the policing oversight mechanism as envisaged by the Independent Commission's Report and as taken forward first by Tom Constantine and then Al Hutchinson and their colleagues was an important and valuable part of the confidence-building process within Northern Ireland that nurtured and sustained not just the specific police reform programme but also the wider political rapprochement culminating in Sinn Féin's endorsement of the arrangements and joining of the Policing Board. While similar results could arguably have been achieved with a smaller budget and a less intrusively extensive performance-monitoring procedure, those very features were themselves integral parts of the success of the process.

It is also worth noting that the North American background and contacts of the Oversight Commissioners and their team provided their progress reports with greater credibility in America and with other international audiences that might have been more sceptical of positive accounts of the pace of change implementation had the authors been from within the United Kingdom or even Europe. To quote a specific example, the Policing Board Chairman found it helpful on visits to Washington DC to refer to Commissioner Constantine and his oversight reports, knowing that his audience in the White House or on Capitol Hill would be au fait with the Commissioner's expertise and his role.

References

Chan, Janet, 'Governing police practice: limits of the new accountability', *British Journal of Sociology*, 50:2, 1999, pp. 251–270

Kersten, Joachim, 'Police powers and accountability in a democratic society: introductory report', *Journal of Educational Administration*, 38:3, 2000, pp. 288–298

Reiner, Robert, *The Politics of the Police*, 3rd edition, Oxford University Press, Oxford, 2000

Cramphorn, Colin, 'Human Rights and policing – Accountability', *Police Research and Management*, 5:3, 2001, pp. 29–36

Halachmi, Arie, 'Performance measurement: a look at some possible dysfunctions', *Work Study*, 51:5, 2002, pp. 230–239

Bolton, Mike, 'Public sector performance measurement: delivering greater accountability', *Work Study*, 52:1, 2003, pp. 20–24

Progress in Action, PSNI, September, 2003

Hutchinson, Al, '*Independent Oversight: a mechanism of effective governance assurance for the policing reforms in Northern Ireland*', unpublished, 2003

Bayley, David, 'Post-conflict Police Reform: is Northern Ireland a Model?', *Policing*, 5 June 2008, pp. 1–8

Doyle, John (ed.), *Policing the Narrow Ground*, Royal Irish Academy, Dublin, 2010

Appendix 17.A

Terms of Reference of the Oversight Commissioner
(the revised text, as on the Oversight Commissioner's website)

Aim

The Office of the Oversight Commissioner was established as a result of the recommendations in the Report of The Independent Commission On Policing For Northern Ireland. The Oversight Commissioner will be responsible for overseeing the implementation of the changes in policing arrangements and structures decided on in the context of the Patten Report.

Functions

The Commissioner will monitor and review progress achieved in implementing change; receive reports, information and explanations, as required, from the agencies responsible for progress; and provide public assurance about the progress of the implementation process.

As part of the process, the Oversight Commissioner will:

- be provided with periodic reports, which will include objectives and timetables, by the Government, the Police Service and the Policing Board covering the changes in policing arrangements and structures for which they are responsible

- conduct periodic progress review meetings on the implementation of change in policing arrangements, structures and related areas with Government Ministers and officials, the Chief Constable, the Policing Board (and in due course the District Policing Partnerships) and with others as appropriate. Such meetings will take place at least three times a year and each of the specified agencies will:

- report to the Commissioner on progress achieved in implementing the changes for which they are responsible

- provide explanations for any delays or failures to achieve objectives for which they are responsible

- provide a report to the Secretary of State after each periodic review. The Secretary of State will place these reports before Parliament and publish them. Such reports will include:

- an account of the progress which has been achieved in implementing the required changes

- the Commissioner's observations on the extent to which any delays or failures are the responsibility of the agencies themselves or due to matters beyond their control

- meet with the Police Ombudsman and other relevant organisations or agencies, including the political parties and community leaders, to discuss progress with the implementation of the required changes

Support

In carrying out his duties, the Oversight Commissioner will be supported by a permanent Chief of Staff, based in Belfast, and by a team of evaluators. The roles of the Chief of Staff and the Evaluation Team will be to:

Chief of Staff

- Manage the office and staff of the Oversight Commissioner.
- Act as the Commissioner's finance officer.
- Serve as the principal point of contact in the absence of the Commissioner.
- Liaise with NIO/PSNI/Policing Board/Police Ombudsman and other interested parties regarding reports required by the Oversight Commissioner.
- Analyse submissions made to the Commissioner.
- Assist in drafting the Commissioner's periodic reports.
- Carry out any other duties as agreed by the Oversight Commissioner.

Evaluators

- Assist the Commissioner in initially assessing the current position of the NIO/PSNI/Policing Board and other interested parties vis-à-vis implementation.

- Assist the Commissioner to design systems aimed at facilitating the monitoring of implementation.

- Provide advice to the Commissioner thus assisting him in the exercise of his functions.

Assessment of the Security Threat

In undertaking periodic reviews of progress, the Oversight Commissioner will be bound to respect the confidential detail of the assessment of the security threat provided by the Chief Constable.

Accountability

Nothing in these terms of reference should be taken as affecting the responsibilities of the Secretary of State or encroaching on the operational independence of the Chief Constable in controlling and directing the police service, or on the responsibilities of the Policing Board.

CHAPTER EIGHTEEN

The American and International Dimensions

18.1 Introduction

The relationship between Northern Ireland and the United States of America is both multi-layered and multi-faceted. It is also a good deal older than many realise. In 1636 a group of Northern Ireland Presbyterians (principally of Scottish descent) set sail for the Massachusetts Bay Colony in North America from Groomsport in the *Eagle Wing*, although they were beaten back by storms in mid-Atlantic. Subsequently, it is estimated that in the 18th century several hundred thousand people of the Protestant (mainly Presbyterian) persuasion left Ulster for what were then the American colonies, while in the 19th and 20th centuries many Irish people, predominantly Roman Catholic, emigrated to America. No less than 15 American Presidents have been of Ulster stock. There has been an American Consulate in Belfast for over 200 years.

In more recent times the American Government played a significant role in Northern Ireland's *peace* and *political processes*. Successive American Presidents appointed special advisers with particular responsibility for Northern Ireland. The Irish (in particular the green) vote was a significant political influence on Capitol Hill in Washington. During much of the Troubles the Provisional Irish Republican Army (PIRA) and then Sinn Féin garnered direct support from America.

Another strand has related to the development of policing on both sides of the Atlantic. The Royal Canadian Mounted Police (RCMP) was modelled in the 1860s quite largely on the Royal Irish Constabulary. We have foreshadowed earlier in this book the American influence on the development of what became the Police Service of Northern Ireland (the Police Service or the PSNI), both through the Membership of Dr Gerald Lynch, President of John Jay College of Criminal Justice, New York, and Kathleen O'Toole, previously Massachusetts Secretary for Public Safety, on The Independent Commission On Policing For Northern Ireland (the Independent Commission), and through policing good practice from America quoted in the latter's Report.

This link continued during the time of the Northern Ireland Policing Board (the Policing Board or Board), with regular visits to America, including a number of well-publicised visits to the White House during the St Patrick's Day celebrations in March each year. Many American politicians took an interest in developments in policing in Northern Ireland, paying close attention, for example, to the regular reports from the Police Oversight Commissioner. The Policing Board considered that it was important to give a first-hand account in Washington and elsewhere of the progress and the challenges, and to provide accurate information to those with influence in America who were potentially prepared to encourage Sinn Féin to support policing, if they judged that it was warranted by the extent of the progress. On the other side of the coin, developments in policing in America also continued to be of importance to the Policing Board; examples included the theoretical and practical applications of the principles of 'Broken Windows', linkages with academic establishments, and representation of the Board at Conferences, seminars, and on sponsored visits.

Additionally, in recent years the British Government has also looked to American police leaders, techniques, and oversight arrangements as a source of guidance for reshaping policing methods and accountability in Great Britain.

18.2   The Relationship between Northern Ireland and America Prior to the Belfast Agreement of April 1998

There are many sources from which one could draw to describe the relationship between Northern Ireland and America prior to the signing of the Belfast Agreement in April 1998. *The American Presence in Ulster, a Diplomatic History, 1796–1996*, by Francis M. Carroll, puts more recent events in a valuable historical perspective. As Carroll notes, the Irish question did constitute a problem for the American

Government at the time when President Woodrow Wilson, the descendant of Ulster immigrant grandparents from County Tyrone, led the Democratic Party, which drew much of its urban support from the Irish–American community. In Belfast the new Northern Ireland Government consulted the United States Consul on the American educational model. During the Second World War over 100,000 US troops were initially posted to Northern Ireland for training and acclimatisation purposes before moving on to various theatres of war.

In 1969 money was raised by Irish–American groups to provide aid primarily to Catholic families who had lost their homes during rioting in August of that year. Leaders from Northern Ireland's Social Democratic and Labour Party (SDLP) were invited to tour major cities in America raising awareness about the situation in Northern Ireland. (Interestingly, the MP Bernadette Devlin and Rev Dr Ian Paisley also visited America at that time.) A hundred Members of Congress, led by the Speaker of the House, the Irish 'Tip' O'Neill, wrote to President Nixon asking him to do something about the sectarian clashes in Northern Ireland. In America the Irish Northern Aid Committee, known as Noraid, with Michael Flannery as a key figure, emerged as an influential pressure group. It was generally understood, as Carroll records, that Noraid diverted significant amounts of its funds to purchase weapons for the PIRA. In subsequent years the Irish Government as well as the British Government sought to reduce the flow of funds and equipment from America. Within the United States, in the later 1970s Senator Edward Kennedy, Senator Daniel Patrick Moynihan, House Speaker Tip O'Neill, and former Congressman Hugh Carey – the 'Four Horsemen', as they were known – came to support a moderate Nationalist position on cooperation with the British Government.

Political factors also influenced efforts by the Royal Ulster Constabulary (RUC) to improve their equipment on various occasions during the Troubles. A request from the RUC to purchase automatic weapons from America in the late 1970s was denied as a result of Congressional pressure, although an earlier order placed through the State Department had been fulfilled.

Bill Clinton, following his election to the White House, demonstrated a personal interest in Northern Ireland. In 1993 he explored with the British and Irish Governments the appointment of a special envoy to promote peace in Northern Ireland. In April that year Gerry Adams applied – unsuccessfully – for a visa to travel to the United States. Following the Downing Street Joint Declaration, in January 1994 Adams renewed his application for a visa. In the event, at the personal decision of President Clinton, Adams was granted a 48-hour visa.

President Clinton and his wife flew into Northern Ireland on 30 November 1995. One of the purposes of the visit was to promote the *peace process*. In a speech in the Mackie's plant in West Belfast President Clinton stated that:

'Violence has no place at the table of democracy, and no role in the future of this land. By the same token, you must also be willing to say to those who renounce violence and who do take their own risks for peace that they are entitled to be full participants in the democratic process.'

Less than three months later, in February 1996, the IRA broke their ceasefire. Later that year former Senator George Mitchell was appointed as one of the co-chairmen of the plenary sessions of the all-party talks. George Mitchell's sustained commitment and political skills have been fully recorded elsewhere, but they undoubtedly played a major role in the reaching of the Belfast (or Good Friday) Agreement on 10 April 1998. In September that year President Clinton came back to Belfast to demonstrate his support for the Agreement and the opportunity it represented for an acceptable form of self-government for all sectors of the community in Northern Ireland. The newly elected First Minister David Trimble, the deputy First Minister Seamus Mallon, and the British Prime Minister Tony Blair joined the President in making speeches at Belfast's Waterfront Hall. The President condemned the Real IRA bomb at Omagh the previous month and stressed that the opportunity for peace must not be allowed to slip away. Later that evening he said publicly

'Three years ago, I pledged that, if you chose peace, America would walk with you. You made the choice, and America will honour its pledge.'

18.3   The Relationship in the Time of the Policing Board

Members of the newly appointed Policing Board and others involved in policing in Northern Ireland visited various locations in the United States in December 2001 in a programme partly devised by Mediation Northern Ireland. Although the timing conflicted with urgent work that had to be taken forward by the new Board in Belfast, the visit was an early, tangible sign of the importance for the Policing Board of links with America both in terms of contacts with opinion-formers in that country and also in keeping abreast of developments in policing and wider law enforcement there.

Dr Richard Haass had been appointed as the Special Envoy for Northern Ireland by President George Bush in 2001. He visited the seventh meeting of the Policing Board on 6 March 2002. In his opening remarks, welcoming Ambassador Haass, the Policing Board Chairman drew attention to the successes the Board had already achieved through a process of discussion and compromise, and the independence it had demonstrated. He concluded by saying:

'We look to Ambassador Haass and his colleagues for support in our task of delivering for the people of Northern Ireland a police service which can work closely with, and is responsive to, the local communities it serves.'

In his response Ambassador Haass said that policing in Northern Ireland was a key issue for the US Government. He looked forward to assisting the Board in any way possible in delivering a new police service. A colleague explained the training opportunities available for police officers at the FBI National Academy and said that the US Government would be lifting its ban on FBI training for PSNI officers. Specifically, a place would be reserved for a PSNI officer on the 10-week FBI Joint Leadership Development training course in Quantico, Virginia, in June and autumn 2002. In discussion, Dr Haass said that he had called on Sinn Féin privately and publicly to reconsider its position and nominate representatives to serve on the Policing Board. There was discussion also about the opportunity for the authorities in both jurisdictions to learn from each other on tackling drugs and racketeering problems.

In summer 2002 the Chairman of the Policing Board, together with the Police Ombudsman, had a meeting with the US Congressional delegation, led by James Walsh, that visited Belfast. This was an important opportunity to provide Members of Congress with an insight into policing developments. Mr Walsh was Chairman of the Friends of Ireland, having been first named to that post by the Speaker of the House in 1995. He had also accompanied President Clinton on his visits to Northern Ireland and was responsible for the Walsh Visas, passed by Congress in 1998, which as part of the peace process allowed citizens from Northern Ireland to live and work in the United States for five years.

In autumn 2002 the US Congress voted for an in-depth State Department report on Northern Ireland policing and human rights. This was reported in the newspapers as in part being prompted by perceived delays in introducing the Independent Commission's Report, including the lack of secondment of senior Gardaí into the PSNI and the slow progress in introducing a new Police College and the reformation of Special Branch.

There were many two-way visits and exchanges. In early summer 2003 a delegation from the US Committee on International Human Rights met the Policing Board Chairman and Vice-Chairman during their visit to Belfast. The group wrote that they were heartened by the progress in the criminal justice system since their previous visit in 1998. Their report was subsequently published in March 2004. It noted that '*the pace and transparency of policing reforms has been striking in comparison to reforms of other criminal justice agencies*'.

In September 2003 Mediation Northern Ireland was involved in arrangements for a further civic policing project exchange visit to Boston in which they invited representatives of the Policing Board and District Policing Partnerships (DPPs) to participate. It was seen as a tangible opportunity to demonstrate support for DPPs. Separately, Policing Board Members were briefed on contacts that had been established with Queen's University in Kingston, Ontario, which had developed a model of best practice with regard to how police engage with the community to establish a common framework for problem-solving. The Boston programme included a presentation on the concept of community policing from Professor George Kelling of Rutgers University and Paul Evans, the then Police Commissioner in Boston (who was later to hold a senior advisory post in British policing.) Those who went on the study visit included the Policing Board Chairman, two *Political Members* and several members of DPPs.

In December 2003 there was a Belfast leg of the second UK–US Police Chiefs Conference under the heading 'Shared Challenges, Shared Solutions'. The conference was addressed by the Policing Board Chairman and Vice-Chairman. Delegates included the Executive Director of the Police Executive Research Forum (PERF), the chiefs of the Miami, Minneapolis, and Kansas City Police Departments, the Deputy Commissioner of the New York Police Department, and the President of the Association of Chief Police Officers (ACPO).

In March 2004 the Policing Board Chairman and Chief Executive (on behalf of the Vice-Chairman) travelled, at the invitation of the American Special Envoy Dr Mitchell Reiss, who had succeeded Ambassador Haass, to Washington for a programme of events which included a meeting with President Bush at the White House. A major focus of the St Patrick's week had been policing. Two DPP representatives had also taken part in the visit. In a subsequent discussion at the Corporate Policy Committee of the Policing Board it was agreed that there was a need to reflect on the enhancing of the Policing Board's profile in the USA and how this could best be addressed.

Also in March 2004 was a hearing on human rights and police reform in Northern Ireland held by the United States Helsinki Commission, an independent agency of the United States Government charged with monitoring and encouraging compliance with the Helsinki Final Act and other Commitments of the 55 countries participating in the Organisation for Security and Cooperation in Europe. This body, which included Senator Hillary Clinton, took evidence from Mitchell Reiss, the Northern Ireland Police Ombudsman, and other Northern Ireland commentators. The chair, Congressman Chris Smith, observed that this was the eighth hearing that he had chaired on human rights in Northern Ireland and at each policing and police reform had been a central theme. Previous witnesses had included Chris Patten, Maurice Hayes, and Rosemary Nelson. Congressman Smith noted that much had improved since the first hearing in 1997.

Dr Reiss cited Commissioner Constantine's conclusion in his latest Oversight Commission's report that the PSNI was making excellent progress in implementing the programme of change mandated by the Independent Commission. He added that public attitudes towards the police had improved in the years since the establishment of the PSNI. He also stated that Sinn Féin should take up its seats on the Policing Board and influence the future of policing from within. Dr Reiss noted that, since the restrictions had been lifted on FBI training for the PSNI in 2001, two officers had been trained at Quantico and Chief Constable Hugh Orde was to begin executive training there that very month. He also said that there had been an excellent return on the *'investment'* represented by eight exchange programmes in the last few years involving those in the PSNI and its oversight bodies. He noted that Policing Board Members had credited their visit to New York and Washington in late 2001 as helping them to establish their expertise and to develop a common civic vision that had stood them in good stead in tackling controversial issues in early 2002.

Shortly afterwards, in May 2004, the Policing Board Chairman and an *Independent Member* visited Washington and New York, where they held talks with leading politicians and other opinion formers. During the same month over 160 DPP members and senior police officers met leading community and policing representatives from Boston, Massachusetts, at a function in Lisburn organised by the Policing Board. The delegates included the PERF Executive Director Chuck Wexler. Mediation Northern Ireland played a valuable role in facilitating such exchanges, as did Boston College.

Successive United States Consuls General made a significant contribution to the political and peace processes. Outgoing Consul General Barbara Stephenson was invited to attend the *Public Session* of the Policing Board in July 2004. The Board Chairman paid tribute to the great interest that she had taken in the Board and its work, and the very important contribution that she had made. In her response she said:

'Can you remember when everybody who knew anything knew that this Policing Board was going to split on sectarian lines, fail on its first mission and never work? Now here we are years later and you are the one organisation that is really still functioning so you just keep at it. I am so proud of the Policing Board.'

In the following month *Political Member* Mr Joe Byrne (SDLP) represented the Policing Board at the International Law Enforcement Forum conference in Washington DC.

In September 2004 another large group of DPP members and senior police officers met leading policing and community representatives from Canada, with whom they discussed best practice in community policing experiences. Later that month Mitchell Reiss addressed the National Committee on US Foreign Policy in New York. Speaking on policing, he noted that *within the PSNI, a new force is being built, with the new culture, grounded on the philosophy of community policing and the need to respect human rights'*. He noted the role played by the policing community in New York, including Jeremy Travis of John Jay College and Jim McShane, who had spent several days in Northern Ireland in 2002 *'talking with Northern Ireland politicians about community policing, including in his father's home village in South Armagh'*. Referring to the multi-party talks at Leeds Castle that had taken place earlier in the month, which he had attended, Dr Reiss expressed the hope that the talks would signal a change in Sinn Féin's approach to policing. He noted the editorial in the *Boston Globe* the previous week calling on Sinn Féin to join the policing oversight bodies. He believed that Irish-America shared this view.

The Policing Board Chairman and Vice-Chairman accompanied four Policing Board Members, four PSNI District Commanders, and four DPP members on a study visit to Boston and Chicago in March 2005. The theme of the visit was *'communication and community policing'*. The group had the opportunity for discussion with Kathleen O'Toole (a member of the Independent Commission), who pointed to the valuable advice that the PSNI had provided to the Boston Police in relation to crowd control as the city prepared to host the 2004 Democratic Convention. Their approach had greatly assisted in the policing of large and potentially volatile crowds. One of the conclusions drawn by the delegates was the advantage of a single call centre for all emergency services and for greatly improved call-handling.

On 13 March 2006 the Policing Board Chairman received a letter from Henry Hyde, the Chairman of the Committee on International Relations of the House of Representatives of the United States Congress, inviting him to testify at an oversight hearing entitled *'the Northern Ireland peace process: policing advances and remaining challenges'*. This hearing was held jointly by the Committee on International Relations sub-committees on Africa, Global Human Rights and International Operations, and Europe and Emerging Threats, one of which was chaired by Representative Chris Smith. The invitation was to testify just two days later, on 15 March, with the Chairman's written statement to be transmitted to the Committee within 24 hours. As the Policing Board Chairman and Vice-Chairman were in Washington DC for the events of St Patrick's week, they had the opportunity to testify.

Henry Hyde's letter stated that the *peace process* had arrived at yet another crucial turning point:

'*Perhaps no issues are as important as policing reform and the resolution of unsolved killings from the troubles in Northern Ireland. ... This hearing will help the US Congress and others understand the complex situation in Northern Ireland and help guide our efforts to cooperate with the various political groups and communities in Northern Ireland, and with the governments of the United Kingdom and the Republic of Ireland to assist in the realisation of genuine peace and stability in Northern Ireland.*'

Members of the Policing Board had discussed in early February of that year the opportunity that the now traditional visit to Washington in the context of the St Patrick's Day celebrations there would provide an opportunity for the outgoing Board Chairman and Vice-Chairman, and a representative from each political party (Ian Paisley Jnr (Democratic Unionist Party (DUP)), Alan McFarland (Ulster Unionist Party (UUP)) and Joe Byrne (SDLP)) to promote the achievements of the Board in its first term to people of influence in America. The Board representatives met key opinion-formers and advised them of progress in policing in Northern Ireland. Following press enquiries, the Policing Board published a detailed account of the programme (and costs) for the Board Members' visit.

A further visit to Washington and New York was made by the Chairman and the new Vice-Chairman, Barry Gilligan, in July 2006, in response to a request from Mitchell Reiss.

In 2007, around the time of the Sinn Féin Ard Fheis decision in January in relation to policing, Chief Constable Hugh Orde undertook a visit to New York and Washington. This was followed by a visit in early February from the Northern Ireland Police Ombudsman and then a visit from seven Members of the Policing Board, including the Chairman, in the middle of March. Their meetings included one with the new US Special Envoy Dr Paula Dobriansky, who had succeeded Dr

Reiss, and an invitation to the Speaker's lunch on Capitol Hill hosted by the Speaker of the House of Representatives Nancy Pelosi for the Taoiseach. They represented the Policing Board at the St Patrick's Day reception in the White House.

Subsequently, in April 2007, Policing Board representatives and DPP members participated in the PERF annual meeting in Chicago. The Board Chairman and Jane Gordon, the Policing Board's Human Rights Adviser, addressed one of the plenary sessions on the theme of lessons learned from Northern Ireland. The Chairman gave a comprehensive interview to the *Irish American Post* setting out the progress in policing in Northern Ireland.

On 13 November 2007 the Policing Board welcomed the new US Consul General, Susan Elliot. She said:

'In my first few weeks in Northern Ireland, it has become very apparent to me that police reform is one the most significant and remarkable achievements of the peace process. The United States recognises the critical role the Policing Board has played in the transparent, efficient and accountable policing service that is evident throughout Northern Ireland, and I look forward to working with the Board.'

In March 2008 the Policing Board Chairman and Vice-Chairman, plus one representative from each of the political parties (which now included Sinn Féin), represented the Board in Washington. The meetings attended by the delegation included separate discussions with Congressmen Peter King, James Walsh and Richie Neal of the Friends of Ireland Group, and Senator Ted Kennedy's staff. A report of the visit was published on the Policing Board's website.

In May 2008 the Policing Board Chairman attended an in-depth discussion organised by PERF in San Francisco that discussed, in particular, the strengths and weaknesses of different models of police accountability and relations with the community. Those present included police chiefs and Commissioners from several major US cities, such as Bill Bratton, then Chief of the Los Angeles Police Department. This conference again underlined the personal commitment to Northern Ireland policing of Chuck Wexler as Chief Executive of PERF, and the mutual benefits in the links between those responsible for policing in Northern Ireland and in America.

In January 2009 the Chairman attended on behalf of the Policing Board the Transnational Policing Programme held in Boston College and in Tucson, Arizona, covering the approach of American police in combating organised crime and cross-border trafficking.

In March 2009, after careful consideration of the costs and benefits, the Policing Board again agreed that the Chairman and Vice-Chairman, plus one representative from each of the political parties, should travel to Washington. At the *Public Session* of the Policing Board on 2 April the Chairman reported that he and the Chief Constable had briefly met President Obama and the First Lady and the President's words of encouragement for policing and the work of the Policing Board had been very welcome. His message to them had been that *'The United States will always stand with those who work towards peace'*.

18.4   Policing a Divided Society – a Conference

In February 2007 a three-day conference, bringing together 300 delegates from police services and policing accountability and research bodies from around the world, was arranged by the Policing Board and the PSNI with the following objectives:

- to showcase and reflect on the progress which had been made in developing policing in Northern Ireland since the Independent Commission on Policing Report in 1999

- to receive presentations on topics where there were new developments in policing internationally in order to stimulate further thinking on policing improvement in Northern Ireland

- to assist the new Policing Board in establishing its vision and priorities for policing over the next five years

It was most timely, as the conference took place in the period following the St Andrews Agreement and the public decision by Sinn Féin to support policing and criminal justice.

During the first two days of the conference topics covered included *'embedding a human rights ethos'*, oversight and accountability, and *'what gets measured gets done'* (performance management); *'hate*

crime – silence is not golden' and '*policing – a collective responsibility*';
terrorism and organised crime; and '*bridging the gap – managing public
expectations*'.

The contributors included Sir Ian Blair, the Metropolitan Police
Commissioner; Kathleen O'Toole, Chief Inspector, An Garda Síochána
Inspectorate; John Timoney, Police Chief, City of Miami Police;
William Bratton, Chief of Police, Los Angeles; John Mack, President
of the Board of Release Commissioners, Los Angeles; Dr Maurice
Manning, President, Irish Human Rights Commission; Professor Ron
Goldstock, former Director, New York State Organised Crime Task
Force; the chiefs of the police services in Dallas, Providence, Seattle,
Leicestershire, and Cheshire; Chuck Wexler, Executive Director, PERF;
and, from Northern Ireland, Professor Monica McWilliams, Nuala
O'Loan, and Al Hutchinson.

In the session on '*Policing a Divided Society*' the former Vice-
Chairman of the Policing Board, Denis Bradley, offered this
perspective:

'*The policing problem in Northern Ireland started not with "The Troubles", but
in the 1920s and was to do with differing views about the legitimacy of the
State. The first act of genius was the Good Friday Agreement of 1998 which
enabled everybody to engage in a political process through which the issues could
be addressed. Since policing was too difficult politically to handle at the time the
setting up of The Independent Commission On Policing For Northern Ireland –
was the second act of genius. It gave an opportunity to create a policing system
capable of commanding general support.*'

Gil Kerlikowski, the Seattle Chief of Police, said at the conference:

'*The PSNI offers the greatest story of change in policing anywhere in the world
at the present. Police managers in other countries have much to learn from its
experience, including the contribution not only of the Chief Constable and his
senior team but that of those responsible for oversight, of the community and
of politicians.*'

Professor David Bayley, School of Criminal Justice, State University
of New York (and part of the Police Oversight Commissioner's Team),
commented:

'Northern Ireland as a whole has been an international success in ending conflict from which others should learn and the recent experience with policing has enormous implications for the rest of the world. It has done this in three main ways: it has worked through the issues of sovereignty and sectarianism to reach a stable position; it has re-oriented its police service and brought it to one which engages with the community; and it has grappled with the issue of paramilitaries in a post-conflict situation.'

A paper entitled *'Reflections on District Policing Partnerships (DPPs)'* was published to coincide with the conference. It profiled the work of DPPs in the evolution of policing since their establishment in March 2003 and showcased their work to the international audience. A pre-conference seminar focusing on DPPs was held on 19 February 2007.

A brief 'alternative' conference entitled *'Collusion – the elephant in the room?'* was held on 20 February 2007; speakers included Geraldine Finucane and Raymond McCord Senior. This was intended as a 'fringe event' to coincide with the international policing conference, making the point that collusion was not on the agenda at the conference.

The report of the International Policing Conference *'Policing The Future'* was published on 2 August 2007. On the publication of the report, the Policing Board Chairman said:

'The policing service must continue to change, evolve and grow to meet changing society and community needs. With increasing diversity in society, engaging communities and building public confidence in policing must be a priority, particularly where communities have been disaffected.'

18.5   Contacts with Other Bodies and Individuals

From its beginning the Policing Board was of interest to a wide range of visitors, both local and from overseas.

In 2002 the Board received visits from President Bush's Special Envoys – Richard Haass and then Mitchell Reiss – and from the Irish Foreign Minister, Brian Cowen. There were many overseas visitors, some in connection with a wider trip to the United Kingdom, others focusing just on Northern Ireland and its policing arrangements. For example, during 2006 there were visitors from Pakistan, Iraq, Latvia,

Kazakhstan, the Basque Country, and Kashmir. (Such visitors often came first to the Policing Board and then, following their establishment in 2004, to one or more DPPs.) In November 2006 the Policing Board Chairman met David Cameron during a visit by the latter to the PSNI College at Garnerville.

On 11 September 2003, at the Chairman's initiative, the leaders of the four main churches in Northern Ireland visited the Policing Board and met the Chairman and Vice-Chairman for a wide-ranging but informal discussion on the role and work of the Board. Also that autumn, following the attendance by the Board's Chairman at the Police Federation conference, the then Chairman of the Northern Ireland Police Federation was invited to speak to Members at the following Board meeting. In 2004, again at the Chairman's instigation, the Board was to be given a briefing by a senior English journalist on the report into the murder of Stephen Lawrence in London and the subsequent investigation by the Metropolitan Police.

The Policing Board also hosted a number of national and international visitors; for example, at the *Public Session* of the July 2003 Board meeting the Chairman welcomed the Assistant Commissioner of the Victoria Police in Australia. Two months earlier the Chairman and Chief Executive of the Police Complaints Authority in England and Wales met the Board's Chairman, Vice-Chairman, and the Chairman of the Complaints Monitoring Committee when they visited Northern Ireland. The level of visits was sustained over the years; for example, at the Board meeting in October 2008 the Chairman welcomed the Chairman of the (then) National Policing Improvement Authority, senior officers from the Dutch police, and officials from the Scottish government and Strathclyde Police Board, along with members of the Grampian Police and the Scottish Police Authority Convenors Forum.

Sometimes the contacts focused on a specific issue. Two such examples which illustrate the approach of the Policing Board were community policing and improved call-handling.

In September 2003 a group of DPP members and managers were part of a study visit to the United States to look at a number of community-based policing initiatives in Boston. In May the following year there was a reciprocal visit. Later in 2004 the Policing Board worked in partnership with PSNI to bring a group of Canadian police officers and community workers to Northern Ireland, focusing in particular on the work of DPPs and the wider area of policing with the community.

Following the interest in the issue during the 2005 Boston visit, a Member of the Board participated in a study visit to the Chicago Emergency Services Call Management Facility in January 2006, on which he reported to the Board subsequently. This also followed a paper from the PSNI on the extent to which the Service had considered work relating to call management in England and Wales. The Board supported in principle the introduction of a new single non-emergency number and looked forward to an integrated call management system. The Board followed this up in questioning of the PSNI in December 2007. It was explained that the PSNI had established a project to deliver a corporate call management solution which would align the Northern Ireland processes to the ACPO national call handling standards. In response to a question from a Board Member suggesting that in rural areas a lot of people thought there was no point in reporting a crime because nobody would ever turn up, the Chief Constable said that the PSNI were probably unique within the United Kingdom in terms of the number of calls they did respond to physically, rather than taking reports on the telephone, as most other police forces had begun to do.

In June 2008 a presentation was given to the Board's Resources and Improvement Committee by a senior police officer from Lothian and Borders (which followed a visit by Board Members to that force). It was agreed that a paper on the chronology of the call management issue would be circulated to all Members. The PSNI agreed to provide more detailed and regular updates to the Committee from September 2008. While a previous presentation from the PSNI had stated that a two-centre contact management structure, similar to the one operated by Lothian and Borders, would be completely delivered by December 2010, in 2008 the PSNI announced that it would formally adopt the ACPO guidelines on call handling, including the National Call Handling Standards. Given the resource constraints, the PSNI would introduce a distributed rather than the two-centre model. Board Members stressed the importance to the public of this issue, which was an area on which the police would be judged very strenuously.

18.6   In Conclusion

An interesting article by Mary Alice Clancy entitled '*The United States and post-Agreement Northern Ireland 2001–6*' that appeared in Volume 18 of *Irish Studies in International Affairs* flagged up the significant impact that the US President's special envoys to Northern Ireland had had during the Bush administration. This she attributed largely to their autonomy. She further noted that, while both the Clinton and Bush administrations had described their roles as '*honest brokers*' in the *peace process*, in practice '*both administrations displayed a marked preference for supporting Dublin when disputes have arisen between the Irish and British governments*'.

The article also pointed up the impact of the Al Qaeda attacks on 11 September 2001. In the author's view, this major act of international terrorism on American soil undoubtedly hardened attitudes in the United States against a potential return to terrorism by the PIRA. Indeed, the PIRA announced its first act of decommissioning six weeks later.

On the other hand, she noted that US officials had the impression that Richard Haass to an extent backed off his initial demand that Sinn Féin join the Policing Board. She distinguished the position of Mitchell Reiss, for whom, in her words, '*policing would become his central preoccupation as special envoy*'. In March 2005, not long after both the Northern Bank robbery and the murder of Robert McCartney, she noted that Gerry Adams was not invited to the annual St Patrick's Day celebration at the White House, but that Robert McCartney's sisters and partner were guests of honour instead. Again she made a link to a subsequent statement on 6 April 2005 in which Gerry Adams called on the PIRA to considering engaging in purely political and democratic activity. In her view, Mitchell Reiss remained consistent in his view that Sinn Féin's joining up to policing and taking its place on the Policing Board was a precondition for the entry of the DUP into devolved government in Northern Ireland.

Chris Patten's book *What Next? Surviving the Twenty-First Century* was published in 2008. He recalled that, after leaving his job as Chairman of The Independent Commission On Policing For Northern Ireland, he travelled regularly to Washington and other American cities to explain British policy in Ireland and to try to persuade US politicians to stop IRA fundraising in their country. In his words:

'It took 9/11, IRA involvement with Colombian terrorists and the bravery of the McCartney sisters – who refused to allow the sanitisation of their brother's murder at the hands of IRA Members, to change public and political opinion in the US, obliging politicians to recognise that the IRA was not the militant arm of the St Vincent De Paul Society.'

Given the geographical distance, it might seem curious that the Policing Board had so much contact with American politicians and the policing community – indeed, arguably more than with British or Irish counterparts. Certainly, senior Members of the Policing Board or DPP representatives were never invited to Whitehall or to Dublin in the same way as they were to Washington. But, as we have already seen, both the make-up of the Independent Commission and the report itself drew significantly on American policing expertise. It was natural for this connection, once made, to work through in tangible form when the Policing Board was established.

Strategically, the importance of regular visits to Washington and New York in particular lay more in the political than in the straight policing context. As we have seen above, there was very direct interest from elected politicians in the Capitol and from others, such as the President's special envoy, in the progress of the implementation of the Independent Commission's recommendations. Policing was at the heart of the *political process* in Northern Ireland, especially at a time when the Policing Board was the only functioning cross-community organisation during the suspension of the Northern Ireland Assembly. The Policing Board, as indeed did Chief Constable Hugh Orde, had credibility with United States politicians as first-hand participants containing a majority of elected representatives, in a way that the former, unelected, Police Authority could never have. Board Members' plain-speaking accounts of the challenges and indeed shortcomings in some areas, as well as the wider progress made, supplemented the reports of the US Consul General in Belfast and the Police Oversight Commissioner.

In the context of the determination of both the British and the Irish Governments, together with the Chairman and Vice-Chairman of the Policing Board and the Chief Constable, to bring about a situation in which Sinn Féin could and would make a public commitment to support policing and directly participate on the Board, the American dimension was an influential and arguably vital one.

Politics aside, it was undoubtedly valuable too for Members of the Board, and members of DPPs as well, to gain direct insight into approaches to policing and oversight in North America. That they often travelled as part of a wider Northern Ireland group including serving police officers and sometimes other community representatives provided a rare chance for those with different perspectives on policing in Northern Ireland to have informal exchanges outside the local political context. Such exchanges also provided a valuable perspective for participants on the position in their own communities, where, for example, levels of gang or gun crime and indeed homicide in US cities could be significantly higher than those then pertaining in Northern Ireland. It was also not lost on Board Members that across the United States there were cities and States where the proportions of ethnic groupings (in the particular city or State) were not reflected in their police force.

It is striking that there was considerable continuity among the Board personnel who travelled to Washington and elsewhere; this helped to reassure their American contacts that the Board was continuing to thrive. The visits also provided some elected representatives in Northern Ireland who might otherwise not have travelled to the US with a deeper appreciation of what America had to offer to both the *political* and the *peace processes*. In turn, the progress reports provided in America by senior Members of the Policing Board undoubtedly played a significant part in helping US politicians to gain a clearer understanding of policing and accountability reforms in Northern Ireland since the Independent Commission's Report, and consequently to urge support for full participation in policing by both communities in Northern Ireland. While there were, in the later years, some public criticisms of the cost of the annual visit to Washington in March, the Policing Board very deliberately published details of the visits, including a breakdown of the expenses.

In short, the Policing Board has been well served through its varied American contacts, including Presidential invitations, attention from the United States Consul General in Belfast, the commitment of successive Presidential special envoys, and the study visits and exchanges facilitated by academic and policing institutions in North America. In turn the Board has been a valuable model for a range of other countries' governments and international groups wishing to explore policing reform and greater accountability.

References

Carroll, Francis M., *The American presence in Ulster, a diplomatic history, 1796–1996*, Catholic University of America Press, Washington DC, 2005

Clancy, Mary Alice, 'The United States and post-Agreement Northern Ireland 2001–6', *Irish Studies in International Affairs*, 18, 2007, pp. 155–173

Patten, Chris, *What Next? Surviving the Twenty-First Century*, The Penguin Group, London, 2008

CHAPTER NINETEEN

The Irish Dimension

19.1 Introduction

As we have seen in the introductory chapters, relationships between those in authority in the two parts of Ireland have not always run smoothly since their creation as separate entities in 1921. This applied to policing as much as to inter-Governmental relations. As The Independent Commission On Policing For Northern Ireland (the Independent Commission) noted, cooperation between the Royal Ulster Constabulary (RUC) and the Garda Síochána was comparatively ad hoc and '*dependent on personal relationships*'. One important thrust of the Independent Commission's Report was to provide a more systematic structure for cooperation between the new Police Service of Northern Ireland (the Police Service or the PSNI) and the Garda. Interestingly, that same point was a key finding in the report of Judge Smithwick, published in December 2013.

It is significant that there remains to this day no equivalent in the Republic of Ireland to the Northern Ireland Policing Board (Policing Board). The historical justification for this lay partly in the rootedness of the Garda in the community. In addition, it suited successive Irish administrations to be in a position to influence the development of policing directly through the Department of Justice. One by-product of this was that, as cooperation between the PSNI and the Garda developed further during the time of the Policing Board, the Board itself was not able to create the same relationship with Dublin as it had with, say, the Association of Police Authorities in London.

19.2   The Scope For Structured Cooperation In The Island Of Ireland

The terms of reference for the Independent Commission required it to make proposals concerning 'the scope for structured cooperation with the Garda Síochána and other police forces'. The Independent Commission stated in its report that

'The present relationship between the RUC and the Garda Síochána is regarded by both police services as very good ... Each service expressed a high regard for the professionalism of the other.'

Nevertheless, the Independent Commission concluded that more could be done to structure the cooperation, and their Report contained a number of specific recommendations. These related to:

- written protocols covering key aspects of cooperation
- an Annual conference between the two police services
- a programme of long-term personnel exchanges, such as fixed term secondments, and consideration to posting liaison officers
- structured cooperation in training
- joint disaster planning
- pooling of investigative teams after major incidents with a substantial cross-border dimension
- effective communications between the Garda and the Northern Ireland police, both through radio and compatible IT system
- a joint database in all the main areas of cross-border criminality

The Updated Implementation Plan published by the Northern Ireland Office (NIO) in August 2001 accepted these recommendations (with the exception of a caveat in relation to the joint database and data protection) and stated that the British and Irish Governments would address these issues in the framework of the British/Irish Intergovernmental Conference, including a formal Agreement on cooperation between the PSNI and the Garda Síochána. This Agreement would provide a framework for the development of protocols between the PSNI Chief Constable and the Garda Commissioner.

Section 56 of the Police (Northern Ireland) Act 2000 required the Policing Board and the Chief Constable to implement any arrangements made in pursuance of an agreement between the Government of the United Kingdom and the Government of Ireland dealing with cooperation on policing matters between the police and the Garda Síochána. Otherwise, however, there was no specific provision in this Act relating to cooperation between the two police services.

It is worth reiterating in this chapter the point made elsewhere that the Irish Government took a very keen interest in the implementation of the Independent Commission's Report and the drafting of the Police (Northern Ireland) Act 2000. During this period, whereas the British Government sought to preserve 'neutrality' between the Unionist and Nationalist traditions in Northern Ireland, the Irish Government demonstrably espoused the Nationalist cause, principally – though not exclusively – in support of the approach adopted by the Social Democratic and Labour Party (SDLP). Senior officials in the Irish Department of Foreign Affairs, rather than the Irish Department of Justice (who would have been likely to be more informed about the practicalities of policing), were to the fore in the discussions, indeed in the negotiations with NIO officials. As we have seen, policing featured prominently at the Weston Park conference in July 2001; Irish officials, led by the then Foreign Affairs Minister, Brian Cowen, played a prominent part in the detailed negotiations there. In the important discussions in the month following the conference, prior to the SDLP's signing up to support for policing, the Department of Foreign Affairs again played a big role.

19.3   North–South Policing Cooperation Measures

On 13 December 2001 the NIO Minister, Jane Kennedy, published a timetable for the implementation of new North/South policing cooperation measures, including lateral entry and secondment. (Secondment may be broadly defined as an officer being on loan to the other service for a finite period prior to their return, while lateral entry would entail a permanent transfer to the new service.) The accompanying press release stated that both Governments intended to put in place the necessary legislative and administrative measures to allow for movement between the two Police Services in both directions, so that officers in the PSNI would be able to apply for posts in the Garda Síochána and vice versa. An Inter-Governmental Agreement was expected to be signed early in the following year (2002), to be followed by protocols to be agreed by the two Police Services on various aspects of policing cooperation, including lateral entry. Changes to the Police Regulations would follow on thereafter.

It was also announced that a (five-sided) senior level Project Board had been established to provide a strategic framework for these areas of cooperation, involving representatives of both Governments, the PSNI, the Garda Síochána, and the Policing Board. (On behalf of the Policing Board, its Interim Chief Executive had been invited to attend a meeting in Dublin earlier that month on this subject.)

The Independent Commission's Report had recommended (Recommendation 159) that:

> 'There should be a programme of long-term personnel exchanges, such as fixed-term secondments, between the Northern Ireland police and the Garda, in specialist fields where cooperation between the two services is most needed, such as drugs, and in areas such as training.' (Paragraph 18.10)

While lateral entry was already possible between police forces within the United Kingdom, section 45 of the Police (Northern Ireland) Act 2000 provided the basis for a wider degree of lateral entry, including from the Garda Síochána. Regulations were developed by the NIO, in consultation with the PSNI and the Policing Board, to facilitate lateral entry from the Garda at ranks above Inspector. Selection was to be based on open competition and merit. The arrangements were planned to be broadly reciprocal.

In a foretaste of the delays that were to follow in this area it was not until 29 April 2002 that the British and Irish Governments signed an 'Inter-Governmental Agreement on Policing Cooperation'. At the end of March the Northern Ireland Secretary of State had sent a draft to the Policing Board Chairman. The Articles of the Agreement covered eligibility to apply for posts, secondment with policing powers, police protocols, an annual conference, personnel exchanges, liaison, training, disaster planning, joint investigations, and communications. The Policing Board Chairman and Vice-Chairman attended the signing ceremony at Castle Buildings in Belfast.

Mr Eddie McGrady (SDLP), a *Political Member* of the Policing Board, put a question to the Prime Minister in the House of Commons on 23 May 2002 in which he invited the Prime Minister to join him in welcoming the formal agreement between the PSNI and the Garda Síochána, '*which would facilitate the pursuit of terrorists and organised criminals*'. This was a comparatively rare example of a development in Northern Ireland policing, after the passage of the initial legislation in 2000, being commented upon in Westminster.

Separately, on 11 March 2002, the PSNI and the Garda formalised their training links so that officers from both Police Services would be involved on a regular basis in delivering training to students in each other's organisation. That week, three Gardaí were to deliver training at the PSNI College at Garnerville, working in conjunction with PSNI trainers to deliver a series of classes on traffic, crime, and general police duties. During the following month PSNI trainers travelled to the Garda College at Templemore in County Tipperary for a reciprocal visit. (In December 2002 the PSNI reported to the Policing Board that in the previous 12 months, 11 PSNI and ten Garda Síochána Sergeant trainers had taken part in an exchange programme lasting one week. In addition, further secondments without policing powers had been agreed between the two services, beginning with Inspectors (Crime and Road Policing)).

In early April 2002 the Policing Board Chairman had a meeting with Timothy Dalton, the Secretary General at the Irish Department of Justice, and other staff. This was an opportunity to discuss similarities in roles between the Policing Board and the Department of Justice.

On 5 April 2002 the *Irish Times* reported that the Irish Department of Justice had assessed the structures for police accountability in the North, particularly the role of the Ombudsman and the Policing Board, along with similar structures in other European and US police forces. This exercise, which had concluded in 2001, was prompted by '*the perceived effect on public confidence in the Garda over issues such as the alleged corruption in Donegal*'. The article noted that it had been decided that the structure best suited to policing in the Republic was an independent Inspectorate, probably headed by a retired senior judge, with an investigative staff. To an extent, it would combine the roles of the Police Ombudsman in Northern Ireland and Her Majesty's

Inspectorate of Constabulary. The then Irish Minister for Justice, John O'Donoghue, was reported as saying that this dual role would not simply adjudicate on complaints but reduce the risk of their arising in the first place. The proposed Inspectorate could also respond to requests from the Minister to examine particular aspects of policing which had come to his attention. The article also noted that, if the present [Irish] Government was returned to power, the Inspectorate should be in place by the end of that year, but that, if the Labour Party was part of the next Government, it had indicated that it would prefer to see structures like the Policing Board in Northern Ireland and an Ombudsman.

At the *Public Session* of the Policing Board on 3 April 2003 *Political Member* Joe Byrne (SDLP) asked about the working relationship between the Garda and the PSNI in relation to the Omagh bomb investigation. In response, Chief Constable Hugh Orde said that the relationship between the PSNI and the Garda Síochána was in general extremely good. He added that most of the success against the dissident republicans recently, certainly in South Armagh, had been as a direct result of joint cross-border cooperation, using police officers on both sides of the border. Assistant Chief Constable Sam Kinkaid added that the two Police Services' inquiry teams were in regular contact on routine actions.

The meeting of the Policing Board's Human Resources Committee on 27 June 2003 was briefed by NIO officials on a draft Order in Council to modify provisions relating to conduct and membership of staff associations in respect of members of the Garda who would be seconded to the PSNI. The Board was also briefed on two sets of Regulations providing for secondments of officers between the two Services. (This legislation was consequential to the April 2002 Inter-Governmental Agreement.) The Policing Board had previously noted at its July 2002 meeting that all the enabling legislation should be in place by August 2003, but that negotiations were continuing concerning financial allowances for seconded officers, and it was anticipated that the earliest that secondments could take place would be 2004. The Policing Board also noted that the two Services had jointly conducted a cross-border disaster planning operation on 21 May 2003, and that, on the following day, the Garda Síochána had hosted an international conference focusing on joint responses to major incidents.

At the meeting of the Policing Board's Corporate Policy Committee on 24 July 2003 Members considered a Regulation 20 Report from the Northern Ireland Police Ombudsman about a cross-border incident concerning the discharge of a firearm by a PSNI officer in the Republic of Ireland. The Ombudsman reported that she had been unable to complete the report as she would have wished, as there was no mechanism for the necessary information to be obtained from the Garda Síochána. The Policing Board agreed that the Board Chairman should write to the Secretary of State urging him to raise the issue with the Irish Department of Justice.

In another instance of a perceived lack of cooperation between accountability and oversight bodies North and South, in spring 2004, by means of a letter from the Policing Board Chairman to the then Irish Minister for Justice, Michael McDowell, the Policing Board invited a representative from the Criminal Assets Bureau (CAB) in Ireland to brief the Board on its work. (The CAB had a very good reputation for the quality of its work.) This invitation was declined in Dublin, notwithstanding the Chairman's letter emphasising that the Board did not want create the impression it had any remit in respect of the Bureau but saw this meeting as an important information-gathering exercise, not least about process.

On the other hand, cooperation between the two Police Services continued to develop. One example was the lending by the PSNI of two water cannon to the Garda, on which the Chief Constable reported at the *Public Session* of the Policing Board on 3 June 2004.

It was not until 22 February 2005 that Chief Constable Hugh Orde on behalf of the PSNI and Commissioner Noel Conroy on behalf of the Garda Síochána formally signed a joint Protocol '*in respect of personnel exchanges for the further improvement of bilateral cooperation between their respective services*'. This Protocol provided for:

- personnel exchanges for all ranks, without policing powers, for up to one year

- secondments for ranks from Sergeant to Chief Superintendent with policing powers, for up to 3 years

- lateral entry permanent transfer officers for ranks above Inspector and under Assistant Chief Constable

The Protocol stipulated that members of the Garda Síochána would, for the duration of their placement, report to and work with the PSNI; however, the officer placed with the PSNI would remain a full member of the Garda Síochána, subject to the overall direction and control of the Garda Commissioner, and would not exercise any police powers in Northern Ireland; the reciprocal position would apply to PSNI members placed with the Garda. Each officer participating in the exchange programme would retain the terms and conditions to which they were entitled as members of their own Service. So far as practical, each Service would provide a participant of equal rank.

Commenting on the signing, the Policing Board Chairman said:

'Today's protocols will provide further opportunities to share training, compare and develop best practice and enhance working relationships. In addition to benefiting policing in general this will also help ensure the delivery of a more effective and efficient service for the community as a whole.'

On 18 March 2005 the Board Chairman wrote to the Garda Commissioner proposing a joint PSNI/Garda briefing for the Policing Board on issues surrounding police exchanges and secondments. However, the Commissioner suggested that any further consideration of such a joint briefing should await outcomes that were being pursued, including the need for statutory provisions to allow for lateral entry from the PSNI or other overseas Forces to permanent posts within the Garda Síochána.

In July 2005 the British and Irish Governments signed a further Agreement on cooperation on criminal justice matters, providing for closer liaison on issues such as sex offending.

Tangible support was provided by the Irish Government for the new policing institutions in Northern Ireland, especially for those under attack from violence or intimidation. For example, in early 2006 the Irish Foreign Minister, Dermot Ahern, visited Strabane to meet the latter's District Policing Partnership (DPP). He expressed his support for the work carried out by the DPP across the District. The former Vice-Chairman of the DPP, Councillor Tom McBride, said:

'The [Irish] Minister's visit to Strabane DPP endorses the vital role that we have played in making the local police more accountable to the public in

Strabane District. Over the past two and a half years we have been working to get policing right, develop public acceptability and keep local people safe. Substantial progress has been made, but we know that there is still more work to do. We look forward to the challenges that the new term of office holds with renewed vigour and understanding.'

One interesting example of cooperation between the PSNI and the Garda Síochána took place in February 2006. This concerned an innovative cross-border diversity training programme for PSNI and Garda officers that was launched jointly by the Chief Constable Hugh Orde and the Garda Commissioner Noel Conroy. Diversity Works was funded through the EU's PEACE II Programme and was aimed at helping police officers to gain a better understanding of the communities they served. It comprised more than 50 one-day training sessions to be held in Northern Ireland and the Republic of Ireland during 2006. The contents of the programme were devised by a team from the PSNI Equality and Diversity Unit and the PSNI College together with Garda officers from Templemore College, in conjunction with a wide range of key community and voluntary sector groups.

A paper prepared by the NIO in 2006 noted that, in progressing lateral entry, the transfer of pensions between jurisdictions had been identified as a key disincentive. The British Government had commissioned a report on possible options to remove or reduce this disincentive, which should enable the completion of draft Regulations to facilitate lateral entry from the Garda at ranks above Inspector. However, no appointments had been made on this basis to that date, and it was to remain an area of frustration.

In spring 2008 Brian Cowen was elected as leader of Fianna Fail. It was a demonstration of the closeness of the relationship established between members of the Policing Board and senior Irish Ministers that the Policing Board Chairman's letter of congratulations received a warm personal response from Mr Cowen in May 2008.

In March 2009 two members of the Policing Board attended a cross-border fraud, corruption, and European Union financial interest conference held in Dublin Castle.

On 13 December 2010 a Cross-Border Policing Strategy was published. It had been jointly agreed between the PSNI Chief Constable Matt Baggott and the Garda Commissioner Fachtna Murphy, and was introduced by the respective Ministers responsible for policing and justice matters, David Ford and Dermot Ahern. The purpose was to improve public safety throughout Ireland, disrupt criminal activity, and enhance the policing capability of both Police Services on the island of Ireland. The strategy contained a number of initiatives set out under a range of headings, including operations, cross-border investigations, intelligence sharing and security, communications and information technology, training, human resources, and emergency planning. (It is interesting to note that, over ten years on, these were still broadly the same areas identified by the Independent Commission in its Report.)

19.4   Policing Developments in the Republic of Ireland

On 23 December 2005 the Garda Síochána Act 2005 Implementation Review Group, chaired by Dr Maurice Hayes, presented its report to the Minister for Justice, Michael McDowell. The Review Group had been established by the Minister for Justice to review preparations for the timely implementation of the 2005 Act. That legislation represented the first major revision of the operation of the Garda Síochána since the foundation of the Irish State, providing a new legal framework for policing in the Republic of Ireland. In particular, the Act defined the respective roles of the Garda Commissioner and the Minister for Justice, which, for example, enabled the latter to set policing priorities.

The Review Group concluded that, on the three main items which they had been tasked to monitor, and on three others which they regarded as important, substantial and satisfactory progress had been made as follows:

- *Ombudsman Commission*: preparations for the formal appointment of the Ombudsman Commission were well in train, with an expected start date of early 2007
- *Garda Inspectorate*: the search was then underway to recruit a Chief Inspector, after which the two other Inspectors would be recruited; it was expected to become operative by the summer of 2006
- *Revised Code of Discipline*: the Disciplinary Code was under preparation,

and a Code of Ethics based on Human Rights principles was being
prepared to be finalised before the Ombudsman Commission opened
for business

- *Joint Policing Committees*: guidelines for Joint Policing Committees
  had been drafted; the Review Group recommended that there should
  be up to 12 pilot schemes before the system was rolled out across the
  Republic nationwide

- *Accounting Officer*: the transfer of Accounting Officer responsibilities
  to the Garda Commissioner was scheduled for 1 July 2006

- *Civilian Staff*: civilian staff then employed by the Department of
  Justice were to transfer to Garda management in October 2006

Unlike the Northern Ireland Ombudsman model, three inde-
pendent members were appointed to the Ombudsman Commission.
The first person appointed to head the Garda Inspectorate as the
Chief Inspector was Kathleen O'Toole, a distinguished law enforce-
ment officer from the United States who had been a member of The
Independent Commission On Policing For Northern Ireland. The role
of the Inspectorate was seen by the Review Group as benchmarking
Garda practice against best international standards.

The Garda Síochána Act 2005 also provided for the establishment by each local authority and the Garda Commissioner of a Joint
Policing Committee to serve as a forum for consultations, discussions,
and recommendations on matters affecting the policing of the local
authority's administrative area. A decision was taken to begin with a
number of pilot schemes, before moving to nationwide implementation in all 114 local authority areas.

In additional remarks, the Review Group noted that the Act obliged
the Garda to manage a process of modernisation on a significant scale,
requiring new management skills. They highlighted the transfer of
the Accounting Officer role to the Garda Commissioner as potentially
the most profound of all the proposed changes, in that it would lead
to a better focus on budgeting and efficiency. They urged too that the
Department of Justice *'must withdraw to a degree if Garda management
is to be free to manage and to develop the capacity to carry out their new
responsibilities'*.

Recognising that the Department would be required in a new

role to perform functions that in some other jurisdictions would be assigned to a Policing Board or Authority, it recommended that those involved have appropriate training, preferably in the environment of a business school with reference to best practice in the private sector. Within the Garda, they recommended the appointment of a dedicated change management team headed by a new post equivalent to Deputy Commissioner.

The Review Group noted that for 80 years the Garda Síochána had recruited at a single entry level, and with few opportunities for lateral entry by way of transfer from other forces or organisations. While this could be a strength in developing a sense of common purpose, that same consolidation of a culture could also isolate an organisation from mainstream developments elsewhere and make it more difficult to introduce new ideas. They commended the action of the Minister in changing the language requirement so as to encourage applications from ethnic minorities and new immigrant communities in Ireland. They also expressed the view that the senior posts, including the most senior, should be opened up to allow for the consideration of international candidates, to provide for new blood and new ideas. They emphasised the need for training, citing the importance attached to it in the Report of The Independent Commission On Policing For Northern Ireland.

The Northern Ireland Policing Board's Human Resources Committee noted in November 2006 that senior police officers from the Garda could apply for promotion opportunities within the PSNI – the Board had invested a great deal of effort and time to reach this position – but there was no reciprocal agreement for PSNI officers to apply for positions in the Garda. (It was not until 2012 that such positions in the Garda were publicly advertised.) It was agreed that a letter should be sent to the Irish Minister for Justice seeking a reciprocal agreement. In December 2006 an offer to meet with the Minister for Justice and the Secretary General of the Department of Justice was received, although this meeting did not take place owing to Mr McDowell's diary pressures. In the same month the Board Chairman wrote to the Secretary of State inviting him to assist them in seeking an urgent resolution to this issue. The letter noted that pension difficulties were delaying the actual implementation of lateral entry and that this was unlikely to be resolved in the near future. Following limited progress, the Policing Board Chairman, on the Board's behalf, wrote to the Irish Minister for Justice in May 2007 regarding advertising of senior appointments within the Garda Síochána.

The *Irish Times* noted in an article on 14 March 2012 that: '*Recruitment drives to fill senior positions within An Garda Síochána are for the first time to be open to those working in the Police Service of Northern Ireland.*' The Irish Minister for Justice, Alan Shatter, had said that the new, more open recruitment system had been provided for in the Inter-Governmental Agreement on Policing Cooperation signed a decade previously, which had in turn resulted from recommendations in the Independent Commission's Report. With immediate effect, when vacancies arose at the rank of Inspector, Superintendent, Chief Superintendent, or Assistant Commissioner, the competition to fill them would be open to PSNI members as well as serving Gardaí. (Subsequently, in an article in the *Belfast Telegraph* dated 27 September 2012, it was reported that PSNI officers had now been invited to apply for permanent senior policing posts in the Garda Síochána following the signing of new regulations by the Irish Justice Minister, Alan Shatter.)

In April 2012, at their annual conference, it was reported in the *Irish Times* that the Association of Garda Sergeants and Inspectors had repeated their call for an Irish police authority. The Association's general secretary said that the establishment of an independent police authority would remove political control from the promotion of senior officers and for budgeting issues for the Garda. He added '*You have to make the system as open and transparent as possible*'. The Garda Commissioner, Martin Callinan, denied that there was political interference in policing:

'*I am accountable to the Minister, but I have never, ever, come across a situation where the Minister tried to influence me in terms of how I conduct my business with the control and governance of An Garda Síochána.*'

On 3 December 2013 the comprehensive report by Judge Smithwick was published. He had chaired the Tribunal of Inquiry which had been set up by the Irish Government in 2005 to look into allegations of collusion between members of the Garda Síochána and the Provisional IRA (PIRA) in the killing of the two senior RUC officers,

Chief Superintendent Harry Breen and Superintendent Bob Buchanan, on their return from a meeting at the Dundalk Garda station on 20 March 1989. (The formal terms of reference of this Tribunal were to enquire into suggestions that members of An Garda Síochána or other employees of the State colluded in the fatal shootings.) Previously, in October 2003, Judge Peter Cory had concluded in his 'Collusion Inquiry Report – Chief Superintendent Breen and Superintendent Buchanan' of 7 October 2003:

'I have considered carefully all the relevant material ... I have concluded that the documents reveal evidence that, if accepted, could be found to constitute collusion. As a result there must be such a public inquiry.'

While Judge Smithwick did not uncover direct evidence of collusion, he found that one or more unidentified members of the Garda Síochána operating in Dundalk did collude with the IRA, providing information that helped lead to the deaths of the two policemen.

Three of the Judge's seven recommendations in his report related specifically to systematising cooperation between the Garda Síochána and the PSNI. They covered procedures allowing for structured exchange of intelligence (rather than ad hoc decision-making), a programme of personnel exchanges, including posting liaison officers from each service to the central headquarters of the other, and the establishment of protocols providing legal structures for the seamless investigation by joint police teams of crimes with a cross-border element.

Three other recommendations related to tackling the culture within the Garda Síochána, which the Judge characterised as *'failing adequately to address suggestions of wrongdoing ... [which] either for reasons of political expediency or by virtue of misguided loyalty has been a feature of life in this State'*. Elsewhere in the report he said:

'I regret to say that this suggests to me that there prevails in An Garda Síochána today a prioritisation of the protection of the good name of the force over the protection of those who seek to tell the truth. Loyalty is prized above honesty.'

In not tolerating unethical behaviour by any of its members, he recommended that vetting procedures should be reviewed to comply with international best practice, and that the disciplinary code should be enforced effectively, including after the resignation of an officer from the force.

In responding on the day of publication, the Irish Minister for Justice, Alan Shatter, said that the Government would to give *'very careful consideration'* to the Tribunal's recommendations and in relation to cooperation between the Garda and the PSNI. In the view of the Tánaiste, Eamon Gilmore, the actions documented in the report were a betrayal of the values and the very ethos of the Garda as the guardians of peace.

In an article in the *Sunday Independent* on 8 December 2013 Colum Kenny compared the position with that in Britain in recent years, where

'Vigorous efforts have been made to make the police more transparent and accountable. Reforms here have been hesitant.'

As an example, he referred unfavourably to the rejection by the Irish Government of the request from the Garda Síochána Ombudsman Commission earlier in 2013 to secure unfettered access to the Garda's system of record-keeping.

In spring 2014 the issue of Garda Síochána accountability again became prominent. A statement issued on 25 March by the Irish Government contained the following passage:

'It also reiterated its commitment to the reform of Garda oversight and accountability. This will include the establishment of an independent Garda authority, which is appropriate to Ireland's needs and which will maintain appropriate democratic accountability to the Oireachtas.

The Government will bring forward the full detail of its comprehensive reform proposals in the coming months.'

The statement added that this would be done following the completion of a number of current enquiries and reviews into the Garda Síochána.

The development that primarily triggered this undertaking was the revelation that several thousand incoming and outgoing telephone calls at Garda stations had been tape-recorded without legislative authorisation. The Government announced the setting up of a statutory Commission of Investigation chaired by a senior serving or retired

member of the judiciary. Also on 25 March 2014 it was announced that
the Government had agreed to the retirement of Mr Martin Callinan
from the position of Garda Commissioner.

Writing in the *Irish Times* on 26 March 2014 Conor Brady, who had
been a member of the Garda Síochána Ombudsman Commission from
its inception in 2005 to 2011, noted that

*'Extraordinarily, the Garda Síochána's model of governance dates back to 1835
… It was a model that was arguably suited to a fledgeling democracy. But it does
not meet the needs of the criteria of a 21st-century society in which the task of
policing is infinitely more complex.'*

Mr Brady suggested that, in looking for successful models elsewhere, some aspects of the Northern Ireland Policing Board might
be examined, as might some of the boards or authorities that operated successfully in the Irish semi-State sector. He added that it was
doubtful if there was anything that might be emulated in the system
of Police and Crime Commissioners in England and Wales. Mr Brady
emphasised that the role would involve supporting – as well as, where
necessary, challenging – the Garda Commissioner.

In the same edition of the paper the Northern editor, Gerry
Moriarty, quoted the remarks of Independent Commission member
Dr Maurice Hayes to a 'Confidence in Policing' conference being held
in Belfast that week – *'absolutely, there should be a board to hold the
Gardaí to account, just as the Policing Board holds the PSNI to account'*. Mr
Moriarty's assessment of *'why it [the Northern Ireland Policing Board] is
regarded as successful'* concluded:

*'Such a board ensures somebody is guarding the guardians, provides the
nexus between the public and the police, allows contentious issue to be venti-
lated before they detonate, and as Mr Hayes has suggested, if operating in the
Republic could have defused the rows before a head or heads had to roll.'*

The *Irish Times* on the following day quoted the comments of Chief
Constable Matt Baggott at the Belfast conference:

*'We exercise powers, we exercise controls over huge amounts of money, and we
are tasked under Article 2 of the Human Rights Act to keep people safe. So it is*

very, very important that we are held accountable as to how we are carrying out our duties.'

In April 2014 the Garda Representative Association held its annual conference. In the run-up the general secretary, P.J. Stone, was reported in the *Irish Times* to have called for the Garda to be freed from '*the shackles of direct political interference*'.

Issues to do with policing then became even more controversial. On 7 May the Minister for Justice Alan Shatter resigned following a report commissioned by the Irish Government from Mr Seán Guerin, Senior Counsel, into the handling of allegations by a Garda Sergeant. On the following day Frances Fitzgerald was appointed Minister for Justice.

However, a former Minister for Justice, Michael McDowell, was quoted in an article in the *Sunday Independent* on 27 July 2014 (and again in the *Irish Times* on 2 August) criticising the Irish Government's intention to create a new independent police authority. He recalled that the suggestion had been considered in 2005, but

'We came to the conclusion that it was not simply impracticable but that it could do a lot of damage to the Irish State and to the principle of parliamentary accountability by government for the executive power under our Constitution.'

He argued that the Garda Síochána was not some '*regional constabulary*' as existed in the United Kingdom; rather, it was a national police force whose statutory function was to '*provide policing and security services for the State*'. He took the view that no democratic government had ever taken the '*wholly extraordinary*' step of taking control of the national police and/or security service away from government and handing it to a body independent of government. His comments contained only the briefest references to the Northern Ireland Policing Board, in the context of querying whether party political representatives would be allowed to serve on a new independent authority.

Responding to criticisms from Mr McDowell, Frances Fitzgerald was quoted as saying that the authority would not remove political accountability, adding 'it does not mean accountability in the Dáil just goes away'. As Minister for Justice, her duty was to 'stand back' from the Garda Síochána as well as setting the standards, directions, and 'absolute requirements' of the force.

19.5   In Conclusion

Some of the comments made by the Review Group on the implementation of the Garda Síochána Act 2005 are particularly instructive. In their remarks they drew on the experience of the transformation of policing in Northern Ireland with particular reference to training as *'the engine which drives change'*. The pace of change in Ireland proved to be measured and slow; for example, it took seven years before their recommendation on opening up the process of appointments to senior posts was implemented.

The Northern Ireland Policing Board consistently sought – before Sinn Féin joined the Board – to strengthen the links between Belfast and Dublin and between the PSNI and the Garda Síochána. This was another example of the way in which the Policing Board, notwithstanding that its membership included political representatives (and potentially others) traditionally not inclined to this approach, quietly but practically got on with implementing the Independent Commission's agenda. However, as we have noted above, it was hampered by there being no equivalent body in the Republic's jurisdiction and, at times, an apparent lack of vision in the Department of Justice.

It does now seem more likely than not that some form of independent board or authority will be created to hold the Garda Síochána to account. It will be very interesting to see to what extent the model of the Northern Ireland Policing Board will be drawn on, and what regard will be had to the lessons learned in the Policing Board's operation.

In conclusion, it is useful to recall from the opening lines of the report of the Review Group a quotation by the first Garda Commissioner, Michael Staines: *'The Civic Guard will succeed not by force of arms, or numbers, but on their moral authority as servants of the people.'*

References

'Independent Inspectorate to guard Garda standards', *Irish Times*, 5 April 2002

Report, The Garda Síochána Act 2005, Implementation Review Group, published on 23 December 2005

Irish Times, 14 March 2012

Irish Times, 4 April 2012

Report Of The Tribunal Of Inquiry Into Suggestions That Members Of An Garda Síochána Or Other Employees Of The State Colluded In The Fatal Shootings Of RUC Chief Superintendent Harry Breen And RUC Superintendent Robert Buchanan On The 20th March 1989, 3 December 2013

'Smithwick report has shown need for more Garda accountability', *Sunday Independent*, 8 December 2013

Irish Times, 26 and 27 March 2014

'A "quick fix" will not solve Garda problem', *Sunday Independent*, 27 July 2014

'How did Justice get so Rough?', *Irish Times*, 2 August 2014

CHAPTER TWENTY

Dealing with the Past – an Intractable Problem?

20.1   Introduction and Background

In Chapter 1 we set out the scale of the casualties during the Troubles. Issues from that time, including criminal reinvestigations, the needs of victims, allegations of collusion, and public inquiries, and the wider matter of how society might address the past collectively, were all concerns that to a greater or lesser degree came before the Northern Ireland Policing Board (the Policing Board or Board). Members had to work out how, and how far, they should engage in these various issues, either as an organisation or individually. *Political Members*, of course, had to take account of the views of their parties.

This chapter is drawn from the longer note, entitled '*Dealing With The Past*', that the two authors submitted to the Panel of Parties in Northern Ireland chaired by Dr Richard Haass and which was published in book form in December 2013. Readers wishing to have a fuller analysis will find it there.

As this chapter highlights, dealing with the past was a preoccupation of the Chairman almost from the beginning of the Policing Board and it was the one topic in the whole of his tenure in respect of which the Chairman sought and obtained the permission of the Board to address on his own behalf. Almost from its beginning the Board was faced with issues arising from atrocities in the Troubles, not least those relating to victims.

In the policing context the Chief Constable Hugh Orde drew up proposals to set up a Serious Crime Review Team, based initially within the Police Service of Northern Ireland (the Police Service or the PSNI), that was resourced to focus solely on reinvestigating previous murders. The team was later to be recast as the Historical Enquiries

Team (HET), in part to free up the bulk of the PSNI to focus on current policing challenges.

In respect of societal issues, the Board Chairman brought forward proposals in 2003 in a paper entitled *'Seeking To Hold The Past In Healthy Balance with The Future'*. Having obtained the endorsement of the Vice-Chairman, Denis Bradley, he sought to initiate a debate at the Board. It would appear that the paper, although the Board were not persuaded by its proposals, played a significant part in shaping the thinking of Secretaries of State for Northern Ireland in setting up the subsequent review jointly led by the Rt Reverend Robin Eames and Denis Bradley. The resulting *'Report of the Consultative Group on the Past'*, published in January 2009, noted that, as a result of the conflict between 1969 and 2001,

- 3,523 persons were killed
- of this total, 2,055 (58%) were attributed to Republican paramilitary groups, 1,020 (29%) to Loyalist paramilitary groups, 368 (10%) to Security Forces, and 80 (2%) to persons unknown
- The breakdown of those killed was as follows: civilians (1,855); members of the Security Forces (1,123); Republican paramilitary group members (394); and Loyalist paramilitary group members (151)
- In addition, some 47,000 people in Northern Ireland sustained injuries in 16,200 bombing and 37,000 shooting incidents
- In total, 19,600 individuals received a sentence of imprisonment for scheduled offences: that is, crimes that the legislation determined were related to terrorism.

Readers may wish to refer back to Chapter 1 of this book, in which we additionally listed 19 of the most serious incidents during the Troubles, of which 16 took place in Northern Ireland, two in England, and one in the Republic of Ireland.

Chapter 3 dealt with developments leading up to the establishment of the Policing Board in autumn 2001. By July of that year the Provisional IRA (PIRA) had not decommissioned and David Trimble had resigned as First Minister. Dixon and O'Kane record:

'That the two governments tried to re-launch the "peace process" with a "final",

"non-negotiable" plan, which was published in August 2001 after intense all-party talks at Weston Park in mid-July. The proposals sought to appeal to republicans by promising demilitarisation, new police legislation to reflect more fully the [Independent Commission's] Report, an international judge [Cory] to investigate controversial killings [Patrick Finucane, Robert Hamill, Rosemary Nelson and Billy Wright in Northern Ireland and Chief Superintendent Breen and Superintendent Buchanan and Lord Justice and Lady Gibson in the Republic of Ireland], the demolition of British security bases and an undertaking not to pursue on-the-runs (people wanted for offences committed before the PIRA called its ceasefire). The proposals argued that decommissioning was indispensable.'

Part of the background against which the Board came into existence was reflected in the work of Judge Cory. The Foreword to each of the subsequent four 'Cory Collusion Inquiry Reports' (though they were not published until 2003/04) reads:

'*I was asked by the Government of the United Kingdom to investigate allegations of collusion by members of the security forces in the context of the deaths of Patrick Finucane, Robert Hamill, Rosemary Nelson and Billy Wright and to report with recommendations for any further action. These four reports are the product of my investigation.*

I had the preliminary role of assessing whether there is a case to be answered as to possible collusion, in a wide sense, by members of the security forces in these deaths such as to warrant further and more detailed inquiry ...

For the reasons which I have given in my reports, I have found that in each of the four cases the documentary evidence indicates that there are matters of concern which would warrant further and more detailed inquiry.'

For Robert Hamill, Rosemary Nelson, and Billy Wright the further and more detailed inquiries were to be in public. For Patrick Finucane no similar inquiry has yet occurred.

20.2   The Omagh, Claudy and Enniskillen Bombings, to Name but Three

In the Policing Board's second month, on 12 December 2001, the Police Ombudsman for Northern Ireland presented to it

'a highly critical report on the policing investigation of the Omagh bombing. The report was in turn strongly criticised by the [then] Chief Constable.'

On 7 February 2002, after several days of deliberation, the Policing Board issued its considered response to the Ombudsman's report and in particular to its recommendations. At its third meeting, on 12 December 2001, the Policing Board agreed to meet not only with the Police Ombudsman and the Chief Constable but also with the victims of the Omagh bombing to discuss the report and the Chief Constable's response. The Chief Constable met with the victims of the Omagh bombing on 24 January 2002, and, accompanied by Board Members and local MLA Joe Byrne, the Board's Corporate Policy Committee met with them on 28 January 2002. (NB Additionally, over the Christmas period, the Board Chairman and Vice-Chairman made contact with various persons from Omagh.) At the 28 January 2002 meeting with the representatives of the victims their pain was palpable, as it was with victims of other atrocities.

On 19 December 2002 Assistant Chief Constable (ACC) Sam Kinkaid informed the Board that in August 2002 he had *'directed ... that a senior detective review the investigation into the Claudy bombing'*, and that he would brief the injured and the relatives of those who died the following day, when the following statement would be released:

'I have just briefed the injured and the relatives of those killed at Claudy on 31 July 1972, on the initial findings of the review into the investigation.

Three bombs were planted in Claudy. They exploded killing nine people. Over 30 people were injured. Claudy remains one of the worst unsolved atrocities of the troubles.

I commissioned the review in August 2002 following the 30th anniversary of the bombing... The purpose of the review is to see if there are any new or existing lines of enquiry that the PSNI can take forward.

I later amended the terms of reference for the review to include an assessment of a letter purporting to come from a "Father Liam". This spoke of the involvement of a Catholic priest in the bomb attack ...

In a search of 1972 papers, information has been found which clearly indicates that a parish priest in the South Derry area was a member of the Provisional IRA and was actively involved in terrorism. Intelligence also indicates that he was involved in the Claudy bomb. Records show he provided an alibi for a person suspected of playing a prominent role in the atrocity. This priest is now deceased ...

It is clear that the relatives of those who died in the bomb attack on Claudy village and those who were injured have not obtained justice. I regret this very much and in particular that opportunities to arrest and interview all of the suspects were not taken in 1972. I have told the families that my officers are fully committed to doing everything possible to bring those responsible before the courts.'

Also on 20 December 2002 the Chairman issued on behalf of the Board the following release:

'The Claudy bombing on 31 July 1972, which claimed the lives of nine people and injured over 30 was an appalling atrocity and the investigation which followed left many questions unanswered. In August this year, 30 years after the bombing, the PSNI initiated a review into the original investigation.

I have now received details of the initial findings from the PSNI review and have passed this information on to all members of the ... Policing Board.

Whilst the bombing took place over 30 years ago I fully appreciate that the grief of the relatives today, particularly in light of the PSNI findings, will be intense. I recognise that given the information they have received, the families of the victims of the bombing will no doubt be feeling many emotions including bewilderment, hurt and anger.

The Policing Board has responsibility for ensuring that the police service is effective, efficient and impartial. It is also important that the police has the confidence of the community it serves. With that in mind I welcome the frankness of the PSNI statement.

Given that the Board's key function is to hold the PSNI to account I expect it will take the earliest opportunity it has to question the Chief Constable and Assistant Chief Constable Kinkaid further about this matter. It is clear from what has come to light today that people will need reassurance. The Policing Board is an essential contributor to achieving that confidence ...

There is no doubt that the events of 31 July 1972, and in particular the subsequent discussions which took place in November and December 1972 raise serious concerns. I can assure the whole community that the Policing Board will do everything within its remit to ensure that public concerns are fully addressed.'

At the *Public Session* of the Board on 6 February 2003 ACC Kinkaid was asked for an update. He replied:

'The on-going inquiry is a review of the original investigation. At the conclusion of the review, the reviewing officer will bring forward recommendations to myself and the Chief Constable as to whether there is any prospect of advancing the investigation towards criminal charges. 23 next of kin of the deceased have been identified, together with 20 surviving injured and all these people have had contact with the Family Liaison Officer who has been dealing with them ...'.

At the meeting on 7 April 2005 the Board asked in the *Public Session* for an update. ACC Kinkaid concluded as follows:

'As we have done in some of the recent murder investigations, I am happy at a further date, to come with the Senior Investigating Officer to a private session of the Board and to brief members on progress to date.'

Several years later, on 13 October 2010, the Head of PSNI's Serious Crime Branch wrote to the Policing Board as follows:

'The Claudy investigation has recently been transferred from the Historical Enquiries Team (HET) to Serious Crime Branch. The scale and complexity of this investigation can best be progressed by Serious Crime Branch, who have the necessary resources available to conduct such an inquiry.

At this stage it is unclear if the victims wish to be treated as a united victims group or as individual families. I have written to the victim's commissioner in an effort to shed some light on this matter. I have enclosed a copy letter which has been sent to each of the families.'

The *Sunday Independent* reported on 2 February 2014 that PSNI had now told the families of the victims of the Claudy bombing that it had insufficient grounds to revisit the crime. The paper noted that the families were continuing to pursue civil actions in relation to the bombing.

At the meeting of the Policing Board held on 2 June 2005 *Political Member* Mr Sam Foster (Ulster Unionist Party (UUP)), asked the Chief Constable about the Enniskillen bombing:

'Can you give me a report on the situation towards bringing before court, those who murdered 12 citizens in the Cenotaph bomb in Enniskillen on 8 November 1987 – that is almost 18 years ago?'

ACC Kinkaid replied:

'It is recognised that the incidents that led to the murder of the 12 people attending the Cenotaph on the 8 November 1987 were one of the most abhorrent in the history of Northern Ireland and police investigations therefore, have continued to pursue every avenue right up to and including the present day. In 2004 I led the investigation, subject to a further review, to see whether there were any new evidential lines of enquiry and the review officers made a number of recommendations that are now being actively pursued.

Detectives from Crime Operations Department have recently sought to trace and re-interview some 111 people as part of that process and put their recollections into context. Some 80 witnesses have been seen to date and efforts will continue to be made to speak to the remainder and some additional 45 witnesses identified by those already spoken to, these are new witnesses that have come to light. This will be, of course, a painstaking process in which every piece of information will have to be thoroughly analysed. In addition to tracing scores of new witnesses, other investigators were concluding some of the details in liaison with colleagues in An Garda Síochána. This is presently being pursued and we remain committed to ensuring that where there is sufficient evidence to bring charges that those persons responsible for this particular crime are brought to justice.'

At the Board meeting on 1 March 2006 an update was provided by the Chief Superintendent, Crime Operations:

'Our C2 people continue to actively pursue and deal with lines of enquiry in relation to the Enniskillen bombing. Just recently, we have identified some new witnesses and they have been interviewed. When those lines of enquiry

are finished the case will then be handed to the Historical Enquiries Team ... As you know, that has been designed to provide a thorough and independent reappraisal of unsolved cases. They have a family centred approach, obviously to seek to address as far as possible the questions of families and issues that remain outstanding. Their governing principle will be maximum disclosure obviously subject to legal guidelines. Now as a general rule, cases will be examined on a chronological order basis, the only exceptions to that will be where there are cases which are already opened. I can assure you that the Enniskillen case is one that will be treated as a case that is already opened ...'.

20.3   Initiating the Debate at the Policing Board and Beyond

At the Policing Board's Corporate Policy Committee meeting on 17 June 2003 the Chairman sought and received the permission of Members to read them a paper entitled *'Seeking To Hold The Past In Healthy Balance with The Future'*. He had written the paper in the context of (a) the numbers killed and injured in the Troubles; (b) the Chief Constable's estimate of *'2,000 plus unsolved killings'*; (c) the Cory Reports and recommendations; and (d) the need to make political progress. He had discussed the paper with the Board's Vice-Chairman and received his endorsement of it. The paper read as follows:

'Seeking to Hold the Past in Healthy Balance with the Future

Introduction

David Bolton in a recent article posed the following question:

"to what degree is progress dependent on addressing the past?"

Which he answered as follows:

"I am reminded of John Paul Lederach's dictum "remember and change where the past is held in healthy balance with the future", and how people should remember in helpful and creative ways while engaging in positive change. We can either sweep the past under the carpet or engage in endless and divisive forensic purity. A man whose daughter died in the Oklahoma bombing comes to mind. He reached a pivotal moment in his grief when he enquired of himself:

"what would it take to enable me to be reconciled to his loss and to inhabit the future, for his own personal peace of mind, and for our collective good

we need to ask ourselves the same question ... and thereafter agree on a "good enough" way of settling the past"

It would seem a sensible approach:

- *to learn from the past in a positive way;*

- *to understand the present; and*

- *to provide for the future in such a way that we do not regress to the past.*

1. Context

In the Troubles some 3,366 people have been killed, of those 1,525 were Catholics and 1,250 Protestants. 300 police officers were killed, and 9,000 police officers were injured, as were 46,753 lay people.

Many to this day mourn their dead. Many to this day are bruised and hurt. Too many cases are unresolved – some 1,800 – and relatives left without closure. Some families believe, rightly or wrongly, that the killing of their relatives involved collusion with the security forces and want public inquiries.

There have been two processes running concurrently which have sought to address the Northern Ireland conflict:

- *first, **the peace process**; and*

- *secondly, **the political process** (Note: The parameters of the latter are well known and are not the purport of this chapter).*

Sinn Féin has argued that their paramilitary wing, namely PIRA was an army; and

- *was engaged in a war; and*

- *since it was a war the prisoners of war should be released.*

By releasing the prisoners does this not mean that the British Government has implicitly recognised Sinn Féin's argument?

Let us envisage, what we all hope is a possible scenario: election in November. This is likely to lead to a cross party Executive including Sinn Féin.

In June 2002 Peter Cory QC was appointed. His Terms of Reference were as follows:

"to conduct a thorough investigation into allegations of collusion by the security forces in six particular cases to which the two Governments committed themselves following the discussions with the Northern Ireland parties at Weston Park last summer."

Among other things his letter of appointment states:

"in the event that a Public Inquiry is recommended, the relevant Government will implement that recommendation."

Assume when he reports that he recommends one or more inquiries, which in turn lead to cases against police officers, either former or present, being referred to the Director of Public Prosecutions. We could, therefore, have on the one hand a former alleged paramilitary sitting as a Minister, and policemen in the dock.

That situation will create for this society and this Policing Board a number of critical issues:

- an even more divided society than we have at present;
- police time being consumed on investigations going back into the not so recent past; and
- a deterioration in police morale.

2. Alternatives

2.1 Article 2 of the European Convention on Human Rights states that "everyone's right to life shall be protected by the law". On that basis collusion and misdemeanours by the State must never happen and the perpetrators must be pursued through public inquiry to prosecutions; or ...

2.3 Accept that in a war nasty things happen on both sides. While you can argue that more can be expected of a State, it would seem disingenuous to do so if, as Sinn Féin has argued, and the argument appears to have been implicitly accepted, that they were engaged in a war, and not in terrorism ... a middle way involving:

2.3.1 the release of the prisoners should now be extended to an amnesty for _all_;

2.3.2 there should be no more inquiries;

2.3.3 a Truth Commission should be established immediately:

- People could begin voluntarily to tell their stories.
- When the main paramilitary organisations agree to go to the Truth Commission, the United Kingdom Government should agree to do so too.'

Each Member of the Committee expressed his/her view in a wide-ranging discussion covering the following:

- the financial and legal consequences of investigating 1,800 unsolved murders

- the need for an elective commission on the past
- public inquiries
- truth commissions
- resources needed to police the past, the present, and the future

The Committee agreed that a discussion paper should be put to a future Board meeting.

At the Board meeting on 3 March 2004 the Board discussed a radio interview which the Chairman had given to the BBC regarding the contents of his paper. The Board recognised that the Chairman had presented a short paper on the subject at an earlier meeting (see above) and that at that meeting there had been no objections to a proposal that the issues discussed in the paper be discussed more widely, provided that the Chairman emphasised that he was speaking in a personal capacity; it was noted that, in the interview, the Chairman had done so. It was agreed that a copy of the paper referred to during the interview be circulated to all Members.

The Policing Board meeting on 1 December 2004 noted a press release announcing a separate initiative undertaken by the Westminster Parliament's Northern Ireland Affairs Committee (NIAC):

'The Committee has decided to conduct an inquiry into possible ways of dealing with Northern Ireland's past ... The purpose of the inquiry we have announced today is to seek out and illuminate ways which have been used to help resolve similar conflicts elsewhere, and which could assist the process of healing society in Northern Ireland.'

The Board also noted that the NIAC had invited individuals or organisations with an interest in this matter to submit written evidence. The Board discussed the submission of the paper prepared previously by the Chairman and endorsed by the Vice-Chairman. Members indicated that they were content for both to submit the paper to the NIAC in their personal capacities. The minute of the 1 December 2004 meeting adds:

'Whilst members agreed that the general debate on the issue of dealing with Northern Ireland's past should be driven by others outside the policing *environment, members also agreed that there was a need for further debate within the Board.'*

At the Board meeting on 3 February 2005 the Chairman referred to a discussion at the previous meeting and to the consensus among Members that there was need for further discussion within the Board on dealing with the past. A motion was unanimously agreed that a group of Members should consider the issue.

At the Board meeting on 7 April 2005 Members' attention was drawn to a press release of 1 March 2005 by the Secretary of State, Paul Murphy, on the future of services for victims and survivors of the Troubles:

'[I have concluded] that any process for dealing with the past in Northern Ireland cannot be designed in isolation, or imposed by Government. There will need to be broadly-based consultation that allows individuals and groups across the community to put their views on what form any process might take. And that consultation process itself will need broad cross-community support if the ideas it generates are to be constructively received. I am therefore announcing today that the Government intends to put in place a new Victims' and Survivors' Commissioner. I believe that this is necessary both to ensure a real focus on the needs of victims and survivors of the Troubles in Northern Ireland and to ensure that their voices continue to be heard and respected.

The Government recognises that there is a need to address in a systematic way all of the unresolved deaths in Northern Ireland's recent troubled past. As I announced last September, I have been in discussions with the Chief Constable about how the ground-breaking work of the Serious Crime Review Team (SCRT) within the Police Service of Northern Ireland might be expanded to help meet this need. I hope that both we and the PSNI will soon be in a position to say more about the next steps on this ...'.

On 24 October 2005 Secretary of State Peter Hain announced the appointment of Mrs Bertha McDougall as the Interim Commissioner for Victims and Survivors of the Troubles. Subsequently, on 2 June 2008, a Commission for Victims and Survivors was created under the Victims and Survivors (NI) Order 2006.

The NIAC published its interim report *'Ways of Dealing with Northern Ireland's Past: Interim Report – Victims and Survivors'* on 8 April

2005. The report urged the UK Government to increase the support it provided to victims and survivors and, while fully supportive of a consultation on the terms of a formal truth recovery process, concluded that the time for this was not yet right.

At the meeting of the Board's Corporate Policy Committee held on 21 April 2005 the Committee agreed that:

- a response to the NIAC's report on *'Ways of Dealing with Northern Ireland's Past'* should be considered by the Committee at a future meeting
- questions should be drafted to ask the Chief Constable at the next Board meeting regarding the PSNI's response to the NIAC report

At the *Private Session* of the Policing Board on 2 June 2005 Members considered a paper that highlighted issues identified in the NIAC's report. The minutes recorded: *'The Working Group did not develop a response to the Interim Report'*. However, subsequently, on 16 June 2005, at the Board's Corporate Policy Committee, it was noted that:

'The Board Group, which was considering the future role of the Board, had considered the NIAC report on ways of dealing with Northern Ireland's past and had agreed that no further action should be taken by the Board at present.'

Prior to a Trinity College Dublin colloquium the theme of which was *'Telling The Truth In Northern Ireland'* the Chief Constable, the Chairman, and the Vice-Chairman agreed to the contents of a paper very much based on that of 17 June 2003 and of the same title: *'Seeking to Hold the Past in Healthy Balance with the Future'*. However, one substantive change was made to the paper, which was to add to it some important paragraphs on *'the policing context'* and *'the way forward'* which had been prepared by the Chairman, the Vice-Chairman, and the Chief Constable and put to the Board on 1 December 2004.

The *'way forward'* included the following proposal:

'We do recommend that it is for the UK Government, in consultation with Republic of Ireland Government to assume, and to begin to discharge, their rightful duty, and to immediately establish a Cross Community body, which would

- *deliberate on the past;*
- *consult with the Northern Ireland community; and*
- *make proposals to the UK Government as to a more constructive way forward in dealing with the past.'*

The paper was not without its critics from among the *Political Members* on the Policing Board; for example, Ian Paisley Jnr (Democratic Unionist Party (DUP)) argued:

'*The authors should recognise that the Policing Board is **not** the centre of gravity for any of these matters! ... The paper expresses what are essentially political views about the past, its conflict past, and how to deal with its victims. The paper appears ... to be making the case for an amnesty for all crime on the pretext the Belfast Agreement released 'prisoners of war' therefore any future process will be an amnesty for those on the wrong side as well as on the paramilitary side. I have never read such drivel before ...'.*

At the meeting on 30 June 2005 the Board noted that:

'*The Board's Working Group had agreed not to develop a response to the Northern Ireland Affairs Committee Interim Report. The consensus view was that issues concerning dealing with the past would be taken forward by Government and the political parties, rather than the Policing Board.'*

Also at the Trinity College Dublin colloquium on 10 June 2005, Chief Constable Hugh Orde read a separate paper '*War is Easy to Declare, Peace is an Elusive Prize*', in which he argued:

'*We need a comprehensive strategy. [Without the latter,] demands for public inquiries become the order of the day, with a focus on State collusion and conspiracy. [In a later speech he added "it must always be remembered that terrorists killed the vast majority of victims during **the troubles**".] This one-dimensional approach fails to acknowledge the sheer scale of the miserable history, and allows a hierarchy of death to be created where some victims are deemed more important than others. In statistical terms, it is a matter of fact that the majority of re-investigations and enquiries currently underway are focused on victims of alleged state involvement in murder in a context where the majority of deaths and injuries resulted from the actions of paramilitary* *organisations. The impact on other victims is substantial. They feel disenfranchised, and do not see the State pursuing their loved ones' killers with matching vigour ...'.*

In respect of the concluding paragraphs of the *'way forward'* of the paper on *'Seeking to Hold the Past in Healthy Balance with the Future'* (at Appendix A), the Chairman on 15 May 2006 wrote to the then Northern Ireland Office (NIO) Minister of State, Paul Goggins, as follows:

'At the March 2006 meeting of the Police Advisory Board (PAB), the issue of "new initiatives to deal with the past" was discussed. I informed those present of a paper which the then Vice-Chairman of the Board, the Chief Constable and myself had developed and agreed as a way of progressing the debate on dealing with the past. At the end of our discussion at PAB the Minister encouraged those present to get involved in identifying a vehicle for addressing the past and emphasised the importance of finding a resolution to these issues. I wholeheartedly endorse those sentiments and have therefore taken the liberty of circulating the paper which sets out a proposed way forward that Denis Bradley (the then Vice-Chairman), the Chief Constable and I consider help us find resolution.'

At the meeting of the Policing Board of 22 March 2007 the Chairman raised the issue of dealing with the past. Following discussion, Members agreed that *'leadership for "dealing with the past" was a matter for consideration by the Northern Ireland Assembly with the Board having an appropriate contribution to make'.*

20.4   The Consultative Group on the Past

In the *Public Session* of the Policing Board held on 5 July 2007 the Board noted that Secretary of State for Northern Ireland, Peter Hain, had announced on 22 June 2007 the formation of the Independent Consultative Group on the Past (the Group). The Group was asked:

- to consult across the community on how Northern Ireland society can best approach the legacy of the events of the past 40 years

- to make recommendations, as appropriate, on any steps that might be taken to support Northern Ireland society in building a shared future that is not overshadowed by the events of the past

On 20 September 2007 the Policing Board's Corporate Policy, Planning and Performance Committee considered the Group's press release of 6 September 2007 inviting all those affected by the legacy of the events over the past 40 years to share their views with the Group. The Committee considered the issue of the Policing Board making a corporate response to the Group and, following discussion, it was agreed that a discussion paper should be drafted; it was also suggested that Members might meet informally to discuss the development of a corporate response.

At the Policing Board meeting on 1 November 2007 it was, however, resolved that

- the *Political Members* of the Board should engage with the Group through their respective political parties
- *Independent Members*, including the Chairman and Vice-Chairman of the Board, could meet with the Group in an independent capacity to present their own views as individual members
- *Independent Members* would discuss whether to make arrangements for a separate meeting with the Group and advise the Chairman accordingly.

At the Board meeting on 6 December 2007 it was noted that *Independent Members* had met to discuss whether they could develop a consensus view on a presentation to the Group and they were not yet ready to decide whether they should meet as a group with the Consultative Group. At the meeting on 7 February 2008 the Chairman gave a verbal update on contact that he and the Vice-Chairman had had with the Consultative Group on 23 January 2008.

At the meeting of the Policing Board's Corporate Policy, Planning and Performance Committee on 15 May 2008 Members were informed that the co-chairs of the Consultative Group, having completed an extensive public consultation, had delivered a keynote address, the purpose of which 'was to set out what the Group believes are the key issues *society needs to address if we are to move towards a shared future that is not overshadowed by the past'.*

At the Policing Board meeting on 5 February 2009 the Chairman highlighted, under *'publications received'*, the *'Report of the Consultative Group on the Past'*, dated 23 January 2009. (The full Report, including a summary of its main Recommendations, is available on the internet.) The importance of the issue and the thoughtfulness with which it was addressed by the Eames/Bradley team should have ensured at least a constructive debate; however, it didn't ...

20.5   The Reinvestigation of Unsolved Murders

On the back of the Police Ombudsman's recommendations in her *'Report on the Investigation of Matters Relating to the Omagh Bombing of 15 August 1998'*, the Policing Board agreed that Her Majesty's Inspector of Constabulary David Blakey oversee *'The Review of Terrorist Linked Murder Inquiries'*. The eventual title of the report, which was completed in 2003, was *'Report on Murder Investigation for the Chief Constable of the Police Service of Northern Ireland'*. Blakey commented on 'reinvestigations' as follows:

'5.4 the European Court of Human Rights has interpreted Article 2 of HRA (Right to life) as placing a responsibility on the state, including the police to provide a thorough and effective investigation capable of leading to the identification and punishment of those responsible for murders.

5.5 Since the beginning of the Troubles (1969) Northern Ireland has suffered an unprecedented level of violence and murder. The volume and frequency of deaths has created a legacy for policing today. A consequence of this has been an increasing demand by relatives of victims for information concerning the present state of police investigations.

"Many of these cases are protracted in nature, but an encouraging (yet disconcerting) trend is starting to emerge where there is pressure from the relatives of murder victims from the Troubles, to reopen and further investigate "old, unsolved" cases, some going back to the 1970s". (Annual HMIC inspection of PSNI 2002)

5.6 PSNI has received a number of letters from relatives of victims killed during the Troubles requesting an assessment of the progress of the investigation in accordance with Article 2 Human Rights Act. These letters are being received both at DCUs and at Headquarters and the response varies from department to department. Some cases prompt a re-investigation whilst others become subject to a desk top review. There is a need for corporate policy in reacting to these enquiries.'

The Policing Board's Corporate Policy Committee at its meeting on 20 February 2003 noted that the Chief Constable had publicly raised the issue of the allocation of police investigative resources to re-examine 'historical crimes'.

At the *Public Session* of the Board on 6 October 2004 the following question was asked by *Independent Member* Mr Barry Gilligan on 'unsolved murders':

'Chief Constable, the Board notes that Government proposes to allocate a sum of money to the PSNI over a three to four year period in order to fund the Serious Crime Review team in reviewing unsolved murders, the number of which we know is very considerable and still a cause of great hurt in this community. Can you clarify for us how you propose to go about this work and how you propose to staff the team to do it?'

Chief Constable Hugh Orde replied as follows:

'I have a number of points to make on this. First, it is our initiative ... We are very pleased to see as a result of our efforts the NIO is looking to supply us with additional funding to deal with this business so we do not have to draw from the current police budget which is clearly necessary to deal with current policing issues.

This is not any sort of replacement for the wider debate around truth and reconciliation issues and all those sorts of things which are being led by the Secretary of State and are out-with our responsibility. This is simply to get sufficient funding to put another unit in place, in addition to our Serious Crime Review team, to assess all the unsolved crimes, including all our unsolved murders of police officers, to see where we have evidential opportunities that we can then pursue. Currently I have not been made aware of the sum of money available. I am told it will be sufficient for the task. The way of structuring it will be to second a small number of officers from other police services, if I can find them. I think there will need to be an independent element to this [unit] and we will need to staff it with retired high quality detectives to review all the cases we have, to look at the forensic exhibits available and to take advantage of the advances in science specifically, that may well give us evidence we can now pursue through a legal process, which we did not have available to us at the time.'

At the Board meeting on 7 April 2005 Members noted a press release issued on behalf of Secretary of State Paul Murphy regarding the creation of a new unit within the PSNI to review unsolved deaths:

'We believe that Northern Ireland needs a tailored approach to deal with the pain, grief and anger associated with its past. Part of this approach is the need to address, in a systematic and comprehensive way, all of the unresolved deaths that took place during the Troubles.

Today's announcement will allow the Chief Constable to establish a new unit and expand this work to cover all unresolved deaths [estimated to be 1,800 from 1969 up to the signing of the Agreement in 1998] in a way that will command the confidence of the wider community. It also supports the establishment of a dedicated team in Forensic Science Northern Ireland to provide comprehensive forensic advice to the review. This is sensitive, painstaking and complex work and in many cases is unlikely to lead to any prosecutions. But it is important work if we are to provide answers to the questions so many people have about the death of their loved ones.'

The press release contained the following 'Note to Editors':

' • *The new ring-fenced Review Unit created by the Chief Constable will be headed by a recently retired Commander from the Metropolitan Police, Dave Cox. In addition the head of investigation is a seconded Detective Superintendent, Phil James, who previously worked in the Stevens' team;*

• *The Unit will be staffed by a mix of serving and retired officers from PSNI and Great Britain forces on an agency basis;*

• *A key part of the process will involve the disclosure of appropriate information to families of victims;*

• *There will be some mechanism to ensure an effective review process and public confidence ...'.*

At the *Public Session* of the Board on 7 April 2005 *Independent Member* Mrs Pauline McCabe asked the Chief Constable to explain what criteria were applied to the selection of ex-officers to assist with the review of historic cases, and what measures he was implementing to optimise confidence in the reviews of cases where there were particular family or public concerns.

The Chief Constable replied:

'In terms of selection of both serving and ex-police officers, the approach will be, we need to find people who have the integrity and the skills for the posts we are going to advertise. We have just put out an advert as Stage 1 across the United Kingdom and the Republic of Ireland to see what sort of a response we get.

In particular, in terms of part of C8 which will be the Special Cases Unit [This was to be called the Historical Enquiries Team (HET)], we will have a substantial number of seconded officers and agency staff from outside the PSNI to give that independent element to the investigations where there are particular concerns, but I think it is worth remembering, that in many cases, there will not be particular concerns, people just want their cases reviewed.'

Above reference was made to a separate speech, *'War is Easy, Peace is an Elusive Prize'*, of June 2005, in which the Chief Constable argued that in order to focus on the present policing needs – protecting communities from crime – he needed the HET to review old cases. He then went on to note that policing and the HET was *'only part of the complex equation that will sum to a comprehensive solution to the past'*.

At the Policing Board's *Public Session* on 2 June 2005 the Chief Constable replied to a question:

'The critical part of the work at the HET will be how we deal with the families and how we liaise with victims' families whilst we reopen and reinvestigate these cases to see if we can take them forward, or where we cannot take them forward, where we make sure we communicate as much as we possibly can, to those families so at least we bring them some form of closure.'

At the meeting of the Policing Board's Corporate Policy Committee on 20 October 2005 Mr David Cox, Head of HET, and Detective Superintendent Phil James made a comprehensive presentation to members on the purpose of the HET, the extent of its task, its analytical database, the potential areas of opportunity, its prioritisation policy, its critical milestones, and its five-phase process (collection/assessment/review/investigation/closure). The Board visited the HET on 19 October 2006 and received a presentation covering the scale of their task, to whom they were accountable, and how they prioritised cases. In subsequent discussion Board Members raised issues including managing the expectations of families and police officers, access to information, and the need to provide clarity on the role of the Team.

In respect of the issue of prioritisation of cases at the 6 December 2007 Board's *Public Session*, *Political Member* Alex Maskey (Sinn Féin) asked why cases were taken out of historical sequence by the HET. He was given the following response by the Chief Constable:

'*The HET have in place a prioritisation policy, which is underpinned by the general rule of allocating cases on a chronological basis. Exceptions to the rule [occur under the following headings]: previously opened investigations; humanitarian considerations; crimes involving issues of serious public interest; and linked series of murders.*'

At the Policing Board's Corporate Policy, Planning and Performance Committee on 15 June 2006 the Chief Constable gave a detailed briefing in relation to the police managerial resource implications for the PSNI in providing further requirements of Public Inquiries and the casework of the HET. The Committee, having discussed the appointment of an additional ACC, resolved under delegated authority that an additional ACC post be created.

At the *Public Session* of the Policing Board on 5 October 2006 the Chief Constable, having been questioned by *Political Members* in respect of lost files impinging on the work of the HET, replied:

'*[Whilst] we have certainly not recovered everything we had hoped to recover through the searches we have undertaken, ... we have found some relevant documentation for nearly every single case and police documentation for over 92% of the 3,268 cases ... Every family we engage with will be told exactly what we have recovered and what we think is missing ...*'.

With respect to the funding of 'historical enquiries', the Policing Board received the following letter from the NIO dated 22 September 2006:

'On 8 March 2005 based on police research, a total of £32m over a six year period was allocated to the Unresolved Deaths Project with the HET receiving £24.2m. The remainder was allocated to the Forensic Science Agency in Northern Ireland (FSNI) for their necessary forensic input. Following the provision of this funding discussions with the Public Prosecution Service (PPS) resulted in further additional finances being provided, bringing the total funding to £34m over six years.

When initially considering the Chief Constable's case for this initiative, the Government was of the view this work would be carried out by the police. However, following discussions between the Chief Constable and the Police Ombudsman that she should be solely responsible for past deaths, as a result of the actions of a police officer, it was recognised the Ombudsman's office also had a role in this Project.'

On 10 November 2006 Mr Trevor Ringland, a then *Independent Member* of the Policing Board, sent the Chairman a note on *'The Viability of Prosecution Based on Historical Enquiry: Observations of Counsel on Potential Evidential Difficulties'*. In his Introduction he stated:

'At the outset, it is possible to identify three basic sources of difficulty likely to be encountered by the [Historical] Enquiries Team:

- there is the possible diminution of quality of evidence through the passage of time;
- in many cases evidence will simply be unavailable;
- any prosecutions that might arise from the fresh enquiries will be subject to the normal evidential and procedural rules; against the backdrop of such rules, the standard of proof beyond reasonable doubt imposed on the prosecution in criminal cases is an exacting one.'

In the presentation which he gave in November 2006 on the work of the HET to a Sub-Committee of the Joint Committee on Justice, Equality, Defence and Women's Rights at the Oireachtas, Dublin, the Chief Constable said:

'I am very proud of our practical contribution to taking responsibility for what happened to police investigations during the Troubles, in the form of the HET. [However], there is not the capacity to deal with all these cases. Many very serious crimes will never be looked at again as the resources are just not *available. We recognise that the likelihood of solving cases in a judicial sense is slight for a number of reasons. The primary aim of HET is to bring a measure of resolution to families. We have consciously shifted the focus to ensure that the driving force behind the team's effort will be to deliver the outcome the family seek rather than the more formal one-dimensional police approach. This approach is unique in UK policing.'*

At the *Public Session* of the Policing Board on 13 December 2006, in reply to a question from *Political Member* Alex Attwood (Social Democratic and Labour Party (SDLP)), the Chief Constable commented on the funding of historical enquiries as follows:

'Currently, I am confident we can deliver pretty much what we want to deliver with the amount of cash allocated. ... I supervise the HET directly myself and will continue to do so and if I do feel I am in difficulty I will come straight back to the Board.'

At the Board meeting on 13 December 2006, the Chairman informed Members that the Corporate Policy, Planning and Performance Committee on 22 November 2006 had considered a paper on *'Dealing with the Past: Issues Aimed At Providing A Background to Facilitate Discussion'*. Among the issues noted or agreed were:

- The legislation governing the work of the Police Ombudsman (OPONI) permits investigations into incidents which occurred more than two years ago where certain criteria are met;
- The OPONI had identified a total of 75 'past' cases and the availability of resources to adequately investigate these had been identified as an issue by the office;
- The OPONI had also identified the non-cooperation of retired officers as a barrier to effective investigation and ultimate closure for the families of victims in such cases;
- That the Policing Board could assist the PSNI with publicising the role of HET by inviting the Chief Constable and the HET top team to present in a Public Session at a future Board meeting.

(The latter presentation was made in the *Public Session* of the Board on 6 July 2007.)

On 5 July 2007 the then NIO Minister Paul Goggins wrote to the Policing Board as follows:

'I am writing in response to your letters about the proposed stocktake of the HET as well as funding issues arising from the recommendations contained in the Police Ombudsman's report into the murder of Raymond McCord Jnr. I apologise for the delay. I am confident that the recently established panel [the Consultative Group] on the past represents the most constructive way forward in attempting to address many of these issues. While I look forward to reading their report and recommendations, the panel is not expected to complete its work until next year. In the immediate future, therefore, it is important that we proceed with the proposed HET stocktake in order to establish how many cases have been dealt with so far, and at what cost; and what the likely timescale is for completion of the work. I have discussed this idea with both the Chief Constable and the Police Ombudsman and it is hoped to agree terms of reference with the organisations involved in the project and begin the stocktake in the near future. I will of course ensure the Policing Board is kept fully informed of progress.'

On 1 November 2007 the Policing Board considered correspondence dated 17 October 2007 from the NIO Policing Division regarding the HET stocktake; attached to the letter were the terms of reference as agreed with the PSNI, of which the principal one was *'To consider how best to continue to deliver the objectives of the HET project taking into account the experience/knowledge gained to date and the existing budgetary constraints.'* The letter added: *'[We] will be taking forward the stocktake shortly and will continue to keep you informed of progress.'*

It is the understanding of the authors that the 'stocktake' on the HET was not completed.

At the Board meeting on 5 June 2008 *Political Member* David Simpson (DUP) asked the Chief Constable about reported high levels of resignation from the HET and the number of cases that had passed the anticipated completion date. The Chief Constable explained about the level of turnover in staff and said that at that point the Team had completed 363 reviews and had 1,107 cases open. Relationships had been built with many diverse groups over and above the 713 families HET had been working with to date.

In late July 2008 former Police Ombudsman Baroness Nuala O'Loan called for a merger of the HET and the Police Ombudsman's office. She argued that it would be more cost effective because they would not both be investigating the same cases, on occasion in parallel, and the unit would be independent of the PSNI. Later Mr Al Hutchinson, Baroness Nuala O'Loan's successor, said that such a merger should be considered.

The Board's Corporate Policy Committee, at its meeting on 18 September 2008, considered NIAC's report into policing and criminal justice in Northern Ireland, 'The Cost of Policing the Past', which had been published in early July 2008. A paper for the Committee reported that

'The [NIAC] report examines whether the cost of "policing the past" is compromising the PSNI and the Police Ombudsman's Office in carrying out their functions. The report recommends alternative ways for the Historical Enquiries Team (HET) to prioritise caseload in order to manage funding more effectively. Significant additional funding would be required to maintain the HET's current approach. The report also recommends that a mid-term review is conducted to establish the costs and benefits of continuing with the HET's present methods.'

The Policing Board had previously formed the following view, which was passed to NIAC:

' • It is the view of the Board that the effectiveness and efficiency of the PSNI in preventing and detecting crime should not be compromised by dealing with the various commitments to historical inquiries.

• It is the responsibility of Government to ensure that the PSNI be provided with adequate funding to deal with **policing the past**, and the Board is committed to ensuring Government deliver the necessary funding for the PSNI in this area.'

At the Policing Board meeting on 2 October 2008 the Chairman said that a publication by Patricia Lundy, Can the Past be Policed? Lessons from the Historical Enquiries Team, Northern Ireland (Draft), had been received. In her Introduction Dr Lundy stated:

'This article explores how societies in transition might address victims' quest for "the truth", or more specifically micro level information. It does this by using a case study of the Historical Enquiries Team (HET) established by the Police

Service of Northern Ireland (PSNI). The HET is a unique attempt by a police service in a society undergoing transition to "police the past". In September 2005 the Chief Constable of the PSNI, Sir Hugh Orde, granted permission to conduct the research and wide and unfettered access to the HET was permitted. It is notable that in the context of Northern Ireland this was unprecedented access to policing. The article therefore offers a unique insight into a unique process …'.

Under '*Part 4: Structural Impediments, Obstacles and Constraints*' and, in particular, '*Staffing and Independence*', Dr Lundy concluded:

'*From a detailed analysis of various cross-referenced sources, and over two years observation of the HET, the research found that each phase of the HET CARIR process (Collection, Assessment, Review, Investigation, Resolution) has involvement by former long serving RUC officers and cannot be described as having the requisite degree of independence as benchmarked by Brecknell (in Brecknell v the United Kingdom) and required by the ECHR.*'

In respect of the collection phase she added, '*The manner in which [this] phase is conducted casts doubt upon the integrity of the process and the very foundation on which the HET is built.*'

At the Board meeting on 4 December 2008 the Chairperson of the Board's Human Rights and Professional Standards Committee highlighted that the Chief Constable, ACC Jones, the HET Director Dave Cox, and Deputy Director Phil James had attended the Committee's meeting on 12 November 2008 and had briefed the Committee on Dr Lundy's article. The Chief Constable had advised the Committee that,

'*Since the article was still in draft form, he was disappointed that it had appeared on the internet. He expressed disappointment on the content of the paper.*'

As at 5 February 2009 the HET had completed over 500 'reviews' and delivered case reports to 200 families. Over the first four years of its existence the HET had cost over £21m.

In 2012 the Minister of Justice for Northern Ireland, David Ford, commissioned Her Majesty's Inspectorate of Constabulary (HMIC)

to inspect the role and function of the HET with (in summary) the following Terms of Reference:

- Does the HET's approach conform to current policing standards and practices?
- Does the HET adopt a consistent approach to all cases?
- Is the HET's approach to cases with state involvement compliant with the European Convention on Human Rights and Fundamental Freedoms (ECHR)?

HMIC published its report on 9 July 2013. In respect of the first of the Terms of Reference HMIC concluded:

'Our findings indicate an unacceptable large range where the HET's approach does not conform to current policing standards and practices.'

In respect to the second of the Terms of Reference HMIC concluded:

'Our inspection found that the HET, as a matter of policy, treats deaths where there was State involvement differently from those cases where there is no State involvement. State involvement cases appeared to be treated less rigorously.'

In respect to the last of the Terms of Reference HMIC concluded:

'[Our] conclusions lead us to consider that the HET's approach to State involvement cases is inconsistent with the United Kingdom's obligations under Article 2 EHCR ... In addition the deployment of former RUC and PSNI officers in State involvement cases gives rise to the view that the process lacks independence.'

Also on 9 July 2013, the *Belfast Telegraph* reported that the Policing Board had announced that the recommendations made by HMIC would be implemented by a working group.

On 30 September 2013 Chief Constable Matt Baggott announced that Chief Superintendent Tina Barnett would replace Commander Dave Cox as leader of the HET.

20.6   In Conclusion

On 8 August 2007 the Chairman was invited to join a *'West Belfast Talkback'* panel at the West Belfast Festival. The first question was addressed to him:

'Professor Rea, I am Patrick Finucane's son. Your views on "dealing with the past" are well known but where do they leave me and my family?'

In reply the Chairman referred to the paper, *'Seeking to Hold the Past In Healthy Balance With the Future'* (see above). However, he went further:

'First, I sympathise with you, your mother and your family in the death of your father but everywhere I go in Northern Ireland I meet similar pain, be it the relatives of the Omagh bombing or RUC or PSNI widows.
     There can be no hierarchy of death or victims.'

In his response to Mr Finucane, the Chairman continued:

'Second, I have bought into the peace process on Sinn Féin's terms, which I understand to be – and correct me if I am wrong – Sinn Féin has argued that its paramilitary wing, viz PIRA:

- *was an army not terrorists,*

- *was engaged in a war and,*

- *since the Troubles was a war, the prisoners of war should be released.'*

(NB The Chairman was referring to Annex B, Prisoners, in the 10 April 1998 Belfast Agreement: 1. 'Both Governments will put in place mechanisms to provide for an accelerated programme for the release of prisoners ... 2. Prisoners affiliated to organisations, which have not established or are not maintaining a complete and unequivocal ceasefire will not benefit from the arrangements' ....)

For the Chairman this meant that Sinn Féin members elected to the Northern Ireland Assembly, or indeed Progressive Unionist Party members if elected to the Northern Ireland Assembly, should – regardless of record and depending on the size of their membership – be Members of the Policing Board or the Northern Ireland Assembly's Executive.

The Chairman then put to the audience – and the audience included the Leader of Sinn Féin, Gerry Adams – the question: *'Does this not mean that both Governments have accepted Sinn Fein's argument?'* No-one voiced their disagreement.

Third, he added:

'In a war nasty things happen on both sides. I do not challenge that collusion took place. Whilst you can argue that more can be expected from a State (Article 2 of the European Convention on Human Rights), it would seem disingenuous to do so, if as Sinn Féin has argued, and it has been implicitly accepted by both Governments that they were engaged in a war, and not in terrorism. Accordingly:

- *as of, say, the Belfast Agreement, the slate should be wiped clean, and our society and policing should look to the future;*
- *the release of prisoners should be extended to an amnesty for all;*
- *there should be no more inquiries; and*
- *our concern as a society should be for the victims at their point of need.'*

In their submission to the Panel of Parties (see below) in November 2013, the authors added to the above that:

- Northern Ireland should draw a line in a 'national' act of public contrition.
- the above programme should be ratified in a Northern Ireland referendum.

The issue of the continuing work of the HET and the reinvestigation of deaths during the Troubles up to April 1998 are separate but clearly related. The HET has been a unique experiment in the context of international policing – a Northern Ireland solution to a Northern Ireland problem. Given its funding constraints and despite criticism, it has been successful in many ways. While very few of the reinvestigations have led to prosecutions, undoubtedly much comfort has been provided to the relatives of victims in terms of information that was not made available to them at the time of death.

On the other hand, there have been several issues, relating primarily to funding and competence. Perhaps predictably – with hindsight – the original six-year budget of £34m has proved very inadequate. By eight years or so after it was set up the HET had tackled only around half of all the identified cases. Second, there have proved to be issues relating to the currency of its professional expertise. This led to the decision to bring HET more closely into the PSNI structure, with the clear objective of obtaining the best outcome for the relatives in the individual cases. In the summer of 2013 a further issue arose in relation to the legal approach being adopted by the HET towards the investigation of cases where the primary responsibility for the death was attributed to the Army.

In addition, its work has been challenged by the issues of superintendence and the relationship with the Police Ombudsman. As noted above, no separate independent superintendence was put in place when the proposals for what became the HET were brought forward. Such a role could have covered not just the accountability function, as with the Policing Board, but also a more explicitly outward-facing dimension, intended to assist the staff of the HET in their public liaison work. The Policing Board formally had responsibility, as has been demonstrated earlier in this book, although this was in practice carried out with a fairly light touch. The NIAC report published in 2008 recommended that the HET should be managed by an independent agency rather than the PSNI, and Sir Hugh Orde wrote to the Policing Board later that year that he would not oppose the transfer of the HET to another body. In practice, no such change was made.

(It is noteworthy that on 19 May 2014 *The Times* reported Sir Hugh Orde, in his capacity as President of the Association of Chief Police Officers, suggesting that a historical inquiry squad should be set up in England and Wales to deal with the increasing number of historical cases that he concluded were taking police officers away from present-day threats. He was quoted as saying '*To police the future you have to police the present and the past – it's all about public confidence.*' He added that there was much to be learnt from the HET in Northern Ireland.)

In terms of the Policing Board, issues arising from the past were a continuing concern, although, as with the extensions to the 50:50 recruitment rule, Members decided that on the societal (as opposed to the policing) way forward there should be no collective viewpoint. Victims were foremost in many deliberations, but so too was the need to assist the PSNI in focusing as far as possible on meeting the current demands of policing and thereby enhancing community confidence.

In the May 2013 strategy, *'Together Building A United Community'*, the members of the Northern Ireland Executive recognised obstacles that were frustrating the movement to a society based on equality of opportunity, good relations, and reconciliation. In the body of the May strategy the five Executive Parties proposed a way forward involving the establishment of a Panel of Parties to consider parades and protests, flags and emblems, and the past. The First Minister and deputy First Minister invited Ambassador Richard Haass and Professor Megan O'Sullivan to serve as Chair and Vice-Chair of the Panel.

The Haass Panel of Parties, despite intensive meetings in December 2013, failed to give universal support to the draft agreement produced by the Chair and Vice-Chair: *'three in particular – the Alliance Party, the DUP, and UUP – were not prepared to endorse this agreement'*. However, the Chair and Vice-Chair stated that *'the draft agreement makes substantial progress in addressing the past'*. In respect of contending with the past, the draft agreement, inter alia:

- ensures the avenue of justice remains open by establishing a Historical Investigations Unit, with the full investigative function of the PSNI, to take over the cases now being addressed by the HET and the historical unit of the Police Ombudsman
- calls for an Independent Commission for Information Retrieval providing those coming forward with information about the conflict with limited immunity
- calls for public statements of acknowledgements by those involved in the conflict, encouraging them to take responsibility for the pain they have caused

In the spring of 2014 there was a further series of events connected to legacy and policing issues.

On 8 April the Sinn Féin MP for Mid Ulster, Francie Molloy, was reported in the Times to have said that *'the de facto amnesty should apply to "all sides" in the conflict'*. The paper called this a significant move from a Republican politician because it would mean that members of the security forces as well as paramilitaries would face investigations.

It added that Mr Molloy stressed that he was expressing a personal view and not setting out a new Sinn Féin policy.

On 11 April 2014 Seamus Daly appeared in court, having been charged in connection with the Omagh bombing.

On 28 April Mr Justice Treacy allowed an application for a judicial review of the PSNI's policing of Loyalist flag protests which had taken place in Belfast between 8 December 2012 and 14 February 2013. (These protests, which passed the Nationalist Short Strand area of East Belfast, followed Belfast City Council's decision to restrict the flying of the Union Flag at the City Hall to 15 designated days per year rather than every day.)

The judge accepted that operational discretion was important to the police and that no court should unreasonably interfere with operational discretion or make practical policing impossible, but found that the ACC was *'labouring under a material misapprehension as to the proper scope of police powers and the legal context in which they were operating'*. Chief Constable Baggott announced that the PSNI would appeal against the judgment. As Chief Constable in Northern Ireland, he would have been very conscious of the need to balance his responsibility for the safety of his officers and his other human rights obligations. It is worth noting, for all the challenges posed during these flags protests, including the potential for violence, no lives were lost and no member of the public was seriously injured.

On 30 April 2014 the Leader of Sinn Féin, Gerry Adams, voluntarily attended a police station in connection with the PSNI's enquiries into the abduction and murder of mother of ten Jean McConville in December 1972. (This followed the charging earlier in April of Ivor Bell, reputed to be a former PIRA chief of staff, with aiding and abetting the murder.) He was released on 4 May, when the PSNI announced that they would pass a file to the Director of Public Prosecutions, who would decide whether Mr Adams should be charged.

References

A New Beginning: Policing In Northern Ireland, The Report Of The Independent Commission On Policing For Northern Ireland, September 1999

Statement By The Police Ombudsman For Northern Ireland On Her

Investigation Into Matters Relating To The Omagh Bombing On August 15 1998, 12 December 2001

Seeking To Hold The Past In Healthy Balance With The Future, Rea, Desmond and Denis Bradley, 2003

Cory Collusion Inquiry Reports, Judge Peter Cory, 2003 and 2004

Ways Of Dealing With Northern Ireland's Past: Interim Report – Victims And Survivors, Northern Ireland Affairs Committee, 8 April 2005

War Is Easy To Declare, Peace Is An Elusive Prize, Hugh Orde at the Trinity College Colloquium, 10 June 2005

Policing The Past To Police The Future, Hugh Orde at Queen's University, 13 November 2006

Lundy, Patricia, 'Can The Past Be Policed? Lessons from the Historical Enquiries Team, Northern Ireland', *Law and Social Challenges*, 11, 2009, pp. 109–171

The Report of the Consultative Group on the Past, 23 January 2009

Irish Times, Mark Heaney, 23 February 2013

Irish Times, 21 March 2013

Together Building A United Community, May 2003, www.ofmdfmni.gov.uk/together-building-a-united-community

Inspection Of The Police Service Of Northern Ireland Historical Enquiries Team, Her Majesty's Inspectorate of Constabulary, 3 July 2013

Belfast Telegraph, 9 July 2013

Rea, Professor Sir Desmond and Masefield, Robin, *Dealing With The Past*, The Decision Partnership, Belfast, November 2013

Sunday Independent, 2 February 2014

The Times, 8 April 2014

The Times, 19 May 2014

CHAPTER TWENTY-ONE

Some Conclusions

21.1 The Principles of Policing

This concluding chapter starts by addressing two of the fundamental issues – the principles of policing and different approaches to holding the police to account. Underpinning both are the questions of consent and confidence in the police. That has been increasingly called into question in England (and indeed in Ireland, as illustrated in Chapter 19) following recent whistle-blowing, official reports, inquiries into incidents, and failed investigations.

This chapter then brings out some key conclusions from the rest of this book, with a particular focus on those two issues.

Sir Robert Peel, then British Home Secretary, the founder of the first metropolitan force in London in 1829, wrote: '*The police are the people and the people are the police.*' For him, getting out into the community, dealing with the daily issues that concern people, and earning their respect and co-operation in preventing crime were the bedrock of good policing. He also believed it was vital that the people could exert an effective democratic check on the police.

Sir Robert himself (although some police historians believe they were formulated considerably later) is said to have set down nine principles of policing based on the General Instructions issued to every member of the Metropolitan Force, as below:

'*1. To prevent crime and disorder, as an alternative to their repression by military force and severity of legal punishment.*

2. To recognise always that the power of the police to fulfil their functions and duties is dependent upon public approval of their existence, actions and behaviour and on their ability to secure and maintain public respect.

3. To recognise always that to secure and maintain the respect and approval of the public means also securing the willing cooperation of the public in the task of securing observance of laws.

4. To recognise always that the extent to which the cooperation of the public can be secured diminishes proportionately the necessity of the use of physical force and compulsion for achieving police objectives.

5. To seek and preserve public favour, not by pandering to public opinion, but by constantly demonstrating absolutely impartial service to law, in complete independence of policy, and without regard to the justice or injustice of the substance of individual laws, by ready offering of individual service and friendship to all members of the public without regard to their wealth or social standing, by ready exercise of courtesy and friendly good humour; and by ready offering of individual sacrifice in protecting and preserving life.

6. To use physical force only when the exercise of persuasion, advice and warning is found to be insufficient to obtain public cooperation to an extent necessary to secure observance of law or to restore order, and to use only the minimum degree of physical force which is necessary on any particular occasion for achieving a police objective.

7. To maintain at all times a relationship with the public that gives reality to the historic tradition that the police are the public and that the public are the police, the police being only members of the public who are paid to give full-time attention to duties which are incumbent on every citizen in the interests of community welfare and existence.

8. To recognise always the need for strict adherence to police executive functions, and to refrain from even seeming to usurp the powers of the judiciary of avenging individuals or the State, and authoritatively judging guilt and punishing the guilty.

9. To recognise always that the test of police efficiency is the absence of crime and disorder, and not the visible evidence of police action in dealing with them.'

In many ways those principles have underpinned at least the theoretical approach to policing in these islands ever since, although during times of challenge, such as Northern Ireland's Troubles, policing practice has to some extent departed from them.

The principles are curiously modern too. For Peel, policing was predicated on the principle of consent, emphasis was placed on dealing courteously with the public, and the use of force was to be minimised.

Even the test of effectiveness and efficiency, as expressed in the last of the nine principles, was based on substance not 'spin'.

Although Peel's principles were not explicitly referred to in the 1998 Belfast Agreement the thrust of the policing appendix to that document is entirely consistent with them, and they are flagged up early in the first chapter of the Report of The Independent Commission On Policing For Northern Ireland (the Independent Commission). Moreover, they remain the starting point for many commentators on how policing should develop in the twenty-first century. In November 2005 the then Metropolitan Police Commissioner, Sir Ian Blair, delivered the BBC's Dimbleby lecture. In his opening remarks he recognised that *'there may be potential for concern about whether the police service is open enough to outside influence'*. He then went on to refer to two seminal dates earlier that year – 6 July 2005, when London won the opportunity to host the 2012 Olympics, and the following day, 7 July, on which 52 people were killed as a result of terrorist action in the largest single act of murder in modern English history. The Metropolitan Police had participated in the Olympics bid, stressing that it was an unarmed service in a free city. He asked: do we want a 6 July police service or a 7 July police service? He also asked who should decide, and how? He said that it was important for the citizens of Britain to articulate what kind of police service they wanted.

Sir Ian Blair has said that the police had long worked on the assumption that the service the public wanted was *'local, visible, accessible, familiar, accountable, and friendly'*. He commented on Peel's reference to citizens in uniform as *'only members of the public that are paid to give full-time attention to the duties which are incumbent on every citizen'*. He noted too that Sir Richard Mayne, one of the two Commissioners appointed by Peel, had said: *'The primary objects of an efficient [effective] police are the prevention of crime and the preservation of public tranquillity.'*

By contrast, the White Paper on police reform, issued by the then Conservative Government in 1993, stated unequivocally that *'the main job of the police is to catch criminals'*. The succeeding Labour Government took the view that it was:

'To build a safe, just and tolerant society, in which the rights and responsibilities of individuals, families and communities are properly balanced, and the protection and security of the public are maintained.'

Sir Ian Blair, in his 2005 Dimbleby lecture, stated that his view was that:

'Properly to respond [to the Service's widening mission], to move to neighbour-hood policing while responding to terror without losing current mainstream services, the police will have to alter the way we work, change the make-up of our workforce and seek out new partnerships with the public, together with new methods of democratic accountability.'

In this connection he referred to Police Authorities *'whose role is almost entirely unknown to the public'*.

More recently, in November 2013, the Independent Police Commission, chaired by Lord Stevens, which had been set up by the Labour Opposition, produced a report entitled *'Policing for a Better Britain'*. This report was significant in more than one respect – it was almost the first report, ostensibly based in Great Britain, that took due account of the range of developments in policing in Northern Ireland. It included a comparison of accountability models as well as the delivery of policing.

Lord Stevens' Commission noted that, for historical reasons, the Peel principles took no account of concepts such as human rights or the challenge of cross-border crime. It concluded that the original principles are *'necessary but not sufficient to articulate a 21ˢᵗ century vision of effective and legitimate policing'*. The Commission's report states that the objective is to *'create a police service that is profes-sional, democratically accountable and which serves the common good'*. It rewrote Peel's principles, placing greater emphasis on both collabo-ration not just with the public but also with other agencies and the police's role in contributing to social cohesion. One key principle adopted in the Commission's report that resonates with several themes in this book is that *'the police must be organised to achieve the optimal balance between effectiveness, cost-efficiency, accountability and responsiveness'*.

The Commission noted that *'public confidence in the integrity of the police has been damaged by a spate of organisational failures and high profile scandals'*. It recommended the introduction of a Code of Ethics that would set standards of professional behaviour – over a decade after a Code had been brought in for Northern Ireland.

Curiously, there is no explicit reference to the protection of, or compliance with, human rights, and reference to the local community is only implicit. On the other hand, in launching the Commission's report, Lord Stevens was quoted as saying that *'Neighbourhood policing is the bedrock on which the service is built'*. He went on to note that, nearly 10 years previously, he had introduced neighbourhood policing into the Metropolitan Police, responding to Londoners unequivocally stating that they wanted community-based policing providing local solutions to local problems.

Lord Stevens' Commission's report refers not only to the Report of the Independent Commission on Policing in Northern Ireland, whose recommendations it states are relevant beyond the island of Ireland, but also the report of the Northern Ireland Consultative Group on the Past, quoting the Group's observation that:

'But policing, as a reflection of the social mores as a society seeks for just and fair dealing, is emerging as a new concept of great importance as we define the nature of a community in the 21ˢᵗ Century.'

21.2   Contemporary Developments in Accountability in Great Britain and America

In 2012 the long-standing Police Authorities in England and Wales were replaced by Police and Crime Commissioners (PCCs). This was in some ways a fundamental change to the traditional tripartite structure of the Home Secretary, the police, and the Police Authority. *The Economist* pointed out on 25 February 2012 that

'A new breed of elected commissioners to hold Police forces to account is coming into being across England and Wales, and candidates are racing to stake their claim. The Government's least noticed but perhaps most radical service reform is hurtling forward. On November 15ᵗʰ voters in each of the 41 Police Force areas outside London will be able to choose a person to supervise their local bobbies. These Police and Crime Commissioners (PCCs) will set Police Force priorities, run their budgets, and hire and fire Chief Constables ... Operational decisions are to remain with the Chief Constable but the new PCCs will have wide powers.'

The Economist commented on PCCs again on 27 October 2012, using the Kent area as an example:

'*Whoever wins the election in Kent on November 15th will take on a powerful job with an annual salary of £85,000 and responsibility for an area that sends 17 MPs to Westminster. Single elected watchdogs are to replace appointed multi-member Authorities overseeing each of the 41 Police Forces in England and Wales outside London. ... In theory the police should become far more accountable to the people they protect.*'

A further comment in *The Economist*'s edition immediately prior to the election of PCCs stood out: '*A single, visible figure is to become the lightning rod for local discontent [with Police].*'

PCCs soon gathered criticisms:

- '*Sixteen PCCs have appointed deputies on salaries of up to £65,000 without any formal appointments process.*' *The Times*; 7 December 2012.

- '*A Populus poll in the last week in January 2013 showed only 11% could correctly name their local Police Commissioner – fewer even than the 15% who bothered to vote [the lowest turnout in peacetime history.]*' *The Guardian*; 25 February 2013.

- '*The Acting Chief Constable of Lincolnshire was suspended without explanation two weeks ago... by [his] PCC.*' *The Times*; 13 March 2013.

- '*More than a third of PCCs are already costing the public more than the police authorities they were elected to replace.*' *The Times*; 25 May 2013.

- '*A PCC has made, what appears to be a series of political appointments, avoiding legislation that requires posts to be awarded on merit alone.*' *The Times*; 21 June 2013.

- '*Too easy for PCCs to ditch Chief Constable, say MPs.*' *The Daily Telegraph*; 20 July 2013.

- '*Nine out of ten people do not know, cannot remember or have never heard of the politician who holds their police force to account, a poll shows today.*' *The Times*, 14 November 2013.

Each PCC has a statutory duty – and an electoral mandate, albeit a minority one – to hold the police to account on behalf the public. The PCC is the recipient of all funding related to policing and crime reduction for their force, and the allocation of this money is a matter for the PCC in consultation with the Chief Constable. The PCC has a legal duty and power to:

' • *Set the strategic direction and objectives of the force through the Police and Crime Plan (which must have regard to the Strategic Policing Requirements set by the Home Secretary),*

• *Scrutinise, support and challenge the overall performance of the force including against the priorities agreed within the Plan,*

• *Hold the Chief Constable to account for the performance of the force's officers and staff ...*

• *Maintain an efficient and effective police force for the police area.'*

It is important to note that the second bullet point above makes explicit the function of the PCC to '*support ... the overall performance of the force*' – an element missing from the Independent Commission Report On Policing For Northern Ireland and the consequent legislation in Northern Ireland, as we have already observed.

A national body, the Association of Police and Crime Commissioners, has been established (to replace the former Association of Police Authorities), to which all Commissioners have agreed to belong, which will promote networking and good practice. Quarterly collective meetings are arranged for Commissioners with key Government Ministers on matters of mutual interest. Against a background in which the Coalition Government and the Home Office were determined to reduce costs, the budget for 2015–16 announced in July 2013 saw a further real terms cut of 5% compared with 2014–15. As set out in the *Police and Crime Commissioners Bulletin* Issue 19 of July 2013, Commissioners were exhorted to '*drive considerable further savings through improving procurement and collaboration across operational areas and support services*'.

In an article in *The Guardian* on 22 May 2013 it was reported that the House of Commons Home Affairs Select Committee had found that 17 of the 41 PCCs had set budgets for their own costs that were higher than the Police Authorities that they replaced. (In Hampshire, the cost had risen by 133% to £3.5m.)

The report of the Stevens Commission was, perhaps not surprisingly in a document produced for the Labour Party in Opposition, critical of many facets of the new PCCs, suggesting that they were flawed. That said, it proposed neither reinstating the former (allegedly largely invisible) Police Authorities nor returning greater control to Westminster. Rather, the Commission advocated granting a greater say to a lower-level tier of local authorities which would set the priorities for local policing. It recognised a need to retain accountability at the force level and recommended the creation of Policing Boards made up of the leaders of the local authorities within the area. This Board would set the budget and the strategic priorities, and have the power to hire and fire the Chief Constable. The Commission considered this model preferable to two alternatives that it also mooted: one in which the chair of the Policing Board was directly elected, and another in which the whole Policing Board was directly elected. However, one model that it does not seem to have considered specifically was the approach of the Northern Ireland Policing Board, with *Political Members* in a balance with *Independent Members.*

Although in some regards the Police and Crime Commissioners have got off to a rocky start, we consider it is as yet early to reach definitive conclusions about their effectiveness and efficiency. That said, in its edition of 15 March 2014 *The Economist* had an article on policing in England and Wales which concluded with the following *'The police need better oversight. The PCCs are not providing it.'*

While, as we have shown, the British Coalition Government introduced comparatively sweeping changes in this area of oversight and accountability, successive British Governments have struggled to tackle the important question of whether police effectiveness and efficiency would not be better served by a significant reduction in the number of police forces in England and Wales, which has remained at 43 for some 50 years or so. Although the last Labour Government did bring forward proposals for mergers in 2006, in the face of political opposition, nothing tangible was done. In the recent past a handful of individual services, such as West Mercia and Warwickshire, have voluntarily collaborated in a number of areas, such as seeking to share back office capability.

In July 2014 Her Majesty's Inspectorate of Constabulary (HMIC) published a report entitled *'Policing in Austerity, Meeting the Challenge'.* While the overall conclusion was that most police forces in England

and Wales had risen to the challenge of austerity, the report pointed to two areas for concern. One was that there was a need to maintain levels of neighbourhood policing, notwithstanding further anticipated staffing reductions. HMIC also concluded that more could be done to achieve savings in collaboration between individual forces.

The report also noted the continuing low proportions of women and minority ethnic officers and observed that there would be only a limited window of opportunity for recruiting staff and officers, given the continuing era of austerity. It continued:

'Forces must take this opportunity to consider how their workforces can better reflect the diversity of the communities they police as this unrepresentative picture has remained unchanged for too many years.'

Meanwhile, in Scotland, where policing is also a devolved matter, a different approach has been taken. Since 1 April 2013 Scotland has had a single police force, replacing the eight that existed previously. In autumn 2011 Kenny MacAskill, Scotland's Justice Secretary, announced that budget cuts had made the country's policing model unsustainable. In June 2012 the Scottish Parliament passed legislation reforming the police and the accountability structure. The new Scottish Police Authority consists of between 10 and 14 *Independent Members*, all appointed by Scottish Ministers. The Authority's legislative role includes promoting the statutory policing principles, supporting continuous improvement in policing, and holding the Chief Constable to account.

One avowed aim of the Scottish reforms was to save public money. Although the head of the Scottish Police Authority has said that the police will not be treated as a business, the Authority does want to inculcate business principles and ethics into policing. Clearly there is scope for efficiency in terms of centralised procurement and rationalisation of separate human resources departments and information technology systems, for example. Additionally, areas previously served by smaller forces will benefit from the greater expertise in specialist aspects of policing developed by the larger ones.

On the other hand, there is an argument that local accountability has been reduced. Partly to counter that, a policing plan has been drawn up for each of the country's 353 council wards. Police commanders in 32 districts, as in Northern Ireland aligned with local authority boundaries, will determine local needs.

The Scottish example suggests that it is through the more radical option of mergers, not collaboration, that really significant developments in effectiveness and efficiency will come.

The Stevens Commission did not come to a clear view on this issue, though it did not believe that the status quo was tenable. It offered three alternatives – mergers and collaboration, regionalisation, and a national police service, and recommended that public consultation should proceed on the basis of these alternatives.

The position in the United States of America is rather different from the model in much of the world in that policing is predominantly a matter for local, municipal government. Accountability arrangements differ across States and Counties, and in some small police departments police chiefs are elected and answerable directly to the electorate, while others are appointed by the local political administration. Often such police chiefs lack the degree of operational independence enjoyed by their counterparts in the United Kingdom.

There is, similarly, considerable variation in the role of oversight bodies across the United States; while some deal predominantly with police misconduct in a way similar to the Police Ombudsman's Office in Northern Ireland, others have a monitoring role and set strategic objectives for the local service. In 1995 the National Association for Civilian Oversight of Law Enforcement was set up to promote greater police accountability; functions include identifying best practice and organising training to increase skills in oversight staff. Furthermore, individual Commissions are sometimes created following a particular cause célèbre, such as the Independent Commission on the Los Angeles Police Department formed in 1991 in the wake of the Rodney King beating.

More recently, events in America during 2012–13 brought into sharp focus the tension that almost inevitably exists between security and liberty and transparency. Edward Snowden's actions sought to shed light on the warehousing by the National Security Agency (NSA) of private data belonging to millions of American and, indeed, other citizens. This aspect of the work of the NSA was in theory subject to vetting by Congress and a national security court. Interestingly, an opinion poll carried out in July 2013 suggested that more Americans now felt that their Government had gone too far in restricting civil liberties than those who believed it should boost security further. The US President was quoted as saying in June that he 'welcomed' a debate on the trade-off between privacy, security, and convenience.

As *The Economist* observed in a leader on 15 June 2013: '*Some operational efficiency is worth sacrificing, because public scrutiny is a condition for popular backing.*'

It will be interesting to see how far the public debate in America about levels of scrutiny and accountability, and indeed the right of redress, will progress.

21.3   In Conclusion

As we have seen, the Report of the Independent Commission on Policing in Northern Ireland is gaining wider recognition for its lasting value. Concepts such as democratic accountability, consent (including affirmative action), human rights (including a code of ethics), public confidence, and engagement with the local community (including neighbourhood policing) have all been at the heart of the reform of policing in Northern Ireland, and have been shown to have application in many other jurisdictions.

However, in reviewing the achievements of the Northern Ireland Policing Board (the Policing Board, the Board) it needs to be borne in mind both that the Independent Commission's Report came from the Belfast Agreement of 1998, to which the Democratic Unionist Party (DUP) were vehemently opposed, and that the two Nationalist parties in Northern Ireland were sceptical about the sincerity of the British Government towards full implementation of the Independent Commission's (175) recommendations. Moreover, the Northern Ireland Policing Board was set up at a time, in October 2001, when the political structures created under the Belfast Agreement were themselves in suspense, and it was for several years the only central organisation with elected representatives operating on a cross-community basis.

Tony Blair was unique among British Prime Ministers in the personal focus that he sustained on Northern Ireland, for which he deserves great credit. In writing to one of the authors at the time of the creation of the Policing Board in autumn 2001, he noted from his own experience how frustrating the work of implementing policing reforms in Northern Ireland could be. He noted, however, that 'it is a huge achievement to be where we now are'.

Setting up the Policing Board was, however, just the initial step. Its success was by no means guaranteed, and at times it seemed likely to be vulnerable to external pressures and events.

Against this background the Policing Board Chairman consciously decided not to push within the Board for the implementation of the Independent Commission's Recommendations per se, but rather on the basis of the demonstrably sound policing principles they embodied. In some critical areas, for example in regard to the 50:50 recruitment rule, the Board Members were unable to reach consensus on a collective position: the *Political Members* chose to make representations to the Government in line with their respective political parties, while the *Independent Members* explored the scope for reaching a common view among themselves. Nevertheless, the history of the period reviewed in this book shows that, in practice, with an incremental approach allied to determination, the Independent Commission's Recommendations and the new beginning to policing were delivered.

Undoubtedly, in the context of the delicate *political* and *peace processes* in Northern Ireland at that time, having a blend of *Political* and *Independent Members* on the Board served the wider community well. The Policing Board has been in existence for just on 13 years now. As this book has shown, we believe that it has been at its most effective when the *Political Members* are heavyweight politicians whose views carry weight both within their own parties and with the wider public. Equally, the *Independent Members* have demonstrated on a number of critical occasions their ability to act collectively to put a check on the *Political Members* for the good of the whole Board and indeed society at large.

A second tension, which the Policing Board Chairman and the first Vice-Chairman, Denis Bradley, in particular, were conscious of, was the creation of a position in which Sinn Féin would feel able to sign up to support for policing in Northern Ireland and take their seats on the Policing Board. With the benefit of hindsight, this might appear as an almost inevitable step, but it was certainly not felt to be so for the first six years of the Board's existence. Denis Bradley did much to encourage the Nationalist and Republican community into the policing sphere at considerable personal cost.

Sinn Féin joined the Policing Board in summer 2007. This was a key step not just in the Board's evolution but also more widely in the political arena. By that time much of the Independent Commission's agenda had been accomplished; in particular, the:

a. Early achievement of the new emblem for the new police service

b. Policing Board had proved itself as an effective mechanism to hold the Chief Constable – and through him the Police Service of Northern Ireland (the Police Service or the PSNI) – to account

c. Operation of the 50:50 rule was demonstrably bringing closer the attainment of 30% representation of Roman Catholics in the PSNI

d. First comprehensive human rights policing framework had been put in place and was being used as a practical template for policing accountability

e. District Policing Partnerships (DPPs) had been established and local policing plans were being used to deliver community policing

As Chapter 12 demonstrated, Ronnie Flanagan played a critical part in leading the Royal Ulster Constabulary to accept the changes set out in the Independent Commission's Report. Then, from the beginning of his tenure as Chief Constable, Hugh Orde showed his willingness to work with the Policing Board and to give a lead in that regard to his senior colleagues. Inevitably there were tensions in that relationship from time to time, some of them compounded by the particular nature of Northern Ireland society and the closeness between local politicians and the media. It was also important in that relationship that – even though there was no explicit obligation in the legislation – the Board Chairman consistently adopted the principle that the Board should be supportive of the PSNI while, at the same time, maintaining its critical accountability role. It is interesting that this support dimension has now been integrated into the policing accountability legislation in England and Wales.

The early achievement of unanimous support among the Board Members for the new emblem and badges of rank for the police service was very significant. It sent a clear signal to the wider political community in Northern Ireland that the Policing Board was an effective body and that, approached with goodwill, seemingly intractable issues could be resolved. It was also a very practical demonstration of the lead given to their *Political* colleagues by *Independent Members* of the Board.

As noted in Chapter 8, the setting up of the DPPs was Northern Ireland's largest ever selection process to public bodies. It reflected well upon the Policing Board that the arrangements worked so smoothly. It was certainly a challenge to ensure that all parts the community, including age, gender, and disability, as well as political opinion, were reflected in the DPPs' composition.

The Policing Board was extraordinarily well served by its Human Rights Advisers, not only in the unique Monitoring Framework that they devised but also in the unprecedented access that they were able to establish with the PSNI, particularly at times during which any police service would feel itself under challenge. The Annual Human Rights Report was an important component in the overall accountability schema and went a long way to ensuring that human rights were at the heart of the reformed police service, just as the Independent Commission's Report had recommended. In addition, the Advisers' reports on individual contentious parades brought out valuable lessons in relation to the importance of advance discussions between local politicians with a view to reaching at least a degree of informal agreement. Achieving consent was a critical goal to which human rights made a major contribution, as did the practical impact of the 50:50 affirmative action legislation.

The Board Chairman consciously chose to emphasise the importance of police effectiveness as a primary objective, seeking to establish benchmarks through HMIC with similar police forces in England and Wales. That said, Northern Ireland makes unique demands on its police service. The legacy of the past, whether it be unsolved murders from the Troubles or contentious parades and public disorder, inevitably impacts on the overall performance of the PSNI, not least in that it takes away resources from where they are needed for current policing. This makes comparisons with other forces more difficult. Moreover, the effect of the major early severance scheme was especially felt in the weakening of the PSNI's criminal investigation capacity for some years.

Despite these challenges the performance of the PSNI, in terms of driving down and solving crime, has significantly improved over the past ten or so years. In addition, the PSNI itself has directly addressed the issue of consent and confidence, so that local communities right across Northern Ireland are now much more ready to turn to the police as their first response to criminal behaviour. Local representation on DPPs, greater professionalism through training, the role of the Police Ombudsman, and the lead given by elected representatives have all played their part.

The Northern Ireland Code of Ethics, and its centrality to disciplinary proceedings, has served in many ways as a model for England and Wales, following public concern about police integrity in some well-publicised incidents. (On 24 October 2013 the Home Secretary, Theresa May, announced that the College of Policing was launching a consultation on a new Code of Ethics for policing in England and Wales.)

The Omagh bombing tragedy of August 1998 will long continue to resonate, especially for the friends and family of those who were killed and injured. But one important effect was the impact on the PSNI. The Police Ombudsman's report, together with the thrust of her recommendations, and the subsequent reports by and recommendations of Sir John Stevens, Sir Dan Crompton, and David Blakey commissioned by the Policing Board and the Chief Constable led to the reorganisation of Crime Operations within the PSNI and a vastly different approach towards the integration of intelligence with criminal investigations.

On the other hand, tackling organised crime was an area where the Policing Board was constrained in its scope to make a direct proactive contribution, as the Northern Ireland Office largely cut the Board out of a strategic planning role. Major criminal activities such as the Castlereagh break-in and the Northern Bank robbery both buffeted the Board and raised issues about its role in reacting to such incidents. However, the Board showed that, in terms of the Chief Constable's operational accountability, it addressed organised crime effectively.

It is interesting to note how an ostensibly mundane issue such as the police service's estate strategy has political significance in the context of Northern Ireland. Certainly the closure of police stations in the border area of the County Fermanagh was fiercely contested at the local level, even though it tied up scarce resources in static security. The passage of time has suggested that, in practice, following their closure, the PSNI has sustained effective policing in the area, as well as saving on costs.

Perhaps the biggest single failure of delivery of the Recommendations in the Independent Commission's Report has been the Police College. The choice of location was in part a political one, though thereafter the delays cannot be laid at the door of politicians. While the concept which has subsequently emerged of a Joint Community Safety College is attractive, it was certainly not built in time to provide the training location for the recruits who have so radically reshaped the PSNI over the past 12 years.

The Policing Board was, of course, only part of the wider criminal justice landscape impacting on policing. The establishment of the 26 DPPs played a key role in the development of policing with the community. The courage of DPP members and their families in supporting policing, particularly at a time when that was not always the easy or popular option, deserves to be fully recognised.

In addition to the DPPs, both the Police Ombudsman and the Police Oversight Commissioner made a significant contribution to the development of policing in Northern Ireland. Indeed, the regularity of the reviews of progress by the Oversight Commissioner undoubtedly assisted the Board in keeping up the pressure on the PSNI to deliver reform. The choice of the individual Oversight Commissioners brought a great deal of North American experience to the role, which in turn assisted in enhancing the links between the Policing Board and PSNI and US law enforcement agencies and politicians in the administration there. Irish–Americans in particular have shown themselves to be both interested in and supportive of the Policing Board.

It is interesting that it remains the case that no police accountability body in these islands or further afield has – yet – been fashioned directly on the model of the Northern Ireland Policing Board. While there have been indications from time to time that a future Irish Government would set up a similar organisation, none has yet done so. Partly for this reason, the Policing Board in Northern Ireland consistently found it hard to establish working relationships with either police accountability or delivery bodies in the Irish Republic.

It must be acknowledged that the financial cost of the Policing Board was not insignificant. In 2009/10 the annual expenditure was £8.17m – well within the budget of £8.73m. Within this total the cost of DPPs, of which the Board met 75%, was £2.88m.

There are commentators in Northern Ireland who express the view that, now the Stormont Assembly Justice Committee is well established, the role of the Policing Board could be reduced or even ended altogether, with some of its functions transferring to the Justice Committee. Without wishing to comment on the efficacy of the Justice Committee or its ability to take on an executive role not associated with any other Stormont Committee, we would make two observations from the experience in England and Wales cited earlier in this chapter. First, it is recorded that in a significant number of PCCs the annual costs now outstrip those of the previous Police Authorities. Second, the Policing Board has, in our view, proved its worth as an oversight and accountability body. The changes made in England and Wales have, according to the above account, diminished that capacity.

Throughout his tenure the Chairman was at all times conscious that the two Permanent Secretaries in the Northern Ireland Office (NIO), Sir Joe Pilling and Sir Jonathan Phillips, and their colleagues David Watkins and Nick Perry, were hugely supportive and had but one desire for the Board, which was that it would be effective. At no time was the Chairman conscious of being leant on by the NIO!

It is important to recognise that many people have contributed to the delivery of the new beginning to policing in Northern Ireland, including past and serving officers and civilian staff throughout the police service, civil servants, and politicians. Credit is due to each and every one of them. But in any account of the history of the Northern Ireland Policing Board it is right to conclude with a tribute to all those who contributed to the Board's achievements. The commitment of successive tranches of Members, including the Vice-Chairmen and Committee Chairs, and its dedicated staff, which included some very capable Chief Executives (Ivan Wilson and Trevor Reaney in particular) and other staff, has ensured that the Policing Board has undoubtedly served Northern Ireland well. Among other staff the first Board Chairman wishes to record his particular debt to Sinead Simpson and Lorraine Calvert, for their industry, wise counsel, and advice, and Veronica Dougherty, who brought some order to it all.

The Policing Board also owes a considerable debt to HMIC and, in particular, Sir Dan Crompton and Ken Williams.

As this book has shown, the Board has not just helped to deliver more effective and efficient policing but also contributed directly to the *political* and *peace processes*.

It may be that certain aspects of the Northern Ireland context made the Policing Board uniquely effective in this jurisdiction, but it is our hope that, through this book, a wider appreciation of how the Policing Board has gone about its business and its record of delivery will be gained outside Northern Ireland.

References

BBC Dimbleby Lecture, Sir Ian Blair, 16 November 2005

The Economist, 25 February 2012

The Economist, 27 October 2012

The Times, 7 December 2012

The Guardian, 25 February 2013

The Times, 13 March 2013

The Times, 25 May 2013

The Economist, 15 June 2013

The Times, 21 June 2013.

The Daily Telegraph, 20 July 2013

The Times, 14 November 2013

'Neighbourhood policing is the bedrock on which the service is built', *The Sunday Telegraph,* 24 November 2013

Policing for a Better Britain, report of the Independent Police Commission, published 25 November 2013

The Economist, 15 March 2014

Policing in Austerity, Meeting the Challenge, a report published by Her Majesty's Inspectorate of Constabulary, July 2014

Index